DESIGN OF MICROPROCESSOR-BASED SYSTEMS

Nikitas Alexandridis

Department of Electrical Engineering and Computer Science

The George Washington University

Prentice Hall
Englewood Cliffs, New Jersey 07632

Library of Congress Cataloging-in-Publication Data

Alexandridis, Nikitas A.,
    Design of microprocessor-based systems / Nikitas Alexandridis.
      p. cm.
    Includes bibliographical references and index.
    ISBN 0-13-588567-1
    1. Microprocessors—Design and construction. 2. System design.
  I. Title.
  TK7895.M5A48 1993
  621.39′16—dc20   92-30941
                  CIP

Acquisitions editor: Don Fowley
Prepress buyer: Linda Behrens
Manufacturing buyer: David Dickey
Supplements editor: Alice Dworkin
Editorial assistant: Phyllis Morgan
Cover design: Design Source

 © 1993 by Prentice-Hall, Inc.
A Simon & Schuster Company
Englewood Cliffs, New Jersey 07632

The author and publisher of this book have used their best efforts in preparing this book. These efforts include the development, research, and testing of the theories and programs to determine their effectiveness. The author and publisher make no warranty of any kind, expressed or implied, with regard to these programs or the documentation contained in this book. The author and publisher shall not be liable in any event for incidental or consequential damages in connection with, or arising out of, the furnishing, performance, or use of these programs.

Printed in the United States of America

10 9 8 7 6 5 4 3 2 1

ISBN 0-13-588567-1

Prentice-Hall International (UK) Limited, *London*
Prentice-Hall of Australia Pty. Limited, *Sydney*
Prentice-Hall Canada Inc., *Toronto*
Prentice-Hall Hispanoamericana, S.A., *Mexico*
Prentice-Hall of India Private Limited, *New Delhi*
Prentice-Hall of Japan, Inc., *Tokyo*
Simon & Schuster Asia Pte. Ltd., *Singapore*
Editora Prentice-Hall do Brasil, Ltda., *Rio de Janeiro*

To the memory of my father Anestis,
and to my wife, Aimy, and daughter, Aneta

Contents

2   MICROPROCESSOR BUS TRANSFERS   51

Preface

This textbook presents advanced microprocessor-based system design concepts and illustrates them through specific examples, using current technology microprocessors and other very large scale integration (VLSI) components. It is intended for advanced undergraduate or beginning graduate students in electrical and computer engineering, computer science, and other related fields. The reader is assumed to have had a course in the design of digital systems (or a first course in microprocessors) and basic knowledge of computer organization and architecture.

The microprocessors are becoming the implementation technology of choice for an increasingly wide range of systems. Rather than giving a quantitative approach and a block diagram view of their architecture, this textbook is more specific and gives a more hardware-oriented approach to the design of such systems. Its purpose is to present ways of building systems using commercial microprocessors; *it is not about* designing the microprocessor chips themselves. (The microprocessor system designer/integrator is much more interested in the speed of the chip rather than on the detailed implementation of its internal CPU.) However, issues that have to do with the design of the microprocessor chip itself impact significantly the *performance* of the overall system as well as how one goes about designing it; therefore, such related internal architectural schemes (e.g., pipelining, on-chip caching, etc.) are presented mainly from the point of view of how they effect system performance. For example, capabilities not provided on-chip will have to be implemented with external chips; the type of external signals and buses the microprocessor has will impact the expense and difficulty of interfacing it to memory and to input/output; the particular microprocessor chip chosen for the design and the particular system bus chosen to interconnect the various boards of the system will influence the interface complexity of each board; other capabilities, such as paging, segmentation, or handling of the internal and external exceptions have similarly significant impact on the design of both the hardware system and the systems software.

This textbook presents a survey of the structure and capabilities of advanced representative microprocessors (both CISC- and RISC-type), and a large number of design examples is given throughout the textbook using commercial chips. It contrasts architectural differences between (primarily) Intel and Motorola microprocessors. An attempt is made throughout to maintain the systems-level design approach (i.e., to look at the global system whose basic building blocks represent complex hardware subsystems, such as microprocessors, buses, memory chips, I/O interface modules, and specialized chips such as MMUs and caches). The text emphasizes that microprocessor-based systems are structured either as a number of chips interconnected through a local bus or as a number of boards interconnected through an industry system bus. The bus is treated here as a basic component of the microprocessor system, which permits alternative system structures and bus-based designs. The reader is considered to be either the designer of boards (microprocessor boards, memory boards, interface boards, etc.) or the board-level microcomputer system designer/integrator. When it comes to software design issues, the reader is considered to be the "systems software designer" who requires knowledge of and access to "all system resources" (i.e., system registers, status bits, and I/O ports).

In designing this textbook, I tried to observe the following guidelines:

a. Instead of directly jumping into the details of how a particular manufacturer has implemented a feature in its microprocessors, explain the issues and trade-offs involved in choosing among different design approaches.

b. Present the various design issues in a unified and generic manner, which would be applicable to all microprocessors irrespective of their particular manufacturer, type (RISC or CISC), word length, and level of integration and then give specific examples of actual implementations.

c. Expose the reader to alternative ways of designing microprocessor-based systems, to the trade-offs involved in putting things together or choosing system components, and to the advantages and disadvantages of the various decisions, rather than to a description of the particular method a manufacturer followed in building a system.

d. Cover a large number of representative microprocessors so that the reader is exposed to various architectural features of microprocessors and how they impact program execution and overall system performance, along with different characteristics and capabilities that impact the way a system is designed. For example, features and capabilities that vary significantly from one microprocessor to another include: RISC versus CISC microprocessors; Harvard architecture with dual external buses; MMU, cache, and floating-point capabilities; on-chip and off-chip implementation of features; microprocessors with instruction and/or data pipelining; reconfigurable microprocessors with advanced data bus transfers; multitasking and virtual memory capabilities based on paging, segmentation, or both; and various control functions that are an integral part of the system design, such as the protected mode in the 80x86 microprocessors, interrupt-driven task switching, and exception handling.

In each chapter, those generic ideas and organizational concepts that exist independent of a particular implementation are presented first, followed by extensive surveys of how specific commercial products have embodied a concept. Although basic principles are presented from a generic point of view to be applicable to the design of systems using a variety of products, descriptions of a large number of specific products and concrete design examples using current components are given throughout the text and are also reflected in the exercises at the end of each chapter to make the text more specific. Important issues and criteria for product selection, as well as alternative hardware and system design choices and trade-offs are also included in each chapter.

Chapter 1 starts with a discussion on the advances in microprocessors and gives an overview of their internal architecture, external I/O signals, and their operation; these are presented in a simplified, generic form here, while details for representative microprocessors are given in the Appendices. Both RISC and CISC microprocessors are discussed and their major differences pointed out, along with other components (such as memory, caches, special coprocessors, and buses) needed to put together a microprocessor-based system. The chapter ends with an introduction to pipelined, superpipelined, and superscalar microprocessors, and a discussion of system design methodology.

Chapter 2 concentrates on the external (local) bus of the microprocessor and how the microprocessor uses it to perform synchronous and asynchronous data exchanges with other units of the system. The chapter starts with a discussion on big- and little-endian ordering of operands in memory and how recent configurable RISC microprocessors handle them dynamically. In addition to the bus timing diagrams for the execution of aligned data transfers on 32- and 64-bit data buses, this chapter presents other advanced data transfer modes, such as "address pipelining," "burst transfers," and misaligned data transfers. It also explains how the recent microprocessors implement "dynamic bus sizing," which allows them to adjust the width of their local data bus to that of the data port they communicate with. The chapter ends with a discussion of the local bus arbitration techniques for performing DMA operations.

Chapter 3 covers the design of the memory subsystem and its interface to the microprocessor. It starts with some basic terms and definitions and presents the various types and characteristics of memory chips. It then gives the details of designing and interfacing memory subsystems of different wordlengths, using various types of static and dynamic RAMs. The more advanced DRAM access modes (page, static column, nibble) are also discussed and an extensive treatment of interleaved memory along with design examples is given. Finally, the chapter presents a quantitative approach to calculating the memory latency time and the memory access time requirements in order to match the processor and memory bandwidths.

Chapter 4 reviews the industry system buses used to interconnect boards from different manufacturers and with different wordlengths in building more powerful microprocessor systems. The three system buses used as examples are the Multibus, the VMEbus, and the Futurebus. Their signals and timings are presented, the way they perform data transfers is explained, and examples are given for interfacing them to processor and memory boards. A section is also devoted to the mad- and sad-endian system buses and how different types of microprocessors are interfaced to them. Both serial and parallel system bus arbitration techniques are presented and the chapter ends with a discussion of trade-offs involved in selecting the system bus.

Chapter 5 covers microprocessor caches. It first discusses system issues, such as different ways of configuring external caches, multilevel caches, and different cache write policies. It then presents the three cache organizations (fully associative, direct mapped, and set-associative) and the cache line format, and gives examples of specific microprocessor on-chip and off-chip cache implementations. An extensive part of the chapter is devoted to the cache coherency problem, the issues involved, and suggested software and hardware solutions. The chapter ends with a discussion of the parameters that affect cache design and gives approximation formulas for measuring cache performance and the cache's impact on the performance of the overall system.

Chapter 6 discusses the design and use of MMUs (Memory Management Units) in advanced multitasking, virtual memory systems. It presents the structure of the logical address space and ways of mapping it into the main memory space. It gives examples of how microprocessors have implemented paging, segmentation, or a combination of both, and discusses the on-chip and off-chip MMU hardware involved.

Chapter 7 contains various relevant topics, which are treated to a limited extent. The scope of this text does not permit devoting a separate chapter to each one. These topics include: protection mechanisms and task switching in various microprocessors, how microprocessors handle external interrupting devices, advanced exception processing in protected mode by various microprocessors, a survey of pipelined microprocessors and a discussion of the pipelining problems, and how segments become "known."

Finally, the *Appendices* survey a number of commercial microprocessors and give their internal organization and a detailed explanation of their I/O pins and signals. Appendix A covers the Intel 80x86 CISC microprocessors, Appendix B covers the 680x0 CISC microprocessors, and Appendix C covers a number of RISC microprocessors (including the Intel i860, the Motorola 88000-series, and the MIPS R-series microprocessors).

I would like to express my appreciation to a number of colleagues for their valuable criticism and comments during the early stages of the manuscript. In addition, I would like to thank the reviewers: Ken Breeding, Ohio State University;   Karan Watson, Texas A&M University;   Michael Chwialkowski, University of Texas, Arlington;   Everett Johnson, Wichita State University;   William Ohley, University of Rhode Island.

Last, but not least, I would like to express my gratitude to my wife and daughter for their support, patience and understanding; their continuous encouragement helped me tremendously in going through the various revisions and rewritings of this text.

Every attempt was made to cover the major issues in designing systems using recent advanced microprocessors, to use a rather large sample of representative RISC and CISC products, and to present design decisions and trade-offs. A notable number of important and powerful microprocessors were not covered in this text because of space limitations. An instructors manual was also prepared with solutions to all the exercises in the text. I would be greatly interested in receiving your comments and criticism, suggestions for improvements to the text, corrections, or contributed exercises. I can be reached at: Dept. of Electrical Engineering and Computer Science, The George Washington University, Washington, DC 20052; tel: 202-994 5251, fax: 202-994 5296, e-mail: alexan @ seas. gwu. edu.

Nikitas Alexandridis
Washington, DC

Microprocessor Architecture and Systems Concepts

1.1 BACKGROUND

In this textbook, the terms *microcomputer, microprocessor-based system,* and *microprocessor system* will mean the same thing: a computer system whose central processing unit (or CPU) is a microprocessor. This chapter discusses the microprocessor chip (its basic internal components and I/O pins and signals), its use in configuring different microprocessor systems, and the various buses used to interconnect the system components. Existing microprocessors differ widely in both their internal structure and in the number and types of I/O pins and signals. Both conventional CISC (complex instruction set computer) and RISC (reduced instruction set computer) microprocessor approaches are explained and contrasted, along with advanced internal architectural features that newer microprocessors have, such as pipelined, superpipelined, and superscalar implementations.

The microprocessor operation is the same as that of any computer CPU: it executes the ''instruction cycle'' through the opcode fetch, decode, read a possible operand, and execute phases; accesses to memory are carried out in terms of ''bus cycles,'' whose total number depends upon the width of the instruction and the operand, the width of the external data bus, and the type of instruction.[1] We give the definition of the ''bus cycle'' and show its relationship to the basic input ''clock cycle,'' explain the ''state transition diagram'' that the processor follows to carry out the bus cycle, and present the most common microoperations executed during each clock cycle. (Additional state transition diagrams, bus timing diagrams, and data transfers for a number of representative microprocessors are given in later chapters and in the Appendices.)

---

[1]Other features that influence this number—such as on-chip caches, a less wide memory port, accessing the operand(s) from internal registers, etc.—will be covered in later chapters.

1.1.1 Advances in Microprocessors

The year 1992 was the twentieth birthday of the microprocessor since the appearance of the Intel 4004. During these 20 years we have witnessed dramatic increases in all facets of design and manufacture of powerful microprocessors. While the first microprocessors that appeared at the end of 1971–beginning of 1972 were very small (only 4 bits), very slow (their input clock frequency was 0.5 MHz), and could access only a 16K-byte main memory, in 1992 the microprocessors are bigger (64 bits), faster (100–200 MHz), and can access a huge memory of $2^{32} = 4$ GB (gigabytes), soon to increase to 2^{64} bytes! Figure 1.1 depicts the chronological evolution of the major characteristics of microprocessors. (The numbers given in parentheses are the exceptional cases rather than the norm that the other numbers represent.)

	1972	1977	1982	1987	1992
Number of I/O pins	16	40	64	100	340 (430)
Transistors/chip (for processors)	2K	20K	100K	500K–800K	>1M
Processor wordlength (bits)	4	8 (16)	16	32	32 (64)
External data bus size (bits)	4	8 (16)	16	32	64 (128)
Input clock frequency (MHz)	0.5–1	5–8	8 (16)	20 (30)	50–100 (200[a])
Average clock cycles per instruction (CPI)	—	—	20	6–2	<1
Maximum main memory (bytes)	$2^{14} = 16K$	$2^{16} = 64K$ (1M)	$2^{24} = 16M$	$2^{32} = 4$ GB	$2^{32} = 4$ GB
Memory chip size (RAM)	1K-bit (1K × 1 bit)	4K-bit to 16K-bit	64K-bit	256K-bit	1M-bit

[a]Recent 64-bit RISC processors.

Figure 1.1 Advances in microprocessor characteristics.

The speed of the microprocessor (which determines the overall system performance) is improved by increasing one or more of the following characteristics:

1. *Processor wordlength*: By making the processor wordlength wider, more bits can be processed internally in parallel.
2. *Input clock*: By using newer, faster technologies, the input driving clock frequency can increase, which in turn increases the speed of program execution by the microprocessor.
3. *Level of integration*: By packing more functional units on the microprocessor chip (such as floating-point units, caches, memory management units, etc.), their interconnection distances and the need for off-chip signaling are decreased, contributing to the increase in the microprocessor operating speed.

4. *Width of external data bus*: The wider the external data bus, the more bits can be transferred to and from a (wider) memory, thus increasing the processor-to-memory bandwidth. Everything else being equal (for example, equal number of clock cycles to do a read/write operation), a microprocessor with a 64-bit external data bus has double the processor-to-memory bandwidth of the microprocessor with a 32-bit external data bus.

5. *Architectural advances*: Finally, internal architectural advances have been incorporated, such as *pipelined, superpipelined,* and *superscalar* implementations (to be discussed later in the chapter), which effectively reduce the average number of clock cycles it takes to execute an instruction (the CPI in Figure 1.1) and therefore increase the microprocessor performance, as we see next.

1.1.2 Microprocessor Performance

There has been a lot of discussion and debate on the differences and advantages/disadvantages between the classical CISC and the more recent RISC processors. Before we present the main issues of the RISC approach and compare it with the CISC approach, we discuss how the processor performance is measured.

The RISC approach (also called "streamlined architecture" [10]) aims at maximizing the performance of the basic CPU by advocating new, simpler, fixed-length, register-oriented instruction sets. The basic principle that drives the RISC approach is that instructions should be kept simple, to increase processor performance. To understand this we should notice that the "processor performance" for a given task in MIPS (million instructions per second) is approximated by the following formula [1]:

$$\text{processor performance (in MIPS)} = \frac{(F)}{(CPI)} \qquad (1.1)$$

where F = *clock rate* in MHz or million cycles per second of the "input clock" to the microprocessor[2] (the reciprocal of the input clock cycle time)

CPI = *average* (*clock*) *cycles per instruction* (it equals the total number of clock cycles needed to execute the task divided by the number of instructions executed).

For example, using Equation 1.1, consider three different processors, each operating from a 40-MHz clock. We say that a microprocessor that under the best-case conditions requires 2 clock cycles to execute an instruction (i.e., it has a *CPI* value of 2) has a peak performance of 20 MIPS; if the second processor can execute one instruction per clock cycle (i.e., *CPI* = 1), it has a peak performance of 40 MIPS; if the third processor can execute 3 instructions per clock cycle (*CPI* = 0.3), it has a peak performance of 120 MIPS.

The processor performance can also be measured by the time it takes to execute a task, called the "processor time," "CPU time," or "time per task" (which is the time the CPU is busy computing for this task, not including the time it waits for I/O), Equation 1.1 can also be written as

$$\text{processor time (per task)} = (NI) * (CPI) * (C) \qquad (1.2)$$

where NI = *number of instructions* executed for a task and C is the clock cycle time or, simply, the *clock cycle*.

[2]Also called the "clock rate of the machine."

The processor performance can be improved by reducing any of these three factors. *C*, the clock cycle time, is technology-driven and depends on the VLSI design of the chip. The clock cycle time is chosen long enough to allow execution of the most simple, basic operations (or *microoperations*) in a single clock cycle; other, more complex operations will require multiple clock cycles for their execution. *NI*, the number of instructions per task, is a function of the instruction set design and how effective the optimized compiler design is. *NI* is usually larger for RISCs, the ratio of the number of instructions for a RISC versus those for a CISC processor being on the average around 1.8 to 2. Finally, *CPI*, the average clock cycles per instruction, is a direct function of the microprocessor internal architecture (instruction pipelining, instruction issue ability, etc.) and the efficiency of the instruction scheduling. Notice that simply increasing the input clock frequency (reducing *C*) may not necessarily make the time needed to perform an instruction shorter, if the number of clock cycles needed to perform the instruction has now increased.

1.1.3 The RISC Approach

The *CPI* is lower for a RISC than for a CISC microprocessor because the RISC approach provides simple, fixed-length instruction formats that permit fast hardwired decoding and greatly simplify the use of internal instruction pipelining; as a result, the number of clock cycles needed to execute an instruction is (on the average) reduced to 1 (i.e., $CPI = 1$). *C*, the clock cycle, is also lower for a RISC than for a CISC processor, because of the former's architectural simplicity and reduced need to access main memory since the majority of RISC instructions are of the register-to-register type. Thus, RISC approaches improve the program performance by minimizing the last two factors in Equation 1.2.

Other additional **common properties** of the RISC approach include [12,14,15]:

1. *Simple load/store architecture*: Most of the instructions are register-based, supported by a large number of CPU registers. References to external memory are minimized: accessing it for operand/result transfer is explicitly done via load and store instructions. While in CISC processors 30–40% of the executed instructions implicitly or explicitly access data memory and 20% are register-to-register operations, in RISC processors less than 20% may be loads and stores and more that 50% are register-to-register operations [13].

2. *Simple instructions*: Instructions have simple fixed format, fixed length, and simple and few addressing modes.

3. *Simple hardwired control*: Because of the RISC instructions' simple and short format, the decoding becomes simpler and this permits implementing the control mechanism using faster hardwired techniques.

4. *Large register set or register windows*: One approach is for RISC processors to have large sets of application-usable registers (larger than in the CISC processors) for quick accessing of operands (which are stored in internal registers rather than in main memory), for subroutine calls, and saving of the processor state during context switches. Large internal registers greatly reduce the need for off-chip memory accesses. CISCs rarely have more than 32 internal registers, while RISCs may have as many as 256.

5. *Faster clocks*: RISCs have faster clock speeds than CISCs (at least twice as fast).

6. *Pipelining and delayed branching*: Although these are not unique RISC characteristics, they are more often found in RISCs than in CISCs. Internal pipelined implementation has been used in RISC processors to achieve the single-clock-cycle-per-instruction goal. The delayed branching technique does not stall the internal pipeline to wait for the instruction at the destination address; instead, the branch instruction is delayed, and will be executed only after one or more instructions immediately following the branch instruction have been executed. It is assumed that the compiler has examined the program and organized it in such a way (for example, by rearranging code and inserting useful instructions in the branch delay slot) to allow the processor pipeline to continue executing instructions during this waiting time.

7. Separate instruction and data buses (*Harvard architecture*): Again, this property is not unique to the RISCs, but it is found more often in RISCs than in CISCs. Because RISC instructions are much simpler than those of CISCs, instructions must be fetched much faster than in CISCs. To allow for that, separate buses and caches are implemented on-chip, one for instructions and one for data. This separation also lowers the CPI per instruction (i.e., improves the performance) because of the overlapping of instruction fetch and data loads/stores.

There are arguments that can be made for and against RISC processors.

RISC Advantages. Reducing the instruction complexity increases the speed, because complex instructions slow down all instructions. The speed is also increased by minimizing memory accesses through register-to-register instruction execution and adapting hardwired techniques for the design of the processor's control section. The instruction simplification reduces circuit complexity (which allows simpler design and faster design and development cycles) and chip area requirements (which allows on-chip implementation of other major functions, such as cache memories, memory management units, floating-point units, etc.).

RISC Drawbacks. RISC programs tend to be lengthier (the *NI* in Equation 1.2 is greater). The managing of internal processor pipelines or caches and implementing delayed branching are concerns that must be taken care of and reflected properly in the design of the compiler (thus the RISC processor's performance relies heavily on compiler design).

In general, however, CISC and RISC are not really two actual, different, specific architectures; instead, they represent two different approaches or paradigms to processor (CPU) design that can be utilized by any microprocessor architecture. A good processor design would have to trade off and select which attributes of RISC and CISC to combine. As a matter of fact, the two approaches and their execution cycle times are now beginning to converge toward the design of hybrid CPUs. Recent CISC processor designs have adopted features which are characteristic of RISCs (such as internal parallelism, Harvard architecture, and pipelined execution units found in the Intel 80486 and Motorola 68040 chips, which allow frequently used instructions to execute in a single clock cycle); on the other hand, RISC processors are becoming more complex, with on-chip MMUs and FPUs, have adopted a higher degree of internal pipelining and parallelism, and have implemented a number of additional not-so-simple instructions.

When it come, however, to the methodology of designing a microprocessor-based system, there are not really too many significant differences when a RISC processor is used instead of a CISC processor. Figure 1.2 shows the interconnection of a conventional micro-processor with a single external bus and that of a RISC microprocessor that has separate external buses for the instructions and data. Two differences that need to be taken into consideration are (1) these are two different external buses that some RISCs may have and (2) the use of faster memory (or memory hierarchy, which includes caches) in order to match the speed of the faster RISC microprocessors. As we will see in the next section, most of the remaining control signals are similar for RISCs and CISCs. It will also become apparent at the end of the chapter, that the current debate is not really between CISCs and RISCs but rather between "superpipelined" and "superscalar" microprocessor implementations.

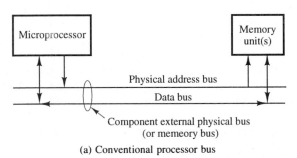

(a) Conventional processor bus

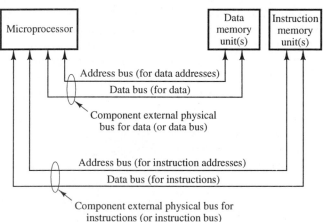

(b) Harvard architecture external processor buses

Figure 1.2 Conventional microprocessor with a single external processor bus (a) and a microprocessor with separate external buses, one for data and one for instructions.

In this textbook we will treat both RISCs and CISCs in a unified fashion for the design of microprocessor-based systems. The **CISC microprocessors** we will use as examples in this textbook will be primarily the 80386[4] and 80486[5] from Intel and the 68030[8] and 68040[9] from Motorola. As example **RISC microprocessors** we will use[3]: from Intel the i860[11], from Motorola the 88000 series (88100 and 88110)[10,3], and from MIPS the R-series (R3000 and R4000)[6,7].

[3]Other notable RISC examples that are not treated in the textbook include SPARC and the IBM RISC System/6000.

1.2 SYSTEM ISSUES

1.2.1 Introduction

Functionally, the modules of a bus-based microprocessor system are divided into two broad classes: bus master and bus slave devices. "Bus master modules" gain control of the bus and are able to initiate data transfers by dividing the address and control lines. To perform these tasks, the bus master is equipped with either a microprocessor CPU or logic capable of initiating bus cycles to transfer data over the bus to and from other destinations. The master identifies the nature of the bus cycle in progress and qualifies the nature of the address on the address bus by issuing proper "status signals" or "function code signals" over the control lines. A module acting as a "bus slave" monitors all bus cycles, and if addressed during a particular bus cycle, it accepts or sends data on the data bus lines. A slave module is not capable of controlling the bus; it simply decodes the address lines and acts upon the control signals it receives from the master. Therefore, a slave always responds to a bus cycle initiated by a master. All data transfer activities between a bus master and a bus slave are carried out in terms of "bus cycles" (see Section 1.5.2).

1.2.2 System Components

Figure 1.3 shows the block diagram of various microprocessor-based systems: Figure 1.3a represents a small, single-board configuration, Figure 1.3b a larger, multiboard system, and Figure 1.3c a multiprocessor system. In addition to the **microprocessor** itself, a microprocessor system must contain as a minimum the following types of components (discussed below in more detail): (1) a **clock** generator, to supply clock signals to the microprocessor and the other components of the system[4]; (2) **main memory** units, usually composed of DRAM (dynamic RAM) chips to store the applications code and the operands/data, with an optional EDCU (error detection–correction unit) to increase the reliability of the information exchange; and (3) some kind of **I/O units** to interface the microprocessor system with external devices, such as keyboards, printers, modems, etc. Sometimes, other optional **coprocessor** chips may be attached to the microprocessor, such as a *math coprocessor* to operate in parallel and execute floating-point arithmetic that the microprocessor does not support. Finally, a system may also incorporate some other special-purpose chips, such as an **MMU** (memory management unit) to implement virtual memory and handle task switching or a **cache memory** composed of SRAMs (static RAM chips) and a cache controller to increase system throughput by providing to the microprocessor information faster than main memory. (As we will see later, most of the microprocessors today have integrated the MMU—and at least a first-level cache—on-chip.)

Microprocessor.   Most microprocessors are single-chip devices, although some consist of more than one chip that make up what is referred to as a "chip set." The microprocessor CPU communicates with memory and I/O subsystems (units) by sending addresses to them (over the *address bus*) and sending to them or receiving from them data

---

[4]In some cases, the microprocessor receives pulses from an external crystal and it is the microprocessor itself that generates the appropriate clock signals distributed to the other components of the system.

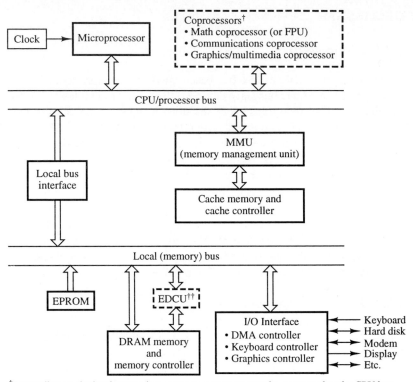

†Depending on the implementation, some coprocessors may be connected to the CPU bus and others to the local bus

††EDCU – error detection – correction unit

(a) Small, single-board, microprocessor-based system (Adopted from [6] courtesy of IDT.)

Figure 1.3 Microprocessor-based systems of various complexities.

(over the *data bus*). All control signals issued by the microprocessor travel over the *control bus*.

Each microprocessor has a *wordlength,* which is characterized by the width of the microprocessor's internal registers and the width of its arithmetic/logic unit or in general its "internal architecture." Although the width of its internal or external buses may or may not be the same, **in this textbook, unless explicitly specified otherwise, we will assume that an *n*-bit microprocessor also has an *n*-bit external data bus.**[5]

The CISC approach follows the classical design of the CPU and its accompanying complex, wider, variable-length instruction set (which results in a more complex structure of the microprocessor's control unit) that supports many different addressing modes. The RISC approach aims at increasing the performance of the microprocessor CPU by providing a different internal processor architecture and simpler, fixed-length, and primarily register-oriented instructions (that simplify the microprocessor's control unit and speed up its operation).

Figure 1.4 shows some of the most important features of our example CISC and RISC microprocessors. It is noticed that—as we move from left to right in the table—newer

[5]Throughout this textbook, a **word** will be 16 bits long and a **doubleword** 32 bits long. In most of the recent RISC processors, a halfword equals 16 bits, a word equals 32 bits, and a doubleword equals 64 bits.

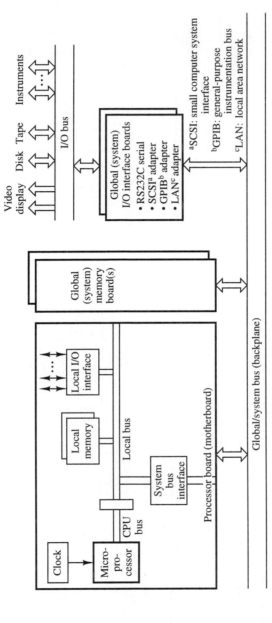

Figure 1.3 (cont.)

(b) Larger, multiboard, microprocessor-based system

System buses: Multibus, VMEbus, Futurebus, EISA, ISA, etc.

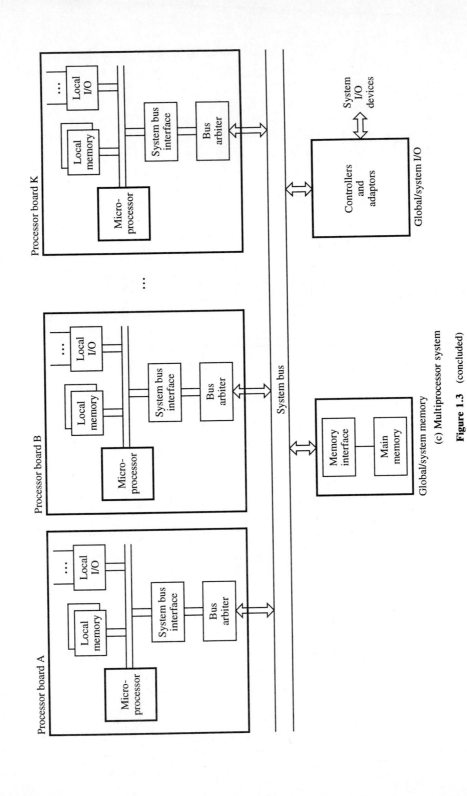

Figure 1.3 (concluded)

(c) **Multiprocessor system**

| | Intel | | | | Motorola | | | | | | MIPS (RISCs) | |
| | 80×86 (CISCs) | | | (RISC) | 680×0 (CISCs) | | | | 88000 series (RISCs) | | R-series | |
	80286	80386	80486	i860	68000	68020	68030	68040	88100	88110	R3000	R4000
Internal architecture (bits)	16	32	32	32	16①	32	32	32	32	32	32	64
External data bus (bits)	16	32	32	64	16	32	32	32	32	64	32	64
Address/main memory (bits/bytes)	24/16MB	32/4GB	32/4GB	32/4GB	24/16MB	32/4GB	32/4GB	32/4GB	32/4GB	32/4GB	32/4GB	36②/64GB
On-chip components	MMU	MMU	•MMU •Cache •FPU	•MMU •Cache •FPU •Graphics unit		ICACHE	•ICACHE •DCACHE •MMU	•ICACHE •DCACHE •IMMU •DMMU •FPU	FPU	•FPU •ICACHE •DCACHE •IMMU •DMMU •Graphics unit	MMU	•MMU •ICACHE •DCACHE
Other characteristics			5-stage pipelined	4-stage pipelined				6-stage pipelined		Super-scalar	5-stage pipelined	8-stage super-pipelined

	386SX	386SL	386DX	486SX	486DX③
Internal architecture (bits)	32	32	32	32	32
External data bus size (bits)	16	16	32	32	32
Address/main memory (bits/bytes)	24/16MB	25/32MB	32/4GB	32/4GB	32/4GB
Other differences	16-20 MHz	•20-25 MHz •On-chip cache controller	20-33 MHz	16-25 MHz (no FPU)	25-50 MHz

① 32-bit internal registers of which only 16 bits are used.

② May go up to 64 bits in future versions.

③ 486DX2 has an internal clock which is double the input clock frequency.

Figure 1.4 Major characteristics of example CISC and RISC microprocessors.

and more advanced microprocessors have increased their wordlengths, bus sizes, addressing capabilities, and input clock frequencies, and have integrated more features on the microprocessor chip. For example, the major difference between the Intel 32-bit CISC microprocessors[†] 80386[4] and 80486[5] is that the latter has integrated a cache and an FPU (Floating Point Unit) on-chip. In the 32-bit Motorola CISCs, the earlier 68020 had on-chip only an I-cache (instruction cache), the 68030[8] has included a separate D-cache (data cache) and an MMU, while the 68040[9] has integrated on-chip the FPU and split the MMU into an IMMU (instruction MMU) and a DMMU (data MMU). Comparing the latest RISC microprocessors in the table, we notice that all of them have a 64-bit external data bus but only the R4000[7] also has an internal 64-bit architecture; most of them have on-chip MMUs, caches, and FPUs, and the Intel and Motorola RISCs also include a graphics unit. Also, most of the latest microprocessors have incorporated pipelined implementations: the 80486, i860, 68040, and R3000 are pipelined; the R4000 is superpipelined; and the 88110 is superscalar. (These terms are explained later in the chapter.)

Finally, the Intel 386 and 486 chips come in several versions, as depicted at the bottom of Figure 1.4; their major difference is that some of them have a 16-bit external data bus and, secondarily, they may be operating from faster input clocks. In this textbook, whenever we refer to the Intel 32-bit 80x86 microprocessors (the 80386 and 80486), we will mean the microprocessors with 32-bit external data buses (i.e., the 386DX and 486DX).

Memory units.   Whenever we use the word "memory," we will mean main memory implemented outside the microprocessor, on separate memory chips; for larger systems, memory chips will be arranged on one or more memory boards. *Static RAMs* (**SRAMs**) hold stored information as long as power is being applied to them. SRAMs are quite often used for special-type high-speed memories called "cache memories" (to be discussed in Chapter 5). On the other hand, *dynamic RAMs* (**DRAMs**) are cheaper, have greater densities, and require less standby power. However, the DRAM only provides for temporary storage of data and requires special circuits to refresh its contents periodically. This periodic refresh requirement makes dynamic memories slower than static memories. The main memory in Figure 1.2a is referred to as an "n-bit memory" if the maximum data it can transfer in parallel is n bits per access, and data exchange between the processor and main memory is done on the n-bit basis (over an n-bit data bus). (The design of the memory subsystem and its interfacing to the microprocessor are covered in Chapter 3.)

I/O interface units.   The I/O interface circuitry implements the communication protocol, converts voltages and currents from the outside world into digital form and presents them to the microprocessor system, or converts digital signals that the microprocessor system generates into the voltages and currents that the external devices require. The microprocessor communicates with an external device through one or more *input or output ports*. The I/O configuration is referred to as **I/O-mapped** if the I/O ports are accessed by special "input" and "output" instructions whose execution generates the "in" and "out" control signals. An alternative configuration is the **memory-mapped I/O;** in this case, memory-type instructions are used to perform the input and output operations, the I/O ports occupy memory locations, and the I/O ports are accessed with (wider) memory addresses. All

[†]These are also referred to as the 386 and 486 microprocessors.

Motorola microprocessors have no separate I/O instructions, forcing the designer to interface the peripheral devices through "memory-mapped" schemes only. All Intel microprocessors have separate I/O instructions permitting either I/O-mapped or memory-mapped configurations.

I/O interfacing may also involve higher-complexity peripheral devices such as magnetic disks. In such cases, the VLSI chips used to interface these devices are more complicated than just a number of I/O ports. One such complex VLSI interface chip is the direct memory access controller (DMAC), which is able to start its own bus cycles to access main memory in order to support high-speed data exchange directly between the external device and the system's main memory with no intervention of the microprocessor CPU. A DMAC chip may support more than one high-speed peripheral device by providing more than one "DMA channel," one channel per I/O device. Other VLSI chips, called "I/O processors," are even more complex interface devices, which remove yet another level of control from the CPU. They contain a number of DMA channels, have processor-like capabilities for executing their own instruction sets, and operate independent of the microprocessor CPU.

Special coprocessor chips. Microprocessor systems may also be configured to include other special-purpose support chips. These are compatible and easily interfaceable to the microprocessor CPU (using the processor's I/O pins), and—acting like satellite processors—free it from a complex task that formally required considerable CPU time and software implementations. By themselves they can be quite complex processors with an instruction set of their own, supported by the enhanced instruction set of the CPU. Typical types of external coprocessors include **floating-point units** (or **FPUs**), **communications coprocessors** (for example, to implement the ISDN protocol), **speech processing coprocessors, graphics coprocessors, multimedia coprocessors** (to compress/decompress video images, with large on-chip memories and multiple execution units), etc.

MMUS. A memory management unit (MMU) aided by systems programs, provides a technique for handling a larger address space in a flexible fashion, on behalf of the user. It does this by subdividing the total address space into blocks (pages or segments), defining logical addresses, and translating them at runtime into physical addresses. It also provides protection and management of the virtual and physical address spaces by checking a number of access attributes, such as user vs. supervisor space, out-of-limits access, class of ownership (i.e., which tasks are permitted access to that block), privilege level (the privilege level of the requestor vs. the privilege level of the module to be accessed), mode of access (read-only vs. read-write, execute only, etc.), etc. MMU hardware is also used to prevent problems that result when multiple tasks within a given application contend for limited physical memory, or when users share common data or employ common programs.

When an MMU is off-chip, it functions as an I/O peripheral which is manipulated (i.e., given the attributes of each module, has its registers updated with new values, etc.) in supervisor mode by special privileged I/O instructions. The more the integration increases, the more MMUs are moving on-chip with the rest of the microprocessor hardware.

Caches. A cache memory is a small high-speed memory placed between the microprocessor CPU and main memory to speed up the rate at which instructions and data are supplied to the CPU by keeping copies of the most recently used memory items. For example, since computer programs spend a lot of time executing loops (i.e., exhibit "temporal locality"), the instructions for the second and subsequent iterations of a loop will be found in the cache. Similarly, data structures such as arrays, vectors, etc., frequently exhibit the property of "spatial locality"; thus, access to nearby data items will also find them in the cache. The inclusion of a cache memory in the system allows the microprocessor to operate at cache speeds much of the time rather than at the slower main memory speeds. In this textbook whenever we use the word "cache" by itself we will mean the "cache RAM" used for storage as well as the "cache controller."

1.2.3 Hierarchy of Buses

It is noted from the configurations in Figure 1.3 that a **hierarchy of buses** is used to interconnect the various components of the system. Coprocessors in Figure 1.3a which are directly connected to the microprocessor chip (sometimes referred to as *close coupling*) use the **CPU bus or processor (external) bus,**[6] which is defined by the I/O pins of the microprocessor. The other components of the system are interconnected through a second-level bus, the **local bus.** (If main memory is connected to this local bus, the bus is also called the **memory bus.**) In a number of system designs the local bus and the processor bus may be the same (and in such cases we will be referring to it interchangeably either as the processor bus or the local bus); if these two buses are different, then the proper "local bus interface" hardware is needed between them to adapt one bus to the other.

The whole system shown in Figure 1.3a can be implemented on a single printed-circuit board (a "motherboard"), in which case it is referred to as a *single-board system;* such systems have limited flexibility and make future expansions very difficult. A larger, more flexible, and easily expandable system is configured using a number of PC boards (*multiboard systems*), of different types, and even from different manufacturers, as shown in Figure 1.3b. In addition to the processor board (all of whose components are interconnected through the local bus), the system contains extra memory implemented on memory boards, and special "adapter boards" used to interface the system to particular peripheral devices and instruments that may require their own special "I/O buses." This third level of bus that interconnects all system boards is called the **global** or **system bus.**

While the CPU or processor bus is specific to the individual microprocessor, the system bus is independent of the microprocessor; i.e., it has its own set of specifications that the board manufacturers must satisfy. For that purpose, each board includes the proper hardware, called the "system bus interface," which allows it to interface to the system bus. The "system bus interface" logic included on the processor board of Figure 1.3b is used to convert the processor-dependent local bus to the processor-independent industry system bus. An example of such hierarchical bus configuration may have a microprocessor operating from a 100-MHz input clock, high-speed local peripherals (e.g., graphics) connected to a 33-MHz local bus, and standard low-speed peripherals connected to an 8-MHz system bus.

Bus characteristics, operation, and timing are important factors in memory and peripheral device interfacing; they are used to identify the specific address or data placed on the respective bus lines and the time required to carry out bus transactions. Such identification is valuable to the system designer/integrator, in order to single-step and debug the system under development instruction by instruction, and interface the microprocessor with

---

[6]Also called the *component-level bus.*

memories and peripherals that have different access times. It is also valuable to the software designer, who must also be aware of software compatibility problems arising when a system is built using a certain type of system bus (that may, for example, be transferring data bytes in its own order[7]) and a mix of 16-, 32-, or 64-bit microprocessor boards from different manufacturers, which themselves impose their own ordering of the most and least significant bytes within a 16-bit word, a 32-bit doubleword entity,[8] etc.

Processor and local bus. This bus is made up of the data bus, the address bus, and the control bus. The *data bus* is used to transfer instructions and data (operands/results); as deduced from the microprocessor examples in Figure 1.4, its width may or may not equal the wordlength of the microprocessor's internal architecture. Depending upon the width of the memory or I/O device with which the microprocessor exchanges data, data transfers may use only a portion of the data bus lines; for example, when a 32-bit processor exchanges data with a 16-bit device, only half of its 32-bit data bus will be involved in this data transfer. The *address bus* is used to transfer memory addresses (to select a memory location) or I/O port numbers (to select an I/O port). All 32-bit processors have 32-bit addresses that can directly access up to 4 GB (gigabytes) of main memory. *Memory addressing* refers to the fact that the address issued to memory always specifies the address of the first byte (the lowest byte address) of an operand; this is true regardless of the length of the operand or its byte ordering (big/little endian) in memory. Finally, control and timing signals use the *control bus* lines to synchronize the operation of the various system modules and facilitate their intercommunication activities over the buses.

System bus. Figure 1.3b shows a processor board (composed of the microprocessor, its interface logic that generates the local bus, and some local memory and I/O ports) connected to global (system) memory and global (system) I/O ports via an industry system bus (such as the Multibus, VMEbus, Futurebus, etc.). The complexity of the "system bus interface" circuitry on the processor board will depend on the particular system bus used and the size and complexity of the overall system. As with the processor and local buses, we will divide the system bus functionally into a "system address bus," a "system data bus," and a "system control bus." Physically, depending on the particular system bus, these lines may be separate, nonmultiplexed lines or they may be multiplexed. (Details of the specifications for a number of industry standard system buses and their interfacing are given in Chapter 4.)

Finally, Figure 1.3c shows the more complicated configuration of a multimicroprocessor system. Each processor has its own private memory and I/O resources that no other processor can access. However, the system also provides global (system) memory and I/O that are "shareable"; i.e., a processor on any processor board can request and gain control of the system bus, and use it to access a global memory location or a global I/O port. In this case, the "system bus interface" hardware on each processing board will include a separate component, called a "bus arbiter" (or "bus exchange"), to arbitrate among simultaneous requests of system bus access and determine which board will be given the shared system bus to execute its data transfers. (Bus arbitration is covered in more detail in Chapter 4.)

[7]The ordering of data bytes on the system bus is referred to as either *mad-endian* or *sad-endian* ordering and is discussed in more detail in Chapter 4.

[8]The microprocessor data ordering in memory is referred to as either *big-endian* or *little-endian* ordering and is discussed in more detail in Chapter 2.

1.3 MICROPROCESSOR: EXTERNAL VIEW

Before we discuss the individual I/O signals of a microprocessor, let's first take a look at different example configurations of microprocessors with external caches and/or MMUs. A number of them are shown in Figure 1.5. The figure includes microprocessors with and without external Harvard architecture.

Figure 1.5a shows example CISC microprocessors with an external cache; Figure 1.5b shows a RISC microprocessor with one external bus and separate ICACHE and DCACHE; and Figure 1.5c shows a RISC microprocessor with external Harvard architecture that defines two external buses: one for data (the *data bus*, which includes lines for transferring the address of the data and separate lines to transfer the data itself) and one for instructions (the *instruction bus*, which includes lines for transferring the address of the instruction and separate lines to transfer the instruction itself); these buses require their own separate sets of synchronization signals. The two buses of the Harvard architecture are used solely to sup-

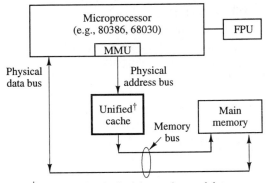

†Unified cache: for both instructions and data

(a) Microprocessor with external cache [10]

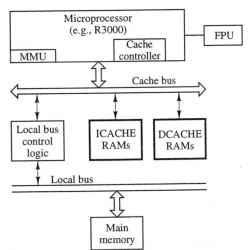

Figure 1.5 Example configurations of microprocessors with external caches and MMUs.

(b) Microprocessor with on-chip cache controller and external instruction and data cache RAMs (Adapted from [6] courtesy of IDT.)

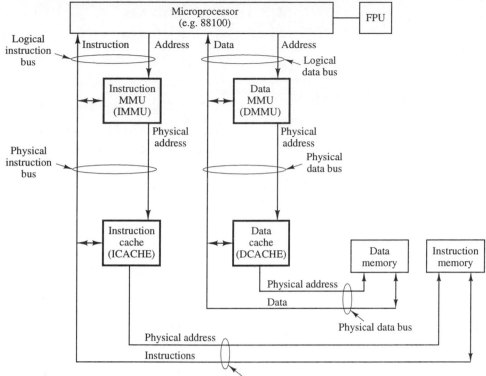

(c) Microprocessor with external MMUs and caches on separate Harvard architecture buses (the IMMU and ICACHE together constitute the Motorola 88200 CMMU chip)[10]

Figure 1.5 (concluded)

port the LOAD and STORE instructions. Since such an instruction takes two cycles to complete, one to calculate the address and one to do the transfer to/from memory, during the second cycle the prefetch unit cannot fetch the next instruction because the data bus lines are busy doing the transfer to/from memory. By providing separate external buses, the microprocessor can now use the data bus to execute the second cycle of the LOAD/STORE instruction and use the instruction bus to simultaneously fetch the next instruction. However, the two buses have different memory bandwidth requirements: instruction fetching requires a much higher memory bandwidth (because RISC-type processors need to fetch a larger number of their simpler instructions in order to implement the same functions that a single complex CISC instruction performs); on the other hand, the data bus bandwidth for a RISC processor is lower than that of a CISC processor (because most of these simple RISC instructions perform internal register-based operations that do not require access to external memory).

1.3.1 I/O Signals

Figure 1.6 shows the external view of CISC and RISC microprocessor chips with their I/O signals. In this section we discuss the address and data buses and some of the most important

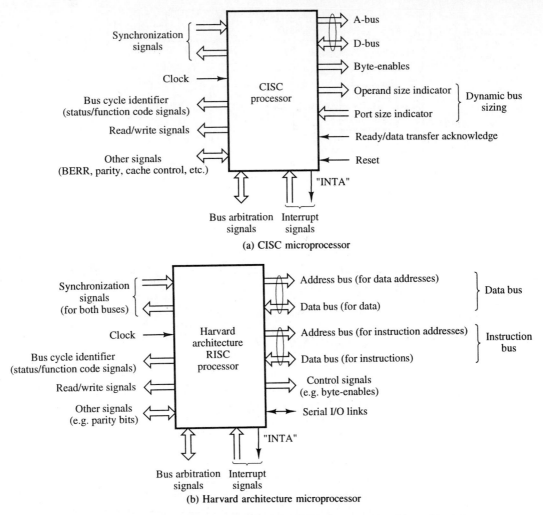

Figure 1.6 External view of CISC and RISC microprocessor chips with their processor (component-level) bus and most important status and control signals.

control signals found in almost all microprocessors. The remaining control signals will be covered in later chapters of the textbook.

Address and data buses. A microprocessor may have either one nonmultiplexed **address bus** (A bus) and a second, separate, **data bus** (D bus), or address and data may be multiplexed on the same lines of one bus called the **address/data bus** (AD bus). Figure 1.7 shows the external address and data buses of the microprocessors listed in Figure 1.4.

A bus is called a (time-) **multiplexed bus** when it transfers different types of information at different, well-defined times during the bus cycle (for example, the R4000 bus). In a multiplexed bus, each transmitter and receiver has one designated time slot. Multiplex-

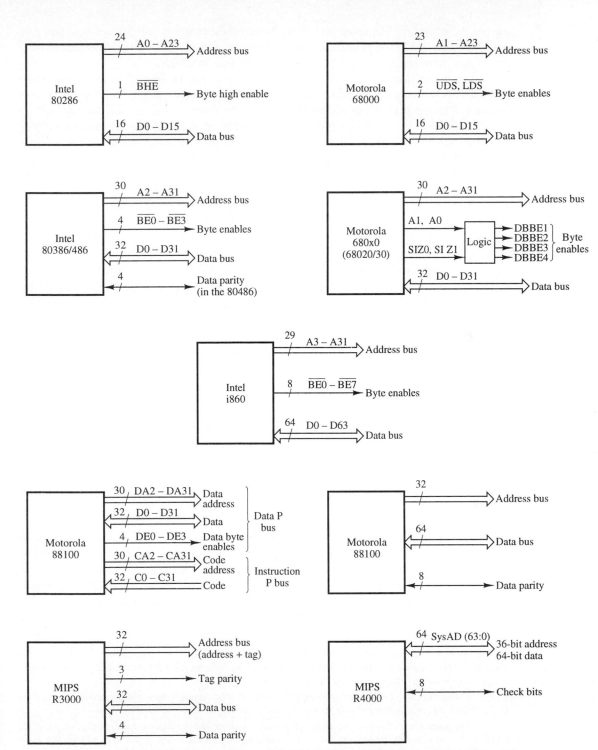

Figure 1.7 External address and data buses of the microprocessors shown in Figure 1.4.

ing has the advantage that fewer pins are required on the chip.[9] A multiplexed bus, however, imposes additional external interface hardware requirements. Most of the recent microprocessors now have separate, *nonmultiplexed* address and data buses.

Another distinction among microprocessor buses has to do with whether the whole byte-address is placed on the address lines or not. For example, all Intel microprocessors of Figure 1.7 do not place all of the address bits on the address bus; instead, they decode internally the lower-order address bits to generate what are called the **byte-enable** signals on separate output pins[10]: the Intel 32-bit 80386/486 microprocessors[11] decode the A1 and A0 bits internally to generate four "byte-enables," BE0#–BE3#, one for each of the two byte-sections of the 32-bit memory[12]; the RISC-type Intel i860 microprocessor places on the address bus the 29 most significant address bits (A3–A31) of the 32-bit address, while it decodes the three least significant bits, A0–A2, to generate eight separate byte enables, BE0#–BE7#, one for each of the eight byte-sections of the 64-bit memory. (The i860 has a 64-bit data bus.) In the Motorola case, the earlier 68000 places on the address bus the 23 most significant bits of its 24-bit address; instead of the A0, it generates two byte enable signals, the upper and lower data strobes (UDS# and LDS#), one for each of the two byte-sections of the 16-bit memory. The Motorola 32-bit 68020/30 microprocessors require external logic to decode bits A1 and A0 (along with the "operand size indicator" bits SIZ0 and SIZ1 to be explained later) in order to generate the four data bus byte enable signals DBBE1–DBBE4 for the 32-bit memory.

As mentioned earlier, some RISC microprocessors define separate processor buses for the instructions and the data (operands) and have dual external bus interfaces. For example, the Motorola 88100 (also see Figure 1.5c) has a *data P bus* (with its own address lines for the data addresses and data lines for the data) and separate *instruction P bus* (with its own address lines for the instruction addresses and data lines for the instructions). Since the data to be transferred may be of any size, the data P bus requires the four data byte enables DE0–DE3. Instructions are always fetched as 32-bit doublewords from doubleword addresses.

Finally, some microprocessors provide extra pins to carry some additional information, such as a parity bit for each byte on the data bus (e.g., the 80486, 88110, and the R3000/4000).

Bus cycle identifiers. At the beginning of a bus cycle, the processor issues a set of signals called the **bus cycle identifiers** (usually in the form or "status" or "function code" signals) to inform the rest of the system modules of the type of bus cycle it has initiated. Figure 1.8a shows the most common types of microprocessor bus cycles, and Figure 1.8b, the "bus cycle identifying" signals of various microprocessors. It is noticed that the

---

[9]That's why earlier microprocessors which could not provide enough pins were forced to muliplex their external bus lines.

[10]As we will see later in more detail, a "byte enable" signal selects one "byte-section" of a memory: For example, a "16-bit memory" is composed of two "byte-sections" that require 2 byte enables; a "32-bit memory" of four "byte-sections" that require four byte enables, etc.

[11]The earlier 16-bit 80286 issues only one "byte high enable" signal, which along with address bit A0 are used to trigger the even and/or odd byte section of a 16-bit memory.

[12]The pound mark (#) after a signal designates negative logic and corresponds to the overbar used over the signal. Quite often, usually for industry standard "system buses," instead of the pound mark (#) the star (*) or slash (/) symbol is used. In this textbook we will be using mainly the pound mark (#) and the overbar interchangeably.

Type of Bus Cycle

Data read cycle (read user data from memory)
Code read cycle (read user program from memory)
Data write cycle (write user data to memory)
Data read cycle (read supervisor data from memory)
Code read cycle (read supervisor program from memory)
Data write cycle (write supervisor data to memory)
Input cycle (read data from an input port)
Output cycle (write data to an output port)
Interrupt acknowledge cycle

(a) Several types of bus cycles. (Some processors also
include a "halt" or "idle" bus cycle.)

INTEL 80386[4]

M/IO#	D/C#	W/R#	Bus cycle type		Locked?
Low	Low	Low	Interrupt acknowledge		Yes
Low	Low	High	Does not occur		—
Low	High	Low	I/O data read		No
Low	High	High	I/O data write		No
High	Low	Low	Memory code read		No
High	Low	High	Halt:	Shutdown:	No
			Address = 2	Address = 0	
			(BEO# High	(BEO# Low	
			BE1# High	BE1# High	
			BE2# Low	BE2# High	
			BE3# High	BE3# High	
			A2–A31 Low)	A2–A31 Low)	
High	High	Low	Memory data read		Some cycles
High	High	High	Memory data write		Some cycles

[4] Reprinted by permission of Intel Corporation. © 1986 by Intel Corp.

MOTOROLA 68020/30[8]

FC2	FC1	FC0	Address space
0	0	0	(Undefined, reserved)[a]
0	0	1	User data space
0	1	0	User program space
0	1	1	(Undefined, reserved)[a]
1	0	0	(Undefined, reserved)[a]
1	0	1	Supervisor data space
1	1	0	Supervisor program space
1	1	1	CPU space
			(see table at right)

A19–A16				CPU space type
1	1	1	1	Interrupt acknowledge
0	0	1	0	Coprocessor communication
0	0	0	1	Access lever control
				(CALLM, RETM)
0	0	0	0	Breakpoint acknowledge

[a]Address space 3 is reserved for user definition, while 0
and 4 are reserved for future use by Motorola.

(b) Bus cycle identifiers

Figure 1.8 (a) Common types of bus cycles; (b) examples of "bus cycle identifiers."
(See the Appendices for the bus cycle identifiers of other microprocessors.)

Intel microprocessors identify the bus cycle by a combination of several control signals, while the Motorola microprocessors use the three output "function code" signals FC2–FC0.

Synchronization signals. **Synchronization** signals are needed to synchronize the operation of the microprocessor with the other components of the system. Output synchronization signals (in the form of an "address strobe" and "data strobe") indicate when address and data are valid on the respective bus lines; input synchronization signals (in the form of a "ready" or "data transfer acknowledge") indicate when the addressed memory or I/O port has responded. Microprocessors that operate asynchronously with their slave devices[13] (like most of the Motorola products) require a pair of "handshake signals" to accomplish their synchronization; for example, a Motorola processor will send to memory the signal "address strobe" to indicate that it has placed an address on the address bus, and the memory will send back to the processor the feedback "data transfer acknowledge" to tell the processor that memory has finished its requested transaction (of either placing data on the data bus or receiving the data that was on the data bus). The 16-bit 68000 uses one feedback signal, the **DTACK#,** while the 32-bit 680x0 microprocessors receive a pair of signals, **DSACK0#** and **DSACK1#**.

Operand size and port size indicators. A number of advanced microprocessors have the capability to dynamically (at run time) adjust the width of the external data bus, according to the size (width) of the memory or I/O port they communicate with. The Motorola products issue an **operand size indicator** (the SIZ0 and SIZ1 pair of signals) to indicate the size of the operand transferred: 00 means 4 bytes (one doubleword), 10 means 2 bytes, 01 means 1 byte, and 11 means 3 bytes (in the case of the 68020/30) or a 16-byte "cache line" (in the case of the 68040). As a feedback signal (called **port size indicator**) that identifies the size of the port attached to the processor, the Intel products sample an input pin called BS16# or BS8# (indicating a port size of 16 or 8 bits, respectively), while the Motorola products interpret the values on their input pins DSACK0# and DSACK1#.

Interrupts and bus arbitration signals. **Interrupt** lines are used by external devices to interrupt the processor and force it to jump to the appropriate interrupt-handling routine whose execution will service the interrupting device. **Bus arbitration** lines are used to allow connecting a number of devices to the same bus (for example, a number of microprocessors, DMA controllers, etc.) so that in an orderly manner only one device will be granted control of the shared bus to start a bus cycle. Interrupts and bus arbitration are discussed in more detail in later chapters.

Other control signals. The **clock input** signal C represents the timing source that defines the input clock cycles and times all activities of the processor external bus. Sometimes it is called the "system clock signal" because it is also supplied to the other modules of the system. Some microprocessor chips require a single-phase clock (the most common situation), whereas others require a two-phase clock (phase 1 and phase 2).

All processors have some kind of **read** and **write** control signals to identify the type of access to memory and I/O. In some processors two processor control signals need to be

---

[13]That is, the processor and the slaves may have their own separate clock sources, each device operating at a different speed.

combined externally to generate the control signal applied to the slave device; for example, to supply to an Intel memory the "memory write" signal, the microprocessors's M/IO# = H and W/R# = H of Figure 1.8b must be combined with external logic. For small systems, the read- and write-type control signals that the microprocessor itself issues are sufficient to be applied to local memory and I/O ports. For larger systems, external circuits in the form of "bus controllers" may be needed to convert the processor's signals to system-wide read and write signals; for example, the Intel external bus controllers generate separate read/write "commands" for memory (called MRDC# and MWTC#) and for input/output ports (called IORC# and IOWC#).

All processors also have a **reset** input pin, which is the highest interrupt that resets the processor to a known internal state. The reset input has different effects on the various microprocessors: in almost all cases, when a reset occurs, the microprocessor address and data buses go to a high-impedance state, all output control signals go to the inactive state, the interrupt system is disabled not to accept external interrupts, and the current bus cycle ends. For those microprocessors that have both user and supervisor modes of operation, the supervisor mode is entered and the appropriate value (the "reset vector") is loaded into the program counter.

The **ready** input signal is used by microprocessors that operate in synchronism with the slave devices[14] (as, for example, in the case of the Intel products) to accommodate memory and I/O devices that cannot transfer data at the processor's fast bus bandwidth. When the microprocessor samples the READY signal asserted, it knows that the action requested has been completed and that the addressed memory or I/O device has placed data on, or accepted data from, the data lines. This allows the microprocessor to end the current bus cycle and advance to the next bus transfer. If it samples the READY signal not asserted, the microprocessor then enters a **wait state**. At the same time it issues appropriate control signals to inform the other system modules that the microprocessor is now in a wait state. While in a wait state, the microprocessor still has control of the local bus.

1.3.2 Local Bus Interface Components

Not all microprocessor chips provide the separate, nonmultiplexed address and data buses required by the slave devices in the system. Furthermore, the required control and timing signals are not always supplied to the slave devices directly from the microprocessor chip itself, because of distance and driving capability considerations. Similarly, not all control signals generated at various points in the system and sent to the master module are applied directly to the microprocessor input pins; in some cases they are applied instead to support components external to the microprocessor chip.

In general, an *interface* is a shared boundary between parts of a microcomputer system, through which information is conveyed. The *interface system* consists of the device-dependent elements (which include all driving and receiving circuits, connectors, and timing and control protocols) of an interface necessary to effect unambiguous data transfers between devices. Information is communicated between devices via the bus, and each device conforms to the interface system definition.

Figure 1.9a shows that interface logic must be included on both the bus master module and the memory slave module. The memory interface logic circuits will be discussed in

---

[14]That is, the microprocessor and slave devices are driven by the same clock source.

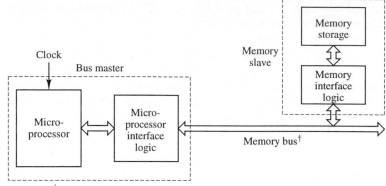

†May be the "component level" or processor bus, the "local bus", or the
"system bus", depending where the memory slave is connected to.

(a) Interface logic on the microprocessor CPU and memory sides

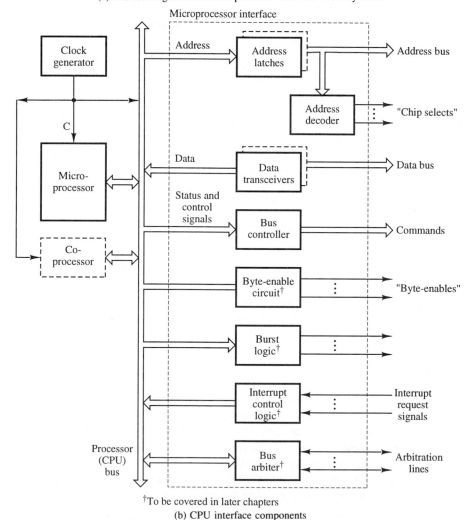

†To be covered in later chapters

(b) CPU interface components

Figure 1.9 Microprocessor-side interface components.

Chapter 3. The "microprocessor interface logic" is circuitry that may be required for several reasons: to demultiplex and/or buffer the CPU's local address and data lines, to interface the microprocessor chip with other system modules by providing them with appropriate system control signals, or to receive from them system control signals and apply them in turn to the microprocessor chip. The complexity of this circuitry (i.e., the number of interface components) depends upon the specific microprocessor chip, and the size and complexity of the final system designed.

Figure 1.9b gives the most common microprocessor interface components; not all of them are needed in each design. We discuss below the clock generator, address latches and address decoder, the data transceivers, the bus controller, and the byte-enable circuitry. The remaining interface components are discussed in later chapters.

Bus drivers or **buffers** are required to place information on the bus. A semiconductor device driving the bus may have either open-collector or tri-state (3ST) outputs. Devices with *open-collector* outputs have only two output states: logic 0 (zero), i.e., the gate pulls the output line to logic 0 (zero), using an active circuit element (the gate's internal output transistor), and logic 1 (one), i.e., the output line is pulled back to logic 1 (one) by a passive circuit element (an external pull-up resistor). Devices that have open-collector outputs allow the logical AND among their outputs simply by having these outputs tied together. For this reason, this connection is also called[15] *wired-AND* or *AND-tied*. The opposite holds for the *tri-state* devices used in bus-based architectures. They prevent excessive loading or driving of the bus lines, and allow many devices to be connected to the bus. Devices connected to the bus must have tri-state outputs: the first two states are the logic 0 and 1 (0.8 and 3.5 volts for TTL); the third state is a high-impedance state or open circuit. A tri-state device has both an active pull-up transistor and an active pull-down transistor in its output [to define the logic 1 (one) and logic 0 (zero) states], but a third, extra input terminal is used to disable the output. When the output is disabled, it is said that the output *floats*. This third state is often called the *high-Z* or *high-impedance state*. When a device is placed in its high-impedance state, it is considered to be electrically disconnected from the bus. Thus, many tri-state devices (drivers) may be connected to the same bus, with their respective outputs forming the logical OR with each other. For this reason this connection is also called *wire-ORed, OR-tied,* or *bus-configuration*. Appropriate control (or select) signals must be applied to select only one of them to drive the bus, while holding all other drivers "disconnected" from the bus.

Address latches (registers with D-type flip-flops) are used to latch the address and hold it as long as required. (We say that the latch operates in a "transparent mode" when the strobe remains active or its "output-enable" OE# pin is grounded to logic 0.) If the processor bus is multiplexed, the external latches are strobed by the ALE or AS signal the processor issues at the beginning of a new bus cycle to demultiplex the bus and provide at their outputs a nonmultiplexed address which remains valid for the duration of the whole bus cycle.

When memory or I/O devices are connected directly to the multiplexed local data bus, it is essential that they be prevented from corrupting the information (usually, an address) present on this bus during the first clock cycle of the bus cycle. Most often, interfacing requirements become simpler if the data bus is buffered. Buffering the data bus also offers

---

[15]When negative logic is used, in which the less-positive level corresponds to logic 1, the open-collector-driven bus lines perform the *wired-OR* function.

both increased drive current capability and capacitive load immunity. For the bidirectional data bus, this buffering is accomplished by using external bidirectional bus drivers (transmitters) and receivers, implemented on the same chip, called the **data transceiver**.

Address decoders are used to receive some address bits off the address bus, decode them, and generate the appropriate "chip-select" signals. Address decoders are also used to identify address ranges and determine whether the current access is for a device connected to the local processor bus or to the global system bus (as we will explain later). Decoders may also be needed to decode status or function code signals (which identify the type of bus cycle).

Another interface circuit shown in Figure 1.9b is the **bus controller** (also called *system controller*) used to convert the microprocessor's control signals to those needed by a system bus. It receives status and control signals from the microprocessor and converts them into system-wide command signals. For example, it may be the bus controller itself that generates the ALE signal to the local address latches and the control signals DT/R# and DEN to the transceivers in the microprocessor interface.

1.4 MICROPROCESSOR: INTERNAL VIEW

In this section we present the common architectural components found inside most microprocessors, while more advanced pipelined microprocessors are discussed in Section 1.6. Figure 1.10 shows what a representative microprocessor chip may contain; dashed lines are used to identify those components found primarily in more advanced microprocessors. The simplified internal block diagrams of a number of representative microprocessors are shown in the Appendices.

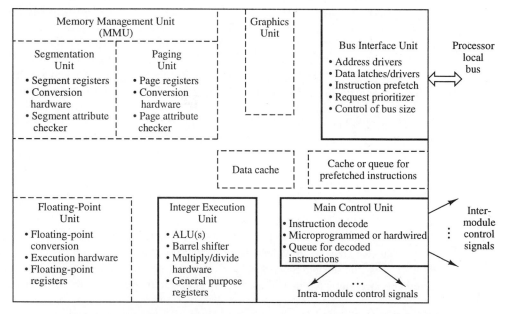

Figure 1.10 Internal components of a microprocessor. (Components within dashed lines are found in some but not all microprocessors.)

Although the different components of these microprocessors will be discussed later in the textbook, we give here a brief overview. For example, it is observed from Figure A.10 in Appendix A that the 80486 has on-chip an 8K-byte cache and an FPU that the 80386 does not have; because of the on-chip cache, the 80486 has a much more sophisticated bus interface unit (with "write buffers" and appropriate hardware to support "burst bus cycles"). Comparing the Motorola 68030 and 68040 in Figure B.8, we notice that the 68040 has placed the FPU on-chip, and split the MMU into a DMMU and an IMMU placed on separate internal buses (an instruction bus and a data bus) to conform with the internal Harvard architecture of the microprocessor. While the above microprocessors have a 32-bit internal architecture and a 32-bit external data bus (also see Figure 1.4), the Intel i860 RISC microprocessor of Figure C.2a has a 32-bit internal architecture and a 64-bit external data bus, has placed on-chip the FPU, the MMU, the ICACHE, and the DCACHE, has introduced an on-chip graphics unit, and internally has a 64-bit and an 128-bit bus. Comparing the Motorola RISC microprocessors of the 88000 series in Figure C.6, we notice that the 88110 has on-chip DMMU and IMMU, a second integer unit, a pair of graphics units, and has replaced the 88100 data and instruction pipes with a DCACHE and an ICACHE, respectively; externally, the 88100 has a Harvard architecture with a pair of buses, while the 88110 multiplexes the addresses and data internally on a single set of external bus lines. Finally, the R4000 in Figure C.12 has a 64-bit internal architecture and a 64-bit external data bus, and has integrated on-chip the FPU, an I-cache, and a D-cache unit that the R3000 had externally.

The three units inside solid lines in Figure 1.10, i.e., the bus interface unit, the control unit, and the integer execution unit, are found in all microprocessors, and are discussed here in more detail. The components inside dashed lines are not found in all microprocessors and are discussed in later chapters.

1.4.1 Bus Interface Unit

The bus interface unit is responsible for all processor bus activities; it works in an independent fashion from the rest of the microprocessor internal components. It initiates external bus cycles when so requested by the CPU and maximizes bus utilization by prefetching instructions from memory whenever the microprocessor external bus is free.

Some of its major logic hardware includes address latches and drivers, data transceivers, a prefetcher circuit that prefetches instructions from memory even before they are needed, hardware to prioritize the various requests for bus cycles that different internal sections of the microprocessor request, and a bus controller. The bus controller can receive input signals from the addressed device to identify the device's width (or size) in order to properly interpret data presented to the microprocessor's input data pins; it also contains multiplexing circuitry to route the incoming data to the correct position in an internal data register, or for a write cycle, to position the data to the correct output data pins. (This is explained in Chapter 2.) The bus controller may operate at the slower speed of the external bus lines while the remaining internal sections of the microprocessor may operate at their own faster speed (as is the case of the 486DX2[†]).

We saw earlier that some RISC microprocessors have a "load/store interface" to provide separate ports for the simultaneous access to instruction- and data-memory spaces. This

---

[†]The 486DX2 operates internally at twice the clock speed of the rest of the system; i.e., the 486DX2/50 operates internally at 50 MHz while the external subsystem still operates at 25 MHz. (Thus the 50-MHz 486DX2 works with existing 25-MHz motherboard designs but performs substantially better than a 25-MHz 486.)

two-port, nonmultiplexed memory access scheme requires separate parts in the bus interface unit, the ''instruction interface unit,'' and the ''data interface unit'' to control these memory modules.

1.4.2 Control Unit

The control unit is used for instruction decoding and sequencing. Its implementation may be either microprogrammed (usually for CISC processors) or hardwired (usually for RISC processors). It contains the proper timing circuitry (driven by basic clock pulses) to provide internal and external timed control signals to facilitate the data transfers. The control unit also contains a control sequencer to control the bus interface unit (by requesting from it instruction prefetches and validating their reception). Recent microprocessors, instead of only a single instruction register, provide a larger instruction buffer or queue to hold a number of instructions prefetched by the bus interface unit. For example, the Intel 80386 has a 12-byte code queue, while the 80486 has a 32-byte code queue; the Motorola 68020 and 68030 have a 3-word-deep instruction pipe. (See the Appendices for the detailed internal structure of these processors.)

To carry out its tasks properly, the control unit must provide for at least the following four capabilities:

1. Establish the state during each machine cycle.
2. Provide logic for determining the correct ''next state''; this next-state selection is done through a proper combination of the present-state information, the microprocessor's external inputs, and certain feedback lines, either from within the microprocessor chip (e.g., flags from the ALU) or from external components in the system.
3. Provide a facility to store the information that identifies the current state.
4. Finally, provide some means for translating this state into proper intra-module and inter-module control signals to be issued by the microprocessor. Since all microprocessors synchronize their events with single- or multiple-phase input clocks, these control signals are issued in synchronism with precise clock pulses. The input clock source, therefore, synchronizes all state transitions of the system.

The control section of a RISC processor is usually hardwired, because speed is much more important than flexibility and compatibility and because RISC instructions have simple and fixed formats. The hardwired implementation results in a smaller control section than that of the microprogrammed approach; however, it is inflexible and presents design difficulties which lead to nonstructured, quite complex configurations. As the complexity of the processor increases, it becomes more expensive than the microprogrammed approach, primarily in terms of development cost. Modifications are also very difficult, since changing the visible machine requires new chip layouts, etc.

Most CISC microprocessors have used microprogrammed implementations for the design of their control section, to allow flexibility, ease of expansion, and upward compatibility. Various groups of microinstructions, forming microroutines, are usually incorporated into a complex system. The (macro) instruction, when properly decoded by the control unit, points to the appropriate microroutine in the control store. Execution of the microroutine corresponds to executing the required microinstruction sequences that implement the needed microoperations. The microprogrammed approach has the advantages of leading to a more "regular" design and providing enhanced instruction flexibility. Future changes and improvements are much easier, since this now requires only changing the microroutines in the control store. Microcoding, however, is slower than random hardwired logic.

1.4.3 Integer Execution Unit

The integer execution unit is responsible for carrying out all the integer arithmetic and logic operations of the CPU. Sometimes it may also be used to perform the computations for generating the "effective address" of an operand. For that purpose, it includes the following hardware: the necessary arithmetic/logic units (adders and a barrel shifter) and hardware multipliers/dividers; general-purpose registers (used for arithmetic/logic operands and results, and for input/output quantities); special registers (that hold intermediate results); and finally, the required local control circuitry.

CISC and RISC microprocessors differ in their typical register structure in that CISC chips generally have small number of registers while RISC chips have much larger number of registers to hold the operands. Increasing the number of internal registers increases (1) the requirements for on-chip real estate needed to implement them, (2) the width of the instructions (to be able to specify the added registers), and (3) the additional hardware needed in the form of multiplexers for storing into or reading data from these registers. When it comes time for the processor to switch from one task to another and needs to save the current task's "context" (i.e., the contents of all its registers) in memory, the larger the number of registers, the longer it will take it to save its context.

The width of the general-purpose registers usually conforms with the basic wordlength of the microprocessor; for example, 32-bit microprocessors have 32-bit registers, with capabilities of addressing an 8- or 16-bit quantity within a register, or concatenating two registers to hold 64-bit quantities.

1.5 SYSTEM OPERATION

1.5.1 Instruction Formats

CISC instruction format. We mentioned earlier that CISC microprocessors have much more complex instructions than RISC microprocessors. As an example consider the general instruction format in Figure 1.11 for the Intel 80386/486 CISC microprocessors [5]. (Not all fields are shown.) These instructions consist of one or two primary opcode bytes, possibly an address specifier consisting of the "mod r/m" byte and "scaled index" byte, a displacement if required, and an immediate data field if required. Within the primary opcode or opcodes, smaller encoding fields may be defined. These fields vary according to the class of operation. The fields define such information as direction d of the operations (to/from), size of the displacements w, register encoding sreg2, sreg3, or sign extension s. The remaining fields of a long instruction and specify register and address mode, address displacement, and/or immediate data.

The complexity of the instruction format and its number of different fields make its decoding cumbersome. Such a complex CISC instruction may specify a large number of addressing modes, including direct, based, base plus displacement, index plus displacement, base plus displacement plus index, etc.

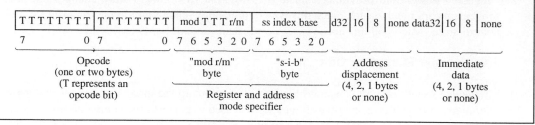

(a) General instruction format

Field name	Description	Number of bits
w	Specifies if data is byte or full size (full size is either 16 or 32 bits)	1
d	Specifies direction of data operation	1
s	Specifies if an immediate data field must be sign-extended	1
reg	General register specifier	3
mod r/m	Address mode specifier (effective address can be a general register)	2 for mod; 3 for r/m
ss	Scale factor for scaled index address mode	2
index	General register to be used as index register	3
base	General register to be used as base register	3
sreg2	Segment register specifier for CS, SS, DS, ES	2
sreg3	Segment register specifier for CS, SS, DS, ES, FS, GS	3
tttn	For conditional instructions, specifies a condition asserted or a condition negated	4

(b) Fields within the instructions

Figure 1.11   Intel 80386/486 CISC instruction formats [5]. Reprinted by permission of Intel Corporation. © 1989 by Intel Corp.

RISC instruction format.   Compared to the long, complex, and many-addressing-mode CISC instruction formats, RISC microprocessors have very simple and short instructions. Figure 1.12 shows the three instruction formats for a RISC-type microprocessor, the R3000/4000 microprocessors. Each instruction consists of a single 32-bit doubleword aligned on a doubleword boundary (i.e., an address evenly divisible by 4). Having a small number of formats simplifies the decoding, shortening the execution time of the instruction. Less frequently used operations and addressing modes can be synthesized by the compiler by using sequences of these simple instructions.

The R3000/4000 instructions can be divided into the following groups [7]:
>   *Load and store* instructions: move data between memory and general registers. They are all I-type instructions, since the only addressing mode supported is base register plus 16-bit signed immediate offset.
>   *Computational* instructions: perform arithmetic, logical, shift, multiply, and divide operations on values in registers. They occur in both R-type (both the operands and the result are stored in registers) and I-type (one operand is a 16-bit immediate value) formats.
>   *Jump and branch* instructions: change the control flow of a program. Jumps are always to a paged, absolute address formed by combining a 26-bit target address with

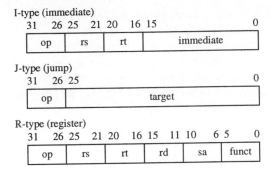

I-type (immediate)

```
31    26 25   21 20   16 15              0
┌──────┬──────┬──────┬──────────────────┐
│  op  │  rs  │  rt  │    immediate     │
└──────┴──────┴──────┴──────────────────┘
```

J-type (jump)

```
31    26 25                             0
┌──────┬────────────────────────────────┐
│  op  │            target              │
└──────┴────────────────────────────────┘
```

R-type (register)

```
31    26 25   21 20   16 15  11 10   6 5   0
┌──────┬──────┬──────┬──────┬──────┬──────┐
│  op  │  rs  │  rt  │  rd  │  sa  │ funct│
└──────┴──────┴──────┴──────┴──────┴──────┘
```

op	6-bit operation code
rs	5-bit source register specifier
rt	5-bit target (source/destination) register or branch condition
immediate	16-bit immediate value, branch displacement or address displacement
target	26-bit jump target address
rd	5-bit destination register specifier
sa	5-bit shift amount
funct	6-bit function field

Figure 1.12 R3000/4000 RISC instruction formats [7].

the high-order bits of the program counter (J-type format) or register addresses (R-type format). Branches have 16-bit offsets relative to the program counter (I-type). "Jump-AndLink" instructions save a return address in internal register 31.

Coprocessor instructions: perform operations in the coprocessors. Coprocessor load and store instructions are I-type.

Coprocessor 0 instructions: perform operations on CP0 registers to manipulate the memory management and exception-handling facilities of the processor.

Special instructions: perform system calls and breakpoint operations. These instructions are always R-type.

Exception instructions: cause a branch to the general exception-handling vector based upon the result of a comparison. These instructions occur in both R-type (both the operands and the result are in registers) and I-type (one operand is a 16-bit immediate value) formats.

1.5.2 Bus Cycles, Clock Cycles, and "States"

A microprocessor carries out the instruction cycle by executing one or more bus cycles, B1, B2, B3, ... **A bus cycle**[16] (also referred to as "local bus cycle" or "external bus cycle") begins whenever the microprocessor needs to access an external memory location or I/O port, i.e., whenever it places an address on the address bus. Therefore, a bus cycle is the sequence of properly timed basic activities required to do a read (or input) cycle, a write (or output) cycle, or a more complex read–modify–write cycle. The simplest possible instruction is the one that can be fetched and executed using only one bus cycle. Once the whole instruction has been fetched, its execution cycle may or may not require additional external

[16]The term "bus cycle" we use here corresponds to what some manufacturers—Intel in particular—refer to as a "machine cycle."

bus cycles (depending upon whether or not it needs to access memory or I/O). This subdivision of an instruction cycle into bus and clock cycles is shown in Figure 1.13.

All basic internal activities of the microprocessor chip (the "microoperations") and all bus cycles that the microprocessor initiates on its external bus must be executed at well-coordinated times. This is accomplished by sometimes using two different clocks, one external and one internal. They are called the "input clock" (which we will denote C) and the "internal processor clock" (which we will denote Cp).

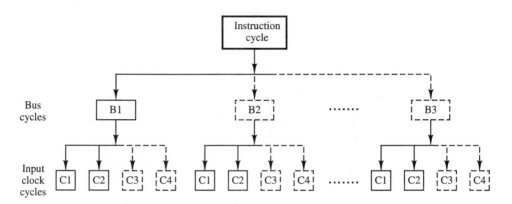

Figure 1.13 An instruction cycle is subdivided into bus cycles B1, B2, . . . (at least one bus cycle). A bus cycle is subdivided into input clock cycles C1, C2, ... (In some microprocessors a bus cycle is made up of a minimum of 2 input clock cycles, in others of 3, and in others of 4 input clock cycles.)

The **input clock C** (also referred to as the "bus clock") is used to drive all bus signal timing; in other words, it establishes the local bus cycle time and controls (clocks) all transfers between the microprocessor and memory or I/O ports. Everything that happens in the system is synchronized to the input clock's rising or falling edges, and for that reason it is also referred to as the **primary, master,** or **system clock.** For example, a microprocessor with an input clock of 16 MHz frequency will have the basic events occur every $C = 62.5$ ns (or even 31.25 ns if the rising and falling edges of the clock are used). This input clock has an **(input) clock cycle** (actually, an "input clock cycle time") equal to the period from positive/negative edge to positive/negative edge; in the above example, the clock[17] cycle is $C = 62.5$ ns.

This input clock C is supplied to the microprocessor from an external *clock generator/driver* chip that acts as a constant frequency source. Figure 1.14a depicts a microprocessor driven by a 16-MHz clock, composed of clock cycles C1, C2, C3, ... Figure 1.14b and c show the clock generators that drive various Intel and Motorola microprocessors. (At the right-hand side of the clock timings we give the actual names the manufacturers use.) The clock generator itself requires an external series-resonant crystal input (or constant frequency source) whose frequency may or may not be the same as that of the generated output clock C. Quite often, the clock generator provides a second clock output, called a **periph-**

---

[17]Whenever we use the word "clock" by itself, we will mean the "input clock"; when a processor has more than one input clock, we will mean the "basic input clock."

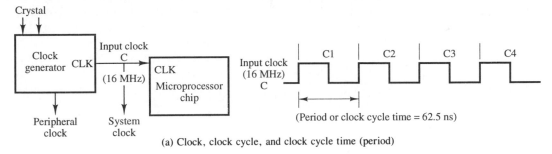

(a) Clock, clock cycle, and clock cycle time (period)

Figure 1.14 Input clock, processor clock, states, and bus cycles for representative Intel and Motorola microprocessors.

eral clock or PCLK, usually at one half the frequency of C. The phase of this "peripheral clock" matches the phase of the internally generated clock (called "processor clock" or Cp), and may be supplied to external support components. The use of this second peripheral clock simplifies system design because it allows the bus interface components to operate at half the speed imposed by the processor's input clock, imposing on them less stringent requirements. For example, consider the clock for the Intel 80386; its external 82384 clock generator produces two clocks: one it calls CLK2, which corresponds to our C, and the other CLK, which has half the frequency of CLK2 and used as a "peripheral clock." The phase of the CLK matches that of the processor clock signal (Cp in Figure 1.14b) generated internally by the 80386.

The internal **processor clock Cp** is distributed throughout the microprocessor chip and used to time all internal logic units. The timing of internal microoperations execution is synchronized to this internal processor clock's rising or falling edges. The processor clock Cp can be either generated internally from the input clock C (the most common case) or supplied externally to the microprocessor along with C (as in the case of the Motorola 68040 of Figure 1.14c). As can be seen from Figure 1.14, some Intel products (for example, the 16-bit 80286 and the 32-bit 80386) divide[18] the input C internally by 2 to generate the internal clock Cp, while others (for example, the 16-bit 8086 and the 32-bit 80486) use C as their internal processor clock Cp, too. In the Motorola case, most products multiply clock C by 2 internally to produce the internal Cp, except for the 32-bit 68040, which receives from the external clock generator both the input clock C (at its pin BCLK) and the double-frequency processor clock Cp (at its pin PCLK). All 68040 external synchronous timing for bus transfers refers to the input BCLK, while internal timing derives from PCLK. (BCLK must be exactly half the frequency of PCLK, and internally, PCLK provides timing reference points within each BCLK period.)

As we said earlier, a **bus cycle** corresponds to the time needed to do a data transfer between the processor and the addressed slave device. A bus cycle is always an integral multiple of the input clock cycle C. The maximum data transfer rate for a bus operation (the **processor bus bandwidth**) is determined not only by the frequency of this input clock C, but also by the width of the microprocessor's external data bus. For example, let's assume that the processor is driven by a 16-MHz input clock and that a bus cycle requires four input

[18]An Intel 80286 or 80386 driven by a 32-MHz clock CLK has an internal processor clock of 16 MHz and, therefore, is usually referred to as a "16-MHz microprocessor."

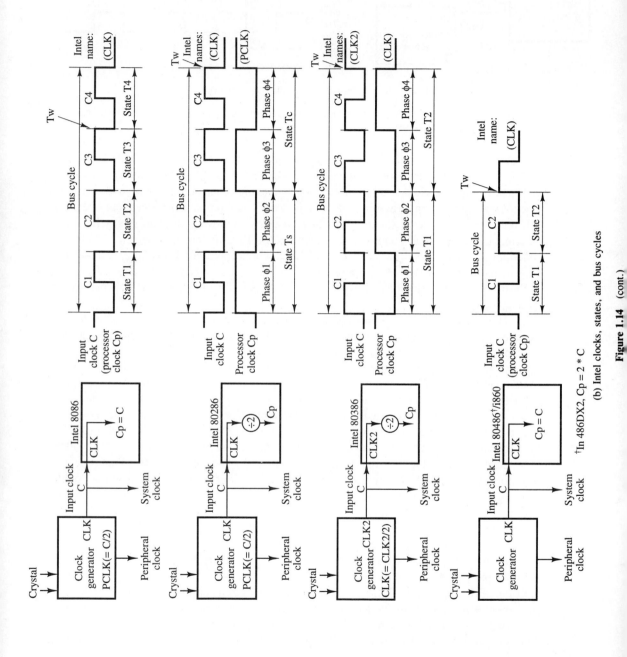

Figure 1.14 (cont.)

(b) Intel clocks, states, and bus cycles

†In 486DX2, Cp = 2 * C

34

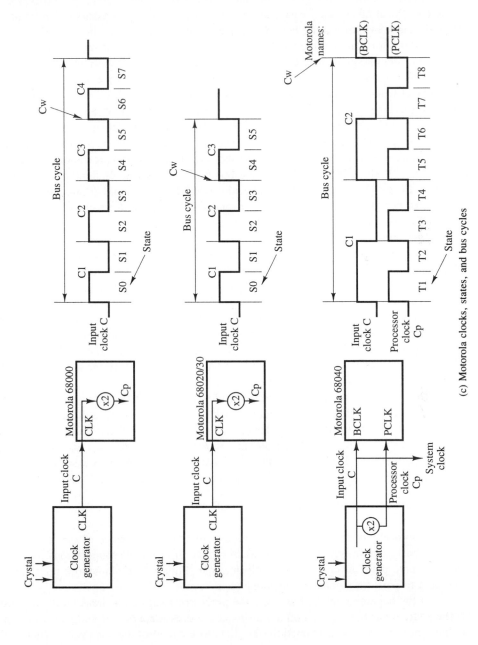

(c) Motorola clocks, states, and bus cycles

Figure 1.14 (concluded)

clock cycles, C1, C2, C3, and C4. Then, if the data bus is 16 bits wide, the *maximum data transfer rate* for this processor would be 2 bytes every four clock cycles, or 8 megabytes per second; if the data bus is 32 bits, the *maximum data transfer rate* would be 16 megabytes per second.

It can be seen from Figure 1.14 that the duration of what each microprocessor calls a **state** (or ''local bus state'') varies among the various microprocessors (even among those from the same manufacturer). For some products the ''state'' is smaller than the input clock cycle time C; for example, the 68040 ''state'' equals one-fourth the input clock cycle, while the 68000 and 68020/30 ''state'' is half the input clock cycle. Asserting and sampling external signals can be done for Motorola products either at clock cycle boundaries (every CLK) or at half clock cycle boundaries (every S state). For other products, the ''state'' is equal to the input clock cycle: for example, the Intel 8086 and 80486 states. Finally, there are products whose ''state'' duration is longer than that of the input clock cycle C; for example, the Intel 80286 and 80386 have a ''state'' which is twice as long as the input clock cycle. Thus, when we compare the Intel 8086, 80286, and 80386 processors of Figure 1.14, we notice that all of them have the same bus cycle, consisting of four input clock cycles, although the 8086 has a ''4-state'' bus cycle, while the 80286 and 80386 have a ''2-state'' bus cycle. For the bus timing calculations one should use the input clock cycle time rather the number of ''states'' used to implement a bus transfer.

The duration of a **wait state** (which is a state inserted[19] to elongate the bus cycle because a slower slave component cannot respond to the processor's request within the allocated time period) also varies among the different products. In all Intel microprocessors, a wait state equals one ''T state''; in all Motorola microprocessors it equals two ''S states,'' except for the 68040, in which it equals four ''T states.'' It is the system designer's responsibility to include the proper external interface logic to force the processor to insert such wait states. For example, let's assume that accessing memory requires one wait state and accessing an I/O port requires three wait states. The design must include the proper external logic to read and decode the address issued on the address bus to determine whether one or three wait states are required for that particular bus cycle.

Most of the basic bus cycles are considered as having fixed length. In some microprocessors, a bus cycle equals four input clock cycles ($4C$), in others three ($3C$), and in the Motorola 68040 two input clock cycles ($2C$). Figure 1.15 shows the minimum duration of a bus cycle for some Intel and Motorola microprocessors. The diagram also summarizes the relationships among the bus cycle, input clock cycle C, internal processor clock cycle Cp, and what various commercial microprocessors call a ''state'' and a ''wait state.''

1.5.3 Microoperations and State Transition Diagrams

All microprocessors carry out a bus cycle by executing a sequence of one or more simultaneous basic operations (referred to as *microoperations*). Microoperations are activities that can take place in one complete clock cycle. Figure 1.16 shows the microoperations executed to perform a generic ''memory read'' cycle.

At the beginning of the bus cycle the processor issues an address on the address bus. If the address has been placed on a multiplexed address/data bus, it will stay valid on these output lines for only the first portion (the first clock cycle) of the bus cycle. When the proc-

---

[19]The actual position in the bus cycle for inserting a wait state depends on the particular microprocessor (as shown in Figure 1.14 and explained later in more detail).

Microprocessor	Minimum duration of a local bus cycle (number of input clock cycles)	Duration of the processor clock (Cp) and input clock (C) cycles	Duration of a local bus "state" (number of input clock cycles)	Duration of a "wait state" (number of input clock cycles)
Intel 8086	4	Equal	T state = 1	1
Intel 80286	4	Cp = 2 input clock cycles	T state = 2	2
Intel 80386	4	Cp = 2 input clock cycles	T state = 2	2
Intel 80486/i860	2	Equal	T state = 1	1
Motorola 68000	4	Cp = 1/2 input clock cycle	S state = 1/2	1
Motorola 68020/30	3	Cp = 1/2 input clock cycle	S state = 1/2	1
Motorola 68040	2	Cp = 1/2 input clock cycle	T state = 1/4	1

Figure 1.15 Relationships among local (or processor) bus cycle, input clock cycle (C), processor clock cycle (Cp), and what various commercial products call a "state" and a "wait state."

essor places an address on the address lines, it asserts an "address strobe" signal [sometimes called "address latch enable" (ALE)] to indicate that a valid address is on the address bus. This ALE can trigger external latching circuitry to latch the address and keep it valid for the remaining part of the bus cycle.

The processor also issues "bus cycle identifiers" (in the form of "status" or "function code" signals listed in Figure 1.8) to inform the rest of the system modules of the type of bus cycle it has initiated.

The Motorola microprocessors also inform the rest of the system modules of the size of the operand to be transferred during the current bus cycle. They do that by issuing a "operand size indicator" in the form of two signals on their output pins SIZ0 and SIZ1 (see, for example, Table B.3 in Appendix B).

Place an address on the address bus (AB←address).
Assert an "address strobe" synchronization signal (AS←H).
Issue a "bus cycle identifier" ("status" or "function code" signals).
Assert a "memory read" signal (R/W#←H, M/IO#←H[a]).
Issue an "operand size indicator" (like the Motorola's SIZ0, SIZ1).
Assert other control signals[b] (DEN, DT/R#, etc.).
Sample the "ready" or "data transfer acknowledge" feedback.
Enter a "wait state" or read input data.
Sample the "port size indicator" (e.g., Intel's BS8# or BS16# or Motorola's DSACK0#/DSACK1#) to determine additional bus cycles.
Negate (deactivate) all signals.

---

[a]For a processor with separate I/O instructions.
[b]Some of them may be generated by external bus controllers.

Figure. 1.16 Basic activities for a generic "memory read" cycle. (Microoperations for completely internal activities are not listed.)

If the cycle were a "write" cycle, then the processor would have to generate "byte enable" signals to indicate which byte lanes of the data bus carry valid data to be stored in the respective "byte sections" of memory. The Intel 32-bit processors issue the BE0#–BE3#, while for the Motorola 32-bit processors these "byte enables" must be generated by external circuitry (see Figure 1.7). For a "read" cycle, these "byte-enable" signals are usually of no importance, because an n-bit memory will always drive all its n output data bus lines, and it is up to the microprocessor to determine how to interpret the signals on its input data pins.

Other control signals are also needed to control external interface devices ("glue logic"). For example, as we will see later, Intel external transceivers require an enabling signal in the form of DEN# (data enable) and a signal to indicate the direction of the data transfer on the data bus, such as DT/R# = L indicating input to the processor, or DT/R# = H indicating output from the processor. Although these may be issued directly from the microprocessor chip itself, most often they are generated from an external "bus controller" chip which receives and decodes the processor's status signals. In such cases, it is the bus controller itself which—in addition to the DEN# and DT/R# signals—also generates the ALE and the read or write command signals to memory (MRDC# or MWTC#) or to I/O ports (IORC# or IOWC#).

During each bus cycle, the processor samples its input "port size indicator" pins to determine the width of the responding slave device (or slave port) and, therefore, to figure out which data bus lines carry valid data and whether or not the whole operand has been received. The outgoing "operand size indicator" and the incoming "port size indicator" pair are used by current microprocessors to implement "dynamic bus sizing" (discussed in the next chapter).

Figures 1.17 and 1.18 depict the simplified state transition diagrams for the Intel 80386 and Motorola 68020/30 microprocessors, along with their most important microoperations needed to execute a memory read and a memory write cycle. (The state transition diagrams and microoperations of other microprocessors are given in the Appendices.)

From Figure 1.14b, we observe that the state transition diagram for an 80386 bus cycle requires four clock cycles C (or two of what Intel calls "T states"). The microoperations in Figure 1.16 have been adjusted for the 80386 signaling and allocated to its four clock cycles as shown in Figure 1.17b and c. In the 80386 case, a wait state corresponds to elongating the bus cycle by two input clock cycles (i.e., repeating state T2).

From Figure 1.14c we observe that the state transition diagram for a 68020/30 bus cycle requires three clock cycles C (or six of what Motorola calls "S states"). The microoperations in Figure 1.16 have been adjusted for the 68020/30 signaling and allocated to its three clock cycles as shown in Figure 1.18b and c. The 68020/30 sample the DSACK1# and DSACK0# signals during S3 and, if needed, insert a wait state of 2 S states between C2 and C3.

1.6 PIPELINED, SUPERPIPELINED, AND SUPERSCALAR MICROPROCESSORS

From Equation 1.1 we observe that to increase the performance of the microprocessor, given a constant clock rate, one needs to reduce the *CPI* value (the average number of clock cycles per instruction). To reduce the average clock cycles per instruction means to introduce

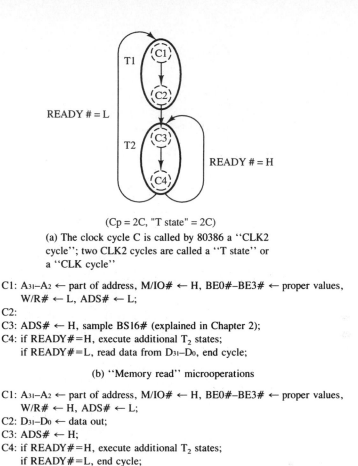

(Cp = 2C, "T state" = 2C)

(a) The clock cycle C is called by 80386 a "CLK2 cycle"; two CLK2 cycles are called a "T state" or a "CLK cycle"

C1: A_{31}–A_2 ← part of address, M/IO# ← H, BE0#–BE3# ← proper values, W/R# ← L, ADS# ← L;

C2:

C3: ADS# ← H, sample BS16# (explained in Chapter 2);

C4: if READY#=H, execute additional T_2 states;
    if READY#=L, read data from D_{31}–D_0, end cycle;

(b) "Memory read" microoperations

C1: A_{31}–A_2 ← part of address, M/IO# ← H, BE0#–BE3# ← proper values, W/R# ← H, ADS# ← L;

C2: D_{31}–D_0 ← data out;

C3: ADS# ← H;

C4: if READY#=H, execute additional T_2 states;
    if READY#=L, end cycle;

(c) "Memory write" microoperations

Figure 1.17 Intel 80386 simplified (nonpipelined) state transition diagram (a), and most important microoperations for 32-bit "memory read" (b) and "memory write" (c) bus cycles.

some kind of internal parallelism so that more than one instruction is executed concurrently which, therefore, increases the number of instructions that may be completed per second.

One way of decreasing the *CPI* value is to introduce to the microprocessor internal, instruction-level parallelism. Two major approaches have been used to achieve this:

1. One is based on the *temporal parallelism*, in which multiple instructions are simultaneously overlapped in execution using one *common hardware* (the pipeline). This leads to **pipelining** (discussed in Section 1.6.1), which yields an (ideal) *CPI* value of 1. The performance of the microprocessor can be increased further by increasing the depth of the pipeline and increasing the clock rate. This leads to **superpipelined** implementations (discussed in Section 1.6.2), which have reduced *CPI* to below 1 (i.e., they execute more than instruction per clock cycle).

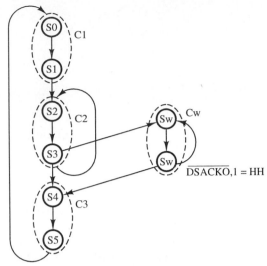

$(C_p = C/2, \text{"S state"} = C/2)$

(a) Two S's make up one input clock cycle C (68030). The 68020/30 call a C a CLK.

C1: A_{31}–A_0 ← address, FC_2–FC_0 ← proper values, SIZ1, SIZ0 ← proper values, $\overline{AS}$ ← L, $\overline{DS}$ ← L, R/$\overline{W}$ ← H;
C2: $\overline{DBEN}$=L, if $\overline{DSACK1}$, $\overline{DSACK0}$=HH, execute additional CW cycles;
            otherwise, advance to C3;
C3: Read data from D_{31}–D_0, negate all asserted signals;

(b) "Read" microoperations

C1: A_{31}–A_0 ← address, FC_2–FC_0 ← proper values, SIZ1, SIZ0 ← proper values, $\overline{AS}$ ← L, R/$\overline{W}$ ← L, $\overline{DBEN}$ ← L;
C2: D_{31}–D_0 ← data out, $\overline{DS}$ ← L,
     if $\overline{DSACK1}$, $\overline{DSACK0}$=HH, execute additional CW cycles;
     otherwise, advance to C3;
C3: R/$\overline{W}$ ← H, D_{31}–D_0 ← 3ST, negate all asserted signals;

(b) "Write" microoperations

Figure 1.18 Motorola 8020/30 simplified state transition diagram (a) and most important microoperations for 32-bit "read" (b) and "write" (c) bus cycles. (Read and write only from/to memory, since memory-mapped I/O.)

2. The second approach to parallelism is based on the *spatial* instruction-level *parallelism* utilizing *separate hardware* (for example, multiple copies of some pipeline stages or functional units). This leads to **superscalar** implementations in which multiple instructions are issued per clock cycle which are executed in separate hardware functional units (discussed in more detail in Section 1.6.3). Superscalars also achieve a *CPI* value of less than 1.

Of the microprocessors in Figure 1.4, pipelined microprocessors are the i860 (4 stages), the 80486 and R3000 (5 stages), and the 68040 (6 stages); superpipelined is the R4000 (8 stages); and superscalar is the 88110.

1.6.1 Pipelining

This technique came about from the observation that, since during execution the instruction is not using the whole microprocessor, the instruction cycle can be broken down into a sequence of steps, each of which takes a fraction of the time needed to complete the entire instruction. Each of these steps is assigned to a different (mutually exclusive) stage of the pipeline. Instructions enter the pipeline at one end, are processed through the stages, and exit at the other end. The pipeline accepts new inputs before previously accepted inputs have been completely processed and exited from it. Also, when a subtask result leaves one stage, the logic associated with that stage becomes free and can accept new results from the previous stage. Thus, the rate at which inputs are fed to the pipeline is chosen in relation to the time required to get an input through one stage, with the main goal of keeping all portions of the pipeline fully utilized. Once the pipeline is full, the output rate will match the input rate.

All stages of the pipeline operate in parallel, each one executing a step from a different instruction. Thus, when an n-stage pipeline is full, it effectively executes n instructions simultaneously.

Each instruction still needs the same amount of time to complete from start to finish, but because n instructions are being processed at a time, once the pipeline is filled, the rate at which instructions are completed in an ideal pipeline (in which each stage takes the same time to execute) is n times as rapid (i.e., the instruction *bandwidth has increased n times*). *The time per instruction on the pipelined microprocessor is equal to the time per instruction divided by the number of pipeline stages.*

More details on how the different microprocessors have implemented pipelining are given in Chapter 7. Here we present only an introduction to the concept.

Most of the recent RISC and CISC microprocessors have implemented internal pipelines with at least 5 stages. In such cases, one machine instruction is broken down to 5 steps, each step requires one clock cycle, and up to 5 machine instructions can be executed concurrently. Consider a hypothetical microprocessor pipeline with the following 5 stages, shown in Figure 1.19:

IF (instruction fetch): The stage accesses the (on-chip) I-cache to fetch the instruction. This involves generating[20] the I-cache address, sending it to the cache, and identifying the cache entry.

ID (instruction decode): This stage involves the actual reading of the instruction from the I-cache[21] (a number of instruction bytes are fetched with a cache access), sending it to the decoder of the control unit, decoding it and determining its length, and accessing the CPU source registers for the operands that may be needed in the operation.

ALU (ALU operations): For an arithmetic/logic instruction, this stage uses the ALU to execute the operation. If it is a load-store instruction, the effective memory address is computed in this stage. (Often, if the instruction is a branch instruction, this stage decides whether the branch is to be taken or not and generates the target address.[22])

---

[20]As we will see in Chapter 6, a translation from virtual to physical address may be required in this step involving part of the MMU hardware. (In RISC processors with paging, this hardware is called the TLB or "translation look-aside buffer.")

[21]We assume here that the instruction was found in the I-cache, i.e., we had a "cache hit."

[22]As in stage IF, the address generation step in this stage may involve a TLB look-up.

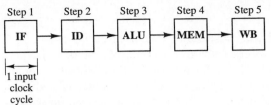

Step 1 Step 2 Step 3 Step 4 Step 5

IF → ID → ALU → MEM → WB

1 input clock cycle

(a) Functional representation of a simplified 5-stage instruction pipeline

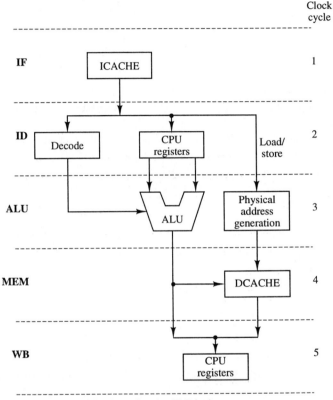

Clock cycle

IF   ICACHE   1

ID   Decode   CPU registers   Load/store   2

ALU   ALU   Physical address generation   3

MEM   DCACHE   4

WB   CPU registers   5

Note: stages IF and ALU may involve TLB look-up

(b) Simplified physical representation of a 5-stage instruction pipeline. (Here we assume the existence of an I-cache and a D-cache on chip.) Adapted from [18].

Figure 1.19 5-stage pipeline with 1 clock cycle per stage. (If this pipeline operates at, say 50 MHz, each stage takes 20 ns to accomplish its task.)

MEM (memory access): This stage is used by load/store instructions to access the D-cache (or main memory) for data load/store.

WB (write back): Update the CPU registers with either the data read from memory/D-cache or with the ALU results.

If the microprocessor depicted in Figure 1.19b operates in a nonpipelined fashion (a nonrealistic assumption), then Figure 1.20a shows the execution of two successive instructions requiring at least 5 clock cycles per instruction. In the 5-deep pipelined execution depicted in Figure 1.20b, it is observed that the pipeline operates at 5 times the rate of the

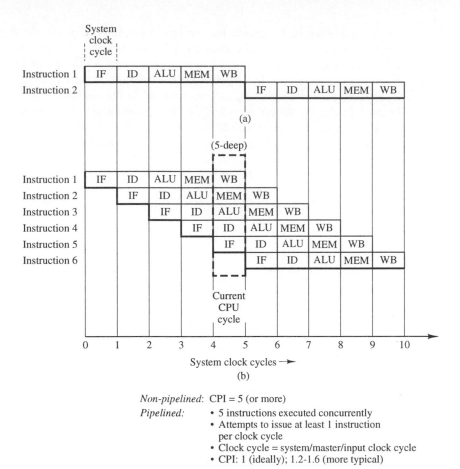

Figure 1.20 Comparing a nonpipelined with a 5-stage pipelined operation (i860 has 4 stages; 80486 and R3000 have 5 stages; 68040 has 6 stages).

nonpipelined scheme, and once the pipeline is filled, ideally it will complete one instruction per clock cycle ($CPI = 1$). Although this average CPI is 1, each instruction cycle (including fetch, decode, store results, etc.) will still take on the average 5 clock cycles (according to the assumptions for Figure 1.20a). Compilers are very crucial to the efficient use of the pipeline by keeping it full with useful instructions.

The above description is referred to ideal operations of pipelines in which all stages require a single clock cycle and instructions are issued to the pipeline in such a way as to keep it always filled. Unfortunately, *data dependencies* and *control hazards,* along with the execution of conditional-branch instructions, present various problems that do not allow such ideal operation.

1.6.2 Superpipelined Microprocessors

Having introduced a pipeline into modern microprocessors, how can the pipeline be modified to further decrease its *CPI* and thus increase its throughput? Superpipelines are used to effectively execute more than one instruction per clock cycle, thus reducing the *CPI* below

1. This is accomplished by increasing the pipeline depth and increasing the pipeline clock rate. Longer pipelines provide finer granularity in instruction execution; for example, a bottleneck stage or a stage that requires longer time to execute can be subdivided into two independent stages. Increasing the pipeline depth, however, requires faster clocks and an increase in the rate at which instructions enter and leave the pipeline.

Figure 1.21a shows the previous 5-stage pipeline operation of Figure 1.20b under the assumption that it operates from a 50-MHz clock. Figure 1.21b depicts its 10-stage superpipelined implementation, in which each previous stage has now been split in two. While the simple 5-stage pipeline of Figure 1.21a has one instruction completed per (system) clock cycle, the 10-stage superpipeline has two instructions completed per (system) clock cycle (using a twofold-faster internal processor clock that allows feeding instructions to the pipe line at twice the rate), thus reducing the *CPI* to 0.5.

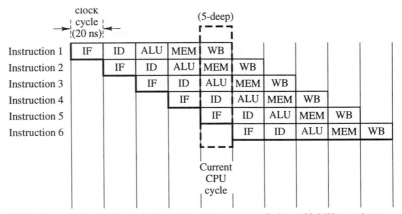

(a) 5-stage *pipeline*: system clock = internal processor clock = 50 MHz, each stage takes 20 ns, one instruction is issued every 20 ns; ideally, *CPI* = 1

Figure 1.21 Five-stage pipelined and 10-stage superpipelined operation [19].

A superpipelined microprocessor requires less complex hardware design than that of a superscalar, but it relies on fast logic that can operate from faster clocks. There is, however, a point of diminishing returns beyond which it does not pay to subdivide the pipeline into more stages.

1.6.3 Superscalar Microprocessors

Superscalar microprocessors are built on the principle that more than one instruction can be issued per clock cycle and dispatched for execution to multiple copies of critical hardware resources (integer execution units, floating-point units, graphics units, etc.). For example, an instruction dispatcher inside the 88110 microprocessor dispatches 2 instructions each clock cycle so that each one executes in one of the concurrently operating duplicate units.

Figure 1.22 shows a hypothetical ''2-way'' superscalar implementation again operating from a 50-MHz clock with 5-stage pipelines of the type shown in Figure 1.20 operating concurrently. Two instructions can now be fetched and decoded together and issued in parallel for execution in two seprate execution units; they will complete in one clock cycle, which reduces the *CPI* to 0.5.

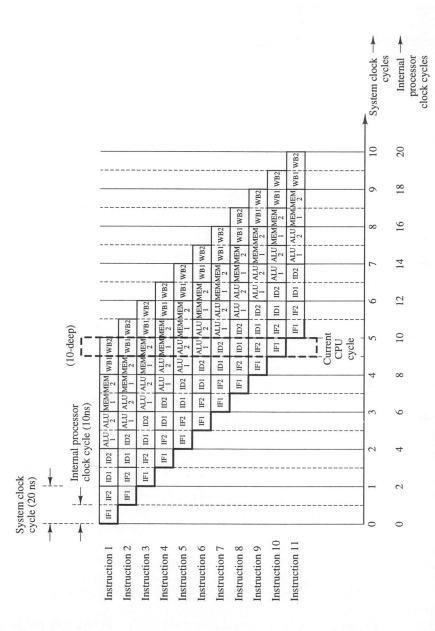

(b) 10-stage *superpipeline*: system clock = 50 MHz, internal processor clock = 100 MHz, each stage takes 10 ns; one instruction is issued every 10 ns; ideally, *CIP*=0.5

Figure 1.21   (concluded)

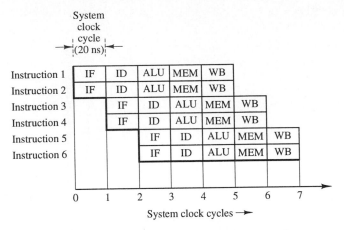

Figure 1.22 Superscalar operation: system clock = internal processor clock = 50 MHz, each stage takes 20 ns, 2 instructions are dispatched simultaneously and executed concurrently in 1 clock cycle; ideally, *CPI* = 0.5 [19].

Comparing an *n*-way superscalar with an *n*-deep superpipelined implementation we notice that they have about equal performance (assuming the same instruction issue restrictions) [2]. However, while the superpipelined implementation requires higher internal clock speeds, the superscalar implementations have much more complex hardware. Of the microprocessors in Figure 1.4 only the 88110 is a superscalar microprocessor[23] [3].

Where a superpipeline cannot increase in depth beyond its maximum, the superscalar approaches can be applied, leading to **superscalar superpipelines**.

1.7 SYSTEM DESIGN METHODOLOGY

Designing and building a microprocessor-based system involves first choosing the appropriate microprocessor to be used as the CPU of the system, selecting the components needed to build the other modules (such as the memory subsystem, the I/O subsystem, caches, buses, etc.), and finally properly interfacing them together to form a *well-balanced* computing system. In this textbook, the design takes the high-level "system approach"; no instruction set design is involved, since it is determined by the particular microprocessor chosen. Most system designs involve a number of stages that correspond to one or more levels of abstraction.

The first stage involves the **specification of requirements** that the system must meet. These include functional requirements (such as the type of applications the system is to execute, the programming language to be used, the type of operating system needed, etc.), other system characteristics (such as upper bounds on cost and lower bounds on performance, expandability objectives, etc.), and the identification of additional constraints (such as existing application software, limitations on power, size, and weight, and other compatibility constraints). This first stage is very difficult and involves both tangible and intangible requirements.

The second stage involves evaluating different alternatives to **establish the architecture** of the system: i.e., identify the subsystems and the way they are to be assembled to-

---

[23]Another superscalar microprocessor not examined here is the IBM RISC System/6000; it has a "forked pipeline" in which the first two stages of "instruction fetch" and "dispatch" are shared, and the dispatcher then dispatches the instruction to either the floating-point path or the integer instruction path inside the microprocessor.

gether. Very rarely, formal notation can be used to describe the architecture; the PMS (processors, memories, switches) notation is a useful structural description.

The most important system module is the microprocessor. Assuming that the architect has a free choice (and various reasons, including company associations and agreements, may restrict this choice), a careful consideration must be given of the type of microprocessor to be used. In this textbook, we not only present the architecture and operation of a number of representative RISC and CISC microprocessors, but also identify their particularities, characteristics, technological constraints, and architectural advances to help the system designer perform a good trade-off analysis among them is selecting the most appropriate microprocessor that meets the requirements of the system to be built.

Then one identifies the characteristics (such as speed and size) of the remaining modules of the system in such a way as to satisfy the overall requirements and present a well-balanced design. With today's high-speed microprocessors, it is imperative to have a well-designed memory hierarchy (an effective *cache and memory architecture*) to match the microprocessor rate of execution. The faster the memory hierarchy can get instructions and data into the microprocessor, the better the overall performance of the system. The faster the microprocessor and the larger the first-level cache it has on-chip, the more necessary it becomes to include large, second-level, external caches. Finally, the designer can then develop the I/O subsystem for interfacing to the outside world. Major subsystem modules and alternative interconnections have already been presented in this chapter, and many more alternatives will be given in the rest of the chapters.

In establishing the most appropriate system architecture, one can do the following:

1. *Analytical methods*: Sometimes analytical approximation methods can be used to evaluate the performance of the microprocessor and the bandwidth of the memory hierarchy (caches and main memory). Parameters that affect the performance of the memory hierarchy (caches and main memory) and approximation formulas used in estimating system performance are discussed in detail in Chapters 5 and 6. Analytical models are difficult to derive and do not represent the behavior of the actual system.

2. *Software simulation*: Commercial software simulators may exist or can be developed (in the form of a computer program) that evaluate the model numerically over a time period [16]. This approach is used to verify the model and gives an insight only in the behavior of the system.

3. *Software prototyping*: A software prototype is an abstract representation of the actual machine, which includes all major subsystems and their interconnections. An interactive software prototype may allow the designer to vary the system parameters effortlessly to assist in the evaluation of the hardware design (e.g., measure utilization and throughput) along with the development of application software (i.e., design and map algorithms onto the actual hardware) [17]. Such software packages may exist at the architecture and the instruction level.

The next stage involves the **development of the hardware and the software** which are usually done in parallel [20]. In this textbook we do not cover the extensive topic of software development. Instead, we concentrate on the hardware design to **construct the hardware prototype;** this involves selecting the basic components (memory chips, I/O, VLSI interface components, cache memories, controllers, buffers, etc.) and designing the various boards of the actual system. We present techniques for designing the main memory subsystem, the cache subsystem, selecting the system bus to interconnect them together, and we discuss approaches for handling external interrupting devices that request service from the system. Quite often, a tradc-off has to be performed in deciding whether functions will be implemented in software or hardware (such as between software-based floating-point and attached hardware FPU). The choice of each component depends on the match **between** the design requirements for that subsystem (that were established with the architecture during the previous design stage) and how well the components fit those requirements.

The next stage is to **test and debug the prototype** and verify it completely before committing to the final system. The prototype is exercised (by executing representative programs—benchmarks—from the kinds of applications the system will run) and modified until it satisfies the given system performance requirements. The prototype construction and verification is an iterative process.

Finally, hardware and software are integrated together, the actual system is built, tested, debugged, and enters the **production** stage.

EXERCISES

1.1. Examine the register structures of the Intel 80386, Intel i860, and Motorola 68030 microprocessors, and discuss their similarities and differences.

1.2. Consider a hypothetical 32-bit microprocessor having 32-bit instructions composed of two fields: the first byte represents the opcode and the remaining the immediate operand or its address.
   (a) What is the maximum directly addressable memory capacity (in number of bytes)?
   (b) Discuss the impact on the system speed if the microprocessor has
      (1) a 32-bit local address bus and 16-bit local data bus, or
      (2) a 16-bit local address bus and a 16-bit local data bus.
   (c) How many bits are needed for the program counter and the instruction register?

1.3. Consider the Intel 8086 (Appendix A) and the instruction ADD DX,1234 whose execution results in adding the 16-bit contents of the specified memory location to the contents of internal register DX and placing the result back into DX. Assume that the internal segment registers contain the following: (CS) = ABCD, (DS) = CDFE, (SS) = D021, and (ES) = CFFF.
   (a) Which memory location does the operand come from?
   (b) If (IP) = 1046, where is the first byte of the instruction stored at? Explain.

1.4. Consider a hypothetical microprocessor generating a 16-bit address (for example, assume that the program counter and the address registers are 16-bit wide) and having a 16-bit data bus.
   (a) What is the maximum memory address space that the processor can access directly if it is connected to a "16-bit memory"?
   (b) What is the maximum memory address space that the processor can access directly if it is connected to an "8-bit memory"?
   (c) What architectural features will allow this microprocessor to access a separate "I/O space"?
   (d) If an "input" and "output" instruction can specify an 8-bit "I/O port number," how many 8-bit I/O ports can the microprocessor support? How many 16-bit I/O ports? Explain.

1.5. Consider the *intersegment* CALL instruction (calling a FAR procedure in a different segment) of the Intel 8086 microprocessor. Assume that this particular instruction is as follows:

   byte1: CALL opcode (assume stored at location 12344)
   byte2: upper half of the target (jump) address
   byte3: lower half of the target (jump) address

byte4: upper half of the new CS register value

byte5: lower half of the new CS register value

Assume that its *execution portion* is given as follows:

$$[(SP)-2] \leftarrow (CS)$$
$$[(SP)-4] \leftarrow (IP)$$
$$(SP) \leftarrow (SP)-4$$
$$(CS) \leftarrow (byte4)(byte5)$$
$$(IP) \leftarrow (byte2)(byte3)$$

where (X) denotes ''the contents of'' and [(X)] denotes ''the contents of the memory location pointed at by the contents of X.'' Assume that initially (CS) = 1000, (SP) = 1000, and (SS) = 6000.

(a) List in the proper sequence all necessary microoperations executed during each input clock cycle during *the execute portion* of the CALL instruction. (*Do not* give those of the fetch portion of the instruction cycle and assume that there is no internal queue in the processor.)

(b) Using the 8086's basic timing diagram shown in Figure A.3, draw the timing diagram for the execution of the above CALL instruction. *Show actual hexadecimal values of the information transferred on the address and data bus byte lanes.*

1.6. Consider the execution of the above Intel 8086 ''intersegment CALL'' instruction (a CALL to a subroutine located in a different code segment in memory). What information is stored in the stack? If the stack pointer register contained the value 1224 before the execution of this CALL, what is its value after the execution? What other internal registers are affected by this instruction's execution?

1.7. When an access to memory is performed for a read operation, how do some microprocessors know how much data the memory sends them? What happens during a write operation?

1.8. Compare and discuss the state transition diagrams of the Intel 80386 and Motorola 68030 microprocessors.

1.9. Consider a 32-bit microprocessor (with a 16-bit external data bus) driven by an 8-MHz input clock. Assume that this microprocessor has a bus cycle whose minimum duration equals 4 input clock cycles. What is the maximum data transfer rate that this microprocessor can sustain? In order to increase its performance, would it be better to make its external data bus 32 bits or to double the external clock frequency supplied to the microprocessor? State any other assumptions you make and explain.

1.10. Compare the data transfer rates of the Intel 80286, the Intel 80386, and the Intel 80486 when each one is driven by a 16-MHz input clock.

REFERENCES

[1] Hennessy, J. L., and D. A. Patterson, *Computer Architecture: A Quantitative Approach*, Morgan Kaufmann Publishers, Inc., San Mateo, CA, 1990.

[2] Jouppi, N., and D. Wall, ''Available Instruction-Level Parallelism for Superscalar and Super-pipelined Machines,'' *Proc. Third Conf. Architectural Support for Programming Languages and Operating Systems*, ACM, Apr. 1989, pp. 272–282.

[3] Diefendorff, K., and M. Allen, ''Organization of the Motorola 88110 Superscalar RISC Microprocessor,'' *IEEE Micro*, Apr. 1992, pp. 40–63.

[4] Intel Corp., *80386 Hardware Reference Manual* (231732-001), Santa Clara, CA, 1986.

[5] Intel Corp., *i486 Microprocessor* (240440-001), Santa Clara, CA, 1989.

[6] Integrated Device Technology, Inc., *R3000/3001 Designer's Guide,* Santa Clara, CA, 1990

[7] MIPS Computer Systems, Inc., *MIPS R4000 Microprocessor User's Manual* (M8-00040), Sunnyvale, CA, 1991.

[8] Motorola Inc., *MC68030 Enhanced 32-bit Microprocessor User's Manual* (MC68030UM/AD), Austin, TX, 1987.

[9] Motorola Inc., *MC68040 32-bit Microprocessor User's Manual* (MC68040UM/AD), Austin, TX, 1989.

[10] Motorola Inc., *MC88100 Technical Data* (BR588/D), Phoenix, AZ, 1988.

[11] Intel Corp., *i860 64-bit Microprocessor Hardware Reference Manual* (CG-101789), Santa Clara, CA, 1990.

[12] Piepho, R. S., and W. S. Wu, "A Comparison of RISC Architectures," *IEEE Micro,* Aug. 1989, pp. 51–62.

[13] Allison, A., "RISCs Challenge Mini, Micro Suppliers," *Mini-Micro Systems,* Nov. 1986, pp. 127–136.

[14] Patterson, D. A., "Reduced Instruction Computers," *Communications of the ACM,* Vol. 28, No. 1, Jan. 1985, p. 189.

[15] Hennessy, J. L., "VLSI Processor Architecture," *IEEE Transactions on Computers,* Vol. C-33, No. 12, Dec. 1984.

[16] Law, A. M., and W. D. Kelton, *Simulation Modeling and Analysis,* McGraw-Hill Book Company, San Francisco, 1982.

[17] Barad, H., *Rapid Prototyping of Massively Parallel Architectures,* Tech. Report 88-10, Tulane University, Electrical Engineering Dept., New Orleans, LA, 1988.

[18] MIPS Computer Systems, *MIPS RISC Architecture,* Lecture Notes, Sunnyvale, CA, Aug. 1991.

[19] MIPS Computer Systems, *RISC Architectures,* Lecture Notes, Sunnyvale, CA, Aug. 1991.

[20] Tabak, D., *Advanced Microprocessors*, McGraw-Hill Book Company, San Francisco, 1991.

2

Microprocessor Bus Transfers

2.1 INTRODUCTION

In the preceding chapter we examined the external view of the microprocessor, defined its input and output pins and signals, presented its basic interface components, and showed how it is configured with other system components to form a working system. This chapter explains how the processor buses are used to implement data transfers. We first present here the big-endian and little-endian ordering of the operands and the alignment of operands and instructions in memory. Then we explain the operation of the local bus and examine the bus timing diagrams that show what signals are placed on the bus lines at each clock cycle of the bus cycle. We cover both synchronous and asynchronous bus operations. We also discuss how recent microprocessors perform address pipelining and burst transfer cycles. The next topic is "misalignment," which is important to both the hardware designers and software system developers. We present misaligned operand transfers to the local bus and explain how different microprocessors handle them. We also discuss the capability that microprocessors have to provide "dynamic bus sizing," i.e., the ability to adjust at run time the width of their local data bus according to the width (or "port size") of the accessed slave device. This allows, for example, 32-bit microprocessors to be easily interfaced with a mix of 8-, 16-, and 32-bit memory modules and I/O peripherals in the same system. Finally, we discuss "bus arbitration": the way that control of the bus is granted to one master when a number of them request access to it simultaneously.

Understanding the bus activities and the timing of the signals placed on it helps the design engineer who develops the system to conduct digital testing or troubleshooting, for example by connecting a logic probe to the bus of a microprocessor or a logic analyzer to display how a microprocessor carries out a particular bus cycle.

2.2 DATA ORDERING AND ALIGNMENT

2.2.1 Big- and Little-Endian Ordering

Most microprocessors follow one of two different ways of storing in memory the data bytes of operands [1,2]: big-endian order and little-endian order. We will be calling these microprocessors *big-endian* and *little-endian* microprocessors, respectively.

In all our discussions here we will assume that the least significant byte of an operand or of an internal register is always referred[1] to as byte 0 or B0, irrespective of the endianess of their storage in main memory. Thus, a 16-bit operand in an internal register will be symbolized as B1,B0, and a 32-bit operand in an internal register will be symbolized as B3,B2,B1,B0. Similarly, throughout this textbook, bit 0 will always denote the least significant (rightmost) bit.

The **big-endian** processor architecture is also called *high-order-byte-first* (H-O-B-F) architecture, because it maps the highest-order byte of an internal register to the lowest memory byte-address. This means that when a multiple-byte data item is stored in memory, its *most significant byte* is stored in the memory location with the lowest address, as shown in Figure 2.1a. The *address* of this data item is the address of its *most significant byte*. When a big-endian processor reads a multiple-byte data item from memory, the byte coming from the lowest address is placed inside into the most significant position of the operand register. Similarly, when bytes arrive at the processor in a sequential fashion, the big-endian processor would treat the first arriving byte as the most significant byte of the operand. This ordering extends to word order as well. Big-endian microprocessors are compatible with the IBM 370 conventions. Representative examples of big-endian microprocessors are the Motorola microprocessors and the SPARC RISC-type microprocessors.

The **little-endian** processor architecture is also called *low-order-byte-first* (L-O-B-F) architecture, because it maps the lowest-order byte of an internal register to the lowest memory byte-address. This means that when a multiple-byte data item is stored in memory, what is stored in the location with the lowest address is now its *least significant byte,* as shown in Figure 2.1b. The *address* of this data item is the address of its *least significant byte*. When a little-endian processor reads a multiple-byte data item from memory, the byte coming from the lowest address is placed inside the least significant position of the operand register. Similarly, for sequentially arriving data, a little-endian processor treats the first arriving byte as the least significant byte of the operand. This ordering applies to word positions as well; for example, little-endians store the least significant 16-bit word (LSW) of a 32-bit doubleword first.[2] Little-endian microprocessors are compatible with DEC VAX conventions. Representative examples of little-endian microprocessors are the Intel processors. The Intel 80486 also uses the little-endian convention but provides two instructions which can convert 16- or 32-bit data between the two byte orderings: BSWAP (byte swap) swaps byte order within a 32-bit register and XCHG (exchange) handles 2-byte items.

A number of RISC processors can operate as **either big-endian or little-endian** processors: they have a control bit (a ''byte-order switch'') in a control register which is set dur-

---

[1]Some products, however, like the Motorola big-endian processors, label the most significant byte of an internal register as BYTE0 or OP0.

[2]As we will see later on, endianess has *nothing to do* with which byte of an operand is *actually transferred first*, because misaligned operands may cause parts of the operand to be transferred in a different order than the normal.

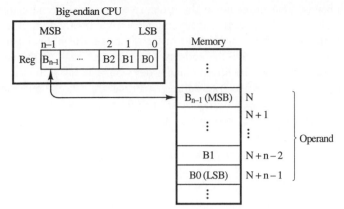

(a) Big-endian (high-order-byte-first) architecture

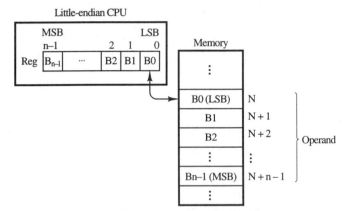

(b) Little-endian (low-order-byte-first) architecture

Figure 2.1 Functional description of data exchange between big- or little-endian processors and memory.

ing system initialization (during RESET) to specify big-endian or little-endian mode of operation. The MIPS R-series (R2000/R3000/R4000) RISC microprocessors are examples of processors that can be configured during RESET to operate either with big-endian or little-endian convention. Other microprocessors even allow dynamic switching between the two byte-ordering conventions by software executing in supervisor mode; one example is the RISC microprocessor Intel i860 (although typically, the i860 will operate in its natural little-endian mode).

A good discussion on historical background of the big- and little-endian processors, their advantages/disadvantages, and reasons for choosing big- versus little-endian processors is given in [2]. A summary of that **comparison** is presented here.

1. In big-endians, *BCD compare* (comparing multiple BCD digits) can be done by using one integer-compare instruction. On the other hand, in little-endians, *byte-wise integer additions* are faster, because they can start while data is being fetched in proper order (with the least significant byte fetched first).

2. There are some functional criteria that distinguish the two. For example, when mixed numbers (having an integer and a fractional part) are stored in memory, accessing the

integer part of the number is done faster when the order is big-endian, because the address already points to the most significant part (the integer) of the operand; in little-endian ordering, which stores the fraction first, in order to access the integer part of the operand a constant must be added to the address. On the other hand, if the access is to fetch the fractional part first, the little-endian order would be faster, because if the order were big-endian, it would require address arithmetic. Also when data are stored in big-endian order, *decimal/ASCII dumps* are easier to read (all values are printed left to right without causing confusion) and *character-string sorting* is done faster.

3. Finally, big-endians have a consistent order in the sense that they store their integer and character strings in the same order (the most significant byte comes first), and a more convenient notation for *fractions,* in the sense that the most significant bit of the signed fraction is at the left and has the index of 0. On the other hand, little-endians have more convenient notations for *integers,* in the sense that the least significant bit of the integer is at the right and has the index of 0.

The type of data ordering influences compiler writing, systems programming, and systems design and interfacing. It must be taken into account when designing multiprocessor systems in which different processors of both types exchange data over the same shared bus or share data bases. When the compiler is not doing it, the user is forced to specify the order (big-endian or little-endian) for data shared among different types of interconnected processors. If the microprocessor has the ability to switch between big- and little-endian modes, it simplifies the data exchange between different types of microprocessors and data bases, and the porting of applications from other types of processors.

2.2.2 16- and 32-bit Microprocessors

Unless otherwise specified, when we refer to an *n*-bit microprocessor we will mean a microprocessor with *n*-bit internal architecture (i.e., *n*-bit general-purpose registers, *n*-bit ALU, etc.) and an *n*-bit external data bus. As we will see in this chapter, versions of *n*-bit processors also exist that support an external data bus of (a) half the size of the processor's wordlength (e.g., the Intel 80386SX has a 32-bit internal architecture and a 16-bit data bus) or (b) twice the size of the processor's wordlength (e.g., the Intel i860 has 32-bit internal registers and a 64-bit external data bus).

16-bit products. Figure 2.2a depicts the aligned 16-bit data reads from a 16-bit memory by a **16-bit big-endian microprocessor.** For big-endian processors, the most significant byte of the operand is stored first in memory (in the lowest memory location), and when transferred to the processor it is placed into the most significant position of the internal register.

It is noticed that a *16-bit memory* is connected to (or can drive) a 16-bit data bus. It is made up of two byte sections, section 0 and section 1, each connected to a separate byte lane of the 16-bit data bus. Section 0 is also called the "even section" or "even byte bank" because it contains all even byte-addresses; section 1 is also called the "odd section" or "odd byte bank" because it contains all odd byte-addresses. An even byte-address will be denoted as 2N (a number evenly divisible by 2), while an odd byte-address will be denoted as 2N + 1.

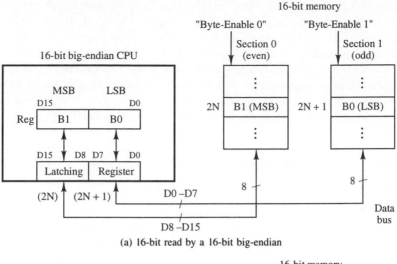

(a) 16-bit read by a 16-bit big-endian

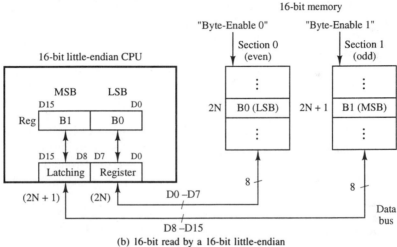

(b) 16-bit read by a 16-bit little-endian

Figure 2.2 Sixteen-bit big-endian and little-endian data transfers.

B1 is the most significant byte (MSB) of the operand; B0 is the least significant byte (LSB) of the operand. (2N) denotes the contents of memory location 2N. As shown, the 16-bit operand is read in one bus cycle (symbolized by the letter 1 in a circle), and—after being latched by the processor in its 16-bit data input latching register—is transferred directly (without byte swapping as in some of the cases to be discussed later) into the processor's internal 16-bit register. This 16-bit word operand is *aligned* in memory because it is stored in locations 2N and 2N + 1 or at a "word address" or "word boundary" (i.e., the operand's address is evenly divisible by 2). For a read operation, memory usually sends a 16-bit operand by driving both byte-lanes of the 16-bit data bus, even though the processor may have requested only a byte. The processor, however, will know which of its input pins received the byte it requested and route it internally to the proper destination. For a *byte write* operation, only one byte-lane of the data bus will carry valid data; this lane is identified by the "byte-enable" signals that the processor issues (which are then used to trigger the corresponding byte-sections of memory to receive the data). (For example, in the case of the Motorola 68000, the control signal UDS# issued by the processor will be used to trigger section 0, while the control signal LDS# is used to trigger section 1.)

For a 16-bit big-endian processor and a 16-bit memory, the most significant byte of an aligned 16-bit word operand is transferred over the most significant lines D8–D15 of the data bus (connected to section 0, the even byte bank), while the least significant byte is transferred over the least significant lines D0–D7 of the data bus (connected to section 1, the odd byte bank).

Figure 2.2b depicts the aligned 16-bit data reads from a 16-bit memory by a **16-bit little-endian microprocessor.** For little-endian processors, it is now the least significant byte of the operand (again symbolized as byte B0) that is stored first in memory (in the lowest memory location) and when transferred to the processor is again placed into the least significant position of the internal register.

When a little-endian processor is used, section 0 now contains the least significant byte of the operand while section 1 contains the most significant. As shown, the 16-bit operand is read in one bus cycle and from the processor's input latching register is transferred directly into the processor's internal 16-bit register. Again, this 16-bit word operand is aligned in memory. As noted earlier, byte transfers will have only one of the two byte-lanes of the data bus carrying valid data.

For a 16-bit little-endian processor and a 16-bit memory, the most significant byte of an aligned 16-bit word operand will again be transferred over the most significant lines D8–D15 of the data bus (which are now connected to section 1, the odd byte bank), and the least significant byte will again be transferred over the least significant lines D0–D7 of the data bus (which are now connected to section 0, the even byte bank). Again, different "byte-enable" signals are applied to the two memory byte-sections during a write operation. [For example, the Intel 8086/286 16-bit processors issue the BHE# (byte high enable) signal which can be used to trigger the odd byte section 1; the even byte section 0 can be triggered by the value A0 = 0.]

32-bit products. Figure 2.3 depicts the 32-bit doubleword and 16-bit word *data load* operations from a 32-bit memory to a **32-bit big-endian microprocessor.** A *32-bit memory* is composed of 4 byte-sections (section 0, section 1, section 2, and section 3), and address 4N is a "doubleword address"; for a big-endian processor, these byte-sections are connected to data bus byte-lanes D24–D31, D16–D23, D8–D15, and D0–D7, respectively.

Figure 2.3a shows the aligned 32-bit doubleword data load. The first or most significant byte B3 of the 32-bit operand (stored in location 4N) is transferred over the most significant byte-lane D24–D31 of the 32-bit data bus, and—after being latched in the processor's input latching register—is placed into the leftmost position of the internal 32-bit register; the least significant byte B0 is transferred over lines D0–D7 and placed into the rightmost position of the internal register. For a 32-bit big-endian processor and a 32-bit memory, the most significant byte of the operand is transferred over the most significant byte-lane D24–D31 of the data bus (connected to memory section 0), while the least significant byte is transferred over the least significant byte-lane D0–D7 of the data bus (connected to memory section 3).

Figure 2.3b shows the two different ways of loading (and storing) aligned 16-bit operands from a 32-bit memory: a word at location 4N and a word at location 4N + 2. A load

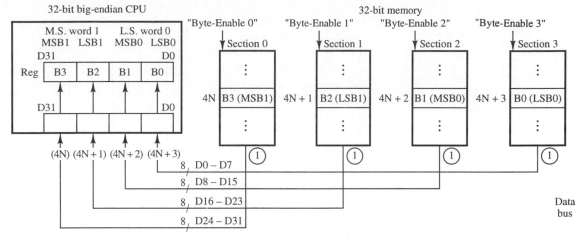

(a) 32-bit load by a 32-bit big-endian processor (load DW from 4N)

Figure 2.3 Thirty-two-bit big-endian processor in 32-bit and 16-bit aligned loads from a 32-bit memory. [*Note:* Solid lines represent the byte-lanes (and processor data pins) that carry *valid data.*]

operation for a smaller operand will place it in the rightmost position of an internal 32-bit register. (Depending on the particular load instruction, the left part of this register may either receive zeros or sign-extend the incoming operand.) The solid lines in Figure 2.3b show which byte-lanes of the 32-bit data bus carry "valid data" in each case. For a read operation, memory usually sends a 32-bit operand by driving all four byte-lanes of the 32-bit data bus, irrespective of the size of the actual operand requested by the processor; the processor, however, will know which of its input pins received the data it requested. In our examples here, the processor will read the 16-bit operand from the respective input pins, and its internal multiplexing hardware will route the operand word to the rightmost position of an internal 32-bit register.

For a *data write,* which byte-lanes of the data bus carry valid data is identified by the "byte-enable" signals used to trigger the corresponding byte-sections of memory to receive the data. These "byte-enables" are either emitted directly from microprocessor output pins (for example, Intel products) or must be generated by external decoding logic (for example, Motorola products) as we will see later. In some microprocessors, when the outgoing operand occupies only part of the data bus, the processor duplicates data on the other data bus byte-lanes. This is done so that the 32-bit processor may be easily connected to 16-bit slave devices (through a 16-bit bus) as well. We will explain this in more detail later.

Figure 2.4 depicts the 32-bit doubleword and 16-bit word read operations from a 32-bit memory to a **32-bit little-endian microprocessor.** For a little-endian processor, byte sections 0, 1, 2, and 3 are connected to data bus byte-lanes D0–D7, D8–D15, D16–23, and D24–D31, respectively. As in the previous paragraph, solid lines represent the byte lanes of the data bus that carry "valid data."

Figure 2.4a shows the aligned 32-bit doubleword data load. The least significant byte of the operand B0 (now stored in location 4N) is placed into the rightmost position of the internal register, while the most significant byte B3 (now stored in location 4N + 3) is routed into the leftmost position of the internal register. For a 32-bit little-endian processor and a 32-bit memory, the most significant byte of the operand will again be transferred over the

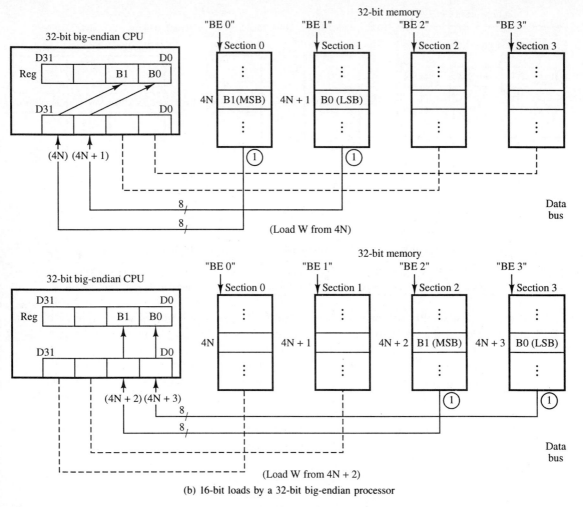

(b) 16-bit loads by a 32-bit big-endian processor

Figure 2.3 (concluded)

most significant byte-lane D24–D31 of the data bus (which is now connected to memory section 3), while the least significant byte will again be transferred over the least significant byte-lane D0–D7 of the data bus (which is now connected to memory section 0).

Figure 2.4b shows the two different ways of loading (and storing) aligned 16-bit operands from a 32-bit memory, at locations 4N and 4N + 2. Again, it is the responsibility of the processor to know which input data pins carry the 16 valid data bits. Internal multiplexing hardware always routes an incoming 16-bit word to the rightmost position of an internal 32-bit register.

One should notice, for example, that the same instruction "load a word from location 4N" will have a microprocessor operating in a big-endian mode expect valid data on input pins D16–D31, while when operating in a little-endian mode will expect the valid data on its input pins D0–D15.

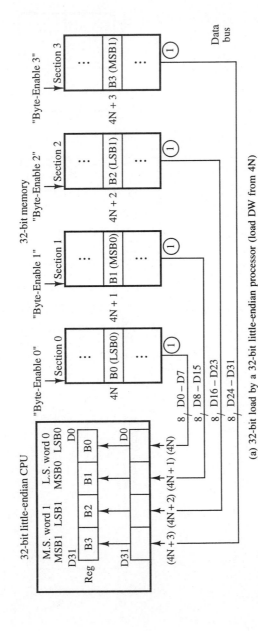

Figure 2.4 Thirty-two-bit little-endian processor in 32-bit and 16-bit aligned loads from a 32-bit memory. [*Note:* Solid lines represent the byte-lanes (and processor data pins) that carry *valid data*.]

(a) 32-bit load by a 32-bit little-endian processor (load DW from 4N)

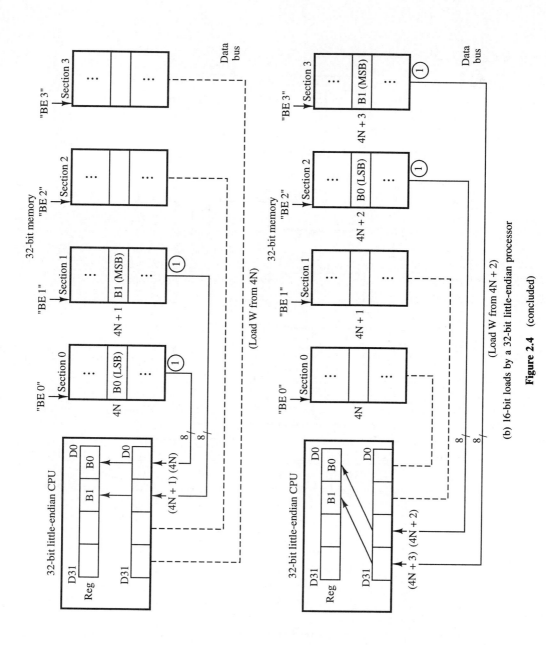

(b) 16-bit loads by a 32-bit little-endian processor

Figure 2.4 (concluded)

2.2.3 RISC Microprocessors with 64-Bit External Data Buses

RISC microprocessors with 64-bit external data buses can have an internal 32-bit architecture, i.e., 32-bit general-purpose registers (for example, the Intel i860 and Motorola 88110), or a 64-bit internal architecture (like the MIPS R4000).[3] If the external bus size matches that of the internal registers, then all the above discussion can be very easily extended to these products also. If, however, the external data bus is 64 bits while the internal register is only 32 bits, the microprocessor first reads 64 bits of data and (while storing them in the on-chip cache) extracts the data bytes needed.

2.2.4 Loads and Stores in Configurable RISC Microprocessors

As we said earlier, some RISC processors are configurable to operate in either big-endian or little-endian mode. We also identified that, for example, for 32-bit processors (see Figures 2.3 and 2.4), although data pins D0–D7 always receive the least significant byte of the 32-bit operand and pins D24–D31 the most significant byte, the specific memory location in which each byte is stored depends on the endianess: if the processor operates in the *little-endian mode*, then the least significant byte (on D0–D7) is stored at location 4N; if it operates in the *big-endian mode*, then the least significant byte (on D0–D7) is stored at location 4N + 3.

Analogous comments can be made for 16-bit transfers. We pointed out earlier that the same *"load a 16-bit word from 4N"* instruction would have the processor expect valid data on different data pins, depending on the endian mode it operates under. For example, if the processor operates in the *big-endian mode* as in Figure 2.3, the above instruction would interpret valid data on pins D16–D31 (and would internally first byte-shift the incoming data bus to the right and then place them in the rightmost positions of the register); similarly for a store operation,[4] the processor would first shift the register data left and then place them as valid data on data bus pins D16–D31. If the processor operates in the *little-endian mode* as in Figure 2.4, the above instruction would interpret valid data on pins D0–D15 (and place the incoming data directly on the rightmost position of the register); similarly for a store operation, the bytes from the rightmost positions of the register would be placed as valid data directly on the data bus pins D0–D15.

From the above we can now generate Figure 2.5 for a 32-bit memory and a 32-bit microprocessor that can operate under both the big- and little-endian modes. Figure 2.5a depicts the data bytes in the internal "data bus latch/driver"; the internal "select/shift logic" will do the proper selection of the data pins (bus byte-lanes) and shifting of the data bytes to transfer them to/from the rightmost positions of the internal register. On loads, the microprocessor internally shifts the incoming data bus to the right before it places data in the register, and on stores, it shifts the register data to the left before it drives the data bus. Figure 2.5b shows the data bytes in the register for big- and little-endian modes for RISC processors with 32-bit external data buses and 32-bit internal registers, such as the MIPS

---

[3]In most of these RISC products, a "word" is 32 bits, a "halfword" is 16 bits, and a "doubleword" is 64 bits.

[4]As we said earlier, some microprocessors may duplicate data on store cycles.

Microprocessor

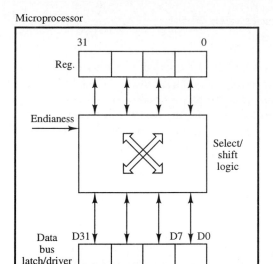

Figure 2.5 Data transfers in RISC processors with little-endian and big-endian operating modes.

(a) Simplified configuration of the internal data alignment (32-bit buses, 32-bit registers)

R2000/R3000 microprocessors. Depending on the type of load instruction, the blank register positions may either receive all zeros or extend the operand's sign.

When it comes to microprocessors with 64-bit external data buses and 32-bit internal registers (i860, M88110) the same comments and rules we mentioned above also apply. Figure 2.5c shows the data transfers for the i860.

Regardless of operand size or byte endianess, the address in a load/store instruction specifies *the byte having the smallest byte address of the addressed field* (which, for a big-endian processor, is the leftmost or most significant byte, while for a little-endian processor, it is the rightmost or least significant byte). Following the above rules, and since the i860 has as default mode of operation the little-endian mode (the memory connected to it so that section 0 is connected to data pins D0–D7), when the microprocessor is switched to operate in big-endian mode it essentially inverts the byte offset addresses in the (load/store) instructions, converting offset 0 into 7 and 7 into 0, 1 into 6 and 6 into 1, etc. [3]

2.2.5 Operand and Instruction Alignment

Operand (data) alignment.   In general, data stored in memory may have different sizes, including bytes (8 bits), words (16 bits), doublewords (32 bits), quadwords (64 bits), and octwords (128 bits, or four doublewords). Data can be located anywhere in memory, starting at any byte address. For maximum performance, when data is stored in memory it must be *aligned*. Data is aligned[5] when it adheres to the following rules:

1. Word operands (16-bit or 2-byte values) are aligned on 2-byte or word boundaries, i.e., the least significant bit A0 of the referencing address must be zero. Such an address will be symbolized in this textbook as 2N (where N is an integer).

[5]Misalignment and misaligned data transfers are treated later.

Figure 2.5 (cont.)

B0 is least significant byte

(b) 32-bit buses, 32-bit registers (e.g., R3000)

Little-endian processor

Storage in memory: 4N | B0 | B1 | B2 | B3 | (D7 – D0 ↔ D31 – D24)

Internal register: 31 ... 0 — B3 B2 B1 B0

Big-endian processor

Storage in memory: 4N | B3 | B2 | B1 | B0 | (D31 – D24 ↔ D7 – D0)

Internal register: 31 ... 0 — B3 B2 B1 B0

Processor data pins (with valid data bytes)†

Access type	Address in load/store instruction	Little-endian D31–D24	D23–D16	D15–D8	D7–D0	LE Internal register	Big-endian D31–D24	D23–D16	D15–D8	D7–D0	BE Internal register
4 bytes	4N	B3	B2	B1	B0	B3 B2 B1 B0	B3	B2	B1	B0	B3 B2 B1 B0
3 bytes	4N		B2	B1	B0	B2 B1 B0	B3	B2	B1		B3 B2 B1
3 bytes	4N + 1	B3	B2	B1		B3 B2 B1		B2	B1	B0	B2 B1 B0
2 bytes	4N			B1	B0	B1 B0	B3	B2			B3 B2
2 bytes	4N + 2	B3	B2			B3 B2			B1	B0	B1 B0
1 byte	4N				B0	B0	B3				B3
1 byte	4N + 1			B1		B1		B2			B2
1 byte	4N + 2		B2			B2			B1		B1
1 byte	4N + 3	B3				B3				B0	B0

†A load always gets a 32-bit doubleword on the processor data pins, but ignores bytes it doesn't need

Little-endian storage in memory (default):

8N | B0 | B1 | B2 | B3 | B4 | B5 | B6 | B7 ←→ D63–D56

←→ D7–D0   ...

B0 is least significant byte

Access type	Address in load/store instruction	Little-endian mode (default) Byte enables (BE#)	Little-endian Processor data pins (D63–D56, D55–D48, D47–D40, D39–D32, D31–D24, D23–D16, D15–D8, D7–D0)	Little-endian Internal register (31 … 0)	Big-endian mode Byte enables (BE#)	Big-endian Processor data pins (D63–D56, D55–D48, D47–D40, D39–D32, D31–D24, D23–D16, D15–D8, D7–D0)	Big-endian Internal register (31 … 0)
4 bytes	8N	0 – 3	B3 B2 B1 B0	B3 B2 B1 B0	7 – 4	B7 B6 B5 B4	B7 B6 B5 B4
	8N + 4	4 – 7	B7 B6 B5 B4	B7 B6 B5 B4	3 – 0	B3 B2 B1 B0	B3 B2 B1 B0
2 bytes	8N	0 – 1	B1 B0	B1 B0	7 – 6	B7 B6	B7 B6
	8N + 2	2 – 3	B3 B2	B3 B2	5 – 4	B5 B4	B5 B4
	8N + 4	4 – 5	B5 B4	B5 B4	3 – 2	B3 B2	B3 B2
	8N + 6	6 – 7	B7 B6	B7 B6	1 – 0	B1 B0	B1 B0
1 byte	8N	0	B0	B0	7	B7	B7
	8N + 1	1	B1	B1	6	B6	B6
	8N + 2	2	B2	B2	5	B5	B5
	8N + 3	3	B3	B3	4	B4	B4
	8N + 4	4	B4	B4	3	B3	B3
	8N + 5	5	B5	B5	2	B2	B2
	8N + 6	6	B6	B6	1	B1	B1
	8N + 7	7	B7	B7	0	B0	B0

(c) 64-bit buses/32-bit registers (for example, the i860 has a little-endian default mode; when operating in big-endian mode, the i860 essentially inverts the byte offset address, converting addresses 7,6,5,4,3,2,1,0 into 0,1,2,3,4,5,6,7, respectively)

Figure 2.5 (concluded)

64

2. Doubleword operands (32-bit or 4-byte values) are aligned on 4-byte or doubleword boundaries, i.e., the two least significant bits A1 and A0 of the referencing address must be zero. Such an address will be symbolized in this textbook as 4N. (Of course, 4N is also a word address.) Thus, for "32-bit memories" (i.e., memories connected to 32-bit data buses), aligned word or doubleword operands will be fetched in a single bus cycle.

3. Quadword operands (64-bit or 8-byte values) are aligned on 8-byte or quadword boundaries, i.e., the three least significant bits A2, A1, and A0 of the referencing address must be zero. Such an address will be symbolized in this textbook as 8N.

4. Octword operands (128-bit or 16-byte values) are aligned on 16-byte or octword boundaries, i.e., the four least significant bits A3–A0 of the referencing address must be zero. Such an address will be symbolized in this textbook as 16N.

Instruction alignment. Since modern microprocessors prefetch code from a 32-bit memory (and place prefetched instructions in an internal buffer/queue or instruction cache), it is assumed that code is always loaded in memory in an aligned form. This means that all instruction words and their extension words reside on word boundaries; when the required instruction begins at an odd word boundary, the microprocessor prefetches the entire 32 bits, although the second word is the required one. Attempting to prefetch an instruction word at an odd byte address would cause a trap or exception.

For 32- and 64-bit processors whose instructions are all 32 bits long, they reside on doubleword boundaries; these microprocessors perform instruction prefetch from a 32-bit doubleword or 64-bit quadword boundary, regardless of port size and alignment.

2.3 ALIGNED BUS TRANSFERS

2.3.1 Synchronous/Asynchronous Buses

All Intel microprocessors have a synchronous local bus. Most Motorola microprocessors have an asynchronous local bus, with the ability to also run synchronous bus cycles. (An exception is the 32-bit Motorola 68040, which has only a synchronous bus.) The MIPS R3000 RISC processor (see Section C3 in Appendix C) has a synchronous local bus when accessing external caches and an asynchronous bus when accessing main memory.[6]

Synchronous bus operation. Memory and input/output synchronization are essentially analogous. In a *synchronous* operation, all events take place within a specified time period in synchronism with a system-wide clock; both the processor master (that initiates the bus cycle) and the memory or I/O slave (that responds to the request) are clocked by the same system clock C.

Synchronous bus protocols time all signals relative to this system clock C, which is propagated to all modules of the system in order to time all address, data, and control information transfers. In other words, a synchronous bus transfer between the microprocessor and memory will have both the microprocessor and memory driven (and synchronized) by

---

[6]As we will see in Chapter 4, from the industry system buses, most of them are asynchronous (Multibus I, VMEbus, Futurebus), while others (Multibus II) are synchronous.

the same input clock C. The information is valid only on a certain clock edge, and assumed to have propagated through the system successfully just before the next clock edge. The clock frequency must be chosen so as to allow enough time for information to transfer from any starting point to every other point in the system. Care must be exercised, because the clock is subject to errors due to skew as distances increase and because there are differences in clock arrival time at different points in the system. A synchronous design may yield a higher speed and lower number of control lines, but it imposes speed constraints on the external devices. Since a bus cycle is made up of a number of clock cycles, its duration will be constrained by the speed of the slowest device connected to the bus (thus a synchronous bus implementation must be based on the "worst case" analysis). To overcome this, synchronous buses use a "wait protocol" that slows down the processor only when it communicates with these slower devices: the processor by default will assume that the slave device responded and advance to its next "state"; it will be slowed down only when it receives a signal in its "ready" input pin which tells it that the addressed device did not have enough time to respond and therefore the bus master must insert a wait state. Synchronous buses are less flexible and, once the design is frozen, they do not allow mixing fast and slow devices to take advantage of newer technology. On the other hand, synchronous buses are easier to understand and use in designing and testing microprocessor-based systems. A synchronous design may yield a higher speed and a lower number of control lines.

Asynchronous bus operation. The asynchronous operation does not use a central clock; in other words, the bus master and bus slave have their own individual input clocks that operate at their own different speeds. Asynchronous bus transfers are based on a handshake process in which the address or data the master places on the bus are accompanied by a corresponding handshake signal: the bus master issues a "strobe" signal to indicate that its corresponding information on the bus lines is valid; the addressed slave device will return a "data transfer acknowledge" signal[7] informing the master that it has responded to the request; i.e., it has either placed data on the data bus (if a read request), or has latched the data off the data bus (if a write request).

The asynchronous data transfer operation on such a bus is described either with a flowchart of the form shown in Figure 2.6 or with a timing diagram of the type shown in Figure 2.7. The description below is the signaling in Figure 2.7 used to synchronize the processor bus master with the slave device.

Read Cycle

1. First, the bus master places the memory address on the address bus.
2. The master allows enough time for the address to stabilize on the address bus and reach the other modules of the system, and then generates an address synchronizing signal (in the form of an address strobe AS#). This signal can be used to trigger and synchronize the addressed slave device. The address will be received and decoded by the slave device.

   The master also generates a "read" command (not shown in the figure). The address must be valid on the address bus for a few nanoseconds prior to the activation of the read command, and must remain valid on the address bus for a few nanoseconds

---

[7]The 16-bit Motorola products use one such signal called "data transfer acknowledge" (DTACK#), while the 32-bit Motorola products use two such signals, called "data and size acknowledge" (DSACK0# and DSACK1#), which are also used as "port size identifiers."

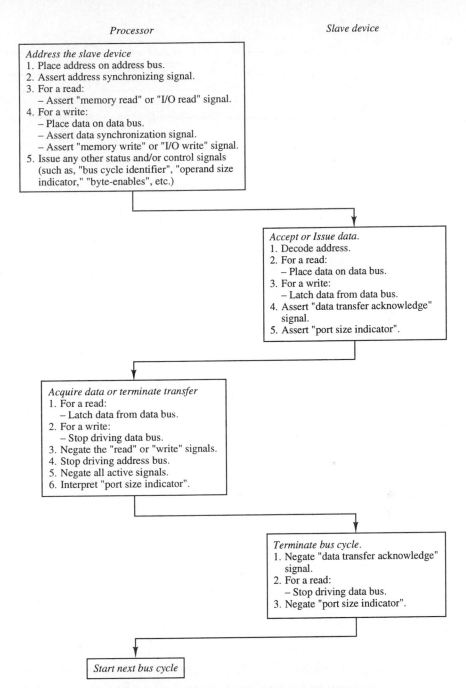

Processor   Slave device

Address the slave device
1. Place address on address bus.
2. Assert address synchronizing signal.
3. For a read:
   – Assert "memory read" or "I/O read" signal.
4. For a write:
   – Place data on data bus.
   – Assert data synchronization signal.
   – Assert "memory write" or "I/O write" signal.
5. Issue any other status and/or control signals (such as, "bus cycle identifier", "operand size indicator," "byte-enables", etc.)

Accept or Issue data.
1. Decode address.
2. For a read:
   – Place data on data bus.
3. For a write:
   – Latch data from data bus.
4. Assert "data transfer acknowledge" signal.
5. Assert "port size indicator".

Acquire data or terminate transfer
1. For a read:
   – Latch data from data bus.
2. For a write:
   – Stop driving data bus.
3. Negate the "read" or "write" signals.
4. Stop driving address bus.
5. Negate all active signals.
6. Interpret "port size indicator".

Terminate bus cycle.
1. Negate "data transfer acknowledge" signal.
2. For a read:
   – Stop driving data bus.
3. Negate "port size indicator".

Start next bus cycle

Figure 2.6   Asynchronous bus read/write flowchart.

after the removal of the read command. At a later time, the master will force a transition of the read command from active to inactive to indicate that the master has received (latched) the data sent by the addressed slave. In response to this read

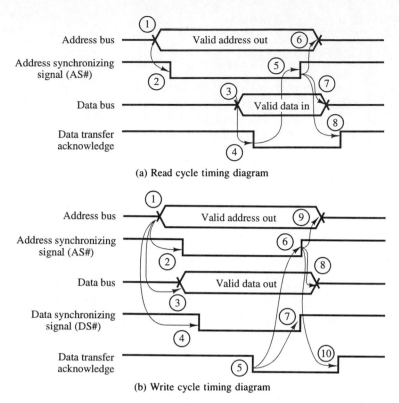

(a) Read cycle timing diagram

(b) Write cycle timing diagram

Figure 2.7 Asynchronous bus read/write timing diagrams.

command, all output buffer circuits of the slave turn toward the bus master (to drive the data bus). Data has not been accessed yet, so the data bus is indeterminate.

3. The design allows enough time for the slave (e.g., memory) access time. The slave then places the data on the data bus lines.

4. Having done this, the slave allows a few nanoseconds for the data to stabilize at the CPU module and then asserts the "data transfer acknowledge" handshake signal, indicating to the master that it has completed the read operation and the data requested is available. The high-to-low transition of the "data transfer acknowledge" signal lets the master know precisely when the data on the data bus is valid.

5. After having received the "data transfer acknowledge," the bus master will latch the data from the data bus, and terminate the read cycle by removing the read command and the address strobe.

6. Some short time thereafter, the processor stops driving the address bus.

7. As a response to the negation of the master's asserted synchronizing and command signals, the slave then terminates its operations by stopping to drive the data bus (some short time after the termination of the read command, to assure that the slave does not take data off the bus prematurely).

8. The "data transfer acknowledge" signal is negated.[8]

Write Cycle

1. The first step in the write cycle is the same as steps 1 and 2 of the read cycle.
2. The master also places the data on the data bus.
3. After a while, a data synchronizing signal (in the form of a data strobe DS#) is generated to indicate that valid data has been placed on the data bus. It also generates the "write" command; (not shown in the figure). Both address and data must be valid on the respective lines a few nanoseconds prior to the activation of the write command; thus, data may be latched by the slave on either the leading or trailing edge of the command. The write command, the address, and the data will not be removed by the master from the bus lines until the master is eventually properly notified by the slave that data has been received.
4. When the slave accepts the data from the data lines, it asserts the "data transfer acknowledge" handshake signal to indicate to the master that it has completed the write operation.
5. After having received the "data transfer acknowledge" from the slave, the bus master will remove the address synchronizing signal and the data synchronizing signal.
6. Shortly thereafter, the master will remove the data from the data lines (i.e., cease driving the data bus) and terminate the write cycle by removing the write command.
7. After a few nanoseconds, the master will also remove the address from the address bus.
8. As a response to the negation of the master's asserted synchronizing and command signals, the slave then terminates its operations by negating its "data transfer acknowledge" signal.

The data transfer acknowledge signal allows bus slaves to synchronize the operations of bus masters with conditions internal to the bus slave (e.g., data not ready) and the external "watchdog timer" will be used to generate the BERR# if the master tries to access an out-of-range address or a nonexistent device. An asynchronous bus design requires somewhat more complex interface logic but allows the use of devices of varying speed in the same system; full advantage is taken of the speed of the faster-responding devices without needing to consider the slow ones.

2.3.2 Intel 80x86 Bus Transfers

Figure 2.8 shows the general interconnection of an Intel 80x86 (80386/486) with a 32-bit memory. The four "byte-enable" signals that trigger these memory sections are BE0#, BE1#, BE2#, and BE3#, respectively, and are issued directly from the microprocessor itself. The 30-bit address A2–A31 supplied to memory points to a doubleword location. Figure 2.4 depicted some examples of how 32-bit and 16-bit operands are stored in the Intel 80x86 little-endian ordering format.

[8]In other cases, the data transfer acknowledge signal may also be removed from the bus within a specified time interval after the (read or write) command has been removed from the bus.

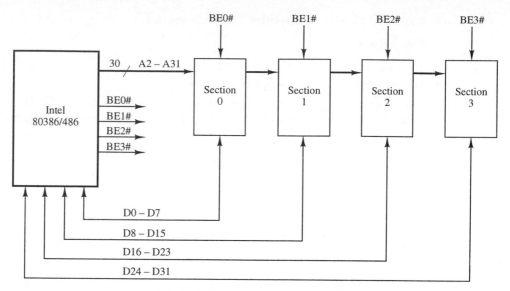

Figure 2.8 Intel 80386/486 connected to a 32-bit memory.

Read cycles. The state transition diagrams and the microoperations executed for aligned 32-bit memory read cycles by the Intel 80386 and 80486 are given in Appendix B. The respective basic timing diagrams that implement the state transition diagrams and microoperations of these processors are shown in Figures 2.9 and 2.10. Depending on the value on the output pin M/IO#, the bus cycle will be accessing either memory or I/O space.

We notice the following similarities and differences. First of all, the 80386 uses a 4-clock-cycle bus cycle, while the 80486 uses a 2-clock-cycle bus cycle. The bus cycle begins with ADS# active (asserted low) in the first clock and ends with "ready" active in the last clock. An 80386 "state" equals two clock cycles, while an 80486 "state" equals one clock cycle. Both processors have nonmultiplexed, synchronous buses. During C1 both processors place the 30 most significant address bits on the address bus lines (pointing to a doubleword address), while they decode bits A1 and A0 internally to generate the BE0#–BE3# control signals. For both of them, the D/C# line distinguishes between data read/write and control cycles.

In the 80386 case, data is read by the processor during C4 (and for a write cycle, the processor places data on the data bus during C2); in the 80486 case, data is transferred during C2 for either read or write cycles (the only difference being that outgoing data appear on the data bus in the middle of C2, while incoming data appear later during C2).

The 80386 can implement "address pipelining" and issue the address for the next bus cycle before the current bus cycle has been totally completed (as will be discussed later); for this purpose, the 80386 has a pin called "next address" (NA#). The 80486 has done away with address pipelining (has no NA# input pin); instead, it implements the "burst transfer" mode (to be discussed later).

Both the 80386 and the 80486 are dynamically reconfigurable processors being able to adjust their bus sizes; they do it by sampling their "port size indicator" input pins. The 80486 has two such pins, bus size BS8# and BS16#, which also allows it to support 8-bit and 16-bit devices; the 80386 has only one such pin (BS16#), which allows it to support

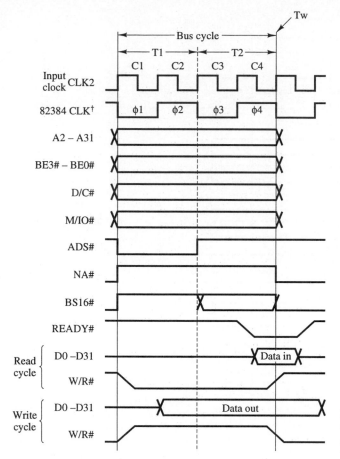

Figure 2.9 Intel 80386 basic bus timing diagram for (memory and I/O) read/write cycles. (Wait states TW repeat state T2.) [4] Reprinted by permission of Intel Corporation. © 1986 by Intel Corp.

†The 82384 CLK is not an input signal, it is generated internally.

only 16-bit devices. As we will see later, depending upon the width of the data operand to be transferred and the size (width) of the accessed slave device, the processor determines whether additional bus cycles are required.

For either product, a 32-bit memory will drive all 32 lines of the data bus during a read cycle.

Write cycles. The 80386 and 80486 handle the memory write cycles or I/O write cycles differently. When the 80386 processor starts a write cycle, then if the operand being transferred occupies **only** the upper 16 bits of the data bus (D16–D31), the 80386 processor *duplicates* that information on the lower half of its data bus (D0–D15). This is done so as to optimize write performance on 16-bit buses (for example, a word write to location $4N + 2$ of a 16-bit slave can be done in a single bus cycle). Figure 2.11 shows in a tabular form the automatic duplication of byte operands or word operands on the respective data bus byte-lanes and the corresponding byte-enables BE0#–BE3# the Intel 80386 asserts.

The 80486, on the other hand, does not duplicate write data; the 80486 always places valid data only on those data bus pins that correspond to byte-enable signals asserted low

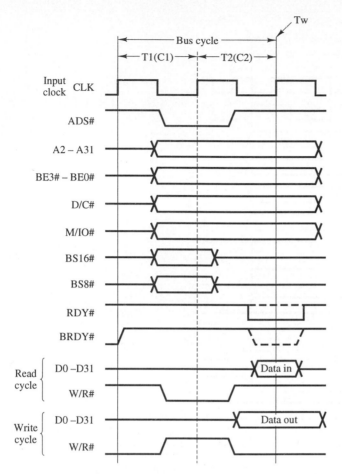

Figure 2.10 Intel 80486 basic bus timing diagram for (memory and I/O) read/write cycles. (Wait states TW repeat state T2.) [8] Reprinted by permission of Intel Corporation. © 1989 by Intel Corp.

during write cycles. (As we will explain later in Section 2.6.2, this requires additional external "byte swap" logic.)

Example 2.1: Intel 80x86 Aligned Bus Transfers

The aligned storage to location 4N of the doubleword operand EFGHIJKL will be done by both the 80386 and 80486 processors in one bus cycle; all four byte enables BE0#–BE3# will be asserted by the microprocessor. The least significant byte KL will be transferred over data bus byte-lane D0–D7 and stored in section 0, while the most significant byte EF will be transferred over data bus byte lane D24–D31 and stored in section 3.

The aligned storage to location 4N of the word operand ABCD will again be done by both Intel processors in one bus cycle and only BE0# and BE1# will be asserted. AB will be transferred over D8–D15 and stored in section 1 and CD will be transferred over D0–D7 and stored in section 0. The values on D16–D31 lines are undefined. (Data duplication does not take place.)

However, the aligned storage of word operand ABCD to location 4N+2 will be done differently by the two processors. In the 80386 case, BE2# and BE3# will be asserted to store this operand transferred over D16–D31 lines (AB to section 3 and CD to section 2). Data duplication now takes place and byte lanes D8–D15 and D0–D7 carry bytes AB and CD, respectively. In the 80486 case, ABCD will be transferred as before over D16–D31 but there will be no data duplication on lines D0–D15.

	80386 Byte-Enables				80386 Write data[a]				Automatic duplication?
	BE3#	BE2#	BE1#	BE0#	D24-D31	D16-D23	D8-D15	D0-D7	
Byte writes	High	High	High	Low	Undef.	Undef.	Undef.	B0	No
	High	High	Low	High	Undef.	Undef.	B0	Undef.	No
	High	Low	High	High	Undef.	B0	Undef.	B0	Yes
	Low	High	High	High	B0	Undef.	B0	Undef.	Yes
Two-byte writes	High	High	Low	Low	Undef.	Undef.	B1	B0	No
	High	Low	Low	High	Undef.	B1	B0	Undef.	No
	Low	Low	High	High	B1	B0	B1	B0	Yes
Three-byte writes	High	Low	Low	Low	Undef.	B2	B1	B0	No
	Low	Low	Low	High	B2	B1	B0	Undef.	No
Four-byte writes	Low	Low	Low	Low	B3	B2	B1	B0	No

[a]Operands are:

   32-bit operand: B3,B2,B1,B0
   16-bit operand: B1,B0
    8-bit operand: B0
   (B0 = least significant byte)

Figure 2.11   Data duplication for the Intel 80386 memory or I/O write cycles and the corresponding byte-enable signals asserted (low) [4]. Reprinted by permission of Intel Corporation. © 1986 Intel Corp.

2.3.3 Motorola 680x0 Bus Transfers

Figure 2.12 shows the general interconnection of a Motorola 680x0 (68020/30/40) processor with a 32-bit memory. The four ''byte-enable'' control signals (DBBE1–DBBE4) that trigger these memory sections are generated by external ''byte-enable'' logic that decodes the two least significant address bits A0 and A1 and the 2-bit ''operand size indicator'' SIZ0 and SIZ1. Figure 2.12 also shows the truth table for this ''byte-enable'' logic. The number of bytes transferred during a read or write bus cycle is equal to or less than the size indicated by SIZ0 and SIZ1 outputs, depending on port size and operand alignment. However, the values SIZ0, SIZ1 = 11 indicate a 3-byte transfer for the 68020 and 68030, while for the 68040 they indicate a ''line transfer,'' i.e., four consecutive doubleword transfers in a ''burst transfer'' (to be explained later). The 30-bit address A2–A31 supplied to memory points to a 32-bit doubleword location. Aligned 32-bit and 16-bit data in a Motorola 680x0 32-bit memory will be stored as shown in Figure 2.3.

Read cycles.   The state transition diagram and the microoperations executed for aligned 32-bit memory read cycles by the Motorola 68020/30 are given in Figure 1.18. The corresponding *asynchronous* timing diagram of these processors is shown in Figure 2.13. (The 68020/30 also support synchronous bus cycles as discussed in Appendix B.) Figure 2.14 shows the state transition diagram and the timing diagram of the 68040.

We notice the following similarities and differences. First of all, all of them have separate 32-bit nonmultiplexed buses (one for addresses, the other for data). The 68040 has a 2- input-clock-cycle bus cycle (a total of 8 ''T states'') as compared to the 3-input-clock-cycle bus cycle of the 68020/30 (a total of 6 ''S states''). Both the 68020 and the 68030 support synchronous as well as asynchronous bus transfers; synchronization between the processor and memory is achieved with the use of the DSACKx# signals. On the other

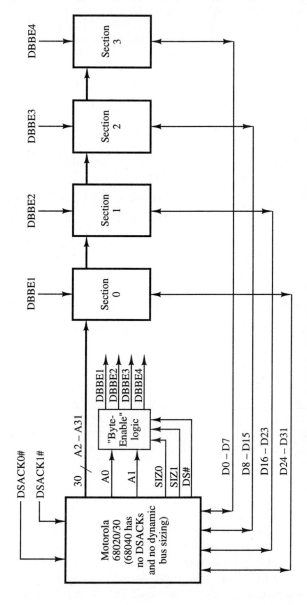

Figure 2.12 Motorola 680x0 (32-bit big-endian) connected to a 32-bit memory [5].

SIZ1	SIZ0	Size		DSACK0#	DSACK1#	Port Width
0	0	4 Bytes		0	1	8 Bits
1	0	2 Bytes		1	0	16 Bits
0	1	1 Byte		0	0	32 Bits
1	1	3 Bytes (for the 68020/30) or a Line (or 4 doublewords, for the 68040)		1	1	Insert wait state

"BYTE-ENABLE" TRUTH TABLE

SIZ1	SIZ0	A1	A0	DBBE1	DBBE2	DBBE3	DBBE4
0	1	0	0	1	0	0	0
		0	1	0	1	0	0
		1	0	0	0	1	0
		1	1	0	0	0	1
1	0	0	0	1	1	0	0
		0	1	0	1	1	0
		1	0	0	0	1	1
		1	1	0	0	0	1
1	1	0	0	1	1	1	0
		0	1	0	1	1	1
		1	0	0	0	1	1
		1	1	0	0	0	1
0	0	0	0	1	1	1	1
		0	1	0	1	1	1
		1	0	0	0	1	1
		1	1	0	0	0	1

Figure 2.12   (concluded)

hand, the 68040 supports only synchronous bus transfers; synchronization is achieved with the use of the "transfer acknowledge" TA# signal that memory sends back to the processor. In the 68040 case, the "operand size indicator" signals SIZ0 and SIZ1 correspond to the specific bus cycle; in the 68020/30 case, they indicate how many bytes are remaining to be transferred.

Both the 68020 and 68030 support dynamic bus sizing; they adjust their bus sizes by issuing SIZ0 and SIZ1 and monitoring the values of the incoming "port size indicator" signals DSACK0# and DSACK1#, which indicate the width of the responding slave device. The 68040, on the other hand, does not support dynamic bus sizing; data transfers between the 68040 and memory or peripheral device is done using a fixed 32-bit data port size. The 68040 has two input pins for clocks (see Figure B.7): BCLK (bus clock signal) and PCLK (processor clock signal). The PCLK signal is exactly twice the frequency of the BCLK signal. In the 68040, an input clock cycle C (or BCLK) consists of 4 "T states," while in the 68020/30 it consists of 2 "S states" (see also Figure 1.14c). Finally, in the 68020/30 a wait state is one clock cycle (or 2 "S states") inserted between C2 and C3; in the 68040, it is again equal to one clock cycle (or 4 "T states") inserted after C2 (repeats C2).

As shown in Figure 2.13a, the 68020/30 processor issues the synchronization signal AS# to indicate to the slave device that a valid address is on the address bus; when the slave

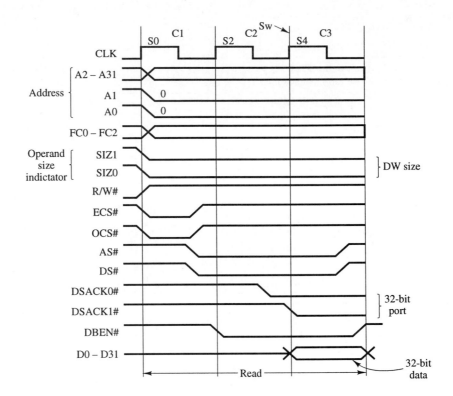

SIZ1	SIZ0	Operand size
0	1	1 Byte
1	0	2 Bytes
0	1	3 Bytes
1	0	4 Bytes

DSACK0#	DSACK1#	Port size
0	1	Byte
1	0	16-bit
0	0	32-bit
1	1	Insert wait state

(a) Asynchronous timing diagram

Figure 2.13 Motorola 68020/30 basic bus timing diagram [5]. (Wait states Sw inserted after S3.)

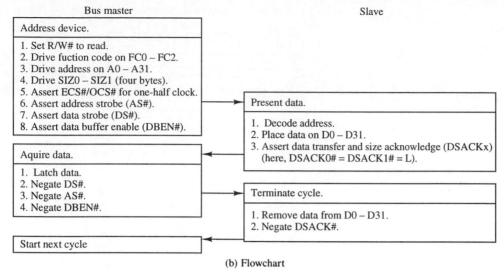

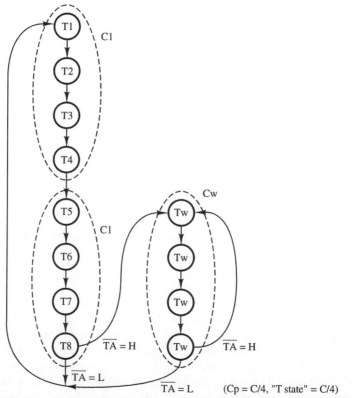

(b) Flowchart

Figure 2.13   (concluded)

$\overline{TA} = H$

$\overline{TA} = H$

$\overline{TA} = L$

$\overline{TA} = L$ (Cp = C/4, "T state" = C/4)

(a) State transition diagram. Four T's make up one input clock cycle C (or BCLK)

Figure 2.14   Motorola 68040 state transition and basic synchronous bus timing diagrams [6].

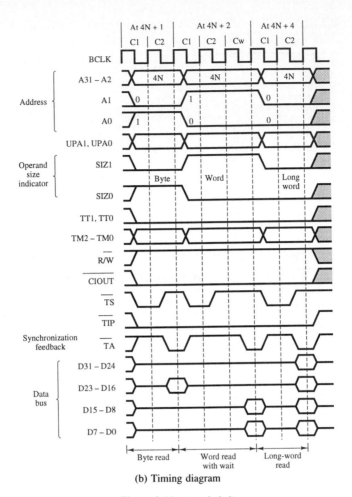

Figure 2.14 (concluded)

device has completed the transaction of placing its data on the data bus (for a read cycle), or latched the data off the data bus (for a write cycle), it will respond back to the processor with the two feedback signals DSACK0# and DSACK1#. If the DSACKx# inputs are not asserted during the sample window of the falling edge of S2, the processor will insert wait states until these signals are sampled asserted. This pair of DSACKx# signals not only synchronize the 68020/30 with memory, they also indicate what the width of the responding slave device is. As we will explain later when we discuss "dynamic bus sizing," if the responding slave device has a width smaller than 32 bits, the processor will have to adjust its data bus width dynamically to interpret the data properly on its input data lines and decide whether it is necessary to execute additional bus cycles in order to complete the operand transfer operation. The timing diagram for the 68020/30 executing asynchronous word and byte read cycles[9] is shown in Figure B.12a in Appendix B. Figure 2.14 shows the 68040 synchronous timing diagrams for byte, word, and doubleword read cycles.

[9]Throughout this chapter, in all timing diagrams for read operations, *only the data bus lines that carry valid information are shown.*

Write cycles. In the 68020/30 case, for a write cycle the processor always drives all four byte-lanes of the data bus at the start of a bus cycle; the rules the processor follows for placing the operand bytes on its external data bus lines during write cycles are shown in Figure 2.15. The entries shown as Bn are the portions of the operand placed on the data bus during that bus cycle and are defined by SIZ0, SIZ1, A0, and A1. An example of using these rules to do data duplication (compare them with the data duplication rules for the Intel 80386 in Figure 2.11) on the data bus when the operand to be written is less than 32 bits is given in Figure B.12b.

Transfer size	Address[a]		Operands on data bus byte-lanes[b]			
	A1	A0	D24–D31	D16–D23	D8–D15	D0–D7
Byte (B)	X	X	B0	B0	B0	B0
Word (w)	X	0	B1	B0	B1	B0
	X	1	B1	B1	B0	B1
Three-byte	0	0	B2	B1	B0	B3[c]
	0	1	B2	B2	B1	B0
	1	0	B2	B1	B2	B1
	1	1	B2	B2	B1[c]	B2
Doubleword	0	0	B3	B2	B1	B0
(DW)	0	1	B3	B3	B2	B1
	1	0	B3	B2	B3	B2
	1	1	B3	B3	B2[c]	B3

[a]X = don't care.

[b]The B's on the data bus refer to a particular byte of the operand written on that byte-lane of the data bus. Operands are:

DW: B3,B2,B1,B0
W: B1,B0
B: B0
(B0 = least significant byte)

[c]On write cycles this byte is output; on read cycles this byte is ignored.

Figure 2.15 Data duplication for the Motorola 68020/30 memory write cycles [5].

The *68040 does not support dynamic bus sizing and does not duplicate data bytes on the data bus during write cycles.* It drives the appropriate byte lanes of the data bus according to the size of the operand and the values of A0 and A1; all other byte lanes are diven with undefined values.

Example 2.2: Motorola 68020/30 Aligned Bus Transfers

Consider the doubleword operand EFGHIJKL to be stored in location 4N. All Motorola 680x0 processors will issue SIZ1, SIZ0 = 00 (doubleword) and do the write operation in one bus cycle. The SIZ1 and SIZ0 signals along with A1A0 = 00 will be decoded externally by the "byte-enable logic" (Figure 2.12) to generate the signals DBBE1−DBBE4 = 1111. The least significant byte KL will again be transferred over D0–D7 but now stored in section 3, while the most significant byte EF will again be transferred over D24–D31 but now stored in section 0.

The aligned storage of the word operand ABCD will be handled differently. In the 68020 and 68030 cases, the storage of ABCD to either location 4N or 4N + 2 will have the operand transferred over both the upper and lower halves of the data bus (AB over D24–D31 and D8–D15 and CD over D16–D23 and D0–D7). In the 68040 case, the storage to location 4N will have ABCD transferred over only D16–D31, while the storage to location 4N+2 will have ABCD transferred over only D0–D15.

2.4 OTHER BUS OPERATING MODES

2.4.1. Address Pipelining

Basic principles. So far we have seen that when the processor is connected to slower devices, their accommodation is accomplished by having the processor insert wait states. This increases the bus cycle time, and thus the available time, so that slower devices can respond. The amount of increase in the bus cycle time depends on the particular product: for example, from Figure 1.14b in Chapter 1 we observe that one wait state in the 8086 increases the bus cycle time by 25%, while it increases the bus cycles of the other Intel products by 50%.

In addition to the wait-state solution, some (mainly Intel) microprocessors are designed to also support another technique, called "address pipelining." For example, in the Intel 80386, address pipelining works only when the microprocessor is so activated by external circuitry (triggering its "next address" NA# input pin). Unlike wait states, the "address pipelining" technique increases the time the addressed slave has to respond without lengthening the bus cycle; *it allows the memory access time for the next bus transaction to overlap the current data transfer time*.

Figure 2.16a shows the basic timing for a nonpipelined bus operation. Consecutive bus cycles N, N+1, N+2, etc. start when the processor issues an address on the address bus and—in this diagram—a bus cycle lasts 4 input clocks. The *memory access time*[10] is 3 clocks. The processor, then, one clock cycle later (assuming no wait states) will latch the data off the data bus, finish the current bus cycle, and start the next cycle by issuing the next address on its address bus lines. In this example, the processor issues an address every 4 clock cycles, receives data every 4 clock cycles, and the memory access time requirement is 3 clock cycles.

Figure 2.16b shows the timing for a pipelined bus operation. The processor places the address of the *next* bus cycle on the address bus *while the current bus cycle is still in progress*. It is observed that, again, the processor issues an address every 4 clock cycles and receives data every 4 clock cycles, but the memory access time requirement has now increased to 5 clock cycles (since the memory subsystem received and started decoding the address earlier). Therefore, pipelined buses allow more time for memory access, without changing the microprocessor bus cycle time (i.e., without slowing down the processor).

Example 2.3: Intel 80286 Address Pipelining

As shown in the 80286 basic timing diagram of Figure A.7 in Appendix A, the 80286 does not wait until the next cycle starts before it issues the next address. For example, consider an "8-MHz 80286"; this means that PCLK = 8 MHz, and the input clock frequency is CLK = 16 MHz. If the processor made available a valid address at the beginning of the bus cycle, then the memory access time requirement would be 218.75 ns (three and a half input CLK clock cycles)

---

[10]The definition of access time here is from the time the address is valid on the address bus (and assumed latched by the slave device) until the slave device responds by placing valid data on the data bus.

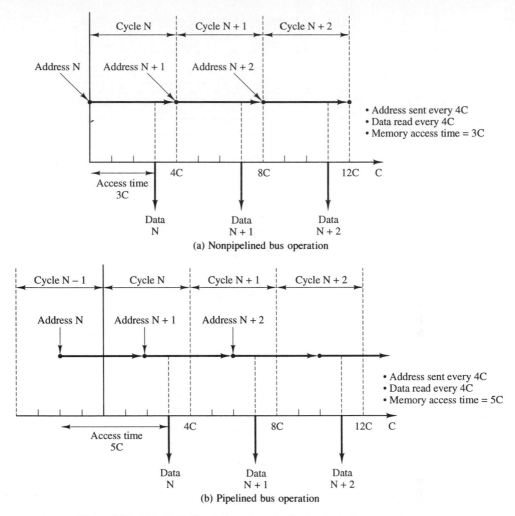

Figure 2.16 Functional description of nonpipelined and pipelined bus operations.

and data will be transferred at a rate of 8 Mbytes per second (2 bytes per bus cycle). Since the issued address becomes valid one clock cycle earlier, a slower memory subsystem with access time of 281.25 ns (four and a half input CLK clock cycles) will still sustain the 8-Mbyte per second transfer rate, without slowing down the processor.

Intel 80386 address pipelining. The 80386 processor has a feature called "pipelined access" and provides an input pin called "next address" NA# that must be asserted in order for the microprocessor to do address pipelining.[11] Consider the nonpipelined case of Figure 2.17a. (This is derived from the 80386 basic timing diagram of Figure 2.9.) It shows that this processor is driven by a 32-MHz input clock C with clock cycle time C = 31.25 ns. (Intel 80386 calls it a "phase.") The responding slave device monitors the ADS# output to confirm that the next address is placed on the address bus, and accesses its data and starts

[11]Address pipelining cannot be used in the Intel 80386 with BS16# bus cycles.

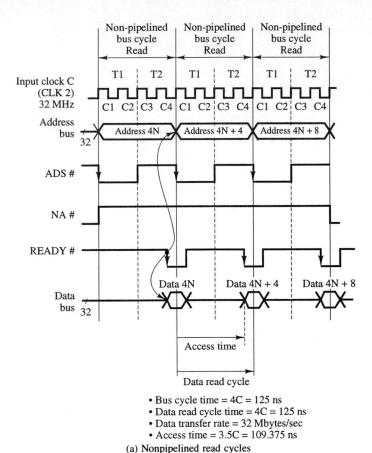

• Bus cycle time = 4C = 125 ns
• Data read cycle time = 4C = 125 ns
• Data transfer rate = 32 Mbytes/sec
• Access time = 3.5C = 109.375 ns

(a) Nonpipelined read cycles

Figure 2.17 Intel 80386 nonpipelined and pipelined bus cycles [4]. Reprinted by permission of Intel Corporation. © 1986 by Intel Corp.

driving the data bus three clock cycles after the processor had issued the address. In this case we say that the access time requirement of the slave device is 3.5*C = 109.375 ns. The READY# signal tells the processor to latch the data and one clock cycle later end the bus cycle for this transfer.

Now consider the timing of Figure 2.17b, which shows the end of the nonpipelined bus cycles followed by the execution of two pipelined cycles. First we notice that unless the "next address" NA# input pin is triggered low by external interface logic, the processor will be executing its normal nonpipelined bus cycles. Whenever the memory subsystem interface is ready to accept the address for the next cycle while the current cycle is still in progress, it sends to the 80386 chip the NA# signal. In our example in Figure 2.17b, this happens during the second bus cycle. During nonpipelined bus cycles, this NA# is sampled at the end of clock cycle 1 (at the end of phase 1) in every T2. When sampled low, the processor will issue the control signals and the address 4N + 8 for the next cycle (as early as the next bus state), and indicate the validity of these signals by asserting low the address status ADS# signal. (In response to the ADS#, the memory subsystem interface latches the address and control signals and starts decoding the operation for the next cycle.) The current

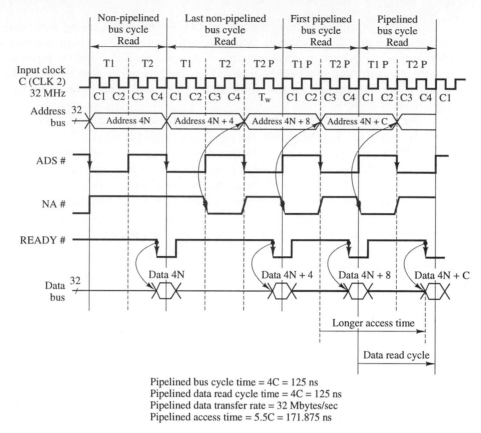

Pipelined bus cycle time = 4C = 125 ns
Pipelined data read cycle time = 4C = 125 ns
Pipelined data transfer rate = 32 Mbytes/sec
Pipelined access time = 5.5C = 171.875 ns

(b) Pipelined read cycles

Figure 2.17 (concluded)

bus cycle is lengthened by one state (two clock cycles) and the processor enters T2P. Then, the memory subsystem concludes its cycle by placing data on the data bus and asserting the READY# line low. As a response to sampling this signal, the processor latches the data and ends the current bus cycle. From there on, consecutive pipelined bus cycles (initiated by the NA# asserted low) will have their respective output addresses become valid before the end of their previous bus cycles.

Example 2.4: Intel 80386 Address Pipelining

In the 80386 nonpipelined operation of Figure 2.17a, consecutive addresses are issued by the microprocessor at the beginning of each bus cycle, i.e., every 4*C = 125 ns. The bus behavior of this diagram imposes on the memory an access time requirement of 3.5*C = 109.325 ns. The 80386 then receives a 32-bit operand every 125 ns; i.e., it sustains a (maximum) data transfer rate (or bandwidth) of 32 Mbytes/sec.

The 80386 address pipelined mode means that the processor is not slowed down (it still reads data every 4 clock cycles and sustains the previous 32-Mbyte/sec data transfer rate), but now it imposes less stringent requirements on the access time of the responding slave, which has increased from 3.5*C = 109.375 ns to 5.5*C = 171.875 ns.

Address pipelining is less effective for I/O devices which, being slow, may require several wait states. If, for example, address pipelining results in saving one wait state (in other words, an I/O access which requires 2 wait states without address pipelining would require one wait state with address pipelining), then the more wait states the I/O device requires, the less significant this elimination of one wait state through address pipelining becomes.

For the 80386, address overlapping can be achieved only between the current and the very next bus cycle. In other words, the pipelining capability triggered by externally asserting the NA# input pin cannot look further than one bus cycle ahead; this is referred to as **1 level of pipelining**. (Asserting NA# more than once during any bus cycle has no additional effects.) The 80386 cannot issue a new address more frequently than every four input clock cycles (CLK2s), as shown in Figure 2.17. (In Section 3.4.1 of the next chapter we give the timing diagram of the address pipelining of the Intel i860, whose NA# input pin can be asserted twice before READY# is asserted, thus supporting **up to 2 levels of pipelining**. In order to accommodate this high data rate, the 4-way interleaved memory design needed is also discussed in that section.)

2.4.2 Burst Transfers

Under the "burst transfer" mode,[12] the microprocessor sends only one address to memory: the starting address of a number of doublewords to be fetched. The memory subsystem interface is required to increment the received address and sequentially send each doubleword back to the processor. The burst transfer mode speeds up the data transfer operation when there is a block of doublewords to be transferred (such as, for example, to fill a line of an on-chip cache memory).

Intel 80486 multiple and burst transfers

The Intel 80486 microprocessor has introduced, in place of the 80386's pipelined address mode, the "multiple bus cycle" and "burst cycle" modes. Figure 2.18a shows the timing diagram of the 80486 normal bus cycles (i.e., nonburst and noncacheable) for a read operation. For any type of cycle (nonburst or burst) the processor places the address on the address bus and asserts the ADS#. Each bus cycle ends with the assertion of the ready signal RDY#. (The input signals "burst ready" BRDY# and "cache enable" KEN# are not asserted.[13]) The output signal "burst last" BLAST# is asserted (low) after each data transfer to indicate the end of the individual 2-state bus cycle.

80486 Multiple Bus Cycles. A multiple bus cycle may be burst or nonburst, and cacheable or noncacheable. The microprocessor executes multiple bus cycles when it needs to do a 128-bit instruction prefetch, a 64-bit floating-point load, a misaligned operand read, or a cache line fill. Multiple cycles may also be caused by the external system if it is a 16-bit or an 8-bit port.

Figure 2.18b shows the timing diagram for a **multiple bus cycle** (nonburst and noncacheable). Notice that for any type of multiple bus cycle the 80486 microprocessor holds

---

[12]Sometimes it is also referred to as "block transfer" mode. When a burst read operation is executed to fill a cache line, it is called "cache line read" or "cache line fill" mode.

[13]When the processor samples RDY# active it ignores BRDY#.

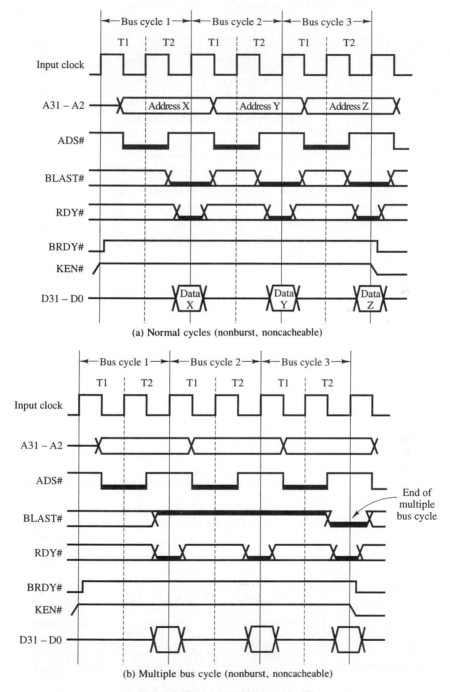

(a) Normal cycles (nonburst, noncacheable)

(b) Multiple bus cycle (nonburst, noncacheable)

Figure 2.18   Intel 80486 bus cycles [8].

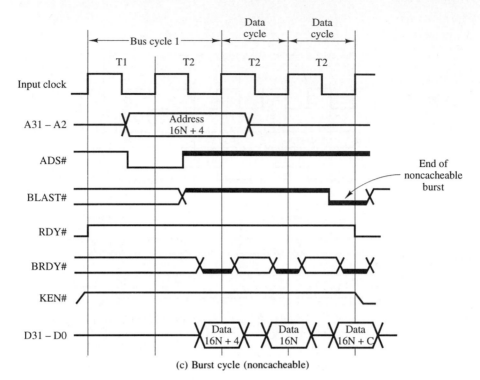

(c) Burst cycle (noncacheable)

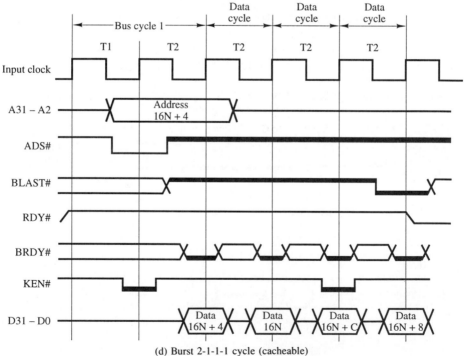

(d) Burst 2-1-1-1 cycle (cacheable)

Figure 2.18 (concluded)

BLAST# high throughout all cycles. It is observed that for such a nonburst multiple cycle, one data item is transferred every bus cycle (the bus cycle composed of 2 states).

For any type of multiple bus cycle, the processor informs the external system that the transfer could take additional cycles and indicates that it is willing to perform a burst transfer by driving the burst last signal (BLAST#) inactive (or high) during the second clock of the first bus cycle. Since in the diagram of Figure 2.18b the external memory system returns RDY# (instead of BRDY#), it indicates to the microprocessor that it will not burst the data; this, therefore, represents a nonburst multiple transfer. The processor then executes whatever number of cycles it needs to complete the multiple transfer it initiated (while continuously driving BLAST# inactive). For each bus cycle, the processor issues a new address and asserts the ADS#. When it finishes all transfers, it indicates the last cycle of the multiple transfer by driving BLAST# active. The total number of cycles that the processor initiates to carry out a multiple transfer depends on the number of bytes the processor needs to complete the internal request (1, 2, 4, 8, or 16), the port size of the accessed slave device (indicated by the BS16# or BS8# inputs), and the alignment of the data to be transferred.

80486 Burst Cycles (Noncacheable). Burst cycles can be cacheable or noncacheable; we first examine the noncacheable burst cycles. As we said earlier, a multiple bus cycle may be converted into a burst cycle if the external system supports bursting. The processor pins used for a burst transfer are the output pin ''burst last'' BLAST# and the input pin ''burst ready'' BRDY#. During any multiple bus cycle, the processor informs the external system that it is willing to do the multiple transfers in a burst mode by holding the burst last signal (BLAST#) inactive in the second clock of the first bus cycle (Figure 2.18c). If the external system supports bursting, it will assert the BRDY# input pin instead of the RDY# pin. With such a burst transfer, the first data item will be fetched in 2 clock cycles, but subsequent data items will be strobed into the 80486 processor every clock cycle. Thus, since the access overhead for these data transfers is eliminated, memory bandwidth is greatly enhanced with the burst mode. During each additional **data cycle**[14] of the burst transfer, the ADS# remains inactive while the processor drives BLAST# inactive to all but the last cycle of the burst transfer. When the processor finally asserts the BLAST# output signal low, it informs the external system that the next time RDY# or BRDY# is returned, the transfer is complete. Burst transfers usually refer to read operations; the 80486 does not support multiple 32-bit burst writes. The only burst writes it supports are to 16-bit or 8-bit ports, and the maximum burst write the 80486 will do in these cases is 32 bits: that is, either four 8-bit operands or two 16-bit operands will be written in a single burst cycle.

In any burst cycle (noncacheable or cacheable) the addresses of the data items will all fall within the same 16-byte aligned block in memory. It is observed in Figure 2.18c that the processor issues the beginning address $16N+4$, which points to the second doubleword of the block. However, the processor expects subsequent data to be received from locations that follow a specific order (and the external address incrementing must follow this rule) in order to fetch all 16 bytes of the block. The order of subsequent access addresses depends upon the first address in the transfer. In order for the 80486 to accommodate both simple 32-bit

---

[14]The term **data cycle** is used here: A bus cycle may contain one or more data cycles and data it transferred to or from the microprocessor during a data cycle.

memories as well as 2-way doubleword interleaved memories, the order of access address sequencing adheres to the following rules[15]:

1. If the first address is 16N, then the next 3 addresses are: $16N+4$, $16N+8$, $16N+C$.

2. If the first address is $16N+4$, then the next 3 addresses are: 16N, $16N+C$, $16N+8$.

3. If the first address is $16N+8$, then the next 3 addresses are: $16N+C$, 16N, $16N+4$.

4. If the first address is $16N+C$, then the next 3 addresses are: $16N+8$, $16N+4$, 16N.

Example 2.5: Intel 80486 Address Ordering To Fill a Cache Line

(If the reader has not studied memory interleaving, he/she may skip the example and come back to it after reading Chapter 3.)

This ''486 address ordering'' can be explained by observing Figure 2.19a, which shows a burst cycle (for example, to fill a line in the on-chip cache) starting from location $16N+A$ form a 2-way doubleword-interleaved memory. The order must be $16N+8$, $16N+C$, 16N, and $16N+4$, or in the following doubleword sequencing: DW2, DW3, DW0, and DW1. Figure 2.19b shows the same cache line fill operation using noninterleaved 32-bit memories. If the same compatible order DW2, DW3, DW0, and DW1 of the interleaved case must be preserved, then the order of bursting the 16-byte cache line from the noninterleaved memory must also be $16N+8$, $16N+C$, 16N, and $16N+4$.

This ordering of addresses is followed for either burst or nonburst cache line fills. An example of the 80486 cache line fill from 16-bit ports is given in Section 2.6.2.

Given the first address in a burst, external hardware can follow the above rules to generate the addresses of subsequent transfers in advance. *For burst cycles, the above ordering*

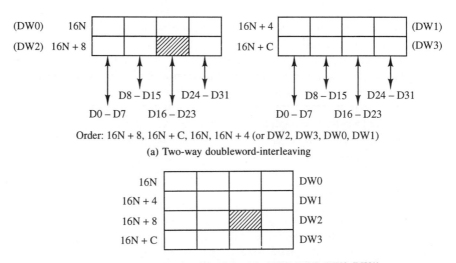

Order: $16N+8$, $16N+C$, 16N, $16N+4$ (or DW2, DW3, DW0, DW1)

(a) Two-way doubleword-interleaving

Order: $16N+8$, $16N+C$, 16N, $16N+4$ (or DW2, DW3, DW0, DW1)

(b) No interleaving, 32-bit memory

Figure 2.19   Intel 80486 burst operation (to fill a cache line) from location $16N+A$ of a 32-bit memory.

[15]This order will guarantee that two successive accesses will fetch data from two different memory banks of a 2-way doubleword interleaved memory, as we will explain in more detail in the next chapter.

of addresses applies to all burst cycles, regardless of their purpose. Burst cycles can be noncacheable or cacheable. For a noncacheable burst, the processor will only burst the number of bytes needed to complete the transfer. Figure 2.20 shows the rules that apply for the four combinations of burst/nonburst and cacheable/noncacheable cycles.

	Nonburst	Burst
Noncacheable	Normal bus cycle	• Address ordering applies (maintained by external hardware) • The 80486 will only burst the number of bytes needed to complete the transfer
Cacheable (cache line fill)	• BE3#–BE0# not interpreted by external hardware during first cycle to a cacheable memory (they are assumed all active) • Always fetches a 16-byte cache line • Address ordering applies (maintained by the processor)	• BE3#–BE0# not interpreted during first cycle to a cacheable memory (they are assumed all active) • Always fetches a 16-byte cache line • Address ordering applies (maintained by memory interface hardware)

Figure 2.20 Rules for 80486 burst/nonburst and cacheable/noncacheable cycles.

In order to support memory systems that may not be able to respond with burst cycles in the order defined here, the 80486 microprocessor allows a burst cycle to be interrupted at any time.

80486 Burst Cycles (Cacheable). **Cacheable burst cycles** are used to fill a (16-byte) line of the 80486's internal cache; these 16 bytes fetched represent a block of main memory aligned on a 16-byte boundary (i.e., its first address has four zeros at the right) and the above mentioned 80486 ''address ordering'' is followed.

The 16 bytes are fist placed temporarily into an internal ''line buffer.'' Figure 2.18d shows the timing diagram for a cacheable burst cycle. During the first bus cycle of a cacheable burst operation, the state of the byte-enables should be ignored; the 80486 expects to receive valid data on its entire 32-bit bus in the first cycle of a cache line fill (i.e., all byte enables should be treated by the external system as if they are all active). The external memory system indicates that this is a cacheable transfer by returning KEN# active one clock before BRDY# during the first cycle of the transfer.[16] When KEN# is driven active in the first clock, the BLAST# is driven inactive in the second clock in response. From there on, the processor will fetch an entire 16-byte cache line regardless of the state of KEN#. The external hardware that receives the first address of a burst cycle can easily calculate in

---

[16]KEN# is ignored during write or I/O cycles (because I/O space is never cacheable in the internal cache). Other types of cycles that are not cacheable are: interrupt acknowledge cycles and locked cycles.

advance the address of subsequent transfers (following the 80486 address ordering rules discussed above) in order to fetch the entire block.

Figure 2.21 shows functionally the steps involved in a cacheable burst read operation to fill a 16-byte line of the on-chip cache. At step 1, the 80486 starts the bus cycle by asserting the address strobe ADS# and sending the address of the first 32-bit doubleword. It also informs the external system that it is willing to perform a burst transfer by holding BLAST# high. At step 2, the external memory system asserts the "cache enable" KEN# signal one clock before RDY# or BRDY# during the first bus cycle of the transfer. (This is issued by external logic[17] to tell the processor that read data should be cached.) The external system then informs the processor at step 3 that it supports bursting for the cache line fill operation by driving BRDY# active (instead of the normal RDY#) at the end of the first bus cycle. A burst read transfer will be executed to fetch four doublewords into the "line buffer." The processor does that by reading one doubleword every input clock cycle (or every T state). During all this time it holds its output BLAST# high, letting the slave interface do the address incrementing itself. Finally, the end of the burst cycle is signaled when the 80486 asserts the output signal BLAST# negative. KEN# must again be returned active (i.e., arrive at its final value in the clock before BRDY#—or before RDY# in the nonburst case—is returned) to indicate that what arrives during the last data cycle of the transfer still is a cacheable data.[18] This will then let internal hardware fill (update) an entire cache line from the 16-byte "line buffer" in 1 clock cycle.

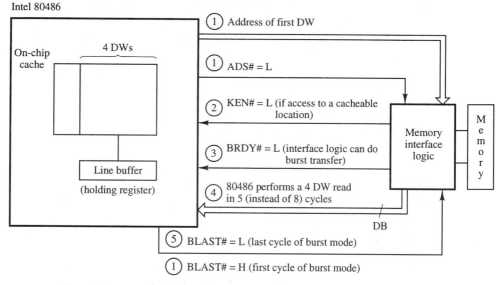

Figure 2.21 Functional description of the Intel 80486 burst transfer mode to fill a cache line of the on-chip cache.

Inside the processor, attribute bits exist in the "translation look-aside buffer" or TLB to identify shared (noncacheable) memory at a page granularity (as will be explained in more

[17]Usually generated by decoding the processor address.

[18]The state of the BLAST# may be changing when a burst transfer is performed with less wide memories (e.g., 16-bit or 8-bit memories).

detail in Chapter 5). For shared (noncacheable) pages and for input ports, a single double-word read operation is performed (KEN# is not asserted, and the internal cache is bypassed).

An example of the 80486 performing a burst (cache line fill) operation from 16-bit memories is given later in Section 2.6.2.

Motorola 680x0 burst transfers

68030 Burst Line Fill Mode. The Motorola 68030 uses the *burst line fill mode* in order to fill a line[19] in its on-chip instruction and data caches; as in the Intel 80386 case, a cache line is filled with a block of 16 bytes (four doublewords) aligned to a 16-byte memory boundary. The 68030 burst line fill[20] mode is done *only with 32-bit ports* and with a *synchronous bus operation.*

A burst fill operation (Figure 2.22) is signaled by the 68030 microprocessor starting a synchronous bus cycle (see Appendix B) and issuing the "cache burst request signal" CBREQ#; this signal is not asserted during any write cycles. The synchronous 32-bit ports should respond with (1) the STERM# (synchronous termination) signal and (2) the CBACK# (cache burst acknowledge) signal, which indicates that the port can support the burst mode. Burst mode operation requires asserting the STERM# low to terminate each of its cycles. As a response to its CBREQ# and after sampling CBACK# and STERM# asserted, the processor maintains its address bus and all output signals in their current state (to a constant value) for the duration of the burst transfer operation, and accepts data on every input clock cycle. The 68030 allows a burst of as many as four doublewords. Conditions that may abort a 68030 burst fill include: cache inhibit is (CIIN#) asserted, bus error (BERR#) asserted, or CBACK# negated prematurely.

The first cycle of any burst cycle must be a synchronous cycle. The minimum cycle time for a 68030 synchronous bus cycle is two input clock cycles (Figure 2.22); i.e., at the beginning of state S2, the processor tests the level of STERM#, and if tested valid the processor latches the data at the end of S2. If a burst fill operation is initiated and allowed to terminate normally, the second, third, and fourth cycles (states S4–S9) latch data on successive falling edges of the clock at a minimum; for this reason this is usually referred to as the "*2-1-1-1 burst protocol.*" The incrementing of the value of the least significant address bits A3 and A2 must be done by memory interface hardware so that all four doublewords of the block are supplied in a "wraparound" fashion.[21]

68040 Line Read. The 68040's burst mode is called "line read." Line read bus cycles are used either to access a 16-byte operand for the MOVE16 instruction or again for filling the microprocessor's on-chip instruction and data caches. As in the 68030, a 68040 line read accesses the 16-byte block from *only 32-bit memory ports* and with a *synchronous*

---

[19]Whether a whole line or a single doubleword is to be fetched from memory on a cache miss, it can be programmed by the supervisor during system initialization. Under the *burst fill mode*, the processor will request to fetch four doublewords and fill an entire cache line; under the *single-entry mode*, the processor will request to fetch one doubleword and update only the invalid doubleword.

[20]The 68020 has only the "single entry" mode, because its cache line is 32 bits (equal to the width of the microprocessor's external data bus) and the cache line has a single "valid bit."

[21]This addressing is compatible with existing "nibble-mode" DRAMs, and can be supported by "page" and "static column" modes (explained in Section 3.3 of the next chapter) with an external modulo-4 counter for A2 and A3.

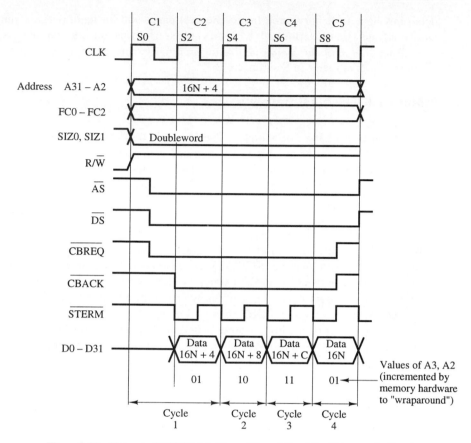

Figure 2.22 Motorola 68030 "2-1-1-1 burst fill mode" to fill a 16-byte cache line (synchronous bus cycles) [5].

bus operation (which is the only type of bus operation the 68040 supports) with the address "wraparound" implemented externally.

Figure 2.23 shows the simplified flowchart and timing diagram of the 68040 line read mode. A "transfer acknowledge" TA# signal is required asserted for each doubleword transfer (on valid clock edges). It can be noted in Figure 2.23b that this input signal TA# stays asserted for the whole duration or the four doubleword reads.

2.5 MISALIGNED DATA TRANSFERS

Since operands may reside at any byte boundaries, they may be misaligned in memory. (See Section 2.2.5 for the alignment rules.) Misalignment is usually associated more with the storage of data (operands) and less with the storage of instructions.

Some microprocessor products *enforce alignment restrictions.* One example is the 16-bit Motorola 68000, which causes an "address error exception" if word operand transfers are attempted at odd byte addresses. Other examples are the RISC processors MIPS R-series and Intel i860, which cause a trap on misaligned transfers. If a misaligned transfer causes a

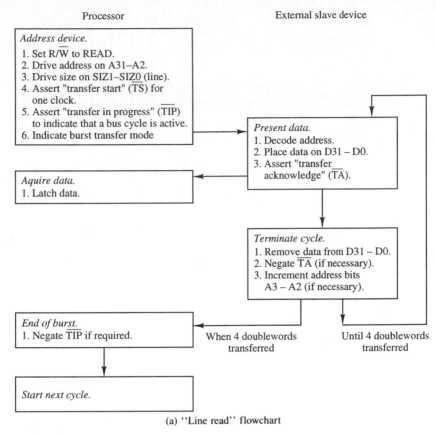

Processor   External slave device

Address device.
1. Set R/W̄ to READ.
2. Drive address on A31–A2.
3. Drive size on SIZ1–SIZ0 (line).
4. Assert "transfer start" (T̄S̄) for one clock.
5. Assert "transfer in progress" (T̄ĪP̄) to indicate that a bus cycle is active.
6. Indicate burst transfer mode

Present data.
1. Decode address.
2. Place data on D31 – D0.
3. Assert "transfer acknowledge" (T̄Ā).

Aquire data.
1. Latch data.

Terminate cycle.
1. Remove data from D31 – D0.
2. Negate T̄Ā (if necessary).
3. Increment address bits A3 – A2 (if necessary).

End of burst.
1. Negate T̄ĪP̄ if required.

When 4 doublewords transferred   Until 4 doublewords transferred

Start next cycle.

(a) "Line read" flowchart

Figure 2.23 Simplified flowchart and timing diagram for a 68040 "line read" mode (not all control signals are shown) [6].

trap/exception, then load or store operations of misaligned data must be handled by a software routine (an inefficient approach).

Other microprocessors *do not enforce alignment restrictions:* this means that they do handle misaligned operand transfers automatically, but they do it by executing possible additional bus cycles. Most of the other processors we cover in this textbook fall in this category. (The total number of bus cycles varies from one product to the other.) This automatic handling of misalignment by the processor is completely transparent to the programmer (except for the increased time the additional bus cycles impose).

The Intel 80486 has a bit in its control register CR0 (the "alignment mask" AM bit 18) whose value determines the enforcement or not of alignment. When the bit is 0, alignment is not enforced and the 80486 operates in the 80386 microprocessor compatible mode. When this bit is 1, a misaligned transfer will cause an interrupt (the "alignment check" AC interrupt).

Alignment is important to many people:

1. To the software and compiler writer, because they must ensure that instructions and operands are properly aligned in memory in order not to degrade the system's performance.

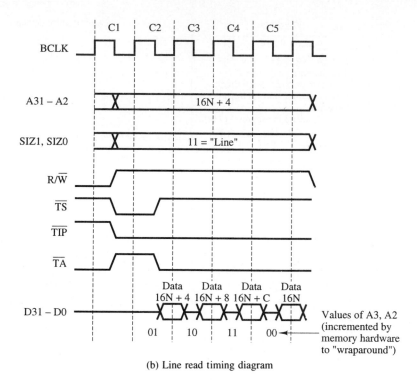

(b) Line read timing diagram

Figure 2.23   (concluded)

2. To the designer of the control section inside the microprocessor chip, which must incorporate features that would allow a processor to execute the required additional bus cycle(s) if it is to be able to take care of misaligned operand transfers automatically.

3. To the designer of the microprocessor chip's external interface, who must also be aware of misalignment issues, because he/she may have to support the microprocessor's misaligned access mode.[22]

4. Finally, both the system designer and programmer must be aware of and account for the effects of misaligned operand transfers, particularly in time-critical applications.

In the following sections we use examples of misaligned storage and data transfers for a number of microprocessors for the word operand ABCD and the doubleword operand EFGHIJKL in 16-bit and 32-bit memories. Both big- and little-endian ordering are covered.

For a 32-bit memory, the 32-bit doubleword operand EFGHIJKL is misaligned when it crosses doubleword boundaries, i.e., it is at either an odd byte address ($4N + 1$ or $4N + 3$) or odd word address ($4N + 2$). Similarly, the 16-bit word operand ABCD is misaligned when it crosses doubleword boundaries, i.e., it is at the $2N + 3$ odd byte address. In any of the above cases, the misaligned transfer will require a second additional bus cycle. Regarding the word operand at the $2N + 1$ odd address of a 32-bit memory, although misaligned, it can

---

[22]For example, when the Motorola 68020 microprocessor chip is connected to the NuBus system bus (as in the case of the Macintosh II [7]), the interface designer must cater so that a 32-bit write to an even-byte address will be routed to the appropriate system bus addresses and performed in only a single NuBus cycle.

be fetched in one bus cycle by most 32-bit processors (except for the Motorola 68040, which treats it as a misaligned operand and fetches it in two bus cycles).

When multiple bus cycles are required to transfer a misaligned multibyte operand, the *most significant bytes are transferred first,* irrespective of the endianess of the processor.

2.5.1 Intel Misaligned Transfers

Consider the 80x86 microprocessors and the 32-bit operand EFGHIJKL stored at location $4N+3$ in a 32-bit memory. Show its placement in the 32-bit memory, the addresses and "byte-enables" that the processor issues to fetch the operand, and draw the 80386 local bus timing diagram (showing the actual address and data values on the respective bus lines and the most pertinent control signals).

Figure 2.24a shows how the 32-bit operand EFGHIJKL is misaligned in the 32-bit memory (stored at location $4N+3$). It is noticed that two bus cycles are required to fetch it, the *most significant part of the operand* transferred during the first cycle. Therefore, during the first bus cycle the 80x86 processors issue the *next-higher doubleword address.* Figure 2.24b shows the addresses and the "byte-enables" the processors issue for the two bus cycles, and the byte lanes of the data bus used to transfer the various parts of the operands per cycle.

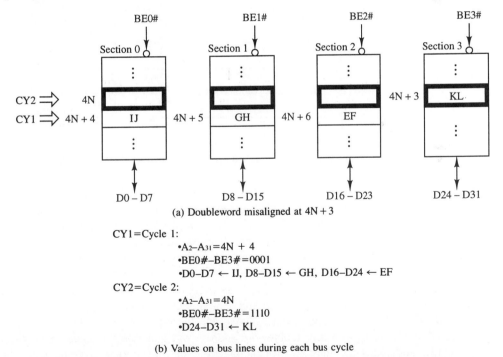

(a) Doubleword misaligned at $4N+3$

CY1=Cycle 1:
- A_2–A_{31}=$4N+4$
- BE0#–BE3#=0001
- D0–D7 ← IJ, D8–D15 ← GH, D16–D24 ← EF

CY2=Cycle 2:
- A_2–A_{31}=$4N$
- BE0#–BE3#=1110
- D24–D31 ← KL

(b) Values on bus lines during each bus cycle

Figure 2.24 Intel 80386/486 misaligned doubleword operand EFGHIJKL (at location $4N+3$).

Figure 2.25 gives the corresponding bus timing diagram for the Intel 80386 micro-processor. Two read bus cycles are executed by the processor. During the first cycle, the

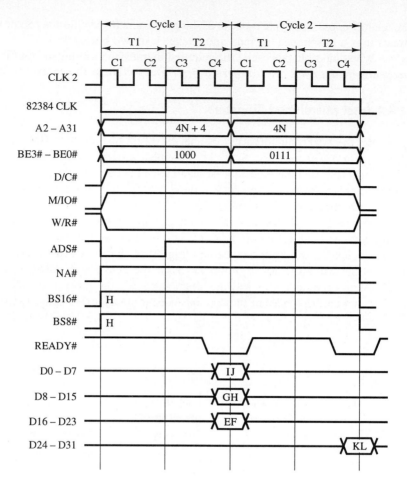

Figure 2.25 Intel 80386: misaligned read cycles to fetch a doubleword from a 32-bit data port (from location 4N + 3).

most significant three bytes, EF, GH, and IJ, are transferred over data bus lanes D16–D23, D8–D15, and D0–D7, respectively. The doubleword address placed on the address bus during this first bus cycle is the *next-higher* doubleword address (actually, its most significant 30 bits) 4N + 4; the two least significant address bits A1A0 = 00, which indicate no offset from this base address, are decoded by the microprocessor internally to generate the four output signals BE0#–BE3# = 0001. The microprocessor then starts a second bus cycle to read the remaining byte of the operand. For this cycle, the microprocessor places on the address bus the *current* doubleword address 4N (the values A1A0 = 11, which indicate that an offset of three from this doubleword address will generate the signals BE0#–BE3# = 1110), and reads the least significant byte KL of the operand over data bus byte lane D24–D31.

In the 80486 case, which has an on-chip cache, when cacheable bus cycles are executed (access to a cacheable location in main memory), misalignment is not an issue because the external memory interface hardware does not interpret BE3#–BE0# (it treats them all as being zeros).

2.5.2 Motorola Misaligned Transfers

Motorola 68020/30. Consider the 68030 and the same 32-bit operand EFGHIJKL stored at location 4N + 3 in a 32-bit memory. Show its placement in the 32-bit memory, the addresses and "byte-enables" that the processor issues to fetch the operand, and draw the 68030 local bus timing diagram (showing the actual address and data values on the respective bus lines and the most pertinent control signals).

Figure 2.26a shows the 32-bit operand EFGHIJKL misaligned in the 32-bit memory (at location 4N + 3). Again, two bus cycles will be required to fetch the misaligned operand, with the most significant part of the operand transferred first during the first cycle. Figure 2.26b lists the control signals supplied to the memory subsystem and the byte-lanes of the data bus used to transfer the various parts of the operand.

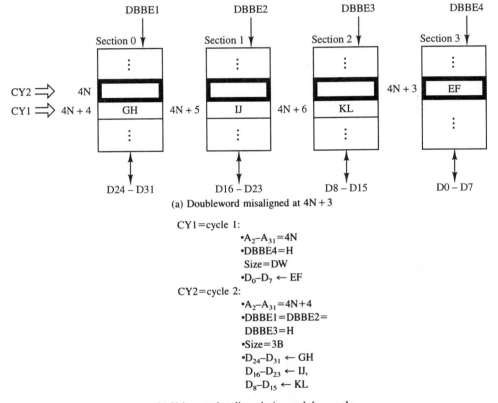

(a) Doubleword misaligned at 4N + 3

CY1 = cycle 1:
- A_2–A_{31} = 4N
- DBBE4 = H
- Size = DW
- D_0–$D_7 \leftarrow$ EF

CY2 = cycle 2:
- A_2–A_{31} = 4N + 4
- DBBE1 = DBBE2 = DBBE3 = H
- Size = 3B
- D_{24}–$D_{31} \leftarrow$ GH
  D_{16}–$D_{23} \leftarrow$ IJ,
  D_8–$D_{15} \leftarrow$ KL

(b) Values on bus lines during each bus cycle

Figure 2.26 Motorola 68020/30 misaligned doubleword operand EFGHIJKL (at location 4N + 3).

Figure 2.27 gives the corresponding bus timing diagram. Two read bus cycles are executed by the processor. During the first cycle, the most significant byte EF of the operand is fetched over data bus lines D0–D7. The doubleword address placed on the 30 lines of the address bus is (the 30-bit) 4N; the values A1A0 = 11 indicate an offset of three from this base doubleword address. The operand size indicator that the processor issues during this

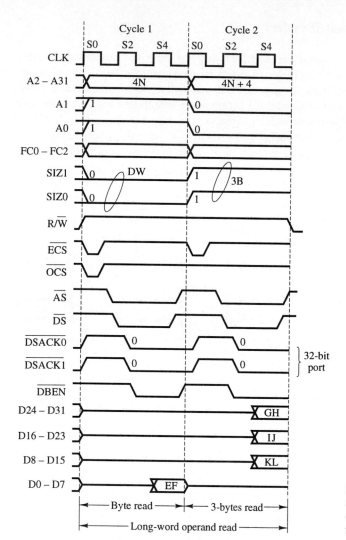

Figure 2.27 Motorola 68020/30: misaligned read cycles to fetch a doubleword (DW) from a 32-bit data port. Adapted from [5].

first cycle indicates a doubleword (i.e., SIZ0SIZ1 = 00). The processor then starts a second bus cycle to read the remaining three bytes of the operand: it places on the address bus the *next-higher doubleword address* 4N + 4 (the values A1A0 = 00 indicate no offset from this doubleword address), issues the values 11 on the output lines SIZ0 and SIZ1 to indicate there are three bytes still remaining to be read, and at the end of the bus cycle, latches bytes GH, IJ, and KL off the bus lanes D24–D31, D16–D23, and D8–D15, respectively.

Motorola 68040. The 68040 handles misaligned transfers differently than do the Motorola 68020 or 68030 processors. In the 68040, misaligned transfers are *converted to a sequence of bus transfers which are always aligned.* (Three-byte transfers are not considered aligned.) Furthermore, the SIZn signals indicate the size of the operand *for the current bus cycle* (not the number of bytes still remaining to be fetched as in the other Motorola 32-bit products). Therefore, a misaligned doubleword fetch from location 4N + 2 will be handled

Microprocessor Bus Transfers   Chap. 2

in two bus cycles, as in the previous 32-bit processors. However, a doubleword fetch from either location 4N + 1 or 4N + 3 will be executed by the 68040 in three bus cycles. Figure 2.28 shows the three bus cycles needed to fetch the doubleword operand EFGHIJKL misaligned at location 4N + 1. Similarly, a word operand stored at 4N + 3 will also be treated as a misaligned operand to be fetched in two aligned bus cycles. In all cases, the bus cycles are executed so that the most significant parts of the operand are fetched first. Because the processor does not support dynamic bus sizing (it always expects the external port to be 32 bits wide), on write cycles it only drives the appropriate byte-lanes of the data bus based on SIZn, A0, and A1 (i.e., depending upon whether the write is for a byte, a word, or a doubleword).

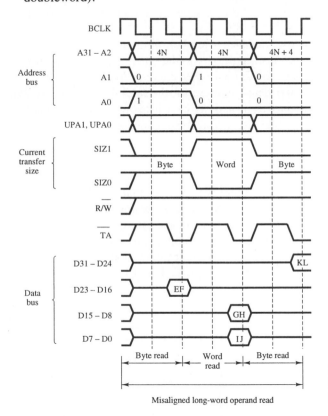

Figure 2.28 Motorola 68040 misaligned fetch of doubleword EFGHIJKL from location 4N + 1 [6].

2.6 DYNAMIC BUS SIZING

A number of microprocessors are dynamically configurable chips. "Dynamic bus sizing" refers to the ability a microprocessor has to dynamically adjust the width of its data bus (more precisely, adjust how and which data bus byte-lanes to use on a per bus cycle basis) according to the width (port size) of the slave port with which it exchanges data. This dynamic bus sizing capability allows transfers of variable-length data, permits 8-, 16-, and 32-bit memory and peripherals to be arbitrarily connected to the same system, and facilitates easy connection to other system buses[23] (i.e., VME, FUTUREBUS, etc.). Dynamic bus sizing is completely transparent to the application programmer.

[23]These bus transfers are also referred to as "8-, 16-, and 32-bit bus transfers."

A pair of control signals are used for this: one outgoing set—which we called the "operand size indicator"—that identifies the width of the operand to be exchanged, and one incoming set—sent by the addressed slave device and called a "port size indicator"—that identifies the size of the responding port. During every bus cycle, the processor samples these feedback signals to determine (1) which data bus byte-lanes carry valid information, and (2) whether the port width is smaller than the width of the requested operand, in which case it must determine the number and type of additional bus cycle(s) to initiate in order to transfer the remaining operand. For Motorola processors, the issued "operand size indicator" are signals SIZ0 and SIZ1, and the received "port size indicators" are the feedback signals DSACK0# and DSACK1#. The Intel processors do not issue "operand size indicator" signals; the "port size indicators" they sample are the input signals at pins BS16# and BS#8.

As we will see in the specific examples given below, the data bus lines used to interface a less wide port vary from one microprocessor to the other: For the Motorola 68020/30, a less wide port must be connected to the *high-order* data bus lines; for the Intel 80386, it must be connected to the *low-order* data bus lines; for the Intel 80486, external *byte swap logic* must be used because the processor expects data bytes always to be received at its correct input pins, no matter what the size of the responding slave device.

2.6.1 Intel 80386

The Intel 80386 has a single "bus size" input pin (BS16#) that a slave port must assert to identify a 16-bit data bus width. Aligned words and doublewords in 16-bit memories would be stored in little-endian order with the least significant byte of the operand stored first. Figure 2.29a shows the Intel 80386 connected to a 16-bit memory subsystem. When a 16-bit port is interfaced to the Intel 80386, it must be connected to the sixteen least significant lines D0–D15 of the data bus. The byte-enable signals (BHE# and BLE#) for the two memory

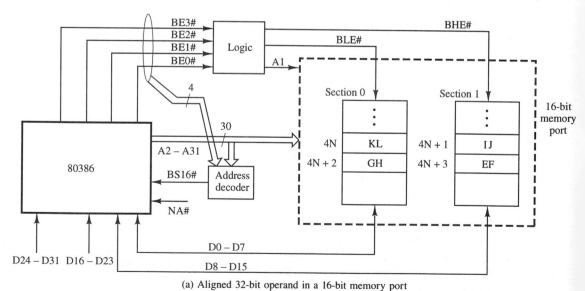

(a) Aligned 32-bit operand in a 16-bit memory port

Figure 2.29 Intel 80386: aligned read cycles to fetch a doubleword from a 16-bit data port.

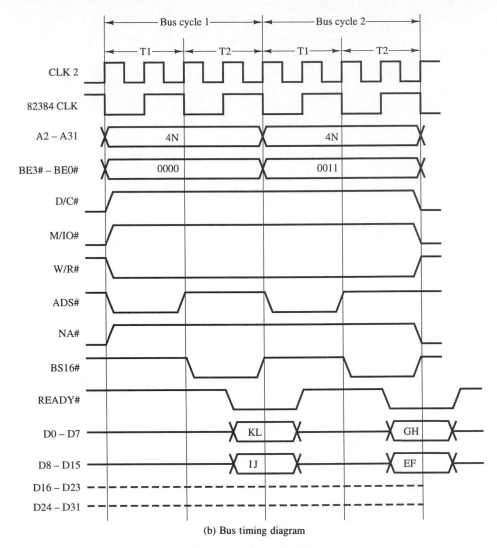

(b) Bus timing diagram

Figure 2.29 (concluded)

sections and signal A1 are generated externally by decoding the four signals BE0#–BE3# according to the table in Figure 2.30.

80386 Aligned transfers with a 16-bit slave device. Figure 2.29b shows how the 32-bit operand EFGHIJKL aligned at location 4N is fetched by the 80386 from a 16-bit port in two cycles. At the beginning of a bus cycle, the microprocessor behaves as if the data bus is 32 bits (issues BE0#–BE3# = 0000). When the bus cycle is acknowledged by the slave port (by asserting the READY# signal at the end of a T2 state to indicate that the current bus cycle is complete), then the most recent sampled value of the input BS16# determines the data bus size for the cycle being acknowledged. If BS16# = H, the physical data bus size is 32 bits; if the BS16# = L, it is a 16-bit data bus and data transfer is valid only over lines D0–D15. It is observed in Figure 2.29b that when the READY# is asserted

i386 & i486 CPU signals				8-, 16-Bit bus signals[a]			
BE3#	BE2#	BE1#	BE0#	A1	BHE#	BLE#(A0)	Comment
H*	H*	H*	H*	X	X	X	X—no active bytes
H	H	H	L	L	H	L	
H	H	L	H	L	L	H	
H	H	L	L	L	L	L	
H	L	H	H	H	H	L	
H*	L*	H*	L*	X	X	X	X—not contiguous bytes
H	L	L	H	L	L	H	
H	L	L	L	L	L	L	
L	H	H	H	H	L	H	
L*	H*	H*	L*	X	X	X	X—not contiguous bytes
L*	H*	L*	H*	X	X	X	X—not contiguous bytes
L*	H*	L*	L*	X	X	X	X—not contiguous bytes
L	L	H	H	H	L	L	
L*	L*	H*	L*	X	X	X	X—not contiguous bytes
L	L	L	H	L	L	H	
L	L	L	L	L	L	L	

Key: X=don't care; H=high voltage level; L=low voltage level; *=non-occurring pattern of Byte Enables; either none are asserted, or the pattern has Byte Enables asserted for non-contiguous bytes.

BLE# asserted when D0–D7 of 16-bit bus is active. BHE# asserted when D8–D15 of 16-bit bus is active. A1 low for all even words; A1 high for all odd words.

[a]8-Bit signals are for 80486 only.

Figure 2.30 Truth table for generating A1, BHE#, BLE# (from the byte enables of the Intel 80386/486) for addressing 8- and 16-bit devices [8]. Reprinted by permission of Intel Corporation. © 1989 by Intel Corp.

during the first bus cycle, the BS16# is sampled low. Therefore, an additional bus cycle will be required to fetch the rest of the operand; IJKL will be transferred during the first cycle and EFGH during the second cycle. In both cases, the lower half of the data bus is used for the transfers. (Remember that address pipelining through NA# cannot be used in the Intel 80386 with BS16# bus cycles.) For an aligned *write operation,* the 80386 microprocessor always drives all four byte lanes of the data bus at the start of each bus cycle and follows the data duplication rules of Section 2.3.2.

In the Intel 80386, aligned operations *transfer the least significant part of the operand first, irrespective of the size of the responding slave device.*

80386 Misaligned transfers with a 16-bit slave device.

As in the case of a 32-bit port, when data is misaligned in a 16-bit port, it must be fetched by the microprocessor in the same order, i.e., the most significant part fetched during the first cycle. (This is the same for both Motorola and Intel microprocessors.) However, because of the earlier 16-bit Intel microprocessors that were fetching first the least significant part of a misaligned operand, the Intel 80386 performs misaligned transfers according to the following rules when a number of *subcycles* are required in a bus cycle:

1. Between two doublewords (i.e., the operand crosses a doubleword boundary), fetch the most significant part first during *subcycle 1* (SCY1).
2. Within a doubleword (i.e., the operand does not cross a doubleword boundary), fetch the least significant part first during *subcycle 1* (SCY1).

Figure 2.31 shows the values of BE3#–BE0# that the "next subcycle" will have (based on their values during the "current subcycle") for 8-bit and 16-bit ports [9].

"Current subcycle"				"Next subcycle" with BS8#				"Next subcycle" with BS16#			
BE3#	BE2#	BE1#	BE0#	BE3#	BE2#	BE1#	BE0#	BE3#	BE2#	BE1#	BE0#
1	1	1	0	n	n	n	n	n	n	n	n
1	1	0	0	1	1	0	1	n	n	n	n
1	0	0	0	1	0	0	1	1	0	1	1
0	0	0	0	0	0	0	1	0	0	1	1
1	1	0	1	n	n	n	n	n	n	n	n
1	0	0	1	1	0	1	1	1	0	1	1
0	0	0	1	0	0	1	1	0	0	1	1
1	0	1	1	n	n	n	n	n	n	n	n
0	0	1	1	0	1	1	1	n	n	n	n
0	1	1	1	n	n	n	n	n	n	n	n

Note: "n" means that another bus cycle will not be required to satisfy the request.

Figure 2.31 Intel 80386/486: the values of BE3#–BE0# when a "next subcycle" is needed for misaligned operands (in 8-bit and 16-bit ports) [4,8]. Reprinted by permission of Intel Corporation. © 1986 and 1989 by Intel Corp.

Example 2.6: 80386 Misaligned Reads from 16-Bit Ports

Consider the 80386 connected to a 16-bit port and the following two cases: (1) the doubleword operand EFGHIJKL misaligned at location $4N + 3$ and (2) the word operand ABCD misaligned at location $4N + 3$. (a) Show their storage in memory and identify the bus cycles needed to fetch them, and (b) Draw the 80386 local bus cycle timing diagram with the most pertinent control signals for case 1.

Solution:

(a) Figure 2.32 shows the two cases of little-endian doubleword and word operands misaligned in the 16-bit memory port, with its two byte sections connected to the lower half of the 80386 data bus. The right-hand side of the diagram identifies the number of bus cycles needed. Figure 2.32a shows that first an access is performed to the *next-higher doubleword address* $(4N + 4)$. Since the part of the operand contained within the "next" doubleword is three bytes, it will be fetched in two subcycles over the 16-bit data bus: During the first subcycle (SCY1) IJ and GH will be fetched over D0–D7 and D8–D15, respectively, and during the second subcycle (SCY2) byte EF will be fetched over D0–D7. Then the microprocessor is to fetch the remaining part of the operand, which is contained inside the doubleword at location $4N$. Only byte KL is found there and it will be fetched during the third cycle (CY3) over data bus lines D8–D15.

(b) Figure 2.33 shows the Intel 80386 bus timing diagram for case (a) of Figure 2.32. As in the aligned case, for a misaligned *write operation*, the 80386 would drive all four byte lanes of the data bus at the start of each bus cycle and follow the data duplication rules of Section 2.3.2.

From all the above, we conclude that in the Intel 80386 microprocessor, misaligned operations with a 32-bit memory port transfer the most significant part first; with a 16-bit memory port, however, most often they also transfer the most significant part of the operand first (but not always).

To avoid a possible conflict between address pipelining and dynamic bus sizing, the 80386 adheres to the following two rules: (1) If NA# has already been sampled asserted, the current data bus size is assumed to be 32 bits (i.e., the 80386 ignores the value of BS16# because it has committed itself to pipeline the next address). (2) If NA# and BS16# are

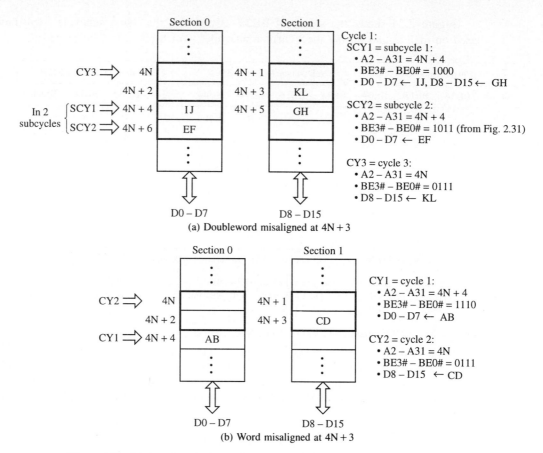

Figure 2.32 Little-endian doubleword operand EFGHIJKL and word operand ABCD misaligned in a 16-bit memory (at location $4N+3$).

both sampled asserted during the last T2 period of a bus cycle, BS16# has priority (i.e., the next address is not pipelined).

2.6.2 Intel 80486

The Intel 80486 does dynamic bus sizing differently from the 80386. First of all, the 80486 has a second input pin, BS8#, to allow interconnecting to its 8-bit slave devices as well. An 80486 may connect to all three bus sizes; if both BS16# and BS8# are asserted, an 8-bit data bus width is selected. Second, the 80486 processor requires that *data bytes be placed on the corresponding data pins*. The table in Figure 2.34 shows the data bus lines where the 80486 expects data to be returned for each valid combination of byte enables, with and without asserting the BS8# or BS16# pins. Finally, unlike the 80386, *the 80486 will not duplicate* during write cycles data on the data bus byte lanes for which the corresponding byte enable is not asserted.

Thus, if the processor is to fetch the aligned operand EFGHIJKL from location 4N of a 16-bit memory port (see Figure 2.34a), it will issue BE3#–BE0# = 0000 and read the

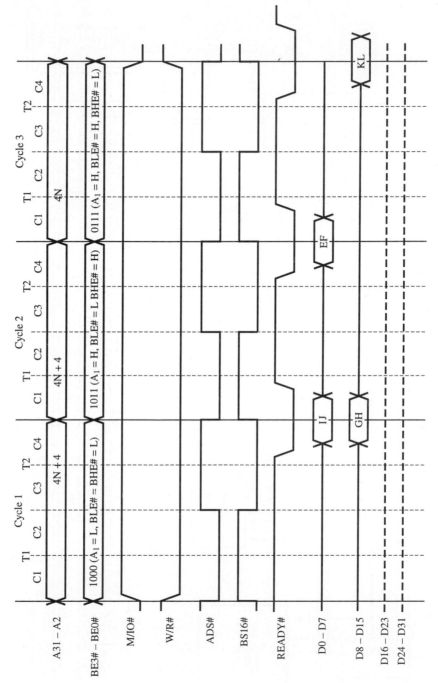

Figure 2.33 Intel 80386: Misaligned read cycles to fetch the doubleword at location 4N + 3 from a 16-bit data port.

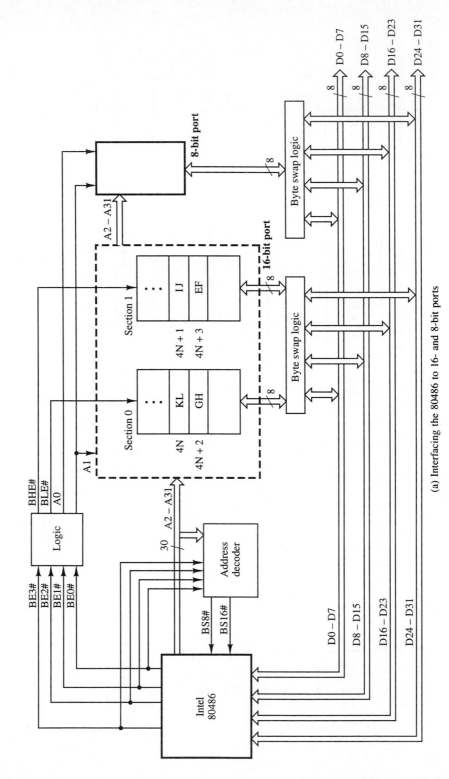

Figure 2.34 Intel 80486 connected to 8- and 16-bit devices.

(a) Interfacing the 80486 to 16- and 8-bit ports

BE3#	BE2#	BE1#	BE0#	w/o BS8#/BS16#	w BS8#	w BS16#
1	1	1	0	D7–D0	D7–D0	D7–D0
1	1	0	0	D15–D0	D7–D0	D15–D0
1	0	0	0	D23–D0	D7–D0	D15–D0
0	0	0	0	D31–D0	D7–D0	D15–D0
1	1	0	1	D15–D8	D15–D8	D15–D8
1	0	0	1	D23–D8	D15–D8	D15–D8
0	0	0	1	D31–D8	D15–D8	D15–D8
1	0	1	1	D23–D16	D23–D16	D23–D16
0	0	1	1	D31–D16	D23–D16	D31–D16
0	1	1	1	D31–D24	D31–D24	D31–D24

(b) Data pins read with different bus sizes [8] Reprinted by permission of Intel Corporation. © 1989 by Intel Corp.

Figure 2.34 (concluded)

first two bytes, KL and IJ (the least significant word), from its input pins D0–D7 and D8–D15, respectively. It will then start a new cycle to read the next two bytes, GH and EF (the most significant word). However, it will now expect these two bytes (GH and EF) to be supplied to its most significant data bus pins D16–D23 and D24–D31, respectively. The table in Figure 2.31 shows the set of byte enables that will be generated on the *next* subcycle (for 8- and 16-bit ports) for all valid possibilities of the byte enables in the current subcycle. Since the 80486 issued BE3#–BE0# = 0000 during the first BS16# subcycle, then from Figure 2.31 it will issue BE3#–BE0# = 0011 during the second BS16# subcycle. It is observed then from Figure 2.34b that the data pins the processor will read during this subcycle are D31–D16. Thus, external logic in the form of "byte swap logic" must be included, as shown in Figure 2.34a, to route the data to the appropriate data pins. The external logic for generating the BLE#, BHE#, and A1 from the BE0#–BE3# is the same as in the 80386 case of Figure 2.29a (implementing the table in Figure 2.30). Similar byte swap logic is also needed for an 8-bit port, because the same routing is needed of the operand bytes to the various input data pins of the 80486.

Misaligned transfers for 16-bit devices are handled by the 80486 in a similar way to the 80386, taking into consideration the fact that the 80486 does not duplicate data on write cycles.

Example 2.7: 80486 Writing a Misaligned Word to a 16-Bit Port

Draw the local bus timing diagram (showing the actual address and data values on the respective bus lines and the most pertinent control signals) for writing the operand ABCD to location 4N + 3 of a 16-bit memory for the Intel 80486.

Solution: The writing of the word operand ABCD to location 4N + 3 will have byte CD stored in location 4N + 3 and byte AB in location 4N + 4. Figure 2.35a shows the interfacing of the 16-bit memory to the Intel 80486 local bus through the "byte swap logic." The two bytes of the word operand will be transferred as follows: during cycle 1, AB over D0–D7 for storage to location 4N + 4; during cycle 2, CD over D24–D31 for storage to location 4N + 3. No data duplication takes place.

Figure 2.35b shows the 80486 local bus timing diagram with the pertinent control signals.

Example 2.8: 80486 Burst (Cache Line) Fill from 16- and 8-Bit Memories

The 80486 cacheable burst line fill operation from 32-bit memories was presented in Section 2.4.2. Here we present the case of 16-bit memories.

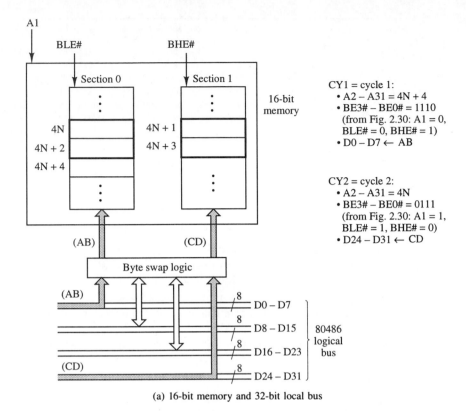

(a) 16-bit memory and 32-bit local bus

Figure 2.35 80486 writing ABCD to location 4N + 3 of a 16-bit memory.

BS8# and BS6# inputs operate during burst cycles in exactly the same manner as non-burst cycles. If the 80486 also received signals on its input pins BS8# or BS16#, which would mean that the burst transfer is with a less wide memory port, then the processor would automatically increase the number of bus cycles needed per burst transfer.

First of all, BS8# or BS16# must be driven active (in the middle of T1, as can be seen in the 80486 basic timing diagram of Figure 2.10) before the first BRDY# is driven active. This forces the 80486 to execute multiple cycles to read the operand. Then, when BRDY# arrives, it will signal the processor that the external system can support bursting of these multiple cycles. Thus, for example, if the BS8# were asserted, each individual 32-bit read would be executed as four 8-bit burst data cycles.

Second, the 80486 order of addressing also applies here. Here, Figure 2.19 is still valid, while the case of the 16-bit port is given in Figure 2.36: the 16-byte cache line is aligned in a 16-bit memory and the line fill starts again from location 16N + A. Even though the port size is now 16 bits, the order in the 32-bit memory of Example 2.5 of reading DW2, DW3, DW0, and DW1 must still be preserved. In order, therefore, to provide compatibility, the cycles should access memory locations in the following order:

16N + A and 16N + 8 (to fetch DW2), 16N + E and 16N + C (to fetch DW3),
16N + 2 and 16N (to fetch DW0), and 16N + 6 and 16N + 4 (to fetch DW1).

Similarly, if for example there is a burst request to location 16N + 4 of the 16-bit memory, then (as explained in Section 2.4.2 and can also be deduced from Figure 2.19a, that now the

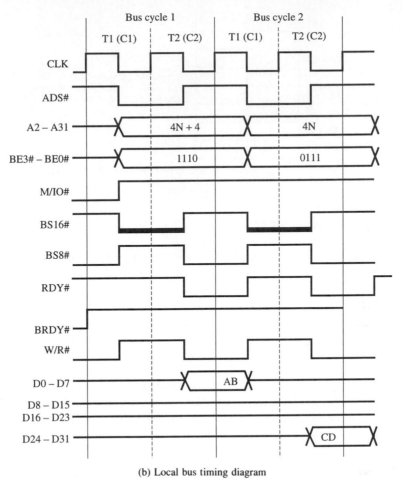

(b) Local bus timing diagram

Figure 2.35   (concluded)

order must be DW1, DW0, DW3, DW2) the accesses will be done to memory locations following the order:

$$16N + 4, \; 16N + 6, \; 16N, \; 16N + 2, \; 16N + C, \; 16N + E, \; 16N + 8, \; \text{and} \; 16N + A$$

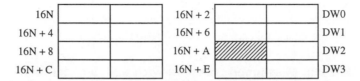

To preserve previous order of DW2, DW3, DW0, DW1, the cycles should be to locations in the order: 16N + A, 16N + 8, 16N + E, 16N + C, 16N + 2, 16N, 16N + 6, 16N + 4

(a) Two-way word interleaving

Figure 2.36   Intel 80486 burst fill operation from location 16N + A of a 16-bit memory.

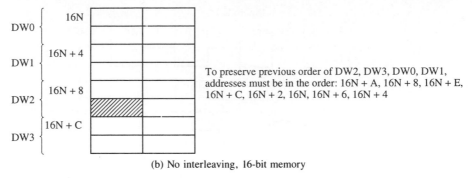

(b) No interleaving, 16-bit memory

Figure 2.36 (concluded)

2.6.3 Motorola 68020/30

In addition to 32-bit ports, the Motorola 68020 and 68030 microprocessors[24] allow the interfacing of 8- and 16-bit memory ports. Contrary to the Intel 80386, less wide ports are interfaced to the Motorola 68020/30 processors using the most significant part of the data bus; 16-bit ports use D16–D31 and 8-bit ports use D24–D31, as shown in Figure 2.37. The individual byte-section enable control signals (for example, the DBBE1 and DBBE2 needed by a 16-bit memory) are generated externally by decoding SIZ0, SIZ1, A0, and A1, according to the table in Figure 2.37b. The feedback handshake signals from the memory port to the microprocessor are DSACK1#,DSACK0# = 01 for a 16-bit memory, and DSACK1#,DSACK0# = 10 for an 8-bit memory.

As we will explain below, the Motorola 68020/30 microprocessors *transfer the most significant part of the operand first, irrespective of the type of alignment in memory or the width of the responding memory port.*

68020/30 Aligned transfers with a 16-bit memory.   Figure 2.38a shows the 32-bit operand EFGHIJKL aligned at location 4N and fetched from a 16-bit memory port in two cycles. Figure 2.38b identifies the cycles needed and gives the values placed on the address and data bus lines. During the first cycle the microprocessor issues an operand size indicator of SIZ1,SIZ0 = 00 (32 bits) and reads the most significant word EFGH over data bus lines D16–D31; during the second cycle it issues a 16-bit size indicator (SIZ1,SIZ0 = 10 for the number of operand bits still remaining to be read) and reads the least significant word IJKL again over data bus lines D16–D31. Figure 2.39 shows the bus timing diagram for the read operation example of Figure 2.37. For an aligned *write operation,* the 68020/30 microprocessors always drive all four byte lanes of the data bus at the start of each bus cycle and follow the data duplication rules of Section 2.3.3.

68020/30 Misaligned transfers with a 16-bit memory.   As in the case of a 32-bit port, when data is misaligned in a 16-bit port, it must be fetched by the microprocessor in the same order, i.e., the most significant part fetched during the first cycle. This

---

[24]The 68040 represents a departure from the 68020 and 68030, because its external bus *does not support dynamic bus sizing;* memory which must be contiguous, such as for code storage or program stacks, must be 32 bits wide.

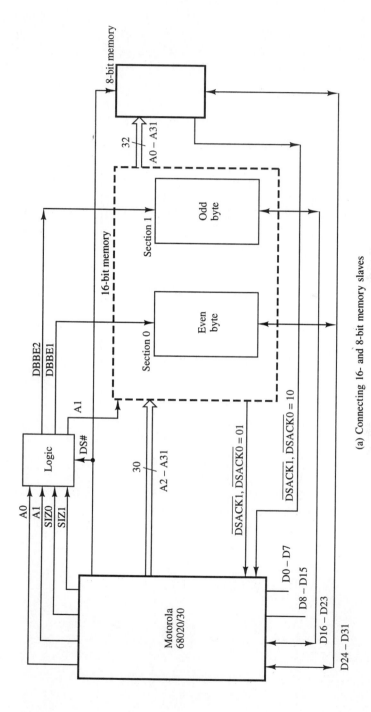

(a) Connecting 16- and 8-bit memory slaves

Figure 2.37 Motorola 68020/30 and 8- and 16-bit memory slaves [10].

Operand size	SIZ1	SIZ0	A1	A0	DBBE1	DBBE2
Byte	0	1	0	0	1	0
			0	1	0	1
			1	0	1	0
			1	1	0	1
Word (16-bit)	1	0	0	0	1	1
			0	1	0	1
			1	0	1	1
			1	1	0	1
3 Bytes	1	1	0	0	1	1
			0	1	0	1
			1	0	1	1
			1	1	0	1
Double word (32-bit)	0	0	0	0	1	1
			0	1	0	1
			1	0	1	1
			1	1	0	1

(b) Decoding SIZ1, SIZ0, A1, A0 to generate DBBE1 and DBBE2

Figure 2.37 (concluded)

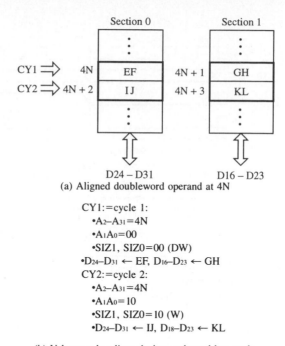

(a) Aligned doubleword operand at 4N

$$CY1 := cycle\ 1:$$
$$\bullet A_2-A_{31}=4N$$
$$\bullet A_1A_0=00$$
$$\bullet SIZ1,\ SIZ0=00\ (DW)$$
$$\bullet D_{24}-D_{31} \leftarrow EF,\ D_{16}-D_{23} \leftarrow GH$$
$$CY2 := cycle\ 2:$$
$$\bullet A_2-A_{31}=4N$$
$$\bullet A_1A_0=10$$
$$\bullet SIZ1,\ SIZ0=10\ (W)$$
$$\bullet D_{24}-D_{31} \leftarrow IJ,\ D_{18}-D_{23} \leftarrow KL$$

(b) Values on bus lines during each read bus cycle

Figure 2.38 Big-endian doubleword operand EFGHIJKL aligned in a 16-bit memory (at location 4N).

happens whether the misaligned operand crosses a doubleword boundary or not (the later is the case of misaligned word completely contained within a doubleword).[25]

Figure 2.40a shows one example of the misaligned doubleword EFGHIJKL in a big-endian 16-bit memory port, and Figure 2.40b the values placed on the address and data bus-lines for each cycle. Figure 2.41 shows the corresponding timing diagram.

This 32-bit misaligned operand will be fetched in three bus cycles. The first three cycles of the operands (EF, GH, IJ) which are contained within the same doubleword at 4N will be fetched with two subcycles. During the first subcycle, an access is performed to doubleword address 4N from which the most significant byte EF is fetched first over data bus lines D16–D23. During the second subcycle, the microprocessor fetches the other two bytes GH and IJ. Finally, the last byte KL, which is in a different doubleword, will have the microprocessor issue the next-higher doubleword address 4N + 4 to fetch it during cycle 3. It must be observed that the microprocessor issues the following operand size indicators: doubleword during subcycle 1, three bytes during subcycle 2, and byte during cycle 3. As in the aligned case, for a misaligned *write operation,* the 68020/30 microprocessors always drive all four byte lanes of the data bus at the start of each bus cycle and follow the data duplication rules of Section 2.3.3.

68030 Misaligned "burst line fill" mode. The 68030 aligned ''burst line fill'' operation from 32-bit memories was presented in Section 2.4.2. The 68030 burst line fill

---

[25]There is no compatibility concern here (as is in the Intel products), because the earlier 16-bit Motorola products did not allow misalignment (they trapped misaligned transfers).

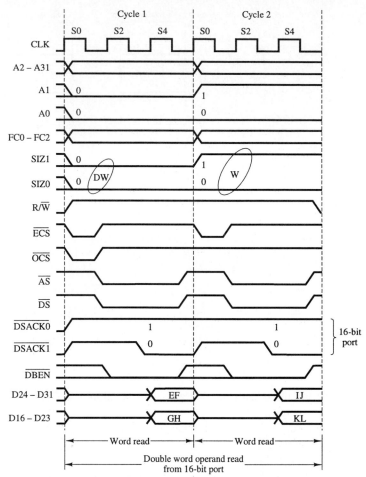

Figure 2.39 Motorola 68020/30: aligned read cycles to fetch the doubleword of Figure 2.37 from a 16-bit data port [5].

(whether aligned or misaligned) is always executed with only 32-bit memories using a synchronous bus operation.

When the doubleword operand the 68030 microprocessor requests on a cache miss is misaligned, two cases are identified: the doubleword operand crosses a doubleword boundary (but not a cache line boundary) and the doubleword crosses a cache line boundary.

1. *Doubleword crosses doubleword boundary (but not a cache line boundary)*: The explanation is given here with the example in Figure 2.42a. Here, the requested doubleword operand ABCDEFGH (that caused a cache miss) is at location 16N + A; it crosses a doubleword boundary, but not a cache line boundary. The 16-byte cache line will be burst-read by following the "wraparound" address order 16N + 8, 16N + C, 16N, and 16N + 4. The four cycles in the burst will be as follows:

cycle 1: request DW at 16N + A, latch DW at 16N + 8, and move it into DW2;
cycle 2: request and latch DW at 16N + C and move it into DW3;

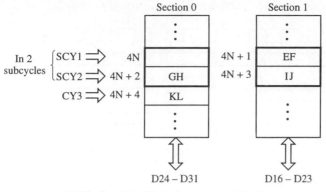

(a) Misaligned doubleword operand at 4N + 1

SCY1=subcycle 1:
  - A_2–A_{31}=4N
  - A_1A_0=01
  - SIZ1, SIZ0=00 (DW)
  - D_{16}–D_{23} ← EF
SCY2=subcycle 2:
  - A_2–A_{31}=4N
  - A_1A_0=10
  - SIZ1, SIZ0=11 (3B)
  - D_{24}–D_{31} ← GH, D_{16}–D_{23} ← IJ
CY3=cycle 3:
  - A_2–A_{31}=4N+4
  - A_1A_0=00
  - SIZ1, SIZ0=01 (B)
  - D_{24}–D_{31} ← KL

(b) Values on bus lines during each bus cycle

Figure 2.40 Big-endian doubleword operand EFGHIJKL misaligned in a 16-bit memory (at location 4N + 1).

cycle 3: request and latch DW at 16N + C and move it into DW0;
cycle 4: request and latch DW at 16N + C and move it into DW1.

2. *Doubleword crosses cache line boundary*: Figure 2.42b shows the doubleword operand at location 16N + E crossing both doubleword and cache line boundaries. The 68030 does not request a burst cycle (i.e., does not assert the cache burst request signal CBREQ#) during the first portion of a misaligned access if the remainder of the access does not correspond to the same cache line. In this case, and since the port is 32 bits, the first access corresponds to the cache entry at address 16N + C (i.e., DW3) which is filled using a *single-entry* load operation. The second access at address 32N corresponds to the second cache line, and the processor asserts the CBREQ# to fill this cache line with a burst mode. Thus the cache fill is done as follows:

a. *Single-entry cycle* 1 to fill DW3 of cache line i cycle 1 is executed to request DW at 16N + E, latch DW at 16N + C, and move it into DW3 of line i.

b. *Burst cycle* 2 to fill cache line j: Cycles 2, 3, 4, and 5 are executed to burst read a 16-byte line from location 32N and fill cache line j.

68030 "Single entry" mode for 16- and 8-bit memories. In this mode, the 68030 fetches a single doubleword. Now asynchronous cycles are executed. The port size

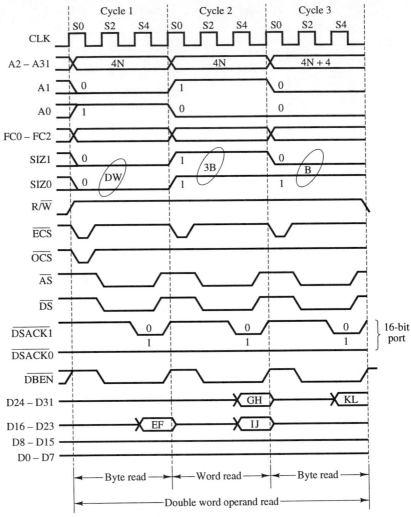

Figure 2.41 Motorola 68020/30: misaligned read cycles to fetch the doubleword of Figure 2.39 from a 16-bit data port [5].

can be 32-, 16-, or 8-bit. Furthermore, all rules of misalignment and dynamic bus sizing described earlier apply.

If the operand is misaligned and crosses a DW boundary, then both DWs of the cache line are updated. Figure 2.43 shows different cases with 32-bit, 16-bit, and 8-bit ports.

2.7 LOCAL BUS ARBITRATION

2.7.1 Processor Arbitration Pins

One set of microprocessor pins used by the interface box called "bus arbiter" in Figure 1.9b are the "bus arbitration pins" usually used for DMA operations. These pins and signals may

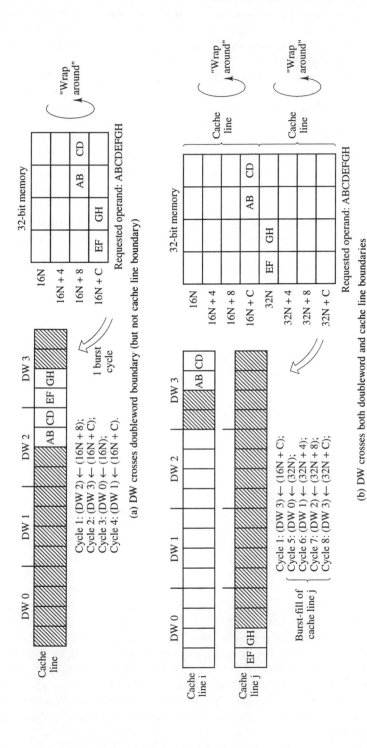

(a) DW crosses doubleword boundary (but not cache line boundary)

Cycle 1: (DW 2) ← (16N + 8);
Cycle 2: (DW 3) ← (16N + C);
Cycle 3: (DW 0) ← (16N);
Cycle 4: (DW 1) ← (16N + C).

Requested operand: ABCDEFGH

(b) DW crosses both doubleword and cache line boundaries

Cycle 1: (DW 3) ← (16N + C);
Cycle 5: (DW 0) ← (32N);
Cycle 6: (DW 1) ← (32N + 4);
Cycle 7: (DW 2) ← (32N + 8);
Cycle 8: (DW 3) ← (32N + C);

Requested operand: ABCDEFGH

Figure 2.42   Motorola 68030: misaligned burst line fill mode.

also be used by other bus masters besides DMA controllers, which request to gain control of the single, shared, local bus in order for them to start their own bus cycles. Figure 2.44 tabulates the names used for these signals by various representative microprocessors. To avoid multiplicity of these names, we will use the generic names HOLD (input) and HLDA (output) to explain their function.

HOLD. The HOLD input line is used by the temporary bus master (such as DMA controllers, I/O processors, etc.) to request control of the local bus from the permanent bus master (the microprocessor). This line may be asserted at certain times only: for example, only if (1) HLDA is not asserted (which means that the permanent master has control of the bus), and (2) HOLD is not already asserted (which means that no other temporary master has requested the bus). The HOLD line may be masked (under hardware or software control) by the permanent bus master to prevent temporary masters from gaining control of the shared bus. As a response to a HOLD signal, the processor enters the "HOLD state" (shown in the various state transition diagrams of the microprocessors) and places all its output pins in their high-Z or high-impedance state, thus relinquishing its local bus and letting the requesting device gain control of the local bus lines. HOLD must remain asserted as long as any other device is the master of the local bus.

HLDA. When the bus master enters the "HOLD state" as a response to the HOLD signal, it asserts the output HLDA signal, thus enabling bus transfer operations for the requestor. If the bus is not granted, the requestor will usually try again. The permanent bus master remains in the HOLD state for an arbitrary number of cycles until the HOLD signal is negated. Upon completion of the hold operation, control of the local bus is returned to the permanent bus master. Hold operations always take priority over interrupt operations.

2.7.2 Serial Arbitration Technique

When many bus requestors are connected to the local bus, proper arbitration is required to resolve simultaneous requests. One technique is to provide a serial nonpreemptive distributed policy implemented by daisy-chaining all requestors to determine which one will become the bus master.

Figure 2.45 shows an implementation in which three bus requestors are connected in a daisy chain configuration. Their bus request signals are wire-ORed together via a common line applied to the HOLD input pin of the microprocessor. To request control of the bus, the requestor asserts its bus request signal (BUSRQ# = L). The processor samples the HOLD after the completion of any bus cycle and asserts its hold acknowledge output signal (HLDA#) to acknowledge release of its local bus. This HLDA# propagates through the daisy chain network; it enters each requestor's BAI# (bus acknowledge input) and leaves via its BAO# (bus acknowledge output). The device that requested control of the local bus becomes the bus master and begins to use it; but this requestor's BAO# remains high, is propagated down the chain, and prevents lower-priority devices from using the bus. When the requestor completes its use of the bus, its BUSRQ# returns to high. One clock cycle later, the processor negates its hold acknowledge (HLDA# = L to indicate that the processor again controls the bus), which is propagated among the bus requestors; any requestor in the daisy chain can now request control of the local bus. Thus, the processor itself is the default bus master.

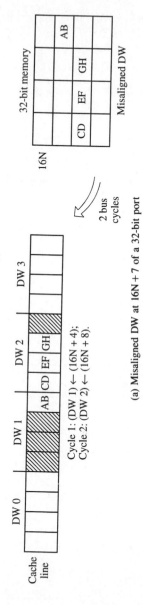

Cycle 1: (DW 1) ← (16N + 4);
Cycle 2: (DW 2) ← (16N + 8).

(a) Misaligned DW at 16N + 7 of a 32-bit port

Figure 2.43 Motorola 68030: misaligned single-entry mode (from 32-, 16-, and 8-bit ports).

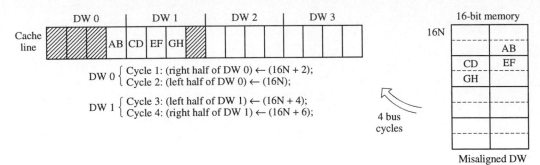

(b) Misaligned DW at 16N + 3 of a 16-bit port

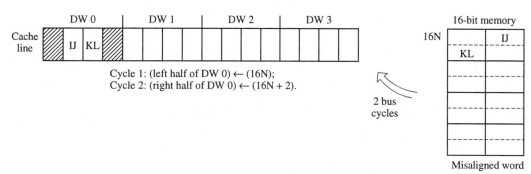

(c) Misaligned word at 16N + 1 of a 16-bit port

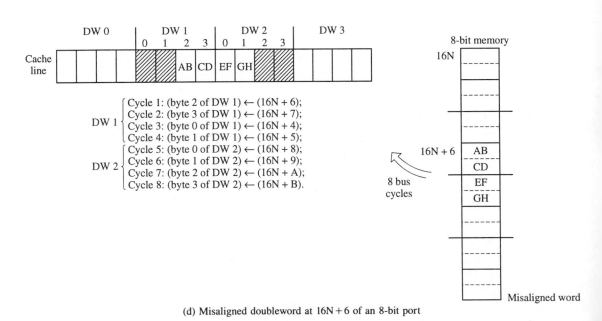

(d) Misaligned doubleword at 16N + 6 of an 8-bit port

Figure 2.43 (concluded)

Intel 8086/286/386	Motorola 680x0	Intel 80486	Intel i860
HOLD (input)	$\overline{\text{BR}}$ (input)	HOLD (input)	HOLD (input)
HLDA (output)	$\overline{\text{BG}}$ (output)	HLDA (output)	HOLDA (output)
Maximum mode (8086):	$\overline{\text{BGACK}}$ (input)	BOFF# (input)	BREQ (output)
$\overline{\text{RQ}/\text{GT}_0}$ (bidirectional)		BREQ (output)	
$\overline{\text{RQ}/\text{GT}_1}$ (bidirectional)			

Figure 2.44 Local bus arbitration signals for several microprocessors.

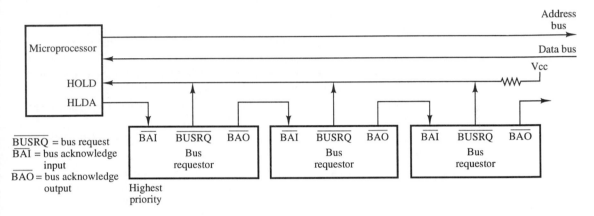

Figure 2.45 Daisy-chaining three bus requestors to the microprocessor [11]. Reproduced by permission. © 1982 Zilog Inc. This material shall not be reproduced without the written consent of Zilog Inc.

When bus requests are issued simultaneously by more than one bus requestor, the one with the highest priority (determined by the requestor's physical proximity to the processor) will become the bus master; its BAO# remains high, aborting any other bus requests farther down the chain, until BUSAK# returns to high. If a bus requestor goes through an unsuccessful bus request attempt, it will usually have to try again after a few cycles.

A second technique is the *parallel bus arbitration technique,* in which an external priority encoder is used to supply the request signal of the highest-priority bus requestor. This more general parallel arbitration technique that uses the bus arbiter among a number of requestors is discussed in Chapter 4 along with system bus issues.

EXERCISES

2.1. Consider the 16-bit Intel 8086 instruction MOV AX,1027, which moves a 16-bit word operand from the memory location specified by the instruction to register AX. Assume that the operand to be transferred is 06F0 (where 06 is the most significant byte) and that the data segment register DS contains the value 3400. Draw the local bus timing diagram for only the execute portion of this instruction and show all appropriate control signals and the values (in hexadecimal) on the address and data buses. (*Hint:* The operand is misaligned.)

2.2. Consider the Intel 8086 (operating in minimum mode) and the 2-byte instruction "ADD AX,[(SI)]," whose execution is as follows:

$$(AX) \leftarrow (AX) + [(SI)];$$

In other words, the content of memory location pointed at by the content of register SI is added to the content of register AX and the result is placed back into AX. The hexadecimal representation of the instruction opcode is 0304. Assume that the operand fetched from memory is 1A3B (1A is the most significant byte). Assume also the following initial contents of registers: $(CS) =$ AA29, $(IP) =$ 5B12, $(AX) =$ 23AD, $(SI) =$ 5122, and $(DS) =$ 42AC.

Assuming that the internal instruction queue is empty, draw the local bus timing diagram for the above instruction cycle. Show the most important control signals, including the BHE#, which is active during the first state of each cycle. Also show the actual hexadecimal values placed on the address and data bus lines. (For the data bus, show explicitly what is transferred over each of the upper and lower halves of the data bus.)

2.3. Consider a microprocessor with a 32-bit address bus and a 16-bit data bus. Also consider the following two cases:

Case 1: The microprocessor uses a synchronous bus and the data lines are multiplexed with the lower portion of the address bus lines. (There are no wait states.)

Case 2: The microprocessor uses an asynchronous bus with no multiplexing on its data and address lines.

For the one-word RET (return) instruction whose execution is: $(PC_L) \leftarrow [(SP)]; (PC_H) \leftarrow [(SP)+2]; (SP) \leftarrow (SP)+4$; and for each of the above two cases:

(a) List the detailed basic activities executed to carry out the instruction execution (only).

(b) Draw the respective timing diagrams that show the local bus lines and the most important control signals, along with the specific information traveling on the bus lines.

State all your assumptions.

2.4. Consider the Intel 80386 and the operand AABBCCDD (where AA is its most significant byte) fetched from location F0000001. Draw the local bus timing diagram showing the most important control signals, the actual hexadecimal address placed on the address bus lines, and the actual hexadecimal bytes transferred over each byte-lane of the data bus, for the following two cases:

(a) When accessing a 32-bit memory.

(b) When accessing a 16-bit memory.

2.5. Consider the Motorola 68030 and the same operand as in Exercise 2.4 but now fetched from location 12345671 of a 32-bit memory. Draw the local bus timing diagram showing the most important control signals (SIZ0–SIZ1, R/W#, AS#, DS#, DSACK0#–DSCACK1#), the actual hexadecimal address placed on the address bus lines connected to the memory subsystem, and the hexadecimal bytes transferred over each of the four data bus byte lanes D0–D7, D8–D15, D16–D23, and D24–D31.

2.6. Consider the 32-bit Intel 80386, which executes a MOV instruction to move a word from location 00003AB7 of a 32-bit memory into an internal register. Assume that the word operand is 1234 (where 12 is the most significant byte). Draw the local bus timing diagram for the execute portion of the above MOV instruction and show all appropriate control signals and the values (in hexadecimal) placed on the address and data bus lines.

2.7. Consider the Motorola 68030 and the operand AABBCCDD (where AA is the most significant byte) fetched from location 12345672. For the following two cases, draw the local bus timing diagram showing the most important control signals (SIZ0–SIZ1, R/W#, AS#, DS#, DSACK0#–DSACK1#), the actual hexadecimal address placed on the address bus lines connected to the memory subsystem, and the hexadecimal bytes transferred over each of the four data bus byte-lanes D0–D7, D8–D15, D16–D23, and D24–D31:

(a) When accessing a 16-bit memory.

(b) When accessing an 8-bit memory.

2.8. Consider a 32-bit memory subsystem into which operands are stored in a little-endian fashion. During any access to memory, the most significant part of the operand is always transferred first. Assume that a 32-bit processor always places a doubleword address on the address bus lines A2–A31 and decodes internally A0 and A1 (along with internal information about the type of memory access, i.e., byte, word, or doubleword) in order to generate the four control signals S0, S1, S2, and S3 for strobing the respective memory section(s) that must respond during the current access:

(a) Explain how bytes, aligned words, and aligned doublewords transfer across the data bus when fetched from main memory over the local bus.

(b) Draw the simplified local bus timing diagrams that show the address and data bus activities (and the respective information transferred on them) and the pertinent control signals issued from main memory for:

(i) A misaligned doubleword operand read (assume that the operand is ABCDEFGH, where AB is the most significant byte)

(ii) A misaligned word operand read (assume that the operand is IJKL, where IJ is its most significant byte)

Assume, finally, that a bus cycle needs 2 input-clock cycles and that the local bus is non-multiplexed and synchronous.

2.9. Give the equivalent figure to that of Figure 2.24 for reading the word operand ABCD from location 4N + 3 of a 32-bit memory by:

(a) A little-endian microprocessor

(b) A big-endian microprocessor

2.10. Draw the local bus timing diagrams (showing the actual address and data values on the respective bus lines and the most pertinent control signals) for the store operation of operand ABCD to location 4N + 2 of a 16-bit memory for the following microprocessors:

(a) Intel 80286

(b) Intel 80386

(c) Intel 80486

(d) Motorola 68020/30

Indicate which data bus-byte lanes carry valid data and which duplicate.

2.11. Draw the local bus timing diagrams (showing the actual address and data values on the respective bus lines and the most pertinent control signals) for the store operation of operand ABCDEFGH to location 4N + 2 of a 16-bit memory for the following microprocessors:

(a) Intel 80386

(b) Intel 80486

(c) Motorola 68020/30

Indicate which data bus byte-lanes carry valid data and which duplicate.

2.12. Repeat Exercise 2.11 for an 8-bit port and the Intel 80486 and Motorola 68030 microprocessors.

2.13. Draw the local bus timing diagram and show the values on the bus lines and the most pertinent control signals for an Intel 80486 nonburst cache line fill operation from location 16N + 4 of a 32-bit memory.

2.14. Repeat Exercise 2.13 when the Intel 80486 is connected to an 8-bit port.

2.15. Give the equivalent figure to that of Figure 2.32a (and the basic operations during each subcycle) for the doubleword EFGHIJKL read from location:

(a) 4N + 1

(b) 4N + 2

2.16. Draw the local synchronous bus timing diagram and show the values on the bus lines and the most important control signals for a Motorola 68030 burst fill operation from location $16N + 7$ of a 32-bit memory with one wait state per data cycle.

REFERENCES

[1] Cohen, D., "On Holy Wars and Plea for Peace," *Computer,* Vol. 14, No. 10, Oct. 1981, pp. 48–54.

[2] James, D. V., "Multiplexed Buses: The Endian Wars Continue," *IEEE Micro,* June 1990, pp. 9–21.

[3] Intel Corp., *i860 64-bit Microprocessor Hardware Reference Manual* (CG-101789), Santa Clara, CA, 1990.

[4] Intel Corp., *Introduction to the 80386* (231746-001), Santa Clara, CA, Apr. 1986.

[5] Motorola Inc., *MC68030 Enhanced 32-bit Microprocessor User's Manual* (MC68030UM/AD), Austin, TX, 1987.

[6] Motorola Inc., *MC68040 32-bit Microprocessor User's Manual* (MC68040UM/AD), Austin, TX, 1989.

[7] Marshall, T., and J. Potter, "How the Macintosh II NuBus Works," *Byte,* Second 1988 Mac Special Edition, pp. MAC39–MAC52.

[8] Intel Corp., *i486 Microprocessor* (240440-001), Santa Clara, CA, 1989.

[9] Intel Corp., *80486 Hardware Reference Manual* (240440-001), Santa Clara, CA, 1989.

[10] Motorola Inc., *MTT20 Course Notes* (MTT20CN), Phoenix, AZ, July 1987.

[11] Zilog Inc., *1982/83 Data Books,* Cupertino, CA, 1982.

3

Memory System Design and Interfacing

3.1 INTRODUCTION

A memory slave communicates with the bus master under a master-slave protocol. It monitors the bus continuously, and when addressed (or selected) by a master during a particular bus cycle, acts upon the control signals provided by the master (i.e., it accepts data from or places data on the data bus lines).

The development of high-density, high-speed semiconductor memory has been the prime cause of the accelerated use of microprocessors. The great variety of memory types and manufacturing technologies forces the designer to know more details and take a more careful look before reaching final decisions. The memory subsystem constitutes a major system expense.

So far in this text we have presented main memory only in a block-diagram form, composed of byte-sections whose total number usually depends on the width of the data bus. We also saw how the operands are stored in main memory in big- and little-endian ordering, which in turn determines which byte lane of the data bus is connected to the respective byte section of memory. Using this block-diagram approach, we also explained what bus cycles are executed in accessing main memory for read and write operations, along with the control signals that various microprocessors generate in order to select (enable) the respective byte section(s) for byte, word, or doubleword access.

In this chapter we get into the details of designing the memory subsystem and interfacing it to the microprocessor's bus lines. From the system designer's point of view, the following questions are of interest:

1. *Wordlength and capacity:* Given the availability of a certain type and size of memory chips, how does one organize them so as to realize a target memory of some desired wordlength and capacity?

2. *Arranging chips on the memory board:* How are all these memory chips arranged on a memory board as an array of rows and columns?

3. *Memory allocation:* What area of the (maximum) addressing space of the microprocessor should this target memory cover? (In other words, what physical addresses should be assigned to this memory?)

4. *Memory interface:* How is this target memory interfaced to the microprocessor external bus lines in a way that meets these assignments?

5. *Memory system speed:* How does one compute the memory latency and memory access time in order to satisfy the microprocessor's speed (i.e., not insert wait states), and how can someone design such a system without necessarily using faster (and more expensive) memory chips?

New microprocessors are capable of addressing large main memory and can be driven by very fast clocks. However, as already mentioned throughout this book, increasing the processor's input clock frequency alone does not guarantee an increase in the overall system performance: the fast processor will be forced to slow down (by inserting wait states) if the data it receives comes from a slower memory. Properly matching the processor and memory bandwidths is the best way of eliminating this performance degradation. Of course, the simplest way to achieve this is to use faster (and more expensive) memory chips. Another technique is to utilize the new accessing modes available in recent large DRAMs. A third technique of increasing memory bandwidth is by designing interleaved memories.

This chapter presents the memory design techniques and provides answers to the above questions with a methodology that is applicable to memories designed using ROM (read-only memory), SRAM (static RAM), or DRAM (dynamic RAM) chips.

3.1.1 Access/Cycle Times and Memory Bandwidth

Besides capacity, another basic memory characteristic is speed. A number of different times are often used to characterize memory speed. One is the **memory access time,** t_a, whose simpler definition is "the time between the receipt by memory of the address bits and memory's response by driving its valid output on the data bus lines." Sometimes, the access time is measured with respect to a specific control signal supplied to memory; for example, *READ command access time* is the time elapsed from the activation of the "READ command."

The **memory cycle time,** t_c, corresponds to "the minimum interval between two consecutive requests for a read operation" (i.e., how often memory can respond to new addresses). As far as SRAMs and ROMs are concerned, the access time constitutes the sole criterion for their speed, because their access time *equals* their cycle time. When it comes, however, to DRAMs, we will see later that their access time *is different* from their cycle time: their cycle time is about twice the access time.[1]

The *memory write time* is the time required from the instant the WRITE command is sent to memory until input data has been stored in memory. It is assumed, of course, that

[1]The terms *full cycle* or *read-modify-write cycle* are also used to denote the memory cycle time for DRAM-type chips, which require periodic refreshing of their contents.

the instant the write signal is supplied, the address has already been decoded and identified the specific memory location, and that the data to be stored have become valid on the data bus. The memory cycle time should last at least as long as the longer of the read or write times.

To evaluate the **performance of the memory subsystem,** the metrics used are the *memory latency* (or memory access[2]) and the *memory bandwidth.* The design strives at reducing the former and increasing the later. At the end of the chapter we present techniques for calculating the required access time so that main memory can match the speed of the microprocessor.

In DRAM memories, where the access and cycle times differ, the access time may be more important because it strongly affects the memory latency time. **Memory latency, L,** is the time it takes to read a ''word'' from main memory and includes address decoding, delays in any other processor-to-memory interface components (such as latches, transceivers, parity checking or error detection and correction hardware, etc.), main memory access time, and possible bus arbitration time when a number of bus masters can access main memory. (In the worst case it may also have to wait for the DRAM precharge time.) The memory latency time is the time the microprocessor has to wait after initiating a memory access request; in the remainder of the memory cycle the microprocessor and memory can operate simultaneously. In simplified situations, all propagation delays are ignored and the memory latency is then the same as the memory access time t_a.

Memory data transfer rate or **memory bandwidth,** b, is the maximum amount of information that can be transferred to and from memory every second and is usually measured in bits/sec or bytes/sec; memory bandwidth depends upon the memory's ''wordlength'' w, its access time, and propagation delays in all interfacing components. Normally, memory bandwidth equals the inverse of its cycle time:

$$\boxed{\text{bandwidth } b \ = \ w/t_c \text{ bits/sec}} \tag{3.1}$$

Since the memory's bandwidth is usually smaller than that of the microprocessor, various techniques have been used to **increase the memory bandwidth:**

1. The simplest way to increase memory bandwidth is to design it using faster memory chips, but this represents the most expensive approach. Even then, however, for today's extremely fast microprocessors, there may not even exist DRAM chips that can handle the microprocessor speeds, at any price.

2. A second approach is to design wider memories. For example, a 32-bit memory delivers 4 bytes per cycle time t_c, yielding a maximum memory bandwidth of $4/t_c$; if the memory width is only 16 bits, then its bandwidth is cut to half. Although the data bus width for a given microprocessor cannot increase, interface logic can be used to latch additional bytes coming from wider memories (such as for a 32-bit processor, data coming from a 64-bit memory, or a 128-bit memory).

3. A third approach is to use newer memory designs that support advanced access modes (nibble, static column, burst transfer, etc.). These are discussed in detail in Section 3.3.

4. More advanced designs interpose between the processor and main memory another type of faster memories, called *cache memories,* which store the most likely information to

---

[2]In Chapter 5 we will modify this definition to the *average memory access time,* taking into consideration the presence of cache memories between the microprocessor and main memory.

be referenced by the processor. In such implementations the processor runs at (the faster) cache speed rather than at (the slower) main memory speed. Cache memories are discussed in detail in Chapter 5.

5. Finally, smarter main memory design and interfacing techniques in the form of *memory interleaving* provide a cheaper solution for matching the higher bandwidth requirements imposed by present-day microprocessors with that provided by slower (and, thus, less expensive) memory chips. Memory interleaving operates on the principle of having several identical but separate memory banks which can operate in parallel. Consecutive data items are stored in different memory banks. This topic is covered in Section 3.4.

One should be very careful when trying to compute the **bus transfer rates** for different microprocessors, because as discussed in Section 1.5.2, the relationships among input clock cycle C, CPU bus cycle, and what is sometimes referred to as a "state," vary from product to product (even from the same manufacturer), as shown in Figure 1.14. For example, consider a 16-MHz external clock (clock period $C = 62.5$ ns) driving the microprocessor chip.[3] In the case of the 16-bit data bus products (Intel 8086 and 80286, and Motorola 68000) which have a 4-clock bus cycle, each sustains a maximum data transfer rate of 8 Mbytes/sec (or 2 bytes per 4*62.5 ns). In the case of a microprocessor with a 4-clock bus cycle but with a wider 32-bit data bus (such as the Intel 80386), it will sustain a maximum data transfer bandwidth of 16 Mbytes/sec (or 4 bytes per 4*62.5 ns). Other processors with 32-bit external data buses that have shorter bus cycles will sustain even higher bandwidths; for example, the Motorola 68020/30 processors have a 3-clock bus cycle and sustain a bandwidth of 21.3 Mbytes/sec, while the Intel 80486 and Motorola 68040 have a 2-clock bus cycle and sustain a bandwidth of 32 Mbytes/sec.

3.1.2 Read-Only Memories

In quite a few microprocessor applications, it is desirable to have the system software and control programs (bootstrap programs, operating system routines, real-time diagnostics, etc.) stored permanently in memory so that they are not lost when power is removed and do not need to be reloaded each time the system is powered on. Such nonvolatile storage is achieved by using ROMs and their alternatives PROMs, EPROMs, and EEPROMs. These memory devices may also be used to hold data that does not change. Some of these memory devices can be programmed only once, while others can be erased and reprogrammed again.

ROMs. The basic type of permanent storage memory is the ROM, also called "masked ROM," which permits only reading of its contents and not writing new information into it. Technologies used for ROM manufacture include bipolar (TTL) and MOS (PMOS, NMOS, CMOS, and FAMOS). ROM memories are "programmed" or "burned" initially during manufacture by using special "masks." They are very fast (have small access times).

PROMs. A variation of ROM is the "programmable ROM" (PROM) or "write-once memory." The time required to write information in a PROM permanently is measured

---

[3]Sometimes, when the input clock is divided internally by 2 to generate the internal "processor clock," such a processor is referred to as an "8-MHz processor."

in milliseconds. PROM memories can be programmed by the customer only once, and are usually manufactured in bipolar technology. PROMs are programmed using special equipment called "PROM programmers or burners." The basic advantage that PROMs have over ROMs is that they do away with the expense of manufacturing the mask. On the other hand, however, PROMs are more expensive. With PROMs, a quick turnaround is accomplished during the system development phase. Low costs are achieved for small system volume productions. Each PROM usually has a pin-compatible counterpart in the form of ROM. However, correcting errors is again not possible with PROMs.

EPROMs/EEPROMs/FLASH memories. The last disadvantage of PROMs can be alleviated by using another type of ROM: the *EPROM* (erasable PROM). These memories are programmable more than once. Their basic difference from RAM memories is that their write time is significantly longer. The contents of an EPROM memory can be erased by exposing the chip to ultraviolet light (for a period of a few minutes), and the memory can then be programmed again. The most attractive technology for manufacturing PROMs is the FAMOS, primarily because of its high speed, low cost, and small size. EPROM memories are widely used for prototype constructions and small-quantity systems, because they allow for corrections of software errors without having to throw away a nonsatisfactory memory chip. Each EPROM also has its counterpart in ROM form. EPROMs are more expensive and slower than bipolar PROMs.

The *EEPROM* (electrically erasable PROM) is a type of PROM which can have selected parts of its memory electrically changed (i.e., erased and rewritten). Electrical erasability implies the potential for programming the device without removing it from the circuit (as is usually done with EPROMs) and without the need for ultraviolet lamps. There exist two types of EEPROMs: (a) metal nitride oxide semiconductors (MNOS EEPROMs), also called **EAROMs** (electrically alterable ROMs), and (b) floating-gate EEPROMs, also called **EEROMs.** Of the two, the EAROMs are most commonly used. The memory parts can be erased in a few milliseconds and rewritten at the rate of a few hundred microseconds. Erasing and writing require threshold voltages of a few volts DC. These electrically erasable PROMs, however, are generally too slow to be used as memories in the final product and are rather expensive.

A more cost-effective and reliable alternative to EPROMs and EEPROMs is the recently introduced *FLASH* memory chips.[4] These chips provide fast read-only nonvolatility along with read/write random access (by having incorporated in-circuit electrical erasure and reprogramming capabilities). Such devices permit periodic updates of code and data and are an innovative alternative to disk, EPROM/EEPROM, and battery-backed SRAMs.

3.1.3 Static and Dynamic RAMs

SRAMs (static RAMs). The main disadvantage of RAM memories is their volatility; i.e, all stored information is lost when power is switched off, and the information must therefore be reloaded after every power-on. RAM chips are manufactured using either bipolar (of smaller density and more expensive) or MOS (of higher density and lower power requirement) technologies.

---

[4] For example, the Intel 28F010 1024K (128K $\times$ 8) [1] and the 28F020 2048K (256K $\times$ 8) [2] CMOS FLASH memories.

Figure 3.1a shows the general block diagram of an SRAM chip with its basic internal structure and I/O pins. Each memory cell is a bistable flip-flop that stores information which can be read with no need to be written back again. (Thus, the SRAM access time equals its

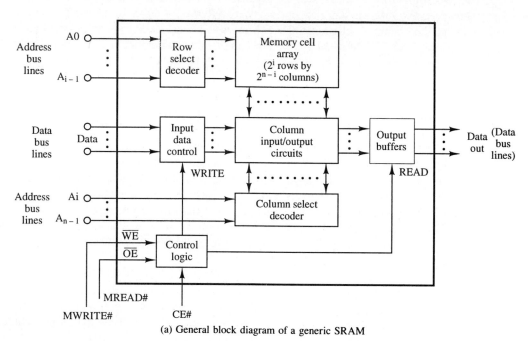

(a) General block diagram of a generic SRAM

256K (or 256K × 1-bit) **DRAM** chip

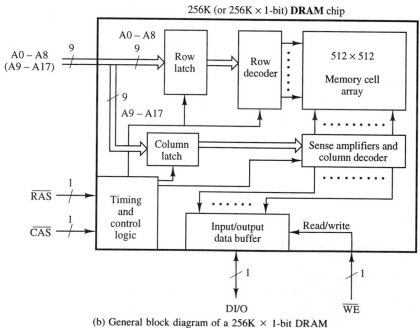

(b) General block diagram of a 256K × 1-bit DRAM

Figure 3.1   Internal structure and I/O pins of SRAM and DRAM chips.

cycle time.) They are faster than DRAMs (that is why the n address bits[5] supplied to them are not multiplexed) and no special clock pulses are required to refresh their contents.

In order to access the chip for any read or write operation, an additional control signal is required, supplied to its CE# (chip-enable) input pin to activate the chip. There are many ways to generate this **chip-enable** or **chip-select** signal,[6] the most common one being by decoding some of the unused most significant address bits (and qualifying them with a "memory read" or "memory write" control signal). Finally, two more control input pins exist on the chip: the WE# (write enable), which triggers the chip to store in an internal location the data bits present at its input data pins, and the OE# (output enable[7]), which triggers the chip to place the data bits from the internally accessed location on its output data pins.

Example 3.1: Interfacing to SRAMs That Have or Do Not Have OE# Pins

Figure 3.2 shows several selection techniques for memory **devices with output enables.** The example devices shown are the Intel 2142[8] 1024 × 4-bit SRAMs, and the signaling is that of the Intel 8086 (or of the 80286, for which only its first 20 address bits are shown). Since each device has a 4-bit "wordlength," a pair of chips must be activated in parallel to drive a byte lane of the data bus; since each device has 1K locations, 10 address bits must be supplied to it as the "word address"; and finally, because it is a 16-bit memory, each pair is connected to either the upper or lower half of the 16-bit data bus to allow for byte transfers on only one byte lane of the data bus (depending on the values of A0 and BHE#).

The interface at the left of Figure 3.2a depicts the case where the microprocessor's WRITE signal (WR#) is combined with the A0 and BHE# to generate the signals to the WE# input pins of the memory chips. The area of memory that these two byte sections cover depends on the output line of the 8206 decoder one connects to the CS1# input pin of the memory chips. The decoder decodes address bits A19–A14. For a read operation, the RD# input signal will trigger both byte sections to drive the data bus (and the processor is responsible for latching the appropriate byte if it had initiated a "byte read" cycle). For a "byte write" cycle, although both byte sections receive the signal CS1#, only the even- or odd-byte section will receive the write strobe (WE#).

The interface in the middle of Figure 3.2a depicts the configuration in which the BHE# and A0 lines now act a "byte-enables" to control byte-section selection directly: A0 = 0 selects section 0 and BHE# = 0 selects section 1. The CS (connected to CS2) is generated as above by decoding the A19–A14 bits. Since the configuration allows connection of the byte enables A0 and BHE# directly to the devices, as well as of the control signals READ (RD#) and WRITE (WR#), byte operations will use the appropriate byte-section.

Finally, the interface of the third diagram in Figure 3.2a again has the A0, WR#, and BHE# signals combined externally before being applied to the memory chips. A read operation always reads 16 bits. The difference from the first design is that individual address bits are now used to condition these memory chips; specifically, they are conditioned with A19A18 = 01, which also define the memory area that these two sections cover.

Figure 3.2b shows the use of external decoders to generate chip-select signals for **devices without output enables.** Separate signals are generated for the even- and odd-byte section devices. The 8205 is a 1-out-of-8 binary decoder.

---

[5]Later on, we will start referring to that part of the microprocessor-issued address which is used by the memory subsystem to do "internal addressing" within its chips as the **word address.**

[6]There exist SRAM chips that have more than one such chip-enable input pin.

[7]Some SRAMs may be calling this OE# pin the RD (read-enable) pin.

[8]The 2142 has instead the "output disable" (OD) input pin for direct control of the output buffers.

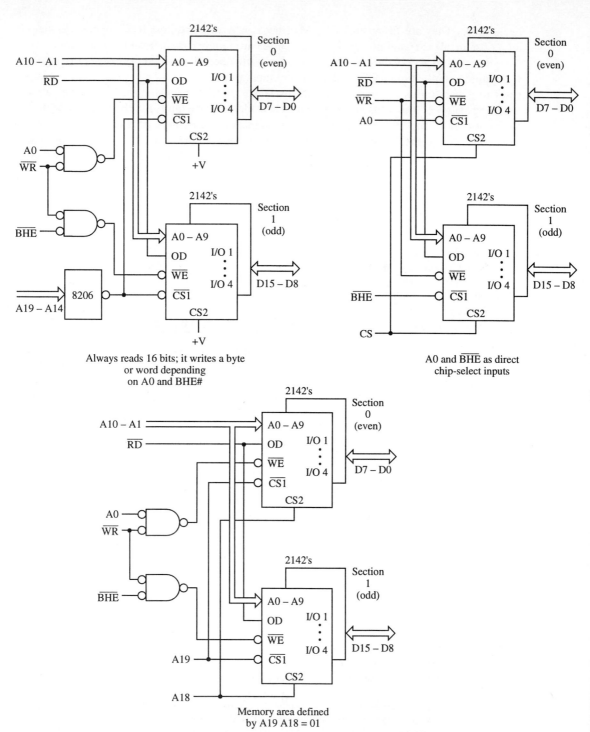

Always reads 16 bits; it writes a byte
or word depending
on A0 and BHE#

A0 and $\overline{BHE}$ as direct
chip-select inputs

Memory area defined
by A19 A18 = 01

(a) Techniques of generating the chip-select signals for memory devices *with* output enables for Intel-based implementations. Courtesy of Intel Corporation [3]. Reprinted by permission of Intel Corporation, Copyright/Intel Corporation 1979. (The 2142 is a 1024 × 4-bit static RAM.)

Figure 3.2 SRAMs with and without output enables pins.

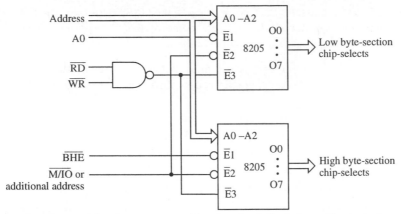

(b) Use of external decoders to generate chip-select signals for devices *without* output enables [4]. Reprinted by permission of Intel Corporation/Copyright Intel Corporation 1983. (The 8205 is an 1-out-of-8 binary decoder.)

Figure 3.2   (concluded)

DRAMs (dynamic RAMs).   In microprocessor systems, SRAMs are used for small-memory designs or for the design of special-purpose memories (such as the external cache memories discussed in Chapter 5). For the larger main memory of the system, usually MOS DRAMs are used because, compared to SRAMs, they have greater densities, are cheaper, and require less standby power. However, they are slower than SRAMs, require data to be written back after being read (thus, their access and cycle times differ), and require periodic refreshing. Highly integrated DRAM chips have a number of special operating modes that significantly decrease access time. We present here the normal *random access mode.*[9]

Structure and Operation.   Figure 3.1b shows the block diagram and internal structure of a 256K × 1-bit DRAM chip. It is observed that these 256K memory cells are internally arranged as a square array of 512 rows and 512 columns. When using DRAMs that have 1-bit input/output capability, if we need to form a 32-bit memory, we would have to use 32 of these DRAMs (each one connected to one of the 32 lines of the data bus D0–D31), all of them triggered to operate in parallel.

Accessing data in a DRAM differs from accessing data in an SRAM. It is observed that DRAM chips have a number of input address pins equal to *half the size* of the total address submitted to them. In the case of the DRAM chip in Figure 3.1b, the memory cell array is accessed by multiplexing the 9 input address lines: first, external memory interface logic (or a "DRAM controller" discussed later) gates the "row address" (the 9 least significant[10] address bits A0–A8) on the DRAM's address input pins and then asserts the RAS# signal[11]; the RAS# will force the DRAM chip to latch the row address, decode it, and select one of the 512 rows. Then, the memory interface logic gates the "column address" (the 9 most significant address bits A9–A17) on the same address input pins of

[9]The faster *page, nibble,* and *static column* modes are discussed later in this chapter.

[10]This order is a design decision.

[11]The RAS# signal is activated after a *row setup time* equal to t_{rs} (see Figure 3.3).

the DRAM and asserts the CAS# signal[12]; the CAS# will force the DRAM chip to latch the column address, decode it, and select one of the 512 columns. The memory cell at the intersection of these two selections is the accessed bit location.

DRAM Access and Cycle Times.   As we can see in the detailed timing diagram of Figure 3.3, DRAMs are characterized by different access times:

Random cycle time (t_{RC}): Minimum time between any two successive reads.

Access time from RAS# (t_{RAC}): The time elapsed from asserting the signal RAS# until valid data is present on the output data pins.

Access time from CAS# (t_{CAC}): The time elapsed from asserting the signal CAS# until valid data is present on the output data pins.

Row setup time (t_{rs}): The time elapsed from the moment the row address is gated to the input pins until the RAS# signal is asserted.

Column setup time (t_{cs}): The time elapsed from the moment the column address is gated to the input pins until the CAS# signal is asserted.

It can be observed that the relationship between the access time from RAS and the (random) cycle time for DRAMs is that *the cycle time is almost twice the access time.* This additional time that must be lapsed before the RAS# can be asserted again is the **precharge time** t_{PR}.

Example 3.2: DRAM Read and Write Timings

DRAM chips have a smaller number of address pins, but the complexity of its interface increases, because it must provide to the chip the address in two steps: a row address followed by a column address. From Figure 3.3, we can then draw the simplified timing diagrams for the read and write cycles to the 256K $\times$ 1-bit DRAM chip of Figure 3.1b as shown in Figure 3.4.

For example, for the READ operation, after presenting the row address to the 9 input address pins of the DRAM chip, the external circuitry must assert the *RAS# (row address strobe)* signal to gate this address into the internal row latch for row decoding; similarly, after presenting the column address to the same 9 input address pins of the DRAM chip, the external circuitry must assert the *CAS# (column address strobe)* signal to gate this address into the internal column latch for column decoding. The time interval from asserting the RAS# until the chip outputs its data is the **DRAM's access time** t_{RAC} (access time from RAS#). It is observed that the chip must precharge for the time interval t_{PR} (called **precharge time,** "RAS# precharge time," "recharge time," or "regenerate time"). The next request to the DRAM cannot be sent before the end of the precharge time and, therefore, the **DRAM cycle time** t_{RC} equals the access time plus the precharge time. If the "write enable" (WE#) control signal remains inactive (i.e., WE# = H as in Figure 3.4a), this bit will automatically appear at the "data output pin" (Dout or Q) of the chip; if, on the other hand, the WE# signal is activated (to signify a write cycle), the bit present at the "data input pin"[13] (Din or D) of the chip will be stored into the selected memory cell (Figure 3.4b).

Because DRAMs have a cycle time which is longer than their access time, advanced memory design techniques must be used to reduce the effect of the precharge time (such

---

[12]The CAS# is asserted after a *column setup time* equal to t_{cs} (see Figure 3.3).

[13]Some 1-bit DRAMs have a single data I/O pin (the DI/O of Figure 3.1b), while others have one data input pin (Din or D) and a separate data output pin (Dout or Q).

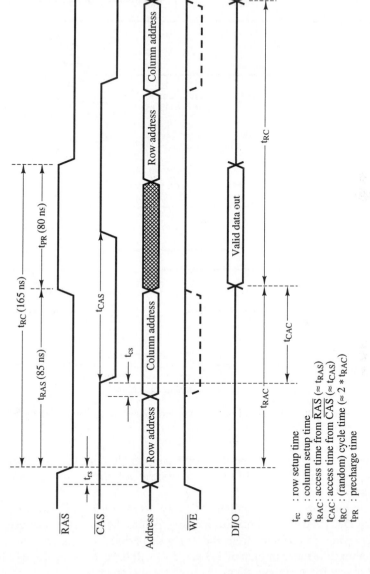

Figure 3.3 Simplified timing diagram of the DRAM "random mode" read cycle (for a 1M × 1-bit 85-ns DRAM device).

t_{rc} : row setup time
t_{cs} : column setup time
t_{RAC}: access time from $\overline{RAS}$ ($\approx t_{RAS}$)
t_{CAC}: access time from $\overline{CAS}$ ($\approx t_{CAS}$)
t_{RC} : (random) cycle time ($\approx 2 * t_{RAC}$)
t_{PR} : precharge time

135

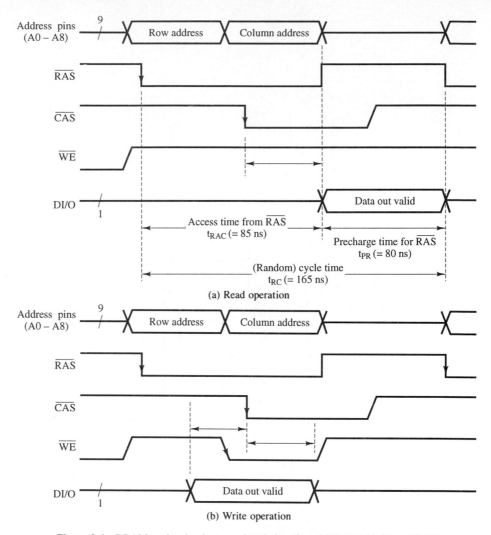

Figure 3.4 DRAM read and write operation timing (for a 256K × 1-bit 85-ns DRAM memory chip).

as memory interleaving, to be discussed later in the chapter) in order to make the access time—and not the cycle time—the metric for the overall DRAM memory system bandwidth.

The precharge time is present in every access to the DRAM; i.e, during every bus cycle the DRAM chips will have to recharge before the processor can use them again. This precharge time is different from the "refresh period" discussed below. Thus, an *85-ns DRAM* chip (like those in Figures 3.3 and 3.4) will have an access time of 85 ns and a cycle time of about 165 ns (about 80 ns are used for the precharge time).

In order to simplify our presentation and the diagrams, unless otherwise stated, the DRAM access time will be the "access time from RAS#" and symbolized as t_a; it will be taken as equal to the precharge time t_{PR}; and each of the access and precharge times will equal half the (random) cycle time, symbolized as t_c.

Example 3.3: DRAM Memory Bandwidth

Under the above simplified assumptions, a "50-ns DRAM" chip will have an access time of $t_a = 50$ ns and a cycle time $t_c = 100$ ns (the other 50 ns are used for the precharge time t_{PR}). Two successive addresses sent to such a memory must be separated by at least 100 ns (its cycle time). Thus the maximum bandwidth that this DRAM can sustain is 1bit every 100 ns or $b = 1/100$ ns $= 10$ Mbits/sec (Equation 3.1).

Constructing a 32-bit-wide memory system using these chips will have a bandwidth of 4 bytes every 100 ns or 40 megabytes per second. A 64-bit memory with the same chips would yield an 80-Mbyte/sec memory subsystem bandwidth.

(More exact memory time requirements—which take into consideration other delays produced by the system bus and interface components that reduce the actual bandwidth—will be discussed at the end of the chapter.)

Refreshing DRAMs.   Information in the DRAM is usually stored as an electrical charge on a capacitor of a single transistor cell, which only provides for temporary storage of data (on the order of msec). Therefore, these DRAMs require special external circuits, counters, and high-voltage pulses to refresh memory periodically. Usually, this is done in a completely transparent operation, between memory accesses, without disturbing the instruction execution. The external refresh circuitry must access each row once within each refresh time interval. A common refresh frequency is one every few milliseconds. (For example, a 256K × 1-bit DRAM may require a refresh operation that cycles through the row address locations every 4 msec.) During memory refresh cycles, the address originates from external address refresh logic and not from the normal address source. Since during refresh periods the memory is not available for processor access, some kind of arbitration circuitry is required at the memory interface to deal with simultaneous requests for access originating from the processor and from the refresh circuitry. In some microprocessor products, the refresh period may be programmable, or refresh can be completely disabled under software control. This periodic refresh is in addition to the precharge time and adds a performance overhead of between 6 and 12%.

3.1.4 Memory Organization

Memory organization has to do with—among other things—determining the "word-length" (or width) of the memory to be designed, figuring out what actual physical addresses will be addressing this memory, and finally, determining out of the total maximum addressing space of the microprocessor which part will be allocated to "local memory" (connected via the local processor bus) and which part will be allocated to "global memory" (connected via the "system bus").

Address spaces.   Some microprocessors (such as those from Intel) have the ability to access two different types of address spaces, the memory address space and the I/O address space. The **memory address space** refers to the maximum size of the directly addressable memory that the processor can access using memory-type instructions. Its size depends on the width of the processor's physical address: e.g., 32-bit processors issue a 32-bit address that can access a 4-Gbyte main memory. The **I/O address space** refers to the maximum number of input/output ports that the processor can access with IN and OUT instructions. For example, if the input/output instruction uses a 16-bit port number, then the processor can access 64K input and 64K output byte-ports.

Two other addressing spaces are distinguished as the "logical address space" and the "physical address space," defined by "logical" and "physical" addresses, respectively.[14] "Logical" and "physical" addresses and the conversion mechanisms required to translate from one to the other type are explained in more detail in Chapter 6. However, for the discussion in this chapter a few introductory comments are appropriate.

All addresses generated by a program are considered "logical addresses," whereas those applied to memory (or I/O devices) are considered "physical addresses." For earlier microprocessors that did not support both logical and physical address spaces, the two addresses are one and the same thing; the address issued by the microprocessor chip is the address applied to memory or I/O slaves. All advanced microprocessors today support both addressing spaces, and an "address conversion mechanism" is required to translate logical addresses to physical addresses. This mechanism comes in the form of what is called an MMU (memory management unit), either outside the microprocessor chip as one or more accompanying chips, or integrated on the same chip with the rest of the microprocessor CPU. In the latter case, the conversion from logical to physical addresses is done inside the processor and the address issued by the microprocessor chip is a physical address. (This is the approach followed by all Intel microprocessors.) In system configurations with the MMUs outside the microprocessor, the logical address issued by the microprocessor chip will not be the same as the physical address transmitted to main memory.

Unless explicitly specified otherwise, for the remainder of this textbook the term "address" by itself will refer to the "physical address" sent to main memory.

Memory wordlength. A byte element is accessed by specifying its address. The byte is the basic addressable element and the smallest unit of information transferred with each access. Data elements or instructions of 16 bits or longer may be placed in memory *starting at any byte address,* and are referenced using an address that designates their first byte in memory[15] and an implicit or explicit indication of their length.

Sixteen-bit memories are composed of the two byte-sections, section 0 and section 1. Such memories are byte addressable, but the basic data transfer may involve a single byte (even or odd) or a 16-bit word. For maximum system efficiency, words and doublewords must be aligned in memory. (Some 16-bit microprocessors, for example the Motorola 68000, enforce such alignment restrictions; others, for example the Intel 80286, do not.) Most 16-bit microprocessors provide at least one extra output signal (such as Intel's BHE# or Motorola's UDS# and LDS# signals), to indicate which byte section(s) will be activated for the byte (or word) transfer. In most 16-bit products, instructions are fetched from memory on a word basis from even addresses.

Thirty-two-bit memories are composed of four byte sections, section 0–section 3. In such memories, although the byte is again the basic addressable element, because the data bus is now 32 bits wide, any two, three, or four consecutive bytes may be grouped together for the transfer. As we saw in previous chapters, the 32-bit microprocessor places on the address bus the 30 most significant bits of the address (thus pointing to a doubleword address), while the 2 least significant bits are used to generate values on the four "byte-enable" control signals that activate the byte sections of the memory. (In other words, these

---

[14]Quite often, the word "virtual" is used instead of the word "logical"; thus, there are "virtual addresses" and a "virtual address space."

[15]Whether this byte is the most significant or the least significant byte depends on the endianess of the stored operands.

2 bits identify an *offset* from the doubleword's base address.) When a 32-bit microprocessor does not enforce memory alignment restrictions, we mean that it automatically initiates additional bus cycles for misaligned elements.

Newer machines (including the MIPS R4000 [13], Intel i860 [11], and Motorola 88110 [14] RISC microprocessors) have 64-bit external data buses that support *64-bit memories* composed of 8 byte sections. In the Intel i860 case, the microprocessor places on the address bus the 29 most significant bits of the address (A3–A31), which identify a quad-word boundary, and outputs on separate pins 8 byte-enable signals (BE0#–BE7#) for the 8 memory sections.

Physical address assignments. In the design of a microprocessor-based system, usually a mixture of RAM and ROM/PROM memories is used. Often ROM/PROM is used to hold the bootstrap and permanent code, while RAM is used for other user programs and data. In such cases, the designer must allocate the address space to ROM and RAM, using a set of memory chips to cover contiguous address ranges in a way that keeps address decoding and memory interface circuits to a minimum. *Physical address assignment* refers to allocating address ranges to the various RAM and ROM memory chips and indicating how other address bits may be used for chip-enable purposes.

Addresses are usually allocated in such a way that one region of addresses belongs to ROM memory, with a separate region to RAM. The specific allocation is often determined by the memory location to which control is transferred when the input RESET signal is applied; in some products the RESET input clears the program counter, while in others it places a specific value in it.

Figure 3.5 shows some examples of memory maps that identify which memory locations have been assigned and the devices at those locations. The map of Figure 3.5c shows the assignment of memory locations to PROM and RAM chips, as well as to input and output ports (in "memory-mapped I/O"). The "comments" column shows the control signals and address bits that may be used as "chip selects."

Address space allocated to the local and system bus. In addition to assigning physical addresses to individual RAM and ROM chips, the address issued by the microprocessor may need to be decoded to identify whether it accesses memory on the local bus or memory on the system bus. Typically, memory resources that reside on the system bus are allocated to particular address windows or address ranges. Of course, the sum of local and global (or system) memory cannot exceed the maximum directly addressable address space of the microprocessor.

Example 3.4: Assignment of Address Spaces to Local and System Buses

Consider, for example, an Intel 80286-based system for which we want to have the addressing space assigned to local and global memory as shown in Figure 3.6a: out of the maximum 16 Mbytes of directly addressable space (that the processor's 24-bit address can access), the first (lowest) 15 Mbytes are to be allocated to local memory, with the remaining 1 Mbyte to global memory. Show the necessary interface hardware and indicate the address formats for accessing the two different memories.

Solution: Figure 3.6b shows the simplified 80286 interface to these local and system resources. The decode logic examines each address issued by the 80286 and determines whether to send it to the local or global bus (by placing the proper value on its output "bus select" to

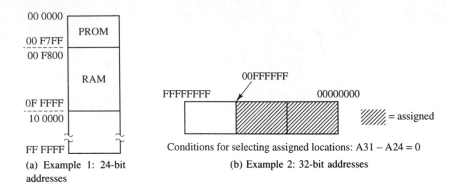

(a) Example 1: 24-bit addresses

(b) Example 2: 32-bit addresses

Device	Memory location(s)	Comments
PROM	000000–00F7FF	MRDC#
RAM	00F800–0FFFFF	MRDC#, MWTC#
8-Bit input ports	100000–10FFFF	MRDC#, A28 = 1 (memory-mapped)
8-Bit output ports	200000–2FFFFF	MWTC#, A29 = 1 (memory-mapped)

(c) Example 3: Memory map with I/O ports and chip-enables

Figure 3.5 Examples of memory allocation maps.

strobe the local or system bus address latches). The bus controller is used to generate the proper commands for the system bus when the processor is to access global memory.

For the above address assignments, Figure 3.6c shows what formats the addresses will have in order to access these two different memories.

3.2 DESIGNING THE MEMORY SUBSYSTEM

3.2.1 Wordlength and Capacity

Since a great variety of memory chips exist, the designer is faced first with the problem of selecting what memory chips to use and then how to connect them properly to form the memory array (which we call the ''target memory''), with the required ''wordlength'' (i.e., number of bits per word) and capacity (i.e., total number of bytes). Having designed this target memory, the designer must then insert the proper circuitry to interface it to the local bus and to the control signals of the microprocessor chip (for small, single-board designs), or to the system bus and its command signals (for larger, multi-board designs).

Quite often, the application at hand may not require the maximum memory that the microprocessor is capable of accessing. The unused address bits can then be used very easily as chip-select signals. Thus, one must also split the total address bits between **word address bits** (those address bits used to access a location inside a memory chip) and **chip-select bits**

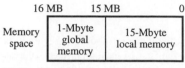

(a) Local and global memory address as-

(a)

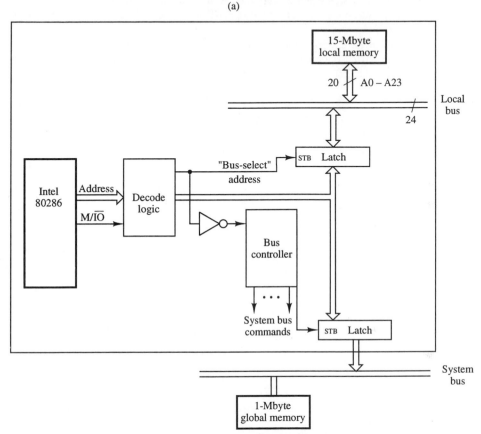

(b) Simplified structure of interfacing the processor to the local and system buses and memories

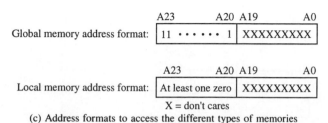

X = don't cares

(c) Address formats to access the different types of memories

Figure 3.6 Assigning address ranges to local and global (system) memory and interfacing the microprocessor to them.

(those address bits used to select which memory chips will be activated to drive/latch their output/input data bus lines).

Example 3.5

Consider, for example, the memory module of Figure 3.7a. Since the memory module has 64K locations, we can use the first 16 least significant address bits and route them to the input address lines for "internal addressing"; i.e., they are used as "word address bits." (Cases where some of the least significant address bits are used as either "byte enables" to select the byte sections of wider memories or "bank selects" in interleaved memories are examined later in the chapter.)

Now we have to solve the memory allocation problem. First of all, we notice that in order to access any byte location in this 64-Kbyte target memory, the module-select input of the memory must also be activated. Second, if we assume that this target memory is to be connected to

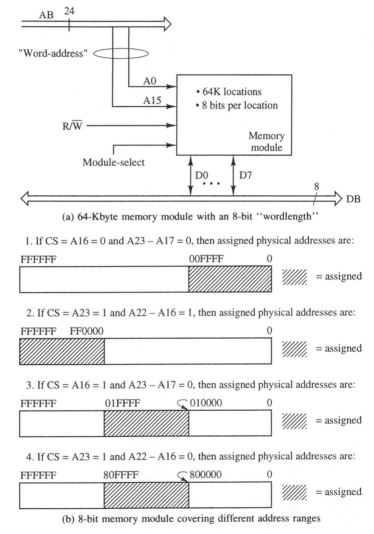

(a) 64-Kbyte memory module with an 8-bit "wordlength"

1. If CS = A16 = 0 and A23 − A17 = 0, then assigned physical addresses are:

2. If CS = A23 = 1 and A22 − A16 = 1, then assigned physical addresses are:

3. If CS = A16 = 1 and A23 − A17 = 0, then assigned physical addresses are:

4. If CS = A23 = 1 and A22 − A16 = 0, then assigned physical addresses are:

(b) 8-bit memory module covering different address ranges

Figure 3.7 64-Kbyte memory module and different assigned address ranges.

a processor whose address bus carries 24-bit addresses (which means that the maximum addressable space is 2^{24} or 16 Mbytes), we have to decide where in this address space this 64-Kbyte area is assigned. This assignment will depend on how we use the remaining (unused) address bits to generate the module-select signal; these address bits will be referred to as "chip-select bits." Figure 3.7b shows different alternatives with which this memory module is assigned to different physical addresses. For example, if the conditions for module select are that all remaining address bits A16–A23 are zeros (ones), then this 8-bit target memory will occupy the lowest (highest) 64K memory locations; if the conditions are CS = A23 = 1 and A16–A22 = 0, then this module covers (is assigned to) memory locations from 800000 through 80FFFF.

From the above discussion and example we can generalize to the following rules for forming the "wordlength" and capacity of the target memory.

Forming the "wordlength" of the target memory. To provide the required wordlength for the target memory, the number of memory chips to be activated/selected in parallel is given by the following simple formula:

$$\text{number of chips} = \frac{\text{wordlength of target memory}}{\text{wordlength of the chip}} \tag{3.2}$$

Thus, if the target memory to be designed is a $2^N \times 2^M$-bit memory using $2^n \times 2^m$-bit chips, then 2^{M-m} chips must be activated in parallel to generate the 2^M-bit "word" of the target memory.

Figure 3.8 depicts the general configuration of the 2^{M-m} memory chips (SRAMs), each of size $2^n \times 2^m$ bits, which are activated in parallel to form the $2^N \times 2^M$-bit target RAM memory. The input and output data to and from this memory is 2^M bits. In this

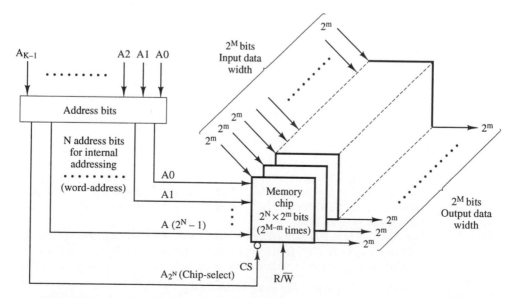

Figure 3.8 Memory module made up of a number of parallel-selected memory chips (SRAMs).

configuration, the 2^N least significant bits from the K-bit address are supplied to *all* memory chips to select the internal location (i.e., they are the "word-address" bits). The next available address bit is used as the "chip-select" (CS) bit applied to the CS input pin of *all* memory chips to activate them in parallel. The way the generation of this CS signal is conditioned on the remaining unused (most significant) address bits will determine what actual physical addresses have been assigned to this target memory.

For example, a memory board with a 64-Kbyte capacity and an 8-bit wordlength (one byte-section) will be made up of eight $64K \times 1$-bit memory chips. Quite often, such a memory module may have a ninth memory chip used as the "parity chip." For each byte written into memory, the memory interface logic in the form of a "parity generator/ checker" will generate the parity bit and store it in the associated parity bit. For each byte read from memory, parity will be generated and compared with the stored parity bit. If a parity error is detected, the access cycle is terminated by sending to the processor an interrupt signal.[16]

Forming the capacity of the target memory. To form the required capacity of the target memory (in number of total locations), the following simple formula is used:

$$\text{number of chips} = \frac{\text{number of locations in target memory}}{\text{number of locations in the chip}} \qquad (3.3)$$

This is also known as "address expansion" or "memory expansion." Thus, if the target memory to be designed is a $2^N \times 2^M$-bit memory using $2^n \times 2^m$-bit chips, then there must be a total of 2^{N-n} chips to form the target memory with 2^N locations.

In practice, the memory chips will be arranged in a two-dimensional array and placed on a printed-circuit memory board. Then for a target memory module of $2^N \times 2^M$ bits, using $2^n \times 2^m$-bit memory chips, the array is computed as follows:

$$\text{number of board columns} = 2^{M-m}, \text{ for a "wordlength" of } 2^M \text{ bits} \qquad (3.4)$$

$$\text{number of board rows} = 2^{N-n}, \text{ for a capacity of } 2^N \text{ "words"} \qquad (3.5)$$

3.2.2 SRAM Memories

Design and interfacing to 16-bit memories

Example 3.6: Functional Design of a 16-Bit Memory

Design the memory subsystem for a generic 16-bit microprocessor (with a 24-bit address) using $64K \times 8$-bit SRAMs. Each memory chip has a single chip-select input. The total capacity of this memory should be 1 Mbytes and assigned to the lowest physical addresses. Show the arrangement of these chips on the printed-circuit board and their interface to the processor's address and data bus lines.

Solution: Figure 3.9a shows the functional design of the 16-bit memory. First of all, since the total target memory is 1 Mbytes we will need sixteen $64K \times 8$ SRAMs. Second, since this is a 16-bit memory, these SRAMs will be assigned 8 of them to section 0 (even bytes) and the

[16]Such as the Motorola's "bus error signal" BERR#.

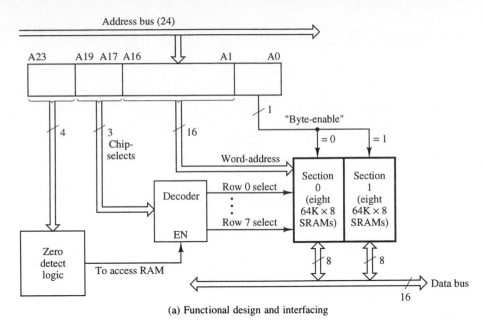

(a) Functional design and interfacing

Figure 3.9 16-bit memory board. (Target total memory = 1M × 8 bits; target section = 0.5M × 8 bits; SRAM chips = 64K × 8 bits.)

other 8 to section 1 (odd bytes), and the least significant address bit A0 will be effectively[17] used as a ''byte enable.'' Since each memory chip has 64K locations, internal addressing requires 16 address inputs; the next 16 bits of the address (A16–A1) are used for this purpose as ''word-address'' and applied to all SRAM chips in the memory. The 8 SRAMs in each section are arranged in a single column (because each chip has the ''wordlength'' of the byte-section), and therefore the next 3 address bits (A19–A17) are decoded to identify the particular SRAM selected (the outputs of the decoder are the ''row-select'' signals that condition the chip-select input pins of all memory chips lying on the corresponding row). Finally, the decoder is enabled only when the remaining address bits (A13–A20) are all zeros (since the 1-Mbyte module must be in low memory).

Figure 3.9b shows the arrangement of these 16 SRAMs on a memory board and Figure 3.9c the real hexadecimal addresses assigned to each of several SRAM chips.

Example 3.7: Interfacing a 16-Bit Memory to the Intel 80286

Show the detailed interfacing of the Intel 80286 to a 16-bit memory bank of total capacity 8 Kbytes composed of 4K × 1-bit SRAM chips.

Solution: Figure 3.10 shows the detailed interfacing. The memory subsystem is composed of sixteen 4K × 1-bit SRAM chips, half of them connected in parallel to form section 0 (the even byte section) and the other half, section 1 (the odd byte section). Since it is a 16-bit memory, A0 along with the BHE# will be used as byte enables. The next 12 address bits A1–A12 are used for addressing inside the memory chips (the word address), while higher-order address bits are decoded to generate the ''bank-select'' signal to assign a physical address range to this memory bank.

[17]In the Intel case, A0 will have to be used along with the microprocessor's signal BHE#. In the Motorola case, A0 will be internally decoded by the microprocessor to generate the signals UDS# (for the even section 0) and LDS# (for the odd section 1).

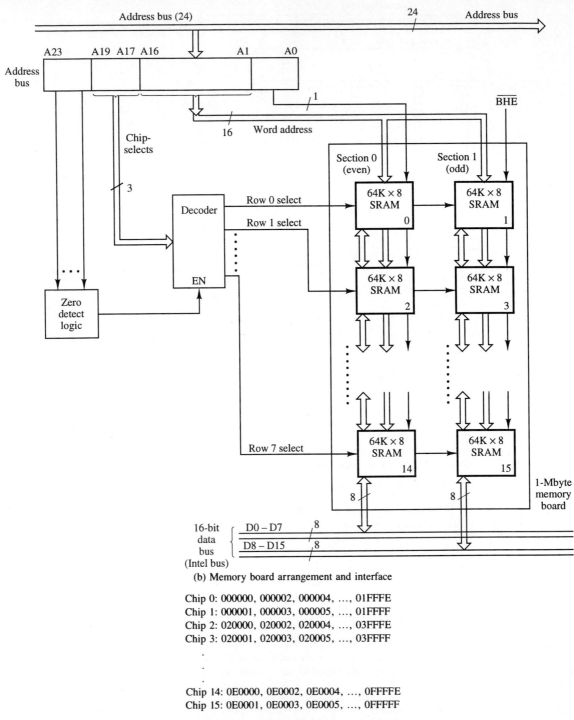

(b) Memory board arrangement and interface

Chip 0: 000000, 000002, 000004, ..., 01FFFE
Chip 1: 000001, 000003, 000005, ..., 01FFFF
Chip 2: 020000, 020002, 020004, ..., 03FFFE
Chip 3: 020001, 020003, 020005, ..., 03FFFF

.
.
.

Chip 14: 0E0000, 0E0002, 0E0004, ..., 0FFFFE
Chip 15: 0E0001, 0E0003, 0E0005, ..., 0FFFFF

(c) Physical addresses (in hex) assigned to the various memory chips

Figure 3.9 (concluded)

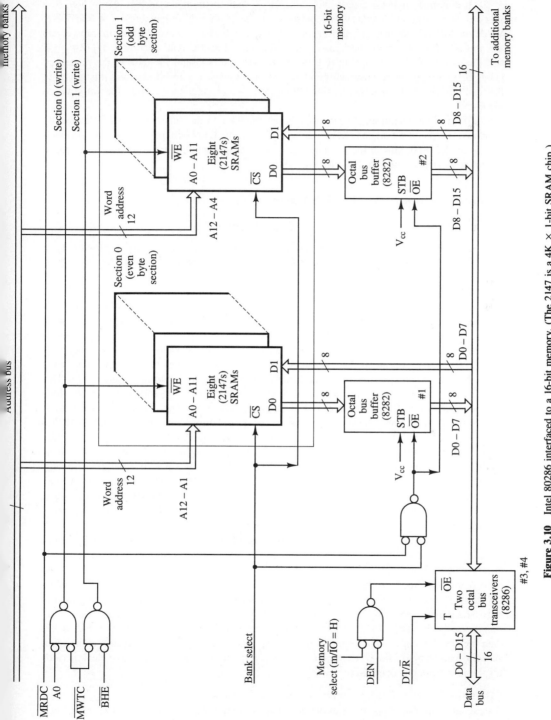

Figure 3.10 Intel 80286 interfaced to a 16-bit memory. (The 2147 is a 4K × 1-bit SRAM chip.) (Adapted from [4]. Reprinted by permission of Intel Corporation, Copyright/Intel Corporation 1983.)

It is noticed that for a read cycle, the 16-bit data at the decoded location in *both byte sections* is read out of memory and buffered at the memory's output buffers #1 and #2. When the MRDC# is asserted, it triggers these two bus buffers to send the data to transceivers #3 and #4. (WE# is high throughout the read cycle.) For this read operation, DT/R# = L and the assertion of DEN will have transceivers #3 and #4 send the data to the processor. (Thus both byte and word reads will send to the microprocessor a 16-bit item and it is left up to the microprocessor to determine which byte lane of the data bus carries the information requested.)

For a write operation, the processor issues the data on the data bus, which is latched by transceivers #3 and #4 when DT/R# is asserted high. The DEN will make this input data available to the DI input pins of the memory chips. Which byte section will store data will depend on the processor's values on lines A0 and BHE#.

Design and interfacing to 32-bit memories

Example 3.8: Interfacing a 32-Bit Memory to Motorola 680x0

Suppose that we want to design a 32-bit memory board of total capacity 1 Mbytes using 64K × 4-bit SRAM memory chips, assigned to the highest memory area of a Motorola 680x0 microprocessor.

Solution: First of all, this 32-bit memory must have four byte sections, section 0, section 1, section 2, and section 3. Thus the arrangement on the board should have four columns, one per byte section. Since the wordlength of each memory chip is 4 bits, a pair of them must always be activated together to form the 8-bit wordlength of the byte section. Therefore, each row on the memory board will have four memory chip pairs. The capacity of this row becomes 4*2*(64K × 4) = 4*(64 Kbytes) = 256 Kbytes. Since the total memory board capacity must be 1 Mbytes, the memory board needs to have 4 such rows, as shown in Figure 3.11a. This design represents a memory board interfaced to a Motorola-type big-endian processor which requires that section 0 be connected to data bus lines D24–D31. The two least significant address bits A0 and A1 are externally decoded to generate the four byte-enable signals DBBE1–DBBE4 to the memory sections; the next 16 address bits are used as a "word address" to access a location inside the memory chips, and bits A18 and A19 are used as "chip selects": their decoding will generate the "row selects" for the board. Finally, since the condition for activating this chip-select decoder is that all remaining most significant address bits A20–A31 be ones, this memory board covers the highest 1-Mbyte of the 2^{32} = 4-Gbyte addressing space. Figure 3.11b shows the ranges of actual hexadecimal addresses covered by the first four pairs of memory chips.

As we mentioned in Chapter 2, a number of Motorola 32-bit processors support both asynchronous and synchronous bus cycles. For the 68020/30 *asynchronous bus cycles*, the processors support byte, word, and doubleword operands to be transferred to/from 32-, 16-, and 8-bit data ports; such cycles are controlled by the data transfer and size acknowledge inputs (DSACK0# and DSACK1#). For the 68040 *synchronous bus cycles,* the processor supports only data transfers to/from 32-bit data ports; such cycles are controlled by the synchronous termination signal (STERM#).[18] The main difference is the STERM# must be asserted earlier than the DSACKs of the asynchronous operation, causing the processor to perform a minimum access time transfer in *two clock periods* (as compared with the minimum of three clock periods for the asynchronous operation).[19]

[18]The 68020/30 synchronous bus transfers are discussed in Appendix B.

[19]As we are doing throughout this textbook, in all the Motorola timing diagrams and unless stated otherwise, we are using the 3-clock cycle asynchronous operation.

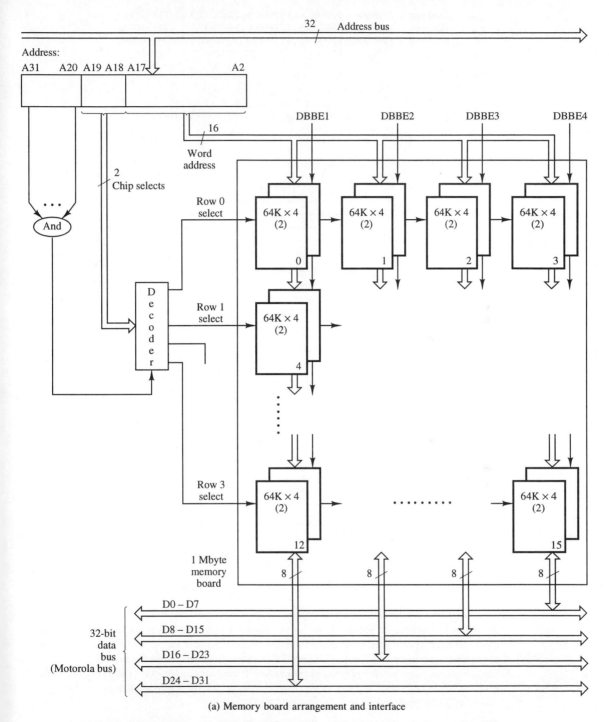

(a) Memory board arrangement and interface

Figure 3.11 32-bit memory board. (Target total memory = 1M × 8 bits; target section = 0.25M × 8 bits; memory chips = 64K × 4 bits.)

Chip pair 0: FFF00000, FFF00004, FFF00008, FFF0000C, ..., FFF3FFFC
Chip pair 1: FFF00001, FFF00005, FFF00009, FFF0000D, ..., FFF3FFFD
Chip pair 2: FFF00002, FFF00006, FFF0000A, FFF0000E, ..., FFF3FFFE
Chip pair 3: FFF00003, FFF00007, FFF0000B, FFF0000F, ..., FFF3FFFF

.
.
.

(b) Physical addresses (in hex) assigned to some of the memory chips

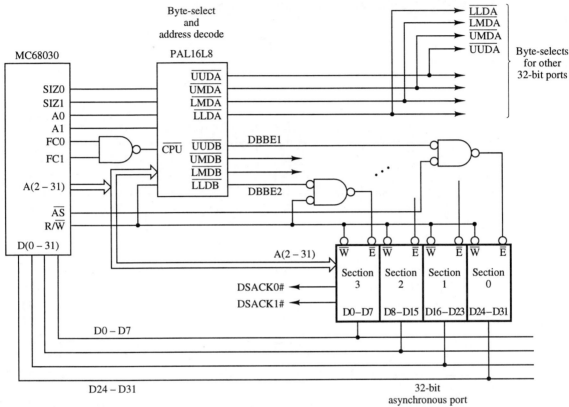

(c) Motorola 68030 interfaced to an asynchronous 32-bit memory port (Adapted from [1])

Figure 3.11   (concluded)

In both cases, it is the selected external slave device that controls the actual length of the bus cycle by sending the above signals to the processor to terminate the cycle. (The bus error signal BERR# is also used to terminate the bus cycle in the absence of DSACKs or STERM# to indicate a bus error condition.) If Figure 3.11a shows the interface on the memory side, Figure 3.11c shows the interface on the Motorola 68030 microprocessor side. The PAL (programmable array logic) device[20] (or an equivalent) is used to provide the byte-enables for the asynchronous 32-bit port.

[20]The PALs are devices used to provide reliable, high-performance substitutes for conventional TTL logic. Their easy programmability allows for quick design of "custom" chips for microprocessor interface and typically results in a more compact board.

Example 3.9: Interfacing a 32-Bit Memory to Intel 80x86

Figure 3.12 shows the simplified diagram of interfacing a 32-bit memory to an Intel 80x86 microprocessor. In this example, each of the four byte sections is made up of one 2K × 8 SRAM chip. The interface bus controller (not shown) provides the read and write commands to memory (MRDC# and MWTC#), the control signals for the address latches (ALE#) and data transceivers (DEN#), and sends back to the processor the READY# active signal to end the bus cycle. Eleven address bits (A12–A2) are routed as "word address" to memory; the four byte enables BE0#–BE3# are also sent to the respective four byte sections of memory, conditioned with the memory write command MWTC#. The input pins OE# of the memory chips are triggered by the MRDC# command, and therefore *all four sections drive the data bus during read operations.* For write operations, the MWTC# is gated with the byte-enable signals to specify which byte sections will store incoming data bytes.

3.2.3 DRAM Memories

8207 DRAM controller. The design and interface of DRAM memories presents more interest because it is the type of main memory most commonly accessed by the processor since it contains the program, data, and information used in processing. The logic used for interfacing to DRAM memory must primarily time-multiplex the two parts of the supplied address, generate the row address (RAS#) and column access (CAS#) strobes, and provide the memory-refresh logic. While earlier designs used a number of different discrete components to implement this interface, the use of the "programmable DRAM controller" chip simplifies this task considerably. DRAM controllers can be used in either noninterleaved or interleaved memory configurations. A number of such DRAM controller chips exist, such as the Intel 8207 [6], which can drive up to 4 banks composed of 256-Kbit DRAM chips each; the TI 74ALS6301 [7], which can drive up to 4 banks composed of 1-Mbit DRAM chips each; the Integrated Devices Technology 79R3721 [8], which supports memories composed of 1-Mbit to 16-Mbit DRAM chips in both noninterleaved and two-way interleaved configurations, in cache burst fill cycles, and in "page mode" operation using on-chip page detection (to be explained at the end of the chapter); etc. All have similar structures, input and output signals, and they function in more or less the same way. In most of our discussion and examples we will be using the Intel 8207. An example using ALS6301 is given at the end of the chapter.

Figure 3.13 shows the detailed internal structure of the Intel 8207 DRAM controller. The 8207 DRAM controller is designed to interface easily with a wide variety of microprocessors to 16K, 64K, and 256K DRAM devices. The 8207 can be used in both single- and dual-port configurations; two internal port interfaces (each havings its own "port enable" input, PEA# and PEB#) allow two independent processors to access a single main memory controlled by one 8207 DRAM controller. Each port can be programmed separately to interface to either synchronous or asynchronous environments; there exist output "data transfer acknowledge" signals (XACKA#/ACKA#, XACKB#/ACKB#, etc.) which can be used for that. Internally the controller has the logic needed to refresh the DRAM chips connected to it. The 9-bit multiplexed address is placed on the output pins AO0–AO8. The controller's LEN output can be used as another "address latch enable" signal, and the chip can be programmed for either internal or external refresh option.[21] Finally, as we

---

[21]Earlier DRAM controller chips required an external "memory timing controller" chip to generate the control signals needed by the DRAM controller (to access and refresh the dynamic memory, and to arbitrate between refresh and access cycles).

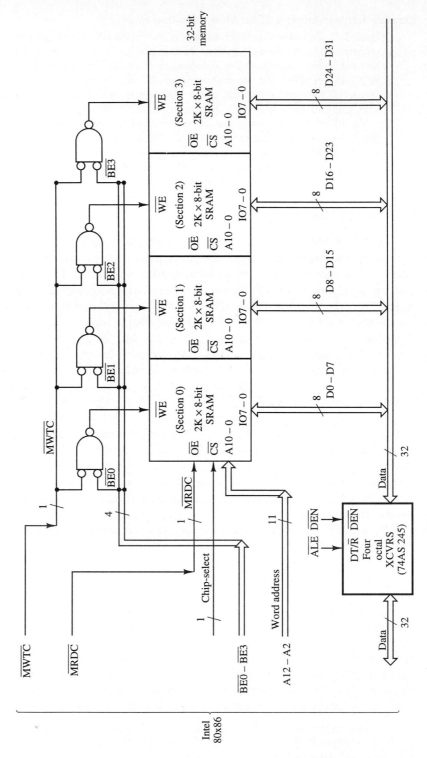

Figure 3.12 Thirty-two-bit SRAM memory interfaced to an Intel 80x86 micro processor. (Adapted from [5]. Reprinted by permission of Intel Corporation, Copyright/Intel Corporation 1986.)

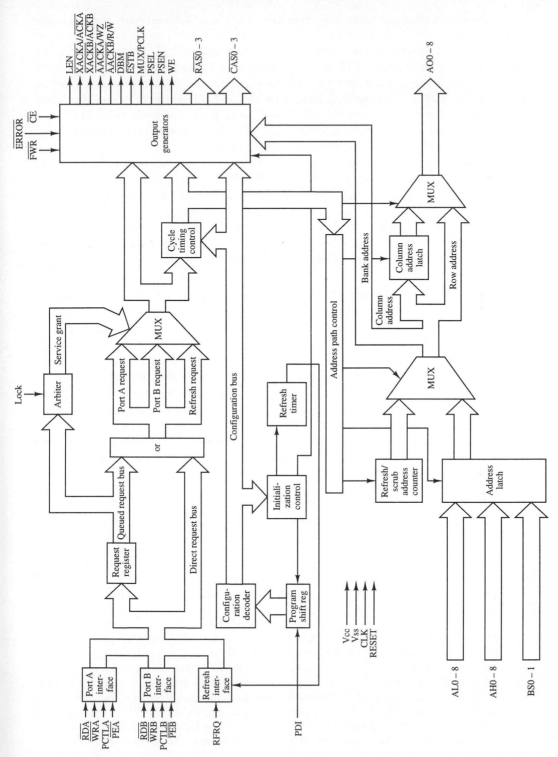

Figure 3.13 DRAM controller (internal structure of the Intel 8207) [6]. Reprinted by permission of Intel Corporation, Copyright/Intel Corporation 1983.

153

will explain in more detail below, the controller issues four different pairs of RAS# and CAS# signals.

The 8207 DRAM controller is interfaced to 16K, 64K, and 256K DRAMs using the address connections of Figure 3.14. If, for example, a 16-bit memory is used, then A0 will be used to effectively generate the DRAM "byte-enable" signal and A1 and A2 will be applied to the 8207's "bank-select" input pins BS0 and BS1 to select one of up to four memory banks that may be connected to the controller (explained below in more detail). The size of the DRAM determines the number of the 8207 input address pins to be used (unassigned address input pins may be strapped to high or low).

We said earlier that the DRAM controller can be programmed to control up to four memory banks, each bank having its own RAS#/CAS# pair. The default condition has the controller control four occupied DRAM banks; in this case, RAS0#/CAS0# will be routed to bank 0, RAS1#/CAS1# to bank 1, RAS2#/CAS2# to bank 2, and RAS3#/CAS3# to bank 3, as shown in Figure 3.15. As another example, we can see from Figure 3.15 that when the controller is programmed for a two-bank configuration, then a pair of RAS# signals and a pair of CAS# signals are activated per bank.

Interfaces using the 8207 DRAM controller. Figure 3.16 shows the simplified block diagram of the 8207 DRAM controller and the way it receives the address, multiplexes it, and supplies it to a 256K $\times$ 1-bit DRAM chip along with the RAS# and CAS# signals. First of all, the controller is assumed here as configured to control 256K locations and receive an 18-bit input address (see Figure 3.14). Each 9-bit half of the address is connected to the respective row address (AL0–AL8) and column address (AH0–AH8) input pins of the DRAM controller. As Note 1 in this figure explains, which 18 address bits one should connect to the DRAM controller input pins depends on the particular design. A multiplexer inside the controller, along with other timing circuitry, will properly sequence in time the two 9-bit halves of the address to the controller output lines AO0–AO8 along with their respective RAS# and CAS# signals. The design here shows applying the RAS0# and CAS0# to the memory chip.

Example 3.10: DRAM Controller Interfaced to a 16-Bit Memory

Figure 3.17 shows the details of an example configuration in which the DRAM controller is used to control a 16-bit DRAM subsystem of total capacity 0.5 Mbytes constructed using 256K $\times$ 1-bit DRAM chips, eight per byte section. Each 256K DRAM chip has nine input address lines requiring multiplexing to produce the 18 address bits needed to access all its 256K cell locations. At the beginning of every bus cycle, the respective RAS# is asserted by the DRAM controller along with the lower 9 address bits to address a row; then CAS# is asserted along with the upper 9 address bits to specify a column.

The figure shows the use of external logic (the "section-select logic") to decode Intel's A0 and BHE# outputs to condition the write-enable signals for the even and odd byte sections. For a read cycle, both byte sections of the 16-bit memory are triggered to drive their respective byte lanes of the data bus. In this example, the next 18 address bits (A1–A18) needed to access a location inside this 0.5M-byte memory are submitted to the DRAM controller. Finally, the remaining 5 most significant bits are used to assign/allocate actual physical addresses to this memory subsystem (via the address decode logic) that triggers the controller's PE# (enable) input pin. Since only one memory bank is connected, the DRAM controller has been programmed (initialized) to operate with only "1 bank occupied"; furthermore, since the bank-

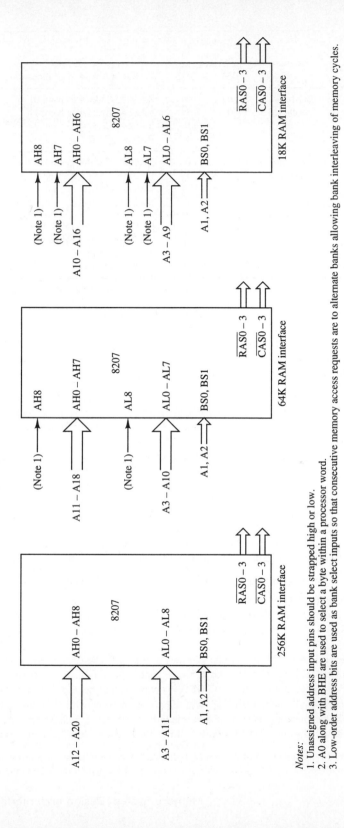

Figure 3.14 Address connections to the 8207 DRAM controller for 256K, 64K, and 16K DRAM devices [6]. Reprinted by permission of Intel Corporation, Copyright/Intel Corporation 1983.

Notes:
1. Unassigned address input pins should be strapped high or low.
2. A0 along with BHE are used to select a byte within a processor word.
3. Low-order address bits are used as bank select inputs so that consecutive memory access requests are to alternate banks allowing bank interleaving of memory cycles.

Programmed mode	Bank-select input BS1	BS0	RAS#/CAS# pair allocation
Four banks occupied	0	0	RAS0#, CAS0# to bank 0
	0	1	RAS1#, CAS1# to bank 1
	1	0	RAS2#, CAS2# to bank 2 Default
	1	1	RAS3#, CAS3# to bank 3
Three banks occupied	0	0	RAS0#, CAS0# to bank 0
	0	1	RAS1#, CAS1# to bank 1
	1	0	RAS2#, CAS2# to bank 2
	1	1	Bank 3 unoccupied
Two banks occupied	0	0	RAS0,1#, CAS0,1# to bank 0
	0	1	RAS2,3#, CAS2,3# to bank 1
	1	0	Bank 2 unoccupied
	1	1	Bank 3 unoccupied
One bank occupied	0	0	RAS0–3#, CAS0–3# to bank 0
	0	1	Bank 1 unoccupied
	1	0	Bank 2 unoccupied
	1	1	Bank 3 unoccupied

Figure 3.15 Bank selection decoding and word expansion on the 8207 DRAM controller [6]. Reprinted by permission of Intel Corporation, Copyright/Intel Corporation 1983.

selects BS0 and BS1 pins of the DRAM controller are connected to logic 0, then from Figure 3.15 it is concluded that all four pairs of RAS# and CAS# strobes will be assigned[22] to this bank 0.

To implement a 1-Mbyte memory, we would need one more memory bank of the type shown on Figure 3.17, for a total of 32 chips, 16 chips per section. Instead of 19 address bits, 20 processor address bits must now be used, and the 8207 programmed to realize that two banks are connected to it. To differentiate between these two banks, an unused address bit must now be connected to pin BS0, while BS1 must be low. (If we connect address bit A19, we will make these two memory banks occupy two contiguous 512-Kbyte memory areas; if we connect address bit A1, we will implement "2-way word interleaving" in which Bank 0 will have the even word locations and Bank 1 the odd word locations, as we will see later.)

Example 3.11: Interface to Four 256-Kbyte Noninterleaved DRAM Banks

Use the 8207 DRAM controller to control a 16-bit DRAM memory of total capacity 16M bytes constructed out of the TMS 4256 (a 256K × 1-bit) DRAM chips. Assume a little-endian microprocessor with a 24-bit address bus and a 16-bit data bus. Show the memory's interface to these bus lines.

Solution: Figure 3.17 showed the interface of the 8207 DRAM controller to one 16-bit memory bank of capacity 512 Kbytes. The 8207 can control up to four such 256-Kbyte memory banks as shown in Figure 3.18a. The 8207 DRAM controller has been programmed to operate with "4 banks occupied" and, therefore, will supply each bank with its own pair of RAS#/CAS# strobes. The memory subsystem's wordlength is 16 bits and address bit A0 is again used (along with the BHE#) to identify the byte. Since this memory has 2 Mbytes capacity, it requires a

[22]If not all banks are occupied, the RAS# and CAS# strobes can be used to allow wider memories ("word expansion") to transfer wider data words without increasing the loading on the RAS# and CAS# drivers.

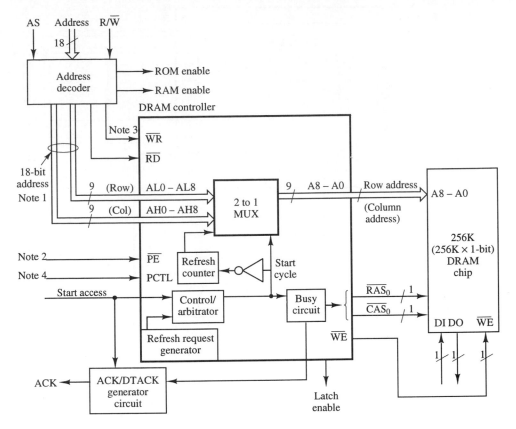

Notes:

1. Which address bits are supplied to the DRAM controller depends on the particular design. (For example : A0 may not be applied to the controller if used to distinguish between even and odd memory sections: or low-order address bits may be used as bank-select inputs in interleaved memory designs.)

2. Usually external logic combines the remaining unassigned address bits to generate the chip-enable (or chip-select) signal.

3. Directly from the microprocessor's output pins or from the bus controller.

4. Port control for configuring one of the two ports to accept command signal (PCTL).

Figure 3.16 Simplified block diagram of a DRAM controller and its interface to a 256K × 1-bit DRAM memory chip.

21-bit address to access any internal byte location; address bits A1–A18 are supplied to the controller's input pins AL0–AL8 and AH0–AH8, while A19 and A20 are connected to the BS0, BS1 inputs. Since the four banks occupy *contiguous* (noninterleaved) 512-Kbyte memory areas, the BS0 and BS1 pins must be driven by bits A19 and A20.[23] Because the DRAM controller is enabled when address bits A21–A23 are zeros (PE receives the number zero output from the decoder), this 2-Mbyte memory is assigned to the lowest 2 Mbytes of the 16-Mbyte maximum main memory space.

[23]Using the high-order bits to select the bank is also sometimes called "high-order interleaving" or "bank switching."

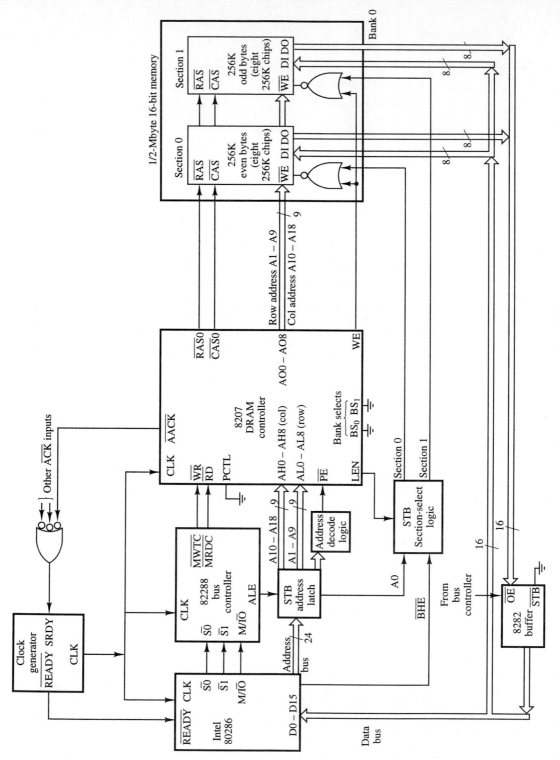

Figure 3.17 Interfacing to a 0.5M-byte memory (wordlength 16 bits) through the 8207 DRAM controller. (Adapted from [6].) Reprinted by permission of Intel Corporation, Copyright/Intel Cor-

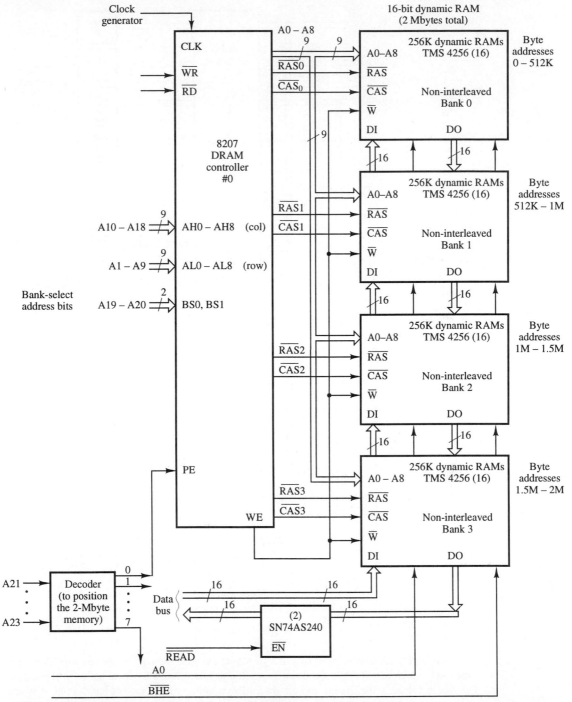

(a) Details of interfacing DRAM controller #0 to four, noninterleaved, 256-Kbyte memory banks. (Adapted from [6] and [7].) Reprinted by permission of Intel Corporation, Copyright/Intel Corporation 1983 and Texas Instruments 1988.

Figure 3.18 DRAM controller chip controlling a 16-Mbyte dynamic memory. (Memory is constructed using 256K × 1-bit DRAM devices.) No interleaving is used.

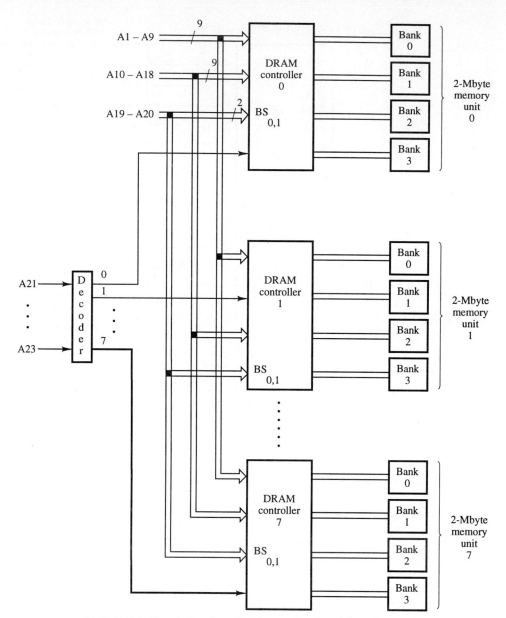

(b) Eight DRAM controllers for a 16-Mbyte noninterleaved dynamic memory

Figure 3.18 (concluded)

Figure 3.18b shows the design of a 16-Mbyte dynamic memory (accessed with 24-bit addresses), which uses 8 DRAM controllers, each one controlling a 2-Mbyte memory of the kind shown in Figure 3.18a. Again, these eight 2-Mbyte memory units are not interleaved; they are contiguous because the selection of the 2-Mbyte memory unit (actually, the selection of its DRAM controller) is done by decoding the most significant address bits A21–A23.

Dual-ported memories.   Dual-ported memories allow two independent units (such as one processor and one graphics controller, or two processors) to access the same memory, for example in situations when the microprocessor is updating (writing to) memory while the graphics controller accesses memory to read data and send them to the graphics display. A DRAM controller that provides two ports can do that by internally queueing each unit's requests, arbitrating between these requests, and directing data to or from the appropriate port. Furthermore, one of the two units can be interfaced synchronously and the other interfaced asynchronously.

Error detection and correction units (EDCU).   Memory error detection and correction can be incorporated in the design by using the DRAM controller and an error detection and correction unit (EDCU). The simplified block diagram of such a design is shown in Figure 3.19. Additional memory is provided to the 32-bit DRAM memory to hold the 8 parity bits. The 8 parity bits are formed here by using a Hamming code (or modified Hamming code) scheme, which allows for single-error correction and double-error detection (SEC-DED). The EDCU works on both read and write cycles, providing corrected data to the rest of the system and to the memory cells.

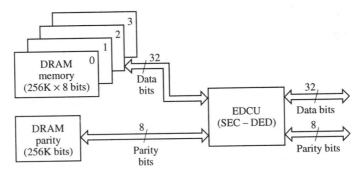

Figure 3.19 DRAM memory with error-detection and error-correction circuitry (EDCU).

On read cycles from memory, the EDCU executes a read-modify-write operation. It uses the 8 parity bits to check and if necessary correct the 32-bit doubleword read out from memory. The corrected 32-bit doubleword and the 8-bit parity are then written back into the DRAM cells and all 40 bits are sent to the rest of the system. On write cycles to memory, the EDCU receives and checks the 32 data bits and the 8 parity bits, corrects any errors, a new 8-bit parity is generated from the new 32-bit doubleword, and all 40 bits are stored into the DRAM cells.

3.3 ADVANCED DRAM ACCESS MODES

In Chapter 2 we covered the *burst transfer mode,* for which, once the initial access to memory occurs, subsequent data can be retrieved more quickly since the overhead of transmitting their addresses is eliminated. Lately, additional circuitry has been added on recent high-density DRAM chips, to provide—in addition to the standard (or random) access mode described earlier—three advanced burst access modes that significantly decrease the access time: the *page, static column* (or video RAM), and *nibble* modes. In all of them, repeated accesses to the same row are allowed without the row-access time overhead. All modes are initiated after a standard read or write is performed.

Although they do not improve system performance as much as caches, these special modes do provide a very useful and less expensive alternative, particularly in applications that require high-speed serial access, such as *video bit map* graphic monitors or *RAM discs*.

Most of the discussion below is from reference [9] and refers to successive read operations from an "85-ns 1M × 1-bit DRAM" chip, structured internally as an array of 1024 rows by 1024 columns of memory cells. In all three cases, the mode is initiated the same way for the standard read or write operation: row address is latched by the RAS# signal asserted low, followed by the latching of the column address with the CAS# signal asserted low. The timing diagrams in Figure 3.20 depict the read operation, but the same comments hold for the write operation.

3.3.1 Page Mode

The page mode refers to accessing within the same row (or page) of the DRAM chip. Page access is performed by holding the row address constant while changing the column address; this provides faster random access to any of the 1024 column bits on a given row. As shown in Figure 3.20a, after the first normal read cycle, the next cycle is a page mode cycle implemented simply by supplying a column address latched by CAS# while RAS# remains asserted. Subsequent page mode cycles are performed with the RAS# held active for a single row address and the CAS# clock cycled while new column addresses are externally supplied for each bit. As long as the microprocessor accesses sequential bits in the same row, the memory chip responds fast since the time normally needed to strobe a new row address is eliminated.

The page mode access time equals t_{CAC}, while its cycle time (how fast successive bits are read) equals t_{PC}. After the first cycle, all read operations are measured *at the t_{CAC} rate*.

3.3.2 Static Column Mode

Static column mode offers roughly the same cycle time as the page mode and a slightly longer access time to any of the (1024) column bits of a given row. However, it operates somewhat differently and is used in applications that require less noise than the page mode. Furthermore, it simplifies the memory interface because the extra CAS# pulses of the page mode are not required. As shown in Figure 3.20b, first the row and column addresses are strobed in the normal manner by taking RAS# and CAS# low. If RAS# and CAS# are kept low, new data can be accessed simply by changing the column addresses, assuming the new address is in the same row; if the new address is not in the same row, then a normal access cycle must be performed. This assumption, that the majority of memory references are sequential, is quite valid; after all, it is this same assumption upon which the widely used cache-based designs are based. Like the page mode, externally supplied column addresses are also required in the static column mode.

Later on we will examine a design that implements this fundamental requirement of the static column mode by using an external component (such as the Texas Instruments

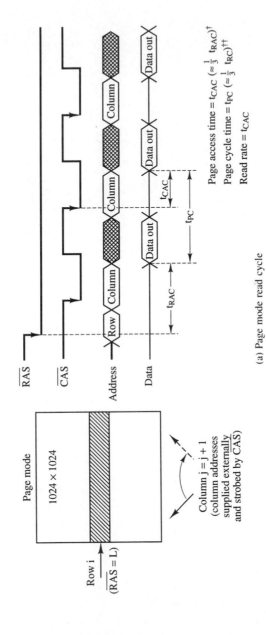

(a) Page mode read cycle

Page access time = t_{CAC} ($\approx \frac{1}{3}$ t_{RAC})[†]

Page cycle time = t_{PC} ($\approx \frac{1}{3}$ t_{RC})[††]

Read rate = t_{CAC}

Figure 3.20 Page, static column, and nibble mode timings [9].

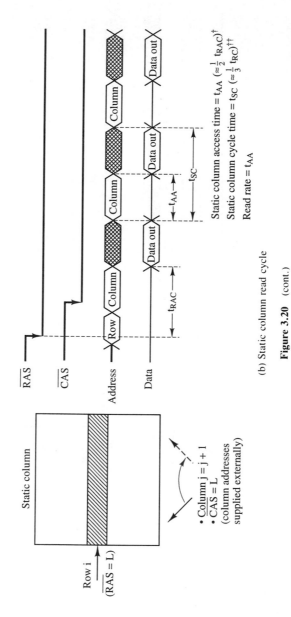

(b) Static column read cycle

Figure 3.20 (cont.)

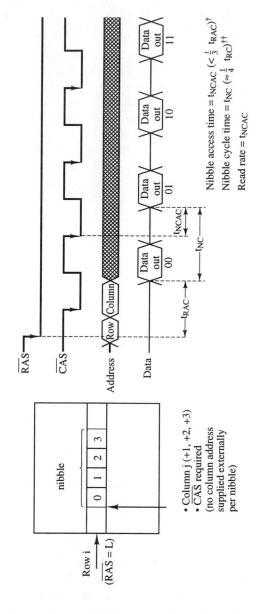

Row i
$(\overline{RAS} = L)$

nibble			
0	1	2	3

• Column j (+1, +2, +3)
• $\overline{CAS}$ required
(no column address
supplied externally
per nibble)

$^{†}t_{RAC}$ = random mode access time
$^{††}t_{RC}$ = random mode cycle time

$\overline{RAS}$

$\overline{CAS}$

Address   ⟨Row⟩⟨Column⟩

Data   ⟨Data out 00⟩⟨Data out 01⟩⟨Data out 10⟩⟨Data out 11⟩

t_{RAC} t_{NC} t_{NCAC}

Nibble access time = t_{NCAC} ($< \frac{1}{3}$ t_{RAC})†

Nibble cycle time = t_{NC} ($\approx \frac{1}{4}$ t_{RC})††

Read rate = t_{NCAC}

(c) Nibble mode read cycle

Figure 3.20   (concluded)

165

ALS6310 "static column detect") to detect whether the currently accessed row is the same as the last row accessed.

The static column access time equals t_{AA}, while its cycle time equals t_{SC}. After the first cycle, all read operations are measured *at the t_{AA} rate*.

3.3.3 Nibble Mode

Nibble mode is different from the other two modes; while the other two allow access to any of the (1024) column bits of a given row, the nibble mode allows access of up to three extra bits of data from sequential locations for every row access, at a much higher rate than in the other two modes; the location of the first bit determines the other bits to be accessed. As shown in Figure 3.20c, after the first normal cycle, nibble mode cycles are implemented by cycling CAS# while holding RAS# asserted, as in the page mode. The difference is, however, that no column address is required to be supplied externally; instead, internal row and column address counters increment at each CAS# cycle. After cycling CAS# three times, the address sequence repeats and the same four bits are accessed again, in serial order.

The nibble mode access time equals t_{NCAC}, while its cycle time equals t_{NC}. After the first cycle, all read operations are measured *at the t_{NCAC} rate*.

3.3.4 Comparing the Three Modes

For each mode, users will typically access most or all of the bits available to that mode. Thus the best measure of speed for nibble mode is the rate at which four bits are read, while for page or static column it is the rate at which 1024 bits are read.

As shown in Figure 3.21, the page mode has access and cycle times that are about one-third those of the standard (random) mode. Page mode is slightly more difficult to interface in a system than static column mode due to the extra CAS# pulses it requires. The nibble mode has access and cycle times that are about one-fourth those of the standard/random mode. The static column mode has the same cycle time as the page mode, but its access time is one-half the standard mode.

3.3.5 Example of 32-Bit Page/Static Column Design

Here we present an example of using a "static column decode" circuit for 1-Mbit DRAM chips. In the static column arrangement, main memory is considered divided into pages (typically, of size 2 Kbytes or 4 Kbytes). In that case, the address is considered as made up of two fields: the most significant field makes up the *page number,* and the least significant field makes up the *offset.* For example, for 4-Kbyte pages, the offset would be 12 bits long. The speed-up occurs (i.e., no wait states are introduced) as long as consecutive accesses are within the same page.[24] This means that the external hardware interface must be designed to be able to detect when two consecutive addresses have the same page number; i.e., it detects whether the currently accessed DRAM row is the same as the last row accessed. (The word *static* refers to this fact that the most significant part of the address does not change.) When the program accesses a location outside the page, the system will run with the normal wait state.

---

[24]This occurs quite often in programming, when for example the program contains loops that fit within a page.

Parameter	Page	Nibble	Static column	Random (standard)
Access time (ns)[a]:				
t_{CAC}	25	—	—	—
t_{NCAC}	—	20	—	—
t_{AA}	—	—	45	—
t_{RAC}	—	—	—	85
Cycle time (ns)[a]:				
t_{PC}	50	—	—	—
t_{NC}	—	40	—	—
t_{SC}	—	—	50	—
t_{RC}	—	—	—	165
Accessible bits	1024	4	1024	All
Order of accessible bits	Random	Fixed	Random	Random
Conditions:				
$\overline{RAS}$	Active	Active	Active	Cycle
$\overline{CAS}$ or $\overline{CS}$[b]	Cycle	Cycle	Active	Cycle
Addresses	Cycle	N/A	Cycle	Cycle
Outputs	Cycle	Cycle	Active	Cycle
Time to read 4 bits (ns)[a]	235	205	235	660
Time to read 1024 unique bits (ns)[a]	51,235	70,400	51,235	168,960

[a]Values for a 1M × 1 85-ns device.

Page: 4-bit read $= t_{RAC} + 3t_{PC}$
                     1024-bit read $= t_{RAC} + 1023t_{PC}$
Nibble: 4-bit read $= t_{RAC} + 3t_{NC}$
                     1024-bit read $= 256 \cdot (t_{RAC} + 3t_{NC} + t_{RP})$
Static column: 4-bit read $= t_{RAC} + 3t_{SC}$
                     1024-bit read $= t_{RAC} + 1023t_{SC}$
Random: 4-bit read $= 4t_{RC}$
                     1024-bit read $= 1024t_{RC}$

[b]$\overline{CS}$ on static column.

Figure 3.21 Page, nibble, static column, and random modes: a comparison of their operating times and characteristics [9].

Figure 3.22 shows the block diagram of a Motorola 68020-based design [7]. Four 32-bit memory banks are controlled by the DRAM controller (this DRAM controller now has ten output pins and therefore can access up to 1M × 1-bit DRAM chips). They cover contiguous areas in physical address space (since the "bank select" is done by decoding address bits A22 and A23), and implement a 16-Mbyte (or 4M-doubleword) memory module: each memory bank is made out of 32 1M-bit DRAM chips of the types used in Figure 3.20. (The A0 and A1 bits are decoded externally to generate the "byte-enable" signals DBBE1–DBBE4 to the four byte sections of each 32-bit memory bank.) This memory is considered subdivided into pages of size 1K doublewords each (or 4 Kbytes).

The design uses the Texas Instruments ALS6310 "static column detect" circuit, which receives the page number that corresponds to the row addresses (bits A12–A21) and

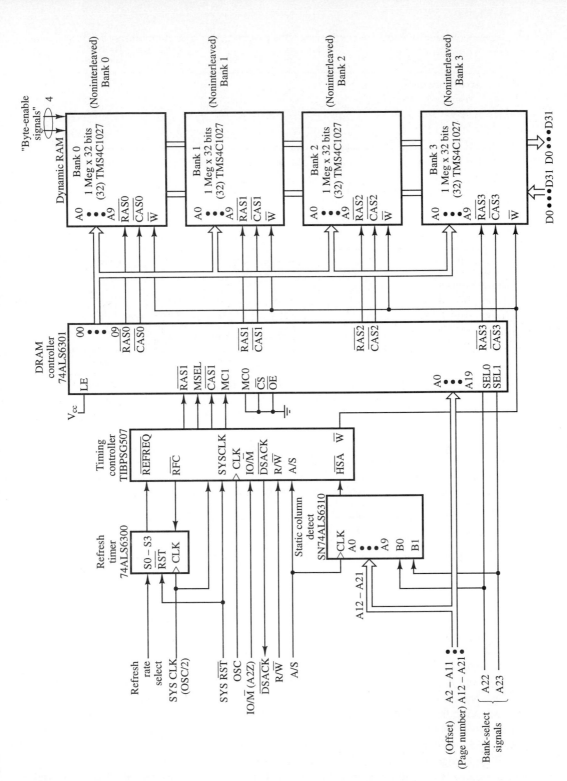

Figure 3.22 *Static column decode* approach of a Motorola 68020-based, noninterleaved, memory design [7].

compares two successive row addresses to check for a match. If they match (and if the bank addresses have not changed), it issues the HSA# = L signal to the timing controller to force it to execute this high-speed static column access sequence. (Notice here that we use the most significant bits A21–A12 from the 68020 as "row addresses" to access within the same memory page, and the least significant bits A11–A2 as "column addresses.") The timing controller is also responsible for generating the required memory timing control signals (RAS#, CAS#, etc.) for the DRAM controller to execute normal DRAM access mode.

The Intel i860 microprocessor has placed this "static column detect" comparator circuit *on-chip;* when the processor detects accesses occurring within the DRAM page, it issues the NENE# (next near) signal to the DRAM controller to facilitate designs using page mode and static column DRAMs. (For an example timing diagram see Figure 3.25b below.)

3.4 MEMORY INTERLEAVING

3.4.1 Basic Concepts

Newer and faster microprocessors demand higher *memory bandwidths:* the maximum number of bits (or bytes) memory can deliver per unit time. For example, a 32-bit memory with a 100-ns cycle time supports a memory bandwidth of 40 Mbytes/sec maximum. Eliminating the speed gap between the microprocessor and main memory is referred to as "bandwidth balancing between processor and memory."

One of the major problems with current DRAM memories is that in recent years we are seeing the microprocessor clock rates rise higher than those of DRAMs; in addition to logic-type delays, DRAMs also incur signal-sensing-type delays. This difference in speeds is even more prominent in high-performance RISC-type microprocessor chips.

The actual memory performance is a function of the degree of memory interleaving (the number of interleaved memory banks), the ratio of "memory access time" to "memory cycle time," and the actual pattern of referencing memory. In this section we present the basic concepts of memory interleaving and give specific examples of designing interleaved memories and interfacing them to microprocessors.

As we mentioned in Chapter 2, the 80386 cannot issue a new address more frequently than every four clock cycles (CLK2s), even with pipeline triggering. The 80486, on the other hand, instead of address pipelining, has the burst transfer mode, in which it issues the first address and can then accept data every single clock cycle (the 2-1-1-1 burst cycle of Figure 2.18d). When executing burst transfers the Motorola 68030 and 68040 can also accept a data item every clock cycle (Figures 2.22 and 2.23). Interleaved memories can be designed to provide these transfer rates.

Memory interleaving is used for the following purposes:

1. To obtain the same memory speed by using slower memory chips.
2. To eliminate the degrading effect of the DRAM precharge time.
3. To permit prefetching of sequential instructions and the execution of burst transfer modes (to fill caches on "cache misses").
4. To increase memory bandwidth, which allows increase in the cache block size without a corresponding increase in the miss penalty, which, therefore, improves cache and system performance. (This will be explained in detail in Chapter 5.)

Memory interleaving relies on the fact that programs tend to access adjacent memory locations. Adjacent addresses are then made to point to different memory banks; the address assignment policy used for that is to assign address i to memory bank j, where $j = i$ (mod N), where N is the total number of banks, an integral power of 2. This approach represents a technique for grouping memory devices into different banks and distributing memory addresses in such a way that consecutive accesses to contiguous locations will be routed to different (interleaved) memory banks, in a way that overlaps the two banks' activities and therefore increases the CPU-memory bus bandwidth. This overlapping means that while one memory bank is busy accessing its data to respond to the processor's request, the other bank is free to receive the next request. Sometimes the interleaving discussed here is called *low-order interleaving*, since the memory interface logic uses the lower address bits to steer the remaining address bits to the proper memory bank.

In the examples presented here we will outline how interleaving is done for memories that use DRAM chips. Noticing that DRAM chips have different access and cycle times, interleaving is used to overlap the access time of one memory bank with the precharge time of another memory bank. To simplify the discussion, we will denote the DRAM "access time from RAS#" by t_a and refer to it as the **access time,** the *precharge time* by t_{PR}, and the **cycle time** by t_c. *Furthermore, we will assume that the access time equals the precharge time, each one being half the DRAM cycle time.*

Two-way interleaving. In all the examples in this section, the DRAM chips will be referred to as "50-ns DRAMs," meaning that their access time t_a is 50 ns (which makes their cycle time 100 ns). The total memory capacity is $M = 2^m$ bytes. Figures 3.23 and 3.24 show the simplified configurations, timing diagrams, and memory bandwidths for both non-interleaved and 2-way interleaved 16-bit and 32-bit memories, referred to as *2-way word-interleaved* and *2-way doubleword-interleaved* designs, respectively. In all these examples the data buses are connected to reflect the use of a big-endian (e.g., Motorola) processor.

16-Bit Word Interleaving. In the case of the 16-bit noninterleaved memory, and for an $M = 2^m$ total memory, there are two byte sections, each having $M/2$ bytes and connected to the two byte lanes of the 16-bit data bus (Figure 3.23a). The timing diagram for the non-interleaved memory indicates that a processor is used whose **bus cycle time** (i.e., how often the processor supplies consecutive addresses to memory) equals the memory's cycle time t_c. Thus, even though DRAM memory responds by issuing data after $t_a = 50$ ns, it will need 50 more ns to precharge before the next address can be applied to it. Thus, data come out from consecutive locations every t_c. If a faster processor is used, whose bus cycle time is, for example, $t_c/2$, the processor will have to be slowed down and issue the next address to location 2N + 2 after t_c instead of after $t_c/2$ time units.

In the 2-way word-interleaving design of Figure 3.23b, there are four byte sections, each one of $M/4$ bytes; but now each pair constitutes a "word bank" connected to the 16-bit data bus. A0 is again used for even/odd section selection; now, however, A1 is also needed to specify access to the even word bank or the odd word bank. In this design, the memory interface will latch the first address to location 2N and route it to the first bank, bank 0, for access. Although bank 0 will respond after t_a time units, it cannot respond to a new request before the end of its memory chip cycle time t_c. While bank 0 is going through the precharge phase of its memory chips, the processor can start the next bus cycle by issuing the next address. (Thus the processor is now issuing successive addresses every $t_a = 50$ ns instead of

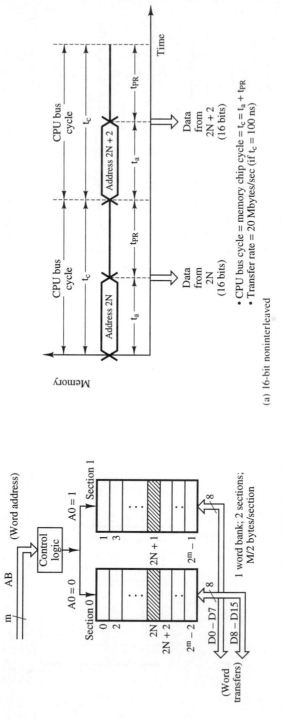

Figure 3.23 Sixteen-bit noninterleaved and 2-way word-interleaved memory and simplified timing diagrams.

(a) 16-bit noninterleaved

- CPU bus cycle = memory chip cycle = $t_c = t_a + t_{PR}$
- Transfer rate = 20 Mbytes/sec (if t_c = 100 ns)

171

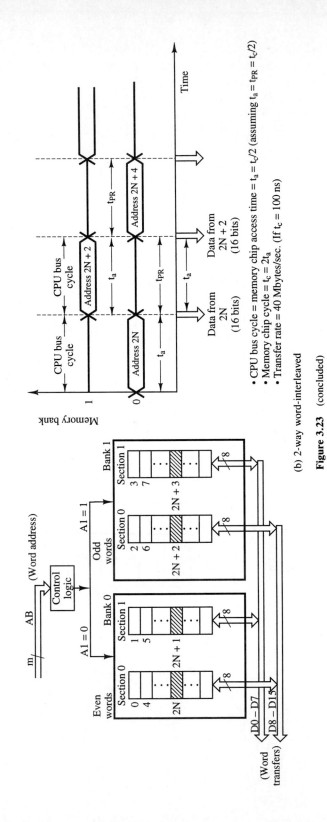

- CPU bus cycle = memory chip access time = $t_a = t_c/2$ (assuming $t_a = t_{PR} = t_c/2$)
- Memory chip cycle = $t_c = 2t_a$
- Transfer rate = 40 Mbytes/sec. (If $t_c = 100$ ns)

(b) 2-way word-interleaved

Figure 3.23 (concluded)

every $t_c = 100$ ns of the noninterleaved case.) If this next address issued is to a location in bank 1 (e.g., location $2N + 2$), the bus controller will route it to bank 1 (which is free) and signal it to start a new access. Thus, the access time of bank 1 completely overlaps the precharge time of bank 0. Bank 1 will also respond after t_a time units. We can observe from the timing diagram in Figure 3.23b that as long as consecutive addresses hit different memory banks (which is usually the case when prefetching instructions, accessing array data, or performing burst transfers), memory accesses will alternate between the two memory banks, matching the processor rate and fetching one word every $t_a = 50$ ns (instead of every t_c of the noninterleaved case). The processor is not slowed down, because memory now operates at the processor speed. For the occasional back-to-back memory cycles to the same memory bank, the memory response would take $t_c = 100$ ns; external address decoding circuitry (interleave logic) is needed to identify these situations and to signal the processor to insert wait states.

With the same 50-ns DRAM chips (i.e., $t_c = 100$ ns), the 16-bit noninterleaved memory will yield a 20-Mbyte/sec maximum transfer rate, while the 2-way word-interleaved memory will yield a 40-Mbyte/sec maximum rate. When 16-bit words are accessed from the same bank (nonsequentially addressed words), referred to as ''back-to-back'' accesses, the performance of the system deteriorates because the processor must now insert wait states and run with a bus cycle equal to t_c instead of equal to t_a. One should be careful not to confuse the 16-bit noninterleaved case of Figure 3.23a with a 2-way byte-interleaved case.

32-Bit Doubleword Interleaving.   In the 32-bit noninterleaved design there are four byte sections, each of $M/4$ bytes and connected to the four byte lanes of the 32-bit data bus (Figure 3.24a). In the 2-way doubleword-interleaved design of Figure 3.24b, there are eight byte sections, each of $M/8$ bytes; but now, each group of four constitutes a ''doubleword bank'' connected to the 32-bit data bus. A0 and A1 are used as before; however, A2 is now also needed to specify access to the even or odd doubleword bank. With the same 50-ns DRAM chips, the 32-bit noninterleaved memory will yield a 40-Mbtye/sec maximum transfer rate, while the 2-way doubleword-interleaved memory will yield an 80-Mbyte/sec maximum rate (the same as with a 4-way word-interleaved memory). One should again be careful not to confuse a 64-bit noninterleaved memory with the 2-way doubleword-interleaved memory of Figure 3.24b.

The above approaches can be extended in any way desirable. For large N-way interleaved memories, it is the responsibility of the memory controller to queue incoming addresses, use an address counter to increment them properly (for example, to support burst transfers), route them to the appropriate memory bank when the bank is ready to proceed with its next access, and provide the necessary buffering on the output data.

i860 Four-way interleaving.   Like the 80386 address pipelining discussed in Section 2.4.1, the Intel i860 also has an input pin NA# to support *address pipelining* for increasing the memory access time without decreasing the bandwidth. Here we discuss the i860 four-way memory interleaving used to support its address pipelining. However, contrary to the 80386, in which the NA# may be asserted only once during any bus cycle, the i860 NA# can be asserted twice before READY# is asserted, thus allowing 3 bus cycles to start before the first one is completed. It is said that **the 80386 provides up to 1 level of address pipelining** (which implies the presence of 2 outstanding bus cycles), while **the i860**

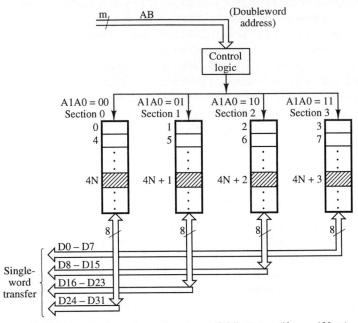

(a) 32-bit noninterleaved; transfer rate = 40 Mbytes/sec (if t_c = 100 ns)

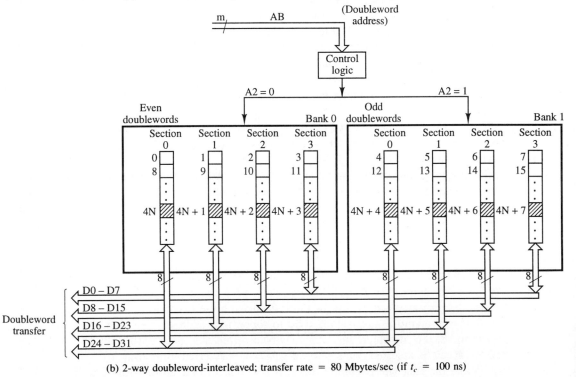

(b) 2-way doubleword-interleaved; transfer rate = 80 Mbytes/sec (if t_c = 100 ns)

Figure 3.24 Thirty-two-bit noninterleaved and doubleword-interleaved memory.

provides up to 2 levels of address pipelining (which implies the presence of 3 outstanding bus cycles, or that three bus cycles operate at one time).

The i860 external bus performs a 64-bit transfer every two clock cycles. Since most read cycles are cacheable, they occur "as cache line fills." Updating the internal instruction or data cache involves the generation of 64-bit read operations. Using the pipelining feature of the bus, the NA# pin can be used to implement 2 levels of pipelining. If the memory is designed with 4-way 64-bit-interleaved memory banks as shown in Figure 3.25a, then the bus activities during pipelining are shown in Figure 3.25b. In Figure 3.25a it is noticed that address bits A4 and A3 are used as "bank selects." (The i860 decodes address bits A2–A0 internally to generate the eight byte enables BE0#–BE7#.) Every bus cycle starts from the assertion of the ADS# signal. The assertion of the NA# signal forces the processor to issue the next address. Each bus cycle ends with the assertion of the READY# signal. (Not asserting the READY# signal forces the processor to insert wait states, not latch data, and not complete the bus cycle.) The order of the data placed on the data bus during read or write cycles must correspond to the order in which the outstanding cycles were initiated. Once fully pipelined, data from the 4-way interleaved banks are received every 2 clock cycles, although the *memory access time* (here, the time between assertion of ADS# and memory driving the data bus) is t_a = clock cycles. (Since a bus cycle takes 2 clock cycles and the 2-level address pipelining can have 3 bus cycles operating at one time, we say that with this address pipelining the maximum data rate[†] 2C of the microprocessor bus can be sustained even if the memory access time is $t_a = 6C$.)

3.4.2 Examples of Designing Interleaved Memories

Interleaved memory designs allow the use of slower—and therefore less expensive—memory chips without reducing the effective memory bandwidth (and, thus, without degrading the overall system performance).

So far in this chapter we presented some introductory material on interfacing to dynamic memories using the DRAM controller and the basic concept of memory interleaving. In this section we expand upon those designs and show more details of memory interleaving schemes interfaced to different example microprocessors. In most cases we will use the Intel 8207 DRAM controller discussed in Section 3.2.3. With the 8207, memory can be designed with up to 4 interleaved banks for a total of 2 Mbytes, with each bank having its own RAS# and CAS# signal pair. To get this maximum 4-way interleaving out of the 8207, one must send to the controller's "bank-select" input pins BS0 and BS1 the bits A1 and A2 of the address.

Two-way word interleaving. Figure 3.26a shows the general configuration of a 2-way word-interleaved memory board. The arrangement consists of a number of 256-Kbit (256K × 1-bit) memory chips on a PC board to implement a 2-way word-interleaved target memory of total capacity 1 Mbyte. Address bit A0 generates the "byte-enable" signals for the byte sections within the selected bank. Each byte section contains 16 memory chips arranged in two rows of 8 chips/row. A 16-bit memory bank is selected by the value of address bit A1 and contains 0.5 Mbyte. The next-higher 18 bits of the address are supplied to all chips of the memory as a "word-address." The value of the unused most significant address

---

[†]Another implementation that can provide this high data rate is by using ordinary static column DRAMs driven by the microprocessor's NENE# output signal (not shown in Figure 3.25b).

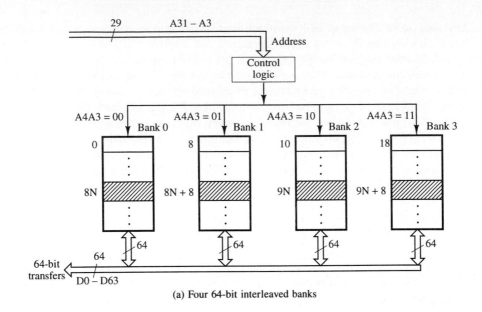

(a) Four 64-bit interleaved banks

Memory access time $t_a = 6C$
Effective throughput (with pipelining) = 2C

(b) Operation

Figure 3.25 Four-way 64-bit-interleaved i860 memory structure and operation. (Adapted from [11]. Reprinted by permission of Intel Corporation, Copyright/Intel Corporation 1989.)

Memory System Design and Interfacing   Chap. 3

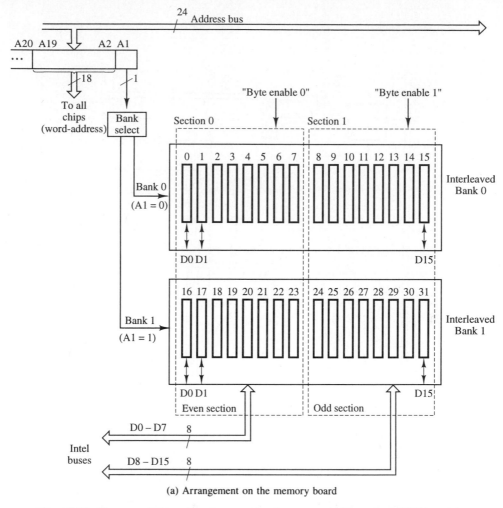

(a) Arrangement on the memory board

Figure 3.26 Two-way word-interleaved memory (total memory = 1 Mbyte; Intel 80286-based design). (Adapted from [6]. Reprinted by permission of Intel Corporation, Copyright/Intel Corporation 1983.)

bits will determine the actual physical addresses that this 1-Mbyte unit occupies within the maximum addressable space of 16 Mbytes.

Figure 3.26b shows an example in which the Intel 80286 microprocessor is interfaced to a 2-way word-interleaved memory. The interleaved arrangement takes advantage of the 80286's address pipelining by letting the early address issued for the next cycle propagate to the next memory bank while the address for the current memory cycle is still valid in the bank. The "interleave logic" identifies whether or not there are back-to-back cycles to the same memory bank: if there are, it will trigger the microprocessor to insert wait state(s); if not, then along with external decoding circuitry it will select the memory bank and send the address to it. The "control signals to banks" logic converts the microprocessor commands to the write-enable (WEH# and WEL#) signals for the byte sections, the output-enable (OE#) signal for the memory chips and data bus octal transceivers (also see Figure 3.10). There are two byte sections within each bank; section 0 is the even byte section (or

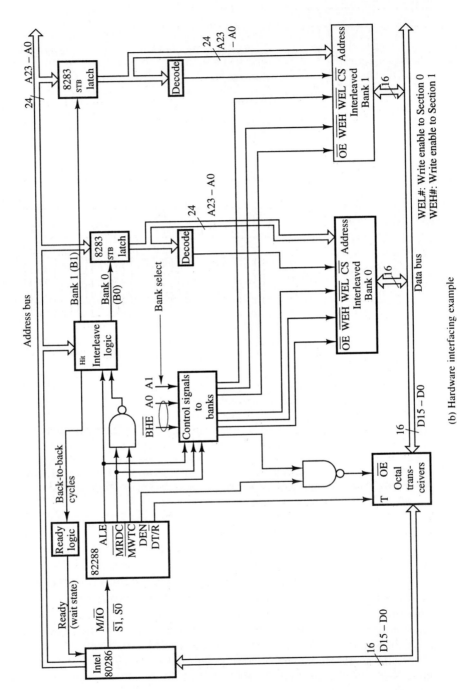

WEL#: Write enable to Section 0
WEH#: Write enable to Section 1

(b) Hardware interfacing example

Figure 3.26 (concluded)

what is called by Intel the "low byte," connected to D0–D7 data bus lines), which is selected when WEL# = 0; section 1 is the odd-byte section (or "high byte," connected to D8–D15), which is selected when WEH# = 0.

Example 3.12: Using the DRAM Controller in a 2-Way Word-Interleaved Memory

Consider a microprocessor with a 16-bit external data bus with a bus cycle time of 50 ns. Design a 1-Mbyte DRAM memory, and show its interface and the timing diagram for its operation.
Solution: Instead of using memory chips with a 50-ns cycle time, we can use slower chips of 100-ns cycle time in a 2-way word-interleaved design as it was suggested by the timing diagram of Figure 3.23b. In that diagram, memory chips were grouped into two 16-bit interleaved banks, the even word bank (bank 0) and the odd word bank (bank 1); address $2N+2$ issued by the processor was routed to the second memory bank while the DRAM chips of the first bank were in their precharge period.

Figure 3.27a shows a 2-way word-interleaved DRAM memory design, which now uses the 8207 DRAM controller to interface the microprocessor to a 1-Mbyte memory. Address inputs to the DRAM controller are bits A19–A2 ("word address") off the address lines. The 8207 is initialized here to recognize that only two 16-bit banks are connected to it; thus, the 8207 will activate two RAS# and two CAS# strobes per bank according the input values applied to the two "bank-select" inputs BS1 and BS0, as suggested in Figure 3.15. In this case, when BS1BS0 = 00, then $RAS_{0,1}$ and $CAS_{0,1}$ will be to bank 0; when BS1BS0 = 01, then $RAS_{2,3}$ and $CAS_{2,3}$ will be to bank 1. By grounding the controller's BS1 input and connecting address bit A1 to pin BS0, the value of A1 will be selecting the particular memory bank (A1 = 0 for bank 0 and A1 = 1 for bank 1). The outputs RAS_2 and CAS_2 are shown connected to bank 1. The signals WEL# and WEH# select the byte section within the word bank, and they may be generated by combining A0 and BHE# (in the Intel case) or they may be the LDS# and UDS# (in the Motorola case).[25] For a read operation, these have no effect since memory will drive all 16 lines of the data bus and the microprocessor will interpret the appropriate input pins according to the type of data it requested. For a write cycle, however, the DRAM controller's write control signal WE to memory is gated with these two signals. Each interleaved bank has a capacity of 0.5 Mbyte and is made up of 16 DRAM chips (the 256K × 1-bit TMS4256 chips).

Figure 3.27b shows the timing diagram of this 2-way word-interleaved memory. (Here we simplified the diagram by assuming that both the row address and the RAS# signal are activated at the same time and that the column address and signal CAS# are also activated at the same time.) Since the cycles are to different memory banks, the RAS2# for the second cycle is overlapped with the RAS0# precharge from the first cycle.

Two-way doubleword-interleaving. Consider again Example 3.12, but now assume that we have a microprocessor with an external 32-bit data bus. The interleaving on memory will now be on a doubleword basis (2-way doubleword interleaving). The wordlength of the memory subsystem is 32 bits and its total capacity is 2 Mbytes, 1 Mbyte per bank, as shown in Figure 3.28. Each byte section is implemented using eight 256K × 1-bit DRAM chips, each bank uses 32 DRAMs, and the total memory requires 64 DRAM chips. Bank 0 (accessed when A2 = 0) is the top half of the pictured memory array; bank 1 (accessed when A2 = 1) is the bottom half. A2 is connected from the processor to the special DRAM control circuitry to control its RAS0# and RAS1# outputs.

The processor-to-memory interface will include the bus interface unit, the buffers and latches, the DRAM control circuitry, etc. (usually implemented using a number of PAL

---

[25]For microprocessors with 32-bit internal architecture and a 16-bit external data bus, the values of A1 and A0 are used to generate the two byte-enable signals for the two byte sections of memory.

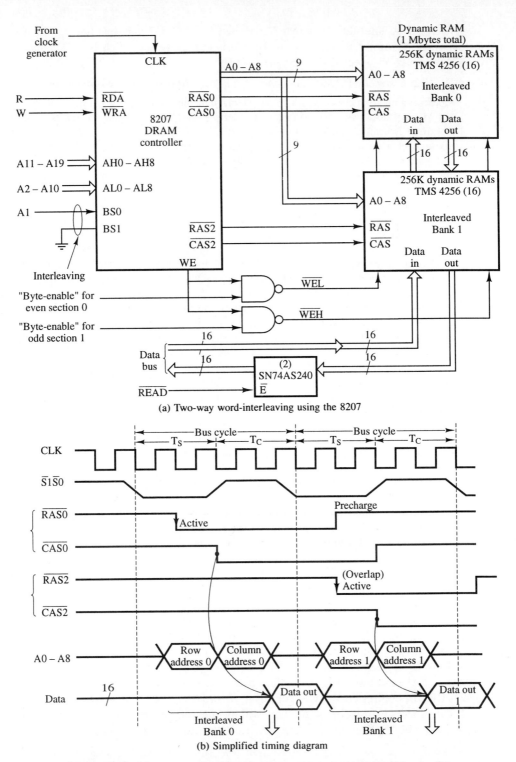

Figure 3.27 Two-way word-interleaved memory using the 8207 DRAM controller. (Adapted from [6]. Reprinted by permission of Intel Corp., ©/Intel Corporation 1983.)

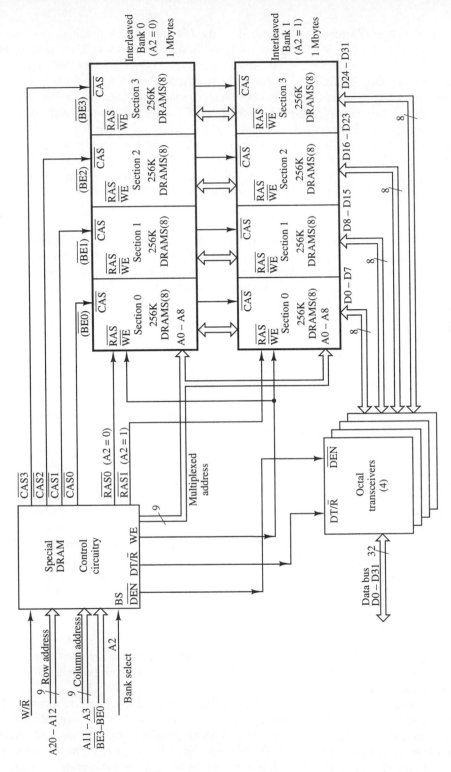

Figure 3.28 Two-way doubleword-interleaved memory. Total capacity is 2 Mbytes; Intel 80386 signaling. (Adapted from [5].)

devices). Two RAS# strobes are generated by the DRAM control circuitry, one for each interleaved memory bank: RAS0# for bank 0 and RAS1# for bank 1. The ''byte enable'' outputs of the microprocessor (BE3#–BE0# in the case of an Intel 80x86 product) are mapped by the DRAM control circuitry directly to the four CAS# strobes (CAS3#–CAS0#), respectively. These CAS3#–CAS0# signals are then used as section-select signals to memory (for example, CAS0# applied to the CAS# inputs of all chips of section 0 in both banks, which for the little-endian 80386 is connected to the lower data bus byte lane D0–D7; CAS1# applied to the CAS# inputs of section 1 in both banks connected to D8–D15, etc). These CAS# signals ensure that only those DRAM byte sections selected for a write cycle are enabled. The write-enable (WE#) signal, the output-enable (OE#) signal, and the multiplexed address signals are connected to every DRAM chip in both memory banks.

Four-way doubleword interleaving. Assume that we want to design a 4-way doubleword-interleaved memory subsystem for the Motorola 680x0 with a total of 2 Mbytes assigned to the highest physical addresses and composed of 64K $\times$ 8-bit memory chips. We want to arrange these chips on a printed circuit board and show the interface lines to the processor's bus. To make things more interesting, let's assume that we also want to figure out what specific physical addresses have been assigned to each chip of memory bank 3.

The design solution is given in Figure 3.29a. There are a total of 32 memory chips, 8 chips/bank; for example, bank 0 is made up of chips 0, 1, 2, 3, 16, 17, 18, and 19. As always for a 32-bit memory, the two least significant address bits, A1 and A0, have been used to generate the four DBBE signals for the four byte sections connected to the respective data bus byte lanes as shown in the figure; section 0 is the leftmost column of chips connected to data bus lines D24–D31; section 3 is the rightmost column of chips connected to data bus lines D0–D7. The next two address bits, A3 and A2, when decoded, will generate the bank-select signals for each of the four banks; for example, A3A2 = 00 selects bank 0, A3A2 = 01 selects bank 1, etc. The next 16 address bits, A19–A4, are applied to all 32 chips as a ''word address'' since each chip has 64K locations. Following the convention we adopted earlier, the next address bit, A20, is used as ''row select'' for one of the two rows within the memory bank selected by A3 and A2: when A20 = 0, the top row is selected; when A20 = 1, the bottom row is selected. Finally, and since the problem specifies that this 2-Mbyte unit should be in the highest memory area, the final condition for accessing any of these 32 chips is that the remaining address bits, A31–A21, must all be ones. Figure 3.29b shows the actual physical addresses assigned to various memory chips in memory bank 3.

3.4.3 Page-Interleaved Designs

We now present an example design of a high-performance *page-interleaved* memory subsystem [10]. The design would require a DRAM control circuitry accompanied by some page-interleaving logic.

The normal 2-way interleaving was discussed earlier and its operation with the newer DRAM devices was given by the timing diagram in Figure 3.27b, whose simplified version is shown in Figure 3.30a. We notice that the RAS0# precharge time of one bank overlaps the RAS1# active time of the other bank. We mentioned that the only drawback of that type of memory interleaving was that back-to-back cycles to the same bank require a wait state.

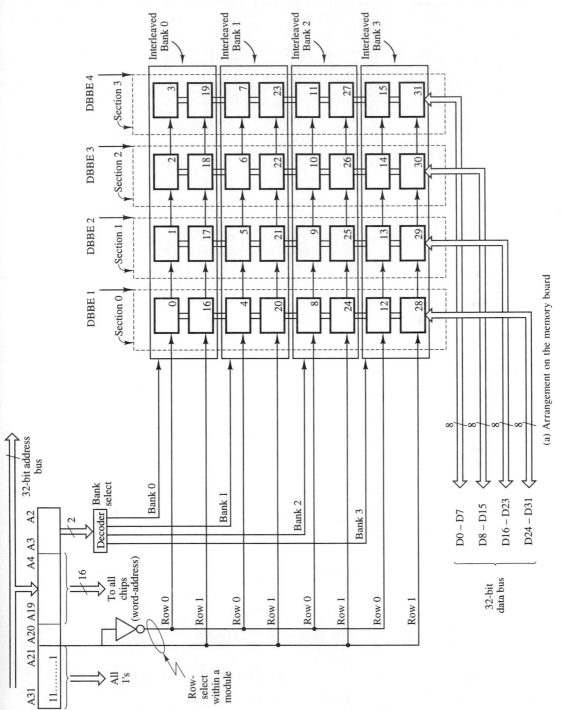

(a) Arrangement on the memory board

Figure 3.29 Four-way, doubleword-interleaved memory: (Motorola 680x0 signaling).

Chip No.	From:	To:
12	FFE0000C	FFEFFFFC
13	FFE0000D	FFEFFFFD
14	FFE0000E	FFEFFFFE
15	FFE0000F	FFEFFFFF
28	FFF0000C	FFFFFFFC
29	FFF0000D	FFFFFFFD
30	FFF0000E	FFFFFFFE
31	FFF0000F	FFFFFFFF

Figure 3.29   (concluded)

(b) Physical addresses assigned to chips in
bank 3

The page-interleaved approach *does allow back-to-back cycles without a wait state*. Keeping in mind the normal page mode operation of Figure 3.20a (repeated here in Figure 3.30b), a 2-way page-interleaved design would then have the operation shown in Figure 3.30c. By overlapping the CAS# precharge time of one bank with the CAS# active time of the other bank, the 2-way page-interleaved approach makes possible zero-wait-state accesses. In this design, the DRAM access time is now determined by the CAS# active delay, which is typically equal to half or less than that of the RAS# access time. The basic idea of the page-interleaved approach is first to lock RAS# and then use successive strobes of the CAS# clock to enter sequential column addresses.

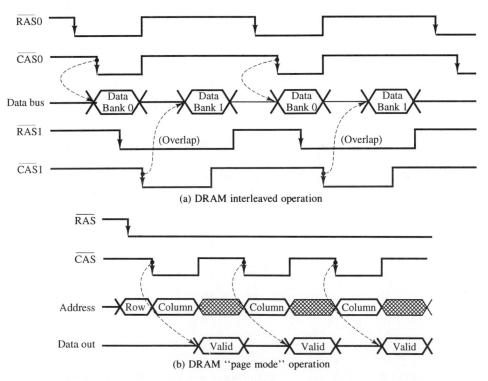

(a) DRAM interleaved operation

(b) DRAM "page mode" operation

Figure 3.30   "Page" and "page-interleaved" DRAM operations. (Adapted from [10]. Used with permission of Advanced Micro Devices, Inc.)

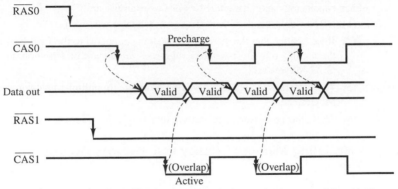

(c) DRAM "page-interleaved" operation (to make it completely compatible with Figure 3.27, replace $\overline{RAS_1}/\overline{CAS_1}$ with $\overline{RAS_2}/\overline{CAS_2}$)

Figure 3.30 (concluded)

3.5 MEMORY TIME COMPUTATIONS

3.5.1 Matching Processor and Memory Speeds

Given:

(a) t_c, the memory cycle time (how often a memory bank can *receive* an address), and

(b) $t_{\text{address-cycle}}$, the microprocessor address-cycle (how often the microprocessor *issues* an address),

Then: In order to match the microprocessor and memory speeds (i.e., introduce no wait states in the processor cycle), we need N-way interleaving, where

$$N = \frac{t_c}{t_{\text{address-cycle}}} \tag{3.6}$$

Example 3.13

Consider an Intel i860 processor driven by an external 32-MHz clock connected to a "125-ns DRAM" memory. Then:

(a) Since the Intel i860 is driven by a 32-MHz clock, we have $C = 1/32$ MHz $= 31.25$ ns. (An i860 "T state" equals one such C clock cycle, i.e., $T = 31.25$ ns.)

(b) Since an i860 bus cycle is made up of 2 clock cycles, then $t_{\text{bus-cycle}} = t_{\text{address-cycle}} = 62.5$ ns. (This bus cycle equals two i860 "T states.")

(c) $t_a = 125$ ns; then the DRAM specifications will suggest that $t_c = 250$ ns (about).

Therefore,

$$N = \frac{t_c}{t_{\text{address-cycle}}} = \frac{250 \text{ ns}}{62.5 \text{ ns}} = 4.$$

In other words, if no wait states are to be introduced, the memory must be 4-way interleaved. (Since the data bus is 64 bits, this memory is 4-way quadword-interleaved of the type shown in Fig. 3.25a.)

Other conclusions and characteristics of this example are:

(1) DRAM chip bandwidth $= 1/t_c = 4$ Mbits/sec.

(2) If we assume that the memory subsystem connected to the Intel i860 is 64 bits wide, then these chips provide a *memory subsystem bandwidth* of 4 million quadwords per second, or 32 Mbytes/sec.

(3) The *processor bandwidth* is $1/62.5$ ns $= 16$ million quadwords per second or 128 Mbytes/sec.

(4) Thus, the processor bandwidth is four times that of main memory.

3.5.2 Calculating Memory Latency and Memory Access Times

We present now a simple model that can be used to compute memory latency L and memory access time requirements in order to satisfy the microprocessor's speed without inserting any wait states. The model to be used is shown in Figure 3.31a and its timing diagram in Figure 3.31b. It shows the microprocessor connected to main memory, along with some of the most commonly used interface components that introduce delays in the memory latency time (L). These delays[26] include the following (numbered in the diagram): (1) ALE active delay: the time between the activation of the ALE by the microprocessor until it is applied to the ALE

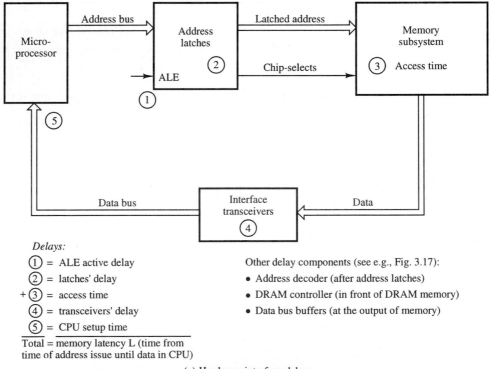

Delays:

① = ALE active delay
② = latches' delay
+③ = access time
④ = transceivers' delay
⑤ = CPU setup time
—————————————
Total = memory latency L (time from time of address issue until data in CPU)

Other delay components (see e.g., Fig. 3.17):
- Address decoder (after address latches)
- DRAM controller (in front of DRAM memory)
- Data bus buffers (at the output of memory)

(a) Hardware interface delays

Figure 3.31 Delays in the processor to memory loop (memory latency L).

[26]In computing the memory response time, the maximum value of these delays is generally used.

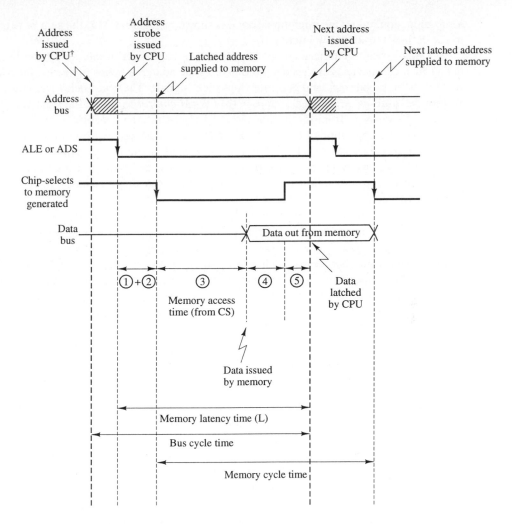

Address issued by CPU†

Address strobe issued by CPU

Latched address supplied to memory

Next address issued by CPU

Next latched address supplied to memory

Address bus

ALE or ADS

Chip-selects to memory generated

Data bus

Data out from memory

① + ② ③ ④ ⑤ Data latched by CPU

Memory access time (from CS)

Data issued by memory

Memory latency time (L)

Bus cycle time

Memory cycle time

† Here we assume that the address is issued at the beginning of the bus cycle. (However, by observing the actual timing diagrams of the microprocessors we can notice that some of them issue the address a little after the start of the bus cycle).

(b) Delays shown in the timing diagram

Figure 3.31 (concluded)

input of the address latches. (2) Latches' delay: the "strobe-to-output" propagation delay of the components used; i.e., the delay with which the outputs appear after the input strobe signal was asserted. (3) Memory subsystem access time: for SRAM memory it is the time from the instant the address is supplied to memory until the memory subsystem responds by driving its output data bus lines; for DRAM memory, it is usually the time from RAS# asserted until the memory subsystem drives its output data bus lines. (4) Transceivers' delay: the propagation delay of the transceiver components used; (5) CPU setup: the minimum data setup time required by the microprocessor. As shown in Figure 3.31a, the sum of delays (1) to (5) defines the **memory latency** *(L)*.

Other possible interface components that may be present in the design and introduce delays include: (a) *Address decoder:* Placed after the address latches to decode the address, route it to the proper bus, and generate chip-select signals. There is a delay from the instant it is strobed until its output signals appear. (b) *DRAM controller:* Placed in front of a DRAM memory. Its delay is from the instant the DRAM controller is enabled until it asserts its output RAS# signal applied to the DRAM chips. (c) *Data bus buffers:* In addition to the interface transceivers, data bus buffers may be placed at the output data bus lines of the memory subsystem (to latch the output data temporarily, and prevent memory and the data bus transceivers from outputting data on the same bus lines simultaneously, for example see Figure 3.10), etc.

In general, in such a closed-loop configuration, the sum of these different delays makes up the memory latency *L*. To simplify the analysis, the memory latency period is measured from the start of the read bus cycle (actually when the "address strobe" is asserted) until the microprocessor latches the data. Then, we can simply say that *memory latency equals the (minimum[27]) bus cycle time[28]* (see, for example, the 80x86 timing diagrams in Figures 2.9 and 2.10). Given the microprocessor's driving clock frequency and knowing how many clock cycles its bus cycle requires, one computes its memory latency *L*. Then, by subtracting from the latency time the sum of all interface component delays (such as delays 1, 2, 4, and 5 in Figure 3.31), one computes the access time required for the memory subsystem. The required memory access time is calculated below using Intel- and Motorola-based system examples.

Example of Intel synchronous buses.   Figure 3.32 presents an example of using the Intel 80286 microprocessor and interfacing it to memory using the ALE output of the bus controller to strobe the address and chip-select latches. The above five delays are numbered on the hardware configuration and on the microprocessor's timing diagram. As shown in this figure, if one uses an "8-MHz 80286 microprocessor" (i.e., one driven by a 16-MHz input clock), then its bus cycle time equals 4*(1/16 MHz) = 250 ns. As shown in Figure 3.32b, (drawn from the 80286's basic bus timing diagram of Figure A.7 in Appendix A), the memory latency (defined here as "the time between the activation of the ALE and the latching of the incoming data by the microprocessor") equals 3 clock cycles or 187.5 ns. Given the actual delays of the interface components as shown at the right-hand side of the diagram, one computes that the memory access time (i.e., the maximum address-to-output delay) must equal 87.5 ns. Thus, if no wait states are to be introduced in the bus cycles, memory must be responding to the microprocessor's request within 87.5 ns.

Motorola example.   As we mentioned earlier, the 32-bit Motorola microprocessors can support both asynchronous and synchronous bus cycles. While for the 68020/30 asynchronous bus cycles the minimum duration is 3 clock cycles (see Figures 2.27 and B.12) and the port size can be 32, 16, or 8 bits, for synchronous bus cycles (see Section

---

[27]Minimum is used if we assume no wait states inserted. In asynchronous buses this means that the "data transfer acknowledge" signal arrives at the time that the microprocessor expects it.

[28]For some microprocessors, however, the memory latency is less than the bus cycle time (for example, the Intel 8086 samples the incoming data at the end of C3 instead of the end of the bus cycle; similarly, the Motorola 68000 samples the input data at the end of S6 and not at the end of its bus cycle which is the end of S8).

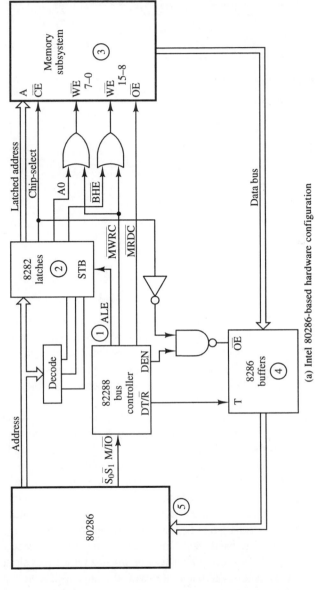

Figure 3.32 Intel 80286 example (timing used to calculate memory access time requirements). (Adapted from [6]. Reprinted by permission of Intel Corporation, Copyright/Intel Corporation, 1983.)

(a) Intel 80286-based hardware configuration

189

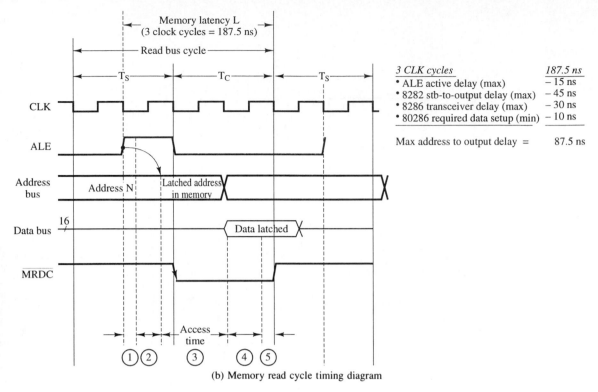

Memory latency L
(3 clock cycles = 187.5 ns)

Read bus cycle

T_S T_C T_S

CLK

ALE

Address bus — Address N — Latched address in memory

16
Data bus — Data latched

MRDC

Access time

① ② ③ ④ ⑤

3 CLK cycles	187.5 ns
• ALE active delay (max)	− 15 ns
• 8282 stb-to-output delay (max)	− 45 ns
• 8286 transceiver delay (max)	− 30 ns
• 80286 required data setup (min)	− 10 ns
Max address to output delay =	87.5 ns

(b) Memory read cycle timing diagram

Figure 3.32 (concluded)

B2.5 in Appendix B) the minimum duration is 2 clock cycles and the port size must only be 32 bits. For any given bus cycle, however, it is the selected slave device itself that determines the actual length of the bus cycle by sending back to the processor the feedback signals that terminate the bus cycle (the DSACKx# signals for asynchronous and the STERM# signal for synchronous operations).

During a read bus cycle, the data is latched by the Motorola processors *on the last falling clock edge* of the bus cycle, i.e., one half clock before the bus cycle ends (to avoid data bus contention with the next bus cycle). Let us consider Figure 3.33, which shows the timing for both asynchronous and synchronous operations, and use it to compute the required access times. (Here we simplify the analysis and do not include delays imposed by other interface devices.) Depending on whether an SRAM or DRAM is interconnected to the processor, different timing paths are the critical ones used in the computations. For example, t_{static} is the memory access time when SRAMs are connected, while $t_{dynamic}$ is the memory access time when DRAMs are used. Static devices use the time between the instant the address becomes valid and the instant the data become valid (since a cycle to SRAM can first be initiated and then that access validated later with the appropriate bus control signal); dynamic devices use the time between address strobe AS# and data valid (because the cycle must be validated before an access can be initiated).

Thus, for an *N*-clock bus cycle these two memory access time requirements are computed by the following simplified formulas:

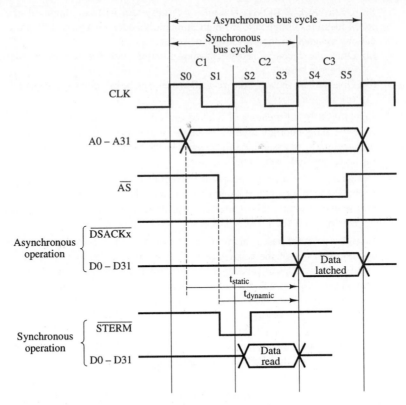

Figure 3.33 Motorola 680x0 example (timings used to calculate memory access time requirements). (Adapted from [12].)

$$t_{\text{static}} \text{ equals } (N*\text{CLK}) - (\text{CLK}) \text{ or about } (N - 1)*\text{CLK} \qquad (3.7)$$

$$t_{\text{dynamic}} \text{ equals about } (N - 0.5)*\text{CLK, also considering the precharge time} \qquad (3.8)$$

where

$N \geq 2$ for synchronous cycles
$N \geq 3$ for asynchronous cycles

EXERCISES

3.1. Construct a 1-Mbyte memory board for the Intel 8086, using 64K × 1-bit SRAM chips.
    (a) Give the array configuration of the chips on the memory board, showing the most important input and output signals and the interface to the address and data bus lines.
    (b) What would the difference be if the above memory chips were DRAMs?

3.2. Design a memory subsystem for a 16-bit microprocessor (you may use as a specific example the Intel 8086) using the following types of memory chips: the 8111 (a 256 × 4 SRAM) and the

8316A (a 2K × 8 ROM). The memory subsystem will be composed of 8-Kbyte contiguous ROM locations assigned to the highest memory addresses and of 1-Kbyte contiguous RAM locations assigned to the lowest memory addresses.

(a) Draw the memory subsystem configuration with the minimum interface to the microprocessor buses.

(b) Give tables showing the real addresses (in hexadecimal) occupied by each 8-bit memory module.

3.3. Construct a 16-bit memory of total capacity 8192 bits using SRAM chips of size 64 × 1 bit. Give the array configuration of the chips on the memory board showing all required input and output signals for assigning this memory to the lowest address space. (The design should allow for both byte and 16-bit word accesses.)

3.4. Design a 4-Kbyte memory board for a Motorola 68000-based system using 1K-bit SRAM chips. Each SRAM has a single CS input pin and the 4-Kbyte memory is to be assigned to the highest area in main memory. Show all 68000 signals applied to this memory. (You do not have to show the hardware for the DTACK signal.)

3.5. Consider a 68000-based microprocessor system with a 2-way word-interleaved memory subsystem. The size of the subsystem is 2^k bytes, it is assigned to low memory, and is designed using memory chips of capacity 2^j locations of 2^i bits per location. Place the necessary number of memory chips to implement the memory subsystem on a printed circuit board and show all necessary signals for interconnecting it to the microprocessor chip.

3.6. Design a 2-way doubleword-interleaved memory module for the Intel 80x86, with a total of 1.5 Mbytes assigned to the highest physical addresses and composed of 32K × 8-bit memory chips. Place these chips on a printed-circuit board and show its interface lines to the microprocessor's bus. Give the real hexadecimal addresses assigned to each memory chip of the first 256K bytes of this module.

3.7. Consider the 32-bit Motorola 680x0 microprocessors driven by an external 32-MHz clock and executing burst transfers from a "62.5-ns DRAM" memory. Assume that 16 Mbytes of this memory are assigned to the lowest address space and made up of 512K × 1-bit DRAM chips. Design the memory, arrange the memory chips on a memory board, and interface it to the microprocessor buses.

3.8. Design a 2-Mbyte memory for the Intel i860 composed of 256K × 4-bit DRAMs assigned to the lowest address space and show its basic interface to the microprocessor buses.

3.9. Draw the Intel 80486 timing diagram for a 2-way doubleword-interleaved SRAM memory.

3.10. Design a 2-way doubleword-interleaved memory for the 32-bit Motorola 680x0. This memory has a total of 2M bytes, is placed on the highest memory addresses, and is composed of 128K × 4-bit SRAM chips. (Each SRAM chip has a single chip-select input.) Place these chips on a memory board and show its interface lines to the microprocessor's buses. Give the real hexadecimal addresses assigned to each memory chip pair of the first 256K bytes of this memory.

3.11. Repeat Exercise 3.10 using 64K × 1-bit DRAM chips.

3.12. Consider a memory design using DRAM chips with access time t_a = 100 ns and precharge time t_{PR} = 80 ns. Draw the timing diagrams (as in Figure 3.22) for:

(a) A 4-way byte-interleaved memory

(b) A 4-way word-interleaved memory

(c) A 2-way doubleword-interleaved memory

Compare their bandwidths.

3.13 Consider the Intel 80286 and a 2-way word-interleaved DRAM memory controlled by the 8207 DRAM controller. Give the actual 80286 bus timing diagrams (include all pertinent control signals) for three memory cycles executed as follows: the first cycle is a read from bank 0, the second is a write to bank 1, and the third is a read from the same bank 1.

REFERENCES

[1] Intel Corp., *28F010 1024 (128KX8) CMOS FLASH Memory* (290207-006), Santa Clara, CA, 1990.

[2] Intel Corp., *28F020 1024 (256KX8) CMOS FLASH Memory* (290245-003), Santa Clara, CA, 1990.

[3] Intel Corp., *The 8086 Family User's Manual* (9800722-03), Santa Clara, CA, Oct. 1979.

[4] Intel Corp., *iAPX286, Hardware Reference Manual* (210760-001), Santa Clara, CA, 1983.

[5] Intel Corp., *80386 Hardware Reference Manual* (231732-001), Santa Clara, CA, 1986.

[6] Intel Corp., *iAPX286 Hardware Reference Manual* (210760-001), Santa Clara, CA, 1983.

[7] Breuninger, R.K., et al., "System Solutions for Static Column Decode," in *Programmable Logic Data Book* (SDZD001C), Texas Instruments, Dallas, 1988, pp. 3.84–3.108.

[8] Integrated Device Technology Inc., *RISC Data Book*, Santa Clara, CA, 1991.

[9] Motorola Semiconductor Products, Inc., Application Note AN986, *Page, Nibble, and Static Column Modes: Speed, Serial-Access Options on 1M-bit + DRAMs*, Phoenix, AZ, 1987.

[10] Bishop, L., "80286 High Performance Memory Interface," 80286 Memory Interface Applications Note, in *Advanced Micro Devices Personal Computer Products*, Advanced Micro Devices, Inc., 1989.

[11] Intel Corp., *i860 64-bit Microprocessor Hardware Reference Manual* (CG-101789), Santa Clara, CA, 1989.

[12] Motorola Inc., *MC68030 Enhanced 32-bit Microprocessor User's Manual* (MC68030UM/AD), Austin, TX, 1987.

[13] Mirapuri, S., et al., "The MIPS R4000 Processor," *IEEE Micro*, Apr. 1992, pp. 10–22.

[14] Diefendorff, K., and M. Allen, "Organization of the Motorola 88110 Superscalar RISC Microprocessor," *IEEE Micro*, Apr. 1992, pp. 40–63.

4

Industry System Buses

4.1 INTRODUCTION

So far in the textbook we covered in detail the component-level or local bus of the microprocessor. Regarding the component-independent backplane or system bus, we only presented some very introductory remarks in Chapter 1. The first half of this chapter here covers the details and operation of some "industry system buses" used in designing larger microprocessor-based systems. Since their operation is not really that much different from that of the local bus, the reader is urged to make frequent references to Chapter 2, which covers the local bus and where terms such as synchronous/asynchronous operation are explained in detail. We focus our discussion in this chapter on three representative industry standard buses: the Multibus, VMEbus, and Futurebus.

The second half of the chapter covers "mad-endian" and "sad-endian" types of system buses, and the general principles of interfacing to them "little-endian" and "big-endian" microprocessors. Specific interfacing design examples are given for the Multibus and VMEbus. We also cover system bus arbitration when a number of masters share the same system bus.

We end the chapter by presenting various characteristics used for trade-off analysis in order to choose the most appropriate system bus for a particular design.

4.2 MICROPROCESSOR SYSTEM BUSES

For small microprocessor-based systems (one or two printed-circuit boards) the microprocessor chip's control signals may themselves be used directly as system commands to interface with memory and I/O devices via the local bus. In larger system configurations (two or more printed-circuit boards) or in multimicroprocessor arrangements, memory and I/O boards are interfaced to the microprocessor board via an industry standard system bus. A simplified block diagram of such an arrangement is shown in Figure 4.1 [1].

The global "system bus" is a general-purpose backbone to which the processor (or processor board), memory, and high-performance I/O are connected [2]. A processor board or module (also called CPU board or motherboard) makes up a small microprocessor-based system in which some local memory and local I/O modules are connected to the microprocessor through its local bus. The system bus implies processor independence; i.e., any type of microprocessor chip can be used on the processor board, thus increasing the flexibility afforded on the type of computer to be constructed. The global memory contains the boards with the system-wide chips, and their interfaces and controller circuits; the I/O section contains the I/O adaptor boards with all the input/output ports and interface circuitry for the connection of system-wide I/O devices.

Peripheral devices are connected to the system via their own "I/O buses." For example, video display terminals may be connected to the system via the EIA (Electronics Industry Association) standard RS-232-C serial links; other special-purpose peripherals such as disks, tapes, and CD-ROMs may be connected via the SCSI (small computer system interface) bus and its standard SCSI adapter boards[†]; measuring and control devices may have their own standard I/O instrumentation bus, such as the IEEE-448 bus interfaced via its GPIB (general-purpose instrumentation bus) adapter boards.

Due to distances and signal driving requirements, a number of interface components are needed to convert the local, processor-specific bus to the standard system bus. It is the responsibility of the system designer to provide the proper interface components on the processor board to adapt the processor-dependent local bus to the industry system bus. The hardware designer is also responsible for designing the memory and I/O boards and interfacing them properly to the selected system bus. Thus the specifications and operation of the system bus are important to the hardware designer and system integrator.

The operation of the system bus is the same as that discussed for the local bus: a master board starts a system bus cycle by placing an address on the system address bus to select one of the slave boards (and maybe a particular part of that slave). The slave board will respond by either driving the system data bus or latching from it data. Similar to the local bus, this operation may be either synchronous or asynchronous, requiring handshake signals. Separate control signals may also be provided on the system bus to specify the address type (memory address or I/O port number).

Figure 4.2 shows some of the most important microprocessor system buses [3–5]. Figure 4.3 gives a table with the major 32-bit system buses and their characteristics [1].

In the sections that follow we present some details on specific industry system buses. We discuss their address and data bus lines, along with those control signals needed for the data transfer cycles and bus arbitration.

Before we begin, let us present some new terms often used in conjunction with the system buses:

Octet:　1 byte of data
Doublet: 2 bytes of data
Quadlet: 4 bytes of data
Octlet:　8 bytes of data, different from octet (8 bits)

[†]SCSI controllers may also be connected to the local bus to interface local I/O devices.

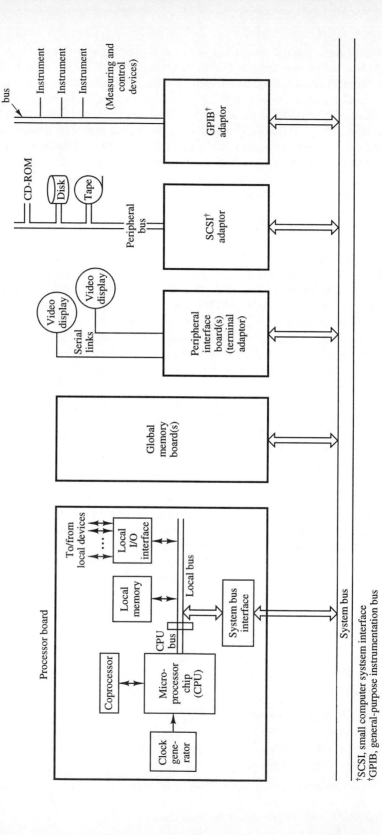

Figure 4.1 Processor, memory, I/O, and peripheral bus interface boards interconnected via the system bus.

†SCSI, small computer systsem interface
†GPIB, general-purpose instrumentation bus

IEEE	896	FutureBus
IEEE	796	Multibus I
IEEE	1296	Multibus II
IEEE	1014	VMEbus
EISA	(Extended Industry	
	Standard Architecture	
IEEE	1196	NuBus
IEEE	960	Fastbus

Figure 4.2 Representative industry microprocessor system buses.

4.3 MULTIBUS

The Multibus I (IEEE 796) has data bus widths of 8 and 16 bits, and address bus widths of 8, 16, 20, and 24 bits. It is an asynchronous (the handshake signals are MRDC*/MWTC* and XACK*), nonmultiplexed bus. The Multibus II (IEEE 1096) has data bus widths of 8, 16, 24, and 32 bits (optimized for 16 bits, low-end justified)[1] and an address bus width of up to 32 bits. It is a synchronous, multiplexed bus. Due to its 16-bit data justification, it does not manage correctly unaligned quadlets, doublets, and 24-bit entities.

We start our system bus coverage of this chapter by first presenting a 16-bit system bus (the Multibus I) and use it as an example for explaining the low-end byte justification and the "byte-switching logic" needed to interface different processor boards to it. Figure 4.4 depicts the lines required for a processor master board to interconnect to the 16-bit Multibus I system bus. We present here the signals needed to do data transfers. It must be noted that the system bus design is modular, and that subsets of these signals may be implemented according to the needs of the particular system design.

4.3.1 Bus Signals

Address bus (A0#–A23#). These 24 lines constitute the system address bus and are used to transfer either memory addresses or I/O device numbers. They define a $2^{24} = 16$-Mbyte memory addressing space, they are driven by tri-state drivers, and are always controlled by the current system bus master.

A 16-bit master in control of the system bus can do input/output by using only the first 16 lines, A0#–A15#, to transmit the 16-bit I/O port number. Therefore, a 16-bit master board can directly access up to $2^{16} = 64$K 8-bit I/O ports.

An 8-bit master board may also be connected to the Multibus I and use either the first 16 address lines, A0#–A15#, to transmit a 16-bit memory address (accessing any of the 64K byte-locations), or use the first eight lines A0#–A7# to transmit an 8-bit I/O port number (accessing any of the 256 8-bit input/output ports). In order to perform such an input/output, the I/O interface board connected to Multibus I must be able to be configured also to decode only the eight lower address lines A0#–A7# and ignore[2] the next eight address lines, A8#–A15#.

Inhibit lines (INH1# and INH2#). The signals INH1# and INH2# are used to prevent a memory slave board from responding to the address on the address bus (i.e., the

---

[1]Bus justification is explained later in the chapter.

[2]In some earlier 8-bit microprocessors the 8-bit port number is duplicated onto the next high-order address lines, A8#–A15#. While this is considered an acceptable procedure, it is not recommended for new designs.

	FutureBus	Multibus II	NuBus	VME32
Support:	IFFF 896	Intel	TI(MIT)	Motorola, Philips, Mostek
System optimization:	32-bit federalist multiprocessor	16-bit autonomous multiprocessor with central service module	32-bit federalist multiprocessor clock module	16-bit centralized multiprocessor; service module optional
Address bits:	32	32	32	32
Address spaces:	MEM, CSR	MEM, message, I/O, intercon	MEM	6 address modifier bits
Data width:	8,16,24,32	8,16,24,32	8,16,24,32	8,16,32
Parity:	Mandatory	Mandatory	Optional	None
Optimized for: (justified)	32-bit	16-bit	32-bit	16-bit
Width steering:	Individual byte strobe	Address + size	Address + size	Address + size + byte strobe within doublet
Sequential transfer:	Yes, unbounded	Yes, unbounded	Yes, bounded	Yes, unbounded
Geographical address:	5 bits, wired	T-pin, needs central service module	5 bits, wired	None
Arbitration:	Decentralized	Decentralized, but needs CSM to initialize	Decentralized	Daisy chain, 4-level
Interrupt:	Memory-mapped or serial bus	Message-space or serial bus	Memory-mapped	7 interrupt levels or destinations or serial bus
Protocol:	Three-way handshake	Synchron 10 MHz	Synchron 10 MHz	Handshaken
Transfer mode:	Multiplex	Multiplex	Multiplex	Simplex
Broadcast:	Yes	No	No	No
Technology:	100-mA OC special drivers	48-mA 3S 60-mA 3S TTL	48-mA 3S 60-mA 3S TTL	48-mA 3S TTL
Maximum speed[a]: (single-read transfer)	200 Mb/s	106 Mb/s	106 Mb/s	152 Mb/s
Board size:	Triple * 280 1024 cm^2 (preferred)	Double * 280 512 cm^2 (preferred)	Triple * 280 1024 cm^2	Double * 160 mm 373 cm^2
Connectors:	1 DIN	1 DIN	1 DIN	2 DIN
Number of slots:	32	20	16	19
Auxiliary buses:	Serial bus (undefined)	Execution iLBX Serial iSSB	None	Execution VMX Serial VMS
Vintage:	1985	1983	1983	1981
Status (in 1989):	Experimental	Few boards, 2 vendors	Only used in NuMachine	About 6 vendors

[a]Maximum estimated speed, based only on time spent in the bus protocol, but not in the logic or in the memory access time. Single read transfer was chosen because it is the most frequent transfer; sequential transfers increase the throughput of all buses and reduce the advantage of the simplex bus VME. A simplex bus is by nature 30% faster than a multiplex bus, but only for single transfers.

Figure 4.3 Major system buses and their characteristics. (Adapted from [1]. © 1989 IEEE.)

signals can be invoked for any memory read or memory write operation). An inhibit signal is generated by the inhibiting slave (identified by decoding the memory address) to inhibit another slave's bus activity. When inhibited this way, the slave disables its drivers from driving all data, address, and acknowledge bus lines (although it may actually perform internal operations).

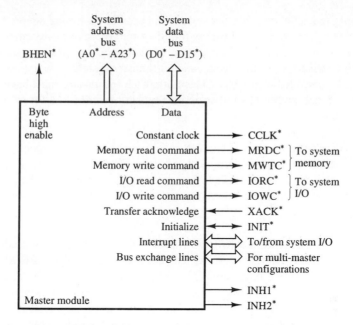

Figure 4.4 Master module signals on the Multibus I (IEEE 796) system bus.

INH1# can be used to inhibit RAM memory devices, and INH2# to inhibit ROM devices. INH1# allows ROM slaves to override RAM slaves when ROM and RAM are assigned the same memory space. INH2# allows auxiliary ROM to override ROM devices when ROM and auxiliary ROM are assigned the same memory space. The two signals INH1# and INH2# may also be used to allow memory-mapped I/O devices to override RAM and ROM devices, respectively.

Thus, a RAM device is considered a bottom-priority slave. A ROM device or a memory-mapped I/O device are considered a middle-priority slave, which may assert INH1# to inhibit the bus activity of a bottom-priority slave. An auxiliary or ''bootstrap'' ROM device is considered a top-priority slave. It may assert INH2# to inhibit the bus activity of a middle-priority slave or INH1# to inhibit a bottom-priority slave as well. When both a middle-priority inhibiting slave and a top-priority inhibiting slave are activated, INH1# will be asserted by (usually, open collector) drivers on both devices.

Data bus (D0#–D15#).   Sixteen bidirectional data lines constitute the system data bus and are used to exchange 8-and 16-bit data with memory and I/O interface boards. Data read and data write are always specified relative to the current master board. Data bus lines are driven by the current master board on write operations, and by the addressed slave board on read operations.

Both memory and I/O cycles can support 8-bit byte and 16-bit word data transfers. This allows both 8-bit master boards and slaves and 16-bit masters and slaves to coexist in a single system. In 8-bit masters, only lines D0#–D7# are valid. The details of the 8-and 16-bit data transfer operations are given in the next section.

Constant clock (CCLK#).   The constant clock provides a clock signal at constant frequency which may be used by master or slave boards as a *master clock*. It is driven by one and only one source within the system and provides a timing source for any or all modules on the bus. The control and timing for all system bus cycles, whether they are cycles of the permanent master module or cycles of the temporary master in control of the system bus, must be derived from this clock. In a multimaster system, only one of the masters will have its clock connected to the bus. (Therefore, each bus master must have the capability of generating an acceptable clock that optionally can be connected to, or disconnected from, the system bus.)

Byte high enable (BHEN#).   This signal is used to specify that data will be transferred on the high-order eight data bus lines D8#–D15#; i.e., it enables the upper byte section of a 16-bit memory board to drive the data bus lines. This signal is used only on systems that incorporate 16-bit slave boards; 8-bit microprocessors do not use this type of signal.

Read commands (MRDC# and IORC#).   The two read commands, memory read command (MRDC#) and I/O read command (IORC#), initiate the same basic type of operation. An active read command line indicates to the slave board that the address lines are carrying a valid address; MRDC# indicates that a memory address is valid on the address lines, while IORC# indicates that an I/O port number is valid on the address lines. A read command additionally indicates that the slave board is to place its data on the data bus.

Write commands (MWTC# and IOWC#).   The two commands, memory write command (MWTC#) and I/O write command (IOWC#), also initiate the same basic type of operation. Similar to the read commands, an active write command line indicates to the slave board that a memory address is valid on the address lines. A write command additionally indicates that the master module has placed valid data on the data bus lines that can be accepted by the addressed slave module.

Transfer acknowledge (XACK#).   Since all exchanges on the Multibus I are asynchronous, they involve handshaking. Therefore, the addressed slave module must provide the master module with an acknowledge signal in response to the transfer control (read or write) command. The signal XACK# is issued by the addressed slave to indicate that the commanded read or write operation is complete, and that the data has been placed on, or accepted from, the data lines. The XACK# allows the master to complete its current bus cycle. If such an XACK# signal is not returned to the master, the bus master normally enters a "wait state," which it leaves when the slave finally asserts XACK#. While in a wait state, the master still has control of the system bus.

To avoid the possibility of an indefinite wait by the master (e.g., a bus master addresses a nonexistent or malfunctioning slave, in which case an acknowledge signal will not be returned to the master), an optional bus time-out function may be implemented on the master board to terminate a bus cycle after a preset interval, even if no acknowledge has been received.

The XACK# line may also be used as a special line commonly used by front-panel devices to stop or single-step a bus master. It is also used in multimicroprocessor systems to force a master to wait for access to the system bus. This XACK# system signal is usually converted to the READY or WAIT local signal (for synchronous, local, component-level buses) and applied directly to the respective input pin of the microprocessor chip.

Initialize (INIT#).   Finally, the signal INIT# is generated to reset the entire system to a known internal state. This signal may be generated by an external source or by any or all of the bus masters. Two external sources that may generate INIT# are:

1. A power-on clear circuit (RC network) that generates an INIT# signal which is held low until the power supplies reach their specific voltage outputs.
2. A (debounced) reset button, usually provided on the system front panel for operator use.

This INIT# system bus signal corresponds to the RESET signal of the local component-level bus applied to the respective input pin of the microprocessor chip. In multimaster configurations, this externally generated INIT# signal resets all bus masters. A master can assert this INIT# line using a software command. The internal state of the master processor is not affected by such an internally generated INIT# signal.

4.3.2 Data Transfers on Multibus I

Figure 4.5 shows a 16-bit master module connected to a 16-bit memory slave module via the Multibus I system bus.[3]

The full 16 data lines are used only for 16-bit transfers. The even byte memory Section 0 is connected (through its buffer) to data bus lines D0#–D7#, the odd byte memory Section 1 is connected to data bus lines D8#–D15#.

We present below various cases involved in *byte transfers* (in which data justification is imposed), where the processor may be either an 8-bit or a 16-bit master. In either case, we consider the memory or I/O slaves to be 16 bits wide.[4] As we will see, a "byte-switching logic" is required on all 16-bit master and 16-bit slave boards to implement data justification and maintain compatibility with 8-bit devices.

8-Bit masters.   The two alternatives are shown in Figure 4.6. For a low (even) byte transfer, in addition to the BHEN# being inactive (high), the A0# is also inactive (high), thus indicating an 8-bit even byte transfer. The data byte is transferred across on data lines D0#–D7# (Figure 4.6a), which is the normal data bus byte lane connected to the even memory section. For a high (odd) byte transfer, BHEN# is inactive (high) but A0# is active (low). Since the Multibus I protocol requires low-end byte justification, the byte-switching logic on the memory board interface is now activated to let the byte from the odd byte memory section transfer across on data lines D0–D7# (Figure 4.6b).

16-Bit masters.   Two alternative configurations are shown in Figure 4.7. For a low (even) byte transfer, again both BHEN# and A0# are inactive (high), thus indicating an 8-bit even byte transfer. The data is transferred across on data lines D0#–D7# (Figure 4.7a), which, as before, is the normal data bus byte-lane connected to the even memory section. For a high byte transfer, however, BHEN# is inactive (high) and A0# is active (low), thus indicating an 8-bit odd byte transfer. Due to the low-end justification requirement

---

[3]In order to simplify our discussion, we assume that the type of microprocessor used (little-endian) matches that of the Multibus I (sad-endian). More complex cases are presented later in the chapter.

[4]Byte transfers to 8-bit slave devices are independent of the CPU.

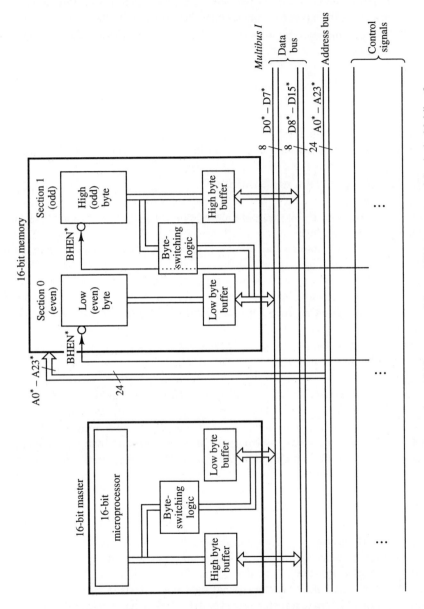

Figure 4.5 Interconnecting a 16-bit master module to a 16-bit memory module via the Multibus I (16-bit transfers: BHEN* = L, AO* = H).

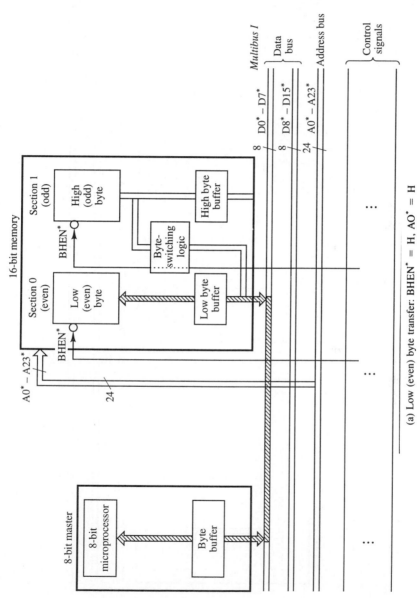

(a) Low (even) byte transfer: BHEN* = H, AO* = H

Figure 4.6 Eight-bit master in even/odd byte transfers.

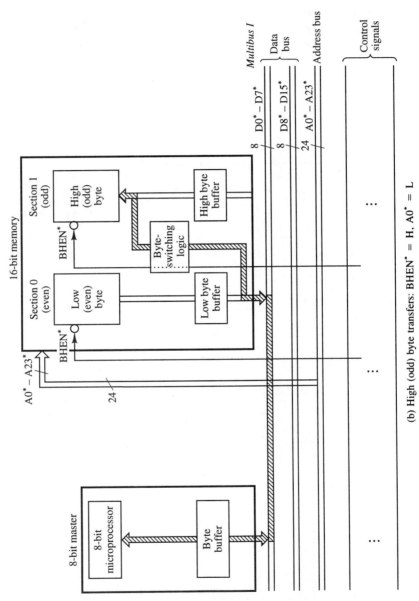

Figure 4.6 (concluded)

(b) High (odd) byte transfers: BHEN* = H, A0* = L

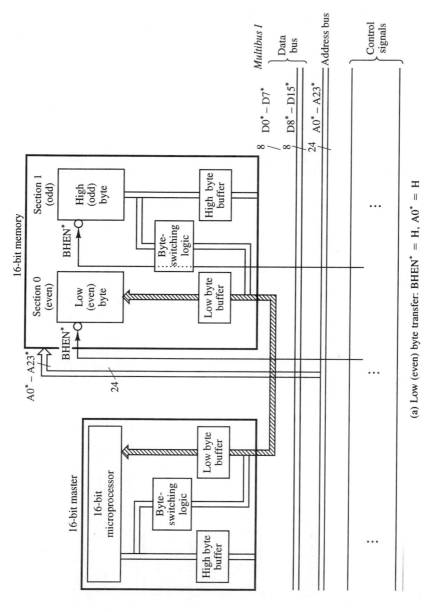

(a) Low (even) byte transfer: BHEN* = H, A0* = H

Figure 4.7 Sixteen-bit master in even/odd byte transfers.

205

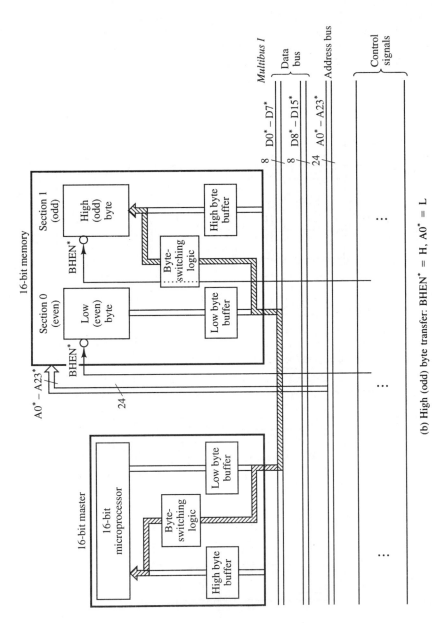

(b) High (odd) byte transfer: BHEN* = H, A0* = L

Figure 4.7 (concluded)

the byte-switching logic on the memory board will again move this byte on data lines D0#–D7# (Figure 4.7b). On the 16-bit processor module, its byte-switching circuit will also be activated now in order to switch the incoming byte from lines D0#–D7# to the high (odd) byte input of the microprocessor chip.

4.3.3 Interfacing to Multibus I

In order to interface a microprocessor to any system bus, the proper hardware logic is required to properly time, encode, and multiplex the signals that pass between the processor and the system bus. As an example, here we again use the Multibus I.

Since the Multibus I allows both 8-bit masters and slaves and 16-bit masters and slaves to coexist in a single system, it allows both 8-bit and 16-bit data transfers. Two signals control the data transfers: BHEN# active indicates that the bus is operating in the 16-bit mode, and the address bit A0# defines an even-byte or odd-byte transfer. For existing devices which maintain only an 8-bit data bus, all 8-bit transfers are performed over the lower half of the 16-bit data bus (regardless of the address). Figure 4.8 shows an implementation of the byte-switching logic using a multiplexer.

4.4 VMEbus

4.4.1 General Concepts

The VME (Versa Module Europe)-16 (one-connector) bus (standard IEEE 1014 [14]) has data bus widths of 8 and 16 bits (and like the Multibus I, it has low-end byte justification) and address bus widths of 8, 16, 20, and 24 bits. It is a nonmultiplexed, asynchronous bus that uses the handshake signals $DS0^*$ and $DS1^*$—decoded from the processor's DS# signal—and the data transfer acknowledge feedback ($DTACK^*$). The VME32 (two connectors) bus has data bus widths of 8, 16, and 32 bits (optimized for 16-bit, low-end justification) and an address bus width of up to 32 bits. It is an asynchronous, nonmultiplexed bus. Sixteen-bit addresses are used for I/O devices in systems that have separate I/O address spaces. Again, like the Multibus II, its 16-bit justification does not allow it to manage correctly quadlets, doublets, and 24-bit entities. (An example of the problems present in interfacing it with even a Motorola 32-bit processor is given later in the chapter.) The VME32 bus has a much stronger bind with the Motorola 680x0 products than Multibus II has with the Intel 32-bit products.

4.4.2 VMEbus Signals

Like we did for the Multibus, we will present here the signals needed to do data transfers (one of the four signal groups referred to as the "data transfer bus" or DTB). The P1 connector includes all signals needed for a standard 16-bit microprocessor, while the second, optional, P2 connector extends the address and data bus lines to accommodate designs based on 32-bit microprocessors. (This second P2 also provides 96 pins for user I/O lines.)

Address bus (A01–A31).   The number of address bits used may be 8 bits (short address, used primarily for accessing I/O ports by microprocessors that include special I/O instructions), 16 bits, 24 bits (standard), and 32 bits (extended).

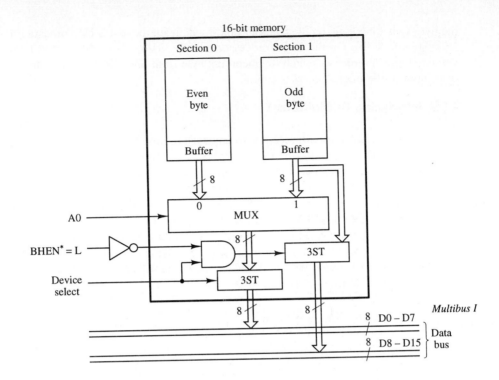

Word transfers: BHEN* = L, A0 = L (A0* = H)
Byte transfers: (1) Even byte (byte across D0 – D7):
 BHEN* = H, A0 = L (A0* = H)
 (2) Odd byte (byte across D0 – D7):
 BHEN* = H, A0 = H (A0* = L)

Figure 4.8 Interfacing to Multibus I in which the byte-switching-logic is implemented with a multiplexer. (3ST is a tri-state buffer/driver). (Adapted from [6].)

Address modifier (AM0–AM5). This is a unique feature of the VMEbus and is used to distinguish among a number of different addressing spaces, such as user (non-privileged) or supervisor (privileged), and code or data spaces. The address modifier bits may also be used to specify the width of the address, such as a 32-bit ("extended"), 24-bit ("standard"), or 16-bit ("short") address. Three of these signals are typically used to transfer the Motorola's function code signals (FC0–FC2), and the designer must include on each processor's interface the appropriate hardware to place an identifying code on these lines. Address modifiers may also be used for what is called "memory map selection": all slave devices examine the address modifier signals and respond only to the codes assigned to them, i.e., different address ranges may be assigned to the various slave devices.

Finally, the address modifiers may be used to specify a *sequential access* (ascending access) to memory, discussed below.

Data Bus (D00–D31). The data transfers over the data bus can be 8, 16, or 32 bits. Data transfers of less than 32 bits must be transferred across the lower end of the data bus (low-end data justification).

AS*, DS0*, DS1*, and DTACK*. The data transfer is done using an asynchronous protocol. The master issues the address strobe (AS*) to inform all slave boards that the address is now stable and may be clocked into latching registers. DS0* and DS1* select the data to be transferred: DSO* = low is the odd byte data strobe signal (byte on data lines D0–D7); DS1* = low is the even byte data strobe signal (byte on data lines D8–D15). For a proper data transfer, the slave responds back with the data transfer acknowledge signal DTACK*. This DTACK* is analogous to the Multibus's XACK* signal.

LWORD*. This signal is asserted by the bus master to indicate a quadlet (or 32-bit longword) transfer. (Actually, the only time a 32-bit doubleword will be transferred across the VME32 bus is when it is aligned on a 32-bit doubleword boundary.)

WRITE*. This is the read/write signal.

BERR*. This line (instead of the DTACK*) is asserted by the slave (or its interface) in the case of an error. Also, when the access port size is not 32 bits wide and the master module starts an aligned 32-bit doubleword transfer, the VME32 bus specifications require of the port to assert the BERR* signal rather than asserting the normal bus cycle termination signal DTACK*.

IACK*. This is the interrupt acknowledge signal. Usually, during a data transfer cycle, the master drives this line high. If IACK* is low, the cycle is not a data transfer cycle but an interrupt acknowledge cycle.

4.4.3 Data Transfers on the VMEbus

The VMEbus operates like the asynchronous local buses discussed in Chapter 2 [7]. Figures 4.9 and 4.10 present in a flowchart form the typical flow of operations for an odd byte read cycle and an even word write cycle. We observe the following: in both cases, since the transfer is not a longword, LWORD* is driven high; in both cases the slave determines whether its address is its own, and while this occurs the master drives WRITE* high or low depending on the cycle type; the master, after verifying that the last cycle is complete and the data bus is available, will then place the proper values on lines DS0* and DS1* to identify the location of the byte/word transfer; for the byte read cycle, the slave places the byte on lines D00–D07; for the word write cycle, the slave latches the data from lines D00–D15; finally, in both cases the slave indicates that it has responded to the transaction by asserting DTACK* low and holding it low as long as the data strobe is driven low.

4.4.4 Sequential Access on the VMEbus

The block transfer mode on the VMEbus is called ''sequential access'' (ascending access) and is specified by the ''sequential-access code'' placed by the bus master on the ''address modifier'' lines AM0–AM5. The first address sent is used to initialize an internal address counter on the addressed memory slave board. From there on, the slave's interface properly increments this address counter (by 1, 2, or 4, for byte, word, or doubleword, respectively), accesses sequential memory locations, and proceeds with the read or write operation. The bus master keeps driving the address strobe AS# low and requests another data transfer by

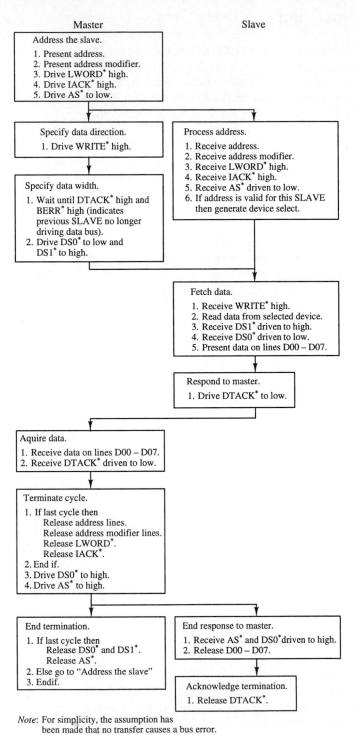

Master | Slave

Address the slave.

1. Present address.
2. Present address modifier.
3. Drive LWORD* high.
4. Drive IACK* high.
5. Drive AS* to low.

Specify data direction.

1. Drive WRITE* high.

Process address.

1. Receive address.
2. Receive address modifier.
3. Receive LWORD* high.
4. Receive IACK* high.
5. Receive AS* driven to low.
6. If address is valid for this SLAVE then generate device select.

Specify data width.

1. Wait until DTACK* high and BERR* high (indicates previous SLAVE no longer driving data bus).
2. Drive DS0* to low and DS1* to high.

Fetch data.

1. Receive WRITE* high.
2. Read data from selected device.
3. Receive DS1* driven to high.
4. Receive DS0* driven to low.
5. Present data on lines D00 – D07.

Respond to master.

1. Drive DTACK* to low.

Aquire data.

1. Receive data on lines D00 – D07.
2. Receive DTACK* driven to low.

Terminate cycle.

1. If last cycle then
   Release address lines.
   Release address modifier lines.
   Release LWORD*.
   Release IACK*.
2. End if.
3. Drive DS0* to high.
4. Drive AS* to high.

End termination.

1. If last cycle then
   Release DS0* and DS1*.
   Release AS*.
2. Else go to "Address the slave"
3. Endif.

End response to master.

1. Receive AS* and DS0* driven to high.
2. Release D00 – D07.

Acknowledge termination.

1. Release DTACK*.

Note: For simplicity, the assumption has been made that no transfer causes a bus error.

Figure 4.9 Odd byte read cycle on the VMEbus.

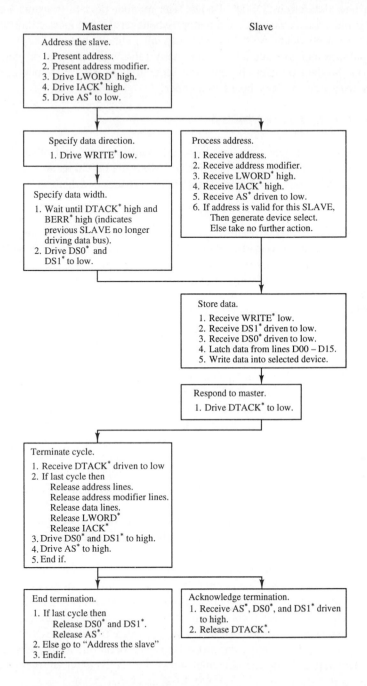

Master   Slave

Address the slave.

1. Present address.
2. Present address modifier.
3. Drive LWORD* high.
4. Drive IACK* high.
5. Drive AS* to low.

Specify data direction.

1. Drive WRITE* low.

Process address.

1. Receive address.
2. Receive address modifier.
3. Receive LWORD* high.
4. Receive IACK* high.
5. Receive AS* driven to low.
6. If address is valid for this SLAVE,
   Then generate device select.
   Else take no further action.

Specify data width.

1. Wait until DTACK* high and BERR* high (indicates previous SLAVE no longer driving data bus).
2. Drive DS0* and DS1* to low.

Store data.

1. Receive WRITE* low.
2. Receive DS1* driven to low.
3. Receive DS0* driven to low.
4. Latch data from lines D00 – D15.
5. Write data into selected device.

Respond to master.

1. Drive DTACK* to low.

Terminate cycle.

1. Receive DTACK* driven to low
2. If last cycle then
   Release address lines.
   Release address modifier lines.
   Release data lines.
   Release LWORD*
   Release IACK*
3. Drive DS0* and DS1* to high.
4. Drive AS* to high.
5. End if.

End termination.

1. If last cycle then
   Release DS0* and DS1*.
   Release AS*.
2. Else go to "Address the slave"
3. Endif.

Acknowledge termination.

1. Receive AS*, DS0*, and DS1* driven to high.
2. Release DTACK*.

Note: For simplicity, the assumption has been made that no transfer causes a bus error.

Figure 4.10 Even word write cycle on the VMEbus.

issuing a new data strobe DS0#, DS1#. The number of data transfers from sequentially increasing addresses is variable, and it stops whenever the bus master that started this block transfer stops driving the AS# low. Actually, all memory boards that have block transfer mode capability increase this address internally (although only one of them at a time participates in the data transfer) because the sequential address incrementing may cross the boundary from one memory board to another.

4.4.5 Interfacing to the VMEbus

We examine here the byte switching logic, the multiplexing, and other hardware circuitry needed to interface the processor (assume the Motorola 68030 as an example) and memory boards to the VMEbus system bus. Most of this discussion here is extracted from reference [8].

Processor-board interface. First of all, the processor's output signals A0 and SIZ0, SIZ1 must be converted to the VME32 system bus signals DS0# and DS1#. The circuit in Figure 4.11a shows the logic for this conversion. Also, the LWORD# control signal (indicating a doubleword or quadlet transfer across the VME32 bus) must also somehow be generated.

Second, we must recall that the VME32 system bus specification dictates low-end justification; i.e., 16-bit word transfers occur on the lower half of the 32-bit system data bus, D0–D15, and byte transfers on the lower byte lane, D0–D7. (This situation arises when either an aligned 32-bit doubleword or an aligned 16-bit word is transferred to a 16-bit port.) The 32-bit Motorola 68030 microprocessor, however, enforces high-end justification; i.e., a word is transferred to a 16-bit port using the upper half of the 32-bit local data bus. Therefore, some multiplexing is required to resolve the differences between the orientation of the local and that of the system bus by switching the word onto the appropriate half of the data bus. As we will explain in more detail below, a MUX signal is required for the multiplexer interface. The generation of the system bus signals DS0#, DS1#, MUX#, and LWORD# needed for multiplex control and selection of the appropriate data path is accomplished by decoding the microprocessor's output signals A1, A0, SIZ1, and SIZ0 using the truth table of Figure 4.11b.

Finally, the DTACK# signal returned from the VME32 bus must be encoded to generate the DSACK0# and DSACK1# signals that the processor requires for proper bus cycle termination.

Figure 4.11c shows part of the actual interface circuitry for converting the Motorola's local bus to that of the VME32 system bus (it shows the logic for generating signals MUX# and LWORD#, but not that for generating signals DS0# and DS1#). The six SN74ALS640 chips are octal bus transceivers that implement the necessary multiplexing logic. The LWORD# asserted active-low indicates a longword transfer across the VMEbus. The MUX# signal is used to select the proper interface octal bus transceivers to enable multiplexing. The left side of the drawing shows the conversion of the system bus signal DTACK# to the local bus signals DSACK0# and DSACK1#.

When the processor starts a 32-bit longword transfer cycle (and asserts the LWORD# signal) it assumes that the accessed port is 32 bits wide. However, when the slave modules connected to the VME32 system bus are not 32 bits wide, the system bus specifications require that when the processor begins an aligned 32-bit longword transfer, the accessed

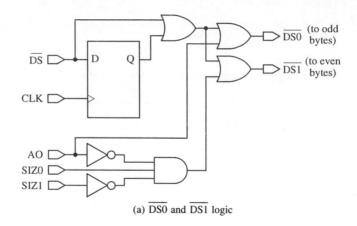

(a) $\overline{DS0}$ and $\overline{DS1}$ logic

	A1	A0	SIZ1	SIZ0	$\overline{DS1}$	$\overline{DS0}$	$\overline{MUX}$	$\overline{LWORD}$
Long	0	0	0	0	0	0	1	0
word	0	0	0	1	0	1	0	1
aligned	0	0	1	0	0	0	0	1
boundary	0	0	1	1	0	0	0	1
	0	1	0	0	1	0	0	1
Word	0	1	0	1	1	0	0	1
misaligned	0	1	1	0	1	0	0	1
	0	1	1	1	1	0	0	1
	1	0	0	0	0	0	1	1
Odd-word	1	0	0	1	0	1	1	1
aligned	1	0	1	0	0	0	1	1
	1	0	1	1	0	0	1	1
	1	1	0	0	1	0	1	1
Byte	1	1	0	1	1	0	1	1
aligned	1	1	1	0	1	0	1	1
	1	1	1	1	1	0	1	1

(b) Truth table for signals

Figure 4.11 Processor-board interface for a 32-bit Motorola 68030-based board connected to the VME32 system bus [8].

slave module assert the BERR# signal rather than the DTACK#. The logic presented in Figure 4.11c includes a "longword retry circuit" (the flip-flop shown at the top along with its associated logic gates) to recover from this situation when it occurs. When an 8- or 16-bit port receives the LWORD# signal, it responds by asserting BERR# to terminate the bus cycle. If BERR# is signaled at the same time that LWORD# is asserted, the interface logic asserts HALT#, which signals the Motorola processor to retry the transfer. The second time the transfer is initiated, LWORD# is blocked and the interface logic will attempt a 16-bit transfer. If the second attempt is terminated with BERR#, then an "exception" will be taken; otherwise, a third bus cycle will be executed by the processor to complete the 32-bit doubleword transfer. Therefore, an aligned 32-bit longword transfer to a 16-bit port will occur in three bus cycles instead of the normal two bus cycles. The logic shown in Figure 4.11

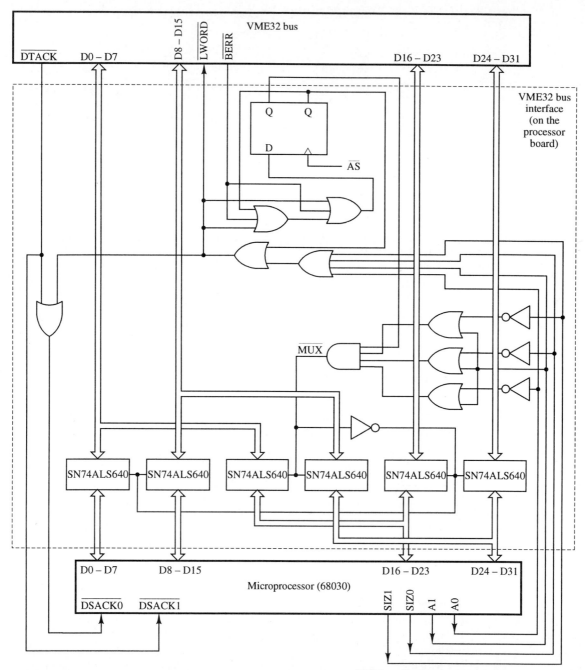

(c) Multiplexing, byte switching, and retry logic (Logic for generating signals $\overline{\text{MUX}}$ and $\overline{\text{LWORD}}$ is shown; logic for generating $\overline{\text{DS1}}$ and $\overline{\text{DS0}}$ is not shown.)

Figure 4.11   (concluded)

allows the transfer of 32-bit doublewords on the VME32 bus, regardless of the size of the slave device selected.

Memory-board interface. Having seen how the Motorola 68030 local bus is converted to the VME32 system bus, let us now examine what interface circuitry is required on the memory board. Figure 4.12a shows a table that includes the width of the information transfers on the VME32 data bus, the respective VME32 bus signals, and the truth table for generating the LW#, W#, EB# (even byte), and OB# (odd byte) control signals needed by the memory board interface.

Information transferred	VME32 bus signals				Memory board interface control signals			
	A1 A0	LWORD#	DS0#	DS1#	$\overline{LW}$	$\overline{W}$	$\overline{EB}$	$\overline{OB}$
32-bits	0 0	0	0	0	0	0	1	0
16-bits	X 0	1	0	0	1	0	1	0
Even byte	X 0	1	1	0	1	1	0	1
Odd byte	X 1	1	0	1	1	1	1	0

(a) Information transfer width, VME32 bus signals, and the truth table for generating signals $\overline{LW}$, $\overline{W}$, $\overline{EB}$, $\overline{OB}$ (logic 1)

Figure 4.12 Memory-board interface for a 32-bit memory board connected to the VME32 system bus. (Adapted from [6].)

Figure 4.12b shows the memory board interface logic for doing a read operation from a 32-bit memory composed of four byte-sections (sections 0–3). One of the data strobe signals DS1# or DS0# is activated for even or odd byte transfers, respectively, while for 16-bit word transfers both lines are activated. For 32-bit longword transfers, the LWORD# is activated by the bus master. 3ST represents a tri-state buffer/driver. Word transfers occur across lines D0–D15. Address bit A1 is used by the multiplexer to select either the most significant or the least significant word. Then, either the even or odd byte of that word is selected for transmission. Byte transfers always occur across lines D0–D7. Another similar multiplexing circuit will be needed for write operations.

4.5 FUTUREBUS

The Futurebus[†] (IEEE 896) was designed by IEEE as a high-performance, high-reliability (and price), truly manufacturer- and technology-independent system bus [9]. It requires no centralized control, meets the designers' needs of future multimicroprocessor systems, and supports cache-based boards and live insertion/withdrawal.[5] All bus lines are driven from open-collector stages and are active-low (the bus lines perform the wired-OR function and, since negative logic is used, binary 1 is represented by the less-positive level).

[†]Actually it is called the Futurebus[+].
[5]Explained at the end of the chapter.

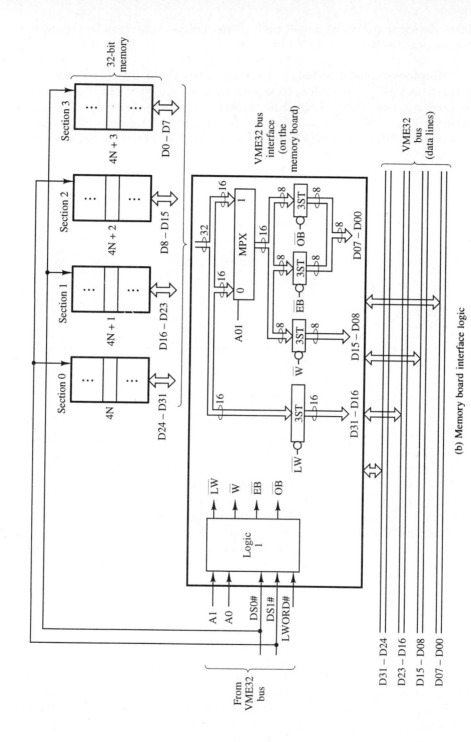

Figure 4.12 (concluded)

(b) Memory board interface logic

The bus is asynchronous and multiplexed. The handshake signals are: address strobe AS* and data strobe DS* from the master, and address acknowledge AK* (and address acknowledge inverse AI*) and data acknowledge DK* (and data acknowledge inverse DI*) from the slave. The asynchronous protocol is even extended to include arbitration. Unlike the other two system buses mentioned earlier, the Futurebus does not dedicate the bus to either a sad-endian or a mad-endian type.[6] Data is multiplexed with 32 bits of address on the same bus. The address/data bus has four additional "CoMmand lines"—the byte-lane-active lines (CM3*–CM0*)—which the master uses to indicate which byte-lane of the bus is used (is active) during the current transfer of either an address or a data. Each byte-lane of the address/data bus has an additional "Error Detection" line (EDx*) which carries the byte's *odd parity* bit used to check the integrity of the information (address or data) transferred on the bus.

The Futurebus has data bus widths of 8, 16, and 32 bits (with future expansions to 64 and 128 bits) and the data bus is *unjustified*. When an address is placed on the address/data bus, lines AD0 and AD1 provide redundant information which, in conjunction with the "byte-lane-active" lines (CM3*–CM0*) which are asserted when data is transferred, allow the slave to ascertain what processor type (big-endian or little-endian) is making the transfer.

4.5.1 Futurebus Signals

Figure 4.13 shows the Futurebus signals [10].

Signal name	Mnemonic	Number	Type of signal	Driven by:
Address/data lines	AD<31..0>*	32	Information	Master/slave
CoMmand lines	CM<4..0>*	5	Information	Master only
STatus lines	ST<2..0>*	3	Information	Slave only
Error Detection lines for AD	ED<3..0>*	4	Information	Master/slave
Command Parity for CM	CP*	1	Information	Master only
Error Valid	EV*	1	Information	Master/slave
Address Strobe	AS*	1	Synchronization	Master only
Address acKnowledge	AK*	1	Synchronization	Slave only
Address acknowledge Inverse	AI*	1	Synchronization	Slave only
Data Strobe	DS*	1	Synchronization	Master only
Data acKnowledge	DK*	1	Synchronization	Slave only
Data acknowledge Inverse	DI*	1	Synchronization	Slave only

Note: "*" means active low

Figure 4.13 Futurebus signals.

Address/data bus, AD<31 ... 0>*.   A 32-bit multiplexed bus (AD31*–AD0*) divided into four byte lanes, called lane W, lane X, lane Y, and lane Z (where lane Z may be thought as the one containing line zero or AD0* of the data bus). Which specific byte of the 32-bit item transfers over which byte lane of the system bus is not defined by the specification; instead, it is left up to the board implementer. During a data transfer, the processor uses four of the five command lines of the Futurebus (CM3*–CM0*) to tell which of the four byte lanes are active. Transferring smaller entities is useful when the microprocessor does a write operation of, for example, a single byte in memory without affecting its neighbors.

---

[6]These are explained in the next section.

Contrary to the Multibus and VMEbus that force low-end data justification (which complicate interfacing due to the need of byte-switching logic), the Futurebus imposes no justification; a byte can transfer over any one of the four lanes W, X, Y, or Z. When 32-bit processor boards and 32-bit memory boards are connected, they require no byte-switching logic. However, when a 16-bit or 8-bit processor board is connected, then byte-switching logic will be required if these processors are required to access all bytes within the 32-bit operand.

Boards that require misaligned quadlet (32-bit) transfers use two system bus transfers to access the misaligned 32-bit operand. Contrary to Multibus and VMEbus, the Futurebus provides the ability to transfer one, two, three, and four bytes in each transfer for the requirements of most 32-bit processors that support misaligned transfers with two cycles.

Command lines, CM<4..0>*.   The master module issues signals on these lines to tell the slave module what operation to perform. Command signals are issued along with either an address or data. When an *address transfer cycle* is executed, each individual command signal is defined as follows:

$CM4^*$*:RD* (*read*)*:* The signal is asserted[7] for a read operation and released for a write operation.

$CM3^*$*:LK* (*lock*)*:* This signal is issued by the master to tell the addressed slave module to lock out all of its other bus interfaces for as long as the master is controlling the system bus (until it releases the LK signal).

$CM2^*$*:BT* (*block transfer*)*:* This signal notifies the slave module that the master is starting a block transfer cycle (see Section 2.4.2).

$CM1^*$*:BC* (*broadcast*)*:* Indicates broadcasting operation with multiple slaves using the three-wire handshake (explained below along with the AS/AK/AI signals).

$CM0^*$*:EC* (*extended command*)*:* Reserved for future definition.

When a *data transfer cycle* is executed, each individual command signal is defined as follows:

$CM4^*$*:* (*read*)*:* As above.

$CM3^*$–$CM0^*$ (*lane W, X, Y, Z*)*:* When released by the master, indicate which lane(s) participate (are active) during this data transfer.

Status lines, ST<2..0>*.   The slave module responds with signals on these lines to indicate to the master module the slave's status. The table in Figure 4.14 shows the encoding of the status signals to yield eight different responses.

Error detection lines, ED<3..0>*.   Signals may be placed on these lines by either the master or the slave (whoever is the transmitter) to provide odd-parity protection for each of the four byte lanes of the address/data bus. Parity protection is optional: error checking is enabled when the EV^* line is asserted by the transmitter.

---

[7]In the Futurebus terminology, *asserted* refers to a signal line driven explicitly to the logic 1 level (if not already in that condition); *released* means to cease driving the signal line.

Signal name			Description
ST2	ST1	ST0	
0	0	0	*Illegal code/reserved.* This code is reserved for future use by the P896 Working Group. If detected by the master, it is treated as an error.
0	0	1	*Valid action.* No difficulty has been detected by the slave.
0	1	0	*Busy.* The slave is busy and cannot accept or send data at this time. The master should try again later.
0	1	1	*Access error.* The master has requested the slave to perform an operation it cannot do, or one that violates one or more of its rules.
1	0	0	*End of data.* The slave is unable to send or receive more data (reached boundary of memory board).
1	0	1	*Illegal code/reserved.* This code is reserved for future use by the P896 Working Group. If detected by the master, it is treated as an error.
1	1	0	*Parity error.* The slave has detected an error condition when checking the address, data, or command against the error detection lines.
1	1	1	*Error code.* An error of unknown type has occurred. This code may occur during broadcasts when multiple slaves are responding.

Note: Although this table uses positive logic, all signals on the P896 bus are driven by inverting, open-collector drivers. Therefore, the codes provided by multiple slaves are wire-0Red on the bus.

Figure 4.14   Status signals issued by the slave connected to the Futurebus [10]. © 1984 IEEE.

Command parity line, CP*.   It is issued by the master and carries the odd-parity bit for the command signals placed on lines CM$<4..0>^*$.

Error valid line, EV*.   When asserted by the transmitter (master or slave), it indicates that the ED* lines are valid and *may* be checked by the receiver (slave or master).

AS*/AK*/AI* lines.   The address strobe (AS*) and the address acknowledge (AK*) are the handshake signals for the transmission of an address. The address acknowledge inverse (AI*) is issued by the slave over a different line to form the three-wire handshake protocol for broadcast operations. (The broadcast mechanism is explained later.)

Once the addressed slave has responded with AK* and AI*, a condition known as *AS/AK lock* has been established, allowing the transfer of data over the AD lines.

DS*/DK*/DI* lines.   The data strobe (DS*) and the data acknowledge (DK*) are the handshake signals for the transmission of data. The data acknowledge inverse (DI*) is used as the third line of the three-wire handshake for broadcast operations. For single-data transfers the "four-edge handshake" is used; for block-data transfers the "two-edge handshake" is used.

4.5.2 Hierarchical Protocol

The data transfer is achieved in the Futurebus following a hierarchical protocol, as shown in Figure 4.15. When the master acquires control of the system bus, it can generate one or

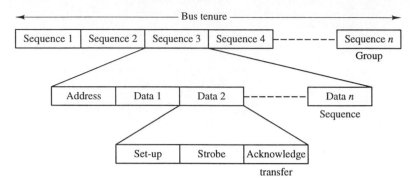

Figure 4.15 Futurebus hierarchical transaction protocol [10]. © 1984 IEEE.

more sequences that make up what is referred to as a *group*. A *sequence* begins with the issuing of an address followed by none or more data transfers (for read or write, to one or more slaves). Along with the address transfer, the signals placed on the five command lines $CM4^*$–$CM0^*$ indicate whether the entire sequence (1) is an unlocked transaction or a locked (indivisible) transaction in the sense that the interfaces of all other modules are locked out from bus access, (2) uses a *single-transfer mode* (a single item—from one to four bytes—is transferred in parallel) or block-transfer mode, (3) is intended for a single slave or multiple slaves (broadcast for writes, or broadcall for reads), or (4) uses standard or extended protocol.

4.5.3 Single-Data-Transfer Cycles

Figure 4.16 shows the simplified bus timing diagram for single-transfer (read and write) cycles on the Futurebus. The numbering shown with the little circles indicates the timing and cause–effect relationships among the rising and falling transitions of the various signals.

    Address cycle. Any cycle starts with the master issuing the address on the address bus along with the address transfer command on the CM^* lines that indicates read vs. write cycle, locked, and single, block, or broadcast transfer modes. The master also asserts the (optional) error valid EV^* line,[8] to indicate that lines ED^* and CP^* are valid; i.e., the master module interface has computed and placed four odd-parity bits, one for each address bus byte lane of the AD^* bus, on lines $ED3^*$–$ED0^*$, and one odd-parity bit on line CP^* that checks the five CM^* lines. (These parity bits *may* be checked by the slave module.) After a skew delay, the master asserts the AS^* to indicate a valid address on the address bus. The addressed slave responds by placing a status on lines $ST2^*$–$ST0^*$, and after a skew delay, the slave drives the address acknowledge line AK^*. As a response to the asserted AK^*, the master releases its AS^*, which will then cause the slave to release its acknowledge AK^* and, after a skew delay, stop driving the status lines. The release of AK^* by the slave signals the master the end of the address cycle transactions. The handshake pair used for the asynchronous address transfer is AS^*/AK^*.

    [8]If the EV^* line is asserted during the address transfer cycle, it indicates that the CP^* line is valid throughout the entire sequence.

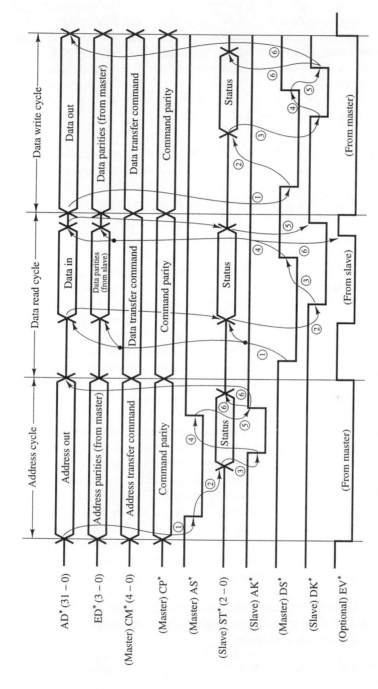

Figure 4.16 Futurebus address, data read, and data write bus cycles.

Data read cycle. The master again issues the command signals (CM4[*9] is asserted to indicate a read cycle) and its parity bit CP^* (if error checking is enabled), and after a skew delay asserts its data strobe DS^* to indicate a data cycle. The addressed slave responds by issuing status signals on lines $ST2^*$–$ST0^*$ and placing valid data on the AD^* bus. If the slave is to enable error checking, it will then compute the four odd-parity bits (one per data bus byte lane), place them on the $ED3^*$–$ED0^*$ lines, and assert line EV^*. The data transfer itself for a (from one- to four-byte) read occurs on the assertion by the slave of the DK^* signal. When data is latched, the master will release its DS^* signal, in response to which the slave will stop driving all AD^*, ED^*, ST^*, DK^*, and EV^* lines. The handshake pair used for the asynchronous data transfer is DS^*/DK^*.

Data write cycle. This cycle is similar to the address transfer cycle except that the information placed by the master on lines AD^* and CM^* is data and a data transfer command, respectively, and the handshake pair now used is DS^*/DK^*. The data transfer itself for a (from one- to four-byte) write occurs on the assertion by the master of the DS^* signal.

4.5.4 Block Transfers on the Futurebus

The block transfer mode (indicated by bit $CM2^*$ placed on the command lines when an address is placed on the AD^* bus) has the master send only one address to the slave followed by the transfer of a number of data items (to or from the slave.) The slave's interface designer must provide a mechanism to properly increment the address locally after each data transfer.

When bit $CM2^*$ is asserted, it also indicates that the more efficient two-edge handshake (instead of the more versatile four-edge handshake used in single transfers) will be in effect for the whole sequence. The *two-edge handshake* allows data transfer to be triggered with either transition of a handshake signal; every transition of AS^*/AK^* or DS^*/DK^* is significant for either strobing the data or providing an acknowledgment for it.[10] The *four-edge handshake* requires a return of each handshake signal to its original state per data transfer operation. Depending on the values on command lines $CM3^*$ and $CM1^*$, the transaction may be indivisible (or locked) as explained above, with a single slave or multiple slaves.

There is no need for the master to indicate the length of the block to be transferred (instead, the master indicates the end of the block transfer by sequencing the two-edge handshake lines DS^* and DK^* in a different time order than is used for the single-transfer mode). Thus, as in the case of the VMEbus discussed above, a block transfer may cross the boundaries of two or more memory boards. In the case of the Futurebus, this is handled by the "end-of-data" status ($ST2^*$–$ST0^*$ = 100) provided by the slaves' interface on the status lines. If a master detects this end-of-data, it drops the AS^*/AK^* lock, puts the next address on the AD^* address lines, and reasserts strobe AS^* to establish a connection with the next slave board.

Figure 4.17 shows the simplified timing diagram of the block-transfer handshake for eight write transfers. (The error detection $ED3^*$–$ED0^*$, the command $CM4^*$–$CM0^*$, and the status $ST2^*$–$ST0^*$ lines are not shown.)

---

[9]The CM4[*] read/write signal may be used directly to control the direction of the bus drivers for read and write transfers.

[10]In the *three-edge handshake* used in the broadcast mode to be discussed next, the AI^* transitions are also used along with the above two handshake signal pairs (as shown in Figure 4.18).

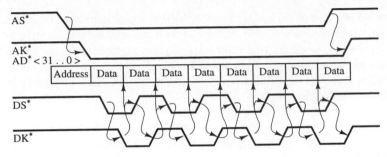

Figure 4.17 Futurebus simplified block transfer mode for eight write transfers [10]. © 1984 IEEE.

4.5.5 Broadcasting Mode

The Futurebus provides a broadcast mechanism that allows a master to write or send data to multiple slaves simultaneously (for example, to maintain cache consistency, to be discussed in the next chapter, or to broadcast an interrupt to multiple boards in a single sequence). The broadcast may also be used to read or receive data from multiple slaves simultaneously, in which case the received data is the logical OR of the data sent by the individual slaves (for example, to perform a fast poll of several boards at a time). Finally, broadcasting may be enabled simultaneously with block-transfer mode.

When the master signals the use of the broadcasting mode, the handshake protocol switches from the two-wire to the three-wire handshake. In the *three-wire handshake protocol*, in addition to the pair AS*/AK* the signal AI* is also used (when an address is transferred), and in addition to the pair DS*/DK* the signal DI* is also used (when data is transferred). The slave responds by asserting the address (AK*) or data (DK*) acknowledge signal, depending on whether an address or data transfer cycle is executed. The address (AI*) or data (DI*) inverse acknowledge line forms the third wire of the broadcast protocol, and it is released by the slave.

Consider Figure 4.18, which depicts the broadcast protocol. The master issues the address and then the address strobe to indicate a valid address [11]. All other bus modules

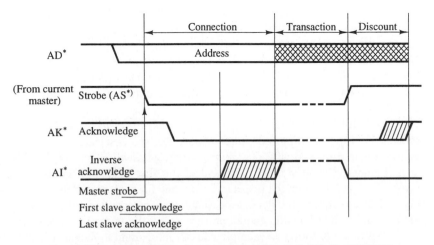

Figure 4.18 Three-wire broadcast handshake (Futurebus) [10]. © 1984 IEEE.

(including the master) assert the acknowledge signal immediately, but each releases AI* and allows it to rise only after it is finished with the address and is ready to go on. The master does not care when the first slave responds and continues to drive the address lines until the last slave is ready to go. To detect acknowledgment of the slowest slave the master watches a rising edge on the AI* signal. Only when AI* has risen may the bus master remove the address from the bus.

4.6 MAD-ENDIAN AND SAD-ENDIAN SYSTEM BUSES AND INTERFACING

Microprocessor system designers and users should be aware of the two types of system buses used in configuring microprocessor-based systems, mad-endian and sad-endian buses, which characterize the relative order of placing addresses and data on the bus. In this section we explain the operation of these system buses and present examples of interfacing to them both big-endian and little-endian processors.

4.6.1 Definitions

Similar to processors that are classified as big-endian and little-endian processors (depending on which end of an internal register they place the byte coming from the lowest memory address), system buses are also distinguished into two classes: mad-endian and sad-endian buses, according to the way data bytes are multiplexed with addresses (in space or time) on the bus [12]. To simplify the interconnection and minimize interface costs, big-endian processors (for example, the Motorola chips) are attached to mad-endian system buses (such as the VMEbus), while little-endian processors (such as the Intel chips) are attached to sad-endian system buses (such as the ATbus, the Multibus II, and the NuBus). However, both big- and little-endian processors should be able to connect to either type of system bus as is the case with the Futurebus, SCI (Scalable Coherent Interface), and Serialbus.

Mad-endian bus (also called a **Type-2** bus) refers to a bus for which, when data is transferred on its multiplexed address/data lines, the first data byte (which has the lowest address) is multiplexed with the *most significant byte* of the address. Big-endian storage ordering formats simplify the interpretation of memory dumps. Also, for high-performance serialized system buses (for which the most significant part of the address is transmitted first to reduce routing delays), data bytes are transmitted to increasing data-byte addresses. For serially transmitted data, the use of mad-endian ordering when assigning byte significance provides consistency at the interface circuitry for demultiplexing address and data bytes.

Sad-endian bus (also called a **Type-1** bus) refers to a bus for which, when data is transferred on its multiplexed address/data lines, the first data byte (which has the lowest address) is multiplexed with the (*small*) *least significant byte* of the address.

Figure 4.19a shows the placement of the first byte, i.e., contents of location 4N—symbolized as (4N)—on the respective byte lane for each one of the two types of buses. For big-endian processors, the byte at location 4N is interpreted as the most significant byte of the operand, while for little-endian processors, as the least significant byte.

Figure 4.19b shows an example of a 32-bit operand in memory starting at location 4N (doubleword alignment) transferred over 32-bit mad-endian and 32-bit sad-endian buses. No-

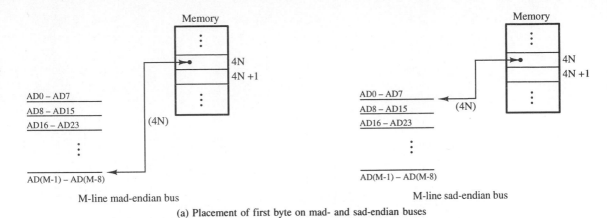

(a) Placement of first byte on mad- and sad-endian buses

Figure 4.19   Data transfers over mad- and sad-endian multiplexed buses (a functional description).

tice that in the case of a mad-endian bus, the content of location 4N is transferred over byte lane AD24–AD31, while in the case of a sad-endian bus, the content of location 4N is transferred over byte lane AD0–AD7. In either case, the 32-bit operand should be properly placed into the internal 32-bit register of the processor so that its least significant byte is positioned at the least significant position of the register.

Figure 4.19b also shows the notation used by the 32-bit version of the Futurebus, where its spatial byte lanes are denoted as W, X, Y, Z, the letter Z indicating the byte containing bit zero. The byte orientation (big-endian or little-endian) is not constrained. (The byte significance within a *quadlet*—a data object of 4 bytes—is beyond the scope of the bus specification and is left up to the implementer.)

The printed-circuit board traces and bus transceivers specify mad- or sad-endian ordering [in Figure 4.19b this is shown by placing (4N) next to the appropriate PC-board traces for the data].

4.6.2 Interfacing Processors to Mad- and Sad-Endian System Buses

Matched types of processors and system buses.   Processors and system buses are matched when either a big-endian processor is connected to a mad-endian system bus or a little-endian processor is connected to a sad-endian system bus. Figure 4.20a depicts an interconnection that represents the case of connecting 32-bit demultiplexed and multiplexed big-endian processor boards to a 32-bit memory board through a mad-endian system bus and performing an aligned read operation from location 4N. Because of the mad-endian system bus, the content of the first location 4N is transferred over the *most* significant address/data bus lines AD24–AD31 (or W in Futurebus notation). Since in this figure big-endian processors communicate with memory, the content of location 4N will be interpreted as the *most* significant byte of the operand, expected by the microprocessor to appear at its 8 most significant data bus pins. The diagram illustrates one demultiplexed CPU executing an aligned 32-bit doubleword read operation from the doubleword address 4N, and a multiplexed CPU executing an aligned 16-bit word read from the same location 4N. (Here we assume that when the processor fetches a word operand it places it in the rightmost position of an internal 32-bit register.)

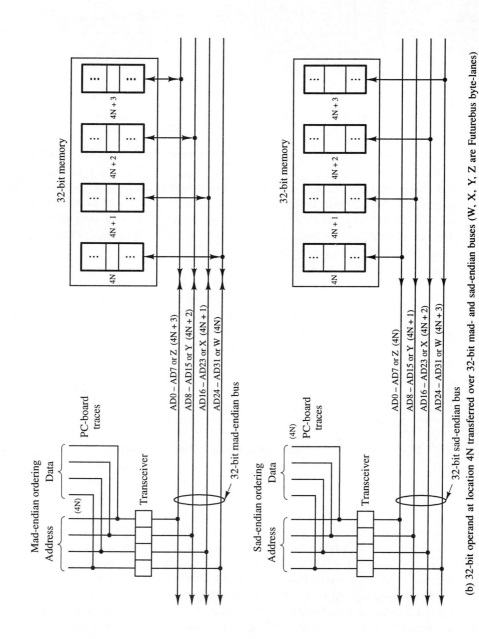

(b) 32-bit operand at location 4N transferred over 32-bit mad- and sad-endian buses (W, X, Y, Z are Futurebus byte-lanes)

Figure 4.19 (concluded)

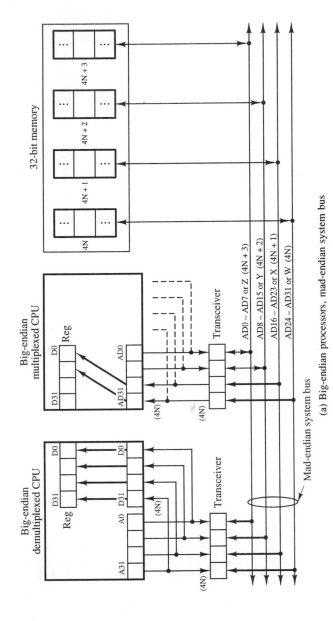

Figure 4.20 Matched processors and system buses for reading 32-bit and 16-bit aligned operands from location 4N.

(a) Big-endian processors and system buses, mad-endian system bus

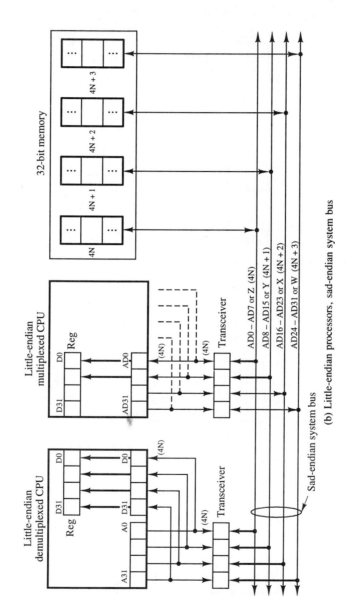

Figure 4.20 (concluded)

(b) Little-endian processors, sad-endian system bus

We already know that dynamically configurable microprocessor chips can be inter-connected to ports of different sizes. As we saw in previous chapters, when the 32-bit Intel 80386 is connected to a 16-bit slave port, their data exchange is done over the least significant half (D0–D15) of the data bus; on the other hand, when the 32-bit Motorola 68020/30 is connected to a 16-bit slave port, their data exchange is done over the most significant half (D16–D31) of the data bus. (In either case, firmware will control an internal multiplexer[11] to route the two incoming bytes off the data bus pins to the proper positions in internal registers.)

Figure 4.20b depicts an interconnection that represents the case of a little-endian processors connected to a sad-endian system bus. Because of the sad-endian system bus, the content of the first location 4N is transferred over the *least* significant address/data bus lines AD0–AD7 (or Z in Futurebus notation). Since in this figure little-endian processors communicate with memory, the content of location 4N will be interpreted as the *least* significant byte of the operand, expected by the microprocessor to appear at its 8 least significant data bus pins. Again, both demultiplexed and multiplexed CPUs are shown aligned doubleword and word data reads.

Unmatched types of processors and system buses. Processors and system buses are not matched when either a big-endian processor is connected to a sad-endian system bus[12] [13], or a little-endian processor is connected to a mad-endian system bus. In such mismatched cases, additional external byte-switching logic is required.[13]

Figure 4.21a depicts an interconnection that represents the case of big-endian processors connected to a sad-endian system bus. Both demultiplexed and multiplexed 32-bit processors are connected to the bus; the content of the first location 4N is transferred over the *least* significant address/data bus lines AD0–AD7 (or Z in Futurebus notation). Since in this example big-endian processors communicate with memory, the content of location 4N represents the *most* significant byte of the operand. The diagram illustrates one demultiplexed CPU executing an aligned 32-bit doubleword read operation from the doubleword address 4N, and a multiplexed CPU executing an aligned 16-bit word read from the same location 4N. It is noticed that since the big-endian CPU expects the content of 4N to be supplied to its 8 most significant data bus pins and this byte is transferred over the least significant byte lane of the sad-endian system bus, external byte-switching logic is required to place the bytes at the correct input data pins of the microprocessor. (As in previous diagrams, we assume that a word read from memory is routed to the rightmost position of an internal 32-bit register.)

Figure 4.21b depicts an interconnection that represents the case of little-endian processors connected to a mad-endian system bus. Both demultiplexed and multiplexed 32-bit processors are connected to the bus; the content of the first location, 4N, is transferred over the *most* significant address/data bus lines AD24–AD31 (or W in Futurebus notation). Since in this figure little-endian processors communicate with memory, the content of location 4N represents the *least* significant byte of the operand. The diagram illustrates one demultiplexed CPU executing an aligned 32-bit doubleword read operation from the

[11]This internal multiplexer is also used to support misaligned data transfers.

[12]Apple's Macintosh II is such an example implementation in which a big-endian processor (Motorola 68020) is attached to a sad-endian system bus (Nubus).

[13]This, however, may fail in the case of misaligned 32-bit doubleword accesses or for processors with an on-chip cache which isolates the bus interface hardware from the processor's knowledge of the data size.

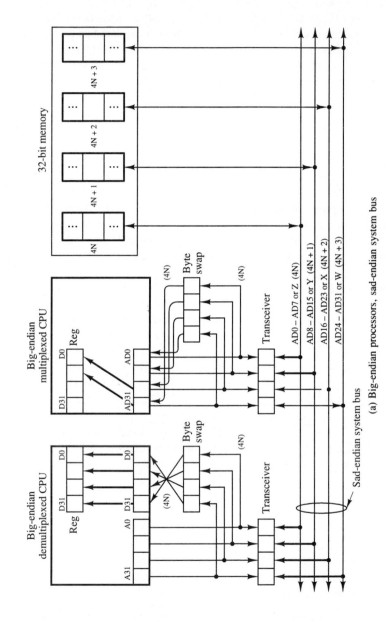

Figure 4.21 Unmatched processors and system buses require external byte-switching logic.

(a) Big-endian processors, sad-endian system bus

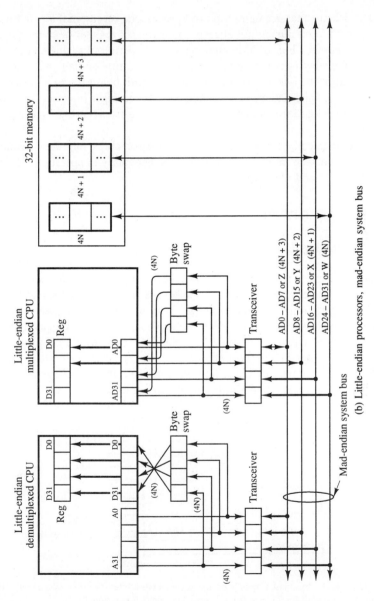

Figure 4.21 (concluded)

(b) Little-endian processors, mad-endian system bus

doubleword address 4N, and a multiplexed CPU executing an aligned 16-bit word read from the same location 4N. Since the little-endian CPU expects the content of 4N to be supplied to its 8 least significant data bus pins and this byte is transferred over the most significant byte lane of the mad-endian system bus, external byte-switching logic is again required.

For designs that use demultiplexed processors, an internal single bit called *byte-order switch* (which is set during initialization in a control register or in the page table and specifies the processor's big- or little-endian mode of operation) is sufficient to support any combination of mad/sad-endian system buses and big/little-endian processors. The hardwired specification of the bus ordering (the printed-circuit board traces and system bus transceivers specify the mad-endian or sad-endian bus ordering), however, necessitates additional byte-switching logic to support *dynamic switching* between big- and little-endian processing options.

As dynamically configurable microprocessor chips migrate to multiplexed address/data buses, two such internal bits will now be necessary to specify the four design environments (big/little and mad/sad).

4.7 SYSTEM BUS ARBITRATION

4.7.1 Arbitration Lines

Although multiple bus masters can share the local processor bus, a more general and flexible design is the one that allows master boards to share the global system bus in a multimaster configuration (see, for example, Figure 1.3c). Each master board now has the general configuration shown in Figure 1.3a. The bus masters request bus control through a "bus arbitration sequence."[14] When a "parallel" bus arbitration priority resolution technique (to be discussed below) is implemented, the bus arbiter interface circuit must be used. Before the details of the bus arbitration are examined, the bus arbiter signals in the IEEE 796 (Multibus) system bus (shown in Figure 4.22) are explained.

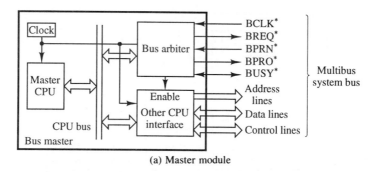

(a) Master module

Figure 4.22 Bus master module equipped with a bus arbiter (Multibus system bus) [16]. Reprinted by permission of Intel Corporation, Copyright/Intel Corporation 1979).

Bus clock (BCLK#). The bus clock is a periodic clock signal used to synchronize the bus arbitration logic; it may be slowed, stopped, or single-stepped. Each bus master must

[14]Quite often, it is referred to as a "bus exchange sequence."

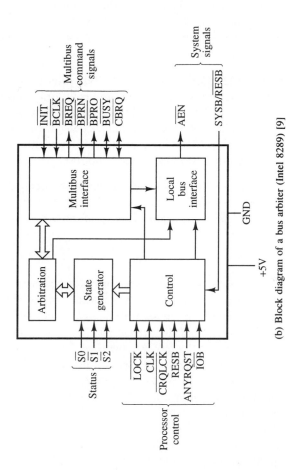

Figure 4.22 (concluded)

(b) Block diagram of a bus arbiter (Intel 8289) [9]

233

have the capability of generating an acceptable clock that optionally can be connected to, or disconnected from, the system bus. In a multimaster system, only one of the masters must have its clock connected to the bus.

Bus request (BREQ#). When a master requests system bus control, it asserts the BREQ# line. This line is used with the parallel priority resolution scheme through the bus arbiter. The highest-priority request enables the BPRN# input of that master, thus allowing it to gain control of the bus.

Bus priority in (BPRN#). The "bus priority in" signal and the next output signal BPRO# are "nonbused" signals. The BPRN# input indicates to a master that no master of higher priority is requesting control of the bus. This signal is daisy-chained when serial priority arbitration is used; when parallel priority arbitration is used, the BPRN# is generated from an external "priority resolving circuit."

Bus priority out (BPRO#). When the "bus priority out"—also a "nonbused" signal—is activated by a bus master, it indicates to the bus master of the next lower priority that it may gain control of the bus (i.e., no higher-priority requests are pending for control of the bus). Like the BPRN#, the BPRO# is daisy-chained when serial priority arbitration is used; BPRO# is fed to the BPRN# input of the next-lower-priority master. When parallel priority arbitration is used, the BPRO# signal is not used.

Bus busy (BUSY#). The "bus busy" signal is a bidirectional signal asserted by the master in control of the bus. All other masters monitor BUSY# to determine the state of the bus, i.e., whether or not they may acquire control of the bus.

4.7.2 Bus Arbitration

To initiate a system bus cycle, the master processor issues appropriate status and/or control signals, irrespective of bus arbiter presence. The master's bus arbiter and the box labeled in Figure 4.22a "other CPU interface" monitor these lines to detect a bus cycle request. If the bus arbiter does not have control of the system bus (i.e., it is not driving BUSY# low), it will issue a control signal to the "other CPU interface" to force all bus-driven outputs into the high-impedance state. Thus, the bus master is "disconnected" from the system bus and the processor enters into wait states. When the bus arbiter acquired access to the system bus, it enables all bus drivers, thus allowing the bus master to access the system bus and the master processor to complete its transfer cycle. At the same time, the bus arbiter asserts BUSY# to other bus masters.

Multiple masters connected via the system bus require priority resolution when the bus is requested simultaneously by more than one master, so that the master with higher priority will take control of the system bus. The synchronization of master requests and the arbitration function are integrated into the bus arbiter. Two bus arbitration priority resolution techniques are used, serial and parallel. Since they are compatible, the two schemes can be combined and used together on the same bus.

Serial arbitration. In this scheme, all master requestors are arranged in a configuration of daisy-chaining their bus arbiters, as shown in Figure 4.23. The bus request lines BREQ# are not used in this configuration. The technique is analogous to the daisy chain

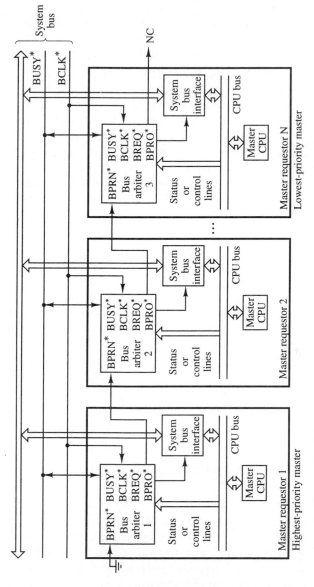

Figure 4.23 Daisy chain or serial system bus arbitration priority resolution technique [16,17]. Reprinted by permission of Intel Corporation, Copyright/Intel Corporation, 1979. (*Note*: BREQ* is not used.)

priority resolution technique discussed in Section 2.7.2 for DMA requestors; here, however, a bus arbiter is included and BPRN# is the master's input from the priority chain. The BPRO# output signal of each master's bus arbiter is connected to the BPRN# input of the next-lower-priority master's bus arbiter. The BPRN# of the highest-priority master in the daisy chain will always be active (grounded), signifying to the other bus arbiters that it always has highest priority when requesting the bus.

Serial priority resolution is accomplished as follows: all masters monitor BUSY# to determine the state of the bus. When a master requests control of the bus (when no other master has control of the bus), it sets its BPRO# high. This signal in turn disables the BPRN# of all lower-priority masters. The BPRO# output for a particular master is asserted if and only if its BPRN# input is active and that master is not requesting control of the bus. The BUSY# line, which indicates an idle or "not busy" status of the system bus, is common to all bus masters. Through this line, a higher-priority master will wait until the current bus master has completed any bus cycles already in progress. Upon completing its transfer cycle, the master in control of the bus determines that it no longer has priority, and surrenders the bus, releasing BUSY#.

The major drawback of this technique is that it can accommodate only a limited number of masters, because of gate delays through the daisy chain. When a parallel priority structure is to be used, the BREQ# of the highest-priority master in the chain should be connected to a priority resolving circuit, which is described next.

Parallel arbitration.   In this scheme, the BPRO# lines are not utilized. An external "parallel priority resolving circuit" is used to resolve the priorities of the bus requests BREQ# from each master (Figure 4.24). Each BREQ# line enters the priority encoder of this external circuit, which generates, as output, the binary address of the highest-priority BREQ# line asserted at its inputs. This address, after being decoded inside the priority resolving circuit, selects the corresponding bus-priority-in line (BPRN#) to be returned to the highest-priority requesting bus master. The bus arbiter receiving this BPRN# signal then allows its associated bus master to access the system bus as soon as the bus becomes available. Thus, the highest-priority request enables the BPRN# input of that master, allowing it to gain control of the bus. The BUSY# line functions in the same way as it does for the serial technique.

4.8 TRADE-OFFS IN SELECTING THE SYSTEM BUS

Selecting the most appropriate system bus is a very important issue. Since there is no "universally best" system bus, the system designer/integrator will have to analyze very carefully the needs and requirements of the type of applications the new product will be used for. Blindly choosing the fastest one, with the widest address and data buses, that can support a number of master boards may be more than is really needed for the application(s). A number of important bus features and characteristics need to be traded-off and evaluated comparatively before reaching a decision.

Given below are some of the most important functional features that characterize a system bus and can be used for its evaluation and comparison with other buses. For the most important system buses their similarities and differences are also given.

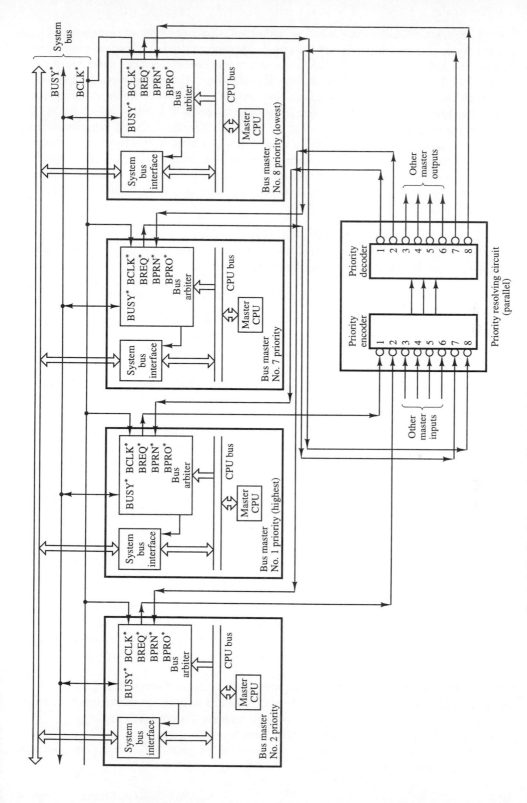

Figure 4.24 Parallel system bus arbitration priority resolution technique [16,17]. Reprinted by permission of Intel Corporation, Copyright/Intel Corporation 1979. (*Note:* BPRO* is not used.)

1. *Synchronous/asynchronous:* The definition and operation of synchronous and asynchronous buses were covered in Chapter 2. Synchronous industry system buses are the NuBus, the Multibus II, and the EISA. Asynchronous industry system buses are the Futurebus, the Fastbus, the VMEbus, and the MicroChannel. For synchronous system buses, for which the final system configuration may not be reached until future expansions are made, the system clock period must be slow enough to cope with a fully loaded system (and with communicating boards positioned at the two ends of the backplane). When evaluating one against the other you should keep in mind that a synchronous bus runs at the speed of the slowest module *attached* to the system, while an asynchronous bus runs at the speed of the slowest module *participating* in bus operations. An asynchronous bus protocol allows the master and slave boards to impose their own timing constraints on the transfer of data over the system bus.

2. *Multiplexed/nonmultiplexed:* Multiplexed system buses are the Futurebus, the Fastbus, the NuBus, and the Multibus II. Nonmultiplexed system buses (which make address pipelining possible) are the VMEbus, the MicroChannel, and the EISA.

3. *Protocols supported:* Refers to the types of transactions supported by the bus.

  a. *Broadcast:* This mode refers to the ability of a master board sending (writing) data to multiple slave boards. The broadcast mechanism is very useful for caches to support the "write-through" scheme fully, a scheme that maintains cache consistency (described in Chapter 5). Both NuBus and Multibus II lack the capability to make broadcast transfers. Futurebus supports the broadcasting mechanism (using the three-wire handshake for communication with multiple slaves, as explained earlier).

  b. *Broadcall:* This mode refers to the ability of a master board executing a read operation which performs a bitwise logical-OR on the data originating from all addressed slave boards. It is supported by Futurebus and Fastbus, but not by VMEbus, Multibus II, or NuBus.

  c. *Message passing:* This corresponds to allowing local-area-network-type transactions over the system bus. It uses write-only block transfers (mainly for sequential blocks) rather than random single transfers over the bus. It is supported by the Futurebus and the Multibus II. It is not supported by VMEbus and NuBus. The Futurebus has built-in hooks at the "link-level protocol" of message passing.

4. *Bus bandwidth:* Bandwidth (measured in megabytes per second) is a useful metric for computer buses. However, companies usually give the raw speed or maximum theoretical data transfer in a peak burst (or under other unrealistic conditions) and, therefore, it is not very useful in practice. Instead, what is of interest is the actual bus bandwidth the actual constructed system provides.

Using a faster system bus does not necessarily mean that the system performance is increased. Architectural means may be needed to utilize fully the available bus bandwidth. As Borrill suggests [1,3], there are two ways to increase system performance:
  a. By reducing the amount of bus traffic each board generates:
    (1) Place cache memories (a transparent to the programmer scheme) between each processor and the bus, or

(2) Use local memories (not a programmer-transparent scheme) located at each board or accessible through some kind of local extension bus.
  b. By reducing the "effective" bus access time:
    (1) Use blocks to communicate across the bus, done by either
       (a) using cache memories, or
       (b) restricting the system to message passing architectures.
    (2) Use static column address or nibble-mode access DRAMs on the memory boards.

5. *Data bus width:* Has to do with the width of a data transferred in parallel over the system bus. The data widths supported by some system buses are as follows: Multibus I (16 bits); Multibus II (16, 32 bits); Futurebus (32, 64, 128, 256 bits); Fastbus (32 bits); VMEbus (16, 32 bits); NuBus (32 bits); MicroChannel (8, 16, 32 bits); EISA (8, 16, 32 bits).

6. *Address bus:* This refers to the maximum width of address that can be placed on the address bus. How the various parts of the address are treated depends on the design. For example, the most significant address bits may be decoded to determine which of several memory boards is to respond, while the least significant bits may identify which memory byte sections within the selected board are to be activated for this transaction. In other cases (such as the "address modifier" of the VMEbus discussed earlier), additional bits may be used to distinguish among a number of different addressing spaces—such as user or supervisor, and code or data—or specify the width of the address issued.

The total number of address lines often limits the amount of memory that can be installed in a system. For example, the Multibus I uses a 24-bit address, while most of the rest of the system buses use 32-bit addresses, although smaller addresses may be used as well.

7. *Addressing:* This refers to the type of addressing supported by the bus. Different types of addressing include:

  a. *Geographical addressing:* The ability to select a slave module at a particular physical position on a bus segment or slot (i.e., by supplying the initial arbitration ID). A portion of the board's physical address space is tied to the slot where that board is physically located. This method allows each module in a computer system to identify itself uniquely by its position along the backplane when the system is powered up. The Futurebus and Fastbus support it with a 5-bit slot ID, the Multibus II uses a T-pin technique with power-up initialization, while the VMEbus does not support it.

  b. *Logical addressing:* This mode specifies a memory location (out of the total of global locations) without explicit regard to its physical position in the system. Each device has a set of logical addresses allocated to it, and if the received address matches one, then the device becomes the responder.

  c. *Broadcast addressing:* As mentioned earlier, this is the ability to select multiple responders.

8. *Data justification:* This refers to the bus specification, imposing that individual data bytes be shifted artificially to either end of the data bus. In this case, boards connected to the bus would require additional byte-switching logic (e.g., byte multiplexers). For example, a 32-bit system data bus, which specifies that 16-bit word transfers always be across the lower half of the data bus, is referred to as having "16-bit justification" or being "16-bit optimized." Buses whose specifications enforce data justification increase the cost and complexity of their interfaces (which now need ''byte-switching'' hardware), and the delay through these interface components. A justified bus is not flexible enough to work well with all system architectures. Data justification is as follows for system buses:

    a. *Multibus:* Has 8-bit low-end justification; i.e., an individual byte always transfers on D0–D7. For Multibus II, a 16-bit word always transfers on D0–D15. The bus allows mixing 8- and 16-bit devices.

    b. *VMEbus:* It also has low-end justification similar to Multibus. (32-bit doublewords must have doubleword addresses, contrary to the Motorola 68000, which allows doublewords to have any even address.) Since the 32-bit VME32 does not provide individual strobes for all four byte lanes, it is impossible to make 24-bit transfers (needed to handle 32-bit misaligned transfers).

    c. *NuBus and Futurebus:* Support nonjustified data transfers; an individual byte can be transferred on any byte lane of the data bus. For example, the Futurebus has separate command lines to indicate which byte lane participates in the current data transfer. In addition to reducing the cost and complexity of bus interfaces, this increases the bus throughput (due to the decrease in the delay through the interface components). Memory boards that have a 32-bit memory organization do not have to have byte-switching interface logic. When it comes to processor boards, then, it depends on the type of microprocessor used: if a 32-bit microprocessor is used, byte-switching interface logic may not be needed; if a 16-bit or an 8-bit processor board is used, it will require byte-switching logic if it must be able to access all bytes within the quadlet.

    9. *Distance:* Refers to the distance between the components that must be connected by a bus. For example, some instrumentation buses can connect measurement equipment within a rack, while others allow distances that are hundreds of feet apart.

    10. *Multilevel device hierarchy:* Multibus I includes two inhibit lines (INH1#, INH2#) that allow devices to be arranged in a 2-level hierarchy. These signals are used to prevent memory slaves from responding to the address on the address bus. An inhibit signal is generated by the inhibiting slave (identified by decoding the memory address lines) to inhibit a lower-level slave's bus activity. An auxiliary or ''bootstrap'' ROM device is considered a top-level slave and may assert these inhibit signals to inhibit the activity of lower-level devices. These two inhibit signals may also be used to allow memory-mapped I/O devices to override RAM and ROM devices. In the case of the VMEbus, each processor's interface places an identifying code in the 6 ''address modifier'' lines; all slave modules examine these lines and respond only to the codes assigned to them.

    11. *Alignment:* Since most of the 32-bit microprocessors support misaligned data transfers (misaligned operations are carried out with two memory references), a number of 32-bit system buses fully support 32/16-bit misaligned operations in which a misaligned quadlet (32 bits) is transferred in two bus cycles. Multibus II, Futurebus, and the latest version of VMEbus fully support 32/16-bit nonaligned operations. Nubus and Fastbus do not.

    12. *Interrupt support:* This has to do with the type and number of interrupt-request lines supported. For example, the Multibus I supports both vectored and nonvectored interrupts, and has 8 interrupt request lines and one interrupt-acknowledge line. Neither Multibus II nor Futurebus have interrupt lines. (In multiprocessor configurations it is difficult for an I/O board to direct its interrupt request to a specific CPU.) In more advanced cases, a normal memory write cycle is used for a board to direct its "interrupt" (or "I want attention") signal to another board.

13. *DMA support:* On these industry system buses a controller board can arbitrate for the bus, act as a bus master, and do DMA directly with memory, with no intervention by the main processor board.

14. *Multimaster capabilities:* This means that any board may gain mastership of the bus via proper bus arbitration mechanisms. Such a capability is useful to allow I/O boards to perform true DMA for accessing main memory independent of the central processor.

15. *Multiprocessing support:* The requirements for supporting efficient multiprocessing include (1) a decentralized interrupt system that lets any board interrupt any other board; (2) a particularly efficient, decentralized, fair arbitration method; (3) for shared memory configurations, a locking mechanism for semaphore operations; (4) a broadcast mechanism which allows implementing a replicated global memory and speeds up the access to shared data; and (5) provisions for supporting multiple boards with caches. There exist different types of multiprocessing configurations [13]:

    a. *Centralized multiprocessing:* One processor runs the kernel and treats the others as slaves; it also has access to the local memory spaces of the slave processors (master-slave mode).

    b. *Autonomous multiprocessors:* The processors do not share a common address space but communicate by messages.

    c. *Federalist multiprocessing:* All processors own a copy of the kernel and communicate over a shared memory; they also have their own private memory.

Implementations adopted by representative industry system buses are as follows: the Multibus I and the VMEbus use arbitration schemes that involve daisy-chained signals. They support 16-bit centralized multiprocessor schemes. (They do not support true multiprocessor architecture very well.) The Multibus II allows a federalist multiprocessor operation, but supports primarily a 16-bit autonomous multiprocessor with central service board. The VMEbus does not support federalistic multiprocessing very well.

16. *Speed of bus arbitration:* This has to do with whether arbitration can be overlapped with the previous data transfer to increase effective bus speed. Providing intelligence on the boards connected to the system bus reduces bus bottlenecks. For example, in the MicroChannel case, a central arbiter device located on the motherboard coordinates bus access. In the EISA, boards compete for bus mastership via a three-way rotating arbitration scheme. A special watchdog timer makes sure that no one entity retains control of the bus for too long. The Futurebus, Multibus II, NuBus, and Fastbus all support distributed arbitration, while the VMEbus supports a 4-level daisy chain arbitration.

17. *Autoconfiguration capabilities:* This refers to a mechanism and a protocol that allows software to configure system parameters automatically. The system polls the boards connected to the system bus to determine which slots are occupied, identifies the boards (by reading a ROM present on each to learn what resources it carries and its configuration), and adjusts the software interface accordingly. Geographical addressing must be in place to achieve this. On the MicroChannel it is possible because of the POS (programmable option select) registers, which are addressed on the slot basis. It is fully supported at any time by the Futurebus, Nubus, and Fastbus, the Multibus II at power-up time only, and not supported by the VMEbus [1,3]. On the Futurebus, Multibus II, and NuBus, the equivalent to POS is called "geographical addressing": a portion of a board's physical address space is tied to the slot where that board is physically located. EISA bus also supports automatic system configuration.

18. *Bus endianess:* The VMEbus has a big-endian byte orientation, and is called a "mad-endian bus." The Multibus II and Nubus have little-endian byte orientation, and are called "sad-endian buses." The Futurebus is not constrained to either orientation.

19. *Parity bits:* Some system buses provide additional parity bits to check the validity of the information transfers. VME has no parity provisions at all. The Multibus II and Futurebus have 1 parity bit per address/data bus byte lane, while the NuBus and Fastbus have 1 bit for all address/data lines. (The Futurebus also has an additional parity bit for its "command lines.") Parity is mandatory for the Multibus II and optional for all other standard buses. (For example, the Futurebus includes a line called "error valid" EV^* which the transmitter asserts to inform the receiver that the error detection mechanism is active.) Such error detection also requires a mechanism for telling the sender that its data was not received correctly and, therefore, they need to be retransmitted. (For example, the Futurebus has the slave send back status signals $ST2 - ST0 = 110$ to the master, indicating parity error.)

20. *Cache coherence:* Cache coherence is discussed in Chapter 5. The Futurebus has a number of lines and rules that must be obeyed by all Futurebus caches [11]. A signal CA^* issued by a master identifies itself as a cache; there is a signal called EC^* (extended command) to invalidate entries in other caches; there is a CH^* (cache hit) signal issued by a cache to indicate a hit (during cache snooping); finally, a DI^* signal can be used to disable the shared memory resource and instead allow a cache to respond.

21. *Monitor/snoop:* The asynchronous VME and Futurebus allow monitoring of the address transfers, while the Fastbus has a wait line to slow handshake for inspection. The synchronous buses Multibus II and NuBus are clocked easily for using a logic analyzer.

22. *Provision for future expansion:* System buses provide reserved lines to allow for future expansion. VMEbus provides 1 reserved line, Multibus II provides 2, and Fastbus provides 5. Futurebus has an extended command mode built-in protocol to ensure compatibility; the bus can be logically extended as well as performance-extended in the future. It provides on its connector "reserved for future" pins.

23. *Converting a local bus to a system bus:* For synchronous system buses, some synchronization circuitry may also be used to synchronize the processor's local clock and the system bus clock in order to transfer the data[15] [1,3]. Usually, the design requires a much better match between the microprocessor chip and its local resources on the same processor board. (This is even more so when caches are placed locally between the microprocessor chip and the system bus, with the effect that only a very small percentage of time the processor makes use of the system bus.) With the updating of the system with a new and faster

---

[15]This is the "clock-latency problem" which on the average will effectively add a half-system-bus-cycle penalty to every transfer on the system bus. Asynchronous buses, of course, do not suffer this "clock-latency problem."

microprocessor chip, the disparity between the processor's clock and that of the system bus would increase.

24. *Cost-effectiveness:* Buses are also compared on their relative cost-effectiveness. That means that the number of active signal lines must be taken into consideration, since they directly affect the bus interface cost-effectiveness. Related to this concern is how much it costs you if you do not make use of all the advanced features of a system bus for your particular design. For cheaper implementations, for example based on 16-bit microprocessor boards, the VMEbus presents definite advantages, while the Futurebus and Nubus become less cost-effective since one must always implement the full 32-bit-wide bus. On the other hand, such a VME-based implementation would definitely raise some compatibility issues with 32-bit-based systems.

25. *Live insertion/withdrawal:* This refers to the ability of add (plug-in) or remove boards while the system is running, and the board newly live-inserted into the bus, establishing synchronism with the other boards already working. This feature is very useful for building fault-tolerant and nonstop systems. Futurebus is the only bus that provides this capability.

26. *Block transfer:* This refers to a multibyte block transfers to RAM, which requires one address cycle followed by a number of data cycles (either read or write cycles). Usually, the address is incremented (on the addressed slave board), data transfer acknowledge signals are still present for each cycle, and cycle-by-cycle error recovery is still possible. The advantage of this scheme is that transaction overhead is amortized across multiple bus transfers. It is useful for interprocessor communications, for cache block exchanges, and for virtual memory paging. Block transfers on the Futurebus were discussed in Section 4.5.4. The VMEbus has the sequential access mode described in Section 4.4.4 ("multiplexed block transfer" or MBLT) and a newer "source synchronous block transfer" (SSBLT) [15].

EXERCISES

4.1. Both the Multibus I system bus and the Motorola 68000 local bus are asynchronous, 16-bit buses. Explain how to take care of any possible problems when a 68000-based processor board is connected to the Multibus I system bus.

4.2. Consider a read operation from an 8-bit memory board. In the first case, the slave board is connected to an 8086-based master board, while in the second case it is connected to a 68000-based master board. In both cases the interconnecting system bus is the IEEE 796. Are there any differences in the data transfers in the above two configurations? Explain.

4.3. Draw all possible bus timing diagrams (showing the most pertinent control signals) for the word write and a byte write cycle for the Multibus I and the Motorola 68000 buses.

4.4. Consider the doubleword operand ABCDEFGH (where AB is its most significant byte) stored at location 4N of a 32-bit memory. Assume that a 32-bit little-endian demultiplexed microprocessor is connected to this memory via a mad-endian system bus with no data justification. Explain how the operand is transferred to the microprocessor for a read cycle.

4.5. Repeat Exercise 4.4 for the same operand now located at $4N + 2$ and the mad-endian bus having low-end justification.

4.6. Consider the word operand ABCD (where AB is its most significant byte) stored at location 4N + 2 of a 32-bit memory. Assume that a 32-bit little-endian demultiplexed microprocessor is connected to this memory via a mad-endian system bus with low-end data justification. Explain how the operand is transferred to the microprocessor for a read cycle.

4.7. Repeat Exercise 4.6 with the operand located at 4N + 1 in a:
(a) 16-bit memory
(b) 8-bit memory

4.8. Illustrate the four mappings (mad-/sad-endian system buses and big-/little-endian microprocessors) for a 2-byte read from location 8N of a 64-bit memory on a 64-bit multiplexed address/data system bus (the 32-bit address is multiplexed with the lower 32 data bus lines D0–D31). (Assume that the system bus imposes no data justification and that the microprocessor internal registers are 64 bits wide.)

4.9. Repeat Exercise 4.8 for a 4-byte operand from location 8N + 4 and assuming that the internal microprocessor registers are 32 bits wide.

4.10. Assume that two 8-bit and one 16-bit microprocessors are to be interfaced to a system bus. Furthermore, the following details are given:
1. All microprocessors have the hardware features necessary for any type of data transfer: programmed I/O, interrupt-driven I/O, and DMA I/O.
2. All microprocessors have a 16-bit address bus.
3. Two memory boards each of 64 Kbytes capacity are interfaced with the bus. The designer wishes to use a shared memory which is as large as possible.
4. The system bus supports a maximum of 4 interrupt lines and one DMA line.

Make any other assumptions necessary and:
(a) Give the system bus specifications in terms of number and types of lines.
(b) Describe a possible protocol for communicating on the bus, i.e., read/write, interrupt, and DMA sequences.
(c) Explain how the above devices are interfaced to the system bus.

4.11. Consider a 2-way interleaved SRAM memory board connected to an 8-bit microprocessor through the IEEE 796 system bus. Assume that the program counter contains the address 123F. Draw the system bus timing diagram to fetch the three-byte instruction CALL ABCD, showing the most pertinent control signals and the actual hexadecimal values of the information placed on the system address and system data bus lines.

REFERENCES

[1] Borrill, P. L., "High-Speed 32-bit Buses for Forward-Looking Computers," *IEEE Spectrum*, July 1989, pp. 34–37.

[2] Gustavson, D. B., "Computer Buses: A Tutorial," *IEEE Micro*, Aug. 1984, pp. 7–22.

[3] Borrill, P. L., "MicroStandards Special Feature: A Comparison of 32-bit Buses," *IEEE Micro*, Dec. 1985, pp. 71–79.

[4] Dawson, W. K., "A Framework for Computer Design," *IEEE Spectrum*, Oct. 1986, pp. 49–54.

[5] White, G., "A Bus Tour," *Byte*, Sept. 1989, pp. 296–302.

[6] Vranesic, Z. G., and S. G. Zaky, *Microcomputer Structures*, Holt, Rinehart and Winston, Inc., New York, 1989, Fig. 11.17, p. 590.

[7] Motorola Semiconductor Products, Inc., *VMEbus Specification Manual* (MVMEBS/D1), Phoenix, AZ, Aug. 1982.

[8] Motorola Inc., *MC68020 Microprocessor to VERSAbus/VMEbus Interconnection Techniques,* EB114 Engineering Bulletin, Austin, TX, 1985.

[9] *IEEE, Specifications for Advanced Microcomputer Backplane Buses,* (IEEE P896 D6.2), Nov. 1983. (Available from the IEEE Computer Society, P.O. Box 80452, Worldway Postal Center, Los Angeles, CA 90080.)

[10] Borrill, P., and J. Theus, "An Advanced Communication Protocol for the Proposed IEEE 896 Futurebus," *IEEE Micro,* Aug. 1984, pp. 42–56.

[11] Sweazey, P., *The Futurebus Caching System,* Tektronix, Inc., Wilsonville, OR.

[12] James, D. V., "Multiplexed Buses: The Endian Wars Continue," *IEEE Micro,* June 1990, pp. 9–21.

[13] Kirrmann, H., "Report on the Paris Multibus II Meeting," *IEEE Micro,* Aug. 1985, pp. 82–89.

[14] IEEE, *IEEE/ANSI Standard 1014, Versatile Backplane Bus: VMEbus,* IEEE Service Center, Piscataway, NJ, 1987.

[15] Regula, J., "The Proposed SSBLT Standard Doubles the VME64 Transfer Rate," *IEEE Micro,* Apr. 1992, pp. 64–71.

[16] Intel Corp., *The 8086 Family User's Manual,* (9800722–03), Santa Clara, CA, Oct. 1979.

[17] N. Alexandridis, *Microprocessor System Design Concepts,* Computer Science Press, Rockville, MD, 1984.

[18] IEEE Task P796/D2, "Proposed Microcomputer System 796 Bus Standard," *Computer,* pp. 89–105, Oct. 1980.

5

Microprocessor Caches

5.1 INTRODUCTION

This chapter is devoted to describing the operation, design, and use of caches. Because some of the terms and issues discussed here may require some background on memory management units (MMUs) covered in the next chapter, the reader is urged to come back to this chapter again after he/she reads the next chapter, too.

A cache memory is a fast RAM-type memory positioned between the relatively fast CPU and slower main memory (usually, DRAM memory) as depicted in Figure 5.1. The cache memory contains the instructions and data (operands) most likely to be needed by the microprocessor. For any read operation, the address that the microprocessor issues is compared by the cache controller with the addresses held in the SRAM cache memory: if one is found in the cache, a **cache hit** occurs and the instruction/data is fetched from the cache rather than from main memory; if there is a **cache miss** (i.e., the requested instruction/data is not in the cache), the address will be sent to memory, a read bus cycle will be executed, and the instruction/data will be fetched to the microprocessor from main memory. In most cases, this instruction/data will also be copied in the cache (called "cache update"). All this comparison logic, and the hardware for controlling and updating the cache and starting main memory bus cycles, are included in the **cache controller.**

Caches[1] improve overall system performance by:

1. Providing information to the microprocessor faster than main memory. (They improve read cycles.)

[1]When we say "caches" or "cache memories" we also include its associated "cache controller" hardware.

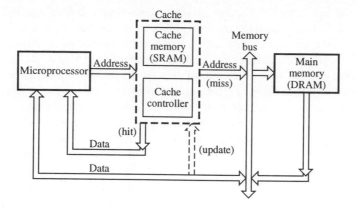

Figure 5.1 Functional block diagram of a smaller and faster cache memory positioned between the microprocessor and slower main memory.

2. Receiving information from the microprocessor at a fast rate and allowing it to continue processing while the cache independently processes the write to main memory as needed. (They improve write cycles.)

3. Improving memory bus utilization by reducing the traffic on the memory bus. (This is particularly important if multiple microprocessors or **bus masters**[2] share the memory bus.) For systems with heavy bus utilization (approaching 100%), caches provide a solution for freeing up the bus to other bus masters. (They improve bus utilization.)

Thus, a cache memory is used to reduce the processor-memory speed-gap by reducing the latency of load and store operations; it is also used to increase the effective memory bus bandwidth (and, therefore, the overall system performance) by reducing the microprocessor's need to access memory bus. As we will explain in detail in this chapter, (1) and (2) above are affected by a number of cache architectural features and (3) can improve by executing burst cycles, using a line buffer to update the cache, or using dual bus (rather than single bus) system architectures. In a more general case, we are interested in minimizing the memory bus utilization *by each microprocessor/cache subsystem* in order to accommodate more bus masters in the system. In most implementations caches can be dynamically disabled for certain types of bus cycles (such as when the processor accesses shared, noncacheable memory areas).

Caches are smaller in size than main memories, but because they are faster they cause the CPU to run effectively at cache speeds rather than at slower (DRAM) memory speeds (fetching from a cache may be done in as low as one clock cycle as compared to a much larger number of clock cycles needed to fetch from main memory). Caches are becoming increasingly important to the design of high-performance small computer systems as the speed and memory requirements of microprocessors have increased. Particularly in RISC microprocessors, the time needed to fetch an instruction often becomes the limiting factor because of the high rate at which RISCs execute instructions (one clock cycle per instruction); if the RISC processor does not have *on-chip caches* (implemented on the same chip

---

[2]The term "bus master" represents any device that can gain control of the bus and be able to initiate bus transfers. Such masters can be: another microprocessor in a multiprocessor system, DMA, a graphics processor, an I/O processor, a SCSI adapter, a LAN interface, etc.

with the rest of the CPU[3]), then *off-chip caches* (implemented externally using industry standard SRAMs and cache controllers) become an absolute necessity.

Cache memories work on the principles of spatial and temporal localities. **Spatial locality** means that a processor is likely in the near future to need the information it is working on at the present, along with information lying nearby in its main memory; i.e., their design is based on the concept of "locality" of program instructions and data structures (such as arrays). **Temporal locality** refers to the fact that programs tend to use recent (rather than older) information, such as in program loops. Caches continuously obtain and temporarily retain informational items that the processor is likely to need in its current operations.

Some main memory accesses cause values to be stored in the cache so that subsequent read operations to those same locations will become "cache hits" that access cache only and do not require an external bus cycle to access main memory. Each cache entry contains both a copy of data (or instruction) that is in main memory as well as its main memory address, which is used to determine whether a cache hit occurs. The items (instructions or data) themselves are stored in that part of the cache called the **data cache** or **cache data RAM**; the item's main memory addresses are stored in that part of the cache called the **cache tag** or **tag RAM**. As will be explained later, these tag fields are treated differently by the cache controller, depending on the way the particular cache memory is organized. Information placed in the cache overlies that in main memory; i.e., some of the information in main memory also resides in the cache (contrary to local memories, which take addressing space away from global main memory); and cache memory is dynamic, i.e., its entries change as the program executes even if they are not explicitly addressed.

Cache performance is often measured by its hit rate: **cache hit rate** (or **hit ratio**) is the percentage of memory requests that are cache hits and is given by the following equation [1]:

$$\text{hit rate } \% = \frac{\text{cache hits}}{\text{total memory requests}} \times 100\% \qquad (5.1)$$

The **miss rate** or (**miss ratio**) is given by: $1 -$ hit ratio. The higher the hit rate, the fewer the accesses to main memory. However, because caches are not operating by themselves but are part of a larger system (part of the memory hierarchy), using the cache miss rate as the lone criterion for evaluating caches is misleading; each cache miss has associated with it a **cache miss penalty** (the time it takes to access main memory, fetch a block, update an entry in the cache, and send the requested item to the microprocessor). When the microprocessor must wait for the memory system to respond, it is said that the processor **stalls.** Thus, the miss rate **and** the miss penalty must be combined together to yield a better measure for evaluating caches. (This is discussed in more detail at the end of the chapter.)

5.2 SYSTEM ISSUES

5.2.1 Configurations

External caches.   Figure 5.2 depicts a number of different configurations using external caches for both CISC and RISC microprocessors. *Instruction caches* are used to

---

[3]In recent RISC processors with vector processing capabilities (e.g., the 64-bit Intel i860 [10]), on-chip data cache can be used as a "vector register set" that holds vectors or their immediate results; compared to small, fixed-length vector registers, the cache-based approach provides more flexibility.

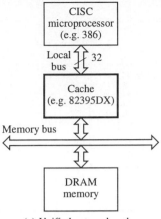

(a) Unified external cache

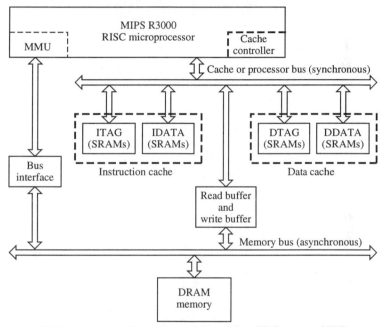

(b) Separate external instruction and data caches ([6] Courtesy of IDT)

Figure 5.2 Example configurations of cache-based microprocessor systems.

store instructions, *data caches* are used to store data (operands), while *unified caches* may hold both instructions and data. For example, the single off-chip cache of Figure 5.2a is a unified cache while those of Figure 5.2c are not. Figure 5.2a is a representative configuration for Intel 80386-based designs[4]; an external cache is required since the 80386 does not have an on-chip cache. Figure 5.2b depicts the configuration with separate external instruction and data caches for MIPS R2000/3000-based implementations [11–13]. The R2000/

---

[4]The 82395DX ''smart cache'' integrates on one chip the cache management logic (cache controller), tag RAM, cache data RAM, and write buffer logic.

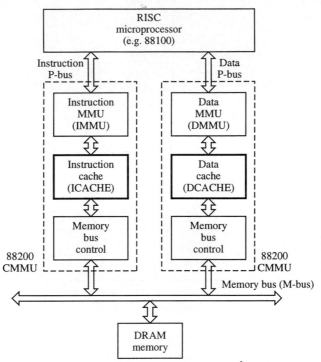

(c) Separate external caches and MMUs (Harvard architecture buses)

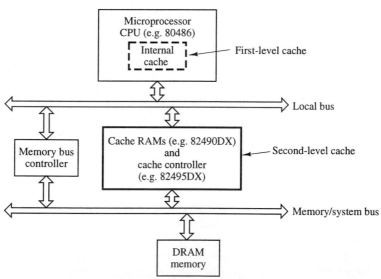

(d) Microprocessors with on-chip (first-level) cache; external cache is a second- level cache

Figure 5.2 (concluded)

3000 microprocessors have integrated the cache controller on the microprocessor chip; this then allows the implementation of the data cache externally using standard SRAM components. Figure 5.2c shows an implementation that uses the Motorola 88100 RISC microprocessor. The 88100 defines two separate external buses, a "data P bus" (for data) and an "instruction P bus" (for instructions). They are considered carrying virtual addresses when the external 88200 CMMU (Cache/MMU) chips are used. Each bus is connected to one 88200 CMMU which contains hardware for both an MMU and a 16-Kbyte cache. The outputs of the two 88200 CMMUs are connected to the "memory bus" (or M bus). Each 88200 also contains the proper hardware control for its internal cache and MMU and for interfacing the chip to the P buses (P-bus control) and to the memory bus (M-bus control). Powerful systems can be configured with up to eight 88200 CMMU chips per processor for a total of 128 Kbytes of cache memory.

A large number of microprocessors have implemented the cache on-chip; e.g., the Motorola 680x0, the Intel 80486 and i860, and the MIPS R4000 shown in Figure 1.4; except for the 80486, which has a unified cache, all others have followed the "split-cache" approach. Because on-chip caches must be extremely fast, they are managed entirely by hardware. On-chip caches reduce the processor's external bus activities and, thus, speed up the processor and increase the overall system performance.[5] On-chip caches are usually not directly accessible by the average user; only systems code can access the cache and its controller's registers, with the processor operating in supervisor/systems mode, executing privileged instructions.

Virtual and physical caches. Functionally, caches are called *real (or physical) caches* when they receive physical addresses, usually from an MMU that has already done the virtual-to-physical address conversion (Figure 5.2b and c). The same argument applies to the on-chip caches; for example, the 68040 and 80486 have on-chip physical caches.

However, some caches are called *virtual (or logical) caches* when they receive unconverted virtual addresses; for example, the Motorola 68020 and 68030, Intel i860, and MIPS R4000 have on-chip virtual caches. Virtual caches have the main problem that two different virtual addresses—called *synonyms* or *virtual address aliases*—can be translated to refer to the same real address (main memory location).

The synonyms problem and other advanced cache coherency schemes are discussed in detail later in the chapter.

Look-through and look-aside configurations. There are two alternatives to placing the cache between the microprocessor and main memory: one is called "look through" (or serial) and the other, "look aside" (or parallel).

Look-Through Architecture. Figure 5.3 shows the look-through configuration (also referred to as **serial cache read** architecture) and its operation. With this approach, first an access to the cache begins, and if a miss occurs, then the address is placed on the memory bus to access main memory. It is noticed that as long as there is a cache hit, data will be coming to the microprocessor at the fast cache rates (while at the same time reducing the

---

[5]Recently, cache memory has been integrated on the same chip with DRAM. DRAM chips have appeared—called "cache DRAM" chips—that have 1-Mbit DRAM for main memory and an 8-Kbit SRAM for cache memory [2,3].

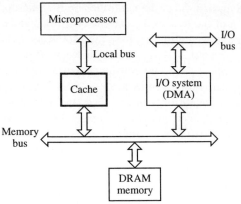

(a) Look-through architecture

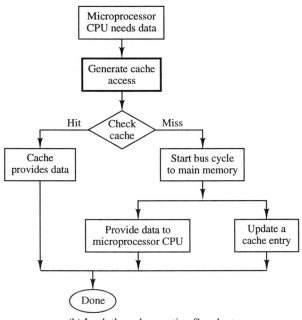

(b) Look-through operation flowchart

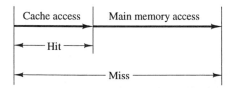

Miss access time = cache access + main memory access

(c) Look-through time delays

Figure 5.3 Look-through caches.

utilization of the memory bus). The existence of separate buses decouples the microprocessor from the rest of the system: the microprocessor can operate out of its cache, while other master modules of the system use the memory bus to access main memory. (This is referred to as "system concurrency.") On the other hand, cache misses impose a total access time which is the sum of the cache access time (referred to as the **lookup penalty** when the cache is checking for a hit) plus that of the main memory access. While main memory is being accessed, the execution flow of the processor stops (the processor executes "stall cycles"), waiting for the memory system to respond with the required data. The other disadvantage is that the existence of two buses makes the cache more complex because it must provide interfaces to two buses: the microprocessor local bus and the memory (system) bus. Usually, such caches implement dual-ported memory to allow concurrent operations on the local and memory bus. Figure 5.4 shows examples of the look-through approach in 80386-based single- and dual-processor system architectures.

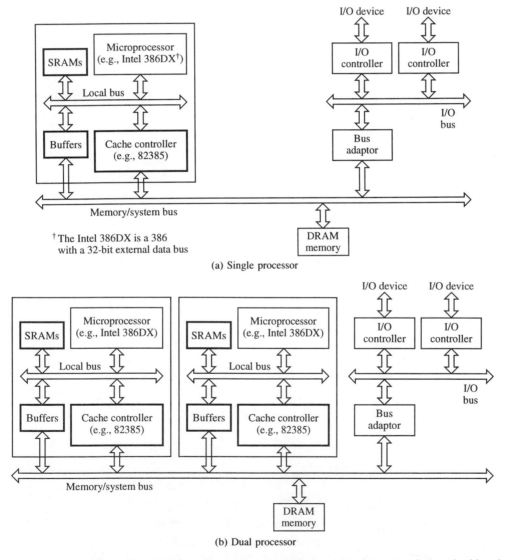

(a) Single processor

(b) Dual processor

Figure 5.4 Look-through external caches in single- and dual-processor designs; Intel-based systems [4]. Reprinted by permission of Intel Corporation, Copyright/Intel Corporation, 1991.

Look-Aside Architecture.   Figure 5.5 shows the look-aside configuration (also referred to as **parallel cache read** architecture) and its operation. With this approach, the microprocessor starts cache and main memory accesses simultaneously. We notice that

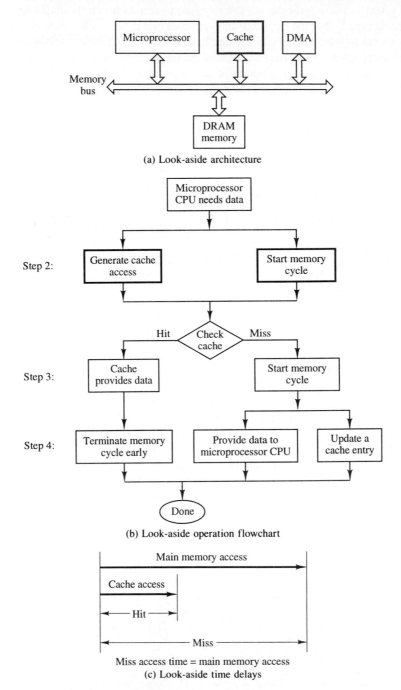

(a) Look-aside architecture

Step 2:

Step 3:

Step 4:

(b) Look-aside operation flowchart

Miss access time = main memory access
(c) Look-aside time delays

Figure 5.5   Look-aside caches.

again, whenever there is a cache hit, data will be coming to the microprocessor at cache rates, and the cache controller will issue a signal to abort main memory access.[6] In the case of a miss, the memory cycle will be allowed to complete; since the memory access started at the same time with the cache access, the total access time will not exceed main memory access time.

In addition to the speed advantage (no ''lookup penalty'' delay is involved), the look-aside architecture has the following **advantages** [4]:

1. It is optional in the design and can be removed at any time without the need to redesign the system.
2. It is a simpler cache since it needs to support only one address and data bus (instead of the two that the look-through architecture requires).

However, it has the following **disadvantages:**

1. No matter whether there is a cache hit or miss, the memory bus and the memory sub-system are kept busy. This means that bus utilization remains high and the access to main memory by other devices in the system is restricted.
2. System concurrency is reduced because it is not possible to operate the microprocessor out of the cache while another master device is accessing main memory.

Multilevel caches. A microprocessor system may have first-level and possibly second-level caches.

First-level caches are usually smaller (typically, 4-Kbyte to 64-Kbyte caches). An example of a first-level cache is the external cache used with the Intel 80386 microprocessor (Figures 5.2a and 5.4).

A *second-level cache* may be an external cache used with a microprocessor that already has an on-chip cache (which corresponds to the first-level cache). The second-level (or secondary) cache typically includes all the instructions/data of the first-level cache and more. It is larger than the first level (typically, of sizes 64 Kbytes to 512 Kbytes). The larger the size of the secondary cache, the greater percentage of memory cycles can be satisfied from cache operations. One example configuration is the one shown in Figure 5.2d (in a look-through architecture); alternatively, the 80486 can use an external 485Turbocache chip (which integrates the cache controller and the SRAM cache on the same chip) in a look-aside architecture similar to that in Figure 5.5a.

Figure 5.6 shows the simplified diagram of an 80486 connected to an external second-level cache memory. There are two output pins in the 80486 that are used for such implementations: PWT (page write-through) and PCD (page cache disable), which are copies of the corresponding attribute bits in the ''page descriptor[7] table'' entry and allow the operating system to control cacheability on a page-by-page basis.[8] PWT = 1 is used to force a

---

[6]Remember from Chapter 2 that, for example, in the case of the Motorola 68020/30 processors (Figure 2.13), the bus cycle will not complete if the ECS# output signal is not validated with the output signal AS# during the first clock cycle.

[7]See Chapter 6.

[8]When paging is enabled, PWT and PCD correspond to bits 3 and 4 in the page descriptor table entry, respectively. When paging is disabled, or for cycles that are not paged when paging is enabled (for example, I/O cycles), PWT and PCD correspond to bits 3 and 4 in the internal control register 3 (CR3).

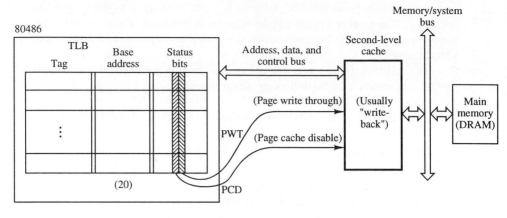

PWT = 1: forces write-through on 2nd level cache which is write-back

PCD =
$$\begin{cases} 1: \text{Internal cache disabled and, thus, 2nd level cache must also be disabled (case of shared or non-cacheable data)} \\ 0: \text{Allows caching of data from that page (case of non-shared or cachable data)} \end{cases}$$

Figure 5.6 Intel 80486 and second-level cache implementations (cacheability on a page basis).

write-through policy (explained below) on the second-level cache (which is normally write-back); PWT has no effect on the internal cache because it is always write-through. PCD is used to disable the second-level cache completely. When PCD = 1, the internal cache is disabled and, therefore, the external cache must also be disabled; this is used for shared, noncacheable data. The value PCD = 0 allows caching of data from that page; it is used for nonshared, cacheable data.

5.2.2 Write Policies

An important decision is which write-to-memory policy to implement? In other words, when should main memory be updated? We discuss three approaches: the write-through, the buffered write-through, and the write-back.

Write-through.   In this approach all memory writes are sent to main memory, even if the desired memory location is in the cache (a "write hit"); i.e., main memory is updated with the data at the same time that this data is used to update an entry in the cache. If the location is not in the cache (a "write miss"), then only main memory is updated. We say that the write-through policy maintains "cache coherency" because both the cache and main memory will always contain the same updated copy of the data. Any other bus master device in the system will have a simpler access since it can read main memory directly and be assured of accessing from it correct data.

This is the simplest, easiest to implement, and most reliable technique. However, it generates more traffic between the processor and main memory and may create a bus bottleneck (especially in a system where several bus masters may be trying at the same time to access main memory).

In configurations with a number of bus masters (where each bus master has its own local cache), this memory update transaction executed by any one of them will be visible on the memory bus. If the writing master broadcasts the new data over the memory bus, the other cache controllers can recognize whether or not their own local caches now have a stale copy of this data. In this case, they may either invalidate that data in their local cache (to indicate that *the cache contains stale data*) or latch the new data off the memory data bus as it becomes available and use it to update the proper entry in their local cache. Of the system buses covered in this textbook, the Futurebus supports an adequate broadcasting mechanism[9] to support the write-through scheme fully.

Buffered write-through.   A second approach is the buffered write-through. This technique uses **write buffers** to decouple the write operations of the CPU (typically done in one clock cycle) from external bus writing to main memory (which typically takes several clock cycles). Without the use of such buffers, a write following another write would have to wait for the first write to memory to complete before it could execute.

The Intel 80486 with its on-chip cache has implemented this approach using 4 internal write buffers to match the CPU's execution of a store in one clock cycle. Figure 5.7 shows diagrammatically the 80486 buffered write-through. If the external bus is busy, the processor uses these four internal write buffers to write to them the data and the destination addresses, in order to complete its write cycle in one clock cycle. When the external bus becomes free, the write to memory can then take place using 2 or 3 clock cycles. Use of the four internal buffers decouples the write operations of the CPU from the external bus activities and allows up to 6 consecutive writes to occur before introducing an instruction stall. To improve performance, the memory write operation can be decoupled from that of its bus, by having memory interface logic latch the write data and address information and implement a "delayed write-memory cycle" to free up the address and data bus lines as quickly as possible.

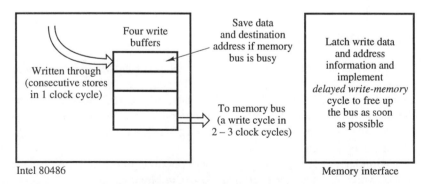

Figure 5.7   Intel 80486 buffered write-through.

Write buffers can also be implemented externally in the form of a FIFO-type device that captures the address and data sent to memory at the processor's high rate, and then send this data to memory at the memory's slower rate.

[9]Explained in Section 4.5.5., Chapter 4.

Write-back (or copy-back). In the write-back approach, if the memory location that is the object of the write is in the cache, the cache controller writes to cache immediately and the data written into the cache is flagged with a "dirty" or "modified" bit. This "dirty" bit indicates that the cache entry has an updated value which has not yet been stored in main memory. (In other words, *main memory now contains stale data* and is said to be *incoherent*.) This data will be sent by the cache controller to main memory at some later time (for example, at the time the cache line that contains this information is to be replaced because of a cache miss, during periods when the processor is busy working on other things and does not use the bus, or when the processor performs context switching which requires "flushing the cache"). When that happens and main memory is updated, the cache controller clears the dirty bit. With the write-back approach, multiple write operations to the same location will not result in needless multiple memory/system bus operations to update main memory.

Write-back is the most complex policy to implement but yields a better overall system performance because it reduces bus traffic and eliminates the bottleneck of waiting for each memory write operation to finish before starting a subsequent memory operation. However, the memory read operation of other bus master devices becomes more involved because they must first check this cache's dirty bit before doing a read operation: if the dirty bit is set, main memory must first be updated and the dirty bit cleared before that master device can continue with its main memory read operation.

When pages can be marked "shared" or "private," writing of shared data can follow the write-through policy (broadcasting the data to other caches), while writing of private data can be done by the write-back policy. Some processors allow software selection between the write-through and write-back mode of operation. For example, the Motorola 68040 can *select the mode on a page basis*[10]: a write-through *allocates* (i.e., updates the cache) only on a cache-read miss; write-back allocates an entry on a miss (read or write) and requests a line read on the bus. Similarly, the external 88200 CMMUs of Figure 5.2c allow the Motorola 88100 processor to select the memory update policy by setting a flag in the page descriptor (inside the 88200's MMU).

5.3 CACHE ORGANIZATIONS

In general, a main memory of size 2^{X+W+B} bytes is subdivided into M **memory blocks,** each block of size 2^{W+B} bytes (Figure 5.8a). To access a "word"[11] in main memory requires submitting an address of $X + W + B$ bits, where the most significant X bits identify the memory block number, the next W bits point to a "word" within the block (the *word displacement within a block*), and the least significant B bits indicate the byte within the "word" (the *byte displacement*).

Similarly, a smaller cache memory contain C lines; each line has a number of fields, two of which are the **cache tag** and the **cache block** (or **sector**), implemented on the "tag RAM" and the "cache data RAM," respectively [5]. The size of the cache block is 2^{W+B} bytes (i.e., equal to the size of a main memory block). A memory block is mapped onto a cache block; thus, cache memory overlies part of main memory. The **cache size** (in bytes)

---

[10]By setting proper values in a field of each "page descriptor" (see Chapter 6).

[11]The "word" within quotes may mean either a 16-bit word or a 32-bit doubleword, depending on the wordlength of the particular cache discussed.

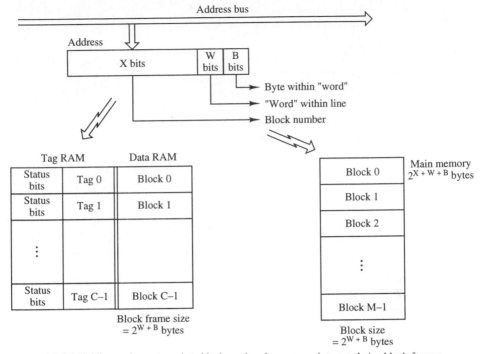

(a) Subdividing main memory into blocks and cache memory into equal-size block frames

Figure 5.8 Cache between the microprocessor and main memory.

is given by the product (number of cache line)*(2^{W+B}), i.e., the tag field and the other non-data bits are not counted.

To access a "word" in the cache, the same $X + W + B$ address bits are submitted to it, but how the cache controller interprets the X most significant bits depends on the way the cache memory is organized, as we will explain below. In general, the most significant address bits are compared with the tag field in the tag RAM to determine whether one of the stored tags matches the incoming one (Figure 5.8b). If the tag matches and the tag is valid (referred to as a "valid cache block" or "valid line"), then there is a *cache hit* and data will be fetched from the cache. Fields W and B are used to specify which data in the cache block will be accessed.

Otherwise, there is a *cache miss;* in such a case (assuming that the validity is on a cache line basis) the cache miss will force an *allocate* (i.e., an update of the cache); an entire block will be loaded from main memory to update one block in the cache (referred to as a **line fill**[12]) and the CPU will receive the data it requested. If the size of the cache block is equal to the width of the data bus (as in the Motorola 68020, whose internal cache has a block size of 32 bits), then a single memory read will suffice to update the cache; if the size of the cache block is bigger than the data bus width (as in most microprocessors whose caches have a block size of 16 bytes or four doublewords), then a "burst read" operation (Section 2.4.2 of Chapter 2) to memory will be needed to fetch the block and update the

---

[12]Unless the cache has been frozen or disabled, either by an external input signal or by the operating system having set the proper bits in the cache's control register.

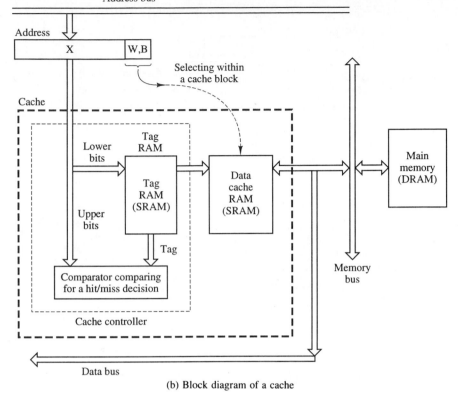

Address bus

Address

| X | W,B |

Selecting within
a cache block

Cache

Tag
RAM

Lower
bits

Tag
RAM
(SRAM)

Upper
bits

Data
cache
RAM
(SRAM)

Main
memory
(DRAM)

Tag

Memory
bus

Comparator comparing
for a hit/miss decision

Cache controller

Data bus

(b) Block diagram of a cache

Figure 5.8 (concluded)

cache. Where in the cache the cache controller will place the incoming block depends on the cache organization and the replacement algorithm implemented. In general, and if there are more than one candidate cache blocks, the cache controller will first look to write the incoming block in one of the invalid cache blocks in the candidate set.

We say that a cache of total capacity 2^d bytes with a cache block size of 2^e bytes will contain C lines, where $C = 2^d/2^e = 2^{d-e}$. If the total number of lines in the cache is C, they may be grouped into S sets of K lines (in this case they are called **ways**) per set. The number of "ways" per set is called the **associativity** K of the cache. When $K = C$, the cache is a *fully associative* cache; when $K = 1$, the cache is a *direct-mapped* cache; otherwise, the cache is a *K-way set-associative* cache. The total number of lines C in the cache always equals the associativity K times the number of sets S:

$$C = K * S$$

Figure 5.9 shows how the X most significant address bits are interpreted in the above three cache organizations.

5.3.1 Fully Associative

In the fully associative organization, a 2^{X+W}-word main memory is subdivided into blocks with 2^W words per block. Since associativity (i.e., the number of lines per set) is $K = C$,

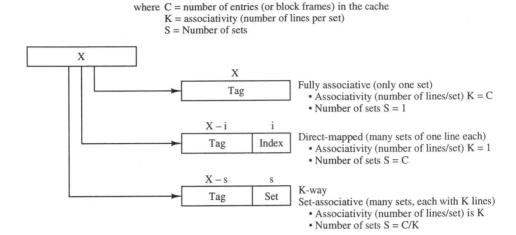

$$C = K*S$$

where C = number of entries (or block frames) in the cache
K = associativity (number of lines per set)
S = Number of sets

X

	X
	Tag

Fully associative (only one set)
- Associativity (number of lines/set) K = C
- Number of sets S = 1

	X – i	i
	Tag	Index

Direct-mapped (many sets of one line each)
- Associativity (number of lines/set) K = 1
- Number of sets S = C

	X – s	s
	Tag	Set

K-way
Set-associative (many sets, each with K lines)
- Associativity (number of lines/set) is K
- Number of sets S = C/K

Figure 5.9 Interpreting the X most significant address bits in the three cache organizations.

then $S = 1$; thus there is only one set with C lines. Because there is only one set, no "set field" is needed in the address, and therefore, as shown in Figure 5.9, all X most significant address bits are interpreted by the cache as the "tag field."

Figure 5.10 shows a simple example of mapping main memory blocks to a fully associative cache of size $C = 8$ lines. Figure 5.10a shows a 64-word or 128-byte main memory and an 8-line fully associative cache. To access any location in this main memory requires a 7-bit address. Main memory is considered divided into 4-word (or 8-byte) blocks; thus, the 3 least significant address bits are needed to access data within a block. The remaining $X = 4$ most significant address bits will then constitute the tag. A cache line is composed of the 4-word cache block of data (the contents of a main memory block), along with the 4-bit tag field (the block's tag). Of the remaining "status bits" in the cache of Figure 5.8a, only one bit is shown here: the line *valid bit* (V). This valid bit indicates that both the cache and main memory contain the same copy of the data. An *invalid* line exists when the block in main memory was modified (for example, with a write operation from another bus master) without at the same time having updated the line in the cache. (In this case *the cache contains stale data.*)

Example 5.1

If main memory (actually, the "cacheable" main memory) is 16 Mbytes, and is considered subdivided into blocks of 4 bytes each, then a fully associative cache line will have a 4-byte block and a 22-bit cache tag.

The cache controller of a fully associative cache includes a number of comparators equal to the number of lines in the cache (its associativity). In Figure 5.10a, when a read operation is executed by the microprocessor, the tag of the incoming address is compared simultaneously in the 8 comparators with all the tags stored in the cache. If a matching tag

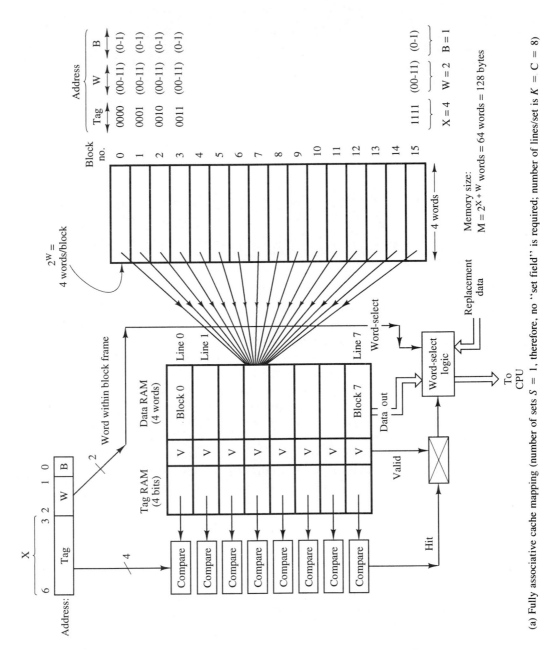

Figure 5.10 Fully associative cache.

(a) Fully associative cache mapping (number of sets $S = 1$, therefore, no "set field" is required; number of lines/set is $K = C = 8$)

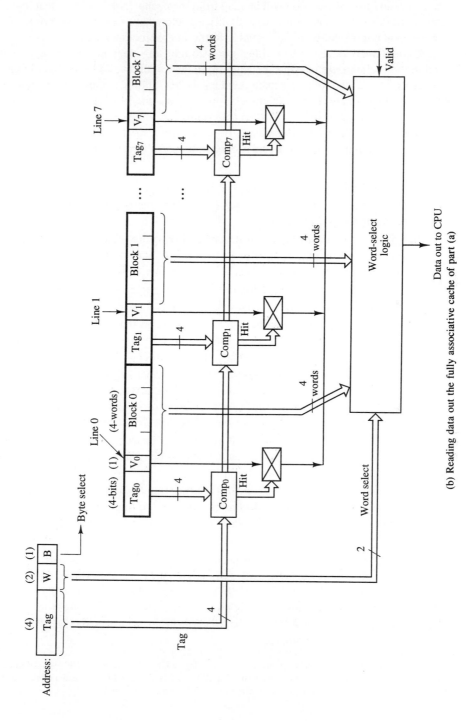

(b) Reading data out the fully associative cache of part (a)

Figure 5.10 (concluded)

263

is found, there is a *tag hit*. If the line's valid bit indicates that its block is valid, then we have a *cache hit,* and the information will be read from the cache. The "word-select logic" in the cache controller will interpret the least significant address bits to read the proper data from the corresponding cache block and send it to the microprocessor CPU.

A *cache miss* occurs when either the incoming tag does not match any of the tags stored in the cache (a *tag miss*) or the valid bit indicates an invalid cache line; in either case bus cycle(s) are needed to access main memory. When a block is moved from main memory into a cache line, in addition to the block's four words, the block's tag (here 4 bits) is also stored in the cache, and the V bit is set to "valid."

Figure 5.10b shows a different way of representing the fully associative cache of Figure 5.10a. The **advantages** and **disadvantages** of the fully associative cache are:

1. All cache tags are compared very fast in parallel. (adv)
2. Although it is the fastest organization, it is the most expensive one because it needs one comparator per entry. (dis)
3. Any block of main memory can be mapped onto any block of the cache, since the search of the cache lines is done in an associative manner. Therefore, any combination of main memory blocks can be in cache at any one time. (adv)
4. The entries in the cache are unordered (and therefore no external decoding is required as in the other organizations to be discussed next). (adv)
5. Since an incoming block can be placed anywhere in the cache, a wide variety of replacement algorithms can be used. (adv) One of the most common ones is the LRU (least recently used) algorithm, to be discussed later.
6. The cost of the cache search depends on the number of tags to be searched simultaneously and the tag field length. Thus, fully associative organizations have been used for relatively small cache memories (of 4 Kbytes or less) and implemented using specialized devices rather than industry standard SRAMs. (dis)
7. There is a low ratio of informational bits (data or instructions within the cache block) to the total number of bits in the cache line (tag bits, plus valid bits, plus cache block bits). (dis)
8. A fully associate cache won't *thrash* (i.e., continually overwrite data that the cache will actually need, as explained in more detail in the direct-mapped organization discussed next), because it uses a replacement policy that saves recently used data. (adv)

Fully associative caches have not been implemented in many microprocessors. Later on we will examine the details of a fully associative cache using as an example the on-chip implementation of the Zilog Z80000. Fully associative organization has been used instead for the structure of the on-chip "address translation cache" (ATC[13]) used in paging (e.g., the Motorola 68030 on-chip ATC and the ATC of the external MC68851 MMU chip used with the Motorola 68020 microprocessors).

---

[13]As will be explained in the next chapter in detail, the "address translation cache" is used in conjunction with the MMU to perform fast address translations. The ATC speeds up logical-to-physical address translations by storing recently used translations. It is also referred to as TLB (table lookeside buffer).

5.3.2 Direct Mapped

In the direct-mapped organization, a 2^{X+W} -word main memory is seen as logically subdivided into pages, each page the size of the data cache RAM. For example, in Figure 5.11, the 64-byte direct-mapped cache at the left would logically see main memory at the right as a collection of 64-byte pages. The data cache RAM and a main memory page are further subdivided into blocks with 2^W words per block; in the example of Figure 5.11 a block equals 8 bytes. Since associativity (i.e., the number of lines per set) is $K = 1$, the number of sets is $S = C$. In a direct-mapped cache, each line corresponds to a set, and block d of main memory will be placed in block f of the cache, where $f = d \pmod{C}$, where C is the number of lines (or sets) in the cache. In other words, all memory locations that have the same low-order address bits (i.e., the *same relative location in all pages*) map onto the same cache line.

Since the cache contains $S = C$ lines, then $i = \log S$ bits in the X field of the address are needed to form what in the direct-mapped approach is called the *index field* that points to one line. Direct mapping is similar to accessing main memory, in the sense that the index field when decoded points to the particular line of the cache. The remaining $X - i$ most significant address bits then make up the tag field stored in the cache along with each data block. The cache controller will have one comparator (since $K=1$).

During a read operation, first the index field of the address is used to specify the particular entry of the cache to be checked. Next, the tag bits of the address are compared to the tag of the selected entry. If there is a match and the valid bit (V) indicates a valid line, a cache hit occurs. The W bits of the address (the "word-select" bits) are then used to select the proper word from this cache block to be delivered to the CPU. If a cache miss occurs (when either the line's tag does not match the incoming tag or the valid bit indicates an invalid line), an external bus cycle(s) will start to access main memory, fetch a block, and update the cache data.

Example 5.2

Assume a 32-bit processor with no on-chip caches. Design a 4-Kbyte direct-mapped external cache for it.

Solution: Off-chip direct-mapped caches may be implemented using standard SRAM chips for the "cache tag RAM" and the "cache data RAM." Since the processor issues a 32-bit address, it can access up to 2^{32} bytes of main memory. For direct-mapped caches, the number of bits in the tag field depends on the size of main memory (actually, the size of the *cacheable* main memory) and the size of the cache, and is given by the following formula (valid only for direct-mapped caches):

$$\text{number of tag bits} = m - n$$

where m is log base 2 of the cacheable main memory size and n is log base 2 of the cache data RAM size. If we assume that the entire address space of 2^{32} bytes is cacheable, then a 4-Kbyte ($= 2^{12}$) cache would require 20 tag bits.

If the block size is 16 bytes, then $W + B = 4$ least significant bits are needed for "word select" within the block. The remaining 8 bits are the index field. Therefore, the cache will have $2^8 = 256$ entries, each with a block size of 16 bytes. Increasing the block size will decrease the number of cache lines.

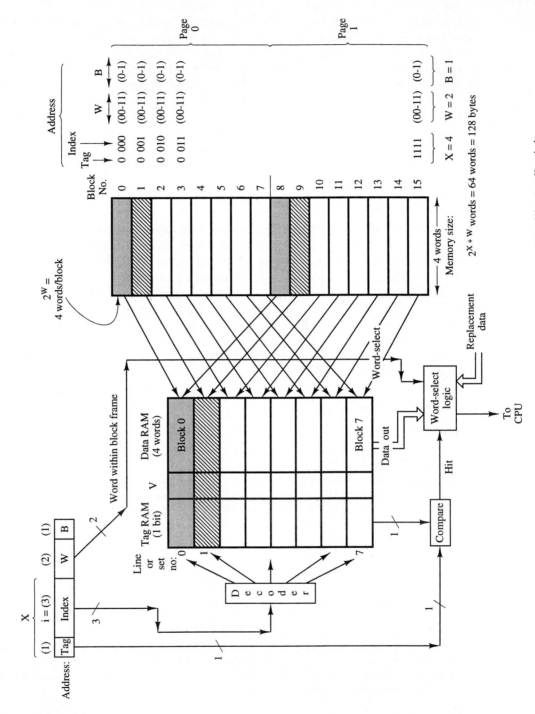

Figure 5.11 Direct-mapped cache mapping (number of sets $S = C$; number of lines/set K = index field i = log S).

If a particular system design has a smaller main memory, or does not cache the total address space, or uses cache sizes larger than 4 Kbytes, fewer tag bits will be required. For example, a 1-Mbyte cacheable main memory and 64-Kbyte caches would require 4 tag bits (bits 19–16 if it is the lowest 1 Mbytes).

When the cache tag RAM is implemented using a separate SRAM chip, the smaller the width of the tag, the smaller the cost of the "cache tag" implementation. The system cost can be further reduced by reducing the *depth* (i.e., number of lines) in the cache tag memory. Without changing the overall size of the cache, the depth of the required tag memory is equal to the cache depth divided by the block size. The depth is reduced by increasing the cache block size. (Later in the chapter we will study the trade-offs involved in increasing the cache block size.) For example, the cache in Figure 5.11 can also be implemented with a cache tag of only 4 entries, if each block in the data RAM becomes 8 words long. This, however, would require more memory read cycles to update the wider (multiword) cache block.

The **advantages** and **disadvantages** of the direct-mapped approach are:

1. The major disadvantage is its bad worst-case behavior: the cache hit ratio drops sharply if two or more memory blocks, used alternately, happen to map onto the same block in the cache. (This contention is much higher in multiprocessor systems.) In this case we say that the system will **thrash.** Thrashing appears when the microprocessor crosses page boundaries in main memory (as, for example, to access, alternatively, the same relative location within different pages).

2. If there is no tag match, output data is suppressed. There is no associative comparison; therefore, the cost is reduced. Their cost is less than that of set-associative caches. (adv)

3. The replacement algorithm is trivial: of all main memory blocks that map onto the same cache block, only one can actually be in the cache at a time. When there is a tag miss, then replace the block in that cache line. (adv)

4. They have worse miss ratios than set-associative caches of the same size. (dis)

Examples of direct-mapped caches are the Motorola 68030 on-chip instruction and data caches and the MIPS R3000 whose on-chip cache controller supports[14] external direct-mapped instruction and data caches implemented using standard SRAMs. These chips implement direct-mapped caches and, therefore, assuming that everything else remains the same, when the cache size becomes larger, the index field increases and the tag field decreases.

5.3.3 Set-Associative

A set-associative cache organization groups a number of cache lines into sets; for example, a 2-way set-associative will have 2 lines or "ways" of the cache per set. In the K-way set-associative organization, associativity (i.e., number of lines per set) is K, and the number of

[14] In addition to implementing direct mapping, the on-chip cache controller of the R3000 allows for a wide range of cache sizes for both the instruction and data caches (*configurable cache sizes* from 0 to 256 Kbytes) and range of block sizes (*configurable line sizes* of 1, 4, 8, 16, or 32 doublewords). These configuration settings are selected during system RESET initialization, and the block size can be selected to be different for the instruction and data caches.

sets is $S = C/K$. For S sets in the cache, the $s = \log S$ rightmost bits of the X field of the incoming address form what is now called the **set field.** The remaining $X - s$ most significant address bits make up the tag field to be stored along with each block. The cache controller will have K comparators. This is the preferred approach by the most recent microprocessors with on-chip caches (4-way set associativity).

Figure 5.12a shows a simple example of mapping the same main memory of Figure 5.11a onto a 2-way set-associative cache. Since associativity is $K = 2$, the $C = 8$ entries of the cache are grouped into $C/K = 4$ sets, each set containing 2 "ways" (or lines). Main memory is again considered logically divided into pages, but each page now has a size equal to the cache size C divided by K, i.e., equal to the number of sets; thus, in the example of Figure 5.12, a page equals now four blocks (32 bytes). A main memory block i, $i = 1$ to C/K, of any page is mapped onto the same set i in the cache, in any of the K "ways" of that set; i.e., all zero blocks from main memory are mapped onto any of the 2 "ways" of set 0 in the cache, all one blocks from main memory are mapped into any of the 2 "ways" of set 1 in the cache, etc.

Figure 5.12b shows how data is read out of the 2-way set-associative cache ($K = 2$). The decoding of the incoming address's set field identifies the particular set. Then K comparators are used to compare the incoming tag simultaneously with the K stored tags of the set's K "ways."

The set-associative organization presents a compromise between fully associative and direct-mapped organizations. It reduces the cost of search because it reduces the number of tags that have to be searched simultaneously. The higher the degree of associativity, the more cache locations are available for each memory location to be written into, which makes the cache more flexible. Set-associative caches tolerate better software that crosses page boundaries of main memory (i.e., multitasking operating systems).

Examples of set-associative caches are: the Motorola 68040 on-chip, physical, 4-way set-associative instruction and data caches; the Motorola 88200 external CMMU with its physical, 4-way set-associative cache; the Intel 80486, physical, 4-way set-associative unified cache; and the Intel i860 on-chip, virtual, 2-way set-associative cache.

5.3.4 General Cache Structure

Three different ways of representing the general organization of a K-way set-associative cache memory are shown in Figure 5.13. As we said earlier, the important parameter in the cache organization is its *associativity* K or *way* (also called "degree of associativity" or "set size"), which gives the number of cache lines in each set and, therefore, the number of comparators in the cache controller. Subscripts in Figure 5.13 identify the cache line or "way" and superscripts the set number. There are $S = 2^r$ total number of sets, each set composed of K lines, and each line containing a block of size 2^W 16-bit words.

A cache of C lines is called **fully associative** (associativity $K = C$) if it contains only one set ($S = 1$, i.e., a main memory block can reside in any block of the cache). A cache of C lines is called **direct mapped** (associativity $K = 1$) if each set contains only one line ($C = S$, i.e., a main memory block can reside in only one block in the cache).

5.3.5 Cache Line Status Bits

In all the above discussion, we assumed the simplest possible format for the cache line, that of Figure 5.8a, which included a "tag field," one "valid bit" for the entire cache line, and

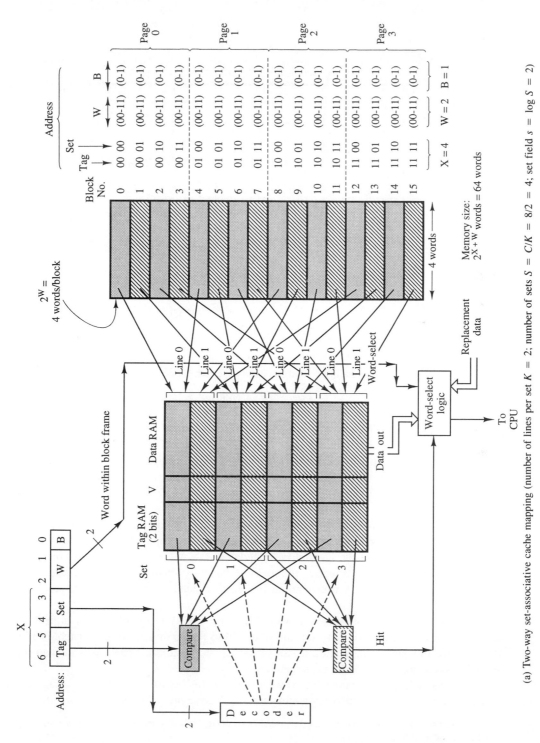

Figure 5.12 Two-way set-associative cache.

(a) Two-way set-associative cache mapping (number of lines per set $K = 2$; number of sets $S = C/K = 8/2 = 4$; set field $s = \log S = 2$)

Memory size:
2^{X+W} words = 64 words

$X = 4$ $W = 2$ $B = 1$

$2^W = 4$ words/block

269

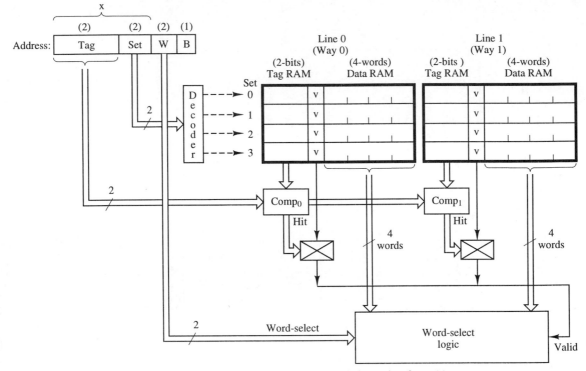

(b) Reading data out of the 2-way set-associative cache of part (a)

Figure 5.12 (concluded)

a "data block" field. Since there was only one valid bit in the line, cache updates were on the entire line basis. More advanced caches include a number of other bits in their tag RAM, which make them more flexible and efficient, and allow control and validity at a higher resolution level (usually at the level of doublewords, or in some cases at the level of words). Discussed below are the various status bits one may find in a tag RAM.

Line valid bit.   The tag or line valid bit means a "valid cache line." An invalid tag means that the corresponding block in main memory has been modified by another bus master, and the data in the cache has not been updated. (As we will explain later, the cache-controller that monitors or "snoops" the memory bus must recognize this updating of main memory and invalidate the corresponding line in the cache.[15]) In this case the cache has stale data.

Some microprocessors have this valid bit (e.g., the Motorola 68040 for both its on-chip instruction and data caches, and the Intel 80486 for its on-chip unified cache); others do not have this single line valid bit (for example, the Motorola 68030 uses instead individual "word valid bits" to be explained next).

If a cache has only a single line valid bit, a "tag hit" exists when there is a tag match and the tag is valid; this also corresponds to a "cache hit." In this case, updating the

---

[15]In some cases, a cache line may also be explicitly invalidated by executing a special cache instruction that sets the tag valid bit to invalid.

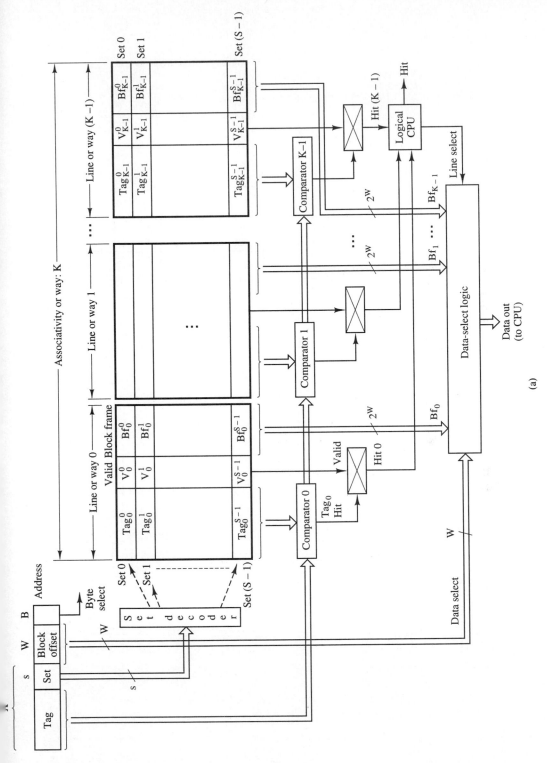

Figure 5.13 Three representations of a K-way "set-associative" cache; superscripts denote the set, subscripts the block or line or "way." (When $S = 1$, then $K = C$ or "fully associative"; when $S = C$, then $K = 1$ or "direct-mapped.")

(a)

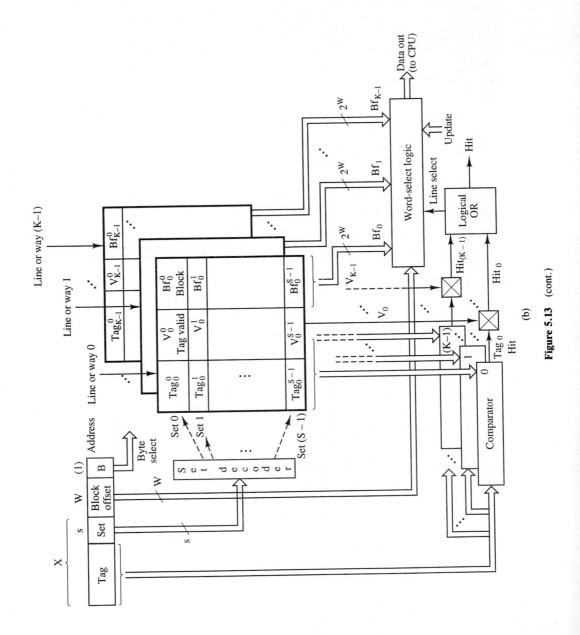

Figure 5.13 (cont.)

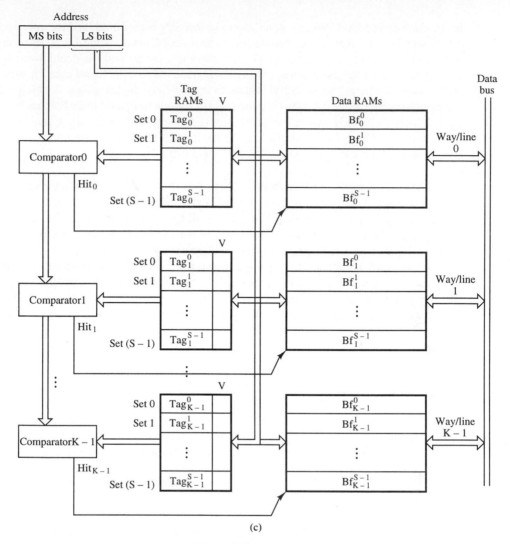

Figure 5.13 (concluded)

cache is done "on a line basis," i.e., a read operation that caused a cache miss will fetch a whole block from memory to update all words in the cache block; furthermore, if the cache line contains no "dirty bits" (to be explained below), only the write-through policy must be followed.

"Word" valid bits. Some microprocessors, instead of a tag valid bit, provide separate valid bits for each 32-bit doubleword or even 16-bit word in the block, called "word" valid bits. In most cases, a "word" valid bit is allocated for each bus-width "word" of data; i.e., on a processor with a 32-bit memory data bus it makes no sense to have valid bits for each 16-bit word because it will not reduce the number of memory transactions on a miss.

For example, the Motorola 68030, instead of a single line valid bit, has four valid bits, one for each of the four doublewords in a block. This provides a higher resolution of validity to the doubleword level. When a doubleword in memory is modified, and the corresponding doubleword in the cache is not updated, then that doubleword's valid bit is set to invalid.

In such caches, a cache hit exists when there is a tag hit **and** the doubleword is valid. If there is a tag hit but the doubleword is invalid (referred to as a "word miss"), such cache misses can execute a "single entry" mode to update only the individual doubleword (it is not necessary to execute a lengthy "burst line fill" mode to update the whole cache line).[16] Again, caches with only "word" valid bits (and no "dirty bits") can support only the write-through policy. Some microprocessors, like the Zilog Z80000 to be examined below, have both a line valid bit and individual "word" valid bits.

"Word" dirty/modified bits. Dirty bits are used only for data caches (which, unlike the instruction caches, support write operations), to signify whether or not the data in the cache is dirty. A "word" in the cache is dirty when the processor has updated it in the cache but the new value has not been written back to main memory yet (as in the write-back mode). In such cases, main memory will contain stale data.

Dirty bits are not used during read operations. For write operations, dirty bits allow implementation of the write-back scheme too; the cache controller uses the dirty bits to identify which entries will have to be copied back to main memory when the proper time arrives (as we said earlier, for example, when the particular cache line is to be replaced or when context switching is to take place).

Example 5.3

Putting together all the above cases, we say that a cache line may be:

Valid, if there is a valid tag and all data items are valid (dirty bits are not inspected during a read).

Dirty, if there is a valid tag and one or more dirty bits (indicating that a line is valid and contains data entries that have not been written into main memory yet).

Invalid, if there is an invalid tag (invalidated by the cache controller which "snoops the bus" and detects another bus master device updating an entry in main memory that is also in the cache). When the line is invalid, a line fill operation is required to update it.

LRU field. A cache memory line may also contain a *least recently used field* (LRU), which is updated with every hit in the cache and used in the pseudo-LRU replacement algorithm (described later in Section 5.4.2).

Exclusive ownership bits. Some cache memories may also contain additional status information to indicate whether the data is exclusive to the cache or resides in other caches of the system, and whether or not the data is modified with respect to memory. For example, the Motorola 88200 CMMU (Figure 5.2c), in addition to the tag invalid indicator (I), contains the following three status indicators: the *exclusive unmodified (EU)* indicator, to indicate that the data in the cache and the corresponding data in memory agree and that this cache has "exclusive ownership" of the data (i.e., the same data does not reside in other caches in the system); the *exclusive modified (EM)* indicator, to indicate that the "exclusive" data in the line has been modified with respect to memory; and the *shared unmodified (SU)*

---

[16]In the Motorola 68030, the "burst line fill" or "single entry" modes (discussed in Section 2.4.2) are programmable.

indicator, to indicate that multiple caches (CMMUs) may be caching the same data, but no copy has been modified with respect to memory. These ownership bits are used to implement "cache coherency protocols." (Another example of a cache coherency protocol, the M.E.S.I. protocol, is given later in Section 5.6.3.)

Access-rights and process-ID fields. Some cache tag RAMs may also contain other fields, such as access-rights and process-ID fields. The **access-rights** field indicates the type of access space the block belongs to; for example, the Motorola products store in this field the function code signals FC0–FC2 to distinguish among code/data and user/ supervisor access spaces. The **process-ID** field distinguishes among cache entries, which belong to different processes (it provides protection).

Parity bits. Finally, some microprocessor caches (e.g., those of the MIPS R3000) have a parity bit for each byte in the data RAM and a parity bit for each byte in the tag RAM.

Example 5.4

(a) Under what conditions is a cache line fetched from memory?

When there is an access-right or process-ID violation.

When there is a cache miss (either no tag match or invalid line).

(b) Under what conditions is a "word" fetched from memory to update a cache entry?

When there is a tag match but a "word" miss (implying the existence of "word valid" bits).

(c) What happens when there is a dirty/modified line and a tag match on a read?

There is a cache hit, because the line in the cache is valid.

(d) What is the difference between an invalid "word" and a dirty "word"?

An invalid "word" means that the "word" in main memory is valid and the one in the cache is stale (invalid); a dirty "word" means that the "word" in the cache is valid and the one in main memory is stale (invalid).

5.4 CACHE UPDATE POLICIES

The cache update policies vary according to the organization of the cache.

In a fully associative cache, any incoming block from main memory can be placed in any block in the cache. The cache controller will first look to replace an invalid line. If all lines are valid, a pseudo-random replacement algorithm (like the LRU algorithm discussed next) may be used to select the cache line to be replaced.

In a direct-mapped cache, block d from main memory will be placed into a specific block f of the cache, such that $f = d \pmod{C}$, where C is the total number of lines in the cache. This means that of all main memory blocks that map onto the same block in the cache, only one can actually be in the cache at a time. Thus the replacement algorithm is very simple: when there is a cache miss, replace the block in that line in the cache.

In a set-associative cache, within a set, a block is mapped fully associatively in any of the lines in the set. Set-associative caches reduce the thrashing problem of the direct-mapped caches since a block is mapped to more than one cache lines.

5.4.1 Cache Allocate

Cache allocate refers to updating the cache. "No cache allocate" is performed on a read hit. Cache allocates are always performed on **read misses.** Whether the read allocate updates a whole line (for example, using a burst read to update a 4-doubleword cache block) or part of it (using a normal 32-bit read cycle to update only one doubleword in the cache block) depends on whether there was a cache miss or just a "word" miss on a particular doubleword. If a cache hit occurs on a write, the line will always be updated. Regarding **write misses,** most microprocessors do not perform cache allocate; others may perform cache allocate. Finally, some microprocessors can do either type of allocate: for example, the Motorola 68030 supervisor can configure the on-chip data cache for either type of allocate on write misses; in the Motorola 68040 case, if the write-through mode is selected, the cache controller allocates only on a cache-read miss; if the copy-back mode is selected, the cache controller allocates a line in the cache on both cache-read and cache-write misses.

5.4.2 LRU Replacement Algorithm

As we said earlier, in the fully associative and set-associative caches, when a line is to be fetched from memory and all cache lines are valid, the cache line to be replaced is decided by the cache controller implementing the LRU (least recently used) algorithm.[17] This algorithm works as follows [7]: Consider, for example, a 4-way set-associative cache (like the on-chip cache of the Intel 80486 and Motorola 68040), and label the four lines or "ways" in each set L0, L1, L2, and L3. When a line needs to be replaced in a set, the cache controller first checks the valid bit in each of the four lines in the set to see if there is an invalid line in this set that can be replaced. The valid bits are checked in the order L0, L1, L2, and then L3. If an invalid line is found, that line is marked for replacement.

If all four lines in the set are valid, then the pseudo LRU algorithm is executed. The LRU algorithm implementation requires an additional field in the cache line (the **LRU field**) composed of three bits B2, B1, and B0. If the most recent access to the set were to lines L0 or L1, B0 is set to 1. B0 is set to 0 if the most recent access were to L2 or L3. If the most recent access to the pair L0:L1 were to L0, B1 is set to 1, else B1 is set to 0. If the most recent access to pair L2:L3 were to L2, B2 is set to 1, else B2 is set to 0.

With this algorithm, the controller first identifies which pair of lines L0:L1 or L2:L3 was least recently used, and then within the selected pair which line was least recently used. This line is the one to be replaced. The decision tree is shown in Figure 5.14.

5.4.3 Cache Line Fill Techniques

When placing a cache between the microprocessor local bus and the memory (system) bus, the performance of the cache and the microprocessor is influenced by the technique used to perform the cache line fill operation.

Often, the cache line has a size which exceeds the memory (system) data bus width; therefore, multiple accesses to memory are required to fill a cache line. One way of doing it is to use **multiple (nonburst) bus cycles** like those described for the Intel 80486 in Section 2.4.2a. For the 80486, which has two clock cycles per bus cycle and an on-chip cache

---

[17]This is really a "pseudo LRU algorithm."

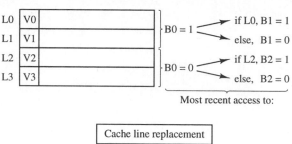

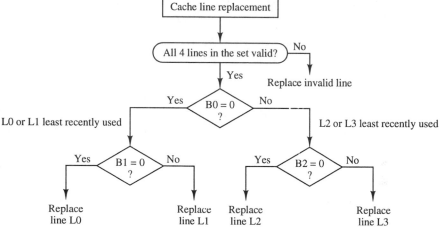

Figure 5.14 Pseudo LRU (least recently used) algorithm.

line of 16 bytes, the nonburst line fill operation would require 2-2-2-2 clock cycles for a total of 8 clock cycles. The 80486 processor can also execute a 2-1-1-1 **burst cycle** to fill the cache line in only 5 clock cycles. In either type of cache line fill (burst or nonburst), the 80486 will follow the specific address ordering discussed in Section 2.4.2a.

Data requested last. The actual instant during the cache line fill operation that the microprocessor CPU receives the requested data coming from main memory depends on the "line fill technique" the cache follows: "data requested last" and "data requested first."

With the **data requested last,** the data item requested is placed in the cache last. This means that all other data items of the cache line are fetched first from memory, then the requested item, and only when the whole line fill operation is completed is the requested item passed to the microprocessor. For example, for a 32-bit microprocessor with a 16-byte cache line requesting a data item from location $16N+4$ of a 32-bit memory, and assuming a line fill with the same order as in the Intel 80486 (see Section 2.4.2a), the cache line will be filled from the following addresses, as shown in Figure 5.15a:

$$16N + 8, \ 16N + C, \ 16N, \text{ and } 16N + 4.$$

This is the simpler to implement but has the drawback that the microprocessor has to stall until the line fill is completed. As we will describe later, this technique has a "high miss penalty."

If we assume this technique applied to a microprocessor with a 2-2-2-2 nonburst cycle and a 2-1-1-1 burst cycle, the first 2 clock cycles needed to access the first doubleword of

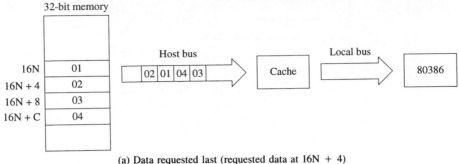

(a) Data requested last (requested data at 16N + 4)

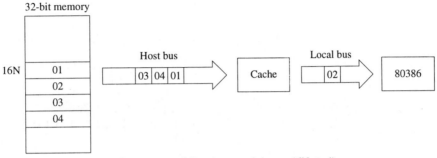

(b) Data requested first (requested data at 16N + 4)

- Location 16N + 4 passed immediately back to microprocessor

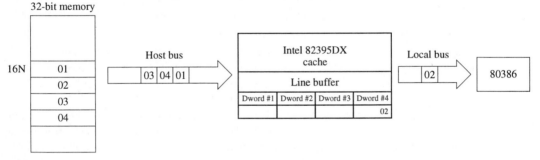

- Location 16N + C passed to microprocessor from the line buffer, before the cache line fill completes

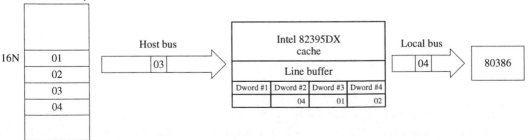

(c) Line buffer caching (requested data at 16N + 4, then at 16N + C)

Figure 5.15 Cache line-fill techniques [4]. Reprinted by permission of Intel Corporation, Copyright/Intel Corporation 1991.

the block are referred to as the **memory latency time** and the remaining clock cycles (6 in the nonburst case or 3 in the burst case) are referred to as the **memory transfer time.** In the data requested last method, the **cache miss penalty** (mentioned in Section 5.1) equals the sum of the memory latency time and memory transfer time. We notice that in this example, nonbursting causes the miss penalty to increase by 3 clock cycles.

Data requested first. In order to improve performance we need to reduce the "cache miss penalty." With the **data requested first,** the line fill first fetches the requested data item and simultaneously passes it to the microprocessor. This means that the microprocessor can continue to operate while the cache completes the remainder of the line fill independently. When the CPU does not have to wait for the entire instruction block to be fetched before restarting its internal pipeline, it is referred to as **instruction streaming.**

Following the same example of requesting a data item from location $16N + 4$, and again assuming an 80486 cache line fill order, the cache line will be filled from the following addresses, as shown in Figure 5.15b:

$$16N + 4, 16N, 16N + C, 16N + 8$$

External caches exist that support either one of the above two cache line fill techniques.[18] Although this is a faster technique, it is more difficult to implement; furthermore, handling a second read while trying to fill the rest of the block becomes tricky.

Line buffer caching. Finally, some microprocessor caches use a read line buffer to implement the **line buffer caching** technique. Figure 5.15c shows the operation: the microprocessor requests memory location $16N + 4$, and then location $16N + C$. With this technique, the microprocessor is allowed to access valid information that has been placed in the line buffer, although the whole line buffer fill operation has not been completed. In other words, when the microprocessor requests data, both the cache data RAM and the line buffer are checked to see if the information is valid. When the cache follows the "data requested first" technique in filling the line buffer, the microprocessor can access the data as soon as it is placed in the line buffer (even though the cache line itself has not yet been updated). The 80486, with its on-chip cache and line size of 16 bytes, has a line buffer and implements the "data requested first" technique; its miss penalty is only 2 clock cycles (equal to the memory latency time). If no line buffering exists, the microprocessor is not allowed to access that line of the cache; this prevents it from receiving stale or invalid information.

5.5 EXAMPLE MICROPROCESSOR CACHES

5.5.1 Fully Associative: Zilog Z80000

Fully associative caches have not been implemented in many microprocessors; they are used primarily to implement the ATC or TLB of paged MMUs. The Zilog Z80000 is one example that has an on-chip, 256-byte fully associative, physical cache. The 256 bytes make up 16

[18]For example, for the Intel 80386 microprocessor, the external Intel 82385 cache controller implements "data requested last," while the external Intel 82395 smart cache implements the "data requested first." The external caches used as secondary caches for the Intel 80486 use the data requested first technique.

cache lines (also called tag lines) with 16 bytes per line, as shown in the functional diagram of Figure 5.16. These 16 bytes are managed as 8 16-bit words, each one having its own word valid bit. Every cache line has a 28-bit tag field, with its own valid tag bit. When a burst load operation is performed (on a tag miss), all 16 bytes are loaded with four consecutive 32-bit transfers. The cache can hold instructions only, data only, or both. Main memory is also subdivided into equally sized blocks of 16 bytes, aligned on a 16-byte boundary for which the rightmost 4 address bits are zero.

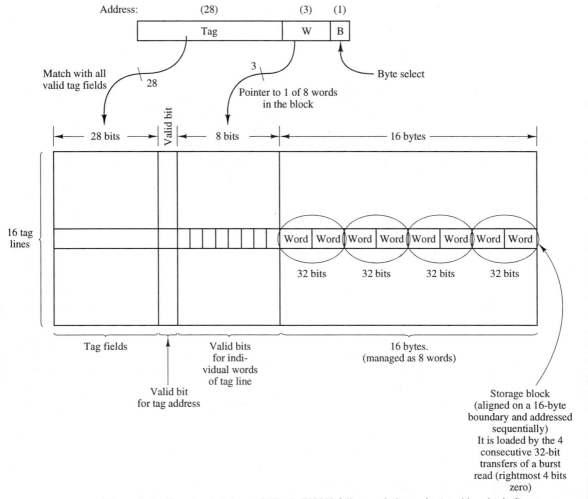

Figure 5.16 Functional diagram of Zilog's Z80000 fully associative cache (on-chip, physical).

The Z80000 cache operates as follows:

1. For both a tag hit (i.e., a tag match and valid tag) and a word hit (i.e., a valid word), and if the operation is a read, then access is from the on-chip cache; otherwise, it is a cache miss, and access is from external main memory.

2. For read operations:
   a. If there is a tag miss, a burst memory access is required to update the cache line; the LRU (least recently used) algorithm is used to choose the line to be replaced.
   b. If there is a tag hit followed by a word miss, one word is read from main memory to update the proper word in the cache.

3. For write operations:
   a. If there is a tag hit, the *write-through* policy is used by which both the internal cache and the external memory are updated.
   b. If there is a tag miss, only main memory is updated.

5.5.2 Direct Mapped: Motorola 68030

The 68030 has followed the *split-cache approach* of providing two separate on-chip caches, one for data and one for instructions. Because of the internal Harvard architecture, separate internal buses are provided for each cache, and a supporting smart bus controller assigns priorities to bus traffic to and from the caches. Each cache is a **virtual cache,** it contains 256 bytes, and is **direct-mapped.** Each cache has the block diagram shown in Figure 5.17 with 16 lines (accessed by decoding a 4-bit index field in the address) composed of the following fields: a 24-bit tag field that contains the 24 most significant virtual address bits, four ''word valid'' bits one for each longword in the cache line, and a block with four longwords, LW0, LW1, LW2, and LW3. Their main difference is their function code field: the instruction cache has only one bit, the FC2, whose value is sufficient to distinguish between user and supervisor code space; the data cache, however, has a 3-bit function code field to distinguish between supervisor data space (FC0–FC2 = 101) and user data space (FC0–FC2 = 001).[19]

The 68030 has a cache hit when (1) there is an access space hit, (2) there is a tag match, and (3) there is a ''word hit.'' A cache miss exists under the following cases: (1) there is an access space miss (or violation), or (2) there is a tag miss, or (3) there is a ''word miss'' (i.e., the requested information is not valid in the cache).

When it comes to write operations, the only concern is with the data cache (since the processor does not write instructions in the instruction cache). The 68030 data cache is a *write-through cache:* on a cache hit, data is written both to the cache and to external memory (provided that the on-chip MMU validates this access), thus keeping main memory coherent; on a cache miss, which one of the two schemes—the *no-write allocation* scheme (in which case no altering of the data in the data cache takes place), or the *write allocation* scheme (in which case the processor always updates the data cache on cacheable write cycles)—is used depends on how the supervisor had initialized the system during RESET (by setting the appropriate bit in the cache's control register). In case the write-through does not allocate on a write miss, the only way new data from memory will be placed in the cache is on a read miss. On a miss, the 68030 microprocessor executes either a *burst line fill cycle* or a *single-entry fill* cycle[20] (see Section 2.4.2).

The 68030 microprocessor has the **CDIS#** (cache disable) input pin that disables both caches, and the **CIIN#** (cache inhibit) input pin that inhibits caching data/instructions on a

---

[19]**Noncacheable entries:** Accesses to the Motorola ''CPU space'' (when FC0–FC2 = 111) are not cached because of possible problems when servicing interrupts from external coprocessors; similarly, accesses to peripheral input/output devices are not cached.

[20]As we will see below, the 68040 does not support the single-entry fill cycle for its cache.

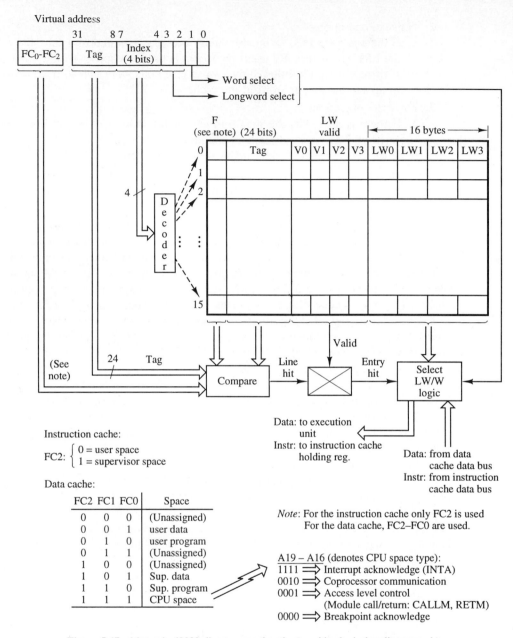

Virtual address

Instruction cache:

$$FC2: \begin{cases} 0 = \text{user space} \\ 1 = \text{supervisor space} \end{cases}$$

Data cache:

FC2	FC1	FC0	Space
0	0	0	(Unassigned)
0	0	1	user data
0	1	0	user program
0	1	1	(Unassigned)
1	0	0	(Unassigned)
1	0	1	Sup. data
1	1	0	Sup. program
1	1	1	CPU space

Note: For the instruction cache only FC2 is used. For the data cache, FC2–FC0 are used.

A19 – A16 (denotes CPU space type):
1111 ⟹ Interrupt acknowledge (INTA)
0010 ⟹ Coprocessor communication
0001 ⟹ Access level control
(Module call/return: CALLM, RETM)
0000 ⟹ Breakpoint acknowledge

Figure 5.17 Motorola 68030 direct-mapped cache (on-chip, logical, split approach).

per-cycle basis.[21] It also has the **CIOUT#** (cache inhibit out) output pin, which is needed due to the fact that the internal caches are virtual caches and this signal could also be used by external hardware to inhibit caching in external caches.

[21]Examples of data that should not be cached are data for I/O devices and data for memory ports with smaller than 32-bit sizes.

Operating system software can also control the cache using two internal CPU registers: the **CACR** (cache control register), used to exercise control over cache operations, and the **CAAR** (cache address register), which contains the address for a cache entry to be cleared. These two registers provide the following software control for the on-chip instruction and data caches: *enable/disable the cache* (where in the second case the processor always fetches from external memory); *clear (invalidate) all valid bits* in the cache; *clear (invalidate) a particular line* of the cache; *freeze the cache* (for example, to lock a critical sequence of code in the cache, in which case, if the cache is enabled, cache hits will always read from the cache but cache misses will not be allowed to update its entries); choose whether a *burst fill cycle* will be used; and choose whether *cache allocate will be performed on write also*.

Example 5.5: Motorola 68030 Instruction Cache

Figure 5.18 shows an example of using the 68030 instruction cache in a cache miss case [8].

The 68030 processor operates in the supervisor mode and the program counter value (the virtual address) 276F1A64 points to instruction 4251, or CLR.W(A1), in the supervisor space. Since the processor operates in supervisor mode, FC2 = 1 in the virtual address. This bit, along with the 24-bit tag of the program counter, is checked against the respective fields of line number 6 (this line is specified by decoding the index field of the program counter address). Since this does not match the FC2 bit in line number 6 in the cache, there is a cache miss. (A cache line miss would have occurred even if the 24-bit tags matched, as we will see in the next example.) To simplify the example, let's assume that the cache filling is done using the "single-entry fill" mode. Then the 68030 on-chip bus controller will initiate a doubleword fetch from main memory, instruction word 4251 (along with the next word) will be fetched in one 32-bit read operation, and LW1 will be updated in the cache. FC2 and the 24-bit tag will be updated with the values of 1 and 276F1A, respectively. The only bit set to valid will be V1, since all the other doublewords left in the cache are invalid (they correspond to the previous *user space* instructions). The bottom of Figure 5.18b shows the new contents of the updated cache line 6.

Example 5.6: Motorola 68030 Data Cache

In Figure 5.19 the processor operates in the supervisor mode (thus, FC2–FC0 = 101) and the executing instruction [MOVE.W (A1),D0] generates the effective address 01F376B8, which points to the data word 1576 in the supervisor data space. Since the processor's FC2–FC0 = 101 does not match the FC2–FC0 field in line number 11 of the cache (this field equals 001), there is a cache line miss. (Because the 24-bit tag matches and V2 indicates a valid entry, the word 1578 in the cache represents an operand item in the same location but in the user space. This is a case where the same virtual address points to two data in two different virtual address spaces.) The bottom part of Figure 5.19b shows the new contents of the updated data cache line 11, using the "single-entry fill" mode.

Example 5.7: Motorola 68030 "Single-Entry Fill" from a 16-bit Port

Explain in detail what happens when the Motorola 68030 attempts to access a doubleword operand at location 16N + A of a 16-bit port and there is a cache miss due to a "word miss." (One way of explaining it is by drawing the local bus timing diagram and showing the values on the bus lines and the most important control signals.)

Solution: Since there is a "word miss," the microprocessor does not necessarily have to read a block from main memory and update the whole cache line (through a "burst fill cycle"). It can also access main memory and perform "single-entry fill cycle." Let's assume that this is the case and that at location 16N + A the operand EFGHIJKL is stored.

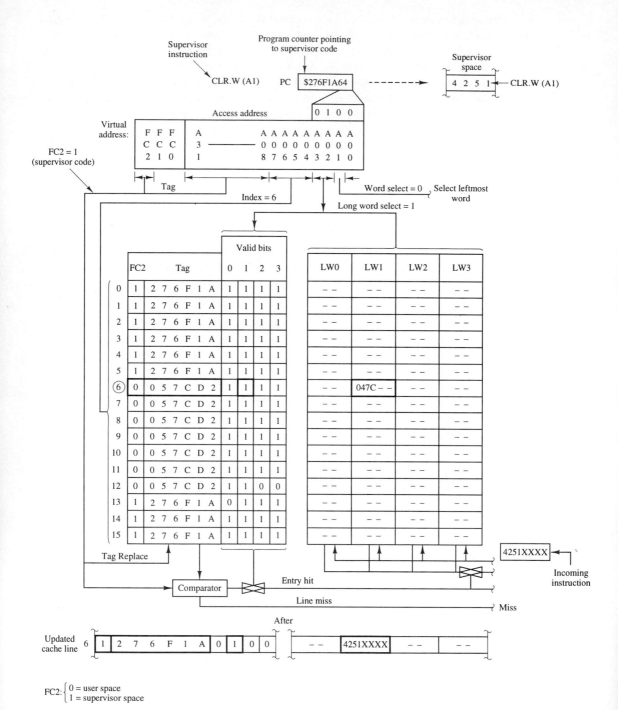

Figure 5.18 Example of instruction miss in the Motorola 68030 instruction cache. On a cache miss we assume here that the ''single-entry fill mode'' is used. Processor is in supervisor mode.

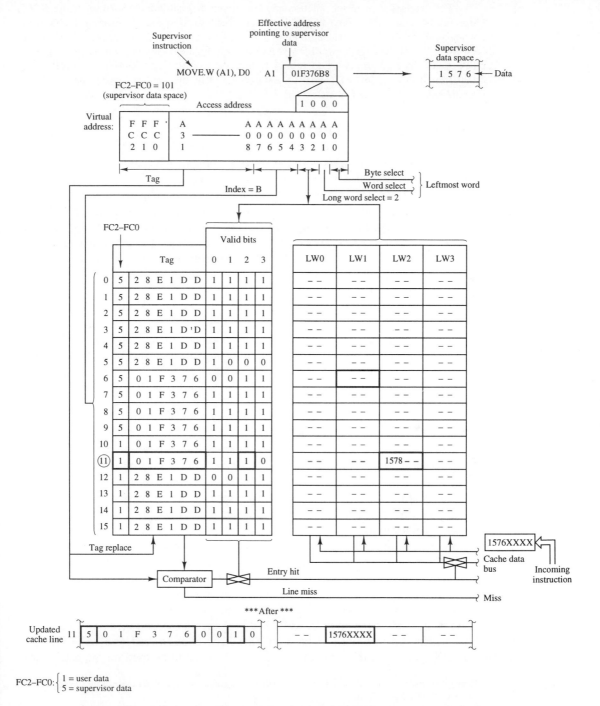

Figure 5.19 Example of a cache miss in the Motorola's 68030 data cache. On a cache miss we assume here that the "single-entry fill" mode is used. Processor is in the supervisor mode.

The detailed steps of the solution and the timing diagram are depicted in Figure 5.20. (Also see Section 2.6.3.) First of all, since the doubleword operand crosses a doubleword boundary, this will result in having both doublewords of the cache be updated: first fill doubleword DW2 and then doubleword DW3. As shown in Figure 5.20a, this will be done in four clock cycles since the memory port is only 16 bits; the words will be fetched in the following order: from $16N + A$, $16N + 8$, $16N + C$, and $16N + E$. The dynamic bus sizing and the valid operand bytes on the data bus are shown in Figure 5.20b.

5.5.3 Set-Associative: Motorola 68040

As in the 68030 case, the 68040 processor has separate, on-chip data and instruction caches, each one now is 4 Kbytes in size. Each cache has a 4-way set-associative organization, composed of 64 sets, each set having 4 lines or "ways," as shown in Figure 5.21. There are 4 lines per set and a total of 64 sets in each 4-way set-associative cache. The low-order 2 bits (B) of the physical address specify the byte displacement within a doubleword, and the next 2 more significant bits (W) specify the doubleword within a line. The set is selected using the 6 bits LA9–LA4 of the logical address. Since these bits do not need to be translated (they are the same for both the logical and physical address), set selection is done in parallel with the address translation (using the address translation cache ATC).

As in the 68030, each line contains 4 doublewords D0, D1, D2, D3 (refillable with one burst access mode[22]), and an address tag field TAG which contains the upper 22 bits of the translated physical address (the 20-bit page frame number and the 2 high bits of the page offset) used by the four comparators. The status field contains the **function code bits** (FC2 for the instruction cache and FC0–FC2 for the data cache). In addition, in both the instruction and data caches, the status field also contains **one valid bit** for the entire line. Finally, in the case of the data cache, which can be written to by the processor, the status field contains four additional **dirty bits,** one for each of the four doublewords in the cache line.

A *cache hit* exists when any of the four tags in the selected set matches the upper 22 bits of the incoming physical address and the tag status is valid. Because there is only one valid bit for the entire line (unlike the 68030) *68040 cache misses always update the entire cache line*.[23] On-chip bus snooping hardware maintains coherency of the two caches. The processor's bus controller prioritizes each cache's external memory requests. Read requests take priority over write requests to ensure that the (instruction, integer, and floating-point unit) internal pipelines remain filled.

Both the instruction and data caches are physical: they receive already translated 32-bit instruction and data physical addresses from the respective on-chip ATC hardware as shown in Figure 5.21.

One of the two data-cache write methods that the processor supports is the cacheable *write-through mode,* which allocates (i.e., updates the cache) only on a cache-read miss[24] (this is the default mode if the on-chip MMU is disabled). The second method is the *write-back mode,* which allocates (i.e., updates the cache) on either a read or a write miss by requesting read cycle(s) on the external bus. The write mode to be used for the data cache

---

[22]Remember that the 68040 does not support dynamic bus sizing and that it always executes synchronous bus operations with only 32-bit ports.

[23]Memory devices unable to support burst accesses can respond by asserting the processor's TBI# (transfer burst inhibit) input pin, forcing the processor to complete the access as a sequence of doubleword accesses.

[24]This is also called "no-write allocate policy."

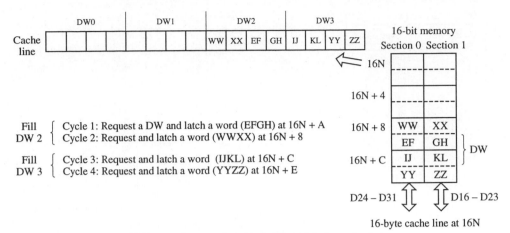

Fill DW 2 { Cycle 1: Request a DW and latch a word (EFGH) at 16N + A
{ Cycle 2: Request and latch a word (WWXX) at 16N + 8

Fill DW 3 { Cycle 3: Request and latch a word (IJKL) at 16N + C
{ Cycle 4: Request and latch a word (YYZZ) at 16N + E

(a) Four cycles to update the doubleword in the cache line

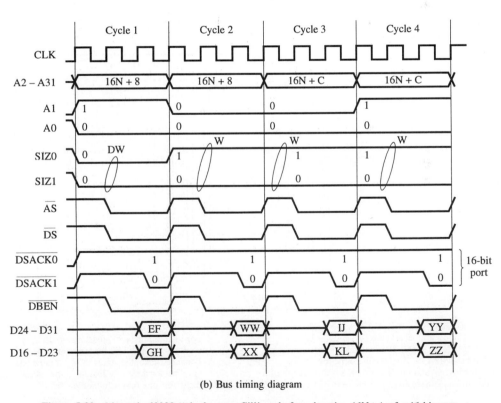

(b) Bus timing diagram

Figure 5.20 Motorola 68030 "single-entry fill" cycle from location 16N+A of a 16-bit port.

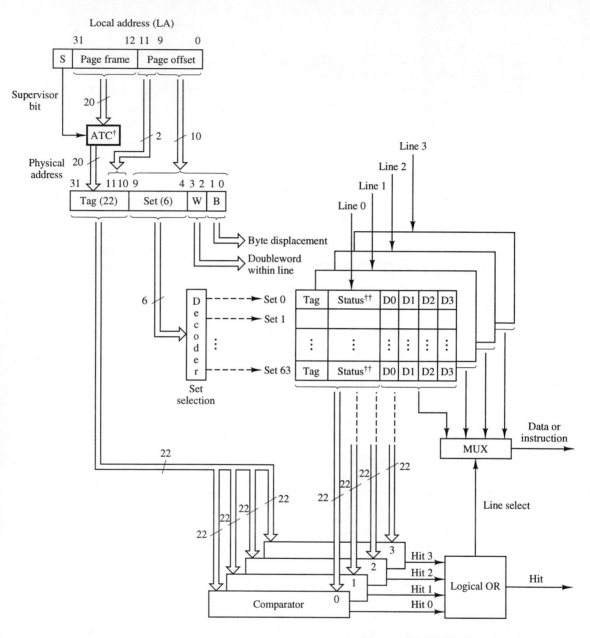

†Actually, only logical address bits LA31 – LA12 pass through the ATC. The remaining least significant address bits LA11 – LA0 are the same for both the logical and physical address. The structure of the ATC and its entries are given in Figure 6.15.

††For instruction cache, the status field contains one valid bit for the entire line. For data cache, the status field contains one valid bit for the entire line, plus four additional dirty bits, one for each doubleword.

Figure 5.21 Motorola 68040 4-way set-associative cache (on-chip, physical, split-cache approach).

is selectable on a per page basis. In addition to the above two modes, two additional cache modes that may be selected (on a per page basis) are the "cache inhibited serialized" mode and the "cache inhibited nonserialized" mode. These two noncacheable modes are used for regions of the address space containing noncacheable targets, such as I/O devices and shared data structures in multiprocessor environments. (Serialization has to do with guaranteeing that accesses to the pages is done in the proper sequence required by the internal integer unit pipeline architecture [9].) The particular one of the above four caching modes is specified on a page basis by the cache mode (CM) bits in the ATC entry (see Figure 6.15). As always, input/output space is noncacheable.

For reads that hit in the caches, the cache half-line (2 doublewords) selected by the physical address bit A3 is multiplexed onto the internal bus (instruction or data bus). For line replacement, the 68040 first locates the first invalid line and then uses it; if no invalid entries are found, the processor uses a pseudo-random replacement algorithm which works as follows: Each cache contains a 2-bit counter which is incremented for each access to the cache; when a replacement is to be done, the line pointed to by the current counter value is replaced, after which the counter is incremented.

5.6 CACHE COHERENCY ISSUES

The problem of cache coherency arises from the fact that data from a given memory location can reside simultaneously in main memory and in one or more caches. Cache coherency problems occur when the cache and main memory do not have the same data; either because another bus master changed the data in main memory without updating its copy in the microprocessor's cache, or the microprocessor changed data in its cache without updating main memory (e.g., when the microprocessor follows the write-back policy). In multiprocessor systems, cache coherency problems may also arise when two different caches have different data; this can happen when more than one bus master device can access shared, writable, memory blocks. Read-only or nonshared data structures can always be safely cached without precautions. In this section we present some of the cache coherency problems and outline their solutions.

5.6.1 The Stale Data Problem

The stale data problem can appear in both uniprocessor and multiprocessor environments. It arises in situations when a data is written into the cache without at the same time also updating main memory (as in a write-back policy); in this case main memory has stale data. In a different situation, a DMA controller or a second processor writes to main memory without at the same time updating the first processor's cache; in this case, the first processor's cache has stale data.

Stale data may appear even in a uniprocessor environment if one is not careful in designing the cache and choosing the appropriate write policy. Figure 5.22 shows a processor reading stale data that this same processor had changed. At step 1, the processor tries to read from location N that causes a cache miss; the data is therefore read from memory and the cache is updated with the new value A. At step 2, the processor updates this data by writing to the same cache location N the value B; if the write-back policy is followed, main memory

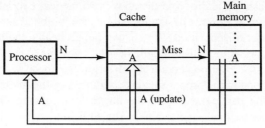

Step 1: Processor reads A from memory.

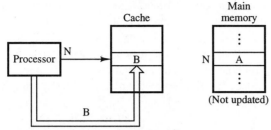

Step 2: Processor writes B to cache only.

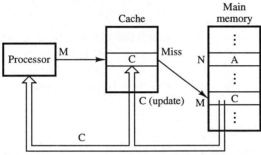

Step 3: A cache miss causes C from main memory to erase B in the cache.

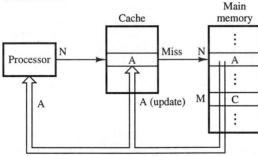

Step 4: Processor reads old stale data A.

Figure 5.22 Example of stale data (write-back mode, no "dirty" bits).

is not updated at the same time and, therefore, memory location N now contains the old stale data A. At step 3, the processor reads from location M that causes a cache miss; the data is therefore read from memory and it is assumed here that when the cache is updated, the new value C overwrites (erases) the old value B. If no "dirty" bits exist, this erasing of value B will not be recorded. Finally, at step 4, the processor tries to read from N the up-dated value B the processor had written earlier; since B was erased from the cache, there is

Microprocessor Caches   Chap. 5

a cache miss and therefore the processor will read from main memory location N the old stale data A.

The above uniprocessor stale data case can be avoided either by choosing the write-through policy or incorporating ''dirty'' bits in the cache. If ''dirty'' bits exist, at step 2 the cache controller would have marked this cache entry as ''dirty.'' Then at step 3, before C overwrites B in the cache, the cache controller would have first copied B back into main memory location N, which allows the processor to read the correct data on the cache miss at step 4.

Handling the stale data problem in a multiprocessor configuration or in a configuration with a processor and an I/O subsystem is discussed below.

5.6.2 Software Solutions

Software solutions involve the compiler marking software code modules and data structures as shared/noncacheable, exclusive, etc. (usually on a page basis). I/O buffer pages (for memory-mapped devices) are also marked ''noncacheable.'' When this page becomes resident, these attributes can be used to control cacheability of the data at a page-level granularity.

The easiest way to avoid the cache coherency problem is by making sure that such ''shared'' pages are never cached. Most recent microprocessors (including the Motorola 68040 and Intel 80486) do attach to each page the shared/nonshared attribute bits (when the page becomes resident) to control cacheability of the page. During paging (or, in general, address translation) these bits are used to disable the internal primary cache or generate control signals to disable the external second-level cache (like the Page Cache Disable signal that the Intel 80486 issues in Figure 5.6) so that the page will not be cached.

Another approach is to cache those pages that are shared but *only for read-only operations,* such as code of critical sections.

A third approach is to cache shared, writable pages *during periods* when they are modified by only one processor (for example, pages marked as being ''exclusive''). If a page is marked exclusive, it indicates that it is exclusively *available in only this cache,* and thus a write transaction need not appear on the memory bus and informing of other caches is not needed.

A final software approach used in multiprocessor systems is to implement a *directory* that keeps the state (invalid, dirty, etc.) of each memory block and includes information about which caches have copies of a memory block.

5.6.3 Hardware Solutions

Although software techniques may be used to maintain cache coherency, more efficient approaches involve hardware-based solutions that make the cache invisible to the operating system and the application software. This is sometimes referred to as **software transparency** and allows the designer to include a cache in the system without having to modify the application software.

Cacheable/Noncacheable memory.　In this hardware solution, certain areas of main memory are designated as ''noncacheable'' and accesses to them are cache misses.

Noncacheable areas of memory are those typically used for I/O registers/ports, ROM code, and I/O buffers.

This implementation requires external hardware decoders to decode the address (or part of it, such as its high-order bits), identify whether an access to such an area is attempted, and route the address to main memory. This is shown in Figure 5.23a. If an access to a cacheable area is detected, these decoders will generate the proper chip-select signals for the cache and send to it the address to check for a hit; if there is a hit, the data will come from the cache; if there is a miss, this address will be routed to main memory.[25]

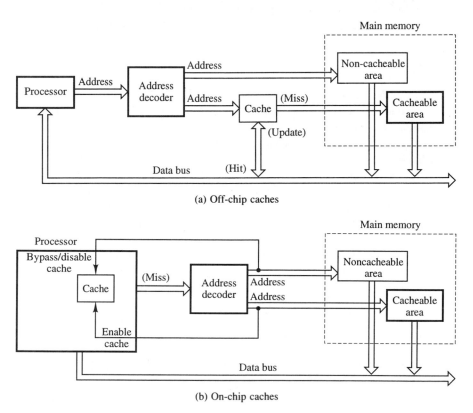

Figure 5.23 Cacheable/noncacheable main memory areas.

Figure 5.23b shows the equivalent configuration when the processor has on-chip caches. If there is a cache miss on a read operation, the external decoder will signal back the processor to *bypass* or *disable* the on-chip cache (i.e., do not update it with a value coming from a noncacheable location of main memory); otherwise, the on-chip cache will be enabled (for example, by triggering the KEN# input pin of the Intel 80486) and updated with the incoming cacheable data.

Instead of completely disabling the on-chip cache, a useful mechanism that some microprocessors have (e.g., the Intel i860) is the "external cache management ability." This

---

[25]A "move string" type of instruction can be used by the software to copy data between noncacheable and cacheable memory.

refs to the ability of the processor to externally *invalidate* cache lines and to specify cache lines as *write-through* or *noncacheable*. (The default cache policy is assumed to be write-back.)

Shared cache. In one approach, accesses of all bus masters are routed to main memory through the same cache (Figure 5.24a). This is usually applied for a small number of masters. We observe that in this case the I/O subsystem interferes with the microprocessor CPU, causing a *CPU to stall for I/O* (loss of CPU performance) and requires the arbitration hardware (Sections 2.7 and 4.7) to decide who accesses the cache.

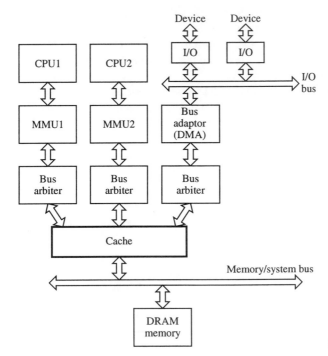

Figure 5.24 Shared cache.

Bus snooping. Figure 5.4 represents the most common case for larger systems or multiprocessor configurations: all bus masters share the same memory/system bus to access DRAM memory. The I/O system is connected to the DRAM memory (without interfering with the microprocessor) and each microprocessor has its own local cache.

Consider the following scenario: First, the microprocessor writes to its local cache with a write-back mode; main memory will be updated with the new data at some later time. What happens, however, if in-between the I/O system wants to read from memory? If this read completes, the I/O system will read old stale data. The solution to this is the following: the cache controller *monitors the memory/system bus for reads;* if the target address is in the cache, it inhibits the I/O system from reading from memory and the cache controller itself provides the data from its cache to the I/O system.

Consider a second scenario: the microprocessor writes to local cache with a write-through mode, i.e., a memory location is also updated at the same time. What happens if the I/O system then writes to the same main memory location? If the write completes, it will be the cache that has old stale data. The solution to this is to have the cache controller *monitor the memory/system bus for writes;* if the target address is in the cache, then either invalidate the cache entry or update it; in the first case, the next microprocessor read operation will read from main memory; in the second case, the next microprocessor read operation will read from the cache.[26] (This case in multiprocessor configurations involves broadcasting the writes on the memory/system bus.)

The above solutions represent the *bus snooping* technique which has the cache controller (or all cache controllers in a multiprocessor configuration) constantly monitor (snoop) all lines of the memory/system bus for each transaction, watch for I/O system or other bus master reads and writes, and compare the address on the memory/system bus to the address tags in its cache. The bus snooping hardware of the cache controller maintains information about the state of every cache line and takes appropriate action to maintain coherency. To minimize interference during tag checking between the snooping hardware and the CPU, the tag RAM portion of the cache is *dual-ported*.

For some products, bus cycles can be marked on the bus as "snoopable" or "non-snoopable." When the cycle is marked as snoopable, the bus snooper checks the caches for a coherency conflict based on the valid and dirty bits of the corresponding cache line and the type of bus cycle.

Bus snooping is activated only for cacheable memory areas or pages. In the case of cacheable/noncacheable memory (discussed in Section 5.6.3), external logic that identifies a noncacheable memory access will inhibit snooping (for example, to reduce performance degradation in a multiprocessor system). In the case of the software solutions (discussed in Section 5.6.2), the snooping controller will need some help from the compiler that assigns ownership information (attribute bits) to each page of code or data.

Example 5.8: Intel 80486 On-Chip Snooping Hardware

The on-chip 80486 cache controller has complete *bus snooping logic* (thus making the 80486 bus different from that of the 80386: the 80486 address bus is input/output, unlike the 80386 address bus, which is output only). Now, as shown in Figure 5.25, the address lines are bi-directional and when another master does a write to memory, the system hardware provides the address at the 80486 pins. At step 1, external system hardware asserts the AHOLD (address hold request) signal, which disables the 80486 address outputs on the next clock cycle (only the address bus is disabled, unlike the HOLD signal, which disables the address and data buses and all control signals). Other normal data activity can still continue while this AHOLD is asserted. At step 2 the external system logic sends the address to the 80486 and asserts the EADS# (external address) signal. Triggered by this signal, the 80486, then at step 3, will perform an "internal cache invalidation cycle" in order to keep the processor's internal cache contents consistent with external memory: the processor will read the address over its address lines and compare it to the cache tags; if a match is found (which means that the other bus master modified that data in main memory), the cache controller will *invalidate* this cache line. (The 80486 has no provision for partially valid lines.) There is a possible degradation because if during this cache invalidation cycle the CPU tries to access the cache simultaneously (either to prefetch an instruction or read data), the CPU will stall for one or more clock cycles.

For a complete flush of the cache contents, the 80486 processor has an input pin (FLUSH#) to invalidate all cache entries (all valid bits for all lines in the cache are cleared). The 80486 cache can also be flushed by the software instructions INVD and WBINVD.

---

[26]As we will see next, under the M.E.S.I. protocol, the cache controller forces this line into the "shared" state.

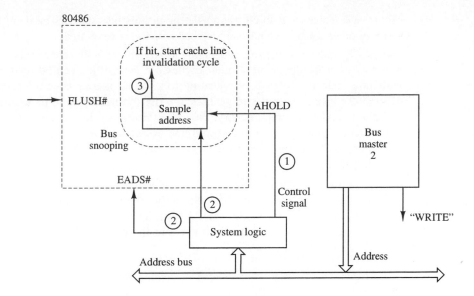

① AHOLD (address hold): 80486 disables its address outputs
on the next clock cycle. (Normal data
activity can continue while
AHOLD is asserted.)

② System logic sends address to 80486 and asserts EADS# (external address).

③ Microprocessor (cache controller) compares address to cache tags and, if a
match, invalidates cache line.

Figure 5.25   Intel 80486 on-chip cache bus snooping.

M.E.S.I. hardware cache coherency protocol.   A hardware-implemented cache coherency protocol is the M.E.S.I. (from the four states a cache line can be in) utilized by Intel's caches.[27] The description that follows is from [4]. Each cache line includes **state bits,** which depend upon what the cache controller is doing during its bus master's data transfer activities and during snooping activities it performs in response to snoop requests generated by other bus masters.

M.E.S.I. States.   M.E.S.I. represents 4 states. They define whether a line is valid (hit or miss), if it is available in other caches (shared or exclusive), and if it is modified (has been modified). The 4 states are:

Modified [M]: This state indicates a line which is available *only* in this cache, and is *modified* (main memory's copy is stale). Such an exclusive modified line can be updated locally in the cache without acquiring the memory bus. Because a modified line is the only up-to-date copy of data, it is the cache controller's responsibility to write-back this data to memory on snoop accesses to it by other cache controllers.

Exclusive [E]: Indicates a line which is exclusively available *only* in this cache, and that this line is *not modified* (main memory also has a valid copy). Writing to an

---

[27]For example, by the Intel 82495DX external cache controller and the 82490DX external cache memory.

exclusive line causes it to change to the modified state and can be done without informing other caches, so no memory bus activity is generated.

Shared [S]: Indicates that this line is potentially shared with other caches. (The same line may exist in one or more other caches.) A shared line can be read by the CPU without a main memory access. Writing to a shared line updates the cache and also requires the cache controller to generate a write-through cycle to the memory bus. In addition to updating main memory, the write-through cycle will invalidate this line in other caches. Since writing to a shared line causes a write-through cycle, the system can enforce a "write-through policy" to selected addresses by forcing those addresses into the [S] state.

Invalid [I]: Indicates that the line is not available in the cache. A read to this cache line will be a miss and cause the cache controller to execute a line fill (fetch the entire line and deposit it into the cache SRAM). A write to this cache line will cause the cache controller to execute a write-through cycle to the memory bus and in some circumstances initiate an allocation.

Basic State Transitions. The states determine the actions of the cache controller with regard to activity related to a line, and the state of a line may change due to those actions. All transactions which may require state changes in other caches are broadcast on the shared memory bus. For example, if a bus transaction requires that a line in another cache be invalidated, the memory bus controller is responsible for asserting an invalidation signal on the bus.

Figure 5.26 shows an example of basic M.E.S.I. state transitions. In Figure 5.26a the "current state" refers to the state of the cache line being accessed either by its CPU or a snoop from another cache on the memory bus. The "action" refers either to a CPU "read," CPU "write," or a "snoop" initiated by another cache attached to the same shared memory bus. The "new state" refers to the state of the current cache line after the action is performed. "Memory bus activity" refers to the action which takes place on the memory bus

Current state	Action	New state	Memory bus activity
M	Read	M	None
	Write	M	None
	Snoop	S	Write back
E	Read	E	None
	Write	M	None
	Snoop	S	None
S	Read	S	None
	Write	E	Write through
	Snoop	S	None
I	Read	E	Line fill
	Write	I	Write through
	Snoop	I	None

(a) Table [21] © 1992 IEEE

Figure 5.26 MESI cache coherency protocol.

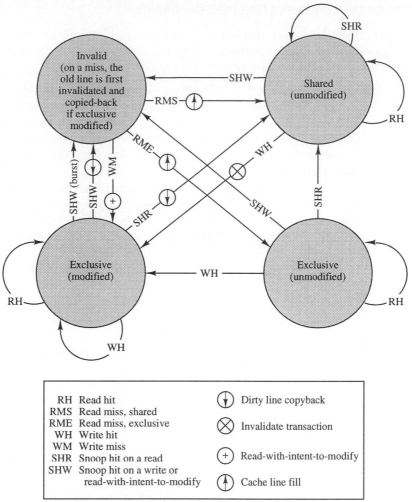

RH   Read hit
RMS Read miss, shared
RME Read miss, exclusive
WH   Write hit
WM   Write miss
SHR Snoop hit on a read
SHW Snoop hit on a write or
        read-with-intent-to-modify

⊕ Dirty line copyback

⊗ Invalidate transaction

⊕ Read-with-intent-to-modify

⊕ Cache line fill

(b) Diagram [4] (Reprinted by permission of Intel Corporation, Copyright Intel Corporation, 1991.)

Figure 5.26   (concluded)

(if any) as a result of the action being performed on the cache line. Note how CPU read and write accesses to the modified and exclusive states cause no memory bus activity.

Figure 5.26b shows the state transition diagram of the MESI cache coherency protocol implemented in the Motorola 88110 superscalar RISC microprocessor [21]. For example, when the snooping hardware of a processor recognizes that another processor starts a bus transaction for a cache line that the processor has it in an (exclusive) modified state, it forces the originator of the transaction off the bus, starts a memory bus cycle and writes the modified line back to memory (write back), changes the state of its line to shared (unmodified), and then allows the original bus transaction to be retried.

The M.E.S.I. model describes a write-back cache. *A write-through cache is a true subset of this model with only the shared and invalid states being implemented.*

5.7 CACHE DESIGN AND SYSTEM PERFORMANCE

A cache must be chosen/designed to *optimize overall system performance*. A cache that works well in one system environment may be a poor fit for a different system environment. Parameters that affect *system performance* include:

1. *Cache performance:* Cache performance is increased when (1) the cache "hit rate" (Equation 5.1) increases, (2) the cache bandwidth increases, and (3) the miss penalty on read misses is reduced (for example, by incorporating a second-level cache). The hit rate usually varies significantly with the software program run. Therefore, in order to determine the overall cache performance, one should look at the hit rate *over a number of programs*.

2. *Cache bandwidth:* Cache bandwidth is dependent upon cache access time, tag comparison time, and propagation delays (of interface components such as address latches and data buffers, processor setup time, etc., discussed in Section 3.5). Smaller cache access and tag comparison times will make cache hits (for both reads and writes) faster.

3. *Memory bus utilization:* Memory bus utilization is improved by improving the following: (1) cache line update (refill) time, which depends upon the burst cycle time, main memory latency, and main memory bandwidth; (2) the write policy, as discussed in Section 5.2.2; and (3) bus architecture features (dual versus single bus architecture, inclusion of line buffers, etc.).

4. *Main memory subsystem:* The performance of the main memory subsystem (usually DRAM) significantly affects the performance of the overall system (see Chapter 3). In the cache-based designs, it affects the amount of time it takes to write data to system memory, the speed with which cache line updates (fills) are performed, and the miss penalty on read misses. A good cache design can compensate for some, but not all, of a poor DRAM memory design. Figure 5.27 shows the impact of DRAM design on systems with first- and second-level caches [18,19].

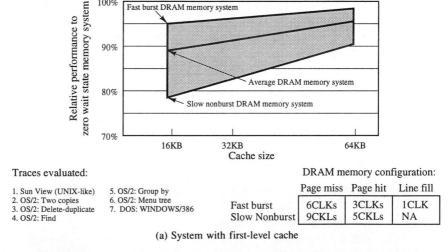

Traces evaluated:

1. Sun View (UNIX-like)
2. OS/2: Two copies
3. OS/2: Delete-duplicate
4. OS/2: Find
5. OS/2: Group by
6. OS/2: Menu tree
7. DOS: WINDOWS/386

DRAM memory configuration:

	Page miss	Page hit	Line fill
Fast burst	6CLKs	3CLKs	1CLK
Slow Nonburst	9CKLs	5CKLs	NA

(a) System with first-level cache

Figure 5.27 Impact of DRAM memory design on systems with first-level cache (a) and second-level cache (b). [4] Reprinted by permission of Intel Corporation, Copyright/Intel Corporation 1991.

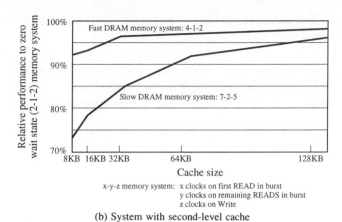

x-y-z memory system: x clocks on first READ in burst
y clocks on remaining READS in burst
z clocks on Write

Figure 5.27 (concluded)

(b) System with second-level cache

Example 5.9

If the bandwidth requirement from the processor to the external cache memory is 120 Mbits per second and the cache can satisfy 92% of the references, then main memory need only satisfy about 8%, which imposes an average main memory bandwidth requirement of 9.6 Mbits per second (8% of 120 Mbits per second). In practice, however, main memory should supply two to three times this required average bandwidth [14].

5. *Cost:* Although not directly associated with performance, cost is always a factor that must be taken into consideration. The cache cost depends primarily on the tag RAM size (number of tags and comparison circuitry are much more expensive than normal SRAMs) and secondarily on the line size (data RAM size). To minimize the cost, one should minimize the number of tags; this is done by having a tag represent multiple bytes of data (i.e., bigger cache block size).

5.7.1 Parameters That Affect Cache Performance

Cache performance is usually measured in terms of the *cache hit/miss ratio*[28]: the ratio of cache hits/misses to the total number of cache requests and it is a function of the cache design (Equation 5.1). However, a minimum cache miss rate does not necessarily mean maximal performance of the overall system. A better metric for judging (estimating) the influence of main memory on the overall system performance is the **average memory-access time,** given by

$$\boxed{\textbf{average memory-access time} = \text{hit rate} * \text{hit time} + \text{miss rate} * \text{miss penalty}}$$

(5.2)

There are a number of trade-offs to be considered and decisions to be made in designing, selecting, and using a cache [15]. For the designer of microprocessor systems, these considerations apply to external off-chip caches or the second-level caches (which invariably

---

[28]The *cache hit/miss rate* is the percentage of references that the cache memory can satisfy/not satisfy, and the sum of the two always equals 100%. For the most common sizes of 4K to 64K bytes, the hit rate ranges from 92 to 98.8% [14].

are always external). Before we discuss how to measure cache performance, let's take a look at the parameters that affect it and their trade-offs.

Miss penalty. **Miss penalty** is the time it takes to access the first "word" of a block in main memory on a miss, transfer the remaining "words" of the block to the cache, and deliver the requested "word" to the CPU. Therefore, it can be expressed by the following equation:

$$\boxed{\begin{aligned} \textbf{miss penalty} &= \text{memory (read) latency } + \text{ transfer time } + \text{ delivery time} \\ &= L + X + D \end{aligned}}$$

(5.3)

where **memory latency**,[29] L = the time to read the first "word" of a block on a cache read miss[30] (which includes address decoding and any other interface logic delays, DRAM memory access time, and possible bus arbitration time when a number of masters can access memory)

transfer time, X = the time to transfer the remaining "words" of a block[31] (which is affected by memory interleaving, page-mode access, etc.)

delivery time, D = time to deliver the requested "word" to the microprocessor CPU

Example 5.10

The main **memory latency** may include the following parameters[32]:

DRAM read access of 100 ns	3 clock cycles
ECC and other logic	4 clock cycles
Address decode and recognition	1 clock cycle
Drive of the backplane bus	2 clock cycles
Processor stall to the drive of memory signals	1 clock cycle
Memory controller to bus interface	2 clock cycles
Total:	13 clock cycles

The **transfer time** has the effect of causing the microprocessor CPU to **stall** waiting for the requested "word" to be fetched from main memory. As we saw earlier, the *data requested first* cache line fill technique can be used to minimize the data cache miss penalty (by minimizing the transfer time). For instruction caches, *streaming* can be used; this is particularly important to the internal pipelines of RISC microprocessors for which instead of stalling until the entire block is first fetched before restarting the pipeline, the pipeline re-

---

[29]Also called *access time, access latency,* or *read latency.* Small latency is more important for RISC microprocessors to reduce the length of the internal pipeline stall.

[30]Usually, the reads or loads are more important than the writes or stores, because in a load operation the CPU stalls until the data is fetched from main memory while on a store operation the CPU continues operation immediately after it presented the address and data (assuming that the interface hardware—usually in the form of a "write buffer"—has already captured them).

[31]This is the case if we assume the *data requested last* cache line fill technique.

[32]The memory latency depends on the system design. These numbers were taken from a 25-MHz R3000-based system with 64 Kbytes of external I-cache, 64 Kbytes D-cache, and a block size of 16 32-bit words [1].

sumes operation as soon as the first instruction "word" causing the miss is fetched from main memory.[33]

If we simplify Equation 5.3 by ignoring the delivery time, we get

$$\textbf{miss penalty} = \text{memory latency} + \text{transfer time}$$
$$= L + X$$

(5.4)

As we will see later, increasing the cache block size may improve the cache miss rate. On the other hand, we can conclude from the above that a bigger block size increases the miss penalty (in the "data requested last" scheme), which has a negative effect on system performance to the point that it may degrade the actual performance.

Besides burst loading and using faster DRAM memories, we can reduce the miss penalty (and thus increase system performance) by including a second-level cache to catch the misses of the first level and provide them with a smaller "second-level cache latency."

Example 5.11: Miss Penalty

Assume a cache-based design with the following timing characteristics on a cache (read) miss:

1 clock cycle to send address to main memory

4 clock cycles to access a 32-bit doubleword from main memory and transfer it to the processor

If the cache block is 1 doubleword, the miss penalty is

$$\text{miss penalty (1 DW)} = L + X = 1 + 4 = 5 \text{ clock cycles}$$

If the cache block is 4 doublewords and assuming a multiple, *nonburst transfer* is executed, the miss penalty is

$$\text{miss penalty (4 DWs)} = 4 * (L + X) = 20 \text{ clock cycles}$$

This demonstrates the *negative effect on the miss penalty that a larger block size has.* If the cache block is 4 doublewords and a *burst transfer* is executed with one doubleword per clock in block refill, the miss penalty becomes

$$\text{miss penalty (4 DWs burst)} = \text{miss penalty for 1 DW} + 3 \text{ clock cycles} = 8 \text{ clock cycles}$$

This demonstrates the *positive effect on the miss penalty that the burst versus nonburst cache fill mode has.*

In all the above cases we assumed that the processor stalls until the entire cache block is fetched ("data requested last" scheme).

Cache size.   A design decision has to do with the size of the cache. The larger the cache, the lower the miss ratio, which usually is translated to a better cache performance. Larger caches, however, are slower because of longer delays at large fan-in and fan-out gates. Locality of reference affects cache size decisions, since trying to increase performance based on increasing cache size is subject to the law of diminishing returns, as shown abstractly in Figure 5.28a.

[33]As an example, the improvement in performance obtained from streaming was measured in the MIPS R3000 microprocessor to be about 5%, depending on the specific application and memory configuration [1].

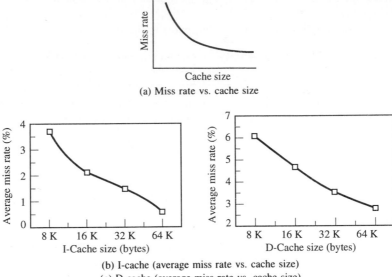

(a) Miss rate vs. cache size

(b) I-cache (average miss rate vs. cache size)

(c) D-cache (average miss rate vs. cache size)

Figure 5.28 (a) Abstract graph of miss rate vs. cache size; (b) and (c) are actually measured plots for average miss rates vs. cache size for the direct-mapped, external, I-cache and D-cache of a MIPS R3000-based configuration [6]. Courtesy of IDT. This average represents the average miss rates for some representative UNIX applications (NROFF, DBX, WOLF, TERSE, HSPICE, and AS1).

Figures 5.28b and c show actual measurements that suggest the following: For I-caches, increasing the cache size from 8K to 16K provides the largest net improvement in miss rates: 3.16%; from 16K to 32K there is only a 0.7% net improvement; at 64K the miss rate shows improvement of about 1.1% over a 32-Kbyte cache. For D-caches, the net improvement in miss rates is higher for 16K and 32K, 1.5%, than for 64K, which is 0.6%. Furthermore, it must be kept in mind that the effect of D-cache miss rate upon performance is not as significant as the I-cache miss rate, because the I-cache is involved in **all** instruction fetches while the D-cache is involved in *just* the load instructions, which are typically 20% of the instruction mix for a given program.

The choice of the cache size may also be dictated by the available area on the board, also keeping in mind that larger caches need more power and more cooling. Reference [16] provides an in-depth discussion on the relation between the cache size and hit ratio for various cache organizations. Because cache performance depends on many other parameters and the locality of the type of software executed, it is not true that a bigger cache always outperforms a smaller cache.

Cache block size. What is the most appropriate size for the cache block? As shown abstractly in Figure 5.29a, as the block size grows, the miss ratio will in general decrease since a miss will fetch more data at a time and is more likely to contain the needed information (spatial locality). Beyond a certain point, however, there are only few blocks in the cache, and the cache misses due to the temporal locality outweigh those due to the spatial locality. With smaller cache blocks, less data is replaced (overwritten) and lost; thus,

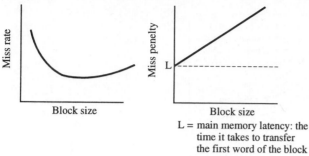

L = main memory latency: the
time it takes to transfer
the first word of the block

(a) Miss rate and miss penalty vs. block size

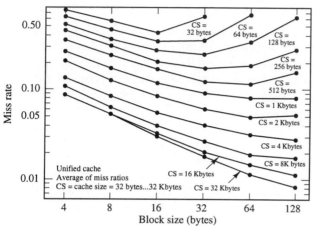

(b) Unified cache (average miss ratio vs. block size for different cache
sizes) [4] (Reprinted by permission of Intel Corporation, Copyright/
Intel Corporation, 1991.)

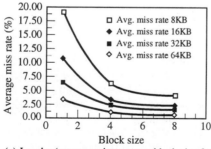

(c) I-cache (average miss rate vs. block size for
different cache sizes) [6]

Figure 5.29 (a) Abstract graph of miss
rate vs. block size; (b) Intel actual measured plots: miss ratio = 1-hit rate; (c)
Actual measured plots for the direct-
mapped, external, I-cache and D-cache of
the MIPS R3000 using the mix of applications in Figure 5.28 [6]. Courtesy of IDT.

data stays longer in the cache and provides a greater chance that it will be there when the
microprocessor needs it.

Although increasing the block size may improve cache performance (improve miss
rate), the actual performance of the system may decrease because other factors tend to con-
tribute to this decrease. For example, the time to service a cache miss also increases (due to
overhead and increased transfer time), which may introduce processor stalls (the miss penalty increases with the increase in block size as shown abstractly in Figure 5.29a).

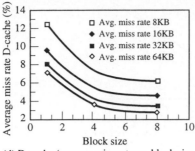

(d) D-cache (average miss rate vs. block size for different cache sizes) [6]

Figure 5.29 (concluded)

Another factor that must be taken into account when deciding the proper block size is the frequency of block crosses and page crosses in main memory, because (a) they take additional time (since they require a second memory bus cycle) and (b) there is a possibility of "page faults" appearing on either half or even on both halves at a time (which introduces delays in swapping a page from the disk into main memory). Increasing the block size increases the likelihood of fetching unnecessary memory.

Finally, bigger blocks correspond to longer tie-ups at the memory interface (increase in memory bus utilization); this can become quite serious in a multiprocessor system since one processor locks out the others from shared memory while it handles a cache miss.

In addition to cache performance, *cache utilization* factors will also have to be taken into consideration. If a 6-byte cache block has a 2-byte tag, then only three-fourths of the line contains useful information; in this case, when the block size increases, this ratio increases.

The instruction cache line size may be different from that of a data cache, because these two caches are used differently. For example, an instruction cache may have a block size of 4 doublewords, while a data cache may be only one doubleword long (since an individual cache doubleword may be written by a software store instruction).[34]

The other graphs in Figure 5.29 depict the behavior of a unified cache, as well as of a separate I-cache and D-cache.

Example 5.12: Miss Rate vs. Miss Penalty

Consider the same case as in Example 5.11. As we saw there, a 4-doubleword (16-byte) cache block yields a miss penalty of 8 clock cycles for a burst transfer.

Let's study the *effect of increasing the block size* from 16 bytes to 32 bytes.

(a) *Miss rate:* If the miss rate is characterized by the behavior in Figure 5.29b, then for a 4-Kbyte cache, the miss rate is *reduced* from (about) 5.5% to 4%; for a 16-Kbyte cache, the miss rate is *reduced* from (about) 3.2% to 1.1%.

(b) *Miss penalty:* If the processor stalls until the entire cache block is burst-fetched, then the miss penalty is *increased* from 8 clock cycles to 12 clock cycles (assuming again one doubleword per clock in cache line refill).

In Section 5.7.2 we will study the effect of *increasing the block size* (which *reduces the miss rate* while at the same time *increasing the miss penalty*) on the overall system performance.

---

[34]This is the implementation of the on-chip caches of the MIPS R3051 processor.

Virtual vs. physical cache.   Another design decision is whether the cache should be a virtual or a physical cache. As we saw in the examples so far, microprocessors have adopted both approaches, although most of the recent products with on-chip caches use the physical cache implementation. For example, of all the Motorola 32-bit microprocessors, the 68020 and 68030 have virtual caches, while the 68040 and 88100 use physical cache implementations. The Intel 80286/386 processors have external physical caches, the Intel 80486 has an on-chip, unified, physical cache, and the Intel i860 has on-chip, split, virtual caches.

Physical caches are those presented with the physical (main) memory address. This implies that the processor's address translation has already been done earlier, or it is done in parallel with the first part of a cache lookup. In the first case, the drawback is that all accesses must suffer the MMU translation delay. The second case limits the size of the cache and constrains mapping of virtual pages to physical page frames. Physical caches allow bus snooping to external caches without the reverse physical-to-logical address translation that virtual caches require.

Virtual caches use the high-order bits of the virtual address to address the cache.[35] Virtual caches are used primarily because they make cache hits faster (and this improves the overall system performance) since information in the cache can be accessed without the address translation delay that the MMU circuitry imposes. (It also permits the virtual-to-physical address translation to be done in parallel with the operation of the cache.) Furthermore, the frequency of address translations is reduced.

On the other hand, however, virtual caches are tricky to design and have a number of problems. One is trying to handle *synonyms* or *aliases:* two different virtual addresses translated to refer to the same physical address in main memory. If that occurs, then the same data element may be present in two different cache locations. Cache incoherency results when one bus master uses one of the two virtual addresses to change the value of that data element in main memory, followed by a second master using the other virtual address used to perform a read operation; the second master will then read old, stale data. Synonyms may appear when two different tasks (one of which may be an operating system task) share a page of data placed in different places in the two tasks' respective virtual address spaces.

Some solutions to the synonyms problem involve either completely disallowing synonyms (by putting shared data at the same relative place in the tasks' virtual address spaces) or adding what is referred to as RTB or reverse translation buffer (hardware that maps physical addresses back to logical addresses). Also, system software can be used to ensure that synonyms cannot occur; since within a context, each physical address must be accessed by only one logical address, during context switches (that cause changes in the virtual addresses) the instruction cache must be invalidated and the data cache flushed.[36] Attaching to each cache line an "address space identifier" or "process ID," reduces the frequency of cache flushes, at the expense of increasing the size and complexity of the cache.

The other problem has to do with I/O. Since virtual caches do not monitor physical addresses, another bus master or the I/O system (which uses physical addresses) can write into an area in main memory which is also accessible to a program, thus causing the cache

---

[35]Similar techniques have been followed by the MIPS R4000 on-chip caches and the Motorola 88200 external CMMUs. This technique is sometimes referred to as *virtually indexed* cache, or *virtually indexed, physically tagged* cache because the specification of the data (in a set-associative cache) is done by decoding the index field directly from the virtual (untranslated) address.

[36]The MIPS R4000 processor solves the logical address synonym problem by flushing the shared data from the on-chip data cache before accessing a physical location by a different logical address [17].

entry to become stale. One solution is for the operating system to guarantee that such an I/O buffer area used for input cannot possibly be in the cache (marked as "noncacheable"). If that is not possible, the operating system must flush the buffer addresses from the cache after an input occurs.

Type of organization. Which of the three types of organization described earlier is the most appropriate one? Their advantages and disadvantages were described earlier. Most of the recent microprocessors have followed the set-associative approach. Increasing the associativity (the number of lines in each set) cuts the miss ratio. However, increasing the associativity requires more components and connections (which, for the on-chip designs, correspond to more silicon area). For small caches, studies have shown that 2-way set-associative organization is the best compared to the other two organizations; going into 4-way set-associative organization adds some more improvement in system performance, but further increases have little extra effect and are not worth their expense. In general, for large external caches of size 64 Kbytes and greater, direct mapping is better. In multiprocessor environments, set associativity presents difficulties since it significantly increases the complexity of snooping. Figure 5.30 shows an example of total miss rates for different cache sizes and degrees of associativity (for a particular system configuration) [20].

Hierarchy of caches. Shall the design incorporate a hierarchy of caches? For those processors that have on-chip caches (whose size is usually restricted), the proper "hooks" in the form of I/O pins and signals are available to let them be connected to external (and larger), second-level, caches. For example, the Intel 80486 of Figure 5.6 has the PWT (page write-through) and PCD (page cache disable) pins; similarly, the R3000 RISC processor of Figures 6.18 and 6.20, which contains on-chip only the cache controller, has the proper I/O pins to interface to external caches implemented using standard SRAMs.

In a two-level cache hierarchy, the primary (or first-level) cache services the CPU requests; on a miss, it obtains its data from the secondary (or second-level) cache rather than from main memory. A secondary cache is much larger than the primary one. The secondary cache only services primary cache misses, and therefore its speed will influence the miss penalty of the first-level cache. Upon a secondary cache miss, data is supplied from main memory; *cache-line forwarding* is used when the line that comes to the secondary cache for updating one of its entries is also forwarded to the primary cache.

Fetching policy. What fetching policy should be implemented? The most common one is *on-demand:* bring in information on a cache miss. Whether the information to be fetched should be a word or doubleword (for replacing an entry only in a cache line) or a whole block through a burst read cycle (for replacing the whole cache line) is another related decision. For example, the Motorola products can be configured for either transfer. Others, like the Intel 80486, always read a whole 16-byte (4-doubleword) line into the microprocessor. An alternative approach is to do a *cache-line prefetch* (as done, for example, in the sequential prefetching of code): main memory can do a prefetch of the next cache line after servicing the current cache line fetch. This is based on the concept that if there is a cache miss in the current line, there is a good chance that there may be a cache miss on the next line, too. Main memory anticipates this, prefetches the next cache line, and holds it in a prefetch buffer in the memory controller. This will increase main memory performance, at the expense of designing a more complex memory controller.

Cache size (KB)	Degree associative	Total miss rate
1	1-way	0.191
	2-way	0.161
	4-way	0.152
	8-way	0.149
2	1-way	0.148
	2-way	0.122
	4-way	0.115
	8-way	0.113
4	1-way	0.109
	2-way	0.095
	4-way	0.087
	8-way	0.084
8	1-way	0.087
	2-way	0.069
	4-way	0.065
	8-way	0.063
16	1-way	0.066
	2-way	0.054
	4-way	0.049
	8-way	0.048
32	1-way	0.050
	2-way	0.041
	4-way	0.038
	8-way	0.038
64	1-way	0.039
	2-way	0.030
	4-way	0.028
	8-way	0.028
128	1-way	0.026
	2-way	0.020
	4-way	0.016
	8-way	0.015

Figure 5.30 Total miss rate for different cache sizes and degrees of associativity (first 3 columns of Figure 8.12 in [20]). From Patterson and Hennessy, *Computer Architecture: A Quantitative Approach.* © Morgan Kaufmann Publishers, 1990.

Replacing policy. When the cache is full, what replacing policy should one implement for choosing the cache line to be replaced? Most often the LRU (least recently used) policy is used (actually, in practice a variation to that is used, called "pseudo LRU"). Other approaches that can also be used are random replacement, or first-in-first-out.

Unified vs. split-cache approach. In designing a cache, a unified or split-cache approach can be followed. The latter refers to implementing a Harvard architecture caching strategy in which there are two separate caches: one contains instructions only (I-cache) and the other contains data (operands) only (D-cache). As we saw earlier, the Motorola 68040, the Motorola 88100, the Intel i860, and the R3000/R4000 processors have chosen the split-cache approach, while the Intel 80x86 processors use the unified approach.

The *unified approach* has the advantages that there is only one cache that communicates with main memory, the CPU components have only one unit to refer to, and it makes more efficient use of the limited resources and thus lowers the average miss ratio. Furthermore, no separate buses are required, as in the split-cache approach, which needs one bus for data and one for instructions. However, it has the disadvantage that data and instruction fetch collisions may arise (something that does not occur in the split-cache approach).

In the *split-cache approach,* the two autonomous caches can perform accesses in parallel (fetching instructions from the instruction cache and reading data from the data cache) and simultaneously operate with a third external access, thus improving overall system performance. The approach also allows the concurrent execution of a number of instructions (that do not require any external access), while the processor is performing an external access for a previous instruction.

5.7.2 Measuring Cache Performance

Choosing the best values of the cache parameters (e.g., cache size, block size, etc.) should be done by measuring the effect they have on the *performance of the overall system* (that they are part of) and selecting those values that *maximize system performance*. As Hennessy and Patterson state [20]: "There tends to be a knee in the curve of memory-hierarchy cost/performance: Above that knee is wasted performance and below that knee is wasted hardware. Architects find that knee by simulation and quantitative analysis."

System performance is measured by the following three methods:

Method 1: Specific application. Since the cache miss ratio does not only depend upon the cache characteristics (such as cache size, block size, etc.) but also upon the degree of locality of the programs being executed, the best way to provide information about the increase or decrease in system performance due to changes in the cache parameters is to measure the execution time of the specific application.

Method 2: Benchmarks. Quite often, method 1 is not practical or possible. Then one uses benchmarks[37] (a suite of programs that are representative of the type of applications the system is to be used for) and measures their run time when they are executed under a cache simulator which allows experiments in varying several cache parameters. (This is referred to as *trace-driven simulation*.) Benchmarks may include "synthetic code" (e.g., Dhrystone, LinPack, Whetstone, etc.) or "real code" for representative applications (e.g., LISP interpreter, Lotus 1-2-3, Paradox 386, NROFF, DBX, HSPICE, etc.). The system architect must choose the benchmark program(s) that best mimic the target application(s).

Method 3: Approximation formulas (or tables). The third method involves use of approximation formulas (and tables) to get an "estimate" on the system performance to be achieved by the various cache miss rates.

Combining the total number of CPU clock cycles time with the frequency of the various instruction types, we define the optimum CPI_o (cycles per instruction) of the system as [20]

---

[37]Actually, their *address traces* are used, which is a recording of every memory address reference obtained by executing a program interpretively [16].

$$CPI_o = \frac{\sum_{i=1}^{n}(CPI_i * I_i)}{\text{instruction count}} \qquad (5.5)$$

where I_i represents the number of times that instruction i is executed in a program and CPI_i represents the average number of clock cycles for instruction i.

This optimum CPI_o assumes ideal conditions (i.e., the value obtained without a cache). The actual, however, CPI is approximated by the formula

actual CPI (due to cache miss)
$= CPI_o +$ total additional clock cycles per instruction
(because of cache misses) $\qquad (5.6)$

If we can estimate the "actual CPI," we can estimate the actual execution time the CPU requires by

actual CPU time $=$ (instruction count)*(actual CPI)*(clock cycle time) $\qquad (5.7)$

Therefore, we need a way of computing the "total additional clock cycles per instruction" in Equation 5.6. A way of developing the formulas for I-caches, D-caches, and unified caches is given in the next Section 5.7.3. For those not interested in all those details, we give here the final approximate formula and use it in the examples that follow.

It turns out that the "total additional clock cycles"[38] are given by the formula

total additional clock cycles per instruction
$=$ (memory accesses per instruction) * (miss rate) * (miss penalty) $\qquad (5.8)$

Example 5.13: Effect of Miss Penalty on *CPI*

Consider a microprocessor cache with a cache miss penalty of 5 clock cycles and that the optimal CPI_o is 2 clock cycles. Assume that on the average there are 3 memory references per instruction.

If we assume that the application is large, floating point intensive such as HSPICE, then we can use existing graphs/tables (like the one shown in Figure 5.31) that show miss rate vs. block size and get the miss rate for this application. Assume a block size of 4 doublewords for which the graph gives us a miss rate of 7.6%. Then from Equations 5.6 and 5.8 we have

$$\text{actual } CPI = 2 + 3 * 0.076 * 5 = 3.14$$

(a) *Increasing the miss penalty:* Let's analyze the impact of changing the miss penalty for a given cache size. Using a cache miss penalty of 10 clock cycles we have a new actual *CPI:*

$$\text{actual } CPI = 2 + 3 * 0.076 * 10 = 4.28$$

For this example, doubling the cache miss penalty from 5 to 10 clock cycles has roughly 35% performance loss.

(b) *Increasing the block size:* If we increase the block size, the miss rate will go down but at the same time the miss penalty will go up. Which one has the greater impact?

Assume that we double the block size to 8 doublewords. Then the graph in Figure 5.31 gives a miss rate of (about) 3%. Furthermore, assume that the earlier miss penalty of 5 clock

---

[38]Hennessy and Patterson call them "memory-stall clock cycles": the clock cycles the CPU spends waiting for the memory system [20].

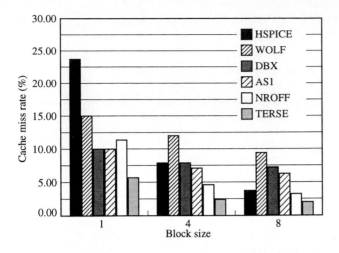

Figure 5.31 Example of a miss rate versus block size (for a particular size cache and a number of representative applications) [6]. Courtesy of IDT.

cycles was for a 2-1-1-1 burst block of the four doublewords (broken down to 2 clock cycles to fetch the first doubleword, followed by 1 clock cycle per doubleword). When the block size becomes now eight doublewords, the new miss penalty becomes 9 clock cycles. Under these assumptions, the new actual *CPI* becomes

$$\text{actual } CPI = 2 + 3 * 0.03 * 9 = 2.81$$

Here, although the miss penalty increased from 5 to 9 clock cycles (because we doubled the cache block size), the overall system performance increased because we had a dramatic decrease in the miss rate.

Example 5.14

Consider the cache characteristics of Example 5.12. We had concluded that

	Block size = 4 DWs		Block size = 8 DWs	
	Miss rate	Miss penalty	Miss rate	Miss penalty
4-Kbyte cache	5.5%	8 clock cycles	4%	12 clock cycles
16-Kbyte cache	3.2%	8 clock cycles	1.1%	12 clock cycles

(a) Consider a microprocessor with CPI_o = 8.5 clock cycles (i.e., without a cache) and assume that there is an average of 3 memory references per instruction.

Then applying the simplified formulas 5.6 and 5.8 we get the actual *CPI* entries in the following table:

	Block size = 4 DWs	Block size = 8 DWs
4-Kbyte cache	CPI = 9.82	CPI = 9.94
16-Kbyte cache	CPI = 9.268	CPI = 8.896

First of all we observe that in all cases of this example, *the inclusion of a cache has increased the actual CPI* (in cache misses) from its original value of 8.5 without a cache. We also observe that while for a 4-Kbyte cache *increasing the block length* from 4 doublewords to 8 doublewords increases CPI, for a 16-Kbyte cache it *decreases the actual CPI* from 9.268 to 8.896. A 16-Kbyte cache has a lower CPI when compared with the 4-Kbyte cache, while the miss penalty remains the same.

(b) Now consider a faster microprocessor with $CPI_o = 2$ clock cycles and an average of 1.3 memory references per instruction. (The remaining characteristics are the same.) Applying the simplified formulas 5.6 and 5.8 we get the actual *CPI* values of the following table:

	Block size = 4 DWs	Block size = 8 DWs
4-Kbyte cache	CPI = 2.572	CPI = 2.624
16-Kbyte cache	CPI = 2.333	CPI = 2.174

Again, in all cache misses the actual *CPI* has increased from the original $CPI_o = 2$ clock cycles. The increase in the CPI is more for the 16-Kbyte cache (0.161) than for the 4-Kbyte cache (0.052).

(c) Comparing (a) and (b) above, we notice that *the faster the microprocessor, the more significant the impact of cache misses.* For the microprocessor with $CPI_o = 8.5$, cache misses in a 4-Kbyte cache (block size 4 DWs) increase the *CPI* by 15%, while for the microprocessor with $CPI_o = 2$, cache misses in the same cache increase the *CPI* by 28%. Analogous behavior is noticed for the 16-Kbyte cache.

5.7.3 Formulas for I-Caches, D-Caches, and Unified Caches

Formulas for I-Caches.   Here no write cycles exist, so only instruction fetch misses in the I-cache are important. If we assume that the CPU will continue executing once the required instruction is read from main memory, even though the whole I- cache line has not yet been updated (this is certainly the case in RISC processors with streaming enabled), then from Equation 5.4 we have

$$\boxed{\text{I-cache miss penalty} = \text{memory (read) latency } (L)} \tag{5.9}$$

Then,

$$\boxed{\begin{aligned}&\text{additional clock cycles for I-cache misses}\\ &= \text{(instruction fetches per program)} * \text{(miss rate)} * \text{(miss penalty)}\end{aligned}} \tag{5.10}$$

Formulas for D-Caches.   Here we have D-cache misses on both reads and writes, and there is a miss penalty for read misses and for write misses. On a read miss in a D-cache, if the CPU can continue execution when the first data arrives even though the entire block is not refilled (as in the "data requested first" line fill technique), then from Equation 5.4 we have

$$\boxed{\text{D-cache miss penalty} = \text{memory latency } (L)} \tag{5.11}$$

If, however, the CPU will resume execution only after the entire block is refilled (as in the "data requested last" technique), then

$$\boxed{\text{D-cache miss penalty} = \text{memory latency } (L) + \text{transfer time } (X)} \qquad (5.12)$$

In general, then, we have

$$\boxed{\begin{aligned}
&\text{additional clock cycles for D-cache misses} \\
&= (\text{reads per program}) * (\text{read miss rate}) * (\text{read miss penalty}) \\
&+ (\text{writes per program}) * (\text{write miss rate}) * (\text{write miss penalty})
\end{aligned}} \qquad (5.13)$$

We can simplify this formula—if we can assume that D-cache misses affect only the execution of reads[39]—to

$$\boxed{\begin{aligned}
&\text{additional clock cycles for D-cache misses} \\
&= (\text{reads per program}^{40}) * (\text{read miss rate}) * (\text{read miss penalty})
\end{aligned}} \qquad (5.14)$$

Then the total additional clock cycles for both I-cache and D-cache misses is the sum of Equations 5.10 and 5.14:

$$\boxed{\begin{aligned}
&\text{total additional clock cycles (due to I-cache and D-cache misses)} \\
&= (\text{instruction fetches/program}) * (\text{I-cache miss rate}) * (\text{I-cache miss penalty}) \\
&+ (\text{data reads/program}) * (\text{D-cache read miss rate}) * (\text{D-cache read miss penalty})
\end{aligned}}$$

$$(5.15)$$

Then the actual *CPI* due to cache misses is

$$\boxed{\begin{aligned}
&\text{actual } CPI = CPI_o + \text{total additional clock cycles} \\
&= CPI_o + (\text{instruction fetches/program}) * (\text{I-cache miss rate}) * (\text{I-cache miss penalty}) \\
&+ (\text{data reads/program}) * (\text{D-cache read miss rate}) * (\text{D-cache read miss penalty})
\end{aligned}}$$

$$(5.16)$$

Formulas for Unified Caches. We simplify the formulas by combining I-cache and D-cache together (such as a "unified" cache with the same miss penalty for instructions and data) and combining the reads and writes together; then Equation 5.15 becomes

$$\boxed{\begin{aligned}
&\text{total additional clock cycles} \\
&= (\text{memory accesses/program}) * (\text{miss rate}) * (\text{miss penalty}) \\
&= \text{number of instructions (memory accesses/instruction)} * (\text{miss rate}) * (\text{miss penalty})
\end{aligned}}$$

$$(5.17)$$

From Equation 5.17 we derived Equation 5.8, which we used in the examples of the preceding section.

---

[39] Since the I-cache miss rate applies to all instructions while the D-cache miss rate just to instructions that need access to memory (mainly for reads), the effects of I-cache miss rates upon system performance are more significant than the D-cache miss rates.

[40] Also referred to as "reads or loads frequency."

EXERCISES

5.1. Consider a 32-bit microprocessor that has an on-chip 16-Kbyte 4-way set-associative physical cache. Assume that the cache has a block frame of 4 doublewords. Draw the block diagram of this cache showing its organization and how the different address fields are used to determine a cache hit/miss. Where in the cache is the doubleword from memory location ABCDE8F8 mapped?

5.2. Given the following specifications for an external cache memory:
   (a) It is a 4-way set-associative cache.
   (b) It has a block of 2 16-bit words.
   (c) It can accommodate a total of 4K doublewords from main memory.
   (d) The cache chip is used with a 16-bit processor that issues 24-bit addresses.
   Design the cache structure with all pertinent information and show how it interprets the processor's addresses.

5.3. The Intel 80486 has an on-chip, unified, physical cache. It contains 8 Kbytes and has a 4-way set associative organization and a block length of 4 doublewords. The 8 Kbytes of the cache are organized into 128 sets. There is a single "line valid bit" (which means that there are no provisions for partially valid lines as in the Motorola 68030) and three bits, B0, B1, and B2 (the "LRU bits"), per line. On a cache miss, the 80486 reads a 16-byte line from main memory (as explained in Section 2.4.2) and follows the "data requested first" technique. Draw the simplified diagram of the 80486 cache and show how the different fields of the address are interpreted.

5.4. Consider the Intel 80486 cache of Exercise 5.3. Explain in detail how the Intel 80486 would perform a nonburst cache line fill operation from address 16N + A of a 16-bit port. (One way of explaining it is by drawing the local bus timing diagram and showing the values on the bus lines and the most pertinent control signals.)

5.5. Consider the Intel 80486 starting a cacheable burst cycle to fill the 16-byte cache line from location 16N + 8.
   (a) How many clock cycles would this cache line fill require if the memory is 16 bits wide? How many if it is 8 bits wide?
   (b) What is the address sequencing (ordering) for this burst transfer for the 16-bit memory case? For the 8-bit memory case?
   (c) Draw the local bus timing diagram with the most pertinent control signals for the 16-bit memory case.

5.6. Explain in detail how the Motorola 68030 would perform a burst fill mode operation from address 16N + 7 of a 32-bit port. (One way of explaining it is by drawing the local bus timing diagram and showing the values on the bus lines and the most pertinent control signals.) How would the Motorola 68040 do the above operation differently?

5.7. Explain in detail how the Motorola 68030 would perform a single-entry mode for the following cases:
   (a) A doubleword read from location 16N + 5 of a 32-bit port
   (b) A doubleword read from location 16N + 5 of a 16-bit port
   (c) A doubleword read from location 16N + 5 of an 8-bit port
   (d) A word read from location 16N + 5 of a 16-bit port
   For each case identify how the cache entries are updated. (One way of explaining it is by drawing the local bus timing diagram and showing the values on the bus lines and the most pertinent control signals.)

5.8. Draw the equivalent to Figure 5.11 for a direct-mapped cache of size 64 Kbytes used to cache a 1-Mbyte cacheable main memory.

5.9. A set-associative cache has a block size of four 16-bit words and a set size of 2. The cache can accommodate a total of 4048 words from main memory. The main memory size that is cacheable is 64K $\times$ 32 bits. Design the cache structure and show how are the processor's addresses interpreted.

5.10. Consider a 32-bit microprocessor physical data cache with the following specifications:
   (a) It has a 128-bit block size.
   (b) Validity is done on a doubleword basis.
   (c) Cache fills can be either on a doubleword basis or on a whole cache line basis.
   (d) It distinguishes among 4 different access spaces.
   (e) It is a 32-line 4-way set-associative cache.
   (f) It supports only the write-back policy.
   Give the block diagram of the cache's structure and indicate how the physical address fields are to be interpreted.

5.11. Consider a cacheable 32-bit main memory of 4K doublewords and a direct-mapped cache with 128 lines and a block length of one doubleword.
   (a) Show how this memory is mapped onto the cache (giving a diagram analogous to that in Figure 5.11).
   (b) If the four doublewords 44556677, 88BB00CC, 55AA55AA, and 00000066 are stored at byte locations 0, 4, 1FC, and 600, respectively, show how they are mapped onto the cache.

5.12. Assume the Motorola 68030 operating in supervisor mode and the instruction cache of Example 5.5. If the processor were programmed to execute the "cache line fill mode," time and describe all on activities that take place when the processor attempts to access a supervisor instruction from location 057CD264.

5.13. The Motorola 68020 has an on-chip 256-byte, direct-mapped cache. The cache stores only instructions (prefetched from memory); on cache hits, instruction fetches into the on-chip instruction pipe are done from the cache. The cache contains 64 lines and has a block length of one doubleword. Each line also contains the function code bit FC2 (to distinguish between user and supervisor code), a tag field, and one valid bit for the entire line.
   Draw the cache's block diagram and the mapping of the 2^{32}-byte main memory blocks onto the cache.

REFERENCES

[1] Lui, I., "R3000 Cache Design Price–Performance Tradeoffs," in *RISC: The MIPS-R3000 Family* (R.-J. Bruss), Siemens Aktiengesellschaft, Munich, 1991.

[2] Asakura, M., et al., "An Experimental 1 Mbit Cache DRAM with ECC," *Symp. VLSI Circuits Digest of Technical Papers,* 1989, pp. 43–44.

[3] Hidata, et al., "The Cache DRAM Architecture: A DRAM with an On-Chip Cache Memory," *IEEE Micro,* Apr. 1990, pp. 14–25.

[4] Intel Corp., *Cache Tutorial* (CG-041691), Santa Clara, CA, 1991.

[5] Hill, M.D., "A Case for Direct-Mapped Caches," *IEEE Computer,* Dec. 1988, pp. 25–40.

[6] Integrated Device Technology, Inc., *R3000/R3001 Designer's Guide,* Santa Clara, CA, 1990.

[7] Intel Corp., *i486 Microprocessor* (240440-001), Santa Clara, CA, Apr. 1989.

[8] Motorola Inc., *MTT20 Course Notes (MTT20CN),* Phoenix, AZ, June 1986.

[9] Motorola Inc., *MC68040 32-bit Microprocessor User's Manual (MC68040UM/AD)*, Austin, TX, 1989.

[10] Intel Corp., *i860 64-bit Microprocessor Hardware Reference Manual (CG-101789)*, Santa Clara, CA, 1990.

[11] Hobbs, M., *RISC/CISC Development and Test Support*, Prentice Hall, Englewood Cliffs, NJ, 1992.

[12] Integrated Device Technology, Inc., *R3000 Family Hardware User Manual*, Santa Clara, CA, Oct. 1988.

[13] Integrated Device Technology, Inc., *1991 RISC Data Book*, Santa Clara, CA, 1991.

[14] Krueger, S., "Are 32 Bits Enough?" *Byte*, Nov. 1989, pp. 299–305.

[15] Smith, A.J., "Cache Memory Design: An Evolving Art," *IEEE Spectrum*, Dec. 1987, pp. 40–44.

[16] Smith, A.J., "Cache Memories," *Computing Surveys*, Vol. 14, No. 3, 1982, pp. 473–530.

[17] MIPS Computer Systems, Inc., *MIPS R4000 Microprocessor Introduction* (M8-00041), Sunnyvale, CA.

[18] Intel Corp., *i486 Microprocessor Data Sheet*, Santa Clara, CA, 1989.

[19] Smith, A.J., "Bibliography and Readings on CPU Cache Memories and Related Topics," *Computer Architecture News*, Vol. 14, No. 1, Jan. 1986, pp. 22–42.

[20] Hennessy J.L., and D.A. Patterson, *Computer Architecture: A Quantitative Approach*, Morgan Kaufmann Publishers, Inc., San Mateo, CA, 1990.

[21] Diefendorff, K., and M. Allen, "Organization of the Motorola 88110 Superscalar RISC Microprocessor," *IEEE Micro*, Apr. 1992, pp. 40–63.

[22] Motorola Inc., *MC68030 Enhanced 32-bit Microprocessor User's Manual*, Phoenix, AZ, 1987.

[23] Motorola Inc., *MTT30 Course Notes*, Phoenix, AZ, Febr. 1988.

6

Microprocessor MMUs

6.1 INTRODUCTION

Main memory is considered the central resource of a microprocessor-based system that must be properly managed by allocating it dynamically to users, programs, or processes (tasks). Today's microprocessors can support very large physical memory spaces, and effective mechanisms must be provided to manage these large amounts of memory.

More important, however, almost all of today's microprocessors further separate the logical address space (virtual memory) from the physical address space (main memory), and provide the capability of developing multitasking, multiuser, and distributed systems in which each task is given its own distinct and protected logical address space. These advanced features require the proper hardware support, which collectively takes the form of what is now referred to as the **MMU (memory management unit).** The more sophisticated the hardware support provided by the MMU, the fewer the functions of the virtual memory management needed to be done by the software.

As shown in previous chapters, MMUs are interposed between the CPU (which issues logical addresses) and main memory (which receives physical addresses). One of the functions of the MMU is to receive logical (or virtual) addresses and translate them into physical (or real) addresses. Like caches, MMUs may be implemented on the same chip with the rest of the CPU, or off-chip on external accompanying chip(s).

Microprocessors with **on-chip MMUs** include the Intel 80386, 80486, and i860, the Motorola 68030 and 68040, and the RISC-type MIPS R2000/R3000 processors (see Figure 1.4 Chapter 1). For example, in the case of the Intel 80386/486 chips, the MMU is made up of two independent units, the segmentation and the paging units; the Motorola 68040 chip with its internal Harvard architecture, which provides two separate internal buses (one for instructions and one for data) has two separate on-chip paged MMUs, one dedicated to translating instruction/code addresses and the other data/operand addresses. As we already saw in earlier chapters, on-chip MMUs may be placed either (1) between the address generating unit of the microprocessor and the on-chip cache (providing the cache with translated physical addresses), as for example in the Motorola 68040, or (2) they may be at the last stage on the chip, sending their output translated addresses to main memory, as in the case of the Motorola 68030. The MIPS R3000 and R4000 RISC processors have an on-chip MMU that implements paging. The advantages of on-chip MMU implementations are that MMU access is faster and allows for the maximum portability of software. Quite often, on-chip MMUs can be disabled by software. On the other hand, the on-chip MMU does take additional transistor count and real estate that could be used for different on-chip functions.

If a microprocessor does not have an on-chip MMU, then the processor's output address may be either a physical address sent directly to memory (if no external MMU chip is used), or a logical address if it first passes through an external MMU (to be converted to a physical address) before being sent to main memory. Microprocessors with **off-chip MMUs** include the 68851 PMMU (paged MMU) chip used with the Motorola 68020 microprocessor and the 88200 CMMU (Cache/MMU) chip used with the Motorola 88100 microprocessor[1] (Figure 6.1). External MMU chips may be positioned between the microprocessor chip and a cache chip (physical cache) or between a cache chip (logical cache) and main memory.

The MMU hardware provides the following **functions:**

1. Supports *dynamic memory allocation* to manage the physical address space efficiently.
2. Supports *virtual memory implementation* and managing of the logical address space.
3. *Maps* a task's logical address space into main memory space for execution (by providing the proper address-translation logic that translates/maps at runtime the task's logical address into a physical address sent to main memory).
4. Provides *memory protection* and task security, by properly isolating one task from the others and checking each memory reference for access rights violations both within a task and between tasks (such as whether the processor is trying to access protected area in memory, trying to execute a write cycle to an area of memory characterized as "read-only," task A tries to access task B's protected space, etc.).
5. Since in virtual memory systems, the executing programs may be only partially resident in main memory, the MMU hardware also *detects missing items that are not resident in main memory* and calls the operating system (by generating an exception) to bring them in. Depending on the type of virtual memory implementation, this is called "demand paging" or "demand segmentation."
6. Permits *sharing* of a single copy of code and data in main memory by a number of concurrently executing tasks.

In this chapter we present the design, operation, and use of MMUs. In order to understand the material better, some related background concepts and useful definitions are

---

[1] The Fujitsu MB86920 chip used with the Sparc (Scalable Processor Architecture) microprocessor (a RISC microprocessor from Sun Microsystems) is another example.

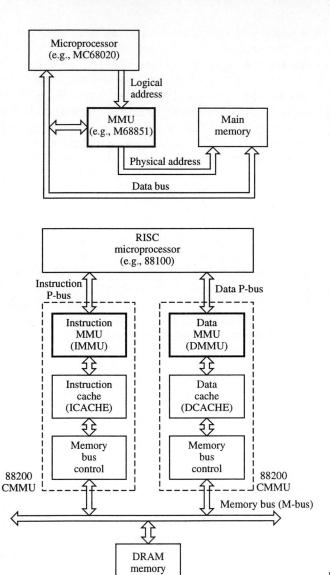

Figure 6.1 Examples of external MMUs.

also included early in the chapter. We start off by briefly reviewing how main memory is managed and then discuss the logical address space: its structure, the rationale for implementing virtual memory, and the hardware support needed for its management and its mapping into main memory. The rest of the chapter presents a survey of how MMUs have been implemented in microprocessors that support segmentation, paging, or combined segmentation and paging.

The topics discussed in this chapter are useful to the hardware system designer, to the programmer of systems code, and to the designer of the operating system. The application programmer, on the other hand, should be aware of the *effect* the MMU hardware may have on his/her programs.

6.2 LOGICAL (VIRTUAL) AND PHYSICAL ADDRESS SPACES

In order to design advanced microprocessor systems with virtual memory, one must clearly separate the logical address space from the physical address space and make logical addresses independent of physical addresses. Furthermore, assigning actual main memory addresses to a task (i.e., performing memory allocation) and allocating the logical address space should be deferred until runtime.

An address used by the programmer or generated by a task to specify a particular informational item is called a **logical address.**[2] The set of all possible logical addresses which can be used by a program to refer to informational items is called the **logical address space.**[3] The address used by main memory to access the location in which the item is stored is called a **physical address**[4]; only physical addresses are supplied to the memory subsystem. The **physical address space**[5] is the maximum addressable main memory that the processor can access directly. Supervisor and user code and data are independent of the actual amount of installed main memory if the above two address spaces are independent. Then, the object code program will contain no physical addresses; it resides in its own logical address space, and any reference it makes to an informational item is done with a logical address. This logical address space (or part of it) must be mapped into (i.e., become resident in) main memory in order for the code to execute.

It must be emphasized once more that *the only space the task is aware of is the logical address space*. (Each task or process has its own logical address space and deals only with logical addresses.) Memory management requires techniques to manage both the physical address space (the actual main memory of the system) *and* the logical address space, and do this dynamically (i.e., at runtime, while the program executes). Usually, the term **virtual memory** is used when the size of the logical address space is larger than that of the physical address space.

6.2.1 Main Memory Allocation

Before a task is executed, real physical main memory space must be allocated to it, i.e., actual physical addresses given to it. In simple cases when only one task runs at a time, the memory allocation problem is easy: a sufficiently large memory area is required to contain all the task's code and data. This placing of the task into main memory is performed by the relocating loader. If several modules are assembled independently and are to be executed together, a linking loader properly links them all together to form a large contiguous *linear logical address space* prior to execution and loads them in main memory as one unit. This allocation of main memory, performed when the task is loaded, is called **static memory allocation**; the ''mapping mechanism'' used to translate logical to physical addresses is the loader itself. The main disadvantage of static memory allocation techniques is that, after being loaded, the task becomes *absolute* or *bounded to physical memory space;* i.e., when the object code is swapped out to the disk and then swapped into main memory, it must be placed in the same memory locations as before.

---

[2] Also called *name* or *virtual address.*

[3] Also called *name space, logical space, logical memory, virtual address space, virtual space, abstract space, addressing space, user address space, task or process address space,* or simply *address space.*

[4] Also called *memory address, real address,* or *absolute address.*

[5] Also called *main memory space, physical memory space, physical space, memory space,* or *real space.*

Similar arguments apply when a **base register** is used into which the loader places the task's starting physical address; since during execution, each logical address of the task will have to use the single base register, we say that the loading process binds the task to this base register. Translating (or mapping) at runtime each logical address to a physical address, then, simply means adding the contents of the base register to the logical address for each memory reference, as shown in Figure 6.2a. During its total execution, the task can be swapped out to the hard disk and then swapped into a different main memory area (without passing through the loader again), simply by having the operating system adjust the *contents* of the base register to point to the task's new starting physical address in memory. In this way, the whole task can be dynamically relocated anywhere in main memory as one unit. The size of the logical address space obtained with the base register technique can never exceed the size of the available main memory space. In the base register approach, we say that the "mapping mechanism" that translates logical addresses to physical addresses is the base register and the adder (Figure 6.2b).

Even if the size of the task allows its whole swapping in and out of main memory, a sufficient large area of contiguous memory locations must be found to contain the task.

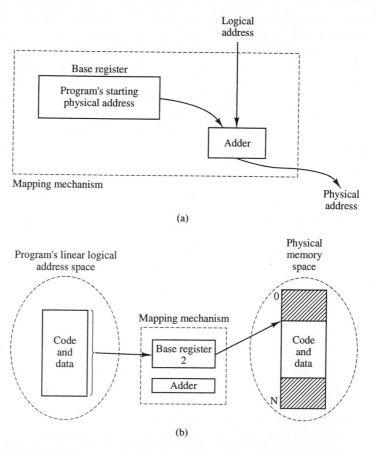

(a)

(b)

Figure 6.2 (a) Mapping mechanism using one base register; (b) with one base register, the entire program can be dynamically relocated anywhere in memory; (c) with two base registers the code and data modules can be relocated independently anywhere in memory.

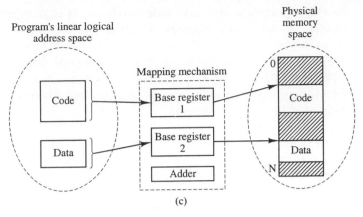

Program's linear logical
address space

Physical
memory
space

Mapping mechanism

Base register
1

Base register
2

Adder

Code

Data

Code

Data

(c)

Figure 6.2 (concluded)

Furthermore, the unit of main memory allocation is nonuniform; it varies in order to suit the needs of the task to be swapped in. Therefore, after a few such swappings, the problem of **external fragmentation** arises; this means that although enough free locations are available in main memory, they are not all in one large enough contiguous main memory block to receive the task swapped in from the disk. In this case, the operating system may perform memory compaction by relocating all resident tasks into one end of the memory, to form a large enough block of free contiguous locations to receive the incoming task.

This memory fragmentation drawback can be reduced somewhat if more than one base register is used. Then the programmer or compiler can split up the task into, for example, code and data modules,[6] and assign a different base register to each (Figure 6.2c). The units of main memory allocation are now reduced in size, and it is easier to find two separate such areas of contiguous memory locations into which to place the two task modules.

However, in more advanced applications, static and base register techniques are not satisfactory because it is difficult (if not impossible) to meet the following requirements:

1. To have *more than one task* coexisting in main memory, so that while one task is being swapped out, another task can start executing.

2. To allow easy *sharing of software modules* (e.g., a compiler, an editor, a questionnaire, a data file, etc.) among concurrently running tasks by having only a single copy of the particular module in main memory rather than providing separate copies of it to each task. Furthermore, two (or more) tasks should be able to share the single copy of a module in memory, by not necessarily using the same name for it (i.e., by referring to it using different logical addresses determined by the operating system at runtime).

3. To permit the separately compiled modules *not to be linked* together to form one complete task *until execution time* (required by program modularity).

4. To allow *varying the task's size* and the size of the data objects it uses dynamically *at runtime*.

5. To allow a *partially loaded task* to execute if the task's logical address space or the sum of several tasks' logical address spaces in a multitasking environment exceeds that of available main memory.

[6] That is, into two blocks of contiguous logical address space locations.

6. To allow system and user tasks and data objects to be *independent of the amount of physical memory.* This simplifies programming, increases software portability between machines with different memory capacities, and allows a system to be expanded easily by adding more main memory or additional disk devices without forcing reprogramming.

7. Finally, to provide the ability to *relocate a task* (or sections of it) anywhere in main memory dynamically *at runtime.*

Since all the above requirements arise at runtime, preplanning the memory allocation strategy is not feasible; instead, memory allocation should be performed by the operating system *dynamically at runtime.*

6.2.2 Structure of the Logical Address Space

As we mentioned earlier, in virtual memory systems, each task or process has its own logical address space and deals only with logical addresses. The structure of the logical address space is therefore of immediate importance to the systems programmer and designer. Although the structure of main memory is always linear (addresses start at location zero and proceed in linear fashion without breaks to the upper limit imposed by the physical address), the logical address space may be linear, nonlinear (segmented), or a combination of the two. Furthermore, it will be shown that logical address contiguity does not necessitate a physical address contiguity.

Linear logical address space.   One common structure of the logical address space is that of the *linear*[7] logical address space, in which permissible logical addresses are the integers 0, 1, . . . , *n.* Such a logical address space is an array of contiguous logical locations (much like main memory) with logical addresses numbered in sequence. A task accesses an item in a linear address space by specifying a single number (rather than a pair of numbers, as required by a segmented address space, to be discussed next). Figure 6.3a shows a 32-bit logical address defining a linear logical address space of up to $2^{32} = 4$ gigabytes (Gbytes). Since such a linear logical space allows direct access to it using a single number, address arithmetic (for example, indexing, etc.) may be done on the entire (in this case, 32-bit) logical address.

The linear addressing scheme is better suited for applications that manipulate large data structures.

Non-linear logical address space.   The second structure that the logical address space may have is nonlinear, or what is most commonly called **segmented.**[8] A segmented logical address space is composed of a number of separate, smaller, linear logical address spaces, called **segments.** Each segment represents a package of logically related information (named by the programmer so that he/she may partition the program along logical boundaries). All addresses within a segment are relative to its base address. To access an item in such a segmented space now requires two logical entities: one to specify the particular segment (usually called the *segment number*), and the other to specify an item within the

---

[7] Also called *one-dimensional, uniform,* or *homogeneous* logical address space.

[8] Also called *nonhomogeneous* or *two-dimensional* logical address space.

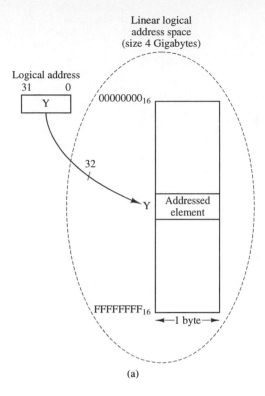

Figure 6.3 Four-gigabyte logical address spaces: (a) a *linear* logical address space addressed by a 32-bit address; (b) a *symbolically segmented* logical address space addressed by the pair "segment number–segment offset."

segment (called the *segment offset*). For example, if a 4-Gbyte logical address space is composed of 64K segments (actually, 65,536 segments) of up to 64 Kbytes per segment, then the two parts of the segmented logical address would be a 16-bit segment number and a 16-bit offset, as shown in Figure 6.3b.

Example 6.1: Intel Logical Addresses

In the Intel products that provide virtual addressing when they operate in "protected mode," the segment number is called *segment selector;* its width is 16 bits but it is only its 14 most significant bits that are used as a segment number, to specify indirectly as many as 16,384 (or 2^{14}) distinct segments, of variable sizes of up to 64 Kbytes each. [The 2 least significant bits of the segment selector in Figure 6.4 are the requested privilege level or RPL bits and are not used in selecting a segment; the value of bit TI (table identifier) indicates indexing into either a "global descriptor table" or a "local descriptor table." Their use will be explained later.]

After a task loads the segment selector into an internal segment register of the microprocessor (see Figures A.5 and A.11 in Appendix A), subsequent references into this same segment in main memory can be done by providing only the segment offset. The 16-bit 80286 has a 16-bit segment offset, while the 32-bit 80386/486 have a 32-bit segment offset. Thus the 286 uses 30-bit logical addresses that can access a logical address space of up to 1 gigabytes or 2^{30} bytes ($= 2^{14} \times 2^{16}$), while the 386/486 use 46-bit logical addresses that can access a logical address space of up to 64 terabytes or 2^{46} bytes ($=2^{14} \times 2^{32}$).[9]

In the more general case, segments have variable sizes (as opposed to pages, which usually have fixed sizes). Contrary to pages, segments are logically independent (i.e., there

---

[9] As we will see later, in all Intel products, half of this logical address space makes up the *global address space* and the other half the *local address space*, a separate local address space allocated to each task.

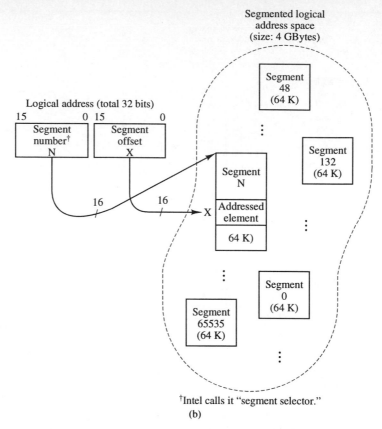

Logical address (total 32 bits)

15   0 15   0

| Segment number† N | Segment offset X |

Segmented logical address space (size: 4 GBytes)

Segment 48 (64 K)

⋮

Segment 132 (64 K)

Segment N

16   16

X

X | Addressed element (64 K) |

⋮

Segment 0 (64 K)

⋮

Segment 65535 (64 K)

⋮

†Intel calls it "segment selector."

(b)

Figure 6.3 (concluded)

are no contiguous addresses across segment boundries) and unordered (i.e., they are not sequential across the logical address space). There is no relationship between the last logical location of segment n and the first location of segment n + 1; in other words, address arithmetic is done *only on the offset part* of the two-part segmented logical address. As a matter of fact, all Intel 80x86 processors will generate an exception (exception 13) if an operand or

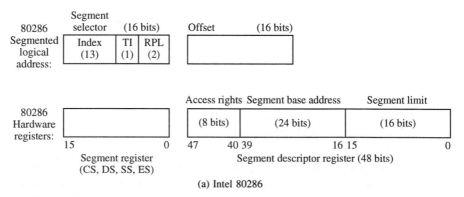

Segment selector (16 bits)			Offset (16 bits)
Index (13)	TI (1)	RPL (2)	

80286 Segmented logical address:

80286 Hardware registers:

	Access rights (8 bits)	Segment base address (24 bits)	Segment limit (16 bits)

15   0   47   40 39   16 15   0

Segment register (CS, DS, SS, ES)   Segment descriptor register (48 bits)

(a) Intel 80286

Figure 6.4 Intel segmented logical addresses and hardware registers (also see figures A.5 and A.11 in Appendix A).

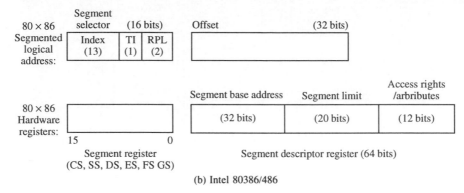

(b) Intel 80386/486

Figure 6.4 (concluded)

instruction fetch occurs past the end of a segment (for example, a word with a low byte at FFFF and the high byte at 0000).

The segmented addressing scheme facilitates programming (enabling the programmer to structure software into modules/segments), and simplifies protection and relocation of objects in memory.

Virtual memory. The size of the logical address space can be smaller than, equal to, or larger than that of physical memory. Various techniques exist that allow expanding the maximum size of either space.

The size of the main memory in a microprocessor system can be expanded by providing external mechanisms (expanded memory boards and software memory managers), which in effect increase the number of address lines applied to memory. But even with the increase in the installed physical memory, the processor's logical address space has not increased and is now smaller than that of physical main memory; the task is still restricted to only a portion of physical memory at any one time; the maximum size of this portion is equal to the processor's maximum possible logical address space.

Advanced microprocessor-based systems require mechanisms that allow the microprocessor's logical address space to be made larger than the size of the actual memory found in any particular system implementation (*virtual memory*). In this case, the logical address space is implemented on both the actual main memory and on the less expensive larger-capacity disk(s). Thus, the user can write large programs without worrying about the physical memory limitations of the system. Furthermore, the incorporation of MMU hardware simplifies the user's programming effort, since the virtual memory scheme frees him or her from worrying about the details of memory management and protection.

6.3 MAPPING

When this distinction between the two address spaces is made, a "mapping table" is required to facilitate going from the logical to the physical address space (i.e., to translate logical addresses generated by the executing task into physical addresses transmitted to main memory). *All address translations are performed at runtime.* This is illustrated conceptually in Figure 6.5a. The mapping table contains the main memory's physical addresses into

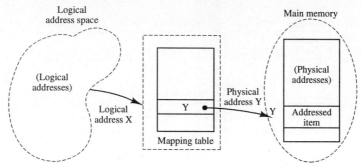

(a) Conceptual operation of the mapping mechanism

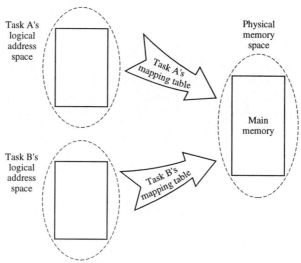

(b) Mapping of linear logical address spaces

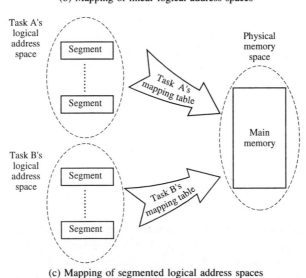

(c) Mapping of segmented logical address spaces

Figure 6.5 Mapping of logical address spaces to physical memory space.

which the task's logical addresses are mapped/translated at any given moment. In practice, mapping tables can be quite large and are stored in main memory.

There are other functions that the mapping mechanism must provide. First, as we will see below in more detail, the task is subdivided into smaller logical blocks which—depending on the virtual memory implementation—are called either *pages* or *segments*. Instead of physical addresses for the task's individual logical addresses, the mapping table size is now reduced because it contains the physical base addresses of pages or segments in memory (i.e., *groups* of logical addresses).

Second, in virtual memory implementations it is not necessary to have the whole task in main memory in order for it to be executed; by taking advantage of the locality of reference exhibited by most programs, only a small subset of pages/segments from each active task may be resident in main memory at any moment. The mapping hardware, therefore, must also be able to indicate automatically whether the addressed item is in a page/segment that resides in main memory or on the external disk. The mapping mechanism receives the logical address X and uses part of it to access an entry in the mapping table. This entry will indicate whether or not the addressed element is in a page/segment that is resident in main memory. If it is in main memory, the mapping mechanism will convert the item's logical address into its physical address in memory, and place it on the address bus to start the memory access cycle. If, however, the addressed item is not in main memory, the mapping mechanism will generate a high-priority exception (called *segment-not-present exception* by Intel, and *page fault* or *bus error exception* by Motorola), the currently executing instruction will be held in abeyance, and the operating system will be invoked to find the page/segment (that contains the addressed item) on the disk, move the page/segment into main memory, and place its physical base address in a mapping table entry. (This is referred to as *updating the tasks' mapping table*). Afterward, the instruction is allowed to complete the access since the mapping mechanism can now proceed with the logical to physical address translation.[10]

Finally, the mapping mechanism must provide protected access to memory; this includes protecting one task from another (*intertask protection*) or within a task, protecting a more privileged software module from a less privileged one, and making sure that no other memory access violations occur (*intratask protection*). For example, the Intel MMU hardware compares the RPL (requestor privilege level) bits of the logical address with the privilege level of the segment to which access is attempted, to block a less-privileged segment from accessing a more-privileged segment.

In multitasking systems where many tasks may be executing concurrently, several mapping tables will exist, one of each task. Each task has its own logical address space (or map), which is independent of the other logical address spaces. When the processor is switched from one task to another, the operating system activates the corresponding mapping table in memory. Figures 6.5b and c depict the mapping of two tasks into main memory: in the first case each task has a linear logical address space; in the second case each task has a segmented logical address space. The sizes of the two tasks' logical address spaces (and therefore their mapping tables) need not necessarily be the same.

---

[10] Two different approaches have been used: One has the hardware keep a copy of the state of the machine before each instruction starts, so that if it is interrupted by the MMU during its execution, it may be restarted when the addressed item has been placed in main memory (*the instruction restart approach*). On the other hand, *the instruction continuation approach* requires the state to be saved before each micro-instruction is executed, to let the instruction continue later from the point it was interrupted.

In the more general case, memory management must manage both main memory and the virtual address space. The first one is also called *main memory allocation* (i.e., assigning main memory to a task during execution time); the second is also called *virtual address space allocation* (i.e., assigning logical address space to a task, again during execution time).

Three methods exist for implementing virtual memory. Each method subdivides the logical address space into blocks of contiguous logical addresses. The three methods are (a) paging, (b) segmentation, and (c) a third method that has recently been implemented by a number of microprocessors which combines segmentation with paging, thus allowing both levels of logical address space subdivision: into variable-sized segments, which are in turn further subdivided into fixed-size pages.

Figure 6.6 shows the sizes of the virtual and physical address spaces for a number of microprocessors, which processors implement segmentation or paging, whether the MMU is implemented on-chip (integrated) or on a separate MMU chip, along with other MMU characteristics to be discussed later in this chapter [1].

6.4 MICROPROCESSORS WITH PAGING

6.4.1 General Concepts

In the first method, *paging,* each task's logical address space is linear. Even if a task consists of a number of independently assembled modules, the linking loader would properly link them together to form a large contiguous *linear* logical address space prior to execution.

In paging, the *task's logical address space* is mechanically subdivided into fixed-size **pages** and a mapping table (called **page descriptor table** or **PDT**[11]) is prepared that has one entry for each logical page of this task. Pages bear no direct relationship to the logical structure of a task. Mapping tables of a task are loaded into memory by the operating system. The *physical main memory* is conceptually organized into same-sized blocks referred to as **page frames.** Contiguous pages of the same task may be placed into noncontiguous page frames in main memory; i.e., items within the task when placed in main memory may be scattered all over and do not retain their logical relationships with each other.

Figure 6.7a shows a 64-Kbyte task, subdivided into thirty-two 2-Kbyte pages, mapped into a 16-Mbyte main memory (organized into 8192 2-Kbyte page frames) through a 32-entry mapping table.

Assume that the maximum size a task can have in this system is 16 Mbytes; if this space is paged into pages with a page size of 2 Kbytes, then it will be made up of 8K (actually, $2^{13} = 8192$) pages, each page identified with a 13-bit page number. A logical address to access an item in this logical address space will have the format shown in Figure 6.7b. The task in Figure 6.7a will be accessing an informational item in its logical space using such a 24-bit logical address. The mapping hardware, in order to translate a linear logical address into a physical one, will interpret each logical address by splitting it into two parts: a 13-bit page number, and an 11-bit offset within the page. The page number will point to one entry in the tasks' mapping table. The content of each table entry is called a **page descriptor** (shown in Figure 6.7c and explained in the next section).

[11] Other names used for this table are *page table, page mapping table* (*PMT*), *page map,* etc.

Feature	80386/i486 Integrated	i860 Integrated	68020/030 68851 MMU/Integrated	68040 Integrated	88000 88200 MMU	Sparc MB86920 MMU	R2000/ R3000 Integrated
Virtual address space (Gbytes)	65.536	4	4	4	4	4	4
Physical address space (Gbytes)	4	4	4	4	4	64	4
Segmentation	Yes	No	No	No	No	No	No
Number of segments	16.384	—	—	—	—	—	—
Segment size	4 Gbytes	—	—	—	—	—	—
Paging	Yes	Yes	Yes	Yes	Yes	Yes	Yes
Page size	4 Kbytes	4 Kbytes	256 bytes–32 Kbytes	4.8 Kbytes	4 Kbytes	4 Kbytes	4 Kbytes
Hierarchical tables	2 levels	2 levels	Up to 5 levels	Up to 3 levels	2 levels	Up to 3 levels	No
Table-walk hardware	Yes	Yes	Yes	Yes	Yes	Yes	No
Combination, segmentation and paging	Yes	Isomorphic	Isomorphic	Isomorphic	Isomorphic	Isomorphic	No
Protection							
Segmentation	Yes	Isomorphic	No	No	Isomorphic	No	No
Paging	Yes	Yes	Yes	Yes	Yes	Yes	Partial
Protection levels	4	2	MMU:8: 030:2	2	2	2	2
Virtual memory support							
Valid bit	Yes	Yes	Yes	Yes	Yes	Yes	Yes
Modified bit	Yes	Yes	Yes	Yes	Yes	Yes	Yes
Referenced bit	Yes	Yes	Yes	Yes	Yes	Yes	No
TLB (paging)							
Number of entries	32	64	MMU:64; 030: 22	128 (64 + 64)	64	64	64
Associativity	Set, 4-way	Set, 4-way	Full	Set, 4-way	Full	Full	Full
Multicontext	No	No	MMU: yes (8); 030:no	No	No	Yes (256)	Yes (64)
Selective flush/lock	—	—	MMU, yes; 030:—	Partial	—	Yes	Partial
Probe	No	No	No	No	Yes	Yes	Yes
Multiprocessor (MMUs) support	386, no; i486, some	Some	Some	Some	Some	Some	Some
Cacheability control	386, no; i486, yes	Yes	Yes	Yes	Yes	Yes	Yes

Figure 6.6   Summary of MMU characteristics [1]. © 1990 IEEE.

In general, the number of bits in the offset field determines the size of each page. The number of bits in the page number field determines the number of entries in the page descriptor table, and, therefore, the size of the task's logical address space. Finally, the number of bits in the physical base address field of a page descriptor determines the number of page frames in main memory.

Since each task runs in its own logical address space, each task has its own PDT. When the system switches from one task to another, a new PDT must be used. Since the starting location of a PDT in memory is pointed at by the contents of a special control register in the MMU hardware (the "control register 3" or CR3 in Intel, or a "root pointer register" in Motorola), when the operating system performs task switching it must place in this special control register a new pointer for the newly activated PDT. In the Motorola case, and since tasks can be user or supervisor tasks, a user PDT will be pointed at by a "user root pointer

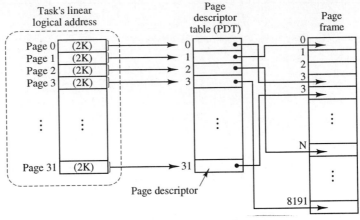

(a) Mapping a 64-Kbyte task into a 16-Mbyte memory

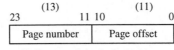

(b) Format of the logical address

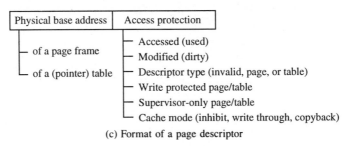

(c) Format of a page descriptor

Figure 6.7 Mapping of a paged task and the formats of its logical address and page descriptor.

register'' in the MMU hardware, and a supervisor PDT by a ''supervisor root pointer register.'' (When the page size is not fixed, the root pointer register in addition to the physical base address of the PDT will also contain a ''limit'' field to indicate the table's size). Like PDTs, pages may be user or supervisor pages. Information about free memory page frames, task control blocks, and other operating system tables and information resides in pages designated as supervisor pages.

6.4.2 Page Descriptors

The pointed-at page descriptor will contain the base physical address of the page frame in memory that holds this logical page (if the page is resident in main memory) and the necessary status or protection bits that provide controlled access to main memory. The format of a page descriptor (modeled after the page descriptors of Motorola) is shown in Figure 6.7c, as composed of two major fields: the ''physical base address field'' and the ''access protection field'' or sometimes called the ''status field.'' (Detailed formats of the actual Intel and Motorola page descriptors are given later in the chapter.)

In most systems, the **physical base address field** contains the high-order bits of the physical base address of the page frame that contains the page. The low-order bits of the physical address required to index into the page frame are supplied by the logical address (as we will see in the next section). In the Motorola microprocessors, this field will contain one of the following: (1) the high-order physical base address of a page frame in memory or (2) the high-order physical base address of a table in memory (called a ''pointer table'') that may contain one of two types of descriptors: (a) ''page descriptors'' that point to page frames in memory or (b) ''table descriptors'' that point to other tables in memory (needed so that the MMU hardware can execute the ''translation table-walkthrough algorithms'' to be explained later in the chapter).

Some of the bits in the **access protection field** include the *accessed or used* bit, which indicates whether or not the page corresponding to the descriptor has been accessed (or, in the case of a pointer table, that the pointer has been accessed as part of the table search); the *modified (or dirty)* bit, which indicates that this page has been modified; the *descriptor type* bits, which indicate whether a descriptor is ''invalid'' (either a nonresident page or a logical address range that is out of bounds), whether it is a ''page'' descriptor or a descriptor in a pointer ''table''; the *write protected* bit, which indicates that a write access to this page or table is not allowed; the *supervisor-only* bit, which indicates that a page (or pointer table) is a supervisor-only page (or pointer table); and finally, the *cache mode* bits, which indicate whether or not caching of items within this page is inhibited (in the Motorola case, when their on-chip cache is bypassed, the processor issues a CIOUT# signal and executes an external bus transfer), and whether cacheable writes will implement the write-through policy (update both the cache and main memory) or the write-back policy (update only the cache line and set its corresponding ''dirty'' bit).

6.4.3 Paged Address Translation

The MMU hardware executes the logical-to-physical address translation, which is depicted functionally in Figure 6.8. We assume here that both the logical and physical addresses are each 24 bits long. In this case, the hardware will interpret the 13 most significant bits of each logical address as a pointer (index) into the task's PDT. As we mentioned earlier, a special control register in the MMU hardware points to the beginning of this PDT in memory. If all the access protection bits of this page descriptor indicate that the page is resident in main memory and no access violations are attempted, the hardware will extract the physical base address Y of the page frame that contains the page and append to its right the 11-bit logical offset L in order to form the physical address sent to memory. Since the logical page and the physical page frame are of equal sizes, the offset in the logical address becomes the offset of the physical address (within the page frame in memory). If either the referenced page is not in main memory, or the memory reference violates the page protection attributes, the processor will generate a page fault exception.

6.4.4 MMUs with ATC or TLB Caches

If things were really happening exactly as in the above simplified presentation, then every memory reference would require two accesses: one to the PDT to fetch the descriptor and the second to fetch the actual item; this involves at least a 50% reduction in the effective memory bandwidth!

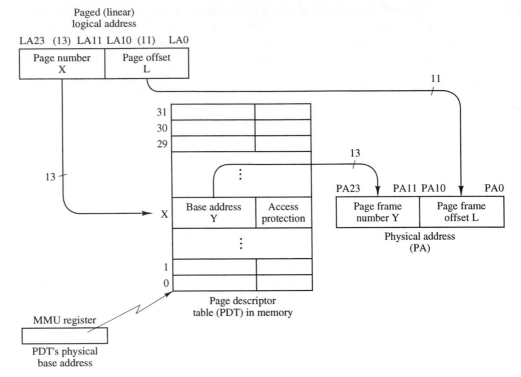

Figure 6.8 Paged address translation. (The example shows logical and physical addresses of 24 bits each.)

What kind of hardware enhancement can be placed in the MMU to reduce this degradation? Well, from the previous chapter on caches we learned that interposing a cache between the address generating hardware and main memory can increase the effective memory bandwidth. Therefore, if a small cache is placed in the MMU *to hold the descriptors of the most recently accessed pages,* then whenever there is a cache hit, the external bus cycle to fetch the descriptor is eliminated.

All of today's microprocessors that implement paging include such a cache. For example, the external paged MMU chip MC68851 used with the Motorola 68020 contains such a 64-entry fully associative cache called **address translation cache** or ATC; the 68030 contains in its single on-chip MMU a 22-entry fully associative ATC [2]; the 68040 chip contains internally two separate MMUs: a data MMU and an instruction MMU, each one with its own private 64-entry 4-way set-associative ATC [3]; finally, the Intel 80386 and 80486, which, in addition to segmentation, also support optional paging, have an on-chip MMU mechanism that contains a 32-entry 4-way set-associative cache called **translation look-aside buffer** or TLB. (The 80486 calls it "page table entry cache" [4] and the 80386 "page-translation cache" [5].) Finally, the RISC-type i860 has an on-chip 64-entry 4-way set-associative TLB, has identical page descriptors with the 80486, and has the 80486's 2-level page translation mechanism [7].

Assume now that we expand our paged address translation mechanism of Figure 6.8 to include a 16-entry 4-way set-associative TLB as shown in Figure 6.9. The two bits of the

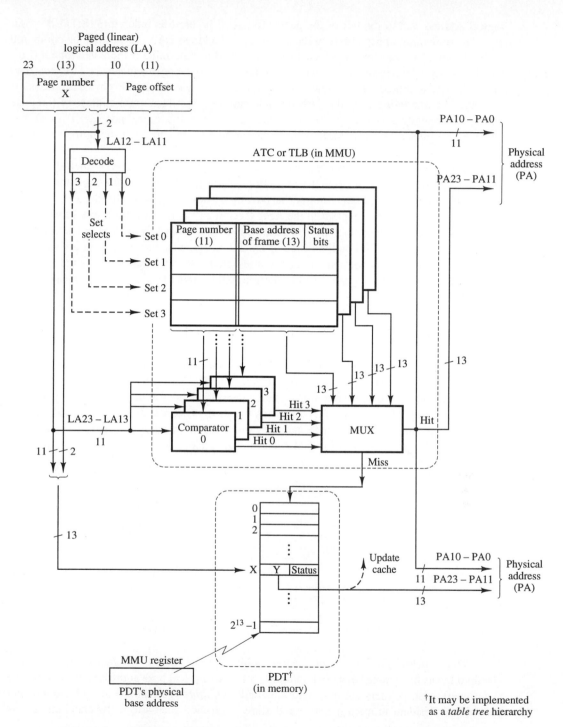

Figure 6.9 The MMU hardware contains a 16-entry, 4-way set-associative TLB to speed up logical-to-physical address translation.

logical address just to the left of the page offset will be used as index into the TLB's four sets. The remaining upper 11 bits of the linear logical address LA23–LA13 will be compared with all four 11-bit tags of the selected set in the TLB to determine if there is a match (i.e., whether a page descriptor for this page is in the TLB). If there is a match (a TLB hit), and the TLB access protection bits check a valid access,[12] then the 24-bit physical address is computed by extracting from the TLB the selected 13-bit physical base address of the page frame and appending to its right the 11-bit page offset from the logical address. This address will then be placed by the MMU on the external address bus to fetch the item from main memory.

However, if the page descriptor were not in the TLB (a "TLB miss"), then the MMU controller hardware will suspend the execution of the instruction, take control of the bus lines, and initiate *without interruption* the previously described access to the PDT in main memory (in what we will explain in the next section as "perform a **table-walkthrough** of the PDT hierarchy") to get the physical base address of the page frame that holds this page. The line read from the PDT will be used to update an entry in the TLB for future accesses. As before, if the item is not resident or the attempted memory reference violated the page protection attributes, then a page-fault exception will be generated and the operating system invoked.

6.4.5 Table-Walkthrough or Table-Search Mechanism

The page descriptor table (PDT) is in practice implemented as a number of smaller tables in a hierarchical or tree structure as shown in Figure 6.10. Only a portion of the tree for the entire logical address space is required to be resident in memory at any time: the portion that translates the logical addresses of the currently executing task. Furthermore, individual page tables become smaller, are easier to manage, and are dynamically allocated as needed. All addresses stored in the translation tables are physical addresses.

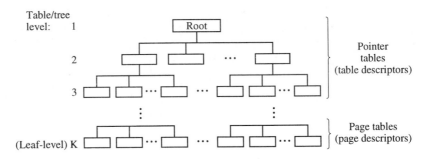

Figure 6.10   Hierarchy of descriptor tables (a table/tree).

The first level is the *root of the tree*, while the last level is the *leaf level*. All intermediate levels have tables that contain pointers to the physical base addresses of tables at the next level; these pointers are descriptors (called now *table descriptors*) to indicate whether the table is resident in main memory and allow controlled access to it (by checking access

---

[12] For example, access protection bits common to both the Motorola 68030 and 68040 MMUs are the *function-code* bits to indicate the access space, the *valid* bit to indicate the validity of the entry, the *write protect*, the *modified*, and the *cache inhibit* bits.

protection bits). Only the leaf tables at the bottom level of the tree (which are the ones called *page tables*) finally contain the page descriptors used to convert the logical address to a physical one.

Different products support different numbers of tree levels. In some products this number is fixed, while in others the number of tree levels is controllable by software and thus able to be tailored to the particular design.

Of the Intel products, the 80286 does not support paging, while the 80386, 80486, and i860 do. The i860 RISC microprocessor's paging unit functions the same and uses the same page table entry formats and TLB as the 80386/486 CISC microprocessors. In the Intel products, the page translation step is optional (it is in effect only when the PG bit in the control register CR0 has been set by the operating system during software initialization). These Intel microprocessors allow a two-level paging scheme: the first level is the **page directory table** (pointed at by the CPU control register CR3) and contains *page table descriptors,* while the second level is made up of the PDTs (page descriptor tables) that contain *page descriptors* as shown in Figure 6.11. The 32-bit input linear logical address has its most significant 20 bits interpreted by the MMU hardware as two fields: a 10-bit index into the page directory table and a 10-bit index into the identified PDT. Two accesses to main memory are performed in order to compute the final physical address of the referenced item: first an access to the page directory table is done to fetch into the CPU the table descriptor (of the PDT), which indicates whether or not this PDT is resident, and contains its physical base address and its access protection bits; the second access is to fetch the page descriptor to be used in calculating the item's physical address. MMU microcode is executed to implement these accesses to main memory and all internal addition operations (for calculating the various physical addresses) *without interruption*.

Example 6.2: Intel Two-Level Paging

Consider a 32-bit Intel microprocessor with paging activated. Intel pages are 4-Kbyte units of fixed size and always located on 4-Kbyte boundaries. Assume that the page descriptor table is placed at byte location A0000 and its first 32-bit entries are XX0X0B00, XX1X0B00, and XX2X0B00. (X's are the 12 "access/protection" bits of the page descriptors in Figure 6.6c. Also remember that values are stored by Intel in little-endian order, and therefore the stored value XX1X0B00 represents the page descriptor 000B1XXX.) Furthermore, assume that locations 000B000C, 000B1010, and 000B2008 have the following hexadecimal contents, respectively: XXMXKLIJ, XX5X3412, and XXEXCDAB. Determine the actual physical addresses for the following three linear logical addresses: 00404ABC, 00802657, 00003123.

Solution: Since the Intel 80x86 page or page frame is 4 Kbytes, the offset is 12 bits. Because pages are located on 4-Kbyte boundaries, these low-order 12 bits of the physical base address are always zero. (For example, the lower 12 bits of register CR3 are always zero to enusre that the Page Directory Table is always page aligned.) From the formats of the Intel page descriptors we observe that the 20 bits 31–12 specify the remaining (upper) bits of the physical base address of a page. Figure 6.12a shows the 2-level Intel tree structure for this example.

The first linear logical address is 00404ABC. Its leftmost 10 bits (the "directory index") are 0000000001; they are added to the left 30 bits of the CR3 to point to the page table descriptor at byte location 000A0004 of the level-1 Page Directory Table. The content of location 000A0004 specifies 000B1 as the upper 20 bits of the physical base address of PDT1 in memory. The processor adds to the 30 most significant bits of base address 000B1000 the 10-bit "page number" 0000000100 of the linear address; the sum points to location 000B1010. The page descriptor in that location specifies as the 20 most significant bits of the page frame physical base address to be 12345. Then the processor appends to them the 12-bit offset ABC to generate

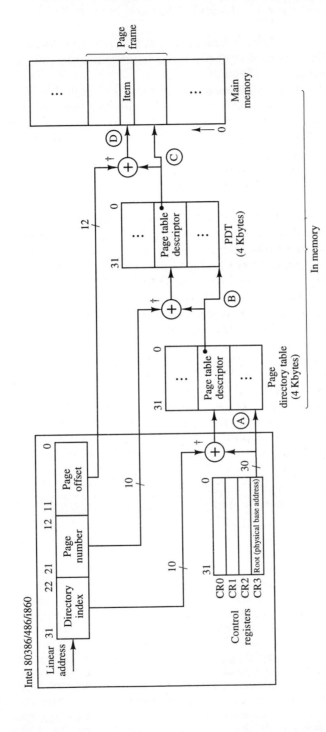

Figure 6.11 Intel 80386/486/i860 two-level paging scheme (executed after a TLB miss) [4]. Reprinted by permission of Intel Corporation, Copyright Intel Corporation 1989.

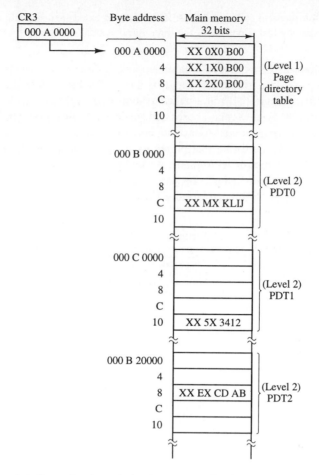

Actual page descriptors in the above memory locations are:
(000 A0000) = 000B0 XXX
(000 A0004) = 000B1 XXX
(000 A0008) = 000B2 XXX
(000 B000C) = IJKLM XXX
(000 B1010) = 12345 XXX
(000 B2008) = ABCDE XXX

(a) Two-level Intel tree structure in memory and its contents

Linear logical address	Physical address
00404ABC	12345ABC
00802657	ABCDE657
00003123	IJKLM123

(b) Logical addresses converted to physical addresses (for example, from the hexadecimal linear logical address 00404ABC, the 10-bit "directory index field" is 0000000001, the 10-bit "page number field" is 0000000100, and the 12-bit "page offset field" is ABC_{16}?

Figure 6.12 Example of address translations in an Intel 2-level paging scheme.

the 32-bit physical address 12345ABC of the addressed item in main memory. Figure 6.12b shows the physical addresses of the three linear logical addresses.

The Motorola 68040 paged system supports a three-level tree structure with either 4K or 8K bytes page sizes; the 68030 supports a tree structure whose number of levels can be as many as five (Figure 6.13) in a paged system with eight page sizes: 256, 512, 1K, 2K, 4K, 16K, and 32K bytes. Separate user and supervisor translation table trees are supported, and the current privilege mode (user or supervisor) selects the user or supervisor root pointer register in the MMU hardware that points to the base address of the first-level table in the respective tree. In a multilevel implementation, the logical address is divided into fields by the systems programmer (using a proper systems register in the MMU called "translation control register"). Both the number and size of these fields can vary; internally, the MMU

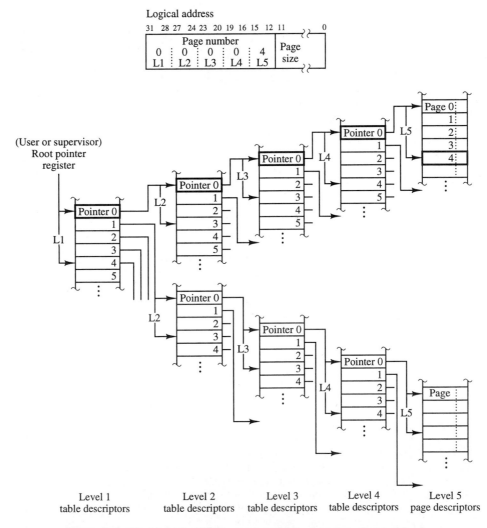

Figure 6.13 The Motorola 68030 supports a table/tree structure of up to 5 levels.

hardware contains a barrel shifter to extract the fields as the table-walk-through algorithm is executing. The five-level implementation in Figure 6.13 shows each such field being 4 bits wide, the first four levels containing table descriptors, and the last (fifth) leaf-level containing page descriptors.

Example 6.3: Motorola Three-Level Table/Tree

Figure 6.14 shows an example of using a Motorola 3-level translation table/tree to convert the supervisor logical address 78543210 into a physical address. The first two fields TIA and TIB each has a 7-bit width (maximum 128 entries in a table in the first two levels), while the third field has only a 5-bit width (maximum 32 entries in the third-level tables).

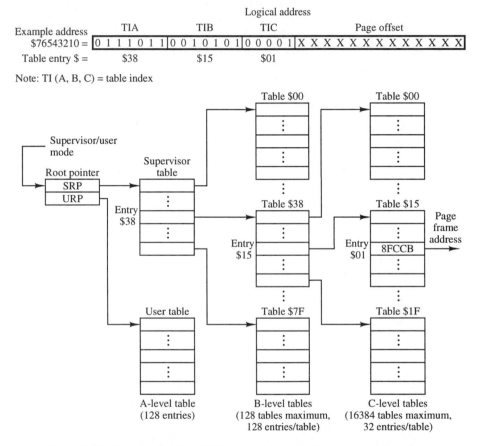

Logical address

	TIA	TIB	TIC	Page offset
Example address $76543210 =	0 1 1 1 0 1 1	0 0 1 0 1 0 1	0 0 0 0 1	X X X X X X X X X X X X X
Table entry $ =	$38	$15	$01	

Note: TI (A, B, C) = table index

A-level table (128 entries)

B-level tables (128 tables maximum, 128 entries/table)

C-level tables (16384 tables maximum, 32 entries/table)

Figure 6.14 Example of a 3-level table/tree to convert the Motorola supervisor logical address 78543210_{16} into the $8FCCB210_{16}$ physical address.

The table search terminates normally when the page descriptor is found, or when an invalid descriptor is encountered (generating an exception), which indicates that either the page is not resident in memory or a portion of the translation table that has not yet been defined.

In general, the larger the number of tree levels, the longer it takes to walk through the translation tables. A balanced system design seeks to optimize the relationship between table-walk time and memory required to hold these mapping tables [7]. For example [2], numerically intensive systems and systems that require large pages and a small amount of virtual memory can be implemented using single-level tables; a two-level paged scheme allows more flexibility in making a trade-off between page size and table size; a three-level implementation is useful when the operating system makes heavy use of shared memory spaces.

6.4.6 Microprocessor Page Descriptor Formats and ATC/TLB Structures

Motorola. Figure 6.15 shows the short formats for the Motorola 68030 page descriptors and table descriptors. In addition to these ''short'' (32-bit) formats, the 68030 has ''long'' 64-bit formats presented in Section B2.6 in Appendix B. That section also shows the page and table descriptor formats for the Motorola 68040 (Figure B.15). Figure 6.16 shows the structure of the 68030 and 68040 ATCs (used as suggested by Figure 6.9).

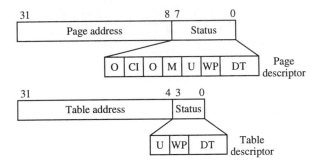

DT: Descriptor type:
  00 = Invalid descriptor
  01 = Page descriptor
  10 = Next table to be accessed contains short descriptors
  11 = Next table to be accessed contains long descriptors

Page address: Physical base address of a page in memory
Table address: Physical base address of a table of descriptors (PDT)

CI: Cache inhibit (processor issues CIOUT# signal)
M: Page has been modified
U: Descriptor has been accessed (used)
WP: Page/table is write protected

Figure 6.15 Motorola 68030 *page descriptor* and *table descriptor* short formats.

In the 68030 case, its ATC has 22 entries and is fully associative (see Section 5.3.1); this ATC is a small on-chip cache in the 68030 MMU hardware, separate from the on-chip instruction and data caches (see Figure B.8b in Appendix B.). The logical address field of an ATC entry (used as a ''cache tag'') is compared with the upper 24 bits (or what is called the ''page number'' in Figure 6.9) of the 32-bit logical address; the physical address field (the cache's ''block frame'') out of the ATC becomes the 24 upper address bits, PA31–PA8, of the physical address; the lower 8 bits, PA7–PA0, are the same with the page offset LA7–LA0 of the 32-bit logical address. The other bits of an ATC entry are explained in Figure 6.16c.

In the 68040 case, the ATC has 64 entries and is organized as a 4-way set-associative cache (see Section 5.3.3). The format of an ATC entry is shown in Figure 6.16b. Since the

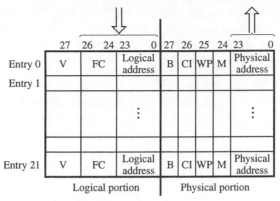

(a) Motorola 68030 ATC (Fully associative cache)

	31	(16)	16								31	(20)	12
V	G	FC	Logical address	U1	U0	S	CM	M	W	R		Physical address	

Tag

(b) Motorola 68040 ATC entry (64-entry, 4-way, set-associative cache)

M: Modified
CI: Cache inhibit (68030)
WP: Write protected (68030)
B: BERR (bus error)
FC: Function code bits (FC2–FC0) indicating access type
V: Valid entry
G: Global entry
U0, U1: User-defined page attribute bits (echoed to the UPA0, UPA1 signals
   if an external bus transfer results from the access)
S: Supervisor-only page/table
CM: cache mode
   00 = cacheable, write-through mode
   01 = cacheable, copy-back mode
   10 = cache inhibited, serialized   } non-cacheable modes
   11 = cache inhibited, nonserialized } (assert CIOUT#)
W: Write protected (68040)
R: Resident
Physical address: Physical address bits A31–A8 for page description (68030);
   Upper 20 bits of physical address (68040)
Logical address: Upper 24 logical address bits (68030);
   Upper 16 logical address bits (68040)

(c) Explanation of the fields

Figure 6.16 Motorola 68030 and 68040 ATCs.

68040 has separate on-chip MMUs (one for instructions and one for data), each MMU has its own ATC (see Figure B.8c in Appendix B). The logical address field of an ATC entry is compared with the upper 16 bits (what is referred to as the ''page number'' in Figure 6.9) of the 32-bit logical address; the physical address field out of the ATC becomes the upper 20 bits, PA31–PA12, of the physical address; the lower 12 bits, PA11–PA0, are the same as the page offset LA11–LA0 of the 32-bit logical address. It is noticed that there are two attribute bits associated with each page (U0 and U1); these are user defined, not interpreted by the

68040, but are echoed on the output pins UPA0 and UPA1; these signals are defined for user code and data accesses only. There are also two bits in the CM (cache mode) field that determine how an access will be handled by the cache on a page basis.[13] A noncacheable mode asserts the cache inhibit output signal CIOUT#, and if the 68040 MMU is disabled, the default caching mode is write-through.

Intel. The formats of the Intel 80386/486 and i860 page directory and page table entries are shown in Figure 6.17. The internal TLB in the page unit of these microprocessors (see Figure 5.6) is a 32-entry, 4-way, set-associative cache[14] of the type shown in Figures 6.9 and 5.21: the tag field (the high-order 20 bits of the linear address), the valid bit, three

31	12	11 9	8 7	6	5	4 3	2	1	0
Upper physical page frame address (A31 – A12)		AVAIL	00	D	A	00	U/S	R/W	P

Note: 0 indicates Intel reserved (do not define)

(a) Intel 80386 format of a page descriptor (in the page directory table or in the page descriptor tables) [5] Reprinted by permission of Intel Corporation, Copyright/Intel Corporation. 1986.

31	12	11 9	8	7	6	5	4	3	2	1	0
Upper physical base address of page table (A31 – A12)		OS reserved	0	0	D	A	PCD	PWD	U/S	R/W	P

Page directory entry (points to a page table)

31	12	11 9	8	7	6	5	4	3	2	1	0
Upper physical page frame address (A31 – A12)		OS reserved	0	0	D	A	PCD	PWD	U/S	R/W	P

Page table entry (points to a page)

Note: 0 indicates Intel reserved (do not define)

(b) Intel 80486/i860 formats of page descriptors (in the page directory table or in the page descriptor tables) [4] Reprinted by permission of Intel Corporation, Copyright/Intel Corporation 1989.

P: Present
R/W: Read/write
U/S: User/supervisor
PWT: Write policy: PWT = 1 write through; PWT = 0 write back
PCD: Cacheability: PCD = 1 disable cache; PCD = 0 enable cache
A: Accessed
D: Dirty
Avail or OS reserved: Software-definable (available for systems programmer use)

(c) Explanation of fields

Figure 6.17 Intel 80386 and 80486/i860 formats of the page descriptors.

[13] These terms are defined in Chapter 5. The two noncacheable modes are for I/O devices and shared data structure pages in multiprocessing systems that are specified as noncacheable by the MMU. The "serialized" access allows all pending writes to complete before beginning the external operand read (to prevent the out-of-order data read and write accesses—that the 68040 normally performs—when accesses are to devices that are sensitive to such accesses).

[14] That is, there are four sets of eight entries each.

attribute bits, the base address field which is 20 bits (contains the high-order 20 bits of the physical address), and the status field bits.

6.4.7 External Paged MMU Chips

Motorola 68851 PMMU.   Since the 68020 does not have an on-chip MMU, virtual memory is implemented with the use of the external 68851 PMMU (paged MMU) chip connected to the microprocessor through its coprocessor interface [8]. The 68851 has its own internal instruction set, the necessary hardware to (1) do address translation, (2) support logical address spaces of up to 4 Gbytes (for user code, user data, supervisor code, and supervisor data spaces), and (3) implement table walking of up to five levels, and an ATC which automatically loads from the tables in main memory. The PMMU provides an eight-level memory protection scheme: user address space is divided into two, four, or eight distinct levels (level 0 is the highest privilege and level seven the lowest). The access level for a bus cycle is encoded in the upper three bits of the logical address generated by the microprocessor. The PMMU compares these bits against the current access level[15] and determines whether the bus cycle is requesting a higher privilege than allowed (in which case it generates a "bus error exception"). Finally, the page size is program-selectable: eight page sizes are available ranging from 256 to 32K bytes.

Figure 6.18 shows the 68851 chip, its internal structure and set of registers, and the block diagram of a system. The internal resources of the PMMU can be accessed by the microprocessor operating in supervisor mode (in "CPU space" denoted by the values FC2–FC0 = 111), and issuing a logical address such that LA19–LA16 = 0010 (i.e., the processor starts a "coprocessor access cycle") and LA15–LA13 = 000 (i.e., the PMMU is accessed as "coprocessor 0"). The PMMU interface register to be accessed is specified by the address bits LA4–LA0.

The 68851 page descriptors can be short (32 bits) or long (64 bits), each one including the standard valid, modified, and referenced bits. The PMMU instruction set includes the instructions necessary for loading and storing of PMMU registers, testing access rights and conditionals based on the results of the test, and providing other PMMU control functions.

The internal ATC is a 64-entry fully associative ATC containing the most recently used logical addresses and their corresponding physical translations. A PMMU ATC entry is similar to that of the 68030 ATC entry (see Figure 6.16a), with the following two additions: (a) there is a "lock entry flag" in the status field used to freeze individual ATC translation entries to avoid replacement and thus speed up the translation of time-critical tasks; and (b) there is an additional 3-bit "task alias" (TA) field in the logical portion of the entry to identify one of eight tasks that may have translation descriptors resident in the ATC simultaneously. Thus, in a multitasking environment, translation descriptors for multiple tasks can reside in the ATC simultaneously. For an ATC hit, the logical address, the FC, and the TA must match.

Motorola 88200 CMMU.   Figure C.4 in Appendix C depicts the MC88200 CMMU (cache memory management unit) connected to the data P bus and the instruction P bus of the Motorola 88100 microprocessor [9]. The 88200 CMMU includes a 88100-compatible P

---

[15] The current access level is specified in the PMMU's current access level (CAL) register.

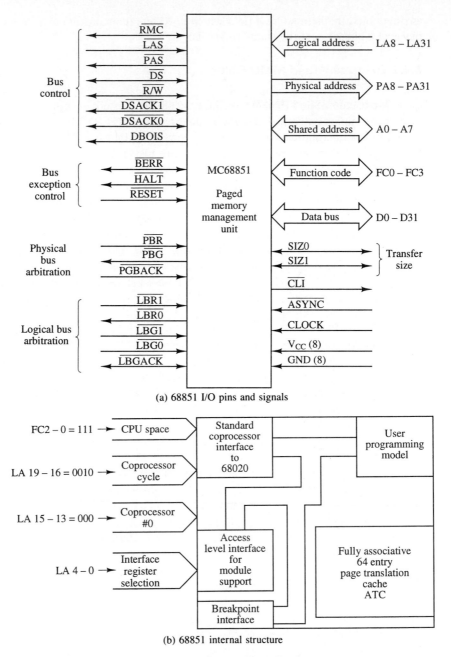

(a) 68851 I/O pins and signals

(b) 68851 internal structure

Figure 6.18 Motorola 68851 PMMU.

bus (processor bus) interface and an M bus (memory bus) interface. An 88100 processor may use two or more CMMUs for increased data cache and ATC sizes and hit rates. The cache part of the 88200 CMMU is discussed in Appendix C2.3. In this section we discuss the MMU part of the chip.

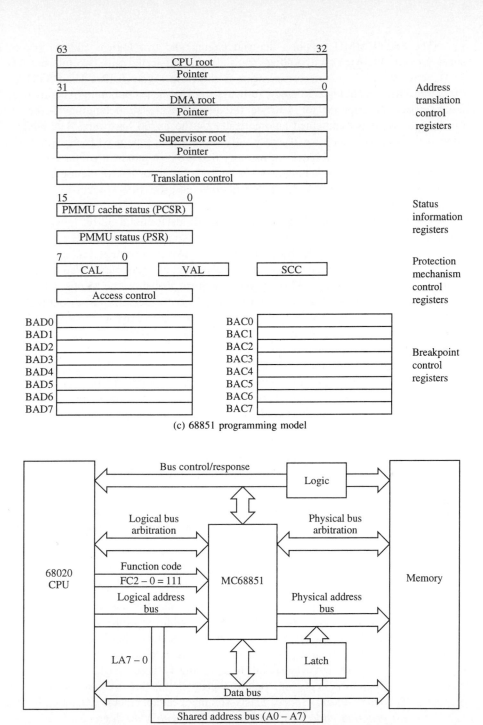

(c) 68851 programming model

(d) 68020-based system block diagram using the external 68851 PMMU

Figure 6.18 (concluded)

The 88200 MMU supports demand paging and two logical address spaces (user/supervisor) of 4 Gbytes each. Address translation is supported with two internal ATCs, the PATC and the BATC, whose organization is shown in Figure 6.19a. The **PATC** (page address translation cache) is a 56-entry, fully associative cache containing recently used translations (page descriptors) for 4-Kbyte fixed-size pages, all belonging to the currently executing task; it is maintained automatically by the 88200 hardware. The **BATC** (block address translation cache) is a 10-entry fully associative cache used to provide translations for ten 512-byte unmapped blocks of memory that are contiguous; it contains memory block descriptors and is software maintained (system software loads it with the logical and physical addresses of the memory blocks); its translations are used for the operating system and its storage of the mapping tables.

The CMMU receives from the processor (on its P bus) a 32-bit logical address and performs address translation first by comparing it simultaneously to all current entries in both ATCs. If there is a cache hit on either ATC, and no privilege violation, the CMMU concatenates the stored physical base address with the low-order word offset from the logical address to form the complete 32-bit physical address placed on the M bus. (If there is a hit in both ATCs, the BATC translation takes precedence.) Checking for an internal cache hit is done in parallel with this address translation operation. Finally, the control field of an ATC entry contains a write protection bit, a modified (or used) bit, a referenced bit, a data cache inhibit indicator, mode (user/supervisor) bit, etc.

If there is a cache miss, the CMMU hardware executes the table-walk algorithm, which searches 2-level translation tables in memory, loads the required descriptor into the PATC, and then proceeds with the logical-to-physical address translation. The tree structure supported by the 88200 contains two distinct levels in the supervisor and user address space, as shown in Figure 6.19b:

1. The first-level mappings are called "segments" (as in UNIX terminology); this level divides each of the two 4-Gbyte logical address spaces into 1024 equivalent 4-Mbyte "segments."

2. The second level (the page level) divides each "segment" into 1024 equivalent page frames, each 4 Kbytes in size. These entries have formats compatible with the 68851 and 68030.

6.4.8 Concluding Remarks on Paging

Since the splitting of the logical address into a page number and an offset is done by the hardware (the software treats both of them as one address/number), the operating system cannot at runtime change the assigned page numbers; page number N will always be referred by this task as page N. Bearing in mind the subdivision of a task through the earlier base registers approach, this then corresponds to assigning a "base register" to each page by the linking loader. Therefore, in paging, the initial program loading is considered to be a *binding process to the logical address space*. This assignment cannot change dynamically at runtime and, thus, *all program addresses are now absolute within the logical address space*. Although the page number—i.e., its assigned index is the PDT—cannot change at runtime, the page can still be dynamically relocated in main memory by *changing the contents* of this PDT index. Therefore, **paging is used to manage the physical address space.** The page is the unit of main memory allocation and of transfer between main memory and the disk.

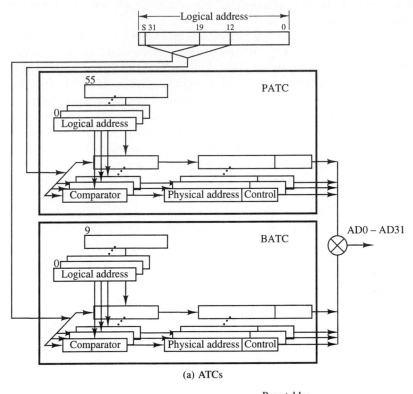

(a) ATCs

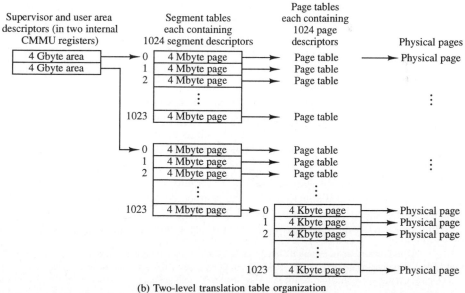

(b) Two-level translation table organization

Figure 6.19   Motorola 88200 (CMMU ATCs and 2-level translation table organization.

While in segmentation the unit of main memory allocation is variable in size, in paging its size is fixed (or may have two distinct values, such as 4K and 8K). Pages are usually much smaller than segments.

Both the *base register* and *paging* schemes yield a linear logical address space. In the single base register approach, all logical addresses are added to the content of the base register in order to produce the physical address; a linear logical address space is produced whose size is smaller than the maximum physical address space. Paging allows a linear logical address space not to have a direct relationship to the set of actual main memory locations and not be limited in size by the physical address space. With paging, the memory fragmentation problem is still not completely eliminated, but its effect is reduced significantly, since it now occurs within the much smaller page frame. As in segmentation, to be discussed next, the entire program does not have to be placed into main memory at the time execution begins. Only those pages required initially can be resident. When a reference is made to a page not in main memory, the operating system intervenes to bring it into main memory and adjusts the page descriptor table to reflect the new situation. (This is called *demand paging*.)

6.5 MICROPROCESSORS WITH SEGMENTATION

6.5.1 General Concepts

An efficient management of the logical address space requires a mechanism to allow the assignment of the entries of the mapping table to blocks of contiguous logical address space locations **at runtime** (not before, during loading). This leads to the segmentation technique.

In *segmentation,* the programmer or compiler subdivides the task's *logical address space* into logically related modules, called **segments;** segments are of arbitrary size, each one addressed separately by its segment number. Segments are much larger in size than pages. A segment is a block of contiguous locations in *logical address space,* representing a package of information (such as a subroutine)[16] which is, as we will see later, accessible in a controlled fashion. Each segment is placed in its entirety into a main memory area of contiguous locations at runtime.

Segments can be named[17] by the programmer, so that he or she may partition the program along logical rather than physical boundaries. For example, the programmer may assign logical modules, subtasks, or *objects* (such as main routines, subroutines, data arrays, symbol tables, stacks, etc.) to individual segments. For the memory management systems that allow variable-sized segments, the user can also specify the size of each segment according to the size of the logical module it contains.

Each of the two distinct parts of the segmented logical address is treated differently. As in paging, the segment number points to an entry in a mapping table in memory prepared by the operating system; this mapping table now contains **segment descriptors** and is called

---

[16] This breaking up of a program into modules, such as main program, subroutines, and data structures, was of course also done on earlier systems. However, in those cases a fixed amount of main memory was allocated to each program module at the time the module was first loaded into memory. The problem we are trying to solve with dynamic memory allocation refers to activities taking place *after* the initial loading has been done and the loader is not in the picture any more.

[17] In Chapter 7 we explain how the operating system associates a segment name with a segment number and "makes a segment known."

the **segment descriptor table** or SDT. Finally, the segment is the unit of main memory allocation and of transfer between main memory and the disk.

Because segments are of larger size, if one wants to speed up the address translation by incorporating an on-chip cache to hold the most recently used segments, the size of this cache would be much smaller than that of the paging's ATC/TLB caches. Because each segment represents a logical entity of its own, items within a segment when placed in main memory retain their logical relationships, and thus there is more determinism in accessing the segments by "type." Finally, because the number of different types of segments supported in today's segmented microprocessors does not exceed six (the four most common ones found in all Intel segmented products being the code, data, stack, and extra segments), then such an on-chip "cache" of four or six registers to hold the active segment descriptors is sufficient.

In all Intel products (whose operation in "protected mode" implements a segmented virtual memory), each entry of this on-chip "cache" is a separate register, into which a corresponding type of segment descriptor is deterministically cached, called a **segment descriptor register.**

6.5.2 Segmentation in the 8086

All advanced 32-bit Intel microprocessors operate in either the "real mode" (to emulate the earlier 16-bit 8086 architecture) or in the "protected mode," which opens up all the hardware capabilities of the newer designs needed to support efficient virtual memory, multitasking system implementations.

Since their segmented operation in "real mode" is exactly the same as that of the 8086 (i.e., the same instructions are executed, an identical addressing mechanism is used to access memory limited to 1 Mbyte, all real-mode segments are exactly 64 Kbytes long and always start on 16-byte boundaries), let us first present the way the 8086 supports segmentation.

The address translation hardware (in the form of the four segment registers and an adder) of the 8086 is implemented on the microprocessor chip itself in its bus interface unit (BIU). Program instructions contain only the offset of the logical address, while the segment to be accessed in the logical address space is determined by the "type" of access performed. This is depicted in Figure 6.20, which shows use of the 16-bit offset[18] to access a data item in the data segment.

As already mentioned, the 8086 provides a 20-bit physical address to memory. Main memory may contain up to 16 segments, each segment having a *fixed size* of 64 Kbytes, and beginning at an address which is evenly divisible by 16.

The address objects that the 8086 manipulates (in address arithmetic) are 16 bits in length. In other words, individual instructions contain a 16-bit *offset address* that can directly access up to 64 Kbytes. The 20-bit physical address issued by the microprocessor is formed internally by combining the 16-bit offset with the 16-bit contents of one of four segment registers in the microprocessor chip. These four segment registers are the code segment register (CS), the data segment register (DS), the stack segment register (SS), and the extra segment register (ES). Segment registers are usually *implicitly addressed* depending on the "type" of memory access performed: instruction fetches are relative to the CS register,

---

[18] In all our discussions here we will be using the 16-bit "long" offset.

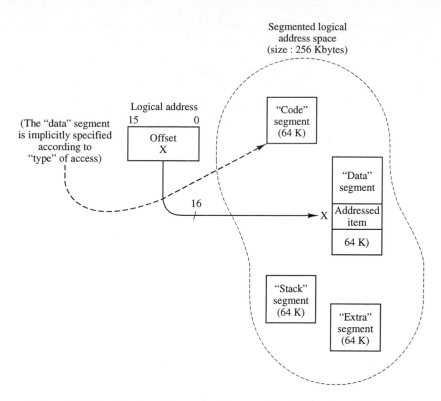

Figure 6.20 Intel "real mode" segmented (segment identified by "type" of access).

operands/data references are relative to the DS register, accesses to the stack in memory are relative to the SS register, and finally, the ES register is used as an extra segment register for accessing data (such as destination data).

Since in any memory reference, both the offset in the instruction and the contents of one of these segment registers are involved, the maximum logical address space that the task (or user) sees at any one instant in time is 4*64K or 256 Kbytes, subdivided into the four fixed-size segments (code, data, stack, extra) of 64 Kbytes each. This logical address space is accessed by a logical address composed of an implicit specification of one of the four segment registers and the offset, as shown in Figure 6.21a. The specified *segment register contains the physical base address of the segment* (actually, its 16 most significant bits); the offset indicates relative location of the addressed element within this segment. Figure 6.21b shows the mapping of the 256-Kbyte logical address space into the 1-Mbyte main memory of the 8086. It can also be noticed that, in this example, the data and stack segments overlap in main memory; if a particular segment does not use all its 64 Kbytes, another segment can be overlaid on top of the unused portion of the preceding segment.

These four segment registers constitute the *segment table* involved in converting logical addresses into physical addresses. The 8086 provides instructions, so that the programmer can manipulate this mapping table (i.e., load, unload, and modify these segment registers). Therefore, he or she can place a segment anywhere in main memory, by modifying its starting address in the corresponding segment register.

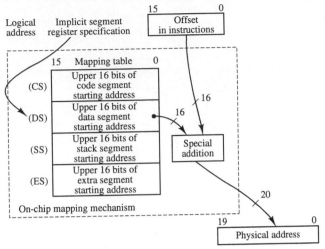

(a) Converting an 8086 logical address into a 20-bit physical address

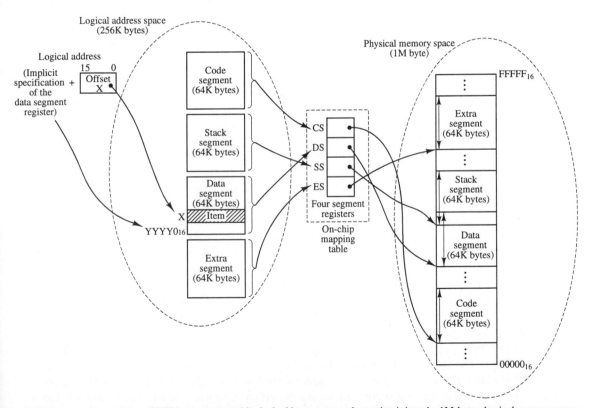

(b) Addressing the maximum 256K-byte segmented logical address space and mapping it into the 1M-byte physical memory space

Figure 6.21 Segmentation in the 16-bit Intel 8086.

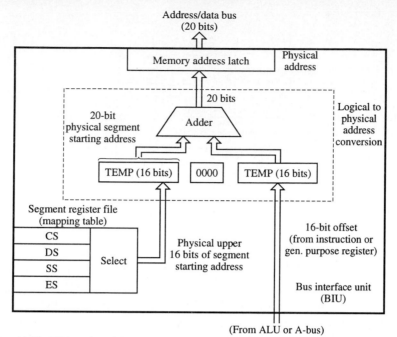

Address/data bus
(20 bits)

(c) The BIU section of the 8086 CPU, containing the logical to physical address conversion mechanism [12]

Figure 6.21   (concluded)

Figure 6.21c shows the block diagram of the on-chip hardware in the BIU of the 8086 that corresponds to the segmented MMU involved in the logical-to-physical address translations. This mapping mechanism combines the 16-bit logical offset from the executing instruction with the 16-bit contents of an implicitly specified segment register to generate the 20-bit physical address sent to memory. It uses the 16-bit contents of a segment register, appends to its right end the four 0s (zeros) (because the starting address of a segment in main memory is always evenly divisible by 16), receives the 16-bit offset-within-segment as an effective address computed by the ALU or from the address field within the executing instruction, and adds them properly in a dedicated adder to generate the 20-bit physical address it places on its output address pins. The delay involved in forming this physical address is minimized by the 8086 performing this segmentation addition for a new memory cycle—when possible—in the last two clock periods of the preceding cycle.

Therefore, it is observed that the 8086 logical address is a combination of a shorter field in the instruction and "typed" specification of an internal segment register. This approach, chosen by the 8086 (and actually all other Intel microprocessors that appeared later) to implement segmentation, results in fewer bits being needed in an instruction to specify an address. The shorter object code saves memory space and executes faster, since the number of memory references to fetch the program instructions is reduced. On the other hand, however, since the mapping table can be under explicit program control and because it has a limited size of only four entries, extra instructions are required to manipulate it (i.e., load and save its registers) when the accessing of more that four segments is needed. These extra instructions will increase the size of the program and the execution time. Furthermore, in the 8086 approach, the four segment registers act as base registers that can have their contents added to the logical offset for each memory operation. This leads to certain inherent problems of main memory allocation.

Programs that do not load or manipulate segment registers are said to be dynamically relocatable at runtime. If dynamic relocatability is required, then the user programs should not be allowed to load or manipulate these segment registers. Since no "privileged" instructions or "supervisor mode" of operation is provided in the 8086, dynamic memory allocation to a number of concurrently running programs cannot be undertaken by an operating system that will trap memory access violations; it is the responsibility of the programmer to trap violations of assigned main memory space. Instead of performing swapping (a system responsibility), a larger physical memory space can be simulated in the 8086 through overlays (a user responsibility).

Finally, it should be mentioned that the 8086 has no protection mode for memory management.

6.5.3 Intel 80x86 On-Chip Segmentation Registers

The Intel on-chip registers that implement segmentation are depicted in Figure 6.22. (Also refer to Figures A.5 and A.11, which show all program-visible and program-invisible registers of the 80286 and 80386/486 processors.) The 16-bit 80286 has four such registers, one for each of the four internal 16-bit segment registers (code or CS, data or DS, extra or ES, and stack or SS segment registers). The 32-bit products 80386 and 80486 have two more 16-bit segment registers that can be used for data segments (the FS and GS segment registers). Each of the six segment registers has its accompanying segment descriptor register. The particular segment descriptor register to be used for the address translation is specified by the "type" of memory access.

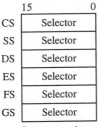

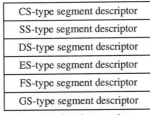

Segment registers

Segment descriptor registers
(Cached automatically)

Note: 1. The 16-bit 80286 has only the first four segment register-segment descriptor register pairs. The size of its segment descriptor registers is 48 bits.
2. In the 32-bit 80386/486 a segment descriptor register is 64 bits long.

(a) Intel segment registers and associated segment descriptor registers

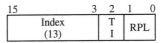

TI: Table indicator
  TI = 0: local descriptor table
  TI = 1: global descriptor table
RPL: requestor's privilege level

(b) 16-bit selector in a segment register

Figure 6.22 Some registers of the Intel's on-chip segmented MMU and the format of a 16-bit selector.

The difference in the use of the segment registers between the real mode and protected mode is that in real mode a segment register contains the (higher) address bits of the *physical base address* of the segment itself in main memory, while in the protected mode it contains an *index (offset) into a descriptor table* in memory. The 13-bit "index" field of the selector in a segment register (see Figure 6.21b) will point to a segment descriptor in one of the two tables in memory (the **global descriptor table** or GDT, or the **local descriptor table** or LDT), depending on the value of the TI bit in the segment register (as shown in Figure 6.23), from which the pointed-at descriptor will be automatically cached into this segment register's descriptor register. The GDT is used to define the global address space (half of the address space) shared by all tasks, while an LDT is used to define the local address space (up to half of the address space) that is unique to each task. The GDT contains descriptors which are possibly available to all of the tasks of the system[19]; the LDT contains descriptors which are associated with a given task.[20] Since each of these two tables is itself a segment (that must be accessed in a protected way), its physical base address, limit, and access attributes are also specified by a segment descriptor which is contained in an internal CPU register called, respectively, either the **GDTR** *segment descriptor register* or the **LDTR** *segment descriptor register.*[21] As long as accesses are done to this same segment in memory, the address translation will be done using the contents of this segment register's descriptor register (as will be explained in more detail below). This holds for any of the six different segment registers in the CPU (CS through GS) and their respective segment descriptor registers. Any time a new selector is placed in a segment register, a new segment descriptor will be automatically cached from one of these two tables into the corresponding segment descriptor register, to be used for all accesses to the new segment. Whenever task switching is performed,[22] a new selector is placed into the LDTR segment descriptor register (from the incoming TSS), which will force the automatic caching of a new descriptor into the LDTR which will now point to the LDT of the newly activated task.

6.5.4 Intel Segment Descriptor Formats

Like the page descriptors, a segment descriptor will have a field that contains the physical base address (usually its most significant bits) of the segment in memory, the "limit" field (since a protected-mode segment has variable sizes), and the "access rights" field (which contains status and attribute bits that provide protected access to memory.) The Intel products have different types of segment descriptors: data, code, gate, TSS, and special system segment descriptors [10,11].

Figure 6.24a shows the format of the Intel 80286 code and data segment descriptors, and Figure 6.24b the format of a special system segment descriptor used to specify the location of an LDT that defines the logical address space and address mapping of an individual task. (The formats of the segment descriptors for the Intel 80386 and 80486 are presented in Section A.2.5, Figures A.13 and A.14.)

The access rights byte differs slightly between code and data segment descriptors. The DPL is the descriptor privilege level that indicates the privilege level of the segment; it is

---

[19] A descriptor pointing to a shared segment is placed in the GDT.

[20] A descriptor pointing to a private segment is placed in the LDT.

[21] There is a third type of descriptor table that an Intel-based system can have, the *interrupt descriptor table* or IDT, which has another register associated with it, the *IDTR segment descriptor register.* The IDT is in effect a relocatable vector table.

[22] By bringing into the CPU the "state" of the new task, called by Intel the *task state segment* or TSS (see Chapter 7).

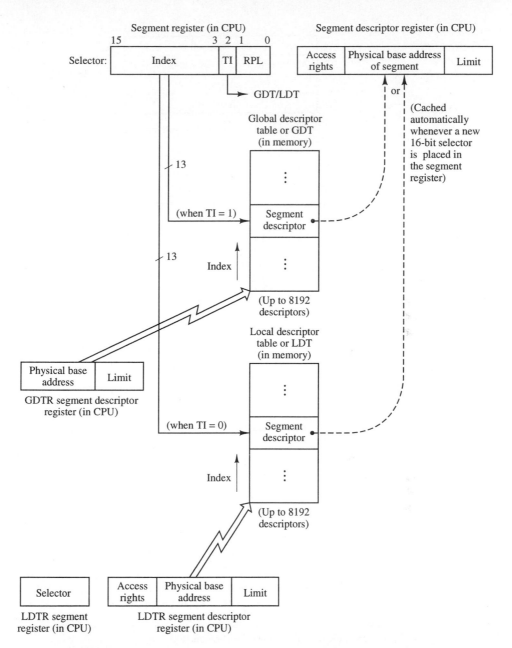

Figure 6.23 Intel protected-mode use of the segment register in specifying the segment descriptor (in either the GDT or LDT table) to be cached automatically into the segment register's segment descriptor register.

compared against the RPL (the requestor privilege level) of the incoming segmented logical address (the part contained in a selector register) to ensure no privilege level[23] violations.

[23] The various Intel privilege levels are explained in the next chapter.

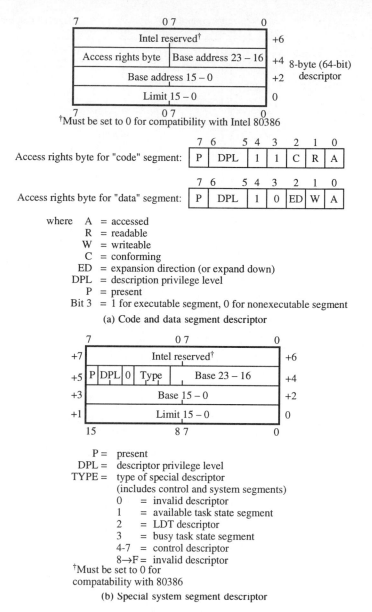

where   A = accessed
         R = readable
         W = writeable
         C = conforming
         ED = expansion direction (or expand down)
         DPL = description privilege level
         P = present
         Bit 3 = 1 for executable segment, 0 for nonexecutable segment

(a) Code and data segment descriptor

     P = present
   DPL = descriptor privilege level
   TYPE = type of special descriptor
           (includes control and system segments)
           0   = invalid descriptor
           1   = available task state segment
           2   = LDT descriptor
           3   = busy task state segment
           4-7 = control descriptor
           8→F = invalid descriptor
†Must be set to 0 for
compatability with 80386

(b) Special system segment descriptor

Figure 6.24 Intel 80286 segment descriptor formats [11] Reprinted by permission of Intel Corporation, Copyright/Intel Corporation 1983.

The ED (expansion direction or expand down) bit is usually set to 0 to allow the data offset to range from 0 to the size of the segment (64 Kbytes); it is set to 1 for stack segments, to allow offsets to be greater than the limit field (the allowed range of offsets within the segment is limit + 1 to 0FFFF). The C (conforming) bit is used for code segments, 1 meaning yes and 0 no (normal case); this allows code at various privilege levels to call a code segment labeled as conforming without causing a privilege level transition (i.e., the current privilege level does not change when executing the conforming code segment). System control and special system segment descriptors have the format shown in Figure 6.24b and the 3-bit field "type" distinguishes among the various types of segments.

6.5.5 Segmented 80x86 Address Translation

Figure 6.25 depicts the functional translation of an Intel segmented logical address into a linear one. (It is called "linear" because in the 80386/486 processors this linear address may be input to the paging unit, which converts it to the final physical address sent to memory.) It is noticed that the segmented logical address is 30 bits for the 16-bit 80286 and 46 bits for the 32-bit 80386 and 486 processors; similarly, the converted physical address for the 80286 is 24 bits, while for the 80386/486 it is 32 bits.

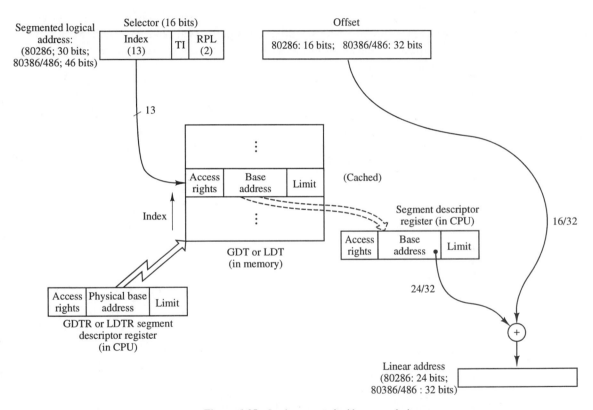

Figure 6.25 Intel segmented address translation.

6.5.6 External Segmented MMU Chips

MMUs that implement segmentation also exist as off-chip, separate, MMU chips. We describe here a way of using such external MMUs and identify their basic components. The specific example we have chosen to develop the concept is that of the external MMU chips used with a 16-bit processor; this processor is of the type in which both the segment number and the segment offset are explicitly specified by the executing instruction (are part of the instruction's "address field").[24]

The processor we are using can access a segmented logical address space of 8 Mbytes, composed of 128 segments that can vary in size from 256 bytes to 64 Kbytes. All the addressing information is contained explicitly *within the instruction itself:* a 23-bit logical address within the instruction contains both the segment number (an unsigned 7-bit segment number to identify one of the 128 segments) and the 16-bit offset within the segment. Only the offset participates in address arithmetic. In general, this offset may be an unsigned 8-bit number, referred to as "short offset," or an unsigned 16-bit number, referred to as "full offset." In our discussions here, we will be using mostly the 16-bit full offset. Six separate 8-Mbyte logical address spaces exist (*code, data,* and *stack,* for both a *supervisor* and a *user* mode of operation) and therefore the processor can support a maximum logical address space of 48 Mbytes.

The microprocessor can be used either alone, or together with a number of external MMUs. When used alone, no address translation is performed, and, therefore, the 8-Mbyte logical address space is equivalent to the 8-Mbyte maximum physical memory space. The 23-bit logical address is the 23-bit physical address transmitted to memory.

To accomplish effective memory management, a separate logical address space must exist. This is implemented when the processor is used with at least one external MMU, as shown in Figure 6.26a. Since the processor and the MMU working together now issue a 24-bit physical address to memory, the maximum addressable main memory increases from the previous 8 Mbytes to 16 Mbytes. The 8-Mbyte segmented logical address space can now be mapped anywhere in the 16-Mbyte physical memory space. What is interesting in this external MMU implementation is that the *whole 128-entry segment descriptor table is con-*

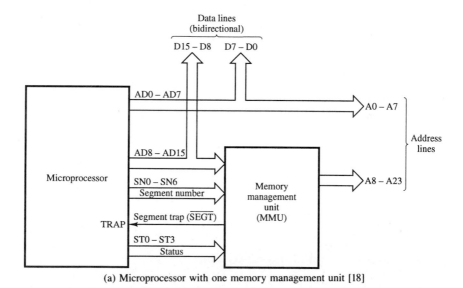

(a) Microprocessor with one memory management unit [18]

Figure 6.26 Microprocessor with one external MMU chip (a), and mapping of the 8-Mbyte logical address space into a 16-Mbyte main memory (b).

[24] The discussion here assumes that the processor is the Zilog Z8001 operating in segmented mode. [18]

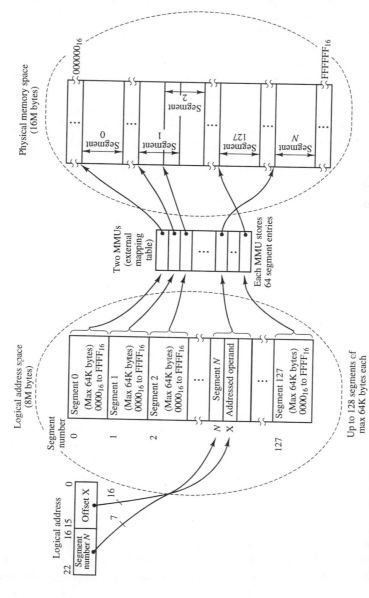

Figure 6.26 (concluded)

(b) Addressing the 8-Mbyte segmented logical address space and mapping the 128 segments into the 16-Mbyte physical memory space

tained in the hardware register file of the external MMU. (Actually, since each external MMU contains a mapping table of only 64 entries, it is capable of mapping only a 4-Mbyte[25] segmented logical address space into the 16-Mbyte physical memory space. Therefore, to support the mapping of the 8-Mbyte maximum logical address space, two[26] such external MMU chips must be used in pair as depicted in Figure 6.26b.) We notice that contiguous (logical) segments need not be mapped into contiguous main memory areas (for example, segment 127 has been mapped before segment N) and that segments may also overlap main memory locations (for example, segments 1 and 2). Segment base values can be changed within the MMU mapping register to provide relocation of code and data is achieved.

The MMU's management scheme places segments in main memory in such a way that the starting physical address of a segment is always evenly divisible by 256; i.e., its rightmost eight bits are always 0 (zero). The MMU contains the mapping table and the hardware to convert segmented logical addresses into physical addresses. The mapping table in the MMU associates the 7-bit segment number with the physical base address of the segment in memory, and the 16-bit offset is concatenated to this base address to obtain the actual 24-bit physical address transmitted to main memory.

Figure 6.27 shows the internal hardware details of an MMU used to convert 23-bit logical addresses into 24-bit physical addresses. A 24-bit base address is associated with each segment. To form a 24-bit physical address, the 16-bit offset is added to the base for the given segment. As seen, the lower half of the 16-bit offset is placed on the address/data bus AD0–AD7 and goes directly to memory. The upper half of the offset on AD8–AD15 and the segment number SN0–SN6 both go to the MMU. The MMU uses the 7-bit segment number to point to an entry in its mapping table from which a 16-bit base address is extracted. This base address is appended to the right with eight 0s (zeros) (because the 24-bit physical base address of a segment is always evenly divisible by 256, and, therefore, each MMU register actually contains the 16 most significant bits of this base address), the upper half of the offset is appended at the beginning with eight 0s (zeros), and the two are added together to form the 16 most significant bits of the physical address. Since the segment number does not participate in address arithmetic, it can be sent out by the processor half a clock cycle ahead of the 16-bit offset address. This compensates for the time delay involved in the use of the MMU; the MMU then functions in parallel with the microprocessor, having essentially no impact on memory access time.

In addition to the mapping table, each MMU also includes a ''protection table'' that contains segment access attributes (given to each segment when it is initially loaded into the MMU). Segment attributes include: segment size and type (read-only, supervisor-only, execute-only, valid DMA, invalid DMA, etc.). When a memory reference is made, the protection mechanism in the MMU checks these attributes against the status information it receives from the microprocessor for the following: user vs. supervisor memory areas; code vs. data and read/write vs. read-only; the absence of a valid entry for the segment; and the size of the segment. When a memory access violation is detected, a write inhibit line guarantees that memory will not be incorrectly changed, and a segmentation trap signal (SEGT#) is sent to the processor. As a response, the program status is saved automatically

---

[25] 64 segments of up to 64 Kbytes each.

[26] Using the status information provided by the microprocessor with each reference, a number of MMU pairs can be enabled dynamically.

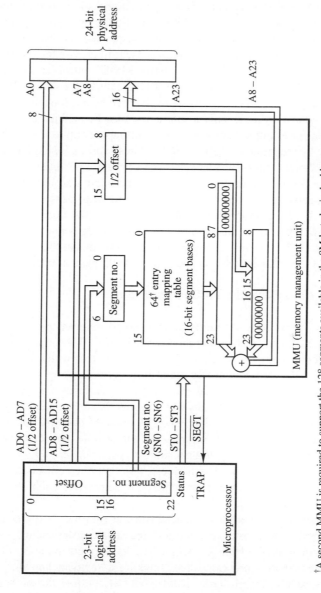

Figure 6.27 Interconnecting the microprocessor with one MMU and the mechanism involved in converting logical to physical addresses.

†A second MMU is required to support the 128 segments available in the 8M-byte logical address space.

361

on the supervisor stack, and this high-priority interrupt informs the operating system of the access violation.

As with paging that is implemented using external PMMU/CMMU chips, the registers of these external segmented MMU chips are accessed as I/O ports (in the supervisor mode, if one exists). Each external segmented MMU chip has chip-select, address strobe, data strobe, and read/write lines, and the operating system can set up the MMU tables using a number of special I/O instructions. These instructions allow loading and unloading of the mapping and protection tables of the MMU. Thus, the operating system may dynamically reload the mapping table as tasks are created, suspended, or changed.

When a single pair of external MMUs is used, to choose the correct MMU chip of the pair, an "upper-range-select" flag in an internal MMU control register is used in connection with bit SN6 of the 7-bit segment number, to indicate that a second MMU is mapping the additional 64 segments. However, several MMUs can be used together to accommodate several mapping tables, although only a single pair may be enabled at any one time.

Consider, for example, a processor that can support up to six MMU pairs, and thus is able to handle six separate 8-Mbyte logical address spaces [12]. Figure 6.28 shows an example of six different tasks, each having its own separate 8-Mbyte logical address space, all of them mapped into the same main memory of maximum size 16 Mbytes. Only one of these MMU pairs is active at any one time. A method similar to bank switching (utilizing control signals issued by the microprocessor) may be used by the operating system to select the appropriate MMU pair (i.e., the appropriate 128-entry segment table that corresponds to the task in control of the system). The operating system can also intervene to load and modify the contents of the segment table of the active MMU pair, to reflect the current situation.

6.5.7 Concluding Remarks on Segmentation

As we already mentioned, **segments** correspond to program modules and have symbolic names usually assigned by the programmer or compiler. The programmer references an informational item using a two-component symbolic address which contains a segment name and the offset of the item within this segment.

The (linking) loader links all these modules to form a *segmented logical address space,* prior to execution. This means that all symbols are retained through the loading process; the actual resolution of these symbols is done *as they are encountered at run time.* Since the loader does not assign a segment descriptor (one table entry) to each specific segment, a segment is not bound to logical address space because all its addresses are relative to the beginning of the segment. Furthermore, objects (when objects correspond to segments with variable size) can be created and deleted dynamically. Each object can have its own protection (or access rights).

Only when the segment is referenced (i.e., at runtime) is it placed in main memory; its starting physical address is inserted into the segment descriptor, and the index of this segment descriptor in the table is assigned as its segment number. (This is done by the operating system with a process called "making a segment known," described in more detail in the next chapter.) In other words, only at runtime do the segment's logical addresses become absolute within the logical address space (i.e., binding to logical address space takes place).

It is seen, therefore, that *segmentation solves the logical address space allocation problem,* since loading does not bind the program to positions in logical address space.

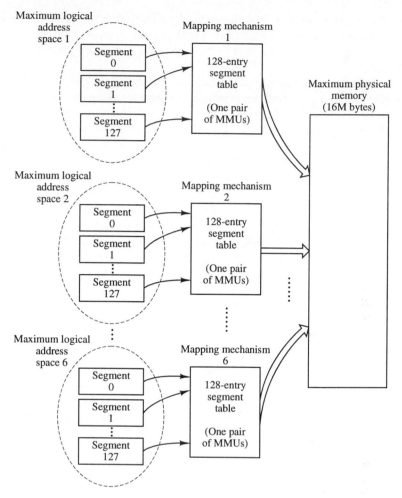

Figure 6.28 Mapping of six separate segmented tasks into the same 16-Mbyte physical memory space of the Z8000 [13].

Thus, on different occasions, a segment can be in different places in the program's logical address space (i.e., their name/number can change at runtime).

The problems of swapping large program modules and of memory fragmentation have not been eliminated completely with segmentation. These problems become even more serious if the system allows for segments of sufficient maximum size that only a few can be entirely resident in main memory at any one time. On the other hand, however, the smaller the maximum allowable segment size, the more segments that can be defined for a logical address space, thus increasing the size of the segment descriptor table required to map the logical address space into main memory.

6.6 COMBINED SEGMENTATION AND PAGING

The concepts of paging and segmentation may be combined to have the advantages of both. This combination allows segments to be partitioned further into pages of equal size.

Similarly, main memory is partitioned into equal-sized page frames. A segment is placed in main memory by placing each of its pages in a different page frame (not necessarily physically contiguous), and the page is the unit of main memory allocation and swapping with the hard disk.

In such an implementation, address translation is performed by a two-step table-lookup scheme, using both segment descriptor tables and page descriptor tables. A separate segment descriptor table is provided for each task, identified by the value in a base register in the CPU (such as the LDTR segment descriptor register in the Intel processors); the table contains an entry for each segment of the task. Since segments are composed of a number of pages, each segment has its own page descriptor table. Thus, a separate page descriptor table is in turn provided for each entry in the segment descriptor table.

Figure 6.29 shows the concept of the translation performed using this technique in the Intel 80x86 processors, which combine segmentation with paging. The logical address is composed of two numbers: the segment selector (its most significant 14 bits) and the 32-bit segment offset. Everything we mentioned earlier for segmentation and paging in these products is still valid (that is, the internal cached segment descriptor registers, the 2-level paged implementation, etc.). The index field of the segment selector points to an entry in a segment descriptor table, and the contents of this entry point to the base address of a segment in memory. The 32-bit linear address is formed by adding this segment base address to the 32-bit segment offset. The 32-bit linear address is interpreted by the system hardware as made up of three fields: a 10-bit index into the page table directory in memory (pointed by the CR3 register of the CPU), a 10-bit page number (used as an index into the selected page descriptor table), and a 12-bit page offset. The page number identifies the proper entry in the selected page descriptor table (containing the physical base address of the page frame in main memory that holds the page, if the page is resident). The 12-bit page offset of the linear address will be added to this base frame address to form the physical address transmitted to

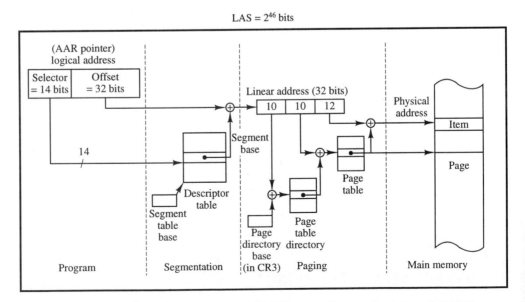

Figure 6.29 Intel 80386/486 address translation (combined segmentation and paging) [17]. © 1985 IEEE.

memory. This combination of segmentation with paging provides solutions to both the logical *and* the physical address space management.

6.7 COMPARING PAGING AND SEGMENTATION

Paging yields a linear logical address space. Since the assignment of a specific entry of the PDT to each logical page is done at load time, we say that *in paging, binding to the logical address space is done at load time*. Once loading is done, a page will always use for its accesses to memory the same table entry; in other words, *the page's addresses are now absolute within the logical address space*. The operating system can at runtime dynamically change the contents of the PDT entry but not the assignment of the entry (the page number).

Because an object (code or data) is mechanically divided into pages by the hardware such that items within the object, when placed in main memory, may be scattered all over and do not retain their logical relationships with each other (even an instruction may cross page boundaries in two different noncontiguous pages), the determinism present in segmentation does exist here. Instead of one descriptor register per page type, the larger ATC/TLB cache memory is now required to contain the most recently used page descriptors and is searched at high speed. When an ATC/TLB miss occurs (i.e., the logical address is not found in the table), then *the MMU hardware* will have to reference the hierarchy of mapping tables in memory to complete the translation and update the ATC/TLB caches. If the ATC/TLB is full, the hardware usually executes the least recently used or LRU policy (see Section 5.4.2) to replace an entry. If the referenced item is not resident in main memory, then the operating system is invoked to find it in the disk and bring it into main memory. *Paging manages the physical address space.*

Paged implementations have the advantage that no external fragmentation exists, but they have internal fragmentation because a whole page frame is always allocated even though the items to be placed in memory are less than a page. This internal fragmentation increases when the size of the page increases. (An increase in the page size reduces the number of page descriptors and thus of the page descriptor tables.) The other advantage is that it is simpler to place a page in main memory (as compared to a segment), and the time to do swapping is shorter for pages that have smaller sizes than segments.

However, a large program or data structure needs larger page descriptor tables as compared to segment descriptor tables. The "thrashing problem" (i.e., the processor spending more time swapping pages than doing actual computations) is more serious in paging than in segmentation. Although paging eliminates the external fragmentation problem, it has some other limitations: (1) it is not able to manage the logical address space as efficiently as segmentation (for example, it cannot increase/decrease the total number of pages dynamically at runtime), (2) it provides less powerful protection, and (3) it presents more difficulties when several concurrently running tasks need to share code and data (for example, it does not allow the shared object to reside in different places in the various logical address spaces).

One advantage of **segmentation** is that internal fragmentation is minimized because the main memory size allocated equals the segment size; on the other hand, however, external fragmentation is more than in paging. Placing a segment in main memory requires large areas, and therefore the placement algorithms are becoming more complex; the larger size of the segment also makes their swapping time longer. Quite often, most of the systems may be posing restrictions as to what physical base address a segment can be starting from. For large programs, however, and data structures, the segment descriptors are fewer and therefore the segment descriptor tables smaller.

Segmenatation manages the logical address space. The programmer or compiler subdivides the program's logical address space into segments. Segment numbers are interpreted and manipulated by the software. Segmentation facilitates easier sharing of code and data, and dynamic shrinkage and expansion of their size as compared to paging.

EXERCISES

6.1. Consider a hypothetical 16-bit microprocessor with an on-chip paged MMU for pages of size 256 bytes each. This MMU works the same way as that of the Motorola 68030, but implements a descriptor table-walkthrough scheme of up to 4 levels maximum. Assume that 24-bit logical addresses are converted to 24-bit physical addresses. Consider the logical address ABCDEF and:

   (a) Give an example diagram for each of the four possible level implementations that shows how the above logical address is translated into a physical one. In each example, use actual hexadecimal digits of your own choice in the page descriptor tables.

   (b) For each of the above 4 cases, identify the number of bytes that must be allocated for the tables in main memory for a task that has only 2 pages.

6.2. Assume a task is divided into 4 equal-sized segments, and that the system builds an 8-entry page descriptor table for each segment. In other words, the system has a combination of segmentation and paging. Assume also that the page size is 2 Kbytes.

   (a) What is the maximum size of each segment?

   (b) What is the maximum logical address space for the task?

   (c) Assume that an element in physical location 00021ABC is accessed by this task. What is the format of the logical address that the task generates for it? What is the maximum physical address space for the system?

6.3. Assume a microprocessor capable of accessing up to 2^{32} bytes of physical main memory. It implements one segmented logical address space of maximum size 2^{31} bytes. Each instruction contains the whole two-part address. External MMUs are used, whose management scheme assigns contiguous blocks of physical memory to segments of fixed size 2^{22} bytes. The starting physical address of a segment is always divisible by 1024. Show the detailed interconnection of the external mapping mechanism that converts logical addresses to physical addresses using the appropriate number of MMUs, and show the detailed internal structure of an MMU (assuming that each MMU contains an 128-entry directly mapped segment descriptor cache) and how each MMU is selected.

6.4. Consider the Zilog Z8001 microprocessor of Section 6.5.6 and a 16-Kbyte task composed of a 10-Kbyte code module and a 6-Kbyte data module. Assume that the code module is segment #2 and the data module segment #4. Also assume that this program is initially loaded into the Zilog's main memory starting at physical location 000100, and that the two segments occupy contiguous areas in main memory. At some instant during its execution, the whole 16-Kbyte task is removed to the disk and then returned to main memory, the code segment occupying memory locations that are (in hexadecimal) 300 higher than those occupied previously, and the data segment occupying memory locations that are (in hexadecimal) 400 higher than those occupied previously.

   (a) Which entries in the mapping table of the external MMU have been affected by this swapping activity?

(b) What are the values contained in these entries before and after the swapping activity?

(c) After this swapping, when an instruction is executed from location 00063A, what is the value (in hexadecimal) contained in the internal 23-bit program counter?

6.5. Consider a paged logical address space (composed of 32 pages of 2 Kbytes each) mapped into an 1-Mbyte physical memory space.

(a) What is the format of the processor's logical address?

(b) What are the length and width of the page table (disregarding the ''access rights'' bits)?

(c) What is the effect on the page table if the physical memory space is reduced by half?

6.6. Assume the Zilog Z8001 microprocessor of Section 6.5.6 with one external MMU. If this configuration is to support five tasks, where each task is given the maximum logical address space of 8 Mbytes, explain how the mapping tables should be handled and serviced by this single MMU.

6.7. Consider a 16-Kbyte program composed of a 10-Kbyte code module and a 6-Kbyte data module. Also assume that this program is initially loaded into the Intel 8086's main memory starting at physical location 00100, and that the two modules occupy contiguous areas in main memory. At some instant during its execution, the whole 16-byte program is removed to the disk and then returned to main memory, the code module occupying memory locations that are (in hexadecimal) 300 higher than those occupied previously, and the data module occupying memory locations that are (in hexadecimal) 400 higher than those occupied previously.

(a) Which segment registers of the processor have been affected by the swapping activity?

(b) What are the values contained in these segment registers before and after the swapping activity?

(c) If a dynamic relocation is to be allowed, what are the restrictions imposed on the above program?

6.8. Consider a Motorola 68030 task with two pages, 0 and FFFFF. Give the two-level tree structure of its table/page descriptors, identify the sizes to be allocated to each table (in bytes), and indicate how would the logical address fields be used. (State all your assumptions.)

6.9. Consider Exercise 6.8. Assume that the level 1 table descriptor table is placed at byte location 00010000 and its first 32-bit entries are 0020000X, 0021000X, and 0022000X. (Assume that the X's have the valid values for the status bits and that the short table descriptor and page descriptor formats are used.) Furthermore, assume that locations 00020000, 00020004, and 0002100C contain the following page descriptors, respectively: 47657XXX, 2BA9CXXX, and 25719XXX.

Determine the actual physical addresses for the following three logical addresses: $403ABC, $123, and $1C5E.

REFERENCES

[1] Milenkovic, M., ''Microprocessor Memory Management Units,'' *IEEE Micro,* Apr. 1990, pp. 70–85.

[2] Motorola Inc., *MC68030 Enhanced 32-Bit Microprocessor User's Manual* (MC68030UM/AD), Austin, TX, 1987.

[3] Motorola Inc., *MC68040 32-Bit Microprocessor User Manual* (MC68040UM/AD), Austin, TX, 1989.

[4] Intel Corp., *i486 Microprocessor* (240440-001), Santa Clara, CA, Apr. 1989.

[5] Intel Corp., *80386 Programmer's Reference Manual* (230958-001), Santa Clara, CA, 1986.

[6] Intel Corp., *i86064-bit Microprocessor Hardware Reference Manual* (CG-101789), Santa Clara, CA, 1989.

[7] Cruess, M., "Memory Management Chip for 68020 Translates Addresses in Less Than a Clock Cycle," *Electronic Design*, May 15, 1986.

[8] Motorola Inc., *MC68851 Technical Summary* (BR299), Austin, TX, 1986.

[9] Motorola Inc., *MC88200 Technical Summary* (BR589/D), Austin, TX, 1988.

[10] Strauss, E., *Inside the 80286*, A Brady Book, Prentice Hall, Englewood Cliffs, NJ, 1986.

[11] Intel Corp., *iAPX286 Programmer's Reference Manual* (210498-001), Santa Clara, CA, 1983.

[12] Roloff, J. J., "Managing Memory to Unloose the Full Power of Microprocessors," *Electronics*, Apr. 10, 1980, pp. 130–134.

[13] Stevenson, D., "Memory Management Rescues 16-bit Microprocessors from Demands of Multiple User's Tasks," *Electronic Design*, Vol. 1, Jan. 4, 1980, pp. 112–116.

[14] Motorola Inc., *MTT30 Course Notes*, Phoenix, AZ. Febr. 1988.

[15] K. Holden, P. Mothersole, and R. Vegrsne, "Memory Management in the 68030 Microprocessor", *AR 248, CMP Publications, Inc.*, Manhasset, NY., 1987, pp. 1–5.

[16] Motorola Inc, *MTT30 Course Notes*, Phoenix, AZ, July 1987.

[17] K. A. (1-Ayat & R. K. Agarwal, "The Intel 80386: Architecture and Implementation", *IEEE Micro*, Dec. 1985, pp. 4–22.

[18] Zilog, Inc., *Z8001 CPU, Z8002 CPU Product Specification*, Cupertino, CA, 1979.

CHAPTER

7

Other Relevant Topics

7.1 INTRODUCTION

In this chapter we cover various other topics that are relevant to the design of microprocessor-based systems. Some of them have to do with architecture and hardware issues (interrupt-I/O), others have to do with systems software design (exception handling and task switching), and others have to do with internal CPU characteristics whose impact on the system performance should be understood (e.g., instruction pipelining).

More specifically, the topics covered in this chapter include the following: We present the various modes of operation at different privilege levels that current microprocessors have and the protection mechanisms these products implement; we examine in more detail the Intel 80x86 protected mode mechanisms. The next topic covers the interrupt-I/O technique and how various microprocessors are interfaced to vectored devices and service them through vectored interrupts. A related issue is covered in the following section: that of advanced exception processing mechanisms in Intel and Motorola 32-bit microprocessors; the concept of "gates" that the Intel products use to provide a protection mechanism and to handle external interrupts that cause a task switch is also covered in that section. The next topic has to do with the internal pipelined architecture that most of the recent RISC and CISC microprocessors have implemented to reduce the processor CPI (clock cycles per instruction) and thus improve the overall system performance. Finally, the topic of "making a segment known" in segmented virtual memory systems is treated briefly at the end of the chapter.

7.2 PROTECTION MECHANISMS

7.2.1 User, Supervisor, and Protected Modes

Advanced microprocessors can operate in a number of "privilege levels," each one separate and completely isolated from the others. Software modules may be distributed among these privilege levels, according to the sensitivity of their function: for example, noncritical user or application functions are usually assigned to the least privileged level and are accessible by all other levels; on the other hand, very critical routines of the operating system kernel are assigned to the most privileged level and are protected from unauthorized access by code in the other less privileged levels. The more privilege the level at which a routine operates, the more system resources its instructions can access and manage.

The minimum number of privilege levels is two, distinguishing the "user level" (the less privileged one) and the "supervisor level" (the more privileged one). Respectively, we say that the processor operates in the *user (normal) mode* or in the *supervisor (system) mode*.[1] The MIPS R3000 calls them the *user* and *kernel* modes.

Newer **Motorola** processors have three levels: one is the usual *user mode*. The other two are the *interrupt state* (into which the system jumps when an external interrupt arrives and this state uses a unique "interrupt stack") and the *master state* (used to separate program-related exceptions from external interrupts, and this state uses a separate "master stack" for each task). Both the interrupt and master states have the system operating in the supervisor mode. The **MIPS R4000** also has three processor privilege levels, called the *user, supervisor,* and *kernel* modes (each one accessing its own address space). The **Intel microprocessors** operate in either the *real-address mode* (emulating the earlier 8086 to provide compatibility with existing software) or the *protected virtual-address mode* (which makes available all Intel's advanced architectural features, such as virtual memory, multitasking, protection, etc.). When operating in the *protected mode,* they can support up to four privilege levels: level 0 is the most privileged and level 3 is the least privileged.

A processor enters the new operating mode either automatically when an exception occurs (covered later in the chapter) or under software control, by setting particular bits in an internal control register; examples of the latter include the S and M bits in the Motorola's "status register," the two KSU (kernel-supervisor-user) bits in the R4000 status register, and the protection enable (PE) bit in Intel's "machine status word" (MSW) register.

This multiple-operating-level mechanism provides security in a computer system and allows memory accesses and special internal registers to be protected. For example, in the 2-mode mechanism, accesses are controlled because programs are allowed to access only their own code and data areas, and are thus restricted from accessing information which they do not need and need not modify. Their access is also limited to certain internal registers of the processor. The operating system and other system-level software, on the other hand, that execute in supervisor mode, have access to all system resources and all internal CPU registers (including those that are user accessible). Most instructions execute the same in user and supervisor mode. However, some instructions which have important system effects are made privileged. *Privileged instructions* are executed only in the supervisor mode (i.e., by systems code) and are therefore not allowed to be used by the normal programmer. Such privileged instructions include instructions which modify some important bits in the CPU

---

[1] These are sometimes referred to as *normal* and *system* modes, respectively.

flags/status register, input and output instructions, enable and disable interrupt instructions, and other special instructions that manipulate critical internal CPU resources. Thus, the handling of interrupts, or traps or exceptional conditions, which uses privileged instructions and accesses critical system resources, is always done in the supervisor mode.

Each mode, besides determining which operations are legal, also differentiates the use of certain special CPU resources. For example, in Motorola products with the 2-level user/supervisor mechanism, there is a "user stack pointer" or USP and a "supervisor stack pointer" or SSP register; these two stack pointer registers are represented by address register A7, which is either the USP or the SSP, depending on the state of the S bit in the processor's status register. If this S bit indicates user mode (S = 0), USP is the active stack pointer, and the SSP cannot be referenced as an address register; the active stack in memory is the "user stack." If the S bit indicates supervisor mode (S = 1), SSP is the active stack pointer, and the USP cannot be referenced; the active stack in memory is the "supervisor stack." The new 32-bit Motorola products with the 3-level user/interrupt/master mechanism (Figures B.9–B.11) have replaced the supervisor stack pointer with two registers: the "interrupt stack pointer" (ISP) and the "master stack pointer" (MSP); they are used when the processor is in the interrupt or master state, respectively. An additional bit (M) in the status register indicates the master/interrupt state. In the Intel case, entering the protected mode opens up the 4-privilege-level model discussed below.

7.2.2 80x86 Protected Mode

The concept of virtual memory management for the Intel products was described in Chapter 6. As we said there, each task has its own virtual address space defined by its LDT (local descriptor table), while all tasks share a common address space defined by the GDT (global descriptor table). In addition to isolating each task from another (by checking limits and access rights), the various distinct objects within the task's virtual address space (the segments) are assigned to different privilege levels to protect both data and code segments. Privilege checks are performed automatically by the hardware to determine which procedures can access a segment. In this section we present the protection provided with Intel's four privilege levels.

The 80x86 protected virtual-address mode (or simply, protected mode) is entered when software sets the protection enable (PE) bit in the "machine status word" register. This initialization involves placing new values in the GDTR and IDTR registers to prepare the system for future task switching, and loading appropriate initial values into the task-specific registers TR and LDTR (for example, place the appropriate segment selector for the initial task).

This protection model is supported by the following four registers shown in Figures A.5 and A.11:

Global descriptor table register (GDTR): contains the linear base address which points to the GDT descriptor table; it also contains a limit field that describes the size of the GDT table (see Figure 6.23). The GDT can have up to 8K descriptors and acts as the mapping table that describes the global/system portion of the virtual address space. Once it has received its values during system initialization, the GDTR does not change (i.e., it is not affected by task switching). It is accessible in both real and protected modes.

Interrupt descriptor table register (IDTR): contains the linear base address of the IDT descriptor table; it also contains a limit field similar to that of the GDTR. The IDT contains a number of ''gates'' (explained later). Like the GDTR, once it has received its values during initialization, the IDTR does not change (it is not affected by task switching). It is accessible in both real and protected modes.

Local descriptor table register (LDTR) and its associated descriptor cache, which contains the linear base address that points to the LDT descriptor table *for the current task* (each task has its own LDT, which identifies the task's separate virtual address space); in addition to the limit field, its descriptor cache also contains an ''access rights'' field to provide protection. The LDT specifies the task-specific, or local, region of the virtual address space that becomes accessible to the task. The LDTR is accessible only in the protected mode. After initialization, its manipulation is automatic; i.e., it is reloaded automatically every time the processor performs a task switch.

Task register (TR) and its associated descriptor cache, which hold information about the current task's TSS (task state segment), i.e., its linear base address, limit, and ''access rights.'' This TSS is the same as what is sometimes called the ''process control block'' and is not accessible by application programs. TR is accessible only in protected mode and like the LDTR, after initialization its manipulation is automatic; it is reloaded automatically every time the processor performs a task switch.

Privilege levels.   The 80x86 processors support four levels of increasing privilege, numbered 3, 2, 1, and 0 (Figure 7.1). A task may have segments in any of these four privilege levels. Level 0, the most privileged level, contains operating system code and data. While code at level 0 may access data at all other levels, code and data at level 0 cannot be directly accessed by code at other privilege levels. The least privileged level, level 3, is used for application programs and data. The other two levels can be used for other systems code and their usage is left up to the system designer. For example, level 1 is used for software that provides high-level functions such as file access scheduling, data communications, resource allocation policy, etc. Level 2 is used for custom operating system extensions that may include data base management, logical file access services, etc.

Programs can access data at the same or outer (less privileged) level, but not at inner (more privileged) levels. In this way, protection is provided for different layers of software within a task, since to allow access, the RPL (the ''requestor's privilege level'' in the virtual address[2] of Figure 6.25) is compared with the privilege level of the segment (the DPL or descriptor privilege level field of the ''access rights byte'' stored in that segment's segment descriptor of Figure 6.24) before access to this segment is permitted.

Interlevel communication.   Each task operates at only one privilege level at any given moment: namely that of the code segment being executed. However, since a task may contain segments at one, two, three, or four levels, all of which are to be used at appropriate times, the 80x86 processors provide a mechanism to traverse privilege levels (perform an interlevel transfer of control). Traversing of privilege levels can be done through either ''intersegment CALLs'' (if the access to that destination is permitted according to the privilege rules) or a CALL instruction, which uses as a target address a ''CALL gate'' (to provide

---

[2] The least significant two bits of the CS register. This RPL is also called the CPL (current privilege level).

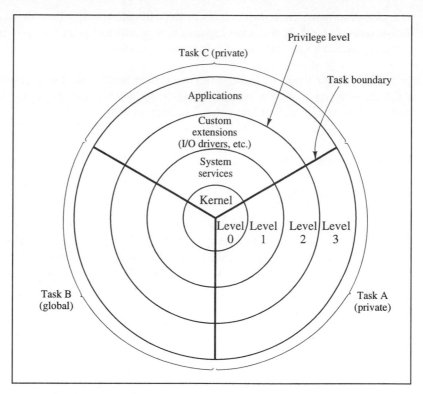

Figure 7.1 Intel four privilege rings (multiple tasks, each one having up to four privilege levels) [1]. Reprinted by permission of Intel Corporation, Copyright/Intel Corporation, 1983.

redirection to a specific entry point in another code[3]). A "gate" is a special descriptor type (residing in either the interrupt descriptor table IDT) which allows programs to use other programs at different privilege levels.

There are various types of gates, to be described in Section 7.4.1; the "call gate" used here, redirects control to a different code segment in the same or a more privileged level or to a different task; most often, however, a call gate specifies a subroutine at a greater privilege level, and the called routine returns via a return instruction. When invoking a subroutine through a gate, the privilege level of the executing routine changes to the level of the code segment to which the gate points. When the subroutine returns, the privilege level is set back to that of the calling procedure. Part of the stack is also copied to a more privileged stack segment.[4]

Call gate descriptors are used by call instructions in the same manner as a code segment descriptor. The hardware automatically recognizes that the destination selector refers

---

[3] They guarantee that transitions will go to valid entry points rather than possibly into the middle of a procedure.

[4] To maintain system integrity, every application must have as many stacks (stack segments) as there are privilege levels in the operating environment under which it is running to permit processing of calls from less privileged levels.

to a gate descriptor. Then the contents of the call gate specify the address of a new destination code segment. If this code segment is at a different privilege level than the current privilege level, an interlevel transfer is being requested.

Task switching.   Moving from one task to another is done by executing a JMP or a CALL instruction with a target address being a TSS (the processor performs a task switch). This is explained in more detail in Section 7.4.1.

7.3 EXTERNAL INTERRUPTS

7.3.1 Interrupt Lines

Every microprocessor has a number of input "interrupt pins" that can be used by external devices to send their interrupt request signals; the microprocessor usually responds to an accepted interrupt by issuing an "interrupt acknowledge" INTA signal. Some microprocessors (like the MIPS R series) rely on the interrupt-handling routine to acknowledge the interrupt. Figure 7.2 lists the interrupt types and pins for various microprocessors.

When an interrupt is detected, the processor context must be saved in order for the software to examine and, if needed, change it, and later be restored to return to the interrupted sequence. The amount of processor context and the way it is saved varies among the various microprocessors. The *Motorola 32-bit CISC microprocessors* will automatically save the processor context on the "active" supervisor stack (which, as we will see later, may be either an "interrupt stack" or a "masters stack"), before jumping into the interrupt handler; the amount of context saved varies depending on the reason that caused the exception. These Motorola microprocessors create and save an "exception stack frame"; depending on the type of exception, a different "exception stack frame" is saved as explained later in Section 7.4.2. For external interrupts, the exception stack frame is 4 words long ("format 0"). The *Intel 32-bit CISC microprocessors* may handle external interrupts with or without task switching. If no task switching is involved, the external stack is used to save the SS:SP, flags, and CS:IP registers; if task switching is involved, the stack is not used but instead a TSS swapping takes place to save the old context in memory and replace it with a new one from a new TSS (as explained in more detail in Section 7.4.1). Other microprocessors, like the RISC *Motorola 88000, Intel i860, and MIPS R series,* copy most of their context information (such as pipeline stages) internally into a large set of shadow registers, and then rely on systems software to decide how much of that information will be saved in an external system memory; at the end, the interrupt handler will restore the entire processor context before returning to the interrupted task.

Nonmaskable interrupts.   All processors have a nonmaskable input. In most cases, this is a single input pin referred to as NMI; in the Motorola products, however, the nonmaskable interrupt is indicated by applying all zeros (which corresponds to the highest-priority interrupt at level 7) to its three interrupt input pins IPL0#–IPL2#.

A *nonmaskable interrupt* cannot be masked off or disabled by software (it is always enabled) and has the highest priority. It is usually intended for "catastrophic events," such as imminent loss of power, memory error detection, etc. Accepting an interrupt request on this line need not generate any INTA signals. The response is usually a transfer to a prede-

Type of Interrupts

Microprocessor	Maskable			Non-maskable
	Nonvectored (interrupt information on data bus is a RESTART instruction)	Vectored (interrupt information on data bus is a vector number)	Auto-vectored (no vector number on the data bus)	(No vector number on the data bus)
Intel 8085	INTR: to handling routines in eight fixed locations 0_{16}, 10_{16}, 18_{16}, 20_{16}, 28_{16}, 30_{16}, 38_{16} RST 5.5: to handling routine in fixed location $2C_{16}$ RST 6.5: to handling routine in fixed location 34_{16} RST 7.5: to handling routine in fixed location $3C_{16}$			TRAP: to handling routine in *fixed* location 24_{16}
Intel 8086, 80x86		INTR: to *variable* vector locations in a vector table (the IDT in protected mode)		NMI: to a vector in the IDT (interrupt descriptor table)
Motorola 68000 and 680x0		Level 1 to level 6: to *variable* vector locations in a vector table	Level 1: to a vector in location 064_{16}. Level 2: to a vector in location 068_{16}.	Level 7: to a vector in location $07C_{16}$. (auto-vectored)

Figure 7.2 Interrupt input pins for various microprocessors. (The RESET input is not included here.)

Type of Interrupts

Microprocessor	Maskable			Non-maskable
	Nonvectored (interrupt information on data bus is a RESTART instruction)	Vectored (interrupt information on data bus is a vector number)	Auto-vectored (no vector number on the data bus)	(No vector number on the data bus)
			Level 3: to a vector in location $06C_{16}$. Level 4: to a vector in location 070_{16}. Level 5: to a vector in location 074_{16}. Level 6: to a vector in location 078_{16}.	
Mips R-Series		INT0#–INT5#: (a) R3000: branches to general exception vector at virtual address 0x80000080 (b) R4000: vectors to locations 0xBFL600200 (vector base) and 0x180 (vector offset) when in 32-bi7 mode or to location 0xFFFF FFFF BFC00200 (vector base) and 0x180 (vector offset) when in 64-bit mode		NMI (in R4000): Vectored to location 0xBFC00000 (in 32-bit mode) or 0xFFFF FFFF BFC00000 (in 64-bit mode)
Intel i860		IN: No INTA signal; trap handler reads from external I/O subsystem		No separate nonmaskable interrupt
Motorola 88100		INT: transfers in an orderly manner to an appropriate exception handler routine		

Figure 7.2 (concluded)

termined location in memory, as shown in the right column of Figure 7.2. For most processors, the nonmaskable interrupt is an "autovectored interrupt," which means that the processor jumps to a predetermined memory location which contains a "vector" (i.e., a pointer which, when loaded into the program counter, will point to another location where the first instruction of the interrupt-handling routine IHR resides). A nonmaskable interrupt can override the maskable interrupts even if they are in progress.

For the remainder of the chapter only maskable interrupts are considered since these are the ones that the system designer uses to interface external interrupting devices.

Maskable or user interrupts. Processors exist with one or more maskable interrupt input pins, as depicted in Figure 7.3. For example, most Intel microprocessors have only one maskable interrupt pin (the INTR). An exception to that is the earlier 8085 shown in Figure 7.3c, which has more than one, *nonencoded,* interrupt input pin; pins RST 5.5, RST 6.5, and RST 7.5 of the 8085 have different priority levels (RST 5.5 is the lowest) and each one transfers control to a different location in memory that contains the first instruction of the respective IHR: the RST 5.5 to location 002C, the RST 6.5 to location 0034, and the RST 7.5 to location 003C. But in all the other Intel products, INTR is the general-purpose interrupt input pin. All Motorola processors (Figure 7.3b) have three *encoded* interrupt priority-level input pins (IPLO#–IPL2#) that receive a 3-bit value representing the priority level of the incoming interrupt (level 7, represented by IPL2#–IPL0# = 000, is the highest level for the nonmaskable interrupt). Examples of recent microprocessors with more than one *nonencoded* maskable interrupt pin are the MIPS R-Series RISC processors, which have 6 pins.

When the microprocessor accepts an interrupt request and this interrupt is enabled, it responds by starting one or more *interrupt acknowledge cycles* and issuing an "INTA" signal. Like the variations in the interrupt input pins, the microprocessors have different ways of generating this "INTA" and also use different names for it. For example, the Intel 80x86 products must externally decode some control signals to generate an INTA signal. From the Motorola products, the 68000 places the values 111 on the output function code pins FC2–FC0, while the 32-bit 68020/30/40 identify the interrupt acknowledge cycle by placing (in addition to the FC0–FC2 = 111) the values 1111 on address bus lines A19–A16.

7.3.2 Vectored Interrupts

In this section we give a brief introduction into vectored interrupts. As examples we use the interrupt structures of the Intel 80x86 (primarily operating in real mode) and Motorola 68000 microprocessors. More advanced issues on exception processing by the Intel processors operating in protected mode and by newer 32-bit Motorola 680x0 processors are given in Section 7.4.

With the interrupt-driven I/O method, data transfer are initiated when an interrupt request signal is issued by the peripheral device requesting service from the microprocessors. *Interrupt signals* or *interrupt request signals* (which we will denote as **IREQ**) are the means by which one or more external slave devices notify the bus master that they require its immediate attention (or service).

Although as we will see later, there exist other external signals applied to special input pins of the processor to interrupt its normal operation (for example, a RESET signal or a "bus error" BERR signal, indicating that the processor issued a nonexisting memory

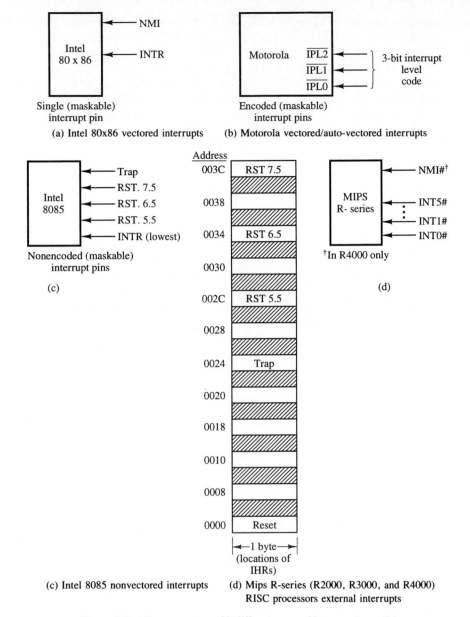

Figure 7.3 Microprocessors with different types of interrupt input pins.

address), with interrupt-driven I/O we will be referring to the interrupt input pins that the designer can use to interface peripheral interrupting devices. (These external hardware interrupts are also referred to as **user interrupts.**)

Because these interrupts can appear at any time, the microprocessor must be capable of "saving" the point at which the execution of the main program was interrupted so that it can return to it later, when it will have finished servicing the peripheral device. Furthermore, when more than one peripheral device is connected to the microprocessor, each with its own interrupt request signal, the following two additional problems arise: (1) the specific one out of the many possible device requesting service must be identified properly; and (2) when several of these devices request service at precisely the same time, a way must exist to prioritize the interrupts so that the devices can be serviced in some logical sequence.

In addition to these external **I/O (or hardware) interrupts,** there are two other classes of interrupts that interrupt the normal operation of the microprocessor: **software interrupts** or **exceptions** (generated by executing ''interrupt-type'' instructions that act as ''supervisor calls,'' requesting service from the operating system) and **internal hardware exceptions** (generated by the internal hardware of the system when it detects anomalous cases such as dividing by zero), which we will discuss later in the chapter.[5]

As we will see later, the various **exceptions** and interrupts have different priorities and therefore must be attended to at different instances of the program execution. External signals of the RESET and BERR type are of the highest priority and therefore must be handled by the processor at the *end of the clock cycle.* Some internal exceptions, such as privilege instructions or illegal instructions, must be handled at the *end of the current bus cycle.* Software interrupts must be handled any time *within the instruction cycle* of the executing instruction that caused the interrupt. Finally, user I/O interrupts are of the lowest priority and can be handled at the *end of the current instruction cycle.* Figure 7.4 shows the various types of Motorola exceptions and the time each exception is recognized by the microprocessor.

1. At end of clock cycle:
   - Reset
   - Address error
   - Bus error (BERR)
2. At end of bus cycle:
   - Illegal instruction
   - Unimplemented instruction
   - Privilege violation
3. At end of instruction cycle:
   - Trace exception
   - Interrupt exception
4. Within an instruction cycle:
   - TRAP
   - TRAPV
   - CHK
   - Zero divide

Figure 7.4 Various types of Motorola exceptions and the instant each is recognized by the processor. [3].

Most advanced microprocessors process exceptions using the vectoring technique. When an exception arises, the processor hardware carries out a number of steps to process it. We will refine these steps for specific microprocessors in later sections of the chapter. In general, however, the vectoring process includes the following steps:

PROCEDURE 7.1: GENERAL SEQUENCE FOR PROCESSING VECTORED EXCEPTIONS

1. Switch to the supervisor mode.
2. Identify the reason for the exception. Distinguish between internal exceptions, software exceptions/interrupts, and I/O hardware interrupts.)

[5] Some products use the term ''exceptions'' to refer to all types of interrupts.

3. Save the current processor context.

4. Branch to the appropriate exception-handling routine.

These steps are explained below in more detail.

1. *Switch to the supervisor mode.* The processor copies internally at least the program counter and the status register,[6] and switches to the supervisor mode. Switching to the supervisor mode is done by the hardware setting the respective "supervisor bit" in its status register.

2. *Identify the reason for this exception.*

a. *Internal hardware exceptions:* Internal logic provides an identifier called the "vector number" and the hardware converts it into a "vector address." Quite often, this conversion is done by multiplying the vector number by 4 (shifting it left by two positions) and the generated vector address points to an entry in a special area of low memory called the "vector table."[7] This is referred to as *autovectoring* since no external hardware was used to provide the vector number.

b. *Software exceptions:* The interrupt-type instruction which caused this exception also provides the vector number in its address field. As before, the hardware will use this vector number and convert it into a vector address.

c. *I/O hardware interrupts:* External interrupt requests arriving at the microprocessor input pins do not force immediate interrupt processing but are made pending. Pending interrupts are detected between instruction executions; i.e., the microprocessor will complete the current instruction execution before recognizing the external interrupt.

An external interrupt may also stay pending if it is *masked* by software (for example, during the period of executing some critical process). For masked interrupt requests, their processing is postponed. (Either external hardware must accumulate them and hold them by priority for the processor or a special interrupt queue routine must be executed to store information for this interrupt in a queue by priority.)

Most often, when an interrupt is accepted, the microprocessor automatically disables all interrupts (and thus they must be enabled again by software, if so desired) or the microprocessor is set to the interrupt level of the current interrupt, thus disabling lower-level interrupts.

If the processor can be interrupted at this point by such an interrupt, the system must first distinguish between autovectored and vectored external interrupts.

Autovectored interrupts are those generated by simple devices that are not themselves capable of generating a vector number. (We call these devices "nonvectored" devices.) For these devices, the processor will itself determine the vector number internally (by examining signals on its input pins), and convert it into a vector address.

---

[6] RISC processors copy internally a larger portion of the processor context than do CISC processors.

[7] These terms are also called "exception number," "exception address," and "exception table."

Vectored interrupts are used by external devices that can provide a vector number to identify themselves ("vectored devices"). In this case, the processor will carry out an "interrupt acknowledge cycle" with which it will read the vector number that the interrupting device had placed on the data bus. Then the processor will multiply it by 4 to convert it into a vector address.

3. *Save the current processor context.* The processor saves the "current processor context."[8] Quite often this is done using the off-chip system stack. The top of the stack location is identified by the contents of the respective supervisor stack pointer register. In simple microprocessors, the processor context is nothing more than the program counter and the (copied internally) old status register. In more complex microprocessors, the processor context is a large number of internal registers. (For example, in the Motorola 680x0 products it is an "exception stack frame," whose size may vary from 4 16-bit words to 46 words, depending upon the type of exception.)

4. *Jump to the appropriate IHR.* Finally, the processor sends the vector address to memory and fetches from it a "vector" (or an "exception vector"). Then, with the next instruction fetch, the processor will use this vector to fetch the first instruction of the IHR (interrupt handling routine) to service this exception.

The above process uses vector numbers to jump indirectly to the corresponding IHRs. Figure 7.5 shows the simplified diagram that describes the activities carried out to process *external I/O vectored interrupts.*

Below we discuss in more detail how the Intel and Motorola products handle vectored interrupts from external devices.

Intel vectored interrupt structures. All newer Intel products support external vectored interrupts. We present here the case of using external PICs (the 8259 programmable interrupt controller) to interface peripheral devices to the Intel microprocessors.

Figure 7.6a shows the simplified diagram of interfacing up to eight interrupting devices to an Intel processor using one external PIC. Figure 7.6b shows the block diagram of the 8259 PIC. The PIC can manage up to eight independent interrupt devices, handles interrupt priority resolution, allows the interrupt requests from these devices to be individually masked (enabled/disabled), and tracks which interrupts are pending and which are currently being serviced to avoid multiple occurrences of interrupts from the same device (nested interrupts). Its three "cascade address" CAS0–2 pins are outputs when the PIC is used as a master (in a cascade configuration to be discussed below for handling more than eight external devices) and are inputs when the PIC is used as a slave.[9] The interrupts at the IR input lines are handled by two internal registers in cascade: the interrupt register (IRR) holds all the IREQ signals of the interrupt devices (pending interrupts), and the in-service register (ISR) stores all the interrupt signals of the devices being serviced. These registers can be read by software to determine which interrupts are currently being serviced and which ones are still pending. The priority resolver circuit selects the highest-priority input signal and strobes that into the corresponding bit of the ISR during INTA# pulse. The PIC

---

[8] This is also called "processor state," "CPU state," "PSW" (program status word), etc.

[9] The PIC is also programmable to operate in other different modes; one of them is when the PIC is to be used with 8-bit Intel microprocessors, in which case it releases a CALL instruction on data bus lines D0–D7 followed by a preprogrammed subroutine address.

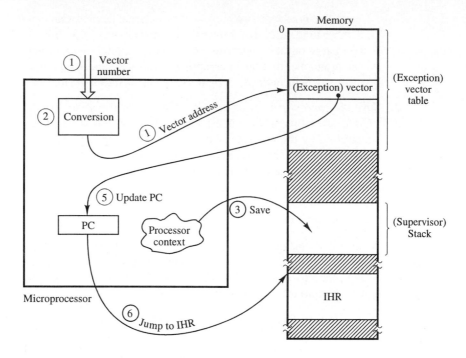

Step 1: Read vector number from data bus D0 – D7.
Step 2: Convert vector number into a vector address
(usually, by multiplying it by 4).
Step 3: Save "Processor context" (a number of internal
registers) on top of the (supervisor) stack.
Step 4: Send vector address to memory (points to an
entry in vector table).
Step 5: Fetch a vector from vector table and update program
counter (at least).
Step 6: Start fetching the first instruction of the IHR.

Figure 7.5 Vectored I/O interrupts and the steps taken to jump to the interrupt handling
routine (IHR).

is used to provide "vectored interrupt" capability: it inputs an 8-bit vector number on data
bus lines D0–D7 whose 3 least significant bits is the 3-bit code of the highest-priority interrupt request input (the other 4 bits are set during initialization). Every time an IHR is
finished, the ISR register must be checked for any pending interrupts. The PIC ensures that
further INTR activations from the current device are disabled until the IHR indicates to it
its completion [usually by sending to the controller an end-of-interrupt (EOI) instruction].

Figure 7.7 shows a simplified diagram of interfacing a cascade of PICs in two levels
(level 1 has the master PIC and level 2 the slave PICs) to accommodate up to 64 interrupt
requests. The numbered circles in the diagram identify the steps followed in handling vectored interrupts according to the procedure described below.

PROCEDURE 7.2: INTEL VECTORED INTERRUPTS FROM CASCADED PICS

1. One or more interrupt devices request service by asserting their IREQ signals to the
slave PICs.

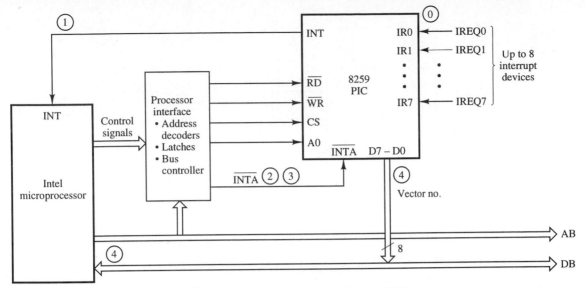

(a) Eight interrupt devices connected through a PIC

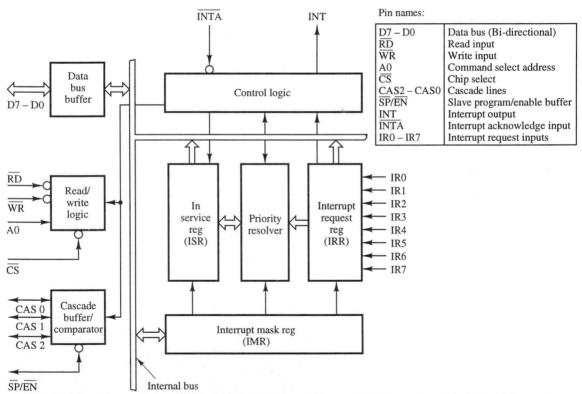

Pin names:

D7 – D0	Data bus (Bi-directional)
$\overline{RD}$	Read input
$\overline{WR}$	Write input
A0	Command select address
$\overline{CS}$	Chip select
CAS2 – CAS0	Cascade lines
$\overline{SP/EN}$	Slave program/enable buffer
INT	Interrupt output
$\overline{INTA}$	Interrupt acknowledge input
IR0 – IR7	Interrupt request inputs

(b) Block diagram and pins of the 8259 PIC [2] (Reprinted by permission of Intel Corporation, Copyright/Intel Corporation, 1979.)

Figure 7.6 8259 PIC (programmable interrupt controller) used to interface 8 external interrupt devices to an Intel microprocessor.

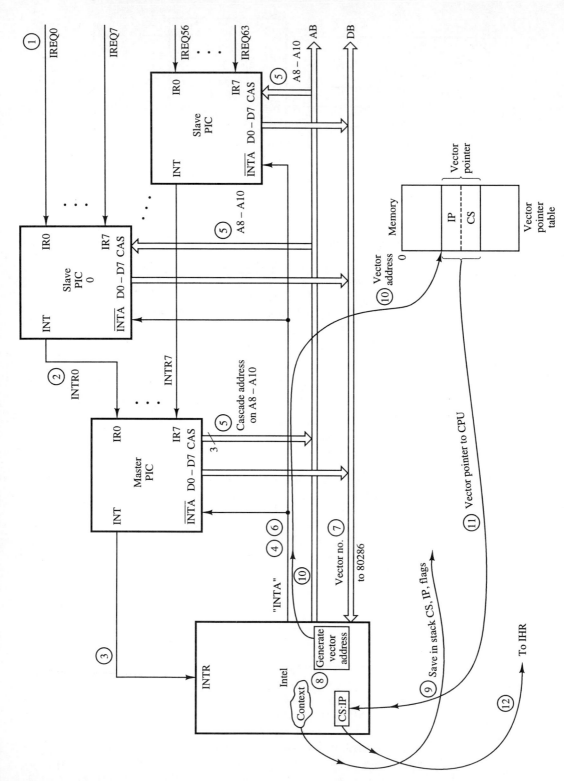

Figure 7.7 Intel microprocessor connected to cascaded PICs. (Steps numbered in circles correspond to those of Procedure 7.2.)

384

2. The INT outputs of all slave PICs are connected to the IR inputs of the master PIC requesting service from it.

3. The master PIC interrupts the microprocessor.

4. If interrupts are enabled, the processor must read a vector number. The Intel processor starts an INTA cycle by issuing two successive "INTA" signals (whichever way each Intel processor generates these "INTA" signals). The first "INTA" signals all PICs that an interrupt has been honored. This freezes the state of the IR input pins in all PICs and moves their higher-priority interrupt from the IRR to the ISR register.

5. The master PIC places on its CAS0–2 outputs the 3-bit cascade address of its highest input signal (identifying its highest-priority interrupting slave PIC). These signals are connected to the address bus lines A8–A10 and sent to the CAS0–2 input pins of all slave PICs to select the slave PIC that is generating the highest-priority INTR.

6. The microprocessor issues the second "INTA" applied to all PICs. During the second "INTA" the PIC with the highest priority pending (addressed by the cascade address on A8–A10) responds and

7. places an 8-bit vector number on the data bus lines D0–D7 to identify its highest-priority input device.

8. The microprocessor latches the vector number and converts it internally to a vector address (by multiplying it by 4).

9. Next, the processor pushes on top of the stack first the CS register, and then the IP and PSW (flags) registers, and

10. sends the generated vector address to the vector table in memory.

11. A doubleword vector is fetched from memory; this vector contains new values for the microprocessor's CS and IP registers.

12. Finally, using the new CS and IP values, the microprocessor starts a new fetch cycle to fetch the first instruction of the IHR for the highest-priority interrupt device.

Motorola vectored interrupt structures. In this section we present the way external devices are connected to the Motorola 68000 microprocessor and how the microprocessor handles exceptional conditions. More advanced exception handling by the 32-bit Motorola 680x0 microprocessors is described in Section 7.4.2.

All Motorola microprocessors have three input pins, called IPL0#, IPL1#, and IPL2#, on which an external encoder must place a 3-bit code to represent the interrupt priority level of the interrupting device. The 68000 uses two other pins to handle an external interrupt: the DTACK# (which signals the processor that a "vectored device" requests service) and the VPA# (which signals the processor that a nonvectored device caused the interrupt and that the processor must itself generate the vector number in an autovectoring mode).

68000 Vector Table. The Motorola 68000 calls all types of interrupts—i.e., internal hardware interrupts (or error conditions), software interrupts due to an instruction execution, and external interrupt requests or error conditions—"exceptions." It calls the vector table, which resides in the reserved lower 1024 words of memory (Figure 7.8), the "exception vector table" and each vector is called an "exception vector." All vectors are one doubleword (32 bits) in length and lie in the "supervisor data space" in memory, except for the RESET vector, which is two doublewords (64 bits) long and lies in the "supervisor

Vector table — lower portion (vector numbers 0–14)

Address (Dec)	(Hex)		Vector number
0	000	Reset (initial SSP)	0
4	004	Reset (initial PC)	
8	008	Bus error	2
12	00C	Address error	3
16	010	Illegal instruction	4
20	014	Zero divide	5
24	018	CHK instruction	6
28	01C	TRAPV instruction	7
32	020	Privilege violation	8
36	024	Trace	9
40	028	Line 1010 emulator	10
44	02C	Line 1111 emulator	11
48	030	(Unassigned, reserved)	12
52	034		13
56	038		14

16 bits

Vector table — upper portion (vector numbers 15–255)

Address (Dec)	(Hex)		Vector Number	
60	03C	Uninitialized interrupt vector	15	
64	04C	(Unassigned, reserved)	16 ⋯ 23	
95	05F			
96	060	Spurious interrupt	24	
100	064	Level 1 interrupt auto-vector	25	⎫
104	068	Level 2 interrupt auto-vector	26	Six external maskable autovectored (VPA)
108	06C	Level 3 interrupt auto-vector	27	
112	070	Level 4 interrupt auto-vector	28	⎭
116	074	Level 5 interrupt auto-vector	29	
120	078	Level 6 interrupt auto-vector	30	⎫ External nonmaskable (autovectored)
124	07C	Level 7 interrupt auto-vector	31	
128	080	16 TRAP instruction vectors	32 ⋯ 47	⎭
191	0BF			
192	0C0	(Unassigned, reserved)	48 ⋯ 63	
255	0FF			
256	100	192 User interrupt vectors (vectored interrupt jump table)	64 ⋯ 255	⎱ External maskable vectored (DTACK#)
1023	3FF			

16 bits

Figure 7.8 The lower 1024 bytes of memory are reserved for the vector table (or "exception vector table" as it is called by the Motorola 68000). Courtesy of Motorola, Inc. [3].

program or code space" in memory. Thus, 256 unique vectors are provided, 192 of which are called "user interrupt vectors" (in locations 000100 through 0003FF) used by external interrupting devices. Whenever an exception arises during the user program execution, the processor switches automatically from the user to the supervisor mode.

Types and Priorities of 68000 Exceptions. The 3-bit applied to the interrupt pins IPL0#–IPL2# indicates the priority level of the interrupt: level 0 (i.e., IPL0#–IPL2# = HHH) is the lowest priority and means "no interrupt," while level 7 (IPL0#–IPL2# = LLL) is the highest priority and is nonmaskable. The microprocessor has in its internal "status register" SR a 3-bit "interrupt mask" which identifies the processor's level. In order for an interrupt to be acknowledged and start exception processing, the level of the incoming interrupt must be greater than the processor's operating level; for example, if the status register interrupt mask is set to level 3, then only interrupt levels 4, 5, 6, and 7 are allowed.

External hardware exceptions include the *user interrupts,* the *reset* signal, and the *bus error* (BERR) signal. The BERR is issued in the following cases: when the processor is accessing nonresident memory; when the external "watchdog timer" detects that the addressed slave device did not respond with the "data transfer acknowledge" signal within the allotted time; when there are parity errors identified in the data transfer; or when an external memory management unit (MMU) identifies an "address translation error" or "protection violation error." (When the BERR is used with the HALT input it forces a rerun of the current bus cycle). **Internal exceptions** include *address error* (such a trying to fetch a 16-bit operand from an odd byte address), *illegal instruction, unimplemented instruction* (see the next section), *privilege violation, trace exception,* and *divine by zero.* Finally, **software exceptions** include those generated by executing instructions *TRAP, TRAPV,* and *CHK.*

For most exceptions, the hardware pushes on top of the supervisor stack (using the internal "supervisor stack pointer" register) first the 32-bit program counter that contains the return address (low half followed by high half), and then the internally copied "old" 16-bit status register.[10] The RESET input provides the highest exception level, by setting the processor interrupt priority mask at level 7; neither the program counter nor the status register is saved, and the reset vector (at location 0 in Figure 7.8) contains new initial supervisor stack pointer and initial program counter values (the reset vector is four 16-bit words long).

68000 Exception Processing Sequence. Figure 7.9 gives the simplified flowchart for the generalized Motorola exception processing sequence. Figure 7.10 shows in detail the various steps that correspond to the following procedure.

PROCEDURE 7.3: MOTOROLA GENERAL EXCEPTION PROCESSING

1. Exception processing is triggered by an external or internal event.
2. The processor copies internally the status register (SR) into a temporary register,
3. sets the privilege state to "supervisor" (by setting the S bit in the SR register to 1), and suppresses tracing (by clearing bit T in the SR).
4. If an *internal exception:* the processor generates the vector number internally *(autovectoring)* and jumps to step 9.

---

[10] As explained later in Section 7.4.2, for the RESET, BERR, and "address error" exceptions the hardware pushes additional processor registers on top of the stack.

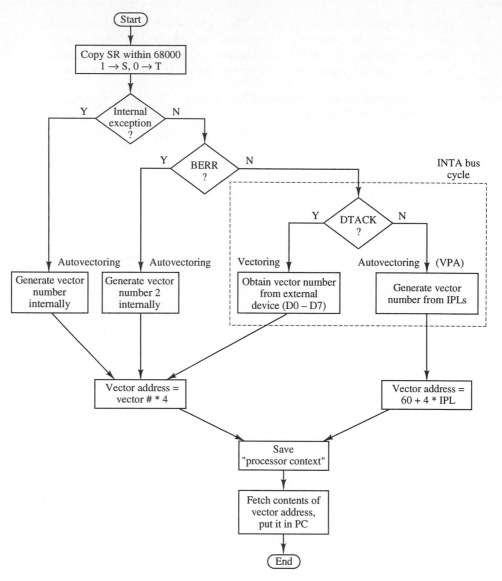

Figure 7.9 Simplified flowchart of the generalized Motorola exception processing sequence [3].

5. If a *BERR exception:* the processor aborts the bus cycle at the end of the current clock cycle, and generates the vector number 2 internally *(autovectoring).* (The processor forces the "spurious interrupt" vector 24 internally when a BERR occurs during an interrupt acknowledge.) Then it jumps to step 9.

6. If *any other external exception:* the processor does the following:
   a. Sets the processor interrupt mask level in the SR register to the (higher) level of the interrupt being serviced (by reading IPL0#–IPL2# inputs).
   b. Starts a bus cycle classifying it as an INTA cycle (by placing all ones on the output function code pins FC0–FC2).

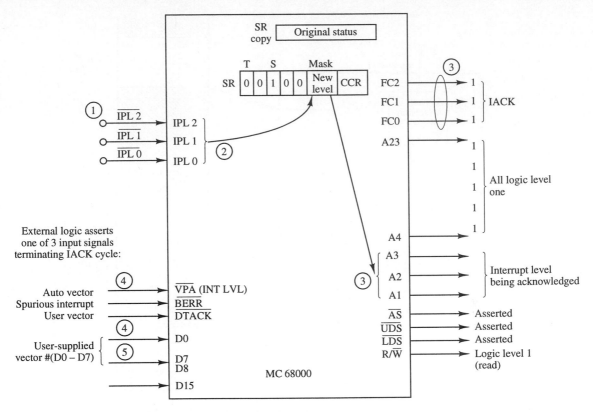

Figure 7.10 Steps of Procedure 7.3 for the Motorola exception processing.

   c. Displays the level number of the interrupt being acknowledged on address pins A1–A3; all other address pins are set to ones.

7. If the *VPA# had been asserted,* the processor generates a vector number from the interrupt level on IPL0#–IPL2# (the interrupting device or its interface does not provide the vector number) and generates the vector address by performing: 60 + 4*IPL. *(Autovectoring)* It then jumps to step 10.

8. If the *DTACK# had been asserted,* the processor obtains a vector number from the external interrupting device or its interface over data bus lines D0–D7. (Regular *vectoring*)

9. The processor converts the ''vector number'' into a ''vector address'' by multiplying it by 4.

10. The processor saves the ''processor context'' by placing the program counter (starting with its lower half first) followed by the internally copied ''old'' status register RS on top of the supervisor stack,

11. fetches the ''vector'' (the ''vector address contents'') from memory and places it into the program counter, and

12. fetches the instruction stream (the first 2 words) of the IHR at the new program counter location.

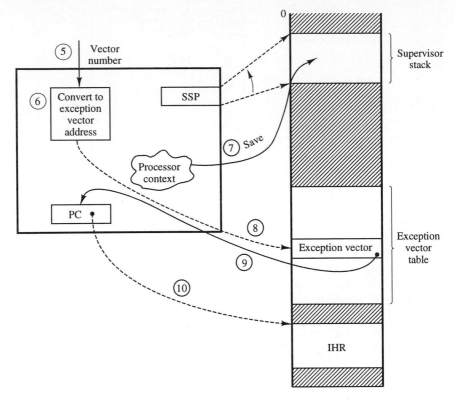

Figure 7.10   (concluded)

Interfacing Vectored and Auto-vectored Devices.   Figure 7.11 shows a number of nonvectored I/O interface chips (such as the PIA and ACIA[11] used for the 6800 peripherals) and the numbering of steps in circles corresponds to the steps of Motorola Exception Processing Procedure 7.3. Their individual interrupt request signals (IRQ) are connected via a priority encoder which performs priority resolution and interrupts the microprocessor by supplying to its IPL0#–IPL2# input pins the 3-bit code of the highest priority. When the microprocessor responds with an "interrupt acknowledge cycle" and issues the signal FC0–FC2 = 111, the external CPU hardware logic uses it to assert the VPA# input pin, indicating to the microprocessor that the interrupting devices will submit no vectors over the data bus and that it is the processor's responsibility to generate a vector number from the interrupt level on IPL0#–IPL2# (step 7 of Procedure 7.3). The interrupt will then be handled by the processor, carrying out the remaining steps of Procedure 7.3.

Assume now that we want to interface to the 68000 both vectored and nonvectored devices. As in Figure 7.11, an external priority encoder will be required to handle up to seven external interrupting devices and provide the 3-bit code to the microprocessor's IPL0#–IPL2# interrupt pins. However, the external CPU hardware logic that receives the "INTA" (FC0–FC2 = 111) signal and the 3-bit code (of the level number of the interrupt being acknowledged) on address lines A1–A3 must now distinguish between a nonvectored

[11] PIA, parallel interface adapter; ACIA, asynchronous communications interface adapter.

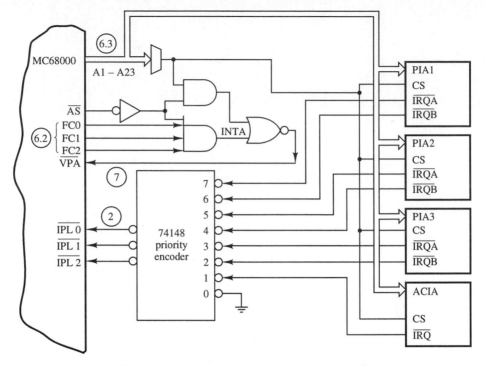

Figure 7.11 68000 auto-vectored external interrupts [3].

interrupting device and a vectored interrupting device. In the first case it will generate a signal to trigger the processor at the VPA# input pin to start auto-vectoring; in the second case, it will generate a signal to trigger the interrupting device to place its vector number on the data bus line D0–D7. Such a design is shown in Figure 7.12 for two interrupting devices, one a nonvectored device that interrupts the processor at level 3 and the other a vectored device that interrupts it at level 5; the vectored device also asserts the DTACK# input pin of the processor. The first decoder that receives the FC0–FC2 outputs makes sure that the second decoder is enabled only during INTA cycles (i.e., when FC0–FC2 = 111). The second decoder receives the level number on lines A1–A3, decodes it, and for interrupt level 3 generates the INTA3# to trigger the VPA# processor pin and start auto-vectoring, and for interrupt level 5 generates the INTA5# to trigger the vectored device's interface to place on the data bus the 8-bit vector number that the processor expects.

7.3.3 Interrupt Latency

The interrupt latency is an important measure of the microprocessor-based system throughput in interrupt-driven configurations. Interrupt latency is the time from the moment an interrupt is asserted until the processor starts handling the interrupt. The more time-critical the application, the smaller this interrupt latency time must be.

The interrupt latency time includes the time delay involved before the external interrupt is recognized (either because the processor is executing a "long instruction" or a long

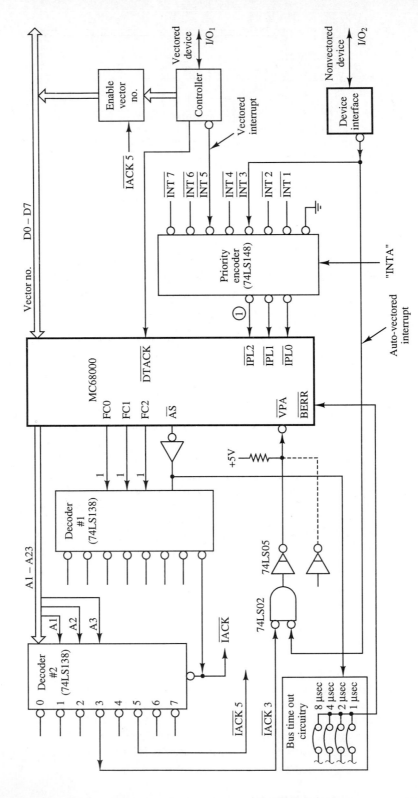

Figure 7.12 68000 auto-vectored and vectored external interrupts [3].

critical sequence of instructions which are executed in a noninterruptible mode), the priority scheme (what is the worst wait time because the processor is handling a higher-priority interrupt), and the overhead in performing context switching (which depends on the number of registers to be saved and the way the processor saves these registers). If interrupts must be polled, an additional delay is introduced by the polling sequence.

7.4 EXCEPTION PROCESSING

7.4.1 Intel Protected-Mode Exceptions

Gates. In the Intel protected mode operation, the vector table is a 256-entry "interrupt descriptor table" (IDT) placed anywhere in memory. Its base address is pointed by the contents of the internal IDTR register. Each of the 256 entries of the IDT (each one of which we earlier called a "vector") is now referred to as a "gate" or "gate descriptor,"[12] is 8 bytes long, and has the format shown in Figure 7.13a. There are three types of gates:

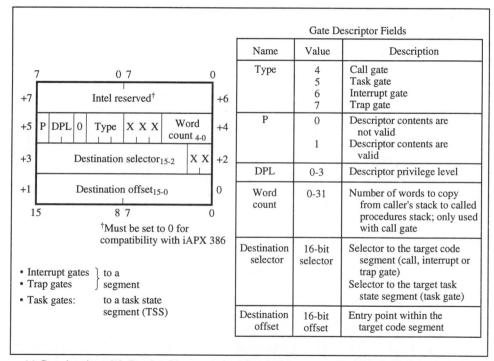

(a) Gate descriptor [1] (Reprinted by permission of Intel Corporation, Copyright/Intel Corporation 1983.)

Figure 7.13 Intel protected-mode gates and handling of an exception without and with task switching.

1. *Interrupt gates* (or descriptor type 6): An interrupt gate is used for external interrupts and points to an executable segment (in the current task) whose execution will take

[12] Descriptors and their use in segmented systems are discussed in Chapter 6.

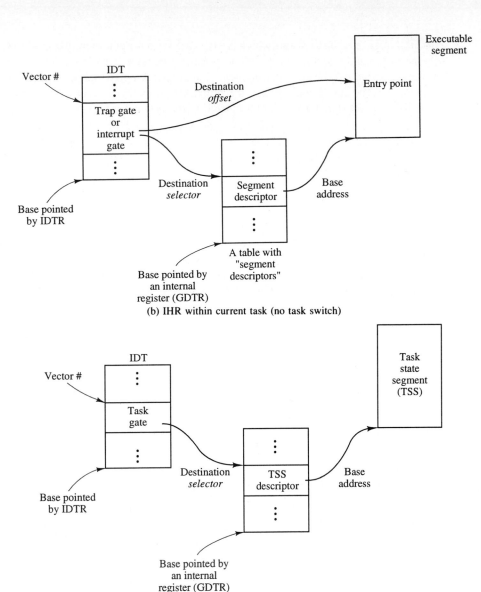

(b) IHR within current task (no task switch)

(c) IHR in a different task (causes task switch)

Figure 7.13 (concluded)

care of the interrupt. No task switching takes place, and the IHR is entered with *interrupts disabled*.

2. *Trap gates* (or descriptor type 7): A trap gate is used for processor-detected exceptions; it also points to an executable segment (in the current task), no task switching takes place, but now the trap handler is entered with *interrupts unchanged*.

In either of the above two ways of handling an interrupt/exception, the stack is used to save the SS:SP, flags, and CS:IP registers. In order to jump to the IHR, both the "destination selector" and the "destination offset" fields of the gate are used (Figure 7.13b).

3. *Task gates* (or descriptor type 5): A task gate can be used for either external interrupts or internal exceptions, and its "destination selector" field, instead of pointing to the IHR, points to the new TSS to be swapped in to replace the old TSS.[13] This TSS swapping implements a "task switch" to get to the IHR that resides in a different task. Since this TSS swapping will have the processor's flags register loaded with new values specified by the new TSS, the IHR is allowed to run with the *interrupts enabled or disabled*. When a task-based interrupt handler is invoked via a task gate, the stack is not used. Instead, a TSS swapping takes place. From the task gate only the "destination selector" field is used (the "destination offset" field is not used) to identify which TSS will be activated with the task switch (Figure 7.13c).

Task switching.   Context or task switching is performed as shown in the simplified diagram of Figure 7.14 by storing in memory the "current TSS" (which then becomes the "old TSS") and swapping into the microprocessor a "new TSS" (which then becomes the "current TSS"). The TSS contains values for the state of the new task, including the address of the next instruction to be executed (i.e., values for the CS and IP registers), the contents of task-variable registers and flags, a pointer that indicates the address space to be activated for the new task, etc.

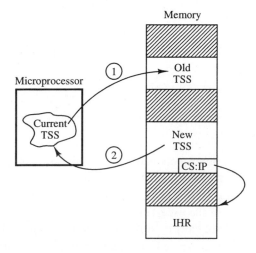

Figure 7.14 Performing task switching (via TSS swapping) to jump to the IHR.

Exception processing.   The Intel protected-mode handling of external and internal interrupts is done according to the procedure given below. The steps of this procedure are numbered in Figure 7.15.

PROCEDURE 7.4: INTEL PROTECTED-MODE INTERRUPT PROCESSING

1. At the beginning, internal CPU registers contain pointers to different tables in memory: the IDTR points to the IDT (or "vector table") that contains the "gates" to be used to jump to the IHR; the GDTR points to the global descriptor table in memory

---

[13] A TSS or task state segment is a segment in memory containing the "processor context" (i.e., values for the processor registers) for the task. In some systems the TSS is called the "process control block" (PCB) or "task control block" (TCB).

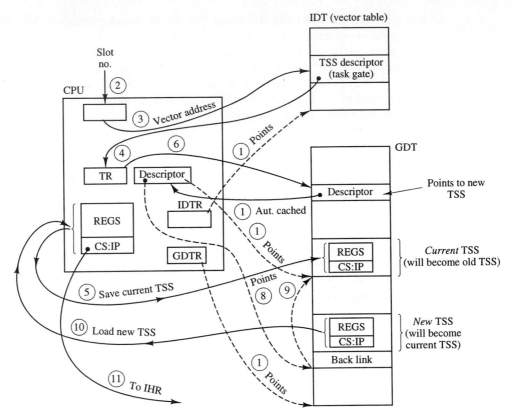

Figure 7.15 Details of the Intel external interrupt processing (via task switching).

that contains operating system descriptors and the various TSSs; and finally, an internal register points to the area of memory that contains the current TSS.

2. The Intel processor performs two INTA bus cycles and reads an 8-bit vector number (also called a "slot number"). If the exception were an internal exception or a software interrupt, the processor will generate this vector number internally.

3. The processor uses the vector number and now multiplies it by 8 (instead of by 4, because each entry in the IDT is 8 bytes long) to generate a vector address to be used as an offset in the IDT table in memory from which

4. a new value will be placed in the TR (task register) of the processor. In other words, the processor reads a gate from the IDT.

   If the gate is an *interrupt gate* or a *trap gate*, the processor will do the following: pushes on stack the SS:SP, flags, and CS:IP registers; disables interrupts; and executes the IHR as indicated within the gate (see Figure 7.13b).

   If the gate is a *task gate* (as is the case in Figure 7.13c), the processor continues the procedure below.

5. The processor automatically saves its current TSS (all CPU registers) in the current TSS in memory and leaves the interrupted task marked busy.

6. It then uses the TR as an offset in the GDT table in memory,

7. from where it reads this descriptor and places it in the internal descriptor register.

8. This register now points to the new TSS in memory.

9. It establishes a "back link" to the previous TSS and

10. new values are placed into the processor's registers from the new TSS.

11. Finally, the new values placed in the CS and IP registers during the previous step will now be used to transfer to the IHR.

7.4.2 Motorola 680x0 Exception Processing

Advanced Motorola 680x0 processors have a more complex exception processing procedure than that of the 68000 described earlier. First of all, when the processor is in the **user mode** (indicated by the status register bits "supervisor/user mode" S equal 0 and "master/interrupt state" M equal either 0 or 1), it will switch to the **supervisor mode** when an external interrupt or internal exception appears (issuing FC0–FC2 = 111), as suggested by Figure 7.16. The processor will create an "exception stack frame" and save it on top of the "active" supervisor stack. Return from the supervisor to the user mode is accomplished by executing the RTE (return from exceptions) instruction or executing an instruction that modifies the S and M bits in the status register (such as a MOVE, ANDI, or EORI to the status register).

When the processor is in the supervisor mode, it can be in one of two states: **interrupt state** (S = 1, M = 0) or **master state** (S = 1, M = 1). When switching from the user mode, it always transfers to the interrupt state. The processor can also enter the interrupt state when—while operating in the master state—an external hardware interrupt appears. In both cases, when the interrupt state is entered, the *interrupt stack* is the active stack (pointed by ISP register A7') into which the exception stack frame is saved.

The only way the processor can enter the master state is from the interrupt state with the execution of the RTE instruction (as will be explained later). When switching to the master state, a *master stack* for the interrupted task is now the active stack (pointed by MSP register A7''). Any exceptions (other than external user interrupts) that may arise while in the master state will not force the processor to switch states. While there is only one "interrupt stack," there is a separate "master stack" for each task (in the task's "task control block"); i.e., the operating system uses the master stack to separate program-related exceptions from interrupts.[14] The interrupt stack and the master stacks are in supervisor memory space.

The 680x0 processors handle external interrupts and other exceptions by executing the following procedure, whose steps are numbered in Figure 7.17a.

PROCEDURE 7.5: MOTOROLA 680x0 EXCEPTION PROCESSING

A. *External Interrupts*
1. IPL0#–IPL2# are asserted by an external interrupting device. The processor compares its current mask level (in its SR register) with the newly arrived one.

---

[14] The operating system assigns a "task control block" or TCB (a special area in memory) to each task, where it saves the task's "context": (1) when task A is suspended, the operating system uses the MSP register (which points to the task's stack in the task's TCB) to push there the task's frame along, possibly, with the task's MSP register; (2) when a new task B is activated, a new value is placed in the MSP register (coming from task B's TCB), which points to the top of task B's stack (in task B's TCB) and is used to move task B's frame into the CPU.

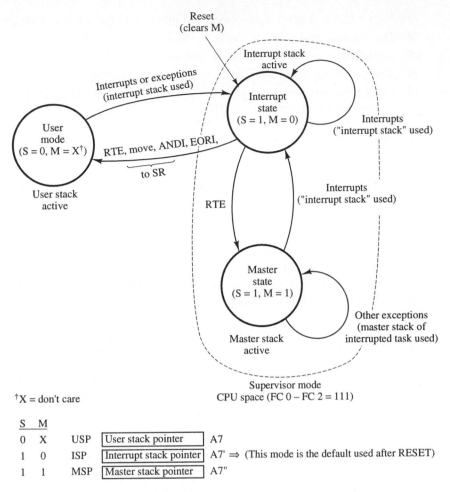

Figure 7.16 Motorola 680x0 user mode and interrupt and master states of the supervisor mode.

[†]X = don't care

S	M			
0	X	USP	User stack pointer	A7
1	0	ISP	Interrupt stack pointer	A7' ⇒ (This mode is the default used after RESET)
1	1	MSP	Master stack pointer	A7"

2. If the new one is of a higher level, it copies the SR register internally into a temporary register TEMP.

3. It sets the S bit to 1 (to indicate supervisor mode), clears the trace bits in the SR, and sets the mask bits in the SR to the interrupt level.

4. The processor then starts a bus cycle, classifying it as an INTA cycle, i.e.:

   asserts the R/W# = H (read signal),
   issues FC0–FC2 = 111 (CPU space),
   issues A16–A19 = 1111 (INTA),
   places the 3-bit "interrupt level" on lines A1–A3,
   sets all other address bits to 1s,
   asserts AS# and DS#, and
   issues SIZ0–SIZ1 = 10 (to indicate that it will read a byte
   vector number over a data bus).

5. Obtains a vector number.

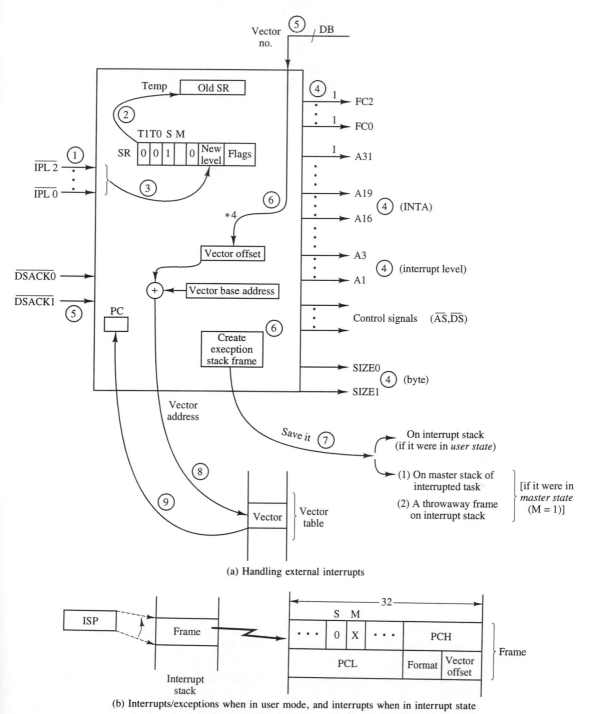

(a) Handling external interrupts

(b) Interrupts/exceptions when in user mode, and interrupts when in interrupt state

Figure 7.17 Motorola 680x0 exception processing.

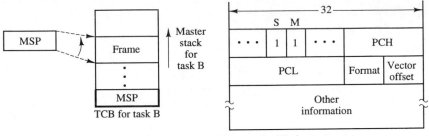

(c) Exception (other than external interrupt) while in master state

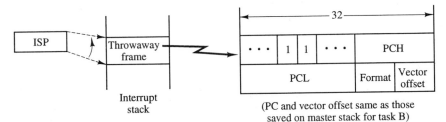

(d) External interrupt while in master state

Figure 7.17 (concluded)

a. *Vectored external interrupts:* DSACKs# are sampled "asserted." The processor asserts IPEND# and obtains a vector number from the selected port as follows:
   (1) FC0–FC2 and A16–A19 are combined externally to form the "port select" signal.
   (2) The selected port places an 8-bit vector number on the proper lane of the data bus (depending on port's size).
   (3) The selected port identifies its width by asserting DSACK0# and DSACK1#.
   (4) The processor goes to step 6.

b. *Autovectored external interrupts:* DSACKs# are sampled "not asserted" and AVEC# is sampled "asserted." The processor generates a vector number internally, and goes to step 6.

B. *Other Exceptions:*
   c. If not an external interrupt, the processor generates the vector number internally, and goes to step 6.

6. The processor multiplies the vector number by 4 (to determine the exception vector offset), and creates an "exception stack frame." As a minimum, an "exception stack frame" is 4 words long and includes the status register, the program counter, the vector offset, and its format or type of frame. Exception stack frames have different lengths depending on what caused the exception, as follows (see Figure 7.18):
   a. *FORMAT $0 (4 words):* for interrupts, format errors, TRAP #n instructions, and illegal instructions.
   b. *FORMAT $1 (4 words):* for throwaway frames.

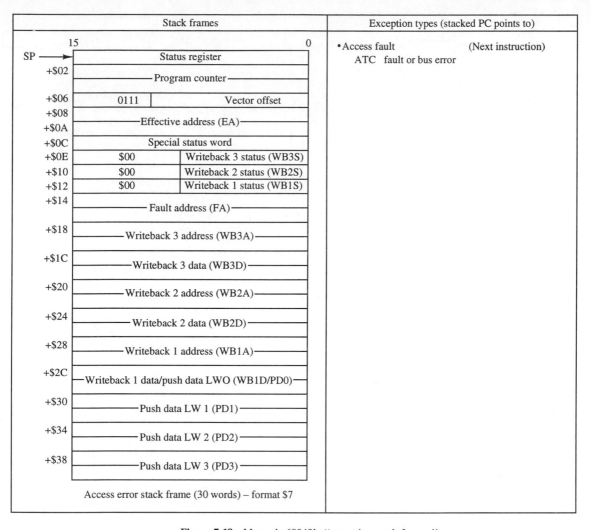

Figure 7.18 Motorola 68040's "exception stack frames."

c. *FORMAT $2 (6 words):* for coprocessor post-instruction exceptions, and CHK, CHK2, cpTRAPcc, TRAPcc, TRAPV, Trace, Zero divide.

d. *FORMAT $A (16 words)* and *FORMAT $B (46 words)* for the 68030; *FORMAT $7 (30 words)* for the 68040 for BERR short and long.

e. *FORMAT $3 (6 words):* for floating-point post-instruction exception in the 68040.

7. The processor saves the exception stack frame on the "active" stack:

a. In *user mode* (S = 0, M = don't care): For either interrupts or exceptions: it sets S = 1, and uses the ISP to save the frame on top of the interrupt stack (Figure 7.17b). Frame will depend on type of interrupt or exception.

b. In *interrupt state* (S = 1, M = 0), which means that the processor was handling an interrupt when the new interrupt arrived: it sets S = 1, and again uses the ISP to save the frame on top of the interrupt stack (also see Figure 7.17b).

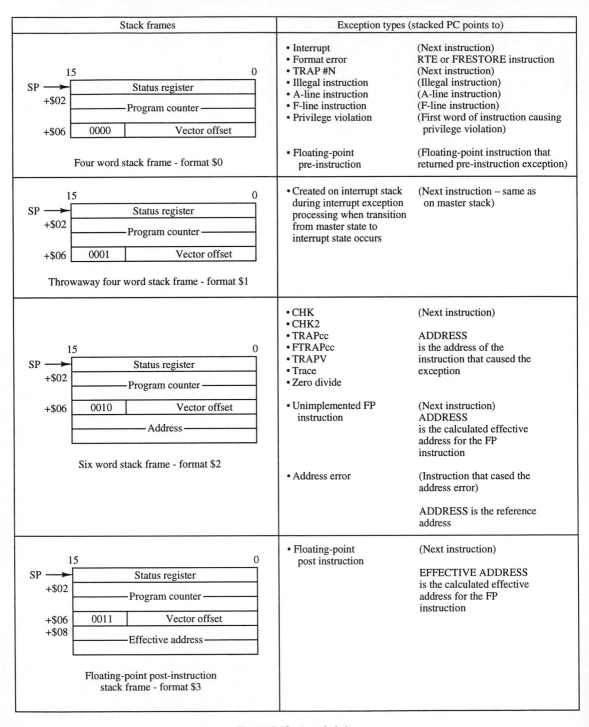

Stack frames	Exception types (stacked PC points to)
Four word stack frame - format $0 15 ... 0 SP → Status register (+$02) Program counter +$06 0000 Vector offset	• Interrupt — (Next instruction) • Format error — RTE or FRESTORE instruction • TRAP #N — (Next instruction) • Illegal instruction — (Illegal instruction) • A-line instruction — (A-line instruction) • F-line instruction — (F-line instruction) • Privilege violation — (First word of instruction causing privilege violation) • Floating-point pre-instruction — (Floating-point instruction that returned pre-instruction exception)
Throwaway four word stack frame - format $1 15 ... 0 SP → Status register (+$02) Program counter +$06 0001 Vector offset	• Created on interrupt stack during interrupt exception processing when transition from master state to interrupt state occurs — (Next instruction – same as on master stack)
Six word stack frame - format $2 15 ... 0 SP → Status register (+$02) Program counter +$06 0010 Vector offset — Address —	• CHK — (Next instruction) • CHK2 • TRAPcc — ADDRESS is the address of the • FTRAPcc — instruction that caused the • TRAPV — exception • Trace • Zero divide • Unimplemented FP instruction — (Next instruction) ADDRESS is the calculated effective address for the FP instruction • Address error — (Instruction that cased the address error) ADDRESS is the reference address
Floating-point post-instruction stack frame - format $3 15 ... 0 SP → Status register (+$02) Program counter +$06 0011 Vector offset +$08 —Effective address—	• Floating-point post instruction — (Next instruction) EFFECTIVE ADDRESS is the calculated effective address for the FP instruction

Figure 7.18 (concluded)

c. In *master state* (S = 1, M = 1):
   (1) If an exception (other than external interrupt) while executing task B: It ensures that S = 1 and uses the MSP to save the frame on top of task B's stack (Figure 7.17c).
   (2) If an external interrupt while executing task B: It (a) ensures that S = 1 and uses the MSP to save the frame on top of task B's stack (Figure 7.17c), and (b) copies the SR register into TEMP register, resets M = 0 (now the active stack is the interrupt stack) to switch to the interrupt state, creates a throwaway frame (FORMAT $1), and uses the ISP to save the throwaway frame on top of the interrupt stack (Figure 7.17d).
8. The processor then adds the vector offset to the vector base register to generate the exception vector address.
9. The processor fetches the contents of vector address and places it into the program counter.
10. The processor prefetches the first three words to fill the instruction pipe (from the IHR).

RTE instruction. RTE examines the stack frame on top of the "active supervisor stack" to determine if it is a valid frame and what type of context restoration should be performed.

1. *For a normal 4-word frame:* The CPU updates the SR and the program counter with the data pulled from the active stack, increments the stack pointer by 8, and resumes normal instruction execution.

2. *For a throwaway 4-word frame:* The CPU reads the SR from throwaway frame FORMAT $1 (usually on the interrupt stack) and increments the active stack pointer by 8 (i.e., it skips the rest of the throwaway frame). This is done so as to read the old M bit, which is 1, and switch the CPU to the master state. In the master state, it begins an RTE processing again. The processor reads a new frame from the top of the active stack (usually, this is the master stack) and performs the proper operations corresponding to that new format.

7.5 PIPELINED MICROPROCESSORS

The general concepts of pipelining were presented in Section 1.6.1 of Chapter 1. In this section we present how pipelining has been implemented in various microprocessors and some of the problems that pipelines present.

7.5.1 Survey of Microprocessor Pipelining

We survey below the way pipelining has been implemented in CISC and RISC microprocessors, using as representative examples the Intel 80486, the Motorola 68040, and the MIPS R-Series microprocessors.

Intel 80486. The 80486 has a 5-stage pipeline, with 1 clock cycle per stage, made up of the following stages (analogous to that shown in Figure 1.19) [4]:

Fetch: This stage corresponds to fetching the instruction from the on-chip cache. However, since a cache line is 16 bytes long, most instructions do not require this stage (because they were already fetched with the previous access). This stage is always required at the target of a branch.

D1: This is the first instruction decoding stage and processes up to 3 instruction bytes. It determines the length of the instruction and the actions that are to be performed during the next stage D2 (the "address generation" stage). A small number of instructions may require 2 clock cycles in stage D1.

D2: This is the address generation stage (needed because of the complexity of the 80486 instructions that intermix computations with accesses to memory). It completes the decoding of the instructions, decodes any displacement or immediate operands, and in parallel computes the effective address. A small number of instructions may require 2 clock cycles in stage D2.

Execute: This is the stage when the ALU is used for internal computations. Instructions that reference memory (including jump instructions) access the on-chip cache in this stage. (Along with the cache lookup, the TLB lookup proceeds in parallel.)

Write-back: This is the register write-back stage, during which the processor updates the register file either with data read from the on-chip cache or main memory, or with the ALU results. Bypass paths are included (to avoid stalling the pipeline) when the WB stage of one instruction writes to a register that is used in the EX stage of the next instruction.

Motorola 68040. The 68040 has a 6-stage integer pipeline (Figure 7.19a). The six stages are explained below [5].

IP: This "instruction prefetching" stage maintains an 128-bit instruction buffer; half of it is loaded, as required, with 64 bits from the on-chip instruction cache.

PCD: This is the "program-counter calculation and decoding" stage. It selects 3 instructions (48 bits) from the buffer for instruction decoding and immediate data extraction. In addition to decoding the opcode, it determines the length of the instruction (and appropriately increments the program counter) to select a new 3-word instruction from the buffer.

EAC: The "effective address calculation" stage calculates the effective addresses for load and store instructions.

EAF: The "effective address fetching" stage is used to fetch the operands (if needed) from the on-chip data cache.

DE: This "data execution" stage uses the ALU for internal calculations, controls the data registers, and can update address registers (to reduce stalls from address register blockage).

WB: This "write-back" stage initiates a store to the data cache. Data to be stored is first placed into a write-back data buffer, which the WB stage reads to then start a store operation. Since both the EAF and the WB stages share the same data cache, priority is given to the EAF stage (when there are simultaneous accesses to the data cache); the WB stage has priority only when the logical address of the load and store match, to avoid the read-before-write hazard.

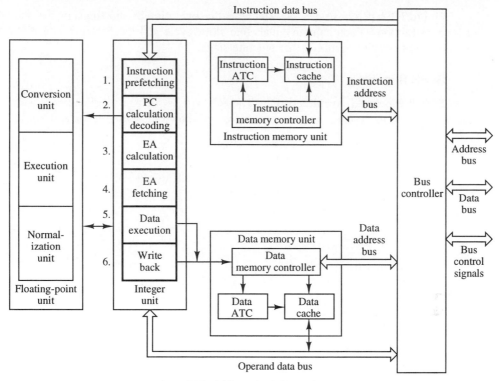

ATC   Address-translation cache
EA   Effective address
PC   Program counter

(a) 68040 CPU with the 6-stage integer pipeline

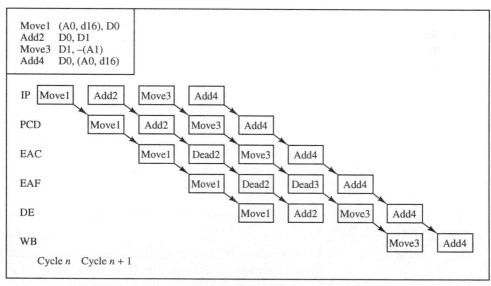

Move1   (A0, d16), D0
Add2   D0, D1
Move3   D1, –(A1)
Add4   D0, (A0, d16)

Cycle n Cycle $n + 1$

(b) Example instructions

Figure 7.19   68040 6-stage pipeline [5].

Figure 7.19b demonstrates the 68040 pipeline operation by showing a typical sequence of four instructions. Each column equals one clock cycle and the notation "dead" means that no useful activity occurs at that pipeline stage.

MIPS R series

R3000 Pipelined Architecture. The R3000 is a 5-stage pipelined processor. The five stages used to execute integer instructions are shown in Figure 7.20a and are:

IF	instruction fetch
RD	register fetch
ALU	execute a register-to-register instruction
MEM	memory access
WB	write back to register

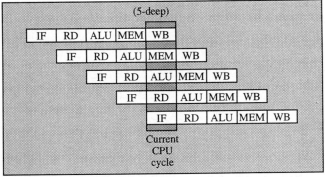

(a) Five-stage instruction pipeline [6] (Gerry Kane/Joe Heinrich, MIPS RISC ARCHITECTURE, © 1992, pp. 2-2, 2-3, 2-6, 2-7, 2-20. Reprinted by permission of Prentice Hall.)

Figure 7.20 R3000 pipelined operation.

(b) Two phases per step and overlapping of operations [6] (Kane/Heinrich, MIPS RISC ARCHITECTURE © 1992. Reprinted by permission of Prentice Hall.)

Each cycle is further divided into separate phases, named phase 1 and phase 2, as shown in Figure 7.20b [6].

IF	$\phi1$	Uses the micro-TLB to translate instruction virtual address to physical address (after branch decision in ALU $\phi1$).
IF	$\phi2$	Sends the physical address to the instruction cache.
RD	$\phi1$	Returns instruction from the instruction cache, whereupon tags are compared and parity is checked.

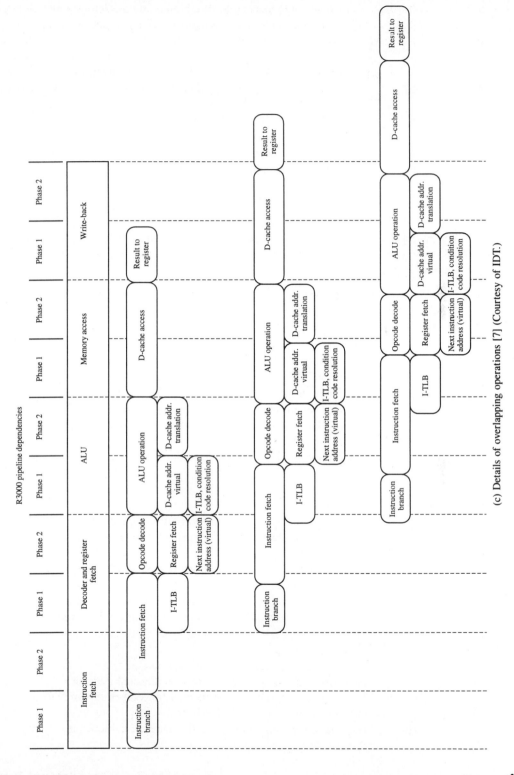

(c) Details of overlapping operations [7] (Courtesy of IDT.)

Figure 7.20 (concluded)

RD	φ2	Reads the register file. If a branch, then calculates branch target address. Latches coprocessor condition input.
ALU	φ1 + φ2	Bypasses operands from other pipeline stages and calculates add, logical, shift, etc., results. Shifts store data and starts integer multiply/divide, or floating-point operation.
ALU	φ1	If a branch, decides whether the branch is to be taken or not. If a load or store, then calculates virtual address.
ALU	φ2	If a load or store, translates virtual address to physical using TLB.
MEM	φ1	If a load or store, sends physical address to data cache.
MEM	φ2	If a load or store, returns data from data cache. Compares tags and checks parity, and extracts byte for loads. If an MTCz or MFCz instruction, then transfers data to or from coprocessor.
WB	φ1	Writes the register file.

Each step requires approximately one CPU cycle (Figure 7.20b). Parts of some operations overlap another cycle, while other operations require only half a cycle. Figure 7.20c shows in more detail this overlapping of operations.

R4000 Superpipelined Architecture.   The R4000 has a superpipeline composed of 8 stages; the instruction and data memory references have been split across two stages [8]. The 8 stages are:

IF	Instruction fetch first half. Virtual address is presented to the I-cache and TLB.
IS	Instruction fetch second half. The I-cache outputs the instruction and the TLB generates the physical address.
RF	Register file. Three activities occur in parallel:
	• Instruction is decoded and a check is made for interlock conditions.
	• Instruction tag check is made to determine if there is a cache hit or not.
	• Operands are fetched from the register file.
EX	Instruction execute. One of three activities can occur:
	• If the instruction is a register-to-register operation, an arithmetic, logical, shift, multiply, or divide operation is performed.
	• If the instruction is a load and store, the data virtual address is calculated.
	• If the instruction is a branch, the branch target virtual address is calculated and branch conditions are checked.
DF	Data cache first half. A virtual address is presented to the D-cache and TLB.
DS	Data cache second half. The D-cache outputs the instruction and the TLB generates the physical address.
TC	Tag check. A tag check is performed for loads and stores to determine if there is a hit or not.
WB	Write back. The instruction result is written back to the register file.

Figure 7.21a shows the instruction execution in the 8-stage pipeline. It is noted that under optimal conditions, one instruction is completed every *internal* clock cycle. The internal, or pipeline, clock is twice the external input, or master, clock.

As in the R3000 case, taking into consideration the two phases per clock cycle, the detailed activities of the R4000 pipeline are shown in Figure 7.21b, while Figure 7.21c

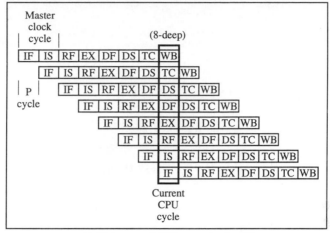

(a) Eight-stage R4000 superpipeline [8]

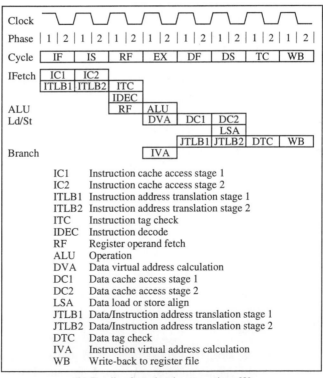

IC1	Instruction cache access stage 1	
IC2	Instruction cache access stage 2	
ITLB1	Instruction address translation stage 1	
ITLB2	Instruction address translation stage 2	
ITC	Instruction tag check	
IDEC	Instruction decode	
RF	Register operand fetch	
ALU	Operation	
DVA	Data virtual address calculation	
DC1	Data cache access stage 1	
DC2	Data cache access stage 2	
LSA	Data load or store align	
JTLB1	Data/Instruction address translation stage 1	
JTLB2	Data/Instruction address translation stage 2	
DTC	Data tag check	
IVA	Instruction virtual address calculation	
WB	Write-back to register file	

(b) Details of overlapping operations [8]

Figure 7.21 R4000 superpipelined operation.

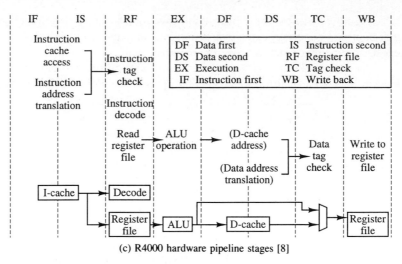

(c) R4000 hardware pipeline stages [8]

Figure 7.21   (concluded)

shows the distribution of the processor hardware to the pipeline stages. Figure 7.21b shows the activities occurring during each pipeline stage for ALU, load and store, and branch instructions. Below we describe the activities during each stage in more detail [8,9].

Instruction fetch, first half (IF).   An instruction address is selected by the branch logic and the instruction cache fetch begins. The instruction translation look-aside buffer (ITLB) begins the virtual-to-physical address translation.

Instruction fetch, second half (IS).   The instruction cache fetch and the virtual-to-physical address translation are completed.

Register fetch (RF).   The instruction decoder (IDEC) decodes the instruction and checks for interlock conditions. The instruction cache tag is checked against the page frame number obtained from the ITLB. Any required operands are fetched from the register file.

Execution (EX).   For register-to-register instructions, the ALU performs the arithmetic or logical operation. For load and store instructions, the ALU calculates the data virtual address. For branch instructions, the ALU determines whether the branch condition is true and calculates the virtual branch target address.

Data fetch, first half (DF).   For load and store instructions, the data cache fetch and the data virtual-to-physical translation begin. For branch instructions, the branch instruction address translation and TLB update begin. Register-to-register instructions perform no operations during the DF, DX, and TC stages.

Data fetch, second half (DS).   For load and store instructions, the data cache fetch and data virtual-to-physical translation are completed. The shifter aligns the data to the word or doubleword boundary. For branch instructions, the branch instruction address translation and TLB update are completed.

Tag check (TC).   For load and store instructions, the cache performs the tag check. The physical address from the TLB is checked against the cache tag to determine if there is a hit or a miss.

Write back (WB).   For register-to-register instructions, the instruction result is written back to the register file. Load and store, and branch instructions perform no operation during this stage.

The more finely grained pipeline of the R4000 results in a branch delay of three cycles and a load delay of two. The branch delay of three is easily observed by noting that the branch comparison logic operates during the EX pipestage of the branch, producing an instruction address which is available for IF stage of the fourth subsequent instruction. The branch delay is illustrated in Figure 7.22.

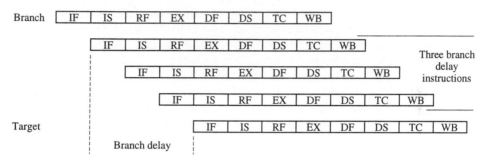

Figure 7.22   R4000 pipeline branch delay [8].

Similarly, the load delay of two is evident in that the completion of a load at the end of the DS pipestage of a load, produces an operand which is available for the EX pipestage of the third subsequent instruction. The load delay is illustrated in Figure 7.23.

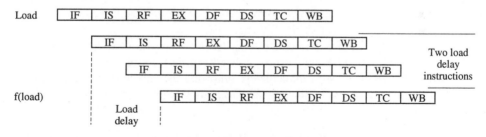

Figure 7.23   R4000 pipeline load delay [8].

7.5.2 Pipelining Problems

In this section we give only a brief introduction to the type of problems that may arise because of internal pipelining. One interlock problem arises when *an instruction depends on previous ALU results;* in this case, the instruction should not be started before these results are available. Problems also arise (referred to as *destination–source conflicts)* when an attempt is made to fetch operands that have not reached storage yet or the result of a pipeline stage has not been stored before a succeeding pipeline stage requires it. A solution to this problem is to have the results of the ALU return first to an internal data buffer before being sent to storage. Another data dependency conflict (the *source–destination conflict)* is when two stages of the pipeline share the same resource, one stage wanting to write into it and the other to read from it. To avoid the read-before-write hazard, the hardware must give priority to the write stage, as done in the 80486 pipeline, whose EAF and WB stages share the data cache (as explained ins Section 7.5.1).[15] Another problem is when an attempt is made to *modify an instruction by a preceding store operation.* This can be handled by the control section if the control section tests the instruction as soon as it is loaded to see whether it is a store-type instruction. If it is, the fetch sequence must wait until the effective address has been prepared to see whether it is going to modify a successive instruction.

To reduce the effect that different pipeline stages may require different amounts of time (for example, for complex instructions that require access to operands in memory), RISC processors have incorporated a large number of registers, simple instructions, and implemented the load/store architecture: all operations are performed on operands held in internal registers, and main memory is accessed explicitly only by load and store instructions. However, this gives rise to the *load delay problem:* because memory is slower than the processor pipeline, the loaded operand is not immediately available to subsequent instructions in the pipeline. For example, consider Figure 7.20a. Assume that the first instruction is a load instruction; the data from the load will not be available until the end of this instruction's MEM cycle, which is too late for the second instruction to use it in its ALU stage.

The load delay problem must be solved without stalling the flow of instructions through the pipeline when a load is executed. The two approaches followed are to let the software (compiler) take care of it (as done by the MIPS R-series microprocessors) or have the processor hardware handle it (as done by the 80486). In the software solution, the compiler is required to reorder instructions so that an unrelated instruction that can do something useful is executed during the "delay slot" (between a load instruction and an instruction that uses the loaded data), or if no other instruction is available, insert a noop (no operation) instruction into the slot. In the case of the 8-stage superpipelined R4000, there is a load delay slot of 2, as shown in Figure 7.23. In the hardware solution, the 80486 has eliminated the load delay by rearranging the pipeline so that memory addresses be computed in the D2 stage of the pipeline before the EX stage [4].

Finally, problems arise when a *conditional branch instruction* is encountered and the previous instruction has not been completed yet; the control section will not know whether to prefetch the instruction immediately following the conditional branch instruction or the instruction at the target of the branch. There are three basic hardware ways for handling the problem of conditional branching:

1. The control section can stop the flow of instructions (stall the pipeline) before fetching the next instruction, until the preceding operation is finished and the results (upon which the branch decision is to be taken) are known. No matter whether the branch is taken or not, this always causes a delay.

2. The second way, branch prediction, makes a guess as to which way the branch is going to go before it is taken, follows this path, and continues preparing instructions; if the guess later proves to be wrong, the pipeline must be flushed clean and started again with the correct instruction. The 80486 follows this approach and assumes that the

[15] The i860 and 88000 microprocessors use a hardware *scoreboarding technique,* which ensures that a source operand is not fetched from a register that is currently waiting for a result.

branch is taken, and in parallel with the operation of the pipeline stages, the CPU runs a speculative fetch cycle to the target of the branch. If the CPU evaluates the condition as true, the fetch to the target address refills the pipeline; otherwise, the 80486 loses three clock cycles.

3. The control section can fetch the instructions immediately following the conditional branch as well as instructions at the target of the branch simultaneously, and when the ALU generates the conditions, then determine which of the two groups of prepared instructions to use.

Most of RISC processors have *delayed branches* so that the processor can execute something useful until the branch address is available. An approach similar to that used for the load instructions is used: branch instructions are delayed and do not take effect until one or more instructions immediately following the branch instruction have been executed. Figure 7.22 shows the insertion of 3 instructions in the R4000 branch delay slot of three. The compiler is placing in the branch delay slot one or more carefully selected instructions; this way the pipeline is not cleared, and the instructions that are in it are allowed to finish.

7.6 MAKING A SEGMENT "KNOWN"

We said in Chapter 6 that a segment does not become bound to the logical (virtual) address space until runtime. In general the sequence is as follows:

1. Only when the segment is referenced (i.e., at runtime), the operating system searches what is referred to as a "known segments table" (KST), which contains pairs of symbolic name-logical address (logical address is the segment number) of known segments.
2. When the name is found in the known segments table, the operating system searches the table to find the name's logical address.
3. If a logical address is found, then the "segment descriptor table" is searched to find the logical address' physical address for the translation. If a physical address is not found, that means that the segment is not resident in main memory. The operating system will place the segment in main memory, insert its starting physical address in the segment descriptor table, and place the index of that entry (which is now the segment's logical address) next to the segment symbolic name in the "known segments table." This will make the segment "known." Only then binding to the logical address space takes place.

Let us take a look at this procedure though the following example.

7.6.1 Translating Segment Names to Physical Base Addresses

Here we assume resident segments.

1. Assume that task i references symbolic segment name $<$name $j>$.
2. The "known segment table" (KST) for task i is searched by the operating system. If the name $<$name $j>$ is found, its segment number (or logical address) $<$number $j>$ is

used to search the "segment descriptor table" (SDT) to find its physical base address for the translation, as shown in Figure 7.24.

3. If the entry in the descriptor table indicates that the segment is not resident, a procedure must be started to find and load the segment and make it "known" to the task.

4. If no segment number is found in the "known segment table," which will happen when a segment name <name j> is initially referenced in task i, a global table referred to as "active segment table" (AST) is used to make the segment "known" to task i.

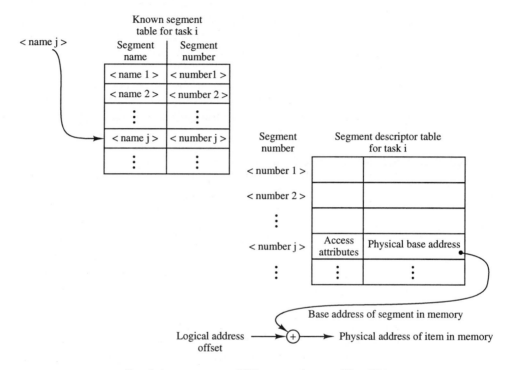

Translation: < name > $\Rightarrow$ KST $\Rightarrow$ < number > $\Rightarrow$ ST $\Rightarrow$ PBA

Figure 7.24 Translating a segment name to a physical base address.

7.6.2 Making a Segment "Known"

1. When a segment name <name j> is initially referenced in task i, its segment number (or logical address) <number> has not yet been established. A global table is maintained by the operating system, called an "active segment table" (AST). This AST is shared by all tasks and contains all active (or resident in main memory) segments, as shown in the functional schematic of Figure 7.25a. For example, the segment whose symbolic name is <name 1> has already been referenced by task 1, it is resident in main memory, and has a physical base address already assigned to it; the same segment has not yet been referenced by task 2 and, therefore, no physical base address entry exists. Segment [name 2] has not yet been referenced by any task.

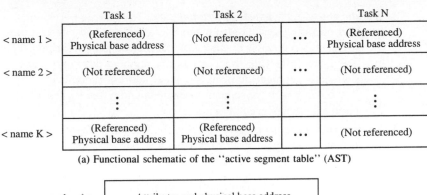

	Task 1	Task 2		Task N
< name 1 >	(Referenced) Physical base address	(Not referenced)	•••	(Referenced) Physical base address
< name 2 >	(Not referenced)	(Not referenced)	•••	(Not referenced)
	⋮	⋮		⋮
< name K >	(Referenced) Physical base address	(Referenced) Physical base address	•••	(Not referenced)

(a) Functional schematic of the "active segment table" (AST)

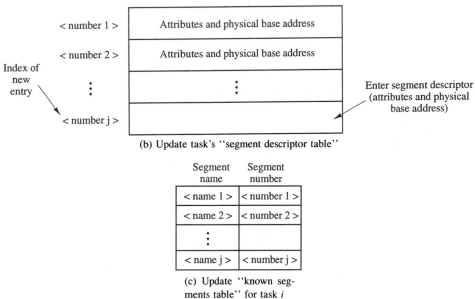

< number 1 >	Attributes and physical base address
< number 2 >	Attributes and physical base address
⋮	⋮
< number j >	

Index of new entry ↘

Enter segment descriptor (attributes and physical base address) ↙

(b) Update task's "segment descriptor table"

Segment name	Segment number
< name 1 >	< number 1 >
< name 2 >	< number 2 >
⋮	
< name j >	< number j >

(c) Update "known segments table" for task i

Figure 7.25 Steps in "making a segment known" to a task.

2. *Update the AST.* The AST is searched to see whether the segment is active (or resident in main memory):

   a. If the segment is resident,[16] then its attributes and physical base address in the AST are used to make an entry in the AST table for this task i, to indicate that task i is also using this segment.

   b. If the segment is not resident (it is not found in the AST table),[17] then the operating system will have to use the segment name <name *j*> as a directory path name, and initiate a file directory search to find the segment in the disk and place it in main memory. It then uses its attributes and its (absolute) physical base address and enters them into the AST table for task *i*.

[16] If it is resident but not yet referenced by task *i*, when it is a *shared segment*—some other task has already referenced it.

[17] If not resident, it could still be a shared segment, which, however, has not yet been referenced yet by any task, or it could be a nonshared segment belonging only to task *i*.

3. *Update the task's segment descriptor table.*

    a. The operating system also enters the attributes and physical base address of this segment into a *newly created entry* of the segment descriptor table for that task *i*.

    b. The index (offset) of this entry in the segment descriptor table now becomes the segment's segment number or logical address <number *j*> as shown in Figure 7.25b. Only now the segment became bound to the logical address space; segment numbers are assigned at runtime.

4. *Update known segments table.* Finally, the known segments table for task *i* is updated by finding an entry in it and inserting the pair <name *j*>-<number *j*> in Figure 7.25c.

Since each task has its own "known segments table," which contains entries for the segments known to the task, and since during the process of making a segment known to a task each task may find a different entry in its "segment descriptor table" into which to enter the segment's segment descriptor (i.e., assign different logical address or segment number), then two tasks, A and B, may share the same segment whose symbolic name is <name *j*> but use different segment numbers (for example, <number *j*> versus <number *k*>) in other words, the same segment with the symbolic name <name *j*> occupies different relative positions in the logical address spaces (or segment descriptor tables) of the two tasks, A and B.

In segmentation, dynamic linking is performed at runtime; the segment numbers become part of the invoking process rather than part of the code. External references must remain symbolic: the first time of access to external reference will be symbolic (to allow retrieval of the segment by the file system, protection checking, and segment number assignment); when the segment thus becomes "known," subsequent references will be done through the assigned segment number. Each segment is given a "linkage section" and transfer of control and external data references occur by indirect addressing through such "linkage sections."

EXERCISES

7.1. Consider the 68030 interfaced to 13 external 16-bit vectored interrupting devices DEV0-DEV12. These 13 devices have the following priorities for servicing (0 is the highest priority):

DEVICE	PRIORITY
0	1
1	9
2	12
3	6
4	5
5	4
6	10
7	11
8	2
9	3
10	0
11	7
12	8

We want priority resolution to be done with external hardware for which we have only one priority encoder chip for the incoming interrupt requests. The smallest possible response time should be given to as many devices as possible of the highest-priority ones.

(a) Draw the interface for interconnecting these devices to the microprocessor.

(b) Number the steps followed when devices DEV1 and DEV12 issue simultaneous interrupt requests. Indicate the actual values placed on the bus lines.

(c) If the beginning addresses of the interrupt-handling routines for these devices DEV0–DEV12 are stored in contiguous increasing memory locations starting from vector address 000108, list the vector numbers (in hexadecimal) that these devices issue.

7.2. The Intel 8086 is used in a maximum mode configuration to monitor the operation of small installation. Assume that four measuring devices are connected so that they interrupt the processor at its input pin INTR at random times to supply the microprocessor with 16-bit digital measurements. These four devices, #0, #1, #2, and #3, have priorities as follows (from the highest to the lowest): #2 has the highest, then #3, then #1, and finally #0 has the lowest. The configuration does not use any priority encoder chip and the I/O interface supplies vector numbers to the microprocessor so that an interrupt from any device will vector the system directly to the respective interrupt-handling routine. The beginning addresses (also called "vectors" or "pointers") of the interrupt-handling routines for devices #0, #1, #2, and #3 are stored in that order in contiguous increasing memory locations starting from the hexadecimal vector address 000A0.

After 50 measurements have been read from *any* device, the processor computes an average value for the 50 measurements from that device, and clears that device's buffer in memory.

(a) Show the part of the vector table that pertains to these four devices and write the respective interrupt types (in decimal) that these devices generate.

(b) Identify the 8-bit interrupt vector numbers (in hexadecimal) that the interface of each device should be placing on the lower half of the data bus and briefly explain.

(c) Give the detailed flowchart for the software needed for this application.

(d) Design the detailed hardware configuration showing all the interfacing components, as well as all the necessary bus lines and control signals.

State your assumptions clearly.

7.3. Repeat Exercise 7.2 for the Motorola 68000 microprocessor with the following differences:

(a) All four devices interrupt the processor with interrupt level 4.

(b) Instead of address 000A0, use address 001008.

7.4. Consider an 8-bit microprocessor and 16 external interrupting devices connected to it through a cascade of PICs (programmable interrupt controllers) and interrupting the microprocessor at the INTR input pin. The operation of the microprocessor and the PIC is as follows:

1. Upon receiving an INTA from the microprocessor, the master PIC jams a CALL instruction (11001101) on the data bus. The master PIC also controls which of the slave PICs will respond during the next steps.

2. The CALL instruction will initiate 2 more INTA signals to be sent to all PICs:

   a. During the first INTA, the PIC selected places on the data bus the lower 8 bits of its preprogrammed subroutine address (assume 16).

   b. During the second INTA, the PIC selected places on the data bus the upper 8 bits of its preprogrammed subroutine address (assume FA).

(a) Draw the block diagram for interfacing these 16 peripheral devices to the microprocessor.

(b) Show all signals issued and the actual values placed on the bus lines, and number the steps (of the signals issued) in the proper sequence.

(c) Explain how the microprocessor would service these 16 interrupting devices.

7.5. Consider seven 16-bit interrupting devices and the Motorola 68020. These devices are capable of generating vector numbers.

(a) Draw the block diagram of interfacing the devices to the processor.

(b) If the processor were in the master state when device #6 issued the interrupt, show all signals issued and the actual values placed on the bus lines, and number the steps (of the signals issued) in the proper sequence.

7.6. Consider three PPIs (programmable parallel interface) and a UART (universal asynchronous receiver/transmitter) connected to the Motorola 68000. These external chips are capable of generating vector numbers. Each PPI generates 2 interrupt requests (one for each of its two internal registers A and B being "ready"); the UART generates 1 interrupt request. The PPIs have higher priority that the UART.

(a) Draw the block diagram for interfacing these chips to the 68000.

(b) Show all the signals issued and the actual values placed on the bus lines, and number the steps (of the signals issued) in the proper sequence.

(c) Explain how the microprocessor would service these interrupting devices.

7.7. Consider a 32-bit memory subsystem organized into four 8-bit sections, S0, S1, S2, and S3. The four bytes of an aligned 32-bit operand are stored "most-significant-byte-first (i.e., the most significant byte in Section S0, which is connected to data bus lines D31–D24).

Assume that the microprocessor always places 18 bits of the address on the address bus lines A19–A2; the microprocessor decodes address bits A1 and A0 to issue four output control signals S0, S1, S2, and S3, used to strobe the respective byte-sections of the 32-bit memory.

In a particular system design, the lower half of the addressing space is used for main memory implemented using RAM chips of size 4K × 8 bits each. For interfacing to external devices, a memory-mapped I/O configuration is implemented with 32 I/O interface chips that use a total of 128-byte locations in the highest portion of the addressing space.

(a) Explain how byte, words, and doublewords transfer over the data bus.

(b) Show the RAM and I/O chips arrangement, their interface to the microprocessor via the address and data bus lines, and the pertinent control signals applied to them.

(c) Draw the simplified local bus timing diagram that shows the address and data bus activities, and the pertinent control signals. (Assume that a read or write cycle needs 2 input clock cycles or "T states" and that the bus is synchronous.)

7.8. Consider 64 interrupting devices and the Intel 80286. These devices are connected through the Mucirus I and are capable of generating vector numbers.

(a) Draw the block diagram of the system configuration using external hardware for priority resolution.

(b) Show all the signals issued and the actual values placed on the bus lines, and number the steps (of the signals issued) in the proper sequence.

(c) Explain how the microprocessor would service these 64 interrupting devices.

REFERENCES

[1] Intel Corp., *iAPX286 Programmer's Reference Manual* (210498–001), Santa Clara, CA, 1983.

[2] Intel Corp., *The 8086 Family User's Manual* (9800722–03), Santa Clara, CA, 1979.

[3] Motorola Inc., *MTT8 Course Notes* (MTT8CN, Rev. 1), Phoenix, AZ, June 1987.

[4] Crawford, J.H., "The i486 CPU: Executing Instructions in One Clock Cycle," *IEEE Micro,* Feb. 1990, pp. 27–36.

[5] Edenfield, R.W., et al., "The 68040 Processor: Part 1, Design and Implementation," *IEEE Micro,* Feb. 1990, pp. 66–78.

[6] Kane, G., and Heinrich, J., *MIPS RISC Architecture*, Prentice Hall, Englewood Cliffs, NJ, 1992.

[7] Integrated Device Technology, Inc., *R3000/R3001 Designer's Guide*, Santa Clara, CA, 1991.

[8] MIPS Computer Systems, Inc., *MIPS R4000 Microprocessor User's Manual* (M8–00040), Sunnyvale, CA, 1991.

[9] Mirapuri, S., M. Woodacre, and N. Vasseghi, "The MIPS R4000 Processor," *IEEE Micro,* Apr. 1992, pp. 10–22.

[10] Motorola Inc., *MC68040 32-bit Microprocessor User's Manual*, Phoenix, AZ, 1989.

Intel 80x86 CISC Microprocessors*

A.1. INTEL 16-BIT 8086/80286 MICROPROCESSORS

Although the 8086 and 80286 are now considered "older" microprocessors, we have included them here because it was their architecture, characteristics, and operation that later Intel products were based upon. Understanding the 8086/286 will help the reader understand more easily the advanced Intel products described next.

A.1.1 8086 Microprocessor

8086 I/O pins and signals.   Figure A.1a shows the external view of the Intel 8086 microprocessor. First of all, we notice that some signals have dual interpretation; this depends on whether the processor is configured in a minimum (one- or two-board systems) or maximum (multi-board) configuration. The 8086 is equipped with a strap pin (MN/MX#) which defines the system configuration. In minimum configuration (when MN/MX# = H), the pins have the interpretations shown in parentheses (e.g., M/IO#, DT/R#, DEN#, ALE#, etc.); in maximum configuration (when MN/MX# = L), they have the second interpretations (e.g., S2#, S1#, S0#, etc.). The maximum configuration requires an external "bus controller" chip to receive the status signals S2#–S0#, decode them, and generate the control signals to memory and I/O ports, as well as generate the signals DT/R#, DEN#, and ALE.

The 8086 has two separate output pins for the read **(RD#)** and the write **(WR#)** control signals sent to memory or I/O. A separate signal, the "memory-I/O" **(M/IO#),** distinguishes between memory address space (M/IO# = H) and I/O address space (M/

*References cited in Appendices A, B, and C appear at the end of Appendix C.

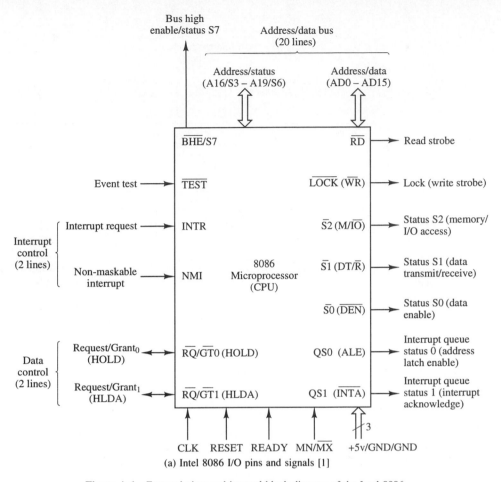

Figure A.1 External view and internal block diagram of the Intel 8086.

IO# = L). Two signals generated by the processor, the **DEN** and **DT/R#,** are used to enable external transceiver chips. These external transceivers buffer the data from the data bus, and are required to satisfy the capacitive loading and drive requirements of larger system configurations. The "data enable" (DEN) signal is used to enable the transceiver. The "data transmit/receive" (DT/R#) signal is sent to the external transceiver to control the direction of the data flow on the data bus: DT/R# = H for data issued by the processor, DT/R# = L for data to be received by the processor. The "address latch enable" (**ALE**) is used to trigger external interface logic to latch the address off the multiplexed address/data bus (on which it is valid for only the first clock cycle of the bus cycle) and maintain it valid for those devices that require a stable address for a longer time. The processor also issues the "byte high enable" (**BHE#**) signal during the first clock cycle of the bus cycle; this signal, along with the A0 address bit, is used to generate "byte enables" for the memory "byte sections," to implement byte or word transfers. The **RESET** input signal causes the processor to terminate its present activity immediately, clear the flags register, the DS, SS, ES segment registers, and the instruction pointer register, and set CS to FFFF, thus forcing the program execution to restart from location FFFF0.

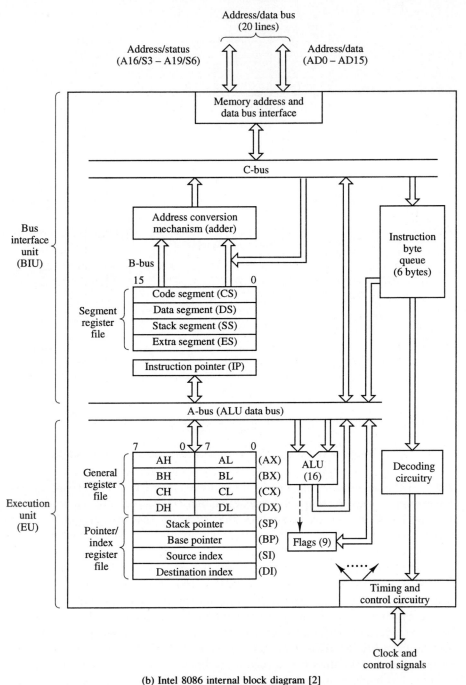

(b) Intel 8086 internal block diagram [2]

Figure A.1 (concluded).

8086 Internal organization. A simplified block diagram of the internal structure of the 8086 microprocessor is shown in Figure A.1b. The architecture of the 8086 microprocessor can be thought of as being partitioned into two independently controlled processing units: the "bus interface unit" or BIU (used to drive/latch the external buses and generate the 20-bit addresses sent to memory) and the "execution unit" or EU (used for arithmetic/logic operations). These units can interact directly, but for the most part they perform as two separate and independent sections of the processor. Having a separate unit devoted primarily to interfacing and managing the external bus lines improves the overall system performance because data transfers on the external bus can be done simultaneously with the internal execution of instructions by the EU unit of the processor (i.e., overlap of internal function with external data transfers).

In addition to keeping the external bus busy, the *bus interface unit* or BIU provides other useful functions. For example, the BIU has the appropriate hardware to take the internally generated 16-bit addresses and convert them to 20-bit addresses before placing them on the address output pins. (This is referred to as "converting the logical addresses to physical addresses.") With a 20-bit address issued, the processor can access physical main memory of up to $2^{20} = 1$ Mbyte capacity. To generate these 20-bit addresses, the BIU contains four special registers, called *segment registers,* along with a special adder. Internal addresses that point to instructions are contained in the instruction pointer and are 16 bits long. Effective addresses of operands computed in the EU hardware are also 16 bits long. Both types of these 16-bit internal addresses[1] are submitted to the address conversion mechanism in the BIU in order to be converted to the 20-bit addresses[2] sent by the microprocessor to memory. Finally, while the EU is busy executing the current instruction, the BIU can also go ahead and "prefetch" the next instruction in the program and place it in its 6-byte queue, assuming that the program execution will proceed sequentially. (When a branch in the program takes place, the BIU resets the queue and immediately begins fetching instructions from the new program location). They are ready to be received by the decoding circuitry whenever the instruction's turn comes up. Every operand fetched from memory or result sent to memory for storage first passes through the BIU.

The *execution unit* or EU includes the 16-bit ALU with its flag register, the instruction decoding and executing circuitry which executes the instruction stream from the internal queue, and the programmer-accessible internal registers. The EU receives prefetched instructions from the BIU queue and provides effective addresses of operands to the BIU for translation. Processing is performed in the EU on operands passed to it from the BIU, and the EU then passes results to the BIU for storage.

8086 State transition diagram. Figure A.2 shows the simplified state transition diagram and the most important microoperations for 16-bit memory read and memory write bus cycles. The 8086 calls its input clock CLK, and each input clock cycle a "T state." The microoperations shown are those executed during each of the four input clock cycles when the processor is operating in the "minimum mode configuration." The processor has a multiplexed address/data bus: the least significant 16 address bits are multiplexed with the 16 data bits, while the remaining most significant four address bits are multiplexed with

---

[1]These addresses correspond to what is called "logical addresses," as explained in more detail in Chapter 6.

[2]These addresses correspond to what is called "physical addresses." The address conversion hardware corresponds to the MMU (memory management unit) discussed in Chapter 6.

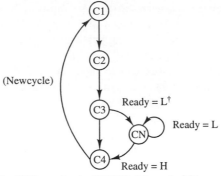

(Newcycle)

Ready = L[†]

Ready = L

Ready = H

[†] The 8086 samples the READY at the end of C2,
but it inserts a wait state between C3 and C4.

(a) Clock cycle C is called by 8086 a "T state"

C1: A_{19}–A_{16} ← part of address, AD_{15}–AD_0 ← part of address, ALE ← H, $M/\overline{IO}$ ← H,
DT/$\overline{R}$ ← L, $\overline{BHE}$ ← L;

C2: A_{19}–A_{16} ← S_6–S_3, $\overline{BHE}$ ← S_7, ALE ← L, $\overline{RD}$ ← L, $\overline{DEN}$ ← L, AD_{15}–AD_0 ← 3ST;

C3: Sample READY: if READY = L, insert wait state(s);
if READY = H, advance to C4;

C4: Read data from AD_{15}–AD_0, negate activated signals;

(b) "Memory read" microoperations (processor in minimum mode[†] with $MN/\overline{MX}$ = V_{cc})

C1: A_{19}–A_{16} ← part of address, AD_{15}–AD_0 ← part of address, ALE ← H,
$M/\overline{IO}$ ← H, DT/$\overline{R}$ ← H, $\overline{BHE}$ ← L, $\overline{DEN}$ = L;

C2: A_{19}–A_{16} ← S_6–S_3, $\overline{BHE}$ ← S_7, ALE ← L, $\overline{WR}$ ← L, AD_{15}–AD_0 ← data out;

C3: sample READY: if READY = L, insert wait state(s);
if READY = H, advance to C4;

C4: AD_{15}–AD_0 ← 3ST, negate activated signals;

(c) "Memory write" microoperations (processor in minimum mode[†] with MN/$\overline{MX}$ = V_{cc})

[†] [In "maximum mode," $MN/\overline{MX}$ = GND. Processor asserts status signals $\overline{S_2}$–$\overline{S_0}$ (to indicate type of bus cycle) during C1. External bus controller decodes status signals and generates control signals ALE, DT/$\overline{R}$, $\overline{DEN}$, $\overline{MRDC}$, $\overline{MWTC}$, $\overline{IORC}$, $\overline{IOWC}$.]

Figure A.2 Intel 8086 simplified state transition diagram (a) and the most important microoperations for a 16-bit "memory read" (b) and a "memory write" (c) bus cycle. (Microoperations for internal activities are not shown.)

status signals S_6–S_3. For a memory read or write, the processor places the proper value (0 or 1) on its output control pin BHE# to indicate whether or not the odd byte memory section (called by Intel a "byte bank") will be activated during the current data transfer. For an input from or an output to a port, BHE# = Low, because the transfers between the processor and the 16-bit I/O port are done on a word basis; I/O port numbers are always 16 bits, on AD0–AD15. Data is read by the processor during C4. In the memory write cycle, the control signal DEN# is asserted earlier during C1, while the data is issued by the processor on the multiplexed address/data bus during C2. Finally, when wait states are needed, they are inserted between C3 and C4.

8086 Bus timing diagram. Figure A.3 shows the 8086 simplified bus timing diagram. It shows the memory read/write cycles and the input/output (or I/O read/write) cycles. The timing diagram results from executing the state transition diagram and the basic operations listed in Figure A.2. An 8086 bus cycle has a minimum of 4 input clock cycles or, as called by Intel, "T states." *Wait states,* if needed, are inserted between states T3 and T4 and they are multiples of an input clock cycle in duration. This means[3] that, for example, an 8-MHz 8086 (processor clock = input clock = 8 MHz and, therefore, input clock cycle = 125 ns) would require a memory access to complete within about three T states (or 3 input clock cycles), i.e., 3*125 ns = 375 ns, if there is to be zero wait states. (The access time with 1 wait state would be 500 ns.) In this zero-wait-state case, the 8-MHz 8086 has a bus cycle equal to 4*125 ns = 500 ns, and a maximum "data transfer rate" of 4 Mbytes per second.

A.1.2 80286 Microprocessor

80286 I/O Signals, internal organization, and register structure. The 80286 is the first Intel processor that can operate in what is called the "protected virtual-address mode" or, for short, "protected mode." (It can still operate in the "real-address mode"; in this mode it behaves exactly like the 8086, i.e., it again accesses an 1-Mbyte main memory through 20-bit addresses.[4]) In "protected mode" the processor can access 16 Mbytes of main memory through 24-bit addresses and can implement virtual memory (see Chapter 6) of size up to 1 gigabyte. Figure A.4 shows the microprocessor pins and signals and its internal block diagram. The 24-bit address bus A23–A0 is nonmultiplexed, and the processor has a separate 16-bit data bus D15–D0. Along with the address, the processor issues the BHE# signal to identify word vs. byte transfer, and the signals COD/INTA#, M/IO#, S1#, and S0#, identify the type of bus cycle the processor starts. The processor has one user maskable, interrupt pin (INTR), and one nonmaskable interrupt pin (NMI).

From the simplified block diagram of the internal structure of the 80286 microprocessor we notice the following differences from the earlier 16-bit 8086. As already mentioned, although the 80286 is also a 16-bit processor (16-bit internal registers, 16-bit ALU, 16-bit external data bus, etc.), it issues to memory a 24-bit address. Another difference is that instead of 8086's two internal independent units (BIU and EU), the 80286 has four independent stages. The *bus unit* or BU contains the appropriate hardware to manage the external bus lines and keep the buses busy. It also includes the 8086 6-byte queue into which the prefetcher places the instruction bytes it prefetches from memory, assuming that the program execution will proceed sequentially. (When a branch in the program takes place, the BU resets the queue and immediately begins fetching instructions from the new program location.) The second unit is the *instruction unit* or IU, which receives opcodes from the BU's queue, decodes them, and prepares them for the next stage in the internal pipeline. Decoded instructions are held in a 3-deep instruction queue. The third stage is the *execution unit* or EU, which contains the ALU, the operand and address registers, and the control section of the microprocessor that coordinates all internal and external activities. Finally, the

---

[3]Also refer to the discussion on the clock cycles and states of Section 1.5.2.

[4]Actually, in this mode the upper four address lines (A23–A20) must be ignored.

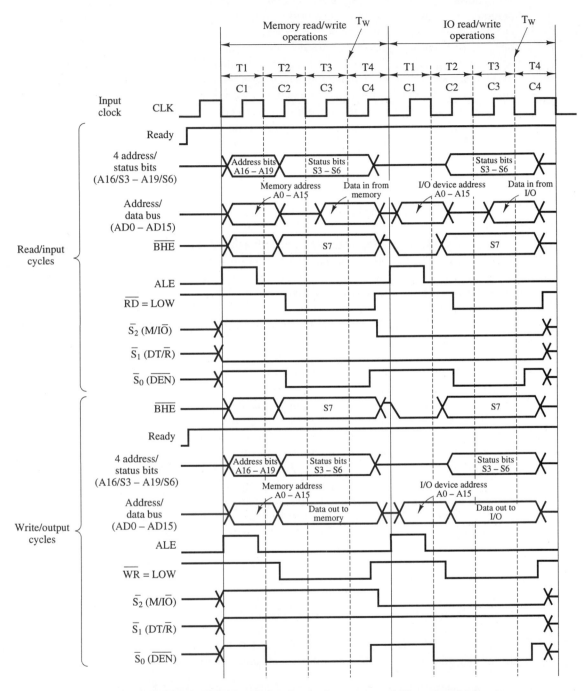

Figure A.3 Intel 8086 simplified bus timing diagram for memory and I/O word read and write cycles. (Wait states T_w inserted after T3.)

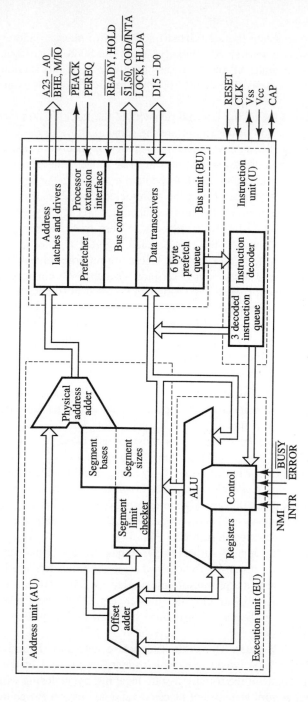

Figure A.4 I/O signals and internal structure of the Intel 80286 [3]. Reprinted by permission of Intel Corporation, Copyright/Intel Corporation 1983.

427

last stage is used to translate logical (virtual) addresses to physical addresses for memory and is called the *address unit* or AU. Finally, while the 8086 was offering no protection capability, the 80286 includes all the necessary hardware in its AU section to provide protection on a per-segment-basis. The 80286 AU, therefore, corresponds to an MMU (memory management unit).

Figure A.5 shows the all the internal registers of the Intel 80286 processor. As can be seen, the registers at the top of the figure are the same as those in the earlier 16-bit 8086. They function in exactly the same way. The four segment registers are again the CS, DS, SS, and ES of the 8086. When the 80286 operates in "real mode," these four segment registers operate similar to those of the 8086, i.e, they contain *a pointer to the beginning of a segment* in memory. When the 80286 operates in the "protected mode," during which the AU implements protected virtual memory through segmentation, these four segment registers contain *selectors* which point to tables in memory; access to segments in memory is done indirectly through the entries of these tables. Each segment register is associated with an individual 48-bit segment descriptor register. These are program-invisible registers and are used to automatically cache a segment descriptor whenever the corresponding segment is loaded with a new selector. Their use is explained in detail in Chapter 6.

Two new program-visible 16-bit segment registers (TR and LDTR) and a number of program-invisible 48-bit registers (called *segment descriptor registers*) are also included in the AU section of the processor to increase its hardware management capability for implementing virtual memory. Their use is explained in more detail in Chapter 7.

80286 State transition diagram.   Figure A.6 shows the simplified state transition diagram and the most important microoperations for the 16-bit 80286 processor. Again, the bus cycle is made up of four input clock cycles, C1, C2, C3, C4, called now by the 80286 "phases phi"; a pair of input clock cycles is called by the 80286 a "state" (T_S = status state and T_C = command state) or "processor clock" PCLK. In order to insert wait states, the processor repeats state T_C. During cycle C1 the whole 24-bit address[5] is placed on nonmultiplexed address lines, and the processor issues the status signals S1#, S2#, which are received and decoded by the external bus controller to generate the control signals needed by memory and I/O. For a read cycle, the 16-bit data is read during C4; for a write cycle, the data is issued during C2.

In addition to the T_S and T_C states the 80286 has two additional states, the T_I (IDLE state) and the T_H (HOLD state). T_I indicates that no data transfers are in progress or requested and is the first state the processor enters after a RESET signal. T_H is entered as a response to a HOLD request by another bus master (e.g., DMA controller) and the 80286 places all its output pins in their high-impedance state, thus relinquishing control of the bus to the requestor bus master.

T_S (*SEND-STATUS* state): This is the first active state after T_I and is signaled by either status line S1# or S2# issued low, which identifies phase 1 of the processor clock PCLK. T_S is the first state of the usually 2-state local bus cycle during which the processor issues the status and control signals and places a valid address on the address bus (if it had not already issued the address prior to entering state T_S). For a write operation, the processor also places the data on the data bus. The bus controller decodes status signals to generate read/write commands and control signals to local transceivers.

---

[5]When the processor operates in "protected mode" with all its capabilities unlocked.

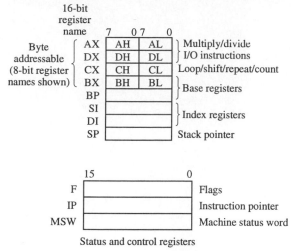

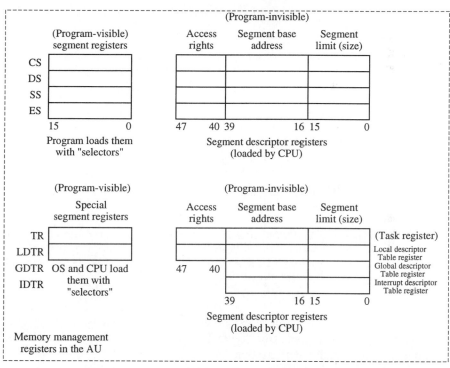

Figure A.5 Program-visible and program-invisible registers of the Intel 80286 [3,4]. (In dashed lines are enclosed the registers in the AU section of the CPU of Figure A.4.) Reprinted by permission of Intel Corporation, Copyright/Intel Corporation 1983.

T_C (*PERFORM-COMMAND* state): After T_S, the perform-command state T_C is entered. This is the state during which the actual data transfer takes place on the bus between the processor and either memory or I/O device ports for a read (input) or write (output) operation. For a read cycle, the addressed device sends data to the processor; for a write cycle, the addressed device accepts data from the processor. When slow memory is connected, the

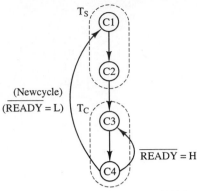

(a) The clock cycle C is called by 80286 a "phi phase"; two phases (or system clock cycles) are called a "state," or "processor clock" PCLK

C1: A_{23}–A_0 ← address[†], $M/\overline{IO}$ ← H, $\overline{S}_1\overline{S}_0$ ← LH (read), $\overline{BHE}$ ← proper value;
C2:
C3: $\overline{S}_1\overline{S}_0$ ← 3ST
C4: Sample $\overline{READY}$: if $\overline{READY}$ = H, execute additional Tc state(s);
                        if $\overline{READY}$ = L, read data from D_{15}–D_0, end cycle;

(b) "Memory read" microoperations

C1: A_{23}–A_0 ← address, $M/\overline{IO}$ ← H, $\overline{S}_1\overline{S}_0$ ← HL (write), $\overline{BHE}$ ← proper value;
C2: D_{15}–D_0 ← data out;
C3: $\overline{S}_1\overline{S}_0$ ← 3ST;
C4: Sample $\overline{READY}$: if $\overline{READY}$ = H, execute additional Tc state(s);
                        if $\overline{READY}$ = L, end cycle;

(c) "Memory write" microoperations (actually, the 80286 issues the next address before the bus cycle starts)

Figure A.6 Intel 80286 simplified nonpipelined state transition diagram (a) and most important microoperations for 16-bit "memory read" (b), and "memory write" (c) bus cycles. (Control signals DT/$\overline{R}$, ALE, DEN, $\overline{MRDC}$, $\overline{MWTC}$, $\overline{IORC}$, $\overline{IOWC}$ are issued by the external bus controller.)

"not ready" signal forces the repetition of state T_C as often as necessary to allow memory to respond. Note that going from T_C to T_S is the ability to execute back-to-back bus operations leading to high bus utilization.

80286 Bus timing diagram. Figure A.7 shows the simplified bus timing diagram for the 16-bit Intel 80286 microprocessor for the memory read/write cycles and the input/output (or I/O read/write) cycles. This timing diagram results from executing the state transition diagram and basic operations listed in Figure A.6. As in the 8086 case, an 80286 bus cycle lasts at least 4 input clock cycles (called by Intel "phi phases" and equal to half of an 80286 state) are needed per bus cycle. *Wait states,* if needed, repeat the execution of input clock cycles C3 and C4 (they repeat state T_C) and, therefore, wait states are now multiples of a *pair* of input clock cycles or of one processor clock PCLK cycle. This

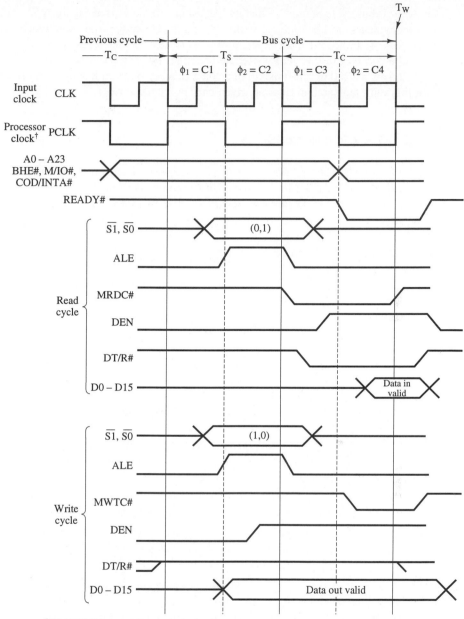

Figure A.7 Intel 80286 simplified bus timing diagram for read and write cycles. (Wait states T_W repeat T_C.)

† The PCLK is not an input clock signal; it is generated internally

means[6] that, for example, an 8-MHz 80286 (processor clock PCLK = 8 MHz, input clock CLK = 16 MHz and, therefore, input clock cycle = 62.4 ns), because it issues the address

[6] Also refer to the discussion on the clock cycles and states of Section 1.5.2.

for the next bus cycle before the current bus cycle completes (see Figure A.7), would require a memory access to be complete within about two states (or four input clock cycles), i.e., 4*62.5 ns = 250 ns, if there is to be zero-wait states. (The access time with 1 wait state would be 375 ns.) In this zero-wait-state example, the 8-MHz 80286 has a bus cycle equal to 4*62.5 ns = 250 ns and a maximum "data transfer rate" of 8 Mbytes per second. (Compare this with the same discussion given earlier for the 8086.)

A.2 INTEL 32-BIT MICROPROCESSORS

The 80386 and 80486 are the 32-bit CISC processors from Intel. Because they are quite similar, they are discussed here together in the same section. We will point out their similarities and differences. Details on their individual characteristics are given throughout the textbook.

A.2.1 80386/486 I/O Pins and Signals

Figure A.8 shows the 80386 I/O pins and signals and Figure A.9 those of the 80486 as described in their respective manuals. The figures also contain tables with the values that the signals M/IO#, D/C#, and W/R# have for the various types of bus cycles that the processor starts. The major "external" differences between the 80386 ad 80486 are as follows:

1. The 80386 divides by 2 its input clock CLK2 to generate the internal processor clock CLK; the period of its processor clock defines a T state made up of two phases, $\phi 1$ and $\phi 2$ (refer to the discussion in Section 1.5.2 and Figure 1.14b). The 80486 has a processor clock which equals its input clock CLK; the period of its processor clock defines a T state.

2. The bus cycle of the 80386 equals 4 input clock cycles, while that of the 80486 equals only 2 input clock cycles. Thus, it takes the 80386 twice as long to fetch a 32-bit operand from memory.

3. The 80386 has the "next address" input pin NA# to implement address pipelining (see Section 2.4.1). The 80486 does not support address pipelining.

4. The 80386 has the input pin BS16# to allow connection of 16-bit peripheral devices. The 80486, in addition to the BS16# pin, has a second input pin BS8# to allow connection of 8-bit peripheral devices as well.

5. The 80486 provides error detection capability for the data being exchanged between the processor and slave devices. It uses its bidirectional data parity input/output pins, one pin for each byte of the data bus, to carry the byte's even parity. The processor has on-chip parity generator and checker.

6. The 80386 has no "burst transfer mode"; the 80486 supports the burst transfer mode (described in detail in Section 2.4.2).

7. The 80486 address bus lines are bidirectional. When its EADS# input pin is triggered, the 80486 will read the external address bus and compare it with the addresses in its internal cache in order to perform an internal cache invalidation cycle to the address indicated when it recognizes a cache hit. (For more details on this cache snooping operation, see Section 5.6.3.)

8. The 80486 provides cache control pins to allow interfacing external (second-level) cache memories.

9. The 80486 has the "address bit 20 mask" (A20M#) input pin, whose assertion causes the 80486 to emulate the 1-Mbyte address wraparound that occurs on the earlier 16-bit 8086.

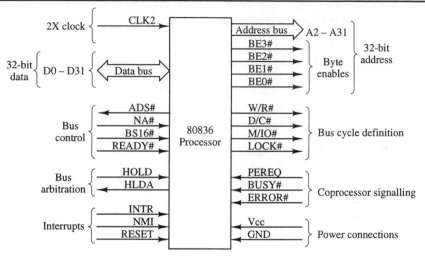

Functional signal groups

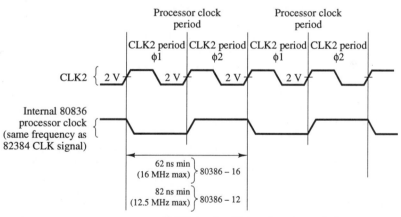

CLK2 signal and internal processor clock

80386 Signal Description

1. Introduction

Ahead is a brief description of the 80386 input and output signals arranged by functional groups. Note the # symbol at the end of a signal name indicates the active, or asserted, state occurs when the signal is at a low voltage. When no # is present after the signal name, the signal is asserted when at the high voltage level.

Figure A.8 80386 I/O pins and signals [23]. Reprinted by permission of Intel Corporation, Copyright/Intel Corporation 1986.

Example signal: M/IO#—High voltage indicates
Memory selected
—Low voltage indicates
I/O selected

The signal descriptions sometimes refer to AC timing parameters, such as "t_{25} reset setup time" and "t_{26} reset hold time."

2. Clock (CLK2)

CLK2 provides the fundamental timing for the 80386. It is divided by two internally to generate the internal processor clock used for instruction execution. The internal clock is comprised of two phases, "phase one" and "phase two." Each CLK2 period is a phase of the internal clock. The figure above illustrates the relationship. If desired, the phase of the internal processor clock can be synchronized to a known phase by ensuring the RESET signal falling edge meets its applicable setup and hold times, t_{25} and t_{26}.

3. Data bus (D0–D31)

These three-state bidirectional signals provide the general purpose data path between the 80386 and other devices. Data bus inputs and outputs indicate "1" when HIGH. The data bus can transfer data on 32- and 16-bit buses using a data bus sizing feature controlled by the BS16# input. Data bus reads require that read data setup and hold times t_{21} and t_{22} be met for correct operation. During any write operation (and during halt cycles and shutdown cycles), the 83086 always drives all 32 signals of the data bus even if the current bus size is 16-bits.

4. Address bus (BE0–BE3#, A2–A31)

These three-state outputs provide physical memory addresses or I/O port addresses. The address bus is capable of addressing 4 gigabytes of physical memory space (00000000H through FFFFFFFFH), and 64 kilobytes of I/O address space (00000000H through 0000FFFFH) for programmed I/O. I/O transfers automatically generated for 80386-to-coprocessor communication use I/O addresses 800000F8H through 800000FFH, so A31 HIGH in conjunction with M/IO# LOW allows simple generation of the coprocessor select signal.

The byte enable outputs, BE0#–BE3#, directly indicate which bytes of the 32-bit data bus are involved with the current transfer. This is most convenient for external hardware.

BE0# applies to D0–D7
BE1# applies to D8–D15
BE2# applies to D16–D23
BE3# applies to D24–D31

The number of byte enables asserted indicates the physical size of the operand being transferred (1, 2, 3, or 4 bytes).

When a memory write cycle or I/O write cycle is in progress, and the operand being transferred occupies **only** the upper 16 bits of the data bus (D16–D31), duplicate data is simultaneously presented on the corresponding lower 16-bits of the data bus (D0–D15). This duplication is performed for optimum write performance on 16-bit buses. The pattern of write data duplication is a function of the byte enables asserted during the write

Figure A.8   (continued).

cycle. Table A.1 lists the write data present on D0–D31, as a function of the asserted byte enable outputs BE0#–BE3#.

TABLE A.1. Write Data Duplication as a Function of BE0#–BE3#

80386 byte enables				80386 write data[a]				Automatic duplication?
BE3#	BE2#	BE1#	BE0#	D24–D31	D16–D23	D8–D15	D0–D7	
High	High	High	Low	Undef.	Undef.	Undef.	A	No
High	High	Low	High	Undef.	Undef.	B	Undef.	No
High	Low	High	High	Undef.	C	Undef.	C	Yes
Low	High	High	High	D	Undef.	D	Undef.	Yes
High	High	Low	Low	Undef.	Undef.	B	A	No
High	Low	Low	High	Undef.	C	B	Undef.	No
Low	Low	High	High	D	C	D	C	Yes
High	Low	Low	Low	Undef.	C	B	A	No
Low	Low	Low	High	D	C	B	Undef.	No
Low	Low	Low	Low	D	C	B	A	No

[a] A = logical write data d0–d7; B = logical write data d8–d15; C = logical write data d16–d23; D = logical write data d24–d31.

5. Bus cycle definition signals (W/R#, D/C#, M/IO#, LOCK#)

These three-state outputs define the type of bus cycle being performed. W/R# distinguishes between write and read cycles. D/C# distinguishes between data and control cycles. M/IO# distinguishes between memory and I/O cycles. LOCK# distinguishes between locked and unlocked bus cycles.

The primary bus cycle definition signals are W/R#, D/C# and M/IO#, since these are the signals driven valid as the ADS# (Address Status output) is driven asserted. The LOCK# is driven valid at the same time as the first locked bus cycle begins, which due to address pipelining, could be later than ADS# is driven asserted. The LOCK# is negated with the READY# input terminates the last bus cycle which was locked.

Exact bus cycle definitions, as a function of W/R#, D/C#, and M/IO#, are given in Table A.2. Note one combination of W/R#, D/C# and M/IO# is never given when ADS# is asserted (however, that combination, which is listed as "does not occur," will occur during **idle** bus states when ADS# is **not** asserted). If M/IO#, D/C#, and W/R# are qualified by ADS# asserted, then a decoding scheme may use the nonoccurring combination to its best advantage.

6. Bus control signals

6.1 Introduction

The following signals allow the processor to indicate when a bus cycle has begun, and allow other system hardware to control address pipelining, data bus width and bus cycle termination.

6.2 Address Status (ADS#)

This three-state output indicates that a valid bus cycle definition, and address (W/R#, D/C#, M/IO#, BE0#–BE3#, and A2–A31) is being driven at the 80386 pins. It is asserted during T1 and T2P bus states.

Figure A.8 (continued).

TABLE A.2. Bus Cycle Definition

M/IO#	D/C#	W/R#	Bus cycle type		Locked?
Low	Low	Low	Interrupt acknowledge		Yes
Low	Low	High	Does not occur		—
Low	High	Low	I/O data read		No
Low	High	High	I/O data write		No
High	Low	Low	Memory code read		No
High	Low	High	HALT:	SHUTDOWN:	No
			Address = 2	Address = 0	
			BE0# High	BE0# Low	
			BE1# High	BE1# High	
			BE2# Low	BE2# High	
			BE3# High	BE3# High	
			A2–A31 Low	A2–A31 Low	
High	High	Low	Memory data read		Some cycles
High	High	High	Memory data write		Some cycles

6.3 Transfer Acknowledge (READY#)

This input indicates the current bus cycle is complete, and the active bytes indicated by BE0#–BE3# and BS16# are accepted or provided. When READY# is sampled asserted during a read cycle or interrupt acknowledge cycle, the 80386 latches the input data and terminates the cycle. When READY# is sampled asserted during a write cycle, the processor terminates the bus cycle.

READY# is ignored on the first bus state of all bus cycles, and sampled each bus state thereafter until asserted. READY# must eventually be asserted to acknowledge every bus cycle, including Halt Indication and Shutdown Indication bus cycles. When being sampled, READY# must always meet setup and hold times t_{19} and t_{20} for correct operation.

6.4 Next Address Request (NA#)

This is used to request address pipelining. This input indicates the system is prepared to accept new values of BE0#–BE3#, A2–A31, W/R#, D/C# and M/IO# from the 80386 even if the end of the current cycle is not being acknowledged on READY#. If this input is asserted when sampled, the next address is driven onto the bus, provided the next bus request is already pending internally.

6.5 Bus Size 16 (BS16#)

The BS16# feature allows the 80386 to directly connect to 32-bit and 16-bit data buses. Asserting this input constrains the current bus cycle to use only the lower-order half (D0–D15) of the data bus, corresponding to BE0# and BE1#. Asserting BS16# has no additional effect if only BE0# and/or BE1# are asserted in the current cycle. However, during bus cycles asserting BE2# or BE3#, asserting BS16# will automatically cause the 80386 to make adjustments for correct transfer of the upper byte(s) using only physical data signals D0–D15.

Figure A.8 (continued).

If the operand spans both halves of the data bus and BS16# is asserted, the 80386 will automatically perform another 16-bit bus cycle. BS16# must always meet setup and hold times t_{17} and t_{18} for correct operation.

80386 I/O cycles automatically generated for coprocessor communication do not require BS16# be asserted. The coprocessor type, 80287 or 80387, is sensed on the ERROR# input shortly after the falling edge of RESET. The 80386 transfers only 16-bit quantities between itself and the 80287, but must transfer 32-bit quantities between itself and the 80387. Therefore, BS16# is a don't care during 80287 cycles and **must not** be asserted during 80387 communication cycles.

7. Bus arbitration signals

7.1 Introduction

This section describes the mechanism by which the processor relinquishes control of its local buses when requested by another bus master device.

7.2 Bus Hold Request (HOLD)

This input indicates some device other than the 80386 requires bus mastership.

HOLD must remain asserted as long as any other device is a local bus master. HOLD is not recognized while RESET is asserted. If RESET is asserted while HOLD is asserted, RESET has priority and places the bus into an idle state, rather than the hold acknowledge (high impedance) state.

HOLD is level-sensitive and is a synchronous input. HOLD signals must always meet setup and hold times t_{23} and t_{24} for correct operation.

7.3 Bus Hold Acknowledge (HLDA)

Assertion of this output indicates the 80386 has relinquished control of its local bus in response to HOLD asserted, and is in the bus hold acknowledge state.

The hold acknowledge state offers near-complete signal isolation. In the Hold Acknowledge state, HLDA is the only signal being driven by the 80386. The other output signals or bidirectional signals (D0–D31, BE0#–BE3#, A2–A31, W/R#, D/C#, M/IO#, LOCK# and ADS#) are in a high-impedance state so the requesting bus master may control them. Pullup resistors may be desired on several signals to avoid spurious activity when no bus master is driving them. Also, one rising edge occurring on the NMI input during hold acknowledge is remembered, for processing after the HOLD input is negated.

In addition to the normal usage of Hold Acknowledge with DMA controllers or master peripherals, the near-complete isolation has particular attractiveness during system test when test equipment drives the system, and in hardware-fault-tolerant applications.

8. Coprocessor interface signals

8.1 Introduction

In the following sections are descriptions of signals dedicated to the numeric coprocessor interface. In addition to the data bus, address bus, and bus cycle definition signals, these

Figure A.8 (continued).

following signals control communication between the 80386 and its 80287 or 80387 processor extension.

8.2 Coprocessor Request (PEREQ)

When asserted, this input signal indicates a coprocessor request for a data operand to be transferred to/from memory by the 80386. In response, the 80386 transfers information between the coprocessor and memory. Because the 80386 has internally stored the coprocessor opcode being executed, it performs the requested data transfer with the correct direction and memory address.

PEREQ is level-sensitive and is allowed to be asynchronous to the CLK2 signal.

8.3 Coprocessor Busy (BUSY#)

When asserted, this input indicates the coprocessor is still executing an instruction, and is not yet able to accept another. When the 80386 encounters any coprocessor instruction which operates on the numeric stack (e.g. load, pop, or arithmetic operation), or the WAIT instruction, this input is first automatically sampled until it is seen to be negated. This sampling of the BUSY# input prevents overrunning the execution of a previous coprocessor instruction.

The FNINIT and FNCLEX coprocessor instructions are allowed to execute even if BUSY# is asserted, since these instructions are used for coprocessor initialization and exception-clearing.

BUSY# is level-sensitive and is allowed to be asynchronous to the CLK2 signal.

BUSY# serves an additional function. If BUSY# is sampled LOW at the falling edge of RESET, the 80386 performs an internal self-test. If BUSY# is sampled HIGH, no self-test is performed.

8.4 Coprocessor Error (ERROR#)

This input signal indicates that the previous coprocessor instruction generated a coprocessor error of a type not masked by the coprocessor's control register. This input is automatically sampled by the 80386 when a coprocessor instruction is encountered, and if asserted, the 80386 generates exception 16 to access the error-handling software.

Several coprocessor instructions, generally those which clear the numeric error flags in the coprocessor or save coprocessor state, do execute without the 80386 generating exception 16 even if ERROR# is asserted. These instructions are FNINIT, FNCLEX, FSTSW, FSTSWAX, FSTCW, FSTENV, FSAVE, FESTENV and FESAVE.

ERROR# is level-sensitive and is allowed to be asynchronous to the CLK2 signal.

ERROR# serves an additional function. If ERROR# is LOW no later than 20 CLK2 periods after the falling edge of RESET and remains LOW at least until the 80386 begins its first bus cycle, an 80387 is assumed to be present (ET bit in CR0 automatically gets set to 1). Otherwise, an 80287 (or no coprocessor) is assumed to be present (ET bit in CR0 automatically is reset to 0). Only the ET bit is set by this ERROR# pin test. Software must set the EM and MP bits in CR0 as needed. Therefore, distinguishing 80287 presence from no coprocessor requires a software test and appropriately resetting or setting the EM bit of CR0 (set EM = 1 when no coprocessor is present). If ERROR# is sampled LOW after reset (indicating 80387) but software later sets EM = 1, the 80386 will behave as if no coprocessor is present.

Figure A.8 (continued).

9. Interrupt signals

9.1 Introduction

The following descriptions cover inputs that can interrupt or suspend execution of the processor's current instruction stream.

9.2 Maskable Interrupt Request (INTR)

When asserted, this input indicates a request for interrupt service, which can be masked by the 80386 Flag Register IF bit. When the 80386 responds to the INTR input, it performs two interrupt acknowledge bus cycles, and at the end of the second, latches an 8-bit interrupt vector on D0–D7 to identify the source of the interrupt.

INTR is level-sensitive and is allowed to be asynchronous to the CLK2 signal. To assure recognition of an INTR request, INTR should remain asserted until the first interrupt acknowledge bus cycle begins.

9.3 Nonmaskable Interrupt Request (NMI)

This input indicates a request for interrupt service, which cannot be masked by software, The nonmaskable interrupt request is always processed according to the pointer or gate in slot 2 of the interrupt table. Because of the fixed NMI slot assignment, no interrupt acknowledge cycles are performed when processing NMI.

NMI is rising edge-sensitive and is allowed to be asynchronous to the CLK2 signal. To assure recognition of NMI, it must be negated for at least eight CLK2 periods, and then be asserted for at least eight CLK2 periods.

Once NMI processing has begun, no additional NMI's are processed until after the next IRET instruction, which is typically the end of the NMI service routine. If NMI is re-asserted prior to that time, however, one rising edge on NMI will be remembered for processing after executing the next IRET instruction.

9.4 Reset (RESET)

This input signal suspends any operation in progress and places the 80386 in a known reset state. The 80386 is reset by asserting RESET for 15 or more CLK2 periods (80 or more CLK2 periods before requesting self test). When RESET is asserted, all other input pins are ignored, and all other bus pins are driven to an idle bus state as shown in Table A.3. If RESET and HOLD are both asserted at a point in time, RESET takes priority even if the 80386 was in a Hold Acknowledge state prior to RESET asserted.

TABLE A.3 Pin State (Bus Idle) During Reset

Pin name	Signal level during reset
ADS#	High
D0–D31	High impedance
BE0#–BE3#	Low
A2–A31	High
W/R#	Low
D/C#	High
M/IO#	Low
LOCK#	High
HLDA	Low

Figure A.8 (continued).

RESET is level-sensitive and must be synchronous to the CLK2 signal. If desired, the phase of the internal processor clock, and the entire 80386 state can be completely synchronized to external circuitry by ensuring the RESET signal falling edge meets its applicable setup and hold times, t_{25} and t_{26}.

Figure A.8 (concluded).

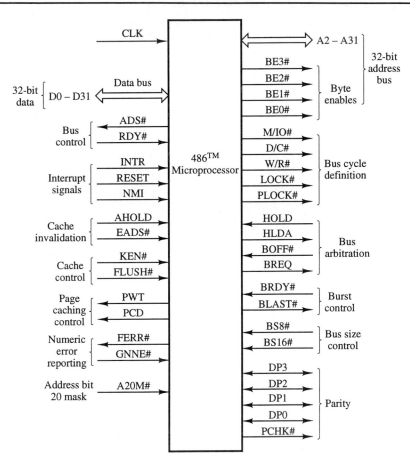

80486 Signal Descriptions

1. Clock (CLK)

CLK provides the fundamental timing and the internal operating frequency for the 486 microprocessor. All external timing parameters are specified with respect to the rising edge of CLK.

The 486 microprocessor can operate over a wide frequency range but CLK's frequency cannot change rapidly while RESET is inactive. CLK's frequency must be stable for proper chip operation since a single edge of CLK is used internally to generate two phases. CLK only needs TTL levels for proper operation. The next figure that follows illustrates the CLK waveform.

Figure A.9 80486 I/O pins and signals [24]. Reprinted by permission of Intel Corporation, Copyright/Intel Corporation, 1989.

2. Address bus (A31–A2, BE0#–BE3#)

A31–A2 and BE0#–BE3# form the address bus and provide physical memory and I/O port addresses. The 486 microprocessor is capable of addressing 4 gigabytes of physical memory space (00000000H through FFFFFFFFH), and 64 Kbytes of I/O address space (00000000H–0000FFFFH). A31–A2 identify addresses to a 4-byte location. BE0#–BE3# identify which bytes within the 4-byte location are involved in the current transfer.

Addresses are driven back into the 486 microprocessor over A31–A4 during cache line invalidations. The address lines are active HIGH. When used as inputs into the processor, A31–A4 must meet the setup and hold times, t_{22} and t_{23}. A31–A2 are not driven during bus or address hold.

The byte enable outputs, BE0#–BE3#, determine which bytes must be driven valid for read and write cycles to external memory.

> BE3# applies to D24–D31
> BE2# applies to D16–D23
> BE1# applies to D8–D15
> BE0# applies to D0–D7

BE0#–BE3# can be decoded to generate A0, A1, and BHE# signals used in 8- and 16-bit systems. BE0#–BE3# are active LOW and are not driven during bus hold.

3. Data lines (D31–D0)

The bidirectional lines, D31–D0, form the data bus for the 486 microprocessor. D0–D7 define the least significant byte and D24–D31 the most significant byte. Data transfers to 8- or 16-bit devices are possible using the data bus sizing feature controlled by the BS8# or BS16# input pins.

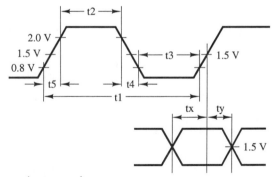

tx = input setup times
ty = input hold times, output float, valid and hold times

D31–D0 are active HIGH. For reads, D31–D0 must meet the setup and hold times, t_{22} and t_{23}. D31–D0 are not driven during read cycles and bus hold.

4. Parity

Data Parity Input/Outputs (DP0–DP3)

DP0–DP3 are the data parity pins for the processor. There is one pin for each byte of the data bus. Even parity is generated or checked by the parity generators/checkers. Even

Figure A.9 (continued).

parity means that there is an even number of HIGH inputs on the eight corresponding data bus pins and parity pin.

Data parity is generated on all write data cycles with the same timing as the data driven by the 486 microprocessor. Even parity information must be driven back to the 486 microprocessor on these pins with the same timing as read information to insure that the correct parity check status is indicated by the 486 microprocessor.

The values read on these pins do not affect program execution. It is the responsibility of the system to take appropriate actions if a parity error occurs.

Input signals on DP0–DP3 must meet setup and hold times t_{22} and t_{23} for proper operation.

Parity Status Output (PCHK#)

Parity status is driven on the PCHK# pin, and a parity error is indicated by this pin being LOW. PCHK# is driven the clock after ready for read operations to indicate the parity status for the data sampled at the end of the previous clock. Parity is checked during code reads, memory reads, and I/O reads. Parity is not checked during interrupt acknowledge cycles. PCHK# only checks the parity status for enabled bytes as indicated by the byte enable and bus size signals. It is valid only in the clock immediately after read data is returned to the 486 microprocessor. At all other times it is inactive (HIGH). PCHK# is never floated.

Driving PCHK# is the only effect that bad input parity has on the 486 microprocessor. The 486 microprocessor will not vector to a bus error interrupt when bad data parity is returned. In systems that will not employ parity, PCHK# can be ignored. In systems not using parity, DP0–DP3 should be connected to V_{CC} through a pull-up resistor.

5. Bus cycle definition

M/IO#, D/C#, W/R# Outputs

M/IO#, D/C# and W/R# are the primary bus cycle definition signals. They are driven valid as the ADS# signal is asserted. M/IO# distinguishes between memory and I/O cycles, D/C# distinguishes between data and control cycles and W/R# distinguishes between write and read cycles.

Bus cycle definitions as a function of M/IO#, D/C# and W/R# are given in Table A.4. Note there is a difference between the 486 microprocessor and 386 microprocessor bus

Table A.4 AD5# Initiated Bus Cycle Definitions

M/IO#	D/C#	W/R#	Bus cycle initiated
0	0	0	Interrupt acknowledge
0	0	1	Halt/special cycle
0	1	0	I/O read
0	1	1	I/O write
1	0	0	Code read
1	0	1	Reserved
1	1	0	Memory read
1	1	1	Memory write

Figure A.9 (continued).

cycle definitions. The halt bus cycle type has been moved to location 001 in the 486 microprocessor from location 101 in the 386 microprocessor. Location 101 is now reserved and will never be generated by the 486 microprocessor.

Bus Lock Output (LOCK#)

LOCK# indicates that the 486 microprocessor is running a read–modify–write cycle where the external bus must not be relinquished between the read and write cycles. Read–modify–write cycles are used to implement memory-based semaphores. Multiple reads or writes can be locked.

When LOCK# is asserted, the current bus cycle is locked and the 486 microprocessor should be allowed exclusive access to the system bus. LOCK# goes active in the first clock of the first locked bus cycle and goes inactive after ready is returned indicating the last locked bus cycle.

The 486 microprocessor will not acknowledge bus hold when LOCK# is asserted (though it will allow an address hold). LOCK# is active LOW and is floated during bus hold. Locked read cycles will not be transformed into cache fill cycles if KEN# is returned active.

Pseudo-Lock Output (PLOCK#)

The pseudo-lock feature allows atomic reads and writes of memory operands greater than 32 bits. These operands require more than one cycle to transfer. The 486 microprocessor asserts PLOCK# during floating point long reads and writes (64 bits), segment table descriptor reads (64 bits) and cache line fills (128 bits).

When PLOCK# is asserted no other master will be given control of the bus between cycles. A bus hold request (HOLD) is not acknowledged during pseudo-locked reads and writes. The 486 microprocessor will drive PLOCK# active until the addresses for the last bus cycle of the transaction have been driven regardless of whether BRDY# or RDY# are returned.

A pseudo-locked transfer is meaningful only if the memory operand is aligned and if it's completely contained within a single cache line. A 64-bit floating point number must be aligned to an 8-byte boundary to guarantee an atomic access.

Normally PLOCK# and BLAST# are inverses of each other. However during the first cycle of a 64-bit floating-point write, both PLOCK# and BLAST# will be asserted.

Since PLOCK# is a function of the bus size and KEN# inputs, PLOCK# should be sampled only if the clock ready is returned. This pin is active LOW and is not driven during bus hold.

6. Bus control

The bus control signals allow the processor to indicate when a bus cycle has begun, and allow other system hardware to control burst cycles, data bus width and bus cycle termination.

Address Status Output (ADS#)

The ADS# output indicates that the address and bus cycle definition signals are valid. This signal will go active in the first clock of a bus cycle and go inactive in the second and subsequent clocks of the cycle. ADS# is also inactive when the bus is idle.

Figure A.9 (continued).

ADS# is used by external bus circuitry as the indication that the processor has started a bus cycle. The external circuit must sample the bus cycle definition pins on the next rising edge of the clock after ADS# is driven active.

ADS# is active LOW and is not driven during bus hold.

Nonburst Ready Input (RDY#)

RDY# indicates that the current bus cycle is complete. In response to a read, RDY# indicates that the external system has presented valid data on the data pins. In response to a write request, RDY# indicates that the external system has accepted the 486 microprocessor data. RDY# is ignored when the bus is idle and at the end of the first clock of the bus cycle. Since RDY# is sampled during address hold, data can be returned to the processor when AHOLD is active.

RDY# is active LOW, and is not provided with an internal pull-up resistor. This input must satisfy setup and hold times t_{16} and t_{17} for proper chip operation.

7. Burst control

Burst Ready Input (BRDY#)

BRDY# performs the same function during a burst cycle that RDY# performs during a nonburst cycle. BRDY# indicates that the external system has presented valid data on the data pins in response to a read or that the external system has accepted the 486 microprocessor data in response to a write. BRDY# is ignored when the bus is idle and at the end of the first clock in a bus cycle.

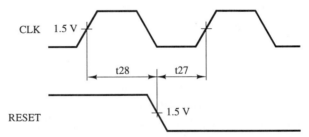

During a burst cycle, BRDY# will be sampled each clock, and if active, the data presented on the data bus pins will be strobed into the 486 microprocessor. ADS# is negated during the second through last data cycles in the burst, but address lines A2–A3 and byte enables will change to reflect the next data item expected by the 486 microprocessor.

If RDY# is returned simultaneously with BRDY#, BRDY# is ignored and the burst cycle is prematurely aborted. An additional complete bus cycle will be initiated after an aborted burst cycle if the cache line fill was not complete. BRDY# is treated as a normal ready for the last data cycle in a burst transfer or for nonburstable cycles.

BRDY# is active LOW and is provided with a small internal pull-up resistor. BRDY# must satisfy the setup and hold times t_{16} and t_{17}.

Burst Last Output (BLAST#)

BLAST# indicates that the next time BRDY# is returned it will be treated as a normal RDY#, terminating the line fill or other multiple-data-cycle transfer. BLAST# is active

Figure A.9 (continued).

for all bus cycles regardless of whether they are cacheable or not. This pin is active LOW and is not driven during bus hold.

6. Interrupt signals (RESET, INTR, NMI)

The interrupt signals can interrupt or suspend execution of the processor's current instruction stream.

Reset Input (RESET)

RESET forces the 486 microprocessor to begin execution at a known state. V_{CC} and CLK must reach their proper DC and AC specifications for at least 1 ms before the 486 microprocessor begins instruction execution. The RESET pin should remain active during this time to ensure proper 486 microprocessor operation. The testability operating modes are programmed by the falling (inactive going) edge of RESET.

Maskable Interrupt Request Input (INTR)

INTR indicates that an external interrupt has been generated. Interrupt processing is initiated if the IF flag is active in the EFLAGS register.

The 486 microprocessor will generate two locked interrupt acknowledge bus cycles in response to asserting the INTR pin. An 8-bit interrupt number will be latched from an external interrupt controller at the end of the second interrupt acknowledge cycle. INTR must remain active until the interrupt acknowledges have been performed to assure program interruption.

The INTR pin is active HIGH and is not provided with an internal pulldown resistor. INTR is asynchronous, but the INTR setup and hold times, t_{20} and t_{21}, must be met to assure recognition on any specific clock.

Nonmaskable Interrupt Request Input (NMI)

NMI is the nonmaskable interrupt request signal. Asserting NMI causes an interrupt with an internally supplied vector value of 2. External interrupt acknowledge cycles are not generated since the NMI interrupt vector is internally generated. When NMI processing begins, the NMI signal will be masked internally until the IRET instruction is executed.

NMI is rising edge sensitive after internal synchronization. NMI must be held LOW for at least four CLK periods before this rising edge for proper operation. NMI is not provided with an internal pulldown resistor. NMI is asynchronous but setup and hold times, t_{20} and t_{21}, must be met to assure recognition on any specific clock.

9. Bus arbitration signals

This section describes the mechanism by which the processor relinquishes control of its local bus when requested by another bus master.

Bus Request Output (BREQ)

The 486 microprocessor drives the BREQ pin active whenever a bus request has been generated internally. External logic can use the BREQ signal to arbitrate among multiple processors. This pin is driven regardless of the state of bus hold or address hold. BREQ is active HIGH and is never floated.

Figure A.9 (continued).

Bus Hold Request Input (HOLD)

HOLD allows another bus master complete control of the 486 microprocessor bus. The 486 microprocessor will respond to an active HOLD signal by asserting HLDA and placing most of its output and input/output pins in a high impedance state (floated) after completing its current bus cycle, burst cycle, or sequence of locked cycles. The BREQ, HLDA, PCHK# and FERR# pins are not floated during bus hold. The 486 microprocessor will maintain its bus in this state until the HOLD is deasserted.

Unlike the 386 microprocessor, the 486 microprocessor will recognize HOLD during reset. Pull-up resistors are not provided for the outputs that are floated in response to HOLD. HOLD is active HIGH and is not provided with an internal pull-down resistor. HOLD must satisfy setup and hold times t_{18} and t_{19} for proper chip operation.

Bus Hold Acknowledge Output (HLDA)

HLDA indicates that the 486 microprocessor has given the bus to another local bus master. HLDA goes active in response to a hold request presented on the HOLD pin. HLDA is driven active in the same clock that the 486 microprocessor floats its bus.

HLDA will be driven inactive when leaving bus hold and the 486 microprocessor will resume driving the bus. The 486 microprocessor will not cease internal activity during bus hold since the internal cache will satisfy the majority of bus requests. HLDA is active HIGH and remains driven during bus hold.

Backoff Input (BOFF#)

Asserting the BOFF# input forces the 486 microprocessor to release control of its bus in the next clock. The pins floated are exactly the same as in response to HOLD. The response to BOFF# differs from the response to HOLD in two ways: First, the bus is floated immediately in response to BOFF# while the 486 completes the current bus cycle before floating its bus in response to HOLD. Second, the 486 does not assert HLDA in response to BOFF#.

The processor remains in bus hold until BOFF# is negated. Upon negation, the 486 microprocessor restarts the bus cycle aborted when BOFF# was asserted. To the internal execution engine the effect of BOFF# is the same as inserting a few wait states to the original cycle.

Any data returned to the processor while BOFF# is asserted is ignored. BOFF# has higher priority than RDY# or BRDY#. If both BOFF# and ready are returned in the same clock, BOFF# takes effect. If BOFF# is asserted while the bus is idle, the 486 microprocessor will float its bus in the next clock. BOFF# is active LOW and must meet setup and hold times t_{18} and t_{19} for proper chip operation.

10. Cache invalidation

The AHOLD and EADS# inputs are used during cache invalidation cycles. AHOLD conditions the 486 microprocessors address lines, A4–A31, to accept an address input. EADS# indicates that an external address is actually valid on the address inputs. Activating EADS# will cause the 486 microprocessor to read the external address bus and perform an internal cache invalidation cycle to the address indicated.

Figure A.9   (continued).

Address Hold Request Input (AHOLD)

AHOLD is the address hold request. It allows another bus master access to the 486 microprocessor address bus for performing an internal cache invalidation cycle. Asserting AHOLD will force the 486 microprocessor to stop driving its address bus in the next clock. While AHOLD is active only the address bus will be floated, the remainder of the bus can remain active. For example, data can be returned for a previously specified bus cycle when AHOLD is active. The 486 microprocessor will not initiate another bus cycle during address hold. Since the 486 microprocessor floats its bus immediately in response to AHOLD, an address hold acknowledge is not required.

AHOLD is recognized during reset. Since the entire cache is invalidated by reset, any invalidation cycles run during reset will be unnecessary. AHOLD is active HIGH and is provided with a small internal pull-down resistor. It must satisfy the setup and hold times t_{18} and t_{19} for proper chip operation. This pin determines whether or not the built-in self-test features of the 486 microprocessor will be exercised on assertion of RESET.

External Address Valid Input (EADS#)

EADS# indicates that a valid external address has been driven onto the 486 address pins. This address will be used to perform an internal cache invalidation cycle. The external address will be checked with the current cache contents. If the address specified matches any areas in the cache, that area will immediately be invalidated.

An invalidation cycle may be run by asserting EADS# regardless of the state of AHOLD, HOLD and BOFF#. EADS# is active LOW and is provided with an internal pullup resistor. EADS# must satisfy the setup and hold times of t_{12} and t_{13} for proper chip operation.

11. Cache control

Cache Enable Input (KEN#)

KEN# is the cache enable pin. KEN# is used to determine whether the data being returned by the current cycle is cacheable. When KEN# is active and the 486 microprocessor generates a cycle that can be cached (most any memory read cycle), the cycle will be transformed into a cache line fill cycle.

A cache line is 16 bytes long. During the first cycle of a cache line fill the byte-enable pins should be ignored and data should be returned as if all four byte enables were asserted. The 486 microprocessor will run between 4 and 16 contiguous bus cycles to fill the line depending on the bus data width selected by BS8# and BS16#.

The KEN# input is active LOW and is provided with a small internal pull-up resistor. It must satisfy the setup and hold times t_{14} and t_{15} for proper chip operation.

Cache Flush Input (FLUSH#)

The FLUSH# input forces the 486 microprocessor to flush its entire internal cache. FLUSH# is active LOW and need only be asserted for one clock. FLUSH# is asynchronous but setup and hold times t_{20} and t_{21} must be met for recognition on any specific clock.

FLUSH# also determines whether or not the tri-state test mode of the 486 microprocessor will be invoked on assertion of RESET.

Figure A.9 (continued).

12. Page cacheability (PWT, PCD)

The PWT and PCD output signals correspond to two user attribute bits in the page table entry. When paging is enabled, PWT and PCD correspond to bits 3 and 4 of the page table entry, respectively. When paging is disabled, or for cycles that are not paged when paging is enabled (for example, I/O cycles) PWT and PCD correspond to bits 3 and 4 in control register 3.

PCD is masked by the CE (cache enable) bit in control register 0 (CR0). When CE = 0 (cache line fills disabled) the 486 microprocessor forces PCD HIGH. When CE = 1, PCD is driven with the value of the page table entry/directory.

The purpose of PCD is to provide a cacheable/non-cacheable indication on a page by page basis. The 486 will not perform a cache fill to any page in which bit 4 of the page table entry is set. PWT corresponds to the write-back bit and can be used by an external cache to provide this functionality.

PCD and PWT have the same timing as the cycle definition pins (M/IO#, D/C#, W/R#). PCD and PWT are active HIGH and are not driven during bus hold.

13. Numeric error reporting (FERR#, IGNNE#)

To allow PC-type floating-point error reporting, the 486 microprocessor provides two pins, FERR# and IGNNE#.

Floating Point Error Output (FERR#)

The 486 microprocessor asserts FERR# whenever an unmasked floating-point error is encountered. FERR# is similar to the ERROR# pin on the 387 math coprocessor. FERR# can be used by external logic for PC-type floating-point error reporting in 486 microprocessor systems. FERR# is active LOW, and is not floating during bus hold.

Ignore Numeric Error Input (IGNNE#)

The 486 microprocessor will ignore a numeric error and continue executing noncontrol floating-point instructions when IGNNE# is asserted. When deasserted, the 486 microprocessor will freeze on a noncontrol floating-point instruction if a previous instruction caused an error. IGNNE# has no effect when the NE bit in control register 0 is set.

The IGNNE# input is active LOW and is provided with a small internal pull-up resistor. The input is asynchronous, but must meet setup and hold times t_{20} and t_{21} to ensure recognition on any specific clock.

14. Bus size control (BS16#, BS8#)

The BS16# and BS8# inputs allow external 16- and 8-bit busses to be supported with a small number of external components. The 486 CPU samples these pins every clock. The value sampled in the clock before ready determines the bus size. When asserting BS16# or BS8# only 16 or 8 bits of the data bus need be valid. If both BS16# and BS8# are asserted, an 8-bit bus width is selected.

When BS16# or BS8# are asserted the 486 microprocessor will convert a larger data request to the appropriate number of smaller transfers. The byte enables will also be modified appropriately for the bus size selected.

Figure A.9   (continued).

BS16# and BS8# are active LOW and are provided with small internal pull-up resistors. BS16# and BS8# must satisfy the setup and hold times t_{14} and t_{15} for proper chip operation.

15. Address bit 20 mask (A20M#)

Asserting the A20M# input causes the 486 microprocessor to mask physical address bit 20 before performing a lookup in the internal cache and before driving a memory cycle to the outside world. When A20M# is asserted, the 486 microprocessor emulates the 1-Mbyte address wraparound that occurs on the 8086. A20M# is active LOW and must be asserted only when the processor is in real mode. A20M# is asynchronous but should meet setup and hold times t_{20} and t_{21} for recognition in any specific clock. For testability, this pin also determines whether or not the external cache test features of the 486 microprocessor will be exercised upon assertion of RESET.

Figure A.9 (concluded).

A.2.2 80386/486 Internal Organization and Register Structures

Figure A.10 shows the internal organization of the 80386 and the 80486 microprocessors together. Figure A.11 combines the internal registers of the 80386 and 80486. We notice that as in the 16-bit 80286, the *program-visible registers* are similar to those of the 16-bit 80286 (i.e., there are 8 general-purpose registers, EAX–ESP, that can be used for data, base, or index registers, and a stack pointer), except that the 80486 registers are now 32 bits wide. The 80486 has an additional set of registers needed by the on-chip floating-point unit: 8 numeric floating-point data registers (R0–R7) with their 2-bit tag fields, a control and status register, a tag register each bit of which marks the content of the respective data register (as valid, zero, infinity, or empty), and an instruction pointer register and data pointer register (that supply the address of the failing numeric instruction and the address of its numeric memory operand when the FPU has detected an error). The flags register and instruction pointer of the 80386/486 are also 32 bits long. The number of code segment registers has now increased to six, the two new ones (the FS and GS) used primarily as additional data segment registers. However, the width of these six segment registers and of the TR (task registers) and LDTR (local descriptor task register) segment registers remains 16 bits, as in the 80286.

The *program-invisible registers* (or *systems registers*) include the segment descriptor registers (one for each of the six segment registers), the TR and LDTR segment registers, and the segment descriptor registers GDTR (global descriptor task register) and IDTR (interrupt descriptor task register). These registers include the three fields they had in the 80286, i.e., the access rights, segment base address, and segment limit fields, but the size of the registers has increased now to 64 bits. The GDTR and IDTR register width has increased to 48 bits. The program-invisible set also includes four 32-bit control registers (CR0–CR3) used to control the on-chip memory management hardware (the segmentation and paging mechanisms of both the 80386 and 80486) and the on-chip cache and on-chip floating-point unit FPU (of the 80486). Both the 80386 and the 80486 include eight 32-bit debug registers that support instruction breakpoints and data brakepoints. Finally, the 486 also contains five test registers (TR3–TR7) used to control the on-chip cache and the TLB (translation lookaside buffer) in its internal paging unit.

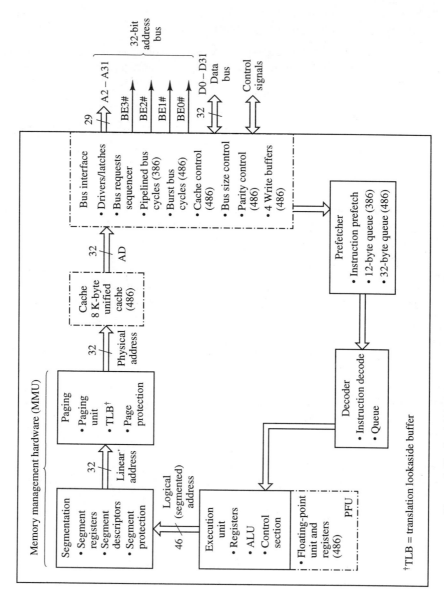

Figure A.10 Intel 80386/486. (Components within dashed lines are found only on the 80486.)

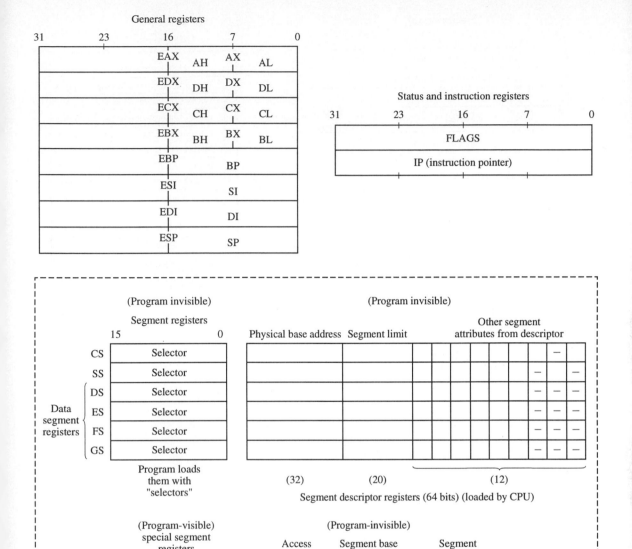

Figure A.11 Program-visible and program-invisible registers of the Intel 80386/486. The registers that only the 486 has are identified by the 486 in parentheses [23,24]. Reprinted by permission of Intel Corporation, Copyright/Intel Corporation 1986, 1989.

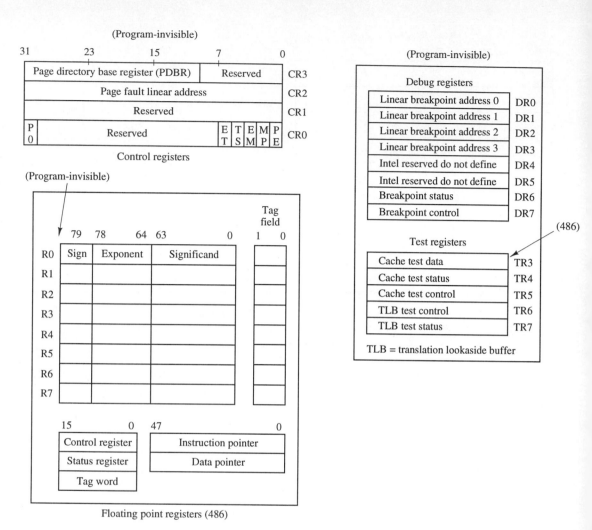

Control registers

Floating point registers (486)

Figure A.11 (concluded).

A.2.3 80386 State Transition and Bus Timing Diagrams

The operation of the 32-bit processor 80386 is similar to that of the 16-bit 80286, except that the 386 now calls the input clock cycle a "CLK2 cycle," and the two states, "T1 state" and "T2 state." The 80386 has two additional states (the T_I and the T_H). All these states correspond to, and behave like, the 80286 states T_I, T_H, T_S, and T_C discussed earlier. An 80386 state lasts two input clock cycles (or two CLK2s) and is equal to what Intel 80386 calls one "82584 CLK." Both the 82584 CLK and the CLK2 are generated by the external 82384 clock generator (see Figure 1.14b). All 80386 inputs are sampled at CLK2 rising edges.

The 80386 nonpipelined state transition diagram and the basic operations that the 386 executes for a read and a write bus cycle are shown in Figure 1.17 of Chapter 1. The processor places during C1 the 30 most significant address bits on the nonmultiplexed address bus lines (thus it always points to a doubleword address), while it internally decodes bits A1 and A0 to generate proper values on its output control pins BE0#–BE3# to indicate which of the four byte sections of memory will be activated during the current bus cycle. The 32-bit data is transferred over the nonmultiplexed data bus lines D31–D0: during C2 for a write, and during C4 for a read. The maximum data transfer rate for a bus operation is 32 bits every four input clock cycles.

Both the Intel 80386 and 80486 are dynamically reconfigurable processors being able to adjust their bus sizes; they do this by sampling their input feedback signals during clock cycle C3 to determine the size of the responding slave device (port); the 80386 has one input pin BS16# (for 16-bit slave devices). Depending upon the width of the data operand to be transferred and the width of the accessed slave device, the processor determines whether additional bus cycles are required.

The simplified timing diagram of the Intel 80386 read and write bus cycles is shown in Figure 2.9 of Chapter 2. (Depending on the value on the output line M/IO#, the bus cycle may be accessing memory space or input/output space.) The timing diagram for this 32-bit product is similar to that of the earlier 16-bit Intel 80286; i.e., a bus cycle is made up of four input clock cycles (or as the Intel 80386 calls them "CLK2 periods"). The two 80286 states T_S and T_C are now called by the 80386, states T1 and T2. The local bus is nonmultiplexed and synchronous. This timing diagram implements the state transition diagram and basic operations listed in Figure 1.17. The D/C# line distinguishes between data and control cycles, such as memory code read, interrupt acknowledge, halt, etc.

Two additional pins are shown in the timing diagrams of the Intel 80386 that were not present in the 16-bit 80286. One of them is the "next address" NA# input pin: it is used by external devices to trigger the processor to implement "address pipelining": it forces the processor to issue the address for the next bus cycle before the current bus cycle has been totally completed. The other additional input pin is the bus size pin BS16#, which is used by an external device to identify that the "port size" is 16 bits.

A.2.4 80486 State Transition and Bus Timing Diagrams

The simplified state transition diagram and basic operations of the 80486 are shown in Figure A.12. An 80486 bus cycle lasts only two input clock cycles (or states T1 and T2). As in the 80386, the 80486 processor places during C1 the 30 most significant address bits on the nonmultiplexed address bus lines, and uses bits A1 and A0 to generate the output control signals BE0#–BE3#. The 32-bit data is transferred over the nonmultiplexed data bus lines

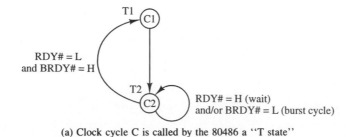

(a) Clock cycle C is called by the 80486 a "T state"

Figure A.12 Intel 80486 simplified state transition diagram (a), and most important microoperations for 32-bit "memory read" (b), and "memory write" (c) bus cycles.

C1: A_{31}–A_2 ← part of address, M/IO# ← H, BE0#–BE3# ← proper values,
  W/R# ← L, ADS# ← L, sample BS16# and BS8#;
C2: ADS# ← H, sample RDY#: if RDY# = H, execute additional T_2 states;
  if RDY# = L, read data from D_{31}–D_0, end cycle;

(b) "Memory read" microoperations

C1: A_{31}–A_2 ← part of address, M/IO# ← H, BE0#–BE3# ← proper values,
  W/R# ← H, ADS# ← L;
C2: ADS# ← H, D_{31}–D_0 ← data out (no automatic duplication),
Sample RDY#: if RDY# = H, execute additional T_2 states;
  if RDY# = L, end cycle;

(c) "Memory write" microoperations

Figure A.12   (concluded).

D31–D0 during C2, for either a read or a write operation (the only difference is that out-going data appear on the data bus in the middle of state T2, while incoming data appear later during T2). The maximum data transfer rate for a bus operation is 32 bits for every two input clock cycles.

The simplified timing diagram of the Intel 80486 read and write cycles is shown in Figure 2.10 of Chapter 2. (Depending on the value on the input pin M/IO#, the bus cycle may be accessing memory space or input/output space). An 80486 bus cycle is now made up of two input clock cycles, called state T1 and state T2. A bus cycle starts by the processor issuing ADS# and terminates when it samples RDY#. Like the Intel 80386, the 80486's local bus is nonmultiplexed and synchronous. This timing diagram implements the state transition and basic operations listed in Figure A.12. The D/C# line distinguishes between data and control cycles (such as memory code read, interrupt acknowledge, halt, etc.). The 80486 does not have the "next address" NA# pin of the 80386, but it has the additional input pin BS8# for 8-bit ports.

A.2.5 80386/486 Segment Descriptor Formats

Figure A.13 shows the general segment descriptor format for either "code" or "data" segments for the Intel 80386. Figure A.14a shows the general format that any of the Intel 80486 segment descriptors may have, while Figure A.14b and c show the segment descriptor format for "code" and "data" segments and the explanation of their "access rights" bits. The format of the page descriptors for the 80386/486 microprocessors is shown in Figure 6.17 and discussed in Section 6.4.6 of Chapter 6.

Descriptors used for applications code and data segments

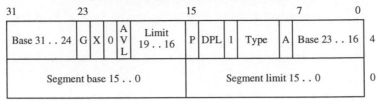

Descriptors used for special system segments

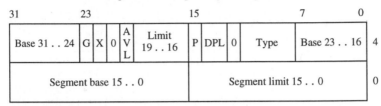

A   Accessed
AVL   Available for use by systems programmers
DPL   Descriptor privilege level
G   Granularity
P   Segment present

Figure A.13   Intel 80386 code and data segment descriptor format [25]. Reprinted by permission of Intel Corporation, Copyright/Intel Corporation 1986.

BASE   Base address of the segment
LIMIT Length of the segment
P   Present bit: 1 = present, 0 = not present
DPL   Descriptor privilege level 0 – 3
S   Segment descriptor: 0 = system descriptor, 1 = code or data segment descriptor
TYPE   Type of segment
A   Accessed bit
G   Granularity bit: 1 = segment length is page granular, 0 = segment length is byte granular
D   Default operation size (recognized in code segment descriptors only):
       1 = 32-bit segment, 0 = 16-bit segment
0   Bit must be zero (0) for compatibility with future processors
AVL   Available field for user or OS

Note: In a maximum-size segment (i.e. a segment with G = 1 and segment
       limit 19 . . 0 = FFFFFH), the lowest 12 bits of the segment base should be zero
       (i.e. segment base 11 . . 000 = 000H).

(a) General format of a segment descriptor

Figure A.14   Intel 80486 segment descriptor formats [24]. Reprinted by permission of Intel Corporation, Copyright/Intel Corporation 1989.

Segment base 15 . . 0					Segment limit 15 . . 0	0
Base 31 . . 24	G	D	0	A V L	Limit 19 . . 16	Access rights byte	Base 23 . . 16	+4

D/B   1 = default instruction attributes are 32-bits,
        0 = default instruction attributes are 16-bits
AVL   Available field for user or OS
G   Granularity bit: 1 = segment length is page granular, 0 = segment length is byte granular
0   Bit must be zero (0) for compatibility with future processors

(b) Format of a code or data segment descriptor

	Bit position	Name	Function	
	7	Present (P)	P = 1	Segment is mapped into physical memory.
			P = 0	No mapping to physical memory exits, base and limit are not used.
	6 – 5	Descriptor privilege level (DPL)		Segment privilege attribute used in privilege tests.
	4	Segment descriptor (S)	S = 1	Code or data (includes stacks) segment descriptor.
			S = 0	System segment descriptor or gate descriptor.
	3	Executable (E)	E = 0	Descriptor type is data segment.
	2	Expansion direction (ED)	ED = 0	Expand up segment, offsets must be ≤ limit.
			ED = 1	Expand down segment, offsets must be > limit.
Type field definition	1	Writeable (W)	W = 0	Data segment may not be written into.
			W = 1	Data segment may be written into.
	3	Executable (E)	E = 1	Descriptor type is code segment.
	2	Conforming (C)	C = 1	Code segment may only be executed when CPL ≥ DPL and CPL remains unchanged.
	1	Readable (R)	R = 0	Code segment may not be read.
			R = 1	Code segment may be read.
	0	Accessed (A)	A = 0	Segment has not been accessed.
			A = 1	Segment selector has been loaded into segment register or used by selector test instructions.

(Right-hand braces: If data segment (S = 1, E = 0); If code segment (S = 1, E = 1))

(c) Access rights byte definition for (b)

Figure A.14   (concluded).

B

Motorola 680x0 CISC Microprocessors*

B.1 MOTOROLA 16-BIT 68000 MICROPROCESSOR

B.1.1 68000 I/O Pins and Signals

The Motorola 68000 is a 16-bit big-endian processor, that can operate either in "user mode" or "supervisor mode." Figure B.1 shows the 68000 I/O pins and signals and its internal block diagram. The processor has a 16-bit data bus and a 23-bit address bus over which the processor sends the 23 most significant bits of the internal 24-bit address. The least significant address bit is used for the processor to issue proper values on the two output control signals UDS# (upper data strobe, to trigger the memory byte section connected to the upper half of the data bus lines) and LDS# (lower data strobe, to trigger the memory byte section connected to the lower half of the data bus lines): (1) to access a word: A0 = 0, and both UDS# and LDS# are asserted[1] or Low; (2) to access an even byte: A0 = 0, and UDS# = L, while LDS# = H; (3) to access an odd byte: A0 = 1, and LDS# = L, while UDS# = H. Like all Motorola products, the 68000 does only "memory-mapped I/O."

Figure B.2 shows the processor connected to 68000-class 16-bit memory and I/O peripherals, through an asynchronous bus (that uses the five control signals R/W#, UDS#, LDS#, AS#, and DTACK#), and to earlier 6800-class 8-bit peripherals through a synchronous bus (that uses the three control signals E, VMA#, and VPA#). The 8-bit peripheral may be connected to either the lower half D0–D7 or the upper half D8–D15 of the 16-bit data bus.

---

*References cited in Appendix B appear at end of Appendix C.

[1]*Assertion:* a signal (pin) is active or true independent of the actual voltage level; *negation:* a signal (pin) is inactive or false independent of the actual voltage level.

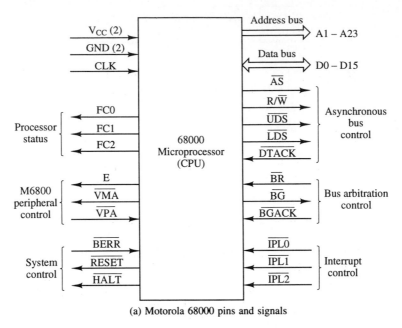

(a) Motorola 68000 pins and signals

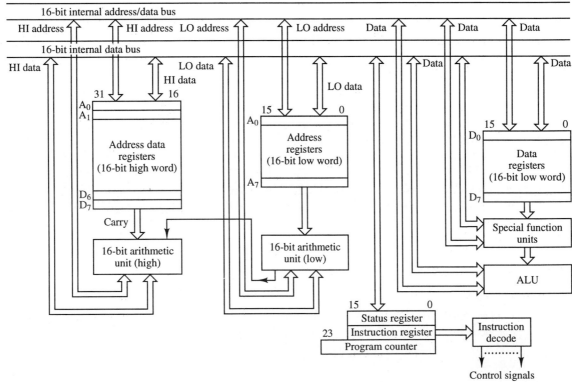

(b) Motorola 68000 internal block diagram

Figure B.1   External view and internal block diagram of the Motorola 68000 [2].

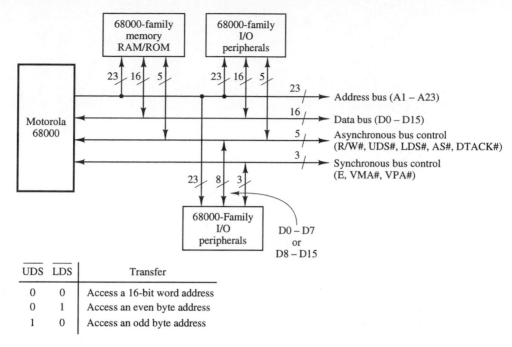

UDS	LDS	Transfer
0	0	Access a 16-bit word address
0	1	Access an even byte address
1	0	Access an odd byte address

Figure B.2   16-Bit Motorola 68000 connected to 16-bit memory and I/O peripherals via an asynchronous bus and to 8-bit peripherals via a synchronous bus [6].

B.1.2 68000 State Transition and Bus Timing Diagrams

The 68000 has a 16-bit nonmultiplexed data bus whose most significant byte lane D8–D15 is connected to Section 0 (the "even section") and the least significant byte lane D0–D7 to Section 1 (the "odd section"). When a "byte write" cycle is executed, *the outgoing byte will be duplicated on both halves of the data bus*, but only one byte section of memory will be triggered by the UDS# or LDS#.

The 68000 "state transition diagram" and the respective "microoperations" are shown in Figure B.3 and its basic bus timing diagram for a read and write cycle in Figure B.4. The 68000 cycle definitions are as follows:

1. *Clock cycle:* The input clock period from positive to positive edge.
2. *Bus cycle:* The sequence of timing events required to do a byte or a word read cycle, a byte or a word write cycle, or a read/modify/write cycle.

We notice that a normal bus cycle consists of four clock cycles C1, C2, C3, and C4; these equal to 8 of what Motorola calls "S states" S0–S7. (One input clock cycle is two S states.)

At the beginning of the bus cycle, the 68000 issues the three function code signals FC0–FC2 to identify the type of bus cycle; it also places on the address bus the 23 most significant address bits A1–A23. Half a clock cycle later, it will issue the proper value on line R/W# to indicate a read versus a write operation. Notice that for a read operation the UDS# and LDS# are issued at the beginning of C2, while for a write cycle at the beginning

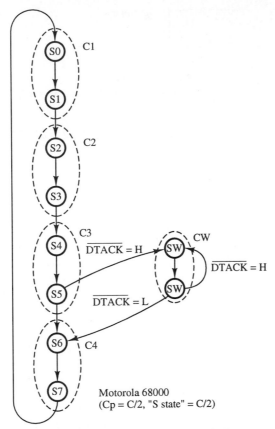

Figure B.3 Motorola 68000 simplified state transition diagram (a), and the most important microoperations for a 16-bit read (b) and a 16-bit write (c) bus cycle [5].

Motorola 68000
(Cp = C/2, "S state" = C/2)

(a) Two S's make up one clock cycle C

of C3. For a read cycle, data is placed on the data bus by the addressed slave in the middle of C3, and the processor will latch this data in the middle of C4 (at the end of S6). For a write cycle the microprocessor places data on the data bus in the middle of C2, and the slave device will latch it after C3.

The local bus is nonmultiplexed and asynchronous (which means that each bus cycle can be of different length): the microprocessor issues at the beginning of C2 the synchronization signal AS# to inform the slave devices that a valid address is on the address bus; when the addressed slave has completed its transaction (of placing data on the data bus for a read cycle or latching the data off the data bus for a write cycle) it will respond back to the processor with feedback signal DTACK#. The DTACK# is expected before the middle of C3 (negative edge of S4). During every bus cycle, the 68000 samples the DTACK# to see whether the addressed slave has responded. If DTACK# has been asserted (low) before the S4 falling clock edge, no wait states are inserted. If the addressed slave is slow in responding, its interface will not assert DTACK# low for one or more system clock cycles; this will in effect cause the microprocessor to lengthen its bus cycle by inserting wait states (each equal to one bus cycle C or a pair of Sw's) after state S5, and allow the slave device to finish its transaction and then assert its DTACK#.

Since different systems require different maximum response times, a "bus error" BERR# input pin of the processor is used. External circuitry (in the form of a "watchdog

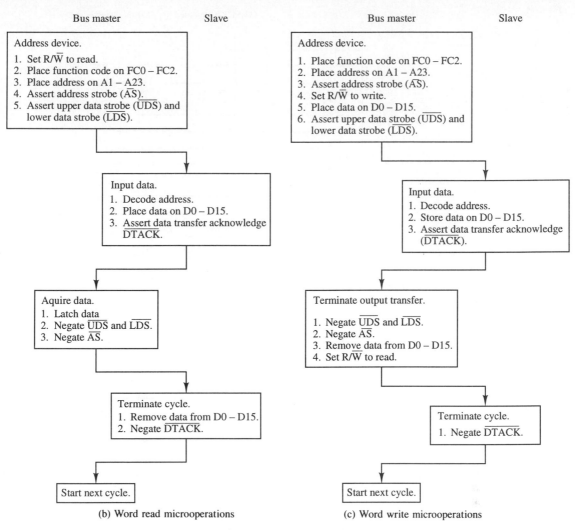

| Bus master | Slave | | Bus master | Slave |

Address device.

1. Set R/W̄ to read.
2. Place function code on FC0 – FC2.
3. Place address on A1 – A23.
4. Assert address strobe (A̅S̅).
5. Assert upper data strobe (U̅D̅S̅) and lower data strobe (L̅D̅S̅).

Input data.

1. Decode address.
2. Place data on D0 – D15.
3. Assert data transfer acknowledge D̅T̅A̅C̅K̅.

Aquire data.

1. Latch data
2. Negate U̅D̅S̅ and L̅D̅S̅.
3. Negate A̅S̅.

Terminate cycle.

1. Remove data from D0 – D15.
2. Negate D̅T̅A̅C̅K̅.

Start next cycle.

(b) Word read microoperations

Address device.

1. Place function code on FC0 – FC2.
2. Place address on A1 – A23.
3. Assert address strobe (A̅S̅).
4. Set R/W̄ to write.
5. Place data on D0 – D15.
6. Assert upper data strobe (U̅D̅S̅) and lower data strobe (L̅D̅S̅).

Input data.

1. Decode address.
2. Store data on D0 – D15.
3. Assert data transfer acknowledge (D̅T̅A̅C̅K̅).

Terminate output transfer.

1. Negate U̅D̅S̅ and L̅D̅S̅.
2. Negate A̅S̅.
3. Remove data from D0 – D15.
4. Set R/W̄ to read.

Terminate cycle.

1. Negate D̅T̅A̅C̅K̅.

Start next cycle.

(c) Word write microoperations

Figure B.3 (concluded).

timer'') must be used to determine the maximum duration between the assertion of the UDS# and LDS# and the DTACK# before issuing the BERR# signal. Similarly, this will trigger the BERR# in case the microprocessor tries to access nonexistent memory. When the BERR# is received, the processor initiates a ''bus error exception sequence'' or retries the bus cycle.

Comparing the 16-bit big-endian here with the 16-bit little-endian of the preceding paragraph we notice that in both cases and for aligned transfers, the least significant byte of the operand is transferred over the least significant byte lane and the most significant byte of the operand over the most significant byte lane.[2]

[2]Keep in mind that memory may always be triggered to send a 16-bit word and it is up to the processor to read the valid byte from its respective 8 input pins.

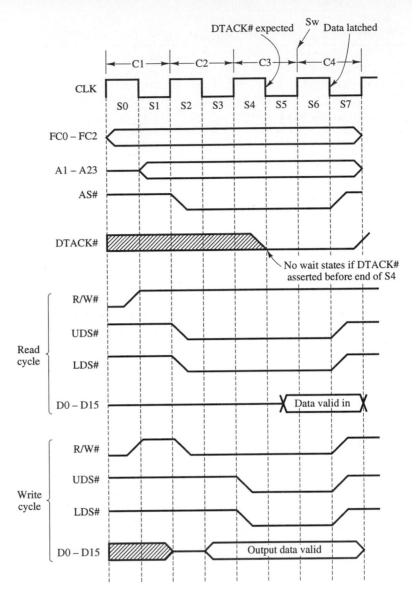

Figure B.4 Motorola 68000 asynchronous bus timing diagram for 16-bit read and write cycles [6]. (Wait states Sw inserted in pairs after S5.)

B.2 MOTOROLA 32-BIT 680x0 MICROPROCESSORS

Figure 2.12 shows the general interfacing of a Motorola 32-bit processor with a 32-bit memory. The memory subsystem is made up of four byte sections and is interconnected (like any 32-bit big-endian processor) to the 68020/30/40 as follows: Section 0 to data bus byte lane D24–D31, Section 1 to byte lane D16–D23, Section 2 to byte lane D8–D15, and Section 3 to byte lane D0–D7. The four control signals (DBBE1–DBBE4) that trigger these memory sections are generated by external logic decoding the two least significant address bits A0–

A1 and the 2-bit "data width identifier" SIZ0–SIZ1. The number of bytes transferred during a write or (noncacheable) read bus cycle is equal to or less than the size indicated by SIZ0 and SIZ1 outputs, depending on port width and operand alignment. However, the values SIZ1,SIZ0 = 1,1 indicate a 3-byte transfer for the 68020 and 68030, while for the 68040 they indicate a "line transfer" (i.e., four consecutive 4-byte transfers for a 4-doubleword burst transfer). The 30-bit address A2–A31 supplied to memory points to a 32-bit doubleword location.

B.2.1 680x0 I/O Pins and Signals

Figures B.5, B.6, and B.7 show the I/O pins and signals and their definitions for the 68020, 68030, and 68040, respectively.

B.2.2 680x0 Internal Organization and Register Structures

Figure B.8 shows the internal block diagrams of the 68020, 68030, and 68040 microprocessors, while Figure B.9, B.10, and B.11 their respective internal register structures.

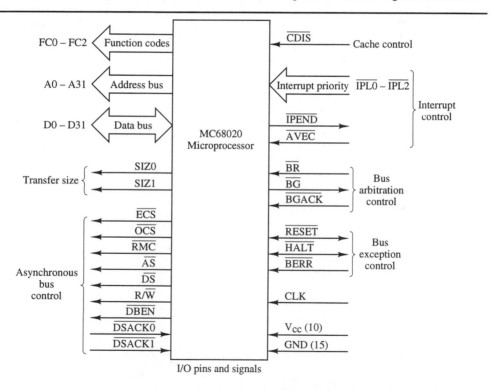

I/O pins and signals

Note

The terms assertion and negation are used extensively. This is done to avoid confusion when dealing with a mixture of "active-LOW" and "active-HIGH" signals. The term

Figure B.5   68020 I/O pins and signals [7].

assert of *assertion* is used to indicate that a signal is active or true, independent of whether that level is represented by a high or low voltage. The term *negate* or *negation* is used to indicate that a signal is inactive or **false.**

1. Function Code Signals (FC0–FC2)

These three-state outputs identify the processor state (supervisor or user) and the address space of the bus cycle currently being executed as defined in Table B.1.

Table B.1 Function Code Assignments

FC2	FC1	FC0	Cycle type
0	0	0	(Undefined, reserved)[a]
0	0	1	User data space
0	1	0	User program space
0	1	1	(Undefined, reserved)[a]
1	0	0	(Undefined, reserved)[a]
1	0	1	Supervisor data space
1	1	0	Supervisor program space
1	1	1	CPU space
			(see table at right)

A19–A16	(CPU space type)
1 1 1 1	Interrupt acknowledge (INTA)
0 0 1 0	Coprocessor communication
	Access level control
0 0 0 1	(Module cam/return: CALLM, RETM)
0 0 0 0	Breakpoint acknowledge

[a]Address space 3 is reserved for user definition, while 0 and 4 are reserved for future use by Motorola.

By decoding the function codes, a memory system can utilize the full 4 gigabyte address range for several address spaces.

2. Address Bus (A0–A31)

These three-state outputs provide the address for a bus transfer during all currently defined cycles except CPU-space references. During CPU-space references the address bus provides CPU related information. The address bus is capable of addressing 4 gigabytes (2^{32}) of data.

3. Data Bus (D0–D31)

These three-state, bidirectional signals provide the general purpose data path between the MC68020 and all other devices. The data bus can transmit and accept data using the dynamic bus sizing capabilities of the MC68020. Refer to **(4) Transfer Size (SIZ0, SIZ1)** for additional information.

4. Transfer Size (SIZ0, SIZ1)

These three-state outputs are used in conjunction with the dynamic bus sizing capabilities of the MC68020. The SIZ0 and SIZ1 outputs indicate the number of bytes of an operand remaining to be transferred during a given bus cycle.

Figure B.5 (continued).

5. Asynchronous Bus Control Signals

The asynchronous bus control signals for the MC68020 are described in the following paragraphs.

5.1 External cycle start ($\overline{\text{ECS}}$)

This output is asserted during the first one-half clock of every bus cycle to provide the earliest indication that the MC68020 may be starting a bus cycle. The use of this signal must be validated later with address strobe, since the MC68020 may start an instruction fetch cycle and then abort it if the instruction word is found in the cache. The MC68020 drives only the address, size, and function code outputs (not address strobe) when it aborts a bus cycle due to cache hit.

5.2 Operand cycle start ($\overline{\text{OCS}}$)

This output signal has the same timing as $\overline{\text{ECS}}$, except that it is asserted only during the first bus cycle of an operand transfer or instruction prefetch.

5.3 Read-modify-write cycle ($\overline{\text{RMC}}$)

This three-state output signal provides an indication that the current bus operation is an indivisible read-modify-write cycle. This signal is asserted for the duration of the read-modify-write sequence. RMC should be used as a bus lock to insure integrity of instructions which use the read-modify-write operation.

5.4 Address strobe ($\overline{\text{AS}}$)

This three-state output signal indicates that valid function code, address, size, and R/$\overline{\text{W}}$ state information is on the bus.

5.5 Data strobe ($\overline{\text{DS}}$)

In a read cycle, this three-state output indicates that the slave device should drive the data bus. In a write cycle, it indicates that the MC68020 has placed valid data on the data bus.

5.6 Read/write (R/$\overline{\text{W}}$)

This three-state output signal defines the direction of a data transfer. A high level indicates a read from an external device, a low level indicates a write to an external device.

5.7 Data buffer enable ($\overline{\text{DBEN}}$)

This three-state output provides an enable to external data buffers. This signal allows the R/$\overline{\text{W}}$ signal to change without possible external buffer contention.

This pin is not necessary in all systems.

5.8 Data transfer and size acknowledge ($\overline{\text{DSACK0}}$, $\overline{\text{DSACK1}}$)

These inputs indicate that a data transfer is complete and the port size of the external device (8, 16, or 32 bits). During a read cycle, when the processor recognizes $\overline{\text{DSACKx}}$,

Figure B.5   (continued).

it latches the data and then terminates the bus cycle; during a write cycle, when the processor recognizes DSACKx, the bus cycle is terminated. See 2.6, **Dynamic Bus Sizing,** for further information on $\overline{\text{DSACKx}}$ encodings.

The processor will synchronize the $\overline{\text{DSACKx}}$ inputs and allow skew between the two inputs.

6. Cache Disable ($\overline{\text{CDIS}}$)

This input signal dynamically disables the on-chip cache. The cache is disabled internally after the cache disable input is asserted and synchronized internally. The cache will be reenabled internally after the input negation has been synchronized internally.

7. Interrupt Control Signals

The following paragraphs describe the interrupt control signals for the MC68020.

7.1 Interrupt priority level ($\overline{\text{IPL0}}$, $\overline{\text{IPL1}}$, $\overline{\text{IPL2}}$)

These inputs indicate the encoded priority level of the device requesting an interrupt. Level seven is the highest priority and cannot be masked; level zero indicates that no interrupts are requested. The least significant bit is $\overline{\text{IPL0}}$ and the most significant bit is $\overline{\text{IPL2}}$.

7.2 Interrupt pending ($\overline{\text{IPEND}}$)

This output indicates that the encoded interrupt priority level active on the $\overline{\text{IPL0}}$-$\overline{\text{IPL2}}$ inputs is higher than the current level of the interrupt mask in the status register or that a non-maskable interrupt has been recognized.

7.3 Autovector ($\overline{\text{AVEC}}$)

The $\overline{\text{AVEC}}$ input is used to request internal generation of the vector number during an interrupt acknowledge cycle.

8. Bus Arbitration Signals

The following paragraphs describe the three-wire bus arbitration pins used to determine which device in a system will be the bus master.

8.1 Bus request ($\overline{\text{BR}}$)

This input is wire-ORed with all request signals from all potential bus masters and indicates that some device other than the MC68020 requires bus mastership.

8.2 Bus grant ($\overline{\text{BG}}$)

This output signal indicates to potential bus masters that the MC68020 will release ownership of the bus when the current bus cycle is completed.

Figure B.5   (continued).

466

8.3 Bus grant acknowledge ($\overline{\text{BGACK}}$)

This input indicates that some other device has become the bus master. This signal should not be asserted until the following conditions are met:

1. $\overline{\text{BG}}$ (bus grant) has been received through the bus arbitration process,
2. $\overline{\text{AS}}$ is negated, indicating that the MC68020 is not using the bus,
3. $\overline{\text{DSACK0}}$ and $\overline{\text{DSACK1}}$ are negated indicating that the previous external device is not using the bus, and
4. $\overline{\text{BGACK}}$ is negated, which indicates that no other device is still claiming bus mastership.

$\overline{\text{BGACK}}$ must remain asserted as long as any other device is bus master.

9. Bus Exception Control Signals

The following paragraphs describe the bus exception control signals for the MC68020.

9.1 Reset ($\overline{\text{RESET}}$)

This bidirectional open-drain signal is used as the systems reset signal. If $\overline{\text{RESET}}$ is asserted as an input, the processor will enter reset exception processing. As an output, the processor asserts $\overline{\text{RESET}}$ to reset external devices, but is not affected internally.

9.2 Halt ($\overline{\text{HALT}}$)

The assertion of this bidirectional, open-drain signal stops all processor bus activity at the completion of the current bus cycle. When the processor has been halted using this input, all control signals will be placed in their inactive state, the R/$\overline{\text{W}}$, function code, and size signals, and the address bus remain driven with the previous bus cycle information. The $\overline{\text{RMC}}$ signal will be driven inactive, if asserted. The data bus is three-stated.

When the processor has stopped executing instructions, due to a double bus fault condition, the $\overline{\text{HALT}}$ line is driven by the processor to indicate to external devices that the processor has stopped.

9.3 Bus error ($\overline{\text{BERR}}$)

This input signal informs the processor that there has been a problem with the bus cycle currently being executed. These problems may be the result of:

1. Nonresponding devices,
2. Interrupt vector number acquisition failure,
3. Illegal accesses as determined by a memory management unit, or
4. Various other application-dependent errors.

The bus error signal interacts with the halt signal to determine if the current bus cycle should be re-run or aborted with a bus error.

Figure B.5 (continued).

10. Clock (CLK)

The MC68020 clock input is a TTL-compatible signal that is internally buffered to develop internal clocks needed by the processor. The clock should not be gated off at any time and must conform to minimum and maximum period and pulse width times.

Figure B.5   (concluded).

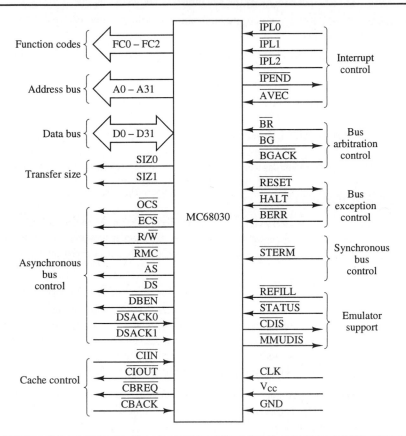

Signal name	Mnemonic	Function
Function codes	FC0-FC3	3-bit function code used to identify the address space of each bus cycle
Address bus	A0-A31	32-bit address bus
Data bus	D0-D31	32-bit data bus used to transfer 8, 16, 24, or 32 bits of data per bus cycle
Size	SIZ0 SIZ1	Indicates the number of bytes remaining to be transferred for this cycle; these signals together with A0 and A1 define the active sections on the data bus
Operand cycle start	$\overline{OCS}$	Identical operation to that of $\overline{ECS}$ except that $\overline{OCS}$ is asserted only during the first bus cycle of an operand transfer
External cycle start	$\overline{ECS}$	Provides an indication that a bus cycle is beginning
Read/write	R $\overline{W}$	Defines the bus transfer as a processor read or write
Read-modify-write cycle	$\overline{RMC}$	Provides an indicator that the current bus cycle is part of an indivisible read-modify-write operation

Figure B.6   68030 I/O pins and signals [8].

Signal name	Mnemonic	Function
Address strobe	$\overline{\text{AS}}$	Indicates that a valid address is on the bus
Data strobe	$\overline{\text{DS}}$	Indicates that valid data is to be placed on the data bus by an external device or has been placed on the data bus by the MC68030
Data buffer enable	$\overline{\text{DBEN}}$	Provides an enable signal for external data buffers
Data transfer and size acknowledge	$\overline{\text{DSACK0}}$ $\overline{\text{DSACK1}}$	Bus response signals that indicate that the requested data transfer operation is completed; in addition these two signals indicate the size of the external bus port on a cycle-by-cycle basis and are used for asynchronous transfers
Synchronous termination	$\overline{\text{STERM}}$	Bus response signal that indicates a port size of 32 bits and that data may be latched on the next falling clock edge
Cache inhibit in	$\overline{\text{CIIN}}$	Prevents data from being loaded into the MC68030 instruction and data caches
Cache inhibit out	$\overline{\text{CIOUT}}$	Reflects the C1 bit in ATC entries or TTx registers; indicates that external caches should ignore these accesses
Cache burst request	$\overline{\text{CBREQ}}$	Indicates a burst request for the instruction or data cache
Cache burst acknowledge	$\overline{\text{CBACK}}$	Indicates that the accessed device can operate in burst mode
Interrupt priority level	$\overline{\text{IPL0-IPL2}}$	Provides an encoded interrupt level to the processor
Interrupt pending	$\overline{\text{IPEND}}$	Indicates that an interrupt is pending
Autovector	$\overline{\text{AVEC}}$	Requests an autovector during an interrupt acknowledge cycle
Bus request	$\overline{\text{BR}}$	Indicates that an external device requires bus mastership
Bus grant	$\overline{\text{BG}}$	Indicates that an external device may assume bus mastership
Bus grant acknowledge	$\overline{\text{BGACK}}$	Indicates that an external device has assumed bus mastership
Reset	$\overline{\text{RESET}}$	System reset
Halt	$\overline{\text{HALT}}$	Indicates that the processor should suspend bus activity
Bus error	$\overline{\text{BERR}}$	Indicates that an erroneous bus operation is being attempted
Cache disable	$\overline{\text{CDIS}}$	Dynamically disables the on-chip cache to assist emulator support
MMU disable	$\overline{\text{MMUDIS}}$	Dynamically disables the translation mechanism of the MMU
Pipeline refill	$\overline{\text{REFILL}}$	Indicates that the MC68030 is beginning to fill pipeline
Microsequencer status	$\overline{\text{STATUS}}$	Indicates the state of the microsequencer
Clock	CLK	Clock input to the processor
Power supply	V_{CC}	Power supply
Ground	GND	Ground connection

Figure B.6 (concluded).

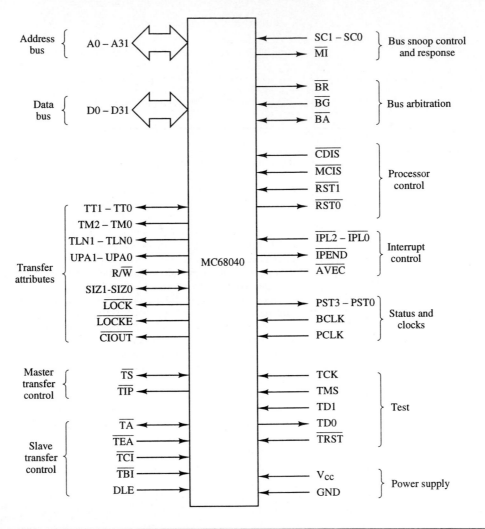

Signal name	Mnemonic	Function
Address bus	A31-A0	32-bit address bus used to address any of 4 Gbytes
Data bus	D31-D0	32-bit data bus used to transfer up to 32 bits of data per bus transfer
Transfer type	TT1, TT0	Indicates the general transfer type: normal, MOVE 16, alternate logical function code, and acknowledge
Transfer modifier	TM2, TM0	Indicates supplemental information about the access
Transfer line number	TLN1, TLN0	Indicates which cache line in a set is being pushed or loaded by the current line transfer
User programmable attributes	UPA1, UPA0	User defined signals, controlled by the corresponding user attribute bits from the address translation entry
Read/write	R/$\overline{\text{W}}$	Identifies the transfer as a read or write
Transfer size	SIZ1, SIZ0	Indicates the data transfer size; these signals, together with A0 and A1, define the active sections of the data bus

Figure B.7   68040 I/O pins and signals [9].

Signal name	Mnemonic	Function
Bus lock	$\overline{\text{LOCK}}$	Indicates a bus transfer is part of read-modify-write operation, and that the sequence of transfers should not be interrupted
Bus lock end	$\overline{\text{LOCKE}}$	Indicates the current transfer is the last in a locked sequence of transfers
Cache inhibit out	$\overline{\text{CIOUT}}$	Indicates the processor will not cache the current bus transfer
Transfer start	$\overline{\text{TS}}$	Indicates the beginning of a bus transfer
Transfer in progress	$\overline{\text{TIP}}$	Asserted for the duration of a bus transfer
Transfer acknowledge	$\overline{\text{TA}}$	Asserted to acknowledge a bus transfer
Transfer error acknowledge	$\overline{\text{TEA}}$	Indicates an error condition exists for a bus transfer
Transfer cache inhibit	$\overline{\text{TCI}}$	Indicates the current bus transfer should not be cached
Transfer burst inhibit	$\overline{\text{TBI}}$	Indicates the slave cannot handle a line burst access
Data latch enable	DLE	Alternate clock input used to latch input data when the processor is operating in DLE mode
Snoop control	SC1, SC0	Indicates the snooping operation required during an alternate master access
Memory inhibit	$\overline{\text{MI}}$	Inhibits memory devices from responding to an alternate master access during snooping operations
Bus request	$\overline{\text{BR}}$	Asserted by the processor to request bus mastership
Bus grant	$\overline{\text{BG}}$	Asserted by an arbiter to grant bus mastership to the processor
Bus busy	$\overline{\text{BB}}$	Asserted by the current bus master to indicate it has assumed ownership of the bus
Cache disable	$\overline{\text{CDIS}}$	Dynamically disables the internal caches to assist emulator support
MMU disable	$\overline{\text{MDIS}}$	Disables the translation mechanism of the MMUs
Reset in	$\overline{\text{RSTI}}$	Processor reset
Reset out	$\overline{\text{RSTO}}$	Asserted during execution of a RESET instruction to reset external devices
Interrupt priority level	$\overline{\text{IPL2-IPL0}}$	Provides an encoded interrupt level to the processor
Interrupt pending	$\overline{\text{IPEND}}$	Indicates an interrupt is pending
Auto-vector	$\overline{\text{AVEC}}$	Used during an interrupt acknowledge transfer to request internal generation of the vector number
Processor status	PST3-PST0	Indicates internal processor status
Bus clock	BCLK	Clock input used to derive all bus signal timing
Processor clock	PCLK	Clock input used for internal logic timing; the PCLK frequency is exactly 2X the BCLK frequency
Test clock	TCK	Clock signal for the IEEEP1149.1 Test Access Port (TAP)
Test mode select	TMS	Selects the principle operations of the test-support circuitry
Test data input	TDI	Serial data input for the TAP
Test data output	TDO	Serial data output for the TAP
Test reset	$\overline{\text{TRST}}$	Provides an asynchronous reset of the TAP controller
Power supply	V_{CC}	Power supply
Ground	GND	Ground connection

Figure B.7 (continued).

Table B.2 Processor Status Encoding

PST3	PST2	PST1	PST0	Internal status
0	0	0	0	User start continue current instruction
0	0	0	1	User end current instruction
0	0	1	0	User branch not taken and end current instruction
0	0	1	1	User branch taken and end current instruction
0	1	0	0	User table search
0	1	0	1	Halted state (double-bus fault)
0	1	1	0	Reserved
0	1	1	1	Reserved
1	0	0	0	Supervisor start/continue current instruction
1	0	0	1	Supervisor end current instruction
1	0	1	0	Supervisor branch not taken and end current instruction
1	0	1	1	Supervisor branch taken and end current instruction
1	1	0	0	Supervisor table search
1	1	0	1	Stopped state (supervisor instruction)
1	1	1	0	RTE executed
1	1	1	1	Exception stacking

Table B.3. Transfer Size Encoding

SIZ1	SIZ0	Requested size
0	0	Long word (4 Bytes)
0	1	Byte
1	0	Word (2 Bytes)
1	1	Line (16 Bytes)

Table B.4 Transfer-Type Encoding

TT1	TT0	Transfer type
0	0	Normal access
0	1	MOVE 16 access
1	0	Alternate logical function code access
1	1	Acknowledge access

Table B.5 Normal and MOVE 16 Access TM Encoding

TM2	TM1	TM0	Transfer modifier
0	0	0	Data cache push access
0	0	1	User data access[a]
0	1	0	User code access
0	1	1	MMU table search data access
1	0	0	MMU table search code access
1	0	1	Supervisor data access[a]
1	1	0	Supervisor code access
1	1	1	Reserved

[a]MOVE 16 accesses only use these encodings.

Figure B.7 (continued).

Table B.6		Alternate Access TM Encoding	
TM2	TM1	TM0	Transfer modifier
0	0	0	Logical function code 0
0	0	1	Reserved
0	1	0	Reserved
0	1	1	Logical function code 3
1	0	0	Logical function code 4
1	0	1	Reserved
1	1	0	Reserved
1	1	1	Logical function code 7

Table B.7	TLN Encoding	
TLN1	TLN0	Line
0	0	Zero
0	1	One
1	0	Two
1	1	Three

Table B.8 Output Driver Control Groups

Signal	Output buffers controlled
$\overline{\text{IPL2}}$	Data bus: D31–D0
$\overline{\text{IPL1}}$	Address bus and transfer attributes: A31–A0, $\overline{\text{CIOUT}}$, $\overline{\text{LOCK}}$, $\overline{\text{LOCKE}}$, R/$\overline{\text{W}}$, SIZ1–SIZ0, TLN1–TLN0, TM2–TM0, TT1–TT0, UPA1–UPA0
$\overline{\text{IPL0}}$	Miscellaneous control signals: $\overline{\text{BB}}$, $\overline{\text{BR}}$, $\overline{\text{IPEND}}$, $\overline{\text{MI}}$, PST3–PST0, $\overline{\text{RSTO}}$, $\overline{\text{TA}}$, $\overline{\text{TIP}}$, $\overline{\text{TS}}$

Note: High input level = small buffers enabled, low = large buffers enabled.

Table B.9 Snoop Control Encoding

		Requested snoop operation	
SC1	SC0	Read access	Write Access
0	0	Inhibit snooping	Inhibit snooping
0	1	Supply dirty data and leave dirty	Sink byte/word/long-word data
1	0	Supply dirty data and mark line invalid	Invalidate line
1	1	Reserved (snoop inhibited)	Reserved (snoop inhibited)

Figure B.7 (concluded).

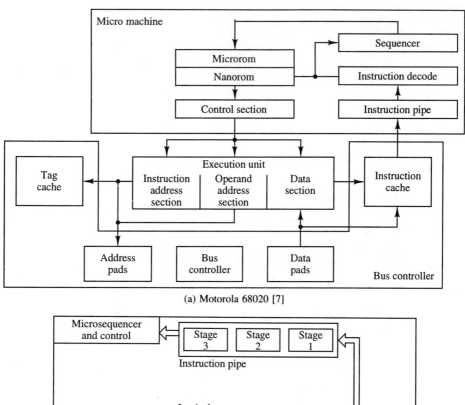

(a) Motorola 68020 [7]

The 68020 does not have the data cache and the MMU/ATC.
(b) Motorola 68030

Figure B.8 Motorola 68020/30/40 internal organizations.

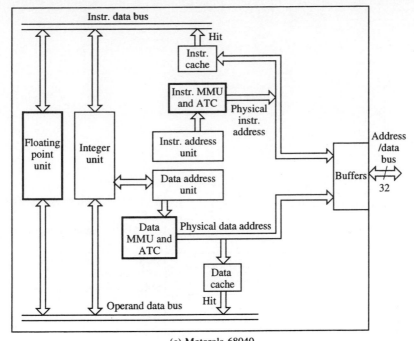

(c) Motorola 68040

Figure B.8   (concluded).

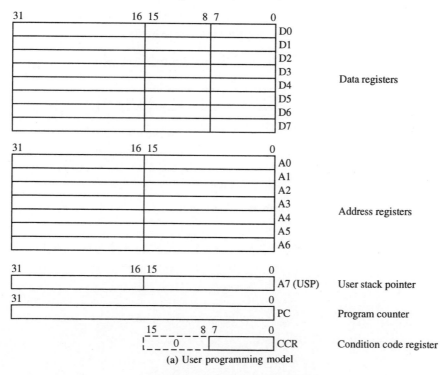

(a) User programming model

Figure B.9   68020 register structure [7].

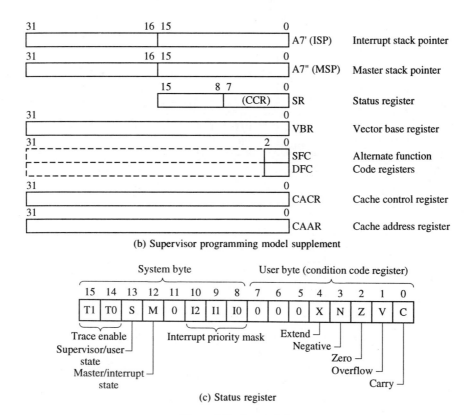

(b) Supervisor programming model supplement

(c) Status register

Figure B.9 (concluded).

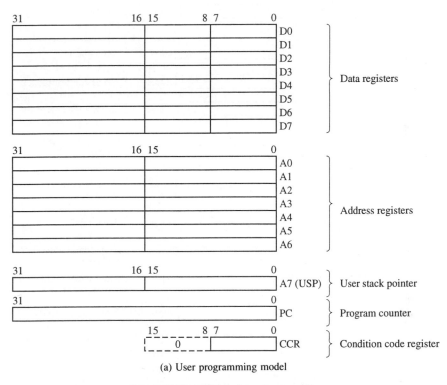

(a) User programming model

Figure B.10 68030 register structure [8].

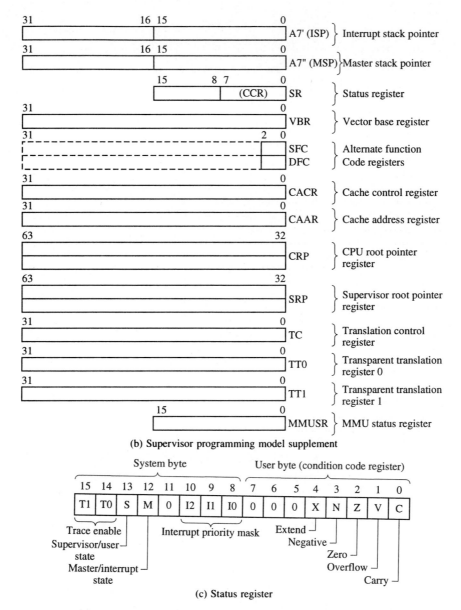

(b) Supervisor programming model supplement

(c) Status register

Figure B.10 (concluded).

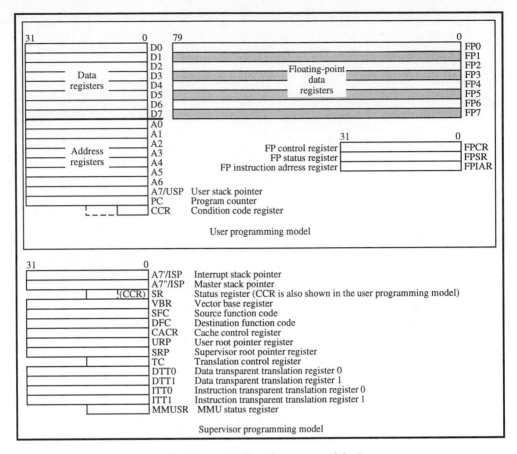

Figure B.11 68040 register structure [a].

B.2.3 680x0 State Transition and Timing Diagrams

The operation of these Motorola 32-bit products is not that much different from that of the 16-bit 68000. They have two separate 32-bit nonmultiplexed buses (one for addresses, the other for data). While both the 68020 and the 68030 support both synchronous and asynchronous bus transfers, the 68040 supports only synchronous transfers. Figure 1.18a in Chapter 1 shows the state transition diagram of the 68020/30, and Figure 1.18b the basic operations for a read and a write cycle: the 68020/30 executes a bus cycle in three input clock CLK cycles C1, C2, C3 (or six states S0–S5), data of 32 bits in width are transferred over the 32-bit data bus D0–D31 during C2 (for a write operation) or during C3 (for a read operation), and wait states are inserted in pairs of Sw (one pair equals one input clock cycle) between S2 and S3. The Motorola 68020/30 microprocessors provide for dynamically reconfigurable buses (the 68040 does not); they adjust their bus sizes by issuing the "data width identifier" SIZ1 and SIZ0 and monitoring the values of the incoming "port width identifier" signals DSACK1# and DSACK0#, which indicate the width of the responding slave device. In the 68020/30, synchronization between the processor and memory is achieved with the use of these DSACKx# signals.

The manifestations of the Motorola 68020/30 state transition diagram of Figure 1.18a in the form of a local bus timing diagram and flowchart are shown in Figure 2.13a and b of Chapter 2; the input clock cycle C corresponds to two S states of the 68020/30. Figure 2.13b shows the flowchart for a doubleword read cycle.

A normal read or write bus cycle is three input clock cycles long C1, C2, C3 (or 6 S states). The 68020/30 local bus is nonmultiplexed and asynchronous. The processor places on the address bus the 30 most significant address bits A2–A31; as depicted in Figure 2.12, the two address signals A0 and A1 will be decoded by external hardware logic along with the two "data width identifier" output signals SIZ0 and SIZ1 to generate the proper values on the four "section select" signals DBBE1–DBBE4 sent to memory.

The microprocessor issues the synchronization signal AS# to indicate to the slave device that a valid address is on the address bus; when the slave device has completed the transaction of placing its data on the data bus (for a read cycle), or latched the data off the data bus (for a write cycle), it will respond back to the processor with the two feedback signals DSACK0# and DSACK1#. If the DSACKx# inputs are not asserted during the sample window of the falling edge of S2, the processor will insert wait states until these signals are sampled asserted. This pair of DSACKx# signals not only synchronizes the processor with the memory slave, it also indicates what the width of the responding memory is ("port width identifier"), as shown in one of the two tables in Figure 2.13a. As we explain in Chapter 2, where we discuss "dynamic bus sizing," if the responding slave device has a width smaller than 32 bits, the processor will have to dynamically adjust its data bus width to interpret properly the data on its input data lines, and decide whether it is necessary to execute additional bus cycles in order to complete the operand transfer operation.

The 68040 is interconnected to main memory like the 68020/30 (Figure 2.12 in Chapter 2). Its state transition and timing diagrams are given in Figure 2.14. The 68040 is a 32-bit big-endian microprocessor, but it has the following *differences* from the 68020/30:

1. The 68040 has a synchronous bus; synchronization is achieved with the use of the "transfer acknowledge" TA# signal that memory sends back to the processor.
2. The value SIZ1,SIZ0 = 1,1 indicates a "line transfer," i.e., four consecutive 4-byte transfers for a 4-doubleword burst transfer. The "data width identifier" signals SIZx correspond to the specific bus cycle and do not indicate how many bytes may be remaining for the operand transfer.
3. The 68040 has a 2-input-clock-cycle bus cycle as compared with the 3-input-clock-cycle bus cycle of the 68020/30.
4. The 68040 does not support dynamic bus sizing; data transfer between the processor and memory or peripheral device is done using a fixed 32-bit data port width.
5. It has two input pins for clocks: BCLK (bus clock signal) and PCLK (processor clock signal). The PCLK signal is exactly twice the frequency of the BCLK signal.
6. In the 68040, an input clock cycle C (or BCLK) consists of 4 T states (instead of the 2 S states of the 68020/30).
7. In the 68040, wait states are inserted in quadruples of T_W (one quadruple equals one input clock cycle BCLK) after C2.

B.2.4 68020/30 Asynchronous Data Transfers

Memory read cycles. The 16-bit operand B1B0 (of which B1 is the most significant byte) will be stored in any of the three locations 4N, 4N + 1, or 4N + 2, and will be fetched in one bus cycle over data bus lines D16–D31, D8–D23, and D0–D15, respectively. The bus cycle at the left-hand side of Figure B.9a shows the timing diagram for a word read cycle from location 4N of a 32-bit memory. The bus cycle at the right-hand side of Figure B.12a shows the timing diagram for a byte read cycle from location 4N + 2 of a 32-bit memory.

Memory write cycles. For a write cycle the processor always drives all four byte lanes at the start of a bus cycle. Figure 2.15 in Chapter 2 gives the table that reflects the rules the processor follows for placing the operand bytes on its external data bus byte lanes during memory write cycles. The entries shown as Bn are the portions of the operand placed on the data bus during that bus cycle and are defined by SIZ0, SIZ1, A0, and A1.

The rules of the table in Figure 2.15 have been used in the write cycles of Figure B.12b. The left-hand side shows a word write cycle: the word is to be written to location 4N + 2 and therefore is transferred over D0–D15 (and duplicated on the upper two byte lanes of the data bus). The right-hand side shows a byte write cycle: the byte is to be written to location 4N + 2 and therefore is transferred over D8–D15 (and duplicated on all other three data bus byte lanes). In these diagrams, the size of the operand to be transferred is identified by the processor issuing output signals SIZ0 and SIZ1 with values 0,1 for a word operand and 1,0 for a byte operand.

B.2.5 68020/30 Synchronous Data Transfers

Both the Motorola 68020 and the 68030 support synchronous bus cycles, but the memory port used must now be 32 bits wide. Instead of the feedback data transfer acknowledge and "port width identifier" signals DSACK0# and DSACK1#, when a bus is terminated by asserting the synchronous termination signal STERM#, that cycle becomes a synchronous cycle, as shown in Figure B.13. (Neither the DSACKx# signals nor the autovector signal AVEC# must be asserted during the cycle to make it a synchronous cycle.) The STERM# signal can be generated by external logic decoding the values on the address bus and the function code FC0–FC2 outputs. Since STERM# can be asserted earlier than the two DSACKx# signals of an asynchronous bus, a synchronous data transfer can be executed in 2 instead of 3 input clock cycles; i.e., the synchronous bus cycle terminates at the end of clock cycle C2. As we see in Chapter 2, the 68020/30 "burst transfer" mode requires synchronous bus cycles.

B.2.6 68030/40 Descriptor Formats

In Section 6.4.6 we discussed the Motorola page descriptor formats. Figure B.14 shows an expanded version of Figure 6.15. Is shows the format of the "root pointer registers" (that point to the root table—supervisor or user—of the page descriptor table tree in memory as

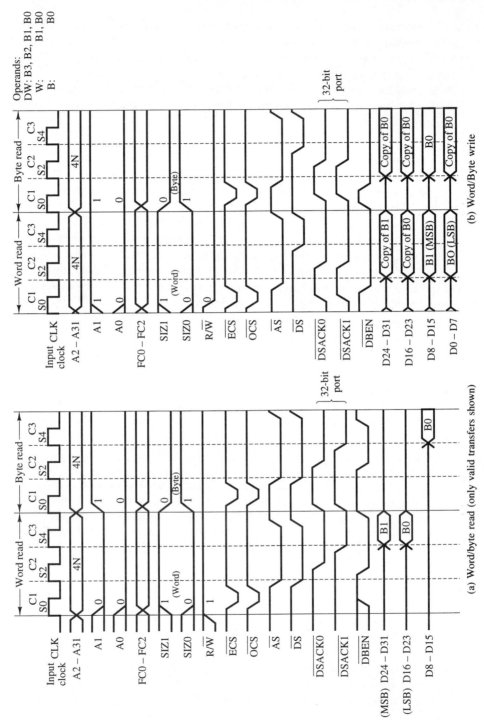

Figure B.12 Motorola 68020/30 word and byte read/write timing diagrams (32-bit port).

(a) Word/byte read (only valid transfers shown)

(b) Word/Byte write

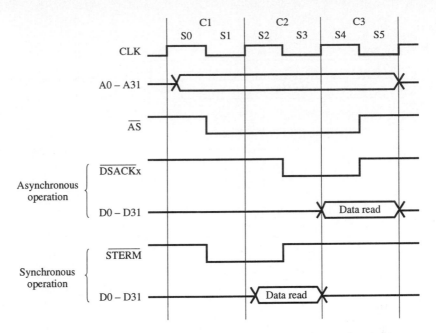

Figure B.13 Motorola 68020/30 32-bit asynchronous and synchronous bus timings.

shown in Figure 6.14), and for the page and table descriptors their short (4 bytes) and long (8 bytes) formats.

Figure B.15 shows the Motorola 68040 page descriptor and table descriptor formats. Figure B.15a shows the 68040 formats of the first-level and second-level table descriptors (two formats are possible at the second-level to support 4K and 8K pages), and Figure B.15b the 68040 page descriptor formats for 4K and 8K page sizes.

The physical address of an "indirect descriptor"[3] contains a pointer to the actual page descriptor. This descriptor indirection is used to facilitate the sharing of pages (allows multiple tasks to access a single page descriptor in order to share a physical page or a table).

The "supervisor-only" bit S and the "write-protected" bit W in the descriptor are used for protection.

---

[3]In the Motorola 68030, the "short" and "long" indirect descriptors do not have a unique descriptor type code as in the 68040. Instead, they reside in the leaf page table and are neither page descriptors nor invalid descriptors.

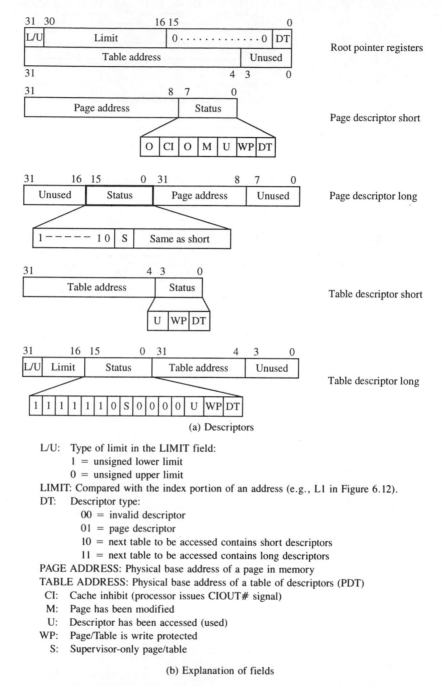

(a) Descriptors

L/U: Type of limit in the LIMIT field:
    1 = unsigned lower limit
    0 = unsigned upper limit
LIMIT: Compared with the index portion of an address (e.g., L1 in Figure 6.12).
DT: Descriptor type:
    00 = invalid descriptor
    01 = page descriptor
    10 = next table to be accessed contains short descriptors
    11 = next table to be accessed contains long descriptors
PAGE ADDRESS: Physical base address of a page in memory
TABLE ADDRESS: Physical base address of a table of descriptors (PDT)
  CI: Cache inhibit (processor issues CIOUT# signal)
  M: Page has been modified
  U: Descriptor has been accessed (used)
WP: Page/Table is write protected
  S: Supervisor-only page/table

(b) Explanation of fields

Figure B.14 Motorola 68030 root pointer, and table and page descriptor formats [8].

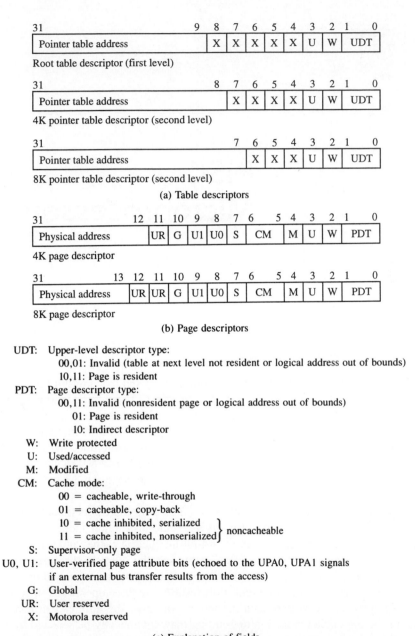

31   **9 8 7 6 5 4 3 2 1 0**

| Pointer table address | X | X | X | X | X | U | W | UDT |

Root table descriptor (first level)

31   **8 7 6 5 4 3 2 1 0**

| Pointer table address | X | X | X | X | U | W | UDT |

4K pointer table descriptor (second level)

31   **7 6 5 4 3 2 1 0**

| Pointer table address | X | X | X | U | W | UDT |

8K pointer table descriptor (second level)

(a) Table descriptors

31   **12 11 10 9 8 7 6 5 4 3 2 1 0**

| Physical address | UR | G | U1 | U0 | S | CM | M | U | W | PDT |

4K page descriptor

31   **13 12 11 10 9 8 7 6 5 4 3 2 1 0**

| Physical address | UR | UR | G | U1 | U0 | S | CM | M | U | W | PDT |

8K page descriptor

(b) Page descriptors

UDT: Upper-level descriptor type:
         00,01: Invalid (table at next level not resident or logical address out of bounds)
         10,11: Page is resident

PDT: Page descriptor type:
         00,11: Invalid (nonresident page or logical address out of bounds)
         01: Page is resident
         10: Indirect descriptor

W: Write protected

U: Used/accessed

M: Modified

CM: Cache mode:
         00 = cacheable, write-through
         01 = cacheable, copy-back
         10 = cache inhibited, serialized ⎫
         11 = cache inhibited, nonserialized ⎭ noncacheable

S: Supervisor-only page

U0, U1:   User-verified page attribute bits (echoed to the UPA0, UPA1 signals if an external bus transfer results from the access)

G: Global

UR: User reserved

X: Motorola reserved

(c) Explanation of fields

Figure B.15   Motorola 68040 table and page descriptor formats [9].

C

RISC
Microprocessors

C.1 INTEL i860

C.1.1 i860 I/O Pins and Signals

The i860 (or 80860) is a RISC-type microprocessor, and has a 64-bit internal and external data bus and 32-bit internal integer registers. Figure C.1 shows the i860 I/O pins and signals and gives a short explanation. The address bus is 32 bits, allowing the processor to directly access 4 gigabytes of memory. Pipelining is used throughout the microprocessor to achieve maximum performance. In addition to its integer processing unit, the i860 has an on-chip MMU with paging (the same paging system of the 80386 and 80486 has been duplicated on the i860), a floating-point unit, a 4-Kbyte instruction cache, an 8-Kbyte data cache, and a 3D graphics unit.

The i860 takes advantage of all these on-chip multiple functional units and issues up to three instructions per clock cycle. In its "dual-instruction mode" the microprocessor fetches two 32-bit instructions from the 64-bit instruction cache, and can route one of them to the integer execution unit (the RISC core) and the other to the floating-point unit for parallel operation [10]. In the best case, a parallel execution of an add and a multiply can be initiated in the floating-point unit, thus resulting in three operations in each clock cycle.

The processor can store data in memory in either the little-endian mode (the default case) or the big-endian mode (an option that may dynamically be selected by software executing in supervisor mode). Code accesses are always done with little-endian addressing.

C.1.2 i860 Internal Organization and Register Structure

Figure C.2a shows the block diagram of the internal structure of the i860 processor and Figure C.2b its register structure [10–12]. The processor includes an integer execution section,

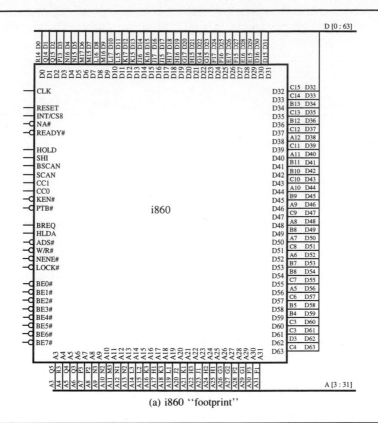

(a) i860 "footprint"

Pin name[a]	Function	Active state	Input/output
Execution Control Pins			
CLK	CLocK		I
RESET	System reset	High	I
HOLD	Bus hold	High	I
HLDA	Bus hold acknowledge	High	O
BREQ	Bus request	High	O
INT/CS8	Interrupt, code-size	High	I
Bus Interface Pins			
A31–A3	Address bus	High	O
BE7#–BE0#	Byte enables	Low	O
D63–D0	Data bus	High	I/O
LOCK#	Bus lock	Low	O
W/R#	Write/read bus cycle	Hi/Low	O
NENE#	Next near	Low	O
NA#	Next address request	Low	I
READY#	Transfer acknowledge	Low	I
ADS#	Address status	Low	O

Figure C.1 Intel i860 I/O pins and signals [12]. Reprinted by permission of Intel Corporation, Copyright/Intel Corporation 1990.

Pin name[a]	Function	Active state	Input/output
	Cache Interface Pins		
KEN#	Cache enable	Low	I
PTB	Page table bit	High	O
	Testability Pins		
SHI	Boundary scan shift input	High	I
BSCN	Boundary scan enable	High	I
SCAN	Shift scan path	High	I
	Intel-Reserved Configuration Pins		
CC1–CC0	Configuration	High	I
	Power and Ground Pins		
V_{cc}	System power		
V_{ss}	System ground		

[a]A # after a pin name indicates that the signal is active at the low voltage level.

(b) i860 pin and signal memory

The external interface of the i860 microprocessor consists of a 64-bit data bus, 29-bit address bus, eight-bit byte-enable control bus, 19 status and control signals, and 48 power and ground pins. This section provides an overview of the services provided by the external interface of the i860 microprocessor.

i860 Microprocessor Buses

The i860 microprocessor communicates with external memory and I/O through a synchronous bus interface that includes a separate data and address bus as follows:

D63–D0   These 64 pins make up the bidirectional data bus external interface. Either 8, 16, 32, or 64 bits of data can be transferred during a bus cycle.

A31–A3   The address bus consists of 29 address pins which address one of 2^{29} 64-bit memory locations.

BE7#–BE0#   The byte-enable bus consists of eight pins that specify which bytes to access within a 64-bit location. These pins are used to enable writing in one, two, four or eight-bytes of the double-word involved in the current write cycle. Read operations should always return 64-bits of data. BE2#, BE1#, BE0# are used as address bits A2, A1, A0 respectively while in CS8 mode.

i860 Microprocessor Output Signals

The i860 microprocessor output signals provide control and status information. The output signals are as follows:

Figure C.1   (continued).

488

ADS#	The i860 microprocessor asserts the address status signal to indicate the beginning of a bus cycle. It identifies the clock period during which it provides a valid address and the other signals required to perform a memory cycle.
W/R#	The write/read# signal indicates whether the current cycle is a write (high state) to or read (low state) from the memory or I/O subsystem.
LOCK#	The lock signal is generated by the processor to indicate locked cycles to external circuitry.
NENE#	The next near signal tells the memory subsystem that a cycle is on the same DRAM row as a previous cycle. This allows the memory subsystem to use page mode or static-column mode features of DRAMs.
PTB	The page table bit signal reflects either the value of the cache disable (CD) bit, or the write through (WT) bit of page table entry during the current cycle. The PBM (page-table bit mode) bit of the EPSR indicates which. If PBM is clear, PTB reflects CD; otherwise, it reflects WT.
HLDA	The hold acknowledge signal indicates that the bus has been released.
BREQ	The bus request signal is asserted when an internal bus request is pending. This signal is used to assist external bus arbitration. Its value is independent of the state of HOLD and HOLDA.
	BREQ is also used as serial output for the boundary scan chain while in boundary scan mode.
INT/CS8	The interrupt and code size signal serves two functions. When the RESET signal is asserted, the CS8 signal can be used to set the code size eight mode to indicate whether the bus performs instruction fetches on the low-order byte of the bus instead of the 64 bit-wide bus. This feature allows booting from a single EPROM. At all other times, this pin serves as the INT signal and functions as the i860 microprocessor's maskable external interrupt. The state of the INT input is sampled on every clock.
KEN#	The cache enable signal enables updates to the processor's instruction and data caches. When paging is enabled, this signal works in combination with the WT, CD, and PTB bits of the current bus cycle. KEN# is sampled on every bus cycle.
HOLD	The bus hold signal floats all output signals except HOLDA and BREQ and causes the processor to relinquish control of the bus. The HLDA signal indicates that the bus has been granted. Instruction execution continues unless required instructions and data cannot be read from the on-chip cache. The state of this pin is sampled every clock.
SHI	The boundary scan shift input signal is used to read boundary scan chain serial data when in boundary scan mode.
BSCN	The boundary scan enable signal enables boundary scan mode for board or component testing.
SCAN	The shift scan is used in conjunction with boundary scan mode to set normal mode (when SCAN is deasserted) or shift mode (when SCAN is asserted).
CC1, CC0	These pins are reserved by Intel and must be strapped low.

Figure C.1   (continued).

i860 Microprocessor Input Signals

Input signals control various i860 microprocessor actions:

CLK — The clock input provides basic timing information for the processor to synchronize internal and external operations. All other signals are sampled relative to the rising edge of CLK. The internal operating frequency is the same as the clock frequency.

READY# — The ready signal indicates to the processor that a bus cycle is finished. For read cycles, the READY# signal indicates that data being read is valid and that the processor can latch the contents of the data bus. For write cycles, it indicates that the data being output to the data bus is being latched by the memory subsystem and is no longer needed to finish the bus cycle. READY# must be synchronous to CLK; it is sampled on every clock after the clock which follows the sampling of ADS#.

NA# — The next address signal allows external data transfers to request pipelining. The signal indicates to the processor that the memory or I/O subsystem is ready to receive a new address and begin a pipelined cycle. NA# is sampled during the second clock after ADS# (further explanation).

i860 Power and Ground Pins

The i860 microprocessor has 24 ground pins and 24 power pins. The *i860 64-Bit Microprocessor Data Sheet* provides pin number assignments, detailed electrical characteristics, and decoupling requirements.

(c) Explanation of the i860 signals

Figure C.1 (concluded).

---

a floating-point execution section, instruction and data caches, an on-chip paged-MMU, and a 3-D graphics unit.

Instructions executed by the 4-stage-pipelined integer unit (in the RISC core) are 32 bits long and have the traditional RISC three-operand load/store format. The floating point unit includes 3-stage-pipelined add and multiply units (there is no hardware floating-point divide unit and, therefore, divide operations must be implemented in software), can perform single- and double-precision arithmetic, and the floating-point instructions support both a scalar and a pipelined mode of operation.

The i860 has two separate virtually addressed caches,[1] one for instructions (4 Kbytes) and the other for data (8 Kbytes). Both caches are implemented as a 2-way set-associative memory, but the instruction cache is 64 bits wide, while the data cache is 128 bits wide. In either case, the block frame is 32 bytes long (four 64-bit quantities) mapping blocks of 32 consecutive bytes loaded from an address having zero for the least significant 5 bits; this cache filling uses a wraparound technique (the processor wraps around to read the first 64-bit quantity of the block after the last one is read). Write operations to the data cache use the write-back policy, and when the data cache writes a bloc to memory, it uses two 128-bit

---

[1]Therefore, software must avoid the aliasing of data; within a context each physical address must only be accessed with one logical address; and during context switches, the instruction cache must be invalidated and the data cache flushed [10].

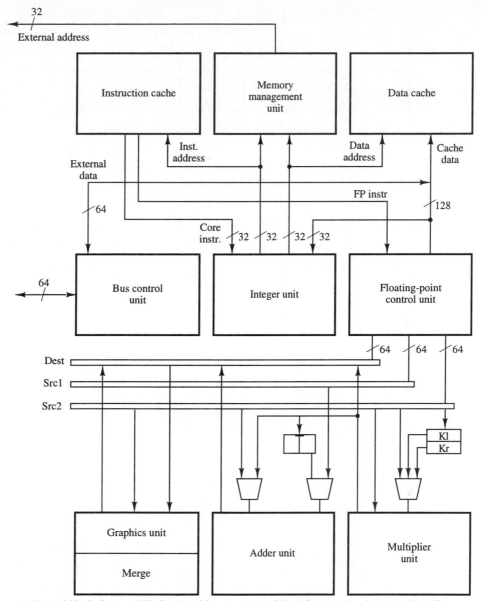

(a) Internal block diagram [12] (Reprinted by permission of Intel Corporation, Copyright/Intel Corporation 1990.)

Figure C.2 Intel i860 internal block diagram and register structure.

wide write buffers. The processor can execute in parallel two instructions by having its control unit fetch two 32-bit instructions from the internal 64-bit wide instruction cache and move one of them to the integer unit and the other to the floating-point unit.

The i860 paged-MMU functions the same and uses the same page table entry formats as the Intel 80386 and 80486 microprocessors. The paged-MMU's operation is optional (can be disabled by software); when enabled, it provides page-level protection based on access

Integer registers		Floating-point registers	
R1		F1	F0
R2		F3	F2
R3		F5	F4
R4		F7	F6
R5		F9	F8
R6		F11	F10
R7		F13	F12
R8		F15	F14
R9		F17	F16
R10		F19	F18
R11		F21	F20
R12		F23	F22
R13		F25	F24
R14		F27	F26
R15		F29	F28
R16		F31	F30
R17			
R18			
R19			
R20			
R21			
R22			
R23			
R24			
R25			
R26			
R27			
R28			
R29			
R30			
R31			

Special-purpose floating-point registers

KR	
KL	
T	
Merge	

Control registers

Fault instruction pointer
Processor status
Extended processor status
Page directory base
Data breakpoint
Floating-point status

(b) i860 programmer model [10] (© 1989 IEEE.)

Figure C.2   (concluded).

rights, as well 2 levels of privilege—user and supervisor. Both logical and physical addresses are 32 bits wide and each consists of a 20-bit page address and a 12-bit offset (thus, a page frame consists of 4 Kbytes of contiguous physical memory starting on a 4-Kbyte boundary). The MMU hardware contains a 64-entry TLB designed as a 4-way set-associative cache; TLB misses has the MMU hardware execute a 2-level page table walk algorithm. Finally, the on-chip graphics unit executes instructions designed to support high-performance 3-D graphics applications.

There are thirty-two 32 integer registers (in what is referred to as "RISC core"); these register may be loaded or stored from 8-, 16-, or 32-bit quantities in memory. A second set of thirty-two 32-bit registers is included in the floating-point section, supporting floating-point and some integer and graphics operations; these registers may be loaded and stored individually, in pairs, or in quads from 32-, 64-, or 128-bit quantities in memory.

C.1.3 i860 State Transition and Bus Timing Diagrams

The 64-bit data bus is fully synchronous, and minimum read and write cycles can be done in two clock cycles. *I/O is "memory-mapped"* (i.e., the processor has no I/O instructions nor separate I/O space). There is one input clock CLK whose clock cycle time determines the duration of the state. The bus cycle has two states, T1 and T11 (Figure C.3a). Figures C.3b and c show both the simplified and complete timing diagrams for an aligned read and an aligned write bus cycle. (The i860 does not allow—i.e., traps—misaligned accesses). A bus cycle begins when the chip's bus controller asserts the ADS# signal and ends when Ready# is sampled active. The address bus A31–A3 carries the upper 29 bits of the physical address of a 64-bit operand.

Eight-, 16-, and 32-bit memory read operations are accomplished by first reading 64 bits of data and extracting the data bytes needed. Data extraction is done by shifting all 64 bits so that the least significant byte of the operand is aligned with bits D7–D0 of the internal register. When placed into a register, 8- and 16-bit integer data are sign-extended to 32 bits. During read operations, the 8 "byte enable" signals BE0#–BE7# are not used to enable memory for specific bytes (BE0# triggers memory byte Section 0 connected the D7–D0 data bus byte lane). These signals are, however, used by memory during write cycles; writing is done by the processor properly aligning the data to be written onto the data bus and writing only on the bytes involved within the 64-bit operand addressed.

The bus optionally allows for bus pipelining[2] (i.e., a new cycle starts prior to the completion of the current one). Instead of the one level that the 80386 allows, the i860 can implement two levels of address pipelining, which is more effective when the memory subsystem is 4-way interleaved (see Figure 3.25).

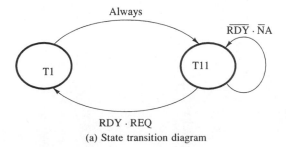

(a) State transition diagram

Figure C.3 i860 State transition and (read and write) bus timing diagrams [12].

[2]This is sometimes called "external pipeline."

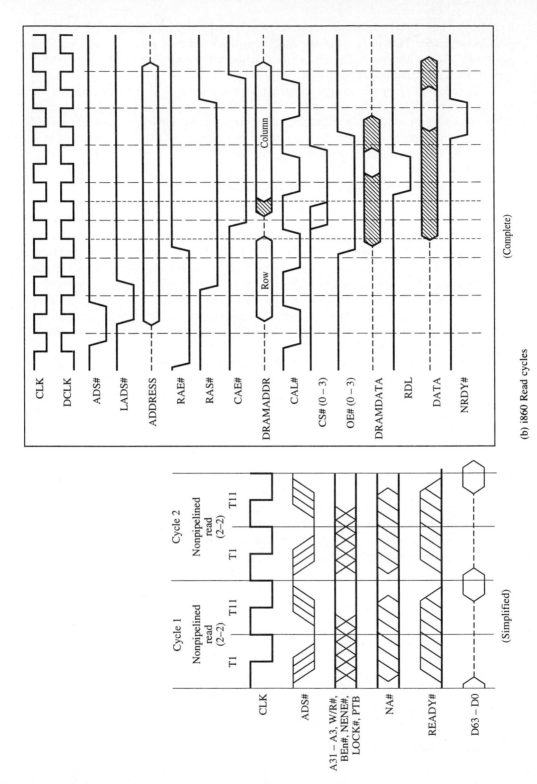

(Complete)

(b) i860 Read cycles

Figure C.3 (continued) [12] (Reprinted by permission of Intel Corporation, Copyright/Intel Corporation 1990.)

494

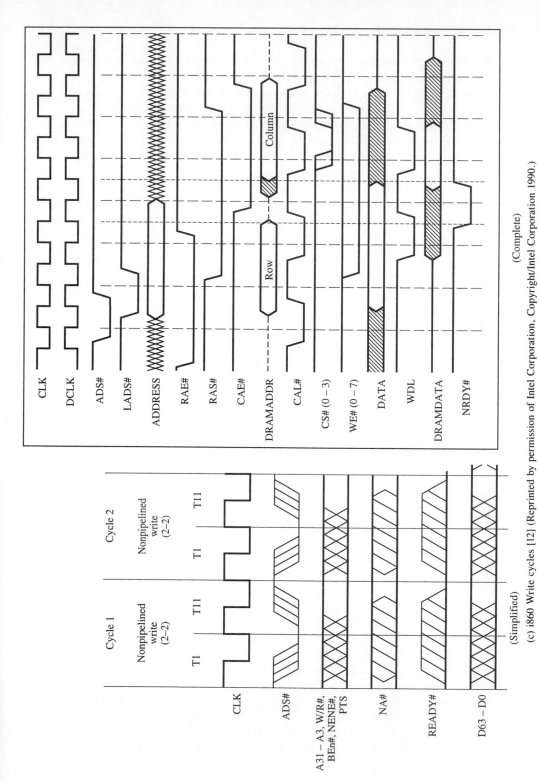

(c) i860 Write cycles [12] (Reprinted by permission of Intel Corporation, Copyright/Intel Corporation 1990.)

Figure C.3 (concluded).

C.2 MOTOROLA 88000-SERIES

The Motorola 88000-series includes the 88100 and the 88100 RISC microprocessors. The 88100 is the first implementation of the 88000 architecture and it is a three-chip set, requiring one CPU (88100) chip and two (or more) cache-MMU chips (88200), one supplying the processor with instructions, the other supplying it with data; the 88100 processor can support up to 8 external CMMUs [13–15]; such a configuration is shown in Figure C.4 (also see Figures 5.2 and 6.1). Although the 88100 can achieve a 1-instruction-per-clock-cycle rate, the superscalar 88110 dispatches multiple instructions each clock cycle and can achieve a throughput of greater than 1-instruction-per-clock-cycle. The 88110 has integrated on the same chip with the rest of the CPU the FPU, an instruction cache, a data cache, and a couple of graphic units. Both the 88100 and 88110 have 32-bit internal general-purpose (integer) registers, but the 88100 has two separate 32-bit external buses in Harvard architecture (one for instructions and the other for data), and the 88110 has one common external bus with a 32-bit address bus and a 64-bit data bus.

C.2.1 88100 I/O Pins and Signals

Figure C.5 gives the definitions of the 88100 I/O pins and signals.

C.2.2 88100/110 Block Diagram and Register Structures

Figure C.4 also shows the internal structure of the 88100 processor, while Figure C.6 shows the internal organization of both the 88100 and 88110 put together. The 88100 contains on-chip fully pipelined integer and floating-point units, a completely hardwired control unit (no microcode), Harvard architecture with separate nonmultiplexed data and instruction memory ports (32-bit data address bus, 32-bit data bus, 30-bit instruction address bus, and 32-bit instruction bus), and selectable big-endian and little-endian ordering. The floating-point unit is implemented as two pipelines—a 5-stage floating-point adder and a separate 6-stage floating-point multiplier pipeline. There is hardware execution of the floating-point divide instructions. These execution units share a common 32-entry multiported register file, and associated with the register file is a register scoreboard for maintaining pipeline coherency among all five execution units. The processor supports both user and supervisor modes.

The 88110 includes 10 concurrent execution units to support the superscalar approach. It includes two integer units, an FPU, a multiply unit, a divide unit, two graphics units, a load/store data unit, and an instruction unit. It uses Harvard architecture for the on-chip caches (one of data and one for instructions); each one is 64 bits wide, with a size of 8 Kbytes, and a 2-way set-associative organization. It has two independent 40-entry, fully associative translation look-aside buffers (TLBs) to support demand paging; each can hold thirty-two 4-Kbyte page address translation entries.

Each 88100 instruction is 32 bits in size. Figure C.7 shows the 88100 instruction formats. All three register instructions use the triadic form. Bit instructions use 10-bit immediate data. General-purpose immediate instructions (Immed) use 16-bit immediate data. Cbr are conditional branch instructions whose destination register field encodes the condition on which to transfer control. Finally, Br are direct branch instructions and Bsr are branch-to-subroutine instructions. The 88110 is upward compatible with the 88100 but with an en-

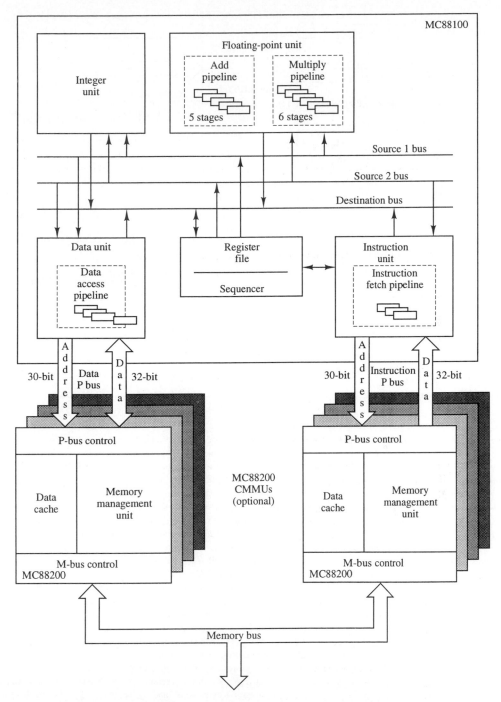

Figure C.4 Motorola 88100 with eight external 88200 CMMUs (cache/memory management units) [16].

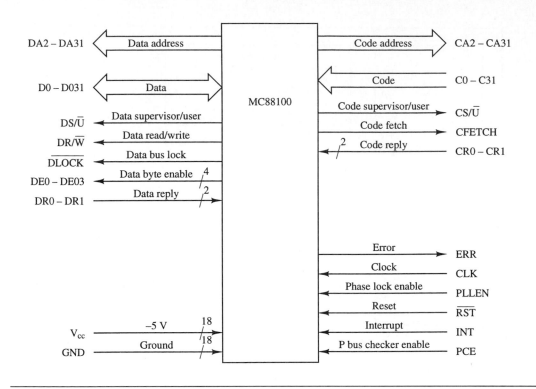

SIGNAL INDEX

Signal name	Mnemonic	Function
Data address bus	DA2–DA31	Provides the 30-bit word address to the data memory space. An entire data word (32 bits) is always addressed; individual bytes or half-words are selected using the data byte strobe signals.
Data bus	D0–D31	32-bit bidirectional data bus interfacing the MC88100 to the data memory space.
Data supervisor user select	DS $\overline{\text{U}}$	This signal selects between the supervisor data address space and the user data address space. DS $\overline{\text{U}}$ is determined by the value of the MODE bit in the processor status register, or by the **usr** option of the **ld** and **st** instructions.
Data read/write	DR/$\overline{\text{W}}$	Indicates whether the memory transaction is a read (DT0 = 1) or a write (DT0 = 0).
Data bus lock	$\overline{\text{DLOCK}}$	The memory lock pin is used by the **xmem** instruction in conjunction with the CMMU. When asserted, the CMMU maintains control of the memory bus during the two **xmem** accesses. Data is guaranteed to be unaccessed between the read and write accesses of the **xmem** instruction.
Data byte enable	DBE0–DBE3	Used during memory accesses, these signals indicate which bytes are accessed at the addressed location. DBE0–DBE3 are always valid during memory write cycles. A memory read is always 4 bytes wide, and the processor uses the enables to extract the valid data. That is, during an **ld** instruction, the

Figure C.5 Motorola 88100 I/O pins and signals. [15].

Signal name	Mnemonic	Function
		memory system should drive all 32 data signals, regardless of whether 1, 2, or 4 byte enables are asserted. When DBE0–DBE3 are negated, the transaction is a null; otherwise, the transaction is a valid load or store operation.
Data reply	DR0–DR1	Indicates the status of the data memory transaction.
Code address bus	CA2–CA31	Provides the 30-bit word address to the instruction memory space. All instructions are 32 bits wide and are aligned on 4-byte boundaries; therefore, the lower two bits of the address space are not required and are implied to be zero.
Code bus	C0–C31	This read-only, 32-bit data bus interfaces the MC88100 to the instruction memory space. Instructions are always 32 bits wide.
Code supervisor user select	CS $\overline{\text{U}}$	Selects between the user and supervisor instruction memory spaces. When asserted, selects supervisor memory and when negated, user memory. This signal is determined by the value of the MODE bit in the processor status register.
Code fetch	CFETCH	When asserted, signals that an instruction fetch is in progress. When negated, the transaction is a null transaction (code P bus idle).
Code reply	CR0–CR1	Signals the status of the instruction memory transaction.
Error	ERR	Asserted when a bus comparator error occurs, ERR indicates that the desired signal level was not driven on the output pin. ERR is used in systems implementing a master checker configuration of MC88100s.
Clock	CLK	Internal clock normally phase locked to minimize skew between the external and internal signals. Since CLK is applied to peripherals (such as CMMU devices), exact timing of internal signals is required to properly synchronize the device to the P bus.
Phase lock enable	PLLEN	Asserted during reset to select phase locking, PLLEN controls the internal phase lock circuit that synchronizes the internal clocks to CLK.
Reset	$\overline{\text{RST}}$	Used to perform an orderly restart of the processor. When asserted, the instruction pipeline is cleared and certain internal registers are cleared or initialized. When negated, the reset vector is fetched from memory, with execution beginning in supervisor mode.
Interrupt	INT	Indicates that an interrupt request is in progress. When asserted, the processor saves the execution context and begins execution at the interrupt exception vector. Software is responsible for handling all recognized interrupts (those between instructions when no higher priority exception occurs).
P-bus checker enable	PCE	Used in systems incorporating two or more MC88100s redundantly. When negated, the processor operates normally and when asserted, the processor monitors (but does not drive) all of its outputs except ERR as inputs.
Power supply	V_{CC}	−5-volt power supply.
Ground	GND	Ground connections.

(b) Definitions of the 88100 I/O signals

Figure C.5 (concluded).

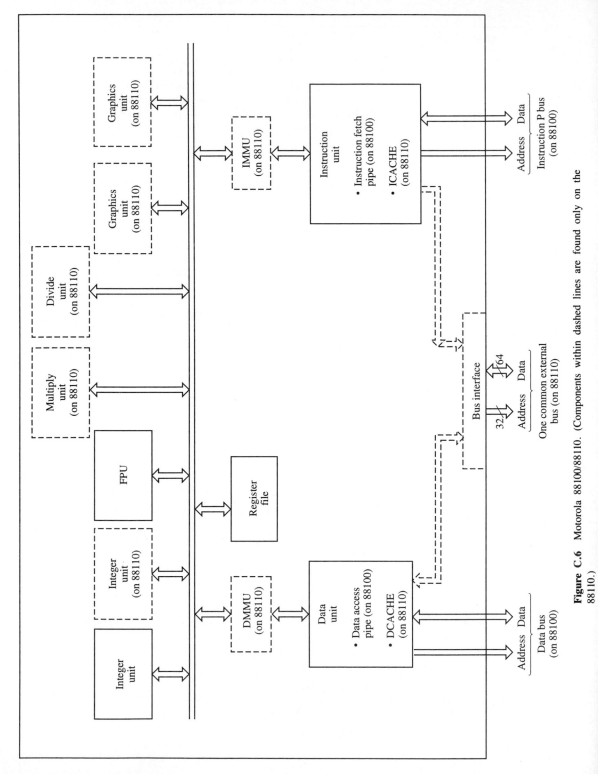

Figure C.6 Motorola 88100/88110. (Components within dashed lines are found only on the 88110.)

6 bits	5 bits	5 bits	11 bits		5 bits
Triadic	D	S1	Op code		S2
Bit	D	S1	Op	Width	Offset
Immed	D	S1	Immediate		
Cbr	M/B	S1	Offset		
Br/Bsr	Offset				

M/B mask or bit

Figure C.7 Motorola 88100 instruction formats. [14]. © 1990 IEEE.

hanced number of integer and floating-point instruction sets and new instructions to support 3D color graphics image rendering.

Figure C.8a shows the internal registers of the 88100. Each register is 32 bits wide, grouped into three types of registers that provide data and execution information to the execution units. As can be seen from the figure, most control registers can be accessed only in the supervisor mode. Figure C.8b shows the internal registers of the 88110; these can be grouped in pairs to hold 64-bit operands whenever necessary—for example, for graphics and double-precision floating-point values. The 88110 also includes new extended 80-bit registers which are used exclusively by the FPU instructions.

C.2.3 88200 Off-Chip CMMU

The Motorola CMMU chip is a combination of a data cache[3] and an MMU and used with the Motorola RISC processor, the MC88100, as shown in the block diagram of Figure C.4: four CMMUs for data caches and four CMMUs for instruction caches. In addition to the cache and the MMU, the 88200 chip contains the interface hardware to the virtual instruction and data buses (the P-bus control) and the hardware interface to the physical memory bus (the M-bus control). Before we describe the MMU, let's first present the 88200 cache.

The CMMU chip contains a 16-Kbyte physical cache. It is organized as a 4-way set-associative memory and is configured as 256 sets of 4 lines each. Each line or block frame contains 4 doublewords and the tag is 20 bits. Like the other Motorola caches discussed in Chapter 5, each cache line also contains status information that indicate whether the data is valid or invalid, exclusive to this CMMU cache, and whether or not the data is modified with respect to main memory.

Like other Motorola products that have on-chip an MMU and a cache, cache access and virtual-to-physical-address-translation are done at the same time. This is feasible because the low-order 12 bits of a virtual address are the same with those of the physical address (i.e., they don't get translated) and, therefore, can be used to index the cache at the

---

[3]We will be using here the term ''data cache,'' although we must keep in mind that this external chip may also be interfaced to the ''instruction bus'' of the MC88100 RISC processor to implement an ''instruction cache'' as well.

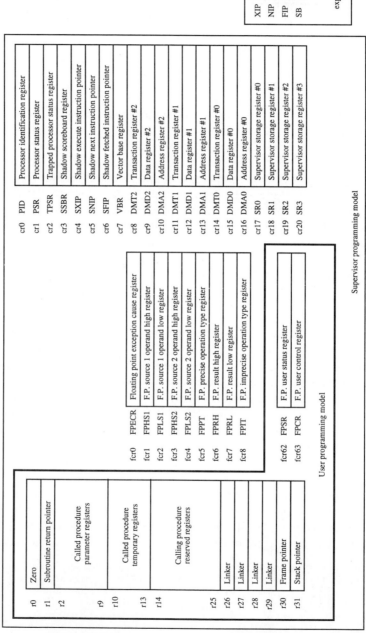

		Processor identification register
cr0	PID	Processor identification register
cr1	PSR	Processor status register
cr2	TPSR	Trapped processor status register
cr3	SSBR	Shadow scoreboard register
cr4	SXIP	Shadow execute instruction pointer
cr5	SNIP	Shadow next instruction pointer
cr6	SFIP	Shadow fetched instruction pointer
cr7	VBR	Vector base register
cr8	DMT2	Transaction register #2
cr9	DMD2	Data register #2
cr10	DMA2	Address register #2
cr11	DMT1	Transaction register #1
cr12	DMD1	Data register #1
cr13	DMA1	Address register #1
cr14	DMT0	Transaction register #0
cr15	DMD0	Data register #0
cr16	DMA0	Address register #0
cr17	SR0	Supervisor storage register #0
cr18	SR1	Supervisor storage register #1
cr19	SR2	Supervisor storage register #2
cr20	SR3	Supervisor storage register #3

Supervisor programming model

(a) 88100 registers

r0		Zero	
r1		Subroutine return pointer	
r2		Called procedure parameter registers	
r9			
r10		Called procedure temporary registers	
r13			
r14		Calling procedure reserved registers	
r25			
r26		Linker	
r27		Linker	
r28		Linker	
r29		Linker	
r30		Frame pointer	
r31		Stack pointer	

fcr0	FPECR	Floating point exception cause register
fcr1	FPHS1	F.P. source 1 operand high register
fcr2	FPLS1	F.P. source 1 operand low register
fcr3	FPHS2	F.P. source 2 operand high register
fcr4	FPLS2	F.P. source 2 operand low register
fcr5	FPPT	F.P. precise operation type register
fcr6	FPRH	F.P. result high register
fcr7	FPRL	F.P. result low register
fcr8	FPIT	F.P. imprecise operation type register
fcr62	FPSR	F.P. user status register
fcr63	FPCR	F.P. user control register

User programming model

XIP		Execute instruction pointer
NIP		Next instruction pointer
FIP		Fetch instruction pointer
SB		Scoreboard register

Internal registers are not explicitly accessible to software

Figure C.8 Motorola 88100 and 88110 internal registers.

502

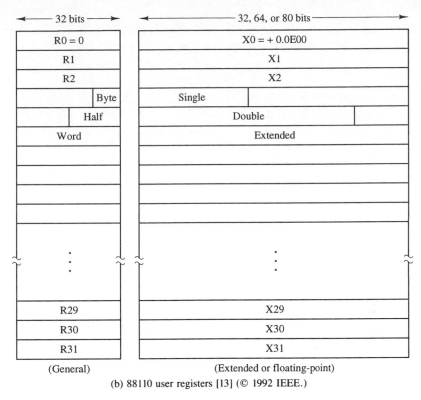

R0 = 0		X0 = + 0.0E00	
R1		X1	
R2		X2	
	Byte	Single	
	Half	Double	
Word		Extended	
R29		X29	
R30		X30	
R31		X31	

(General) (Extended or floating-point)

(b) 88110 user registers [13] (© 1992 IEEE.)

Figure C.8 (concluded).

same time the other 20 most significant logical address bits are sent to the CMMU's ATC for translation.[4] (The operation is analogous to that depicted in Figure 5.21.)

The cache has the ability to designate certain parts of memory as uncacheable, and the memory update policy to be used: write-through or write-back. It has bus snooping capability to maintain cache consistency and for line replacement uses the LRU algorithm in a 4-doubleword burst-mode transfer.

The 88200 MMU supports demand-paging and two logical address spaces (user/supervisor) of 4 Gbytes each. Address translation is supported with two internal ATCs, the PATC and the BATC, whose organization is shown in Figure C.9a. The **PATC** (page address translation cache) is a 56-entry, fully associative cache containing recently used translations (page descriptors) for 4-Kbyte fixed-size pages, all belonging to the currently executing task; it is maintained automatically by the 88200 hardware. The **BATC** (block address translation cache) is a 10-entry fully associative cache used to provide translations for ten 512-byte unmapped blocks of memory that are contiguous; it contains memory block descriptors and is software maintained (system software loads it with the logical and physical addresses of the memory blocks); its translations are used for the operating system and its storage of the mapping tables.

The CMMU receives from the processor (on its P bus) a 32-bit logical address and performs address translation by simultaneously comparing it to all current entries in both

---

[4]Actually, the most significant eight of these 12 bits are decoded to select one of the 256 sets.

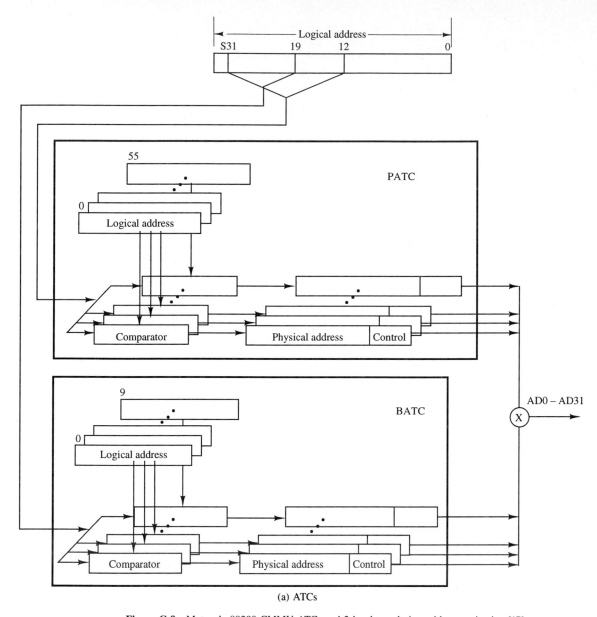

Figure C.9 Motorola 88200 CMMU ATCs and 2-level translation table organization [17].

ATCs. If there is a cache hit on either ATC and no privilege violation, the CMMU concatenates the stored physical base address with the low-order word offset from the logical address to form the complete 32-bit physical address placed on the M bus. (If there is a hit in both ATCs, the BATC translation takes precedence.) Checking for an internal cache hit is done in parallel with this address translation operation. Finally, the control field of an ATC entry contains a write protection bit, a modified (or used) bit, a referenced bit, a data cache inhibit indicator, mode (user/supervisor) bit, etc.

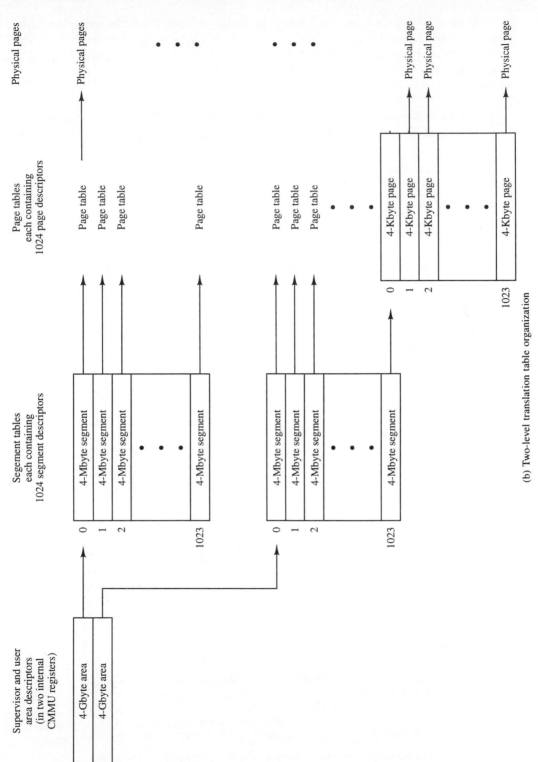

(b) Two-level translation table organization

Figure C.9 (concluded).

If there is a cache miss, the CMMU hardware executes the table walk algorithm, which searches 2-level translation tables in memory, loads the required descriptor into the PATC, and then proceeds with the logical-to-physical address translation. The tree structure supported by the 88200 contains two distinct levels in the supervisor and user address space, as shown in Figure C.9b:

1. The first-level mappings are called segments (as in UNIX terminology); this level divides each of the two 4-Gbyte logical address spaces into 1024 equivalent 4-Mbyte segments.

2. The second level (the page level) divides each segment into 1024 equivalent page frames, each 4 Kbytes in size. These entries have formats compatible with the 68851 and 68030.

C.2.4 88110 On-Chip Address Translation Facilities

The 88110 has on-chip hardware facilities to support paged virtual memory implementations [13]. The processor includes two independent TLBs (as shown in Figure C.10a), one for logical instruction addresses and the other for logical data addresses. Each TLB is a fully associative cache of the type shown in Figure C.10b, and can hold 32 4-Kbyte page address translation entries. Each CAM (content-addressable memory) element is associated with one physical page descriptor. If the memory reference is found in the TLB (a hit) and there is no access rights violation, the address is translated and sent to the respective instruction or data cache. If the memory reference is not found in the TLB (a miss), then usually the hardware will execute a table-walking algorithm to walk though the operating system's page tables and fetch a new page descriptor.

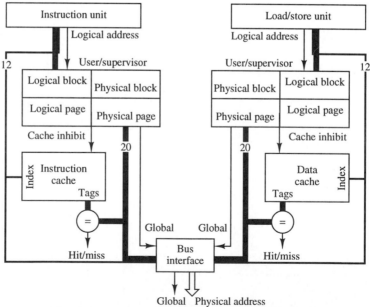

(a) Translating logical to physical addresses for the instruction and data caches

Figure C.10 88110 virtual address translation facilities [13]. © 1992 IEEE.

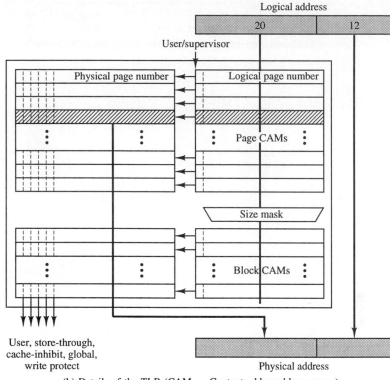

(b) Details of the TLB (CAM = Content-addressable memory)

Figure C.10   (concluded).

C.3 MIPS R-SERIES

The MIPS R-series includes the R2000, R3000, R6000, and R4000 microprocessors. We will include in this section the R3000 and R4000 as examples.

R3000.   The R3000 is a 32-bit RISC processor [18,19]. The processor executes instructions using a 5-stage pipeline, and includes an integer execution unit, a paged MMU, and the necessary on-chip cache hardware controller to interface to external separate SRAM instruction and data caches.

Figure C.11 depicts a system configuration using the MIPS R3000 processor and external instruction (I-cache) and data (D-cache) caches. The processor bus (also called here "cache bus") is a synchronous bus that permits the Harvard architecture on the memories connected to it (separate instruction and data standard SRAM memories used as caches). The processor is able to obtain a 32-bit instruction and data from the cache memory on every clock cycle. The local bus (also called memory bus) is asynchronous and used to interface larger main memory DRAMs, EPROM memory, and peripheral devices. Multiple clock cycles are required to perform data movement in the asynchronous memory.

The R3000 RISC processor has the cache controller and cache interface hardware on-chip to support various cache and main memory sizes. This on-chip control directly generates all of the cache control signals, supports separate external data and instruction physical

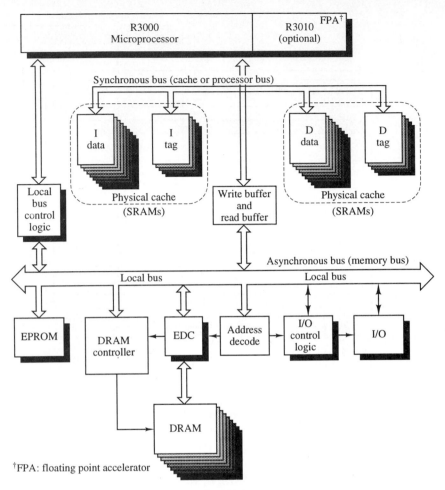

Figure C.11 MIPS R3000-based system with external I-caches and D-caches [20]. Courtesy of IDT.

caches, and permits their implementation using commercially available standard SRAM devices. The cache controller implements direct mapped caches, allows for wide range of cache sizes (both the instruction and data caches can vary from 0 to 256 Kbytes) and line sizes (of 1, 4, 8, 16, or 32 32-bit doublewords[5]), and supports the refilling of the cache when a cache miss occurs in 1, 4, 8, 16, or 32 doublewords blocks. Block refill size can be different for instruction and data caches, and is configured during system RESET initialization.[6] The write policy for the data cache is write-through and, therefore, depending on the particular implementation, a number of external "write buffers" in a FIFO configuration may be required to capture the address and the data from the processor at the processor's speed and retire the data to main memory at the memory's speed. The R3000 has

[5]The 32-bit doubleword is referred to by the R3000 as a word.

[6]The various configuration settings are selected using the six interrupt input pins and decoded internally by different clock cycles.

what is referred to as "instruction streaming" capability, in that it performs simultaneous execution of incoming instructions while the cache is being refilled (updated).

R4000. The R4000 is a full 64-bit RISC processor; i.e., it has a 64-bit external data bus and 64-bit internal general registers. The R4000 is compatible with the R3000 with the following enhancements: it has separate on-chip primary data and instruction caches, an optional cache interface for off-chip secondary cache, and an on-chip floating-point unit. Figure C.12 depicts the simplified internal structure of the R3000 and R4000 microprocessors.

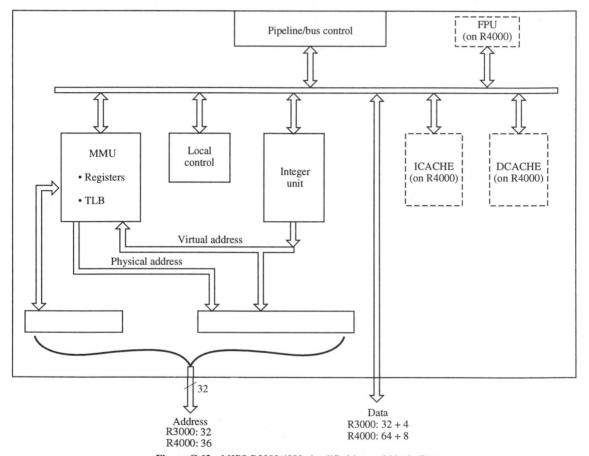

Figure C.12 MIPS R3000/4000 simplified internal block diagram.

Figure C.13 shows the versatility of the R4000 processors in configuring various systems: the first configuration is the simplest, minimal-parts-count design; the second takes advantage of the on-chip cache controller to interface external secondary caches implemented with standard SRAMs; the third corresponds to advanced multiprocessor designs.

In both the R3000 and R4000 the byte ordering is configurable into either big-endian (compatible with Motorola and IBM 370 conventions) or little-endian (compatible with Intel, National, and DEC VAX conventions). The R3000 has two operating modes: user and

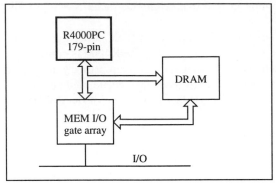

(a) Low-cost configuration

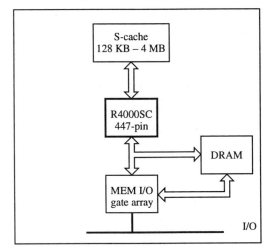

(b) Mid-range configuration

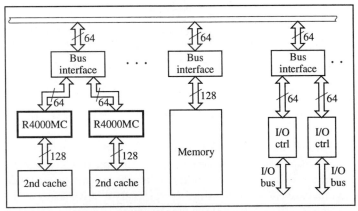

(c) High-end configuration

Figure C.13 R4000-based system configurations [20].

kernel (which is analogous to "supervisor" mode provided by many processors); the R4000 has three operating modes: user mode, an intermediate mode now called supervisor mode, and a high privilege level called by the R4000 kernel mode.

C.3.1 R3000/R4000 I/O Pins and Signals

Figure C.14a depicts the R3000 I/O pins configuration and Figure C.14b gives their definitions. The R4000 is available in three different configurations: the R4000MC and

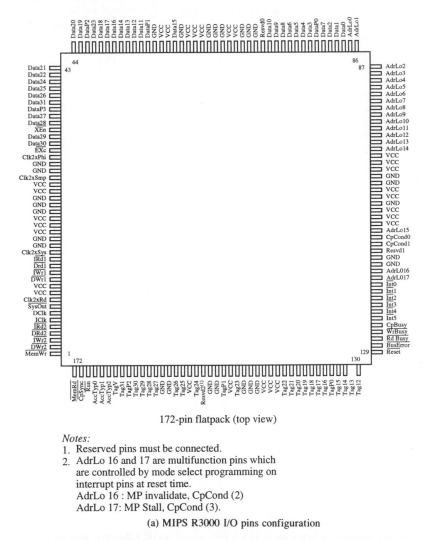

172-pin flatpack (top view)

Notes:
1. Reserved pins must be connected.
2. AdrLo 16 and 17 are multifunction pins which are controlled by mode select programming on interrupt pins at reset time.
   AdrLo 16 : MP invalidate, CpCond (2)
   AdrLo 17: MP Stall, CpCond (3).

(a) MIPS R3000 I/O pins configuration

Figure C.14   MIPS R3000 I/O pins and signal descriptions [19]. Courtesy of IDT.

R4000SC (both with 447 pins), which include a 128-bit wide secondary cache bus, and the R4000PC (with 179 pins), with no secondary cache interface [20,21]. Figure C.15a depicts the R4000SC/MC symbolic pinout and Figure C.15b gives their definitions.

Pin name	I/O	Description
Data (0-31)	I/O	A 32-bit bus used for all instruction and data transmission among the processor, caches, memory interface, and coprocessors.
DataP (0-3)	I/O	A 4-bit bus containing even parity over the data bus.
Tag (12-31)	I/O	A 20-bit bus used for transferring cache tags and high addresses between the processor, caches, and memory interface.
TagV	I/O	The tag validity indicator.
Tag P (0-2)	I/O	A 3-bit bus containing even parity over the concatenation of TagV and Tag.
AdrLo (0-17)	O	An 18-bit bus containing byte addresses used for transferring low addresses from the processor to the caches and memory interface. (AdrLo 16: CpCond (2), AdrLo 17: CpCond (3) set by reset initialization).
$\overline{\text{IRd1}}$	O	Read enable for the instruction cache.
$\overline{\text{IWr1}}$	O	Write enable for the instruction cache.
$\overline{\text{IRd2}}$	O	An identical copy of $\overline{\text{IRd1}}$ used to split the load.
$\overline{\text{IWr2}}$	O	An identical copy of $\overline{\text{IWr1}}$ used to split the load.
IClk	O	The instruction cache address latch clock. This clock runs continuously.
$\overline{\text{DRd1}}$	O	The read enable for the data cache.
$\overline{\text{DWr1}}$	O	The write enable for the data cache.
$\overline{\text{DRd2}}$	O	An identical copy of $\overline{\text{DRd1}}$ used to split the load.
$\overline{\text{DWr2}}$	O	An identical copy of $\overline{\text{DWr1}}$ used to split the load.
DClk	O	The data cache address latch clock. This clock runs continuously.
$\overline{\text{XEn}}$	O	The read enable for the Read Buffer.
AccTyp(0-2)	O	A 3-bit bus used to indicate the size of data being transferred on the data bus, whether or not a data transfer is occurring, and the purpose of the transfer.
$\overline{\text{MemWr}}$	O	Signals the occurrence of a main memory write.
$\overline{\text{MemRd}}$	O	Signals the occurrence of a main memory read.
$\overline{\text{BusError}}$	I	Signals the occurrence of a bus error during a main memory read or write.
$\overline{\text{Run}}$	O	Indicates whether the processor is in the run or stall state.
Exception	O	Indicates that the instruction about to commit state should be aborted and other exception related information.
$\overline{\text{SysOut}}$	O	A reflection of the internal processor clock used to generate the system clock.
CpSync	O	A clock which is identical to $\overline{\text{Sysout}}$ and used by coprocessors for timing synchronization with the CPU.
RdBusy	I	The main memory read stall termination signal. In most system designs RdBusy is normally asserted and is deasserted only to indicate the successful completion of a memory read. RdBusy is sampled by the processor only during memory read stalls.
$\overline{\text{WrBusy}}$	I	The main memory write stall initiation/termination signal.
CpBusy	I	The coprocessor busy stall initiation/termination signal.
CpCond (0-1)	I	A 2-bit bus used to transfer conditional branch status from the coprocessors to the main processor.
CpCond (2-3)	I	Conditional branch status from coprocessors to the processor. Function is provided on AdrLo 16/17 pins and is selected at reset time.
MPStall	I	Multiprocessing Stall. Signals to the processor that it should stall accesses to the caches in a multiprocessing environment. This is physically the same pin as CpCond3; its use is determined at RESET initialization.
MPInvalidate	I	Multiprocessing Invalidate. Signals to the processor that it should issue invalidate data on the cache data bus. The address to be invalidated is externally provided. This is the same pin as CpCond2; its use is determined at RESET initialization.
$\overline{\text{Int}}$ (0-5)	I	A 6-bit bus used by the memory interface and coprocessors to signal maskable interrupts to the processor. At reset time mode select values are read in.

Figure C.14 (continued).

Pin name	I/O	Description
Clk2xSys	I	The master double frequency input clock used for generating $\overline{\text{SysOut}}$.
Clk2xSmp	I	A double frequency clock input used to determine the sample point for data coming into the processor and coprocessors.
Clk2xRd	I	A double frequency clock input used to determine the enable time of the cache RAMs.
Clk2xPhi	I	A double frequency clock input used to determine the position of the internal phases, phase1 and phase2.
$\overline{\text{Reset}}$	I	Synchronous initialization input used to force execution starting from the reset memory address. $\overline{\text{Reset}}$ must be deasseted synchronously but asserted asynchronously. The deassertion of $\overline{\text{Reset}}$ must be synchronized by the leading edge of $\overline{\text{SysOut}}$.

(b) R3000 pin definition

Figure C.14 (concluded).

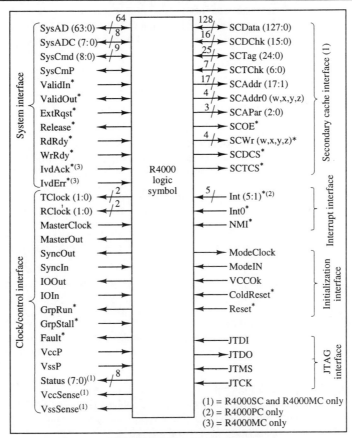

(a) MIPS R4000 symbolic pinout

Figure C.15 MIPS R4000 I/O pins and signal descriptions [21].

System Interface

These signals comprise the interface between the R4000 and other components in the system. Signals IvdAck[*] and IvdErr[*] are available only on the R4000SC and MC. All other signals are available on all three package configurations.

ExtRqst[*]:   **External request**   **Input**
An external agent asserts ExtRqst[*] to request use of the system interface. The R4000 grants the request by asserting Release[*].

IvdAck[*]:   **Invalidate acknowledge**   **Input**
An external agent asserts IvdAck[*] to signal successful completion of a processor invalidate or update request (R4000MC and SC only).

IvdErr[*]:   **Invalidate error**   **Input**
An external agent asserts IvdErr[*] to signal unsuccessful completion of a processor invalidate or update request (R4000MC and SC only).

Release[*]:   **Release interface**   **Output**
In response to the assertion of ExtRqst[*], the R4000 asserts Release[*] to signal the requesting device that the system interface is available.

RdRdy[*]:   **Read ready**   **Input**
The external agent asserts RdRdy[*] to indicate that it can accept processor read, invalidate, or update requests in both overlap and non-overlap mode or can accept a read followed by a potential invalidate or update request in overlap mode.

SysAD(63:0):   **System address/data bus**   **Input/Output**
A 64-bit address and data bus for communication between the processor and an external agent.

SysADC(7:0):   **System address/data check bus**   **Input/Output**
An 8-bit bus containing check bits for the SysAD bus.

SysCmd(8:0):   **System command/data identifier bus parity**   **Input/Output**
A 9-bit bus for command and data identifier transmission between the processor and an external agent.

SysCmdP: **System command/data identifier bus parity**   **Input/Output**
A single, even-parity bit for the SysCmd bus.

ValidIn[*]:   **Valid input**   **Input**
An external agent asserts ValidIn[*] when it is driving a valid address or data on the SysAD bus and a valid command or data identifier on the SysCmd bus.

ValidOut[*]:   **Valid output**   **Output**
The R4000 asserts ValidOut[*] when it is driving a valid address or data on the SysAD bus and a valid command or data identifier on the SysCmd bus.

WrRdy[*]:   **Write ready**   **Input**
An external agent asserts WrRdy[*] when it can accept a processor write request.

Figure C.15 (continued).

Clock/Control Interface

These signals comprise the interface for clocking and maintenance functions.

IOOut: **I/O output**   **Output**

Output skew rate control feedback loop output. Must be connected to IOIn through a delay loop that models the IO path from the R4000 to an external agent.

IOIn: **I/O input**   **Input**

Output skew rate control feedback loop input (see IOOut).

MasterClock: **Master clock**   **Input**

Master clock input establishes the processor operating frequency.

MasterOut: **Master clock out**   **Output**

Master clock output aligned with MasterClock.

RClock(1:0):   **Receive clocks**   **Output**

Two identical receive clocks that establish the system interface frequency.

SyncOut: **Synchronization clock out**   **Output**

Synchronization clock output. Must be connected to SyncIn through an interconnect that models the interconnect between MasterOut, TClock, RClock, and the external agent.

SyncIn: **Synchronization clock in**   **Input**

Synchronization clock input.

TClock(1:0):   **Transmit clocks**   **Output**

Two identical transmit clocks that establish the system interface frequency.

GrpRun*:   **Group run**   **Output**

The R4000 pulses GrpRun* after completing a group of instructions.

GrpStall*:   **Group stall**   **Input**

An external agent asserts GrpStall* to stall the processor after completion of the current group of instructions.

Fault*:   **Fault**   **Output**

The R4000 asserts Fault* to indicate a mismatch output of boundary comparators.

Status(7:0):   **Status**   **Output**

An 8-bit bus that indicates the current operation status of the processor.

VccP: **Quiet VCC for PLL**   **Input**

Quiet Vcc for the internal phase locked loop.

VccSense: **VCC sense**   **Input/Output**

This is special pin used only in component testing and characterization. It provides a separate, direct connection from the on-chip VCC node to a package pin without attaching to the in-package power

Figure C.15 (continued).

planes. Test fixtures treat VccSense as an analog output pin: the voltage at this pin directly shows the behavior of the on-chip VCC. Thus, characterization engineers can easily observe the effects of di/dt noise, transmission line reflections, etc. VccSense should be connected to VCC in functional system designs.

VssP:	**Quiet VSS for PLL**	**Input**

Quiet Vss for the internal phase locked loop.

VssSense:	**VSS sense**	**Input/Output**

VssSense provides a separate, direct connection from the on-chip VSS node to a package pin without attaching to the in-package ground planes. VssSense should be connected to VSS in functional system designs.

Secondary Cache Interface

These signals comprise the interface between the R4000 and the secondary cache. These signals are available only on the R4000MC and SC.

SCAddr(17:1):	**Secondary cache address bus**	**Output**
SCAddr0W:	**Secondary cache address lsb**	**Output**
SCAddr0X:	**Secondary cache address lsb**	**Output**
SCAddr0Y:	**Secondary cache address lsb**	**Output**
SCAddr0Z:	**Secondary cache address lsb**	**Output**

The 18-bit address bus for the secondary cache. Bits 17 through 1 are bidirectional. Bit 0 has four output lines to provide additional drive current.

SCAPar(2:0):	**Secondary cache address parity bus**	**Output**

A 3-bit bus that carries the parity of the SCAddr bus and the cache control lines SCOE*, SCWR*, SCDCS* and SCTCS*.

SCData(127:0):	**Secondary cache data bus**	**Input/Output**

A 128-bit bus used to read or write cache data from and to the secondary cache data RAM.

SCDChk(15:0):	**Secondary cache data ECC bus**	**Input/Output**

A 16-bit bus that carries two Error Checking and Correcting (ECC) fields covering the upper or lower 64 bits of the SCData from and to the secondary cache.

SCDCS*:	**Secondary cache data chip select**	**Output**

Chip select enable signal for the secondary cache data RAM.

SCOE*:	**Secondary cache output enable**	**Output**

Output enable for the secondary cache data and tag RAM.

SCTag(24:0):	**Secondary cache tag bus**	**Input/Output**

A 25-bit bus used to read or write cache tags from and to the secondary cache.

Figure C.15   (continued).

| SCTChk(6:0): | Secondary cache tag ECC bus | Input/Output |

SCTChk(6:0):   Secondary cache tag ECC bus   Input/Output
A 7-bit bus that carries an Error Checking and Correcting (ECC) field covering the SCTag from and to the secondary cache.

SCTCS*:   Secondary cache data chip select   Output
Chip select enable signal for the secondary cache tag RAM.

SCWrW*:   Secondary cache write enable   Output

SCWrX*:   Secondary cache write enable   Output

SCWrY*:   Secondary cache write enable   Output

SCWrZ*:   Secondary cache write enable   Output
Write enable for the secondary cache data and tag RAM.

Interrupt Interface

These signals comprise the interface used by external agents to interrupt the R4000 processor. Int*(5:1) is available only on the R4000PC; Int*(0) and NMI* are available on all three configurations.

Int*(5:1):   Interrupt   Input
Five of six general processor interrupts, bit-wise ORed with bits 5:1 of the interrupt register.

Int*(0):   Interrupt   Input
One of six general processor interrupts, bit-wise ORed with bit 0 of the interrupt register.

NMI*:   Non-maskable interrupt   Input
Non-maskable interrupt, ORed with bit 6 of the interrupt register.

Initialization Interface

These signals comprise the interface by which an external agent initializes the R4000 operating parameters. All of these signals are available on all three processor configurations.

ColdReset*:   Cold reset   Input
This signal must be asserted for a power on reset or a cold reset. The clocks SClock, TClock, and RClock begin to cycle and are synchronized with the de-assertion edge of ColdReset*. ColdReset* must be de-asserted synchronously with MasterOut.

ModeClock: Boot mode clock   Output
Serial boot-mode data clock output at the system clock frequency divided by two hundred and fifty six.

ModeIn: Boot mode data in   Input
Serial boot-mode data input.

Figure C.15   (continued).

Reset*:	**Reset**	**Input**

This signal must be asserted for any reset sequence. It may be asserted synchronously or asynchronously for a cold reset, or synchronously to initiate a warm reset. Reset* must be de-asserted synchronously with MasterOut.

VCCOk:	**VCC is OK**	**Input**

When asserted, this signal indicates to the R4000 that the + 5 volt power supply has been above 4.75 volts for more than 100 milliseconds and will remain stable. The assertion of VCCOk initiates the initialization sequence.

JTAG Interface

These signals comprise the interface by which the JTAG boundary scan mechanism is provided.

JTDI:	**JTAG data in**	**Input**

Data is serially scanned in through this pin.

JTCK:	**JTAG clock input**	**Input**

The R4000 outputs a serial clock on JTCK. On the rising edge of JTCK both JTDI and JTMS are sampled.

JTDO:	**JTAG data out**	**Output**

Data is serially scanned out through this pin.

JTMS:	**JTAG command**	**Input**

JTAG command signal, signals that the incoming serial data is command data.

(b) MIPS R4000 signal descriptions

Figure C.15 (concluded).

C3.2 R3000/R4000 Internal Organizations and Register Structures

R3000.   Figure C.16a depicts the R3000 functional block diagram and Figure C.16b its internal integer general-purpose and multiply/divide registers (used to hold the results of the respective operations), and its program counter. All registers are 32 bits long. Any of the 32 general-purpose register can be used for address pointer, stack pointer, or data pointer; however, register r0 is hardwired to always contain the value "0" (a useful constant) and register r31 is used as the link register in jump-and-link instructions (the return address for subroutine calls). There is a 32-bit program counter, and two 32-bit registers that hold the results of integer multiply and divide operations. The R3000 has no program status word (PSW) register; its functions are provided by the "status" and "cause" registers incorporated within system control coprocessor 0 (CPO).

R4000.   Figure C.17a depicts the R4000 functional block diagram with the additional units integrated on-chip. Each of the on-chip instruction and data caches is 8 Kbytes and has its own 64-bit data path, while the optional secondary cache interface is 128 bits wide to support caches from 128 Kbytes to 4 Mbytes. The on-chip caches are direct-mapped,

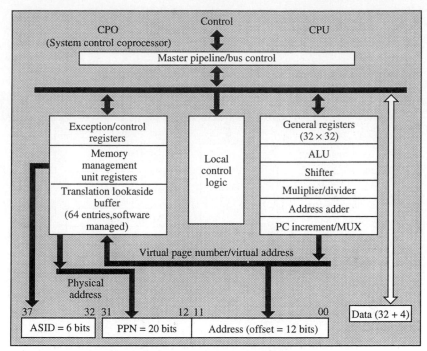

(a) R3000 functional block diagram

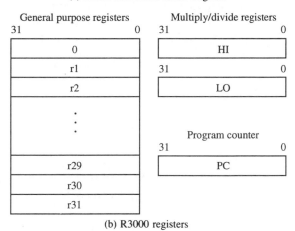

(b) R3000 registers

Figure C.16 R3000 internal structure and registers [22].

virtually indexed, and physically tagged, organized with either a 4-doubleword (16-byte) or 8-doubleword (32-byte) cache line, and the data cache implements the write-back policy. The on-chip paged-MMU is assisted with a 48-entry, fully associative TLB. Each entry maps a pair of variable-size pages, where the page size varies from 4 Kbytes to 16 Mbytes, increasing in multiples of 4.

Figure C.17b shows the R4000 integer unit registers. These are similar to those of the R3000 except that they are 64 bits wide. (When the processor is programmed to operate as a 32-bit processor, these registers are 32-bit wide.)

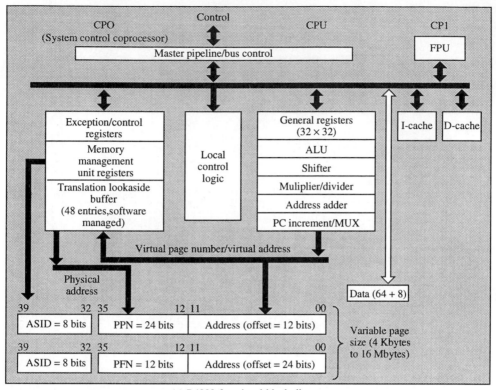

(a) R4000 functional block diagram

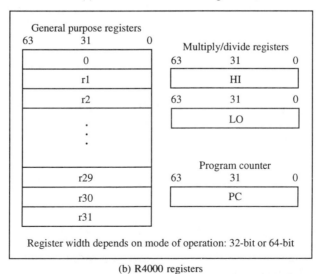

(b) R4000 registers

Figure C.17 R4000 internal structure and registers [22].

C.3.3 R3000/R4000 Instruction Formats

Both the R3000 and R4000 processors have instructions which are 32 bits long. Following the RISC convention, both processors have only three types of instruction formats, shown in Figure 1.12 in Chapter 1: Immediate (I), Jump (J), and Register (R) types. This approach simplifies instruction decoding, thus minimizing instruction execution time. The instruction set is divided into load/store instructions (all are I-type), computational instructions (either I-type or R-type), jump and branch instructions (of any of the above three types), and co-processor and special instructions.

C.3.4 R3000 Off-Chip Cache RAMs

Figure C.18 shows the design and interfacing details of the Harvard architecture cache organization implemented using a single address bus and single data bus, time multiplexed

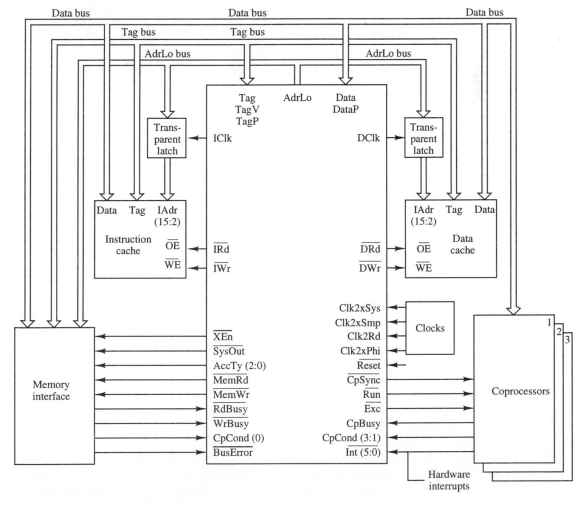

Figure C.18 R3000 interfering details of the Harvard architecture cache organization [19]. Courtesy of IDT.

within the bus cycle. Since the address bus is time-multiplexed, address latches are needed to capture the cache address and allow sufficient time for SRAM access (SRAMs with on-chip latches may also be used). Address bits A15–A2 of the address (offset within a physical page) form the cache address placed on the AdrLo bus; address bits A1,A0 are not physically connected to the cache memories because the transfers are done on a 32-bit double-word basis.

Figure C.19 shows the 60-bit cache line format. There is a parity bit DataP for each byte in the data field and a parity bit TagP for each byte in the PFN and V fields.

```
59   57 56  55                    36 35   32 31              0
 ┌──────┬───┬──────────────────┬───────┬──────────────────┐
 │ TagP │ V │       PFN        │ DataP │       Data       │
 └──────┴───┴──────────────────┴───────┴──────────────────┘
```

Data   cache data
DataP parity over the data field
PFN   page frame number, or the upper
       20-bit address field which form the tags
V   valid bit
TagP   parity over the PFN and V fields

Figure C.19 R3000 cache line format (direct-mapped caches) [20]. Courtesy of IDT.

If each one of the I-cache and D-cache of Figure C.11 is 64 Kbytes, each cache can be implemented using 15 IDT7198s (which are 16K × 4 SRAM chips) as shown in Figure C.20: 8 SRAM chips for the cache line data bits (31:0); one SRAM chip for the DataP; five SRAM chips for the 20-bit PFN; and one SRAM chip for the TagP and V. The first 8 SRAMs make up the *Cache Data* and the other 7 the *Cache Tag*. The figure also shows how the R3000 processor internally converts the VPN (the virtual page number) to PFN (the physical page frame number) and uses the tag comparator to determine a cache hit/miss. The FCT373A are address latches.

As we explained in Chapter 5, like in any direct-mapped cache memory, the number of bits in the PFN tag field depends on the size of the cacheable main memory and the size of the cache.

C.3.5 R3000 Bus Cycles

The R3000 bus (or CPU) cycle is divided in two phases, as shown in the timing diagram of Figure C.21 (for accessing I-cache and D-cache), During **phase 1,** the processor issues the D-cache address on lines AdrLo (which is captured by external latches) if there is a data transaction (load or store) during this cycle. At the same time an instruction and its tag are fetched from the I-cache in the data and tag lines. During **phase 2,** the processor issues the next instruction address for the I-cache (which is externally latched), and completes any data transaction initiated in phase 1. If the data transaction were a load, the data and its tag are fetched from the D-cache; if it were a store, the processor drives the data and tag buses, writing the data and tag into the DCACHE. All clock and control signals for the latches are directly generated by the R3000: IClk, IRd#, IWr# for the ICACHE, and DClk, DRd#, DWr# for the D-cache.

Asynchronous main memory cycles start by the processor on cache misses, identified by the processor itself when its on-chip tag comparator indicates that the item received from the cache was not the desired item. The number of bits received over the tab bus depends on the particular system configuration (at RESET initialization time). For larger caches, low-

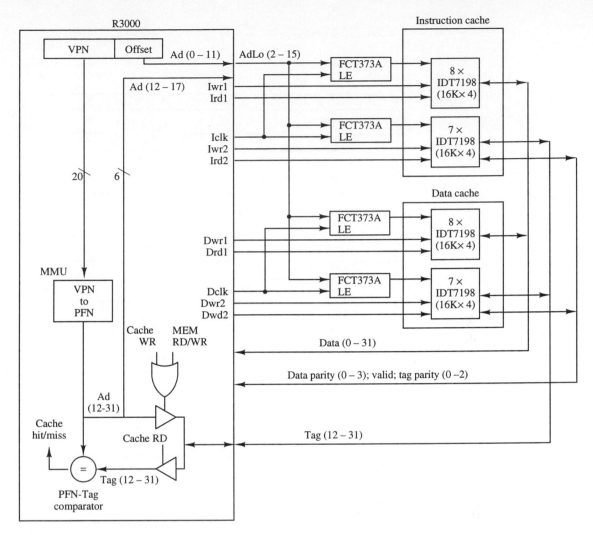

VPN, virtual page number
PFN, physical page frame number

Figure C.20 64-Kbyte external I-cache, a 64-Kbyte external D-cache, the internal conversion of VPN (virtual page number) to PFN (page frame number), and the internal tag comparison [20]. Courtesy of IDT.

order tag bits do not need to be supplied for the tag comparison. The number of high-order tag bits supplied is determined by the system designer, according to the amount of cacheable main memory the system supports. When there is a cache miss, the processor asserts the MemRd# signal and goes into a "stall".[7] It stays in the stall state until the memory system indicates that it is ready to return this data by deasserting the busy signal (RdBusy = L).

[7]In a "stall cycle" the processor stops execution flow (no forward progress of the processor's internal pipeline is made) and waits for the main memory system to respond with the required data.

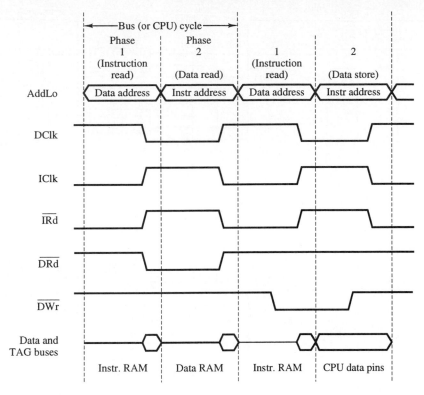

Figure C.21 Timing diagram for R3000 synchronous bus operation (to access I-cache and D-cache) [19]. Courtesy of IDT.

The processor also enters a stall state whenever a read request is made from an uncacheable address. It provides a signal called ACCTyp(2) to differentiate between a cached or uncached read reference. The AccTyp(0) signal indicates instruction or data for cached space and the two AccTyp(1:0) bits indicate the size of data for uncached space.

REFERENCES

[1] Intel Corporation, *The 8086 Family User's Manual*, Santa Clara, CA, 1979.

[2] Alexandridis, N.A., *Microprocessor System Design Concepts*, Computer Science Press, Rockville, MD, 1984.

[3] Intel Corporation, *iAPX286 Programmer's Reference Manual*, Santa Clara, CA, 1983.

[4] Intel Corporation, *iAPX286 Hardware Reference Manual*, Santa Clara, CA, 1983.

[5] Motorola Semiconductor Products, Inc., *16-bit Microprocessor User's Manual*, Prentice Hall, Englewood Cliffs, NJ, 1982.

[6] Motorola Semiconductor Products, Inc., *MTT8 Course Notes* (MTT8CN), Phoenix, AZ, 1987.

[7] Motorola Inc., *MC68020 32-bit Microprocessor User's Manual* (MC68020UM/AD) Prentice Hall, Englewood Cliffs, NJ, 1985.

[8] Motorola Inc., *MC68030 Enhanced 32-bit Microprocessor User's Manual* (MC68030UM/AD) Phoenix, AZ, 1987.

[9] Motorola Inc., *MC68040 32-bit Microprocessor User's Manual* (MC68040UM/AD), Phoenix, AZ, 1989.

[10] Kohn, L. and N. Margulis, "Introducing the Intel i860 64-bit Microprocessor," *IEEE Micro,* Aug. 1989.

[11] Atkins, M., "Performance and the i860 Microprocessor," *IEEE Micro,* Oct. 1991.

[12] Intel Corp., *i860 64-bit Microprocessor Hardware Reference Manual* (240330-002), Santa Clara, CA, 1990.

[13] Diefendorff, K., and M. Allen, "Organization of the Motorola 88110 Superscalar RISC Micro-processor," *IEEE Micro,* Apr. 1992, pp. 40–63.

[14] Alsup, M., "Motorola's 88000 Family Architecture," *IEEE Micro,* June 1990.

[15] Motorola Inc., *MC88100 Technical Summary 32-bit Third-Generation RISC Microprocessor* (BR588/D), 1988.

[16] Hobbs, M., *RISC/CISC Development and Test Support,* Prentice Hall, Englewood Cliffs, NJ, 1992.

[17] Motorola Inc., *MC88200 16-Kilobyte Cache/Memory Management Unit (CMMU), Technical Summary* (BR589/D), Phoenix, AZ, 1988.

[18] Integrated Device Technology, Inc., *R3000/R3001 Designer's Guide* (MAN-RISC-01051), Santa Clara, CA, 1990.

[19] Integrated Device Technology, Inc., *RISC Data Book* (DBK-RISC-00021), Santa Clara, CA, 1991.

[20] MIPS Computer Systems, Inc., *MIPS R4000 Microprocessor Introduction* (M8-00041), Sunny-vale, CA, 1991.

[21] MIPS Computer Systems, Inc., *MIPS R4000 Microprocessor User's Manual* (M8-00040), Sunnyvale, CA, 1991.

[22] Kane, G., and J. Heinrich, *MIPS RISC Architecture,* Prentice Hall, Englewood Cliffs, NJ, 1992.

[23] Intel Corp., *Introduction to the 80386, Including the 80386 Data Sheet,* Santa Clara, CA, April 1986.

[24] Intel Corp., *i486 Microprocessor,* Santa Clara, CA, April 1989.

[25] Intel Corp., *80386 Programmer's Reference Manual,* Santa Clara, CA, 1986.

[26] Motorola Inc., *MC68020 Technical Summary 32-bit Virtual Memory Microprocessor,* Technical Data BR243/D, Dec. 2, 1987.

Index